D1072354

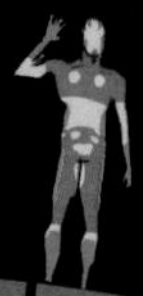

MISTER MIRACLE

TOM KING writer | **MITCH GERADS** artist and colorist | **CLAYTON COWLES** letterer

MITCH GERADS collection cover art | **NICK DERINGTON** original series cover art

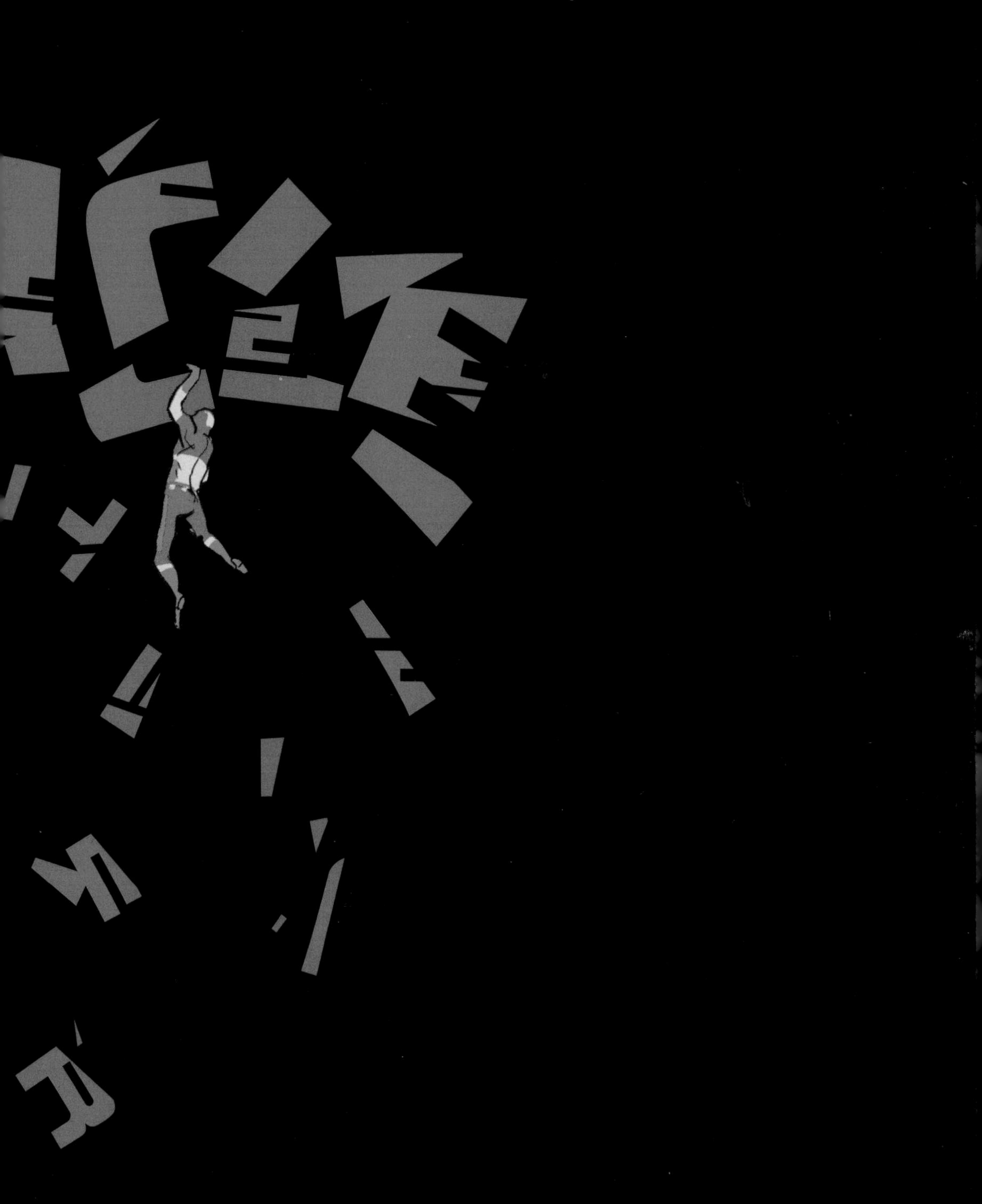

MISTER MIRACLE created by **JACK KIRBY**

JAMIE S. RICH Editor – Original Series
MOLLY MAHAN | BRITTANY HOLZHERR Associate Editors – Original Series
MAGGIE HOWELL Assistant Editor – Original Series
JEB WOODARD Group Editor – Collected Editions
SCOTT NYBAKKEN Editor – Collected Edition
STEVE COOK Design Director – Books / Cover Design
MONIQUE NARBONETA Publication Design

BOB HARRAS Senior VP – Editor-in-Chief, DC Comics
PAT McCALLUM Executive Editor, DC Comics

DAN DiDIO Publisher
JIM LEE Publisher & Chief Creative Officer
AMIT DESAI Executive VP – Business & Marketing Strategy,
          Direct to Consumer & Global Franchise Management
BOBBIE CHASE VP & Executive Editor, Young Reader & Talent Development
MARK CHIARELLO Senior VP – Art, Design & Collected Editions
JOHN CUNNINGHAM Senior VP – Sales & Trade Marketing
BRIAR DARDEN VP – Business Affairs
ANNE DePIES Senior VP – Business Strategy, Finance & Administration
DON FALLETTI VP – Manufacturing Operations
LAWRENCE GANEM VP – Editorial Administration & Talent Relations
ALISON GILL Senior VP – Manufacturing & Operations
JASON GREENBERG VP – Business Strategy & Finance
HANK KANALZ Senior VP – Editorial Strategy & Administration
JAY KOGAN Senior VP – Legal Affairs
NICK J. NAPOLITANO VP – Manufacturing Administration
LISETTE OSTERLOH VP – Digital Marketing & Events
EDDIE SCANNELL VP – Consumer Marketing
COURTNEY SIMMONS Senior VP – Publicity & Communications
JIM (SKI) SOKOLOWSKI VP – Comic Book Specialty Sales & Trade Marketing
NANCY SPEARS VP – Mass, Book, Digital Sales & Trade Marketing
MICHELE R. WELLS VP – Content Strategy

MISTER MIRACLE

Published by DC Comics. Cover, compilation and all new material Copyright © 2019
DC Comics. All Rights Reserved.

Originally published in single magazine form in MISTER MIRACLE 1-12 and MISTER
MIRACLE #1 DIRECTOR'S CUT 1. Copyright © 2017, 2018 DC Comics. All Rights
Reserved. All characters, their distinctive likenesses and related elements featured in this
publication are trademarks of DC Comics. The stories, characters and incidents featured
in this publication are entirely fictional. DC Comics does not read or accept unsolicited
submissions of ideas, stories or artwork.

DC Comics, 2900 West Alameda Ave., Burbank, CA 91505
Printed by LSC Communications, Kendallville, IN, USA. 5/20/19. Second Printing.
ISBN: 978-1-4012-8354-4

Library of Congress Cataloging-in-Publication Data is available.

PEFC Certified
This product is from
sustainably managed
forests and controlled
sources
PEFC
PEFC/29-31-337   www.pefc.org

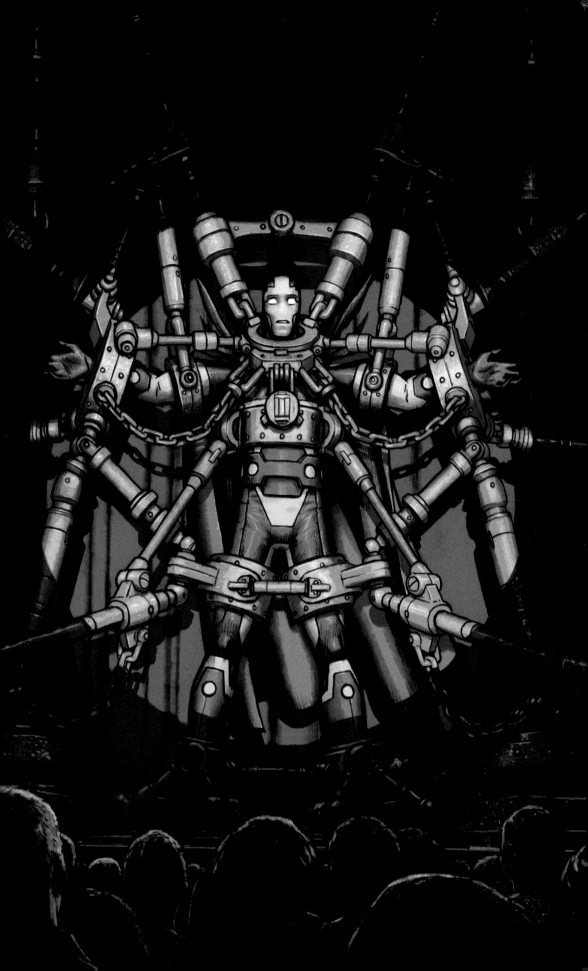

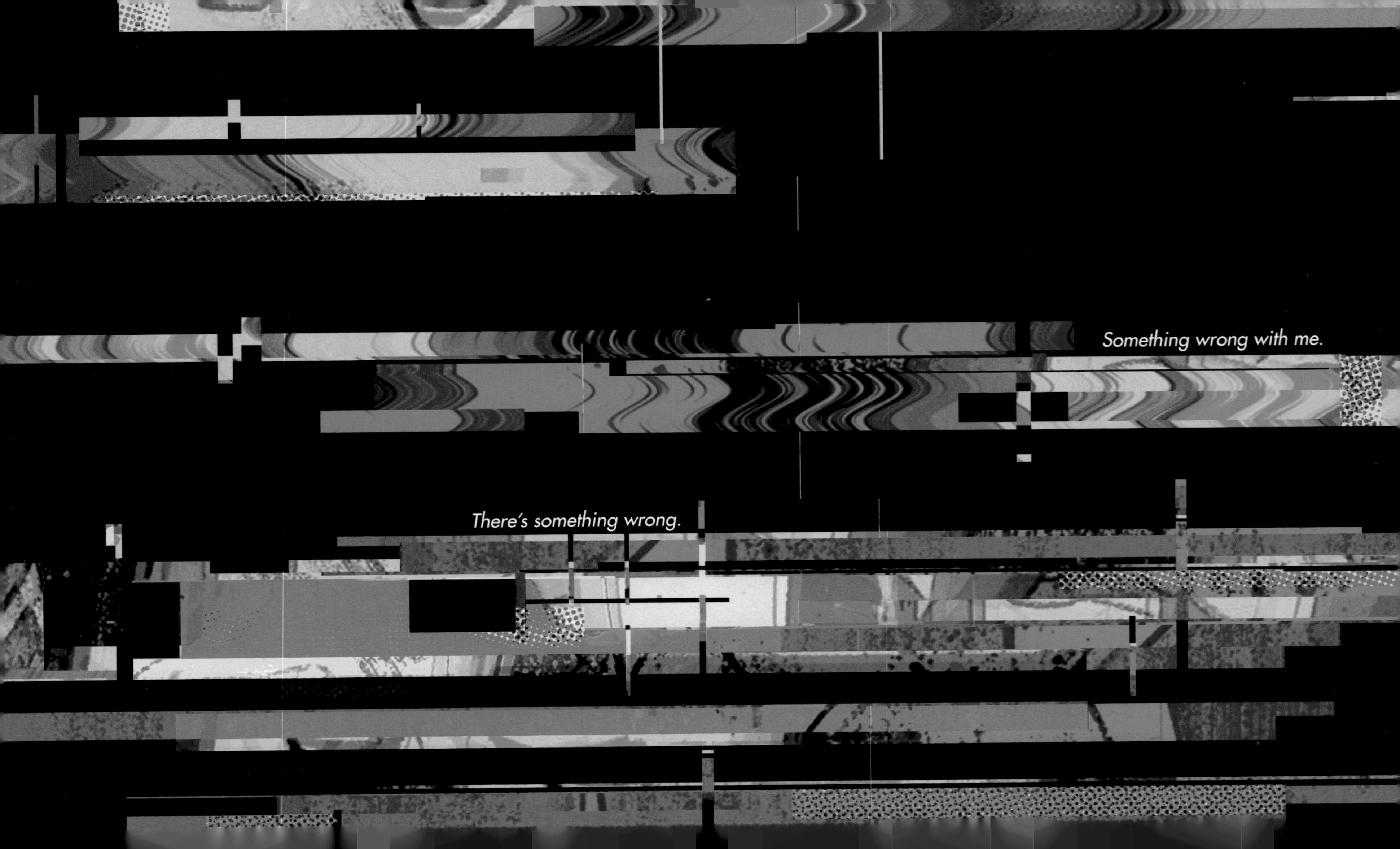

There's something wrong.
Something wrong with me.

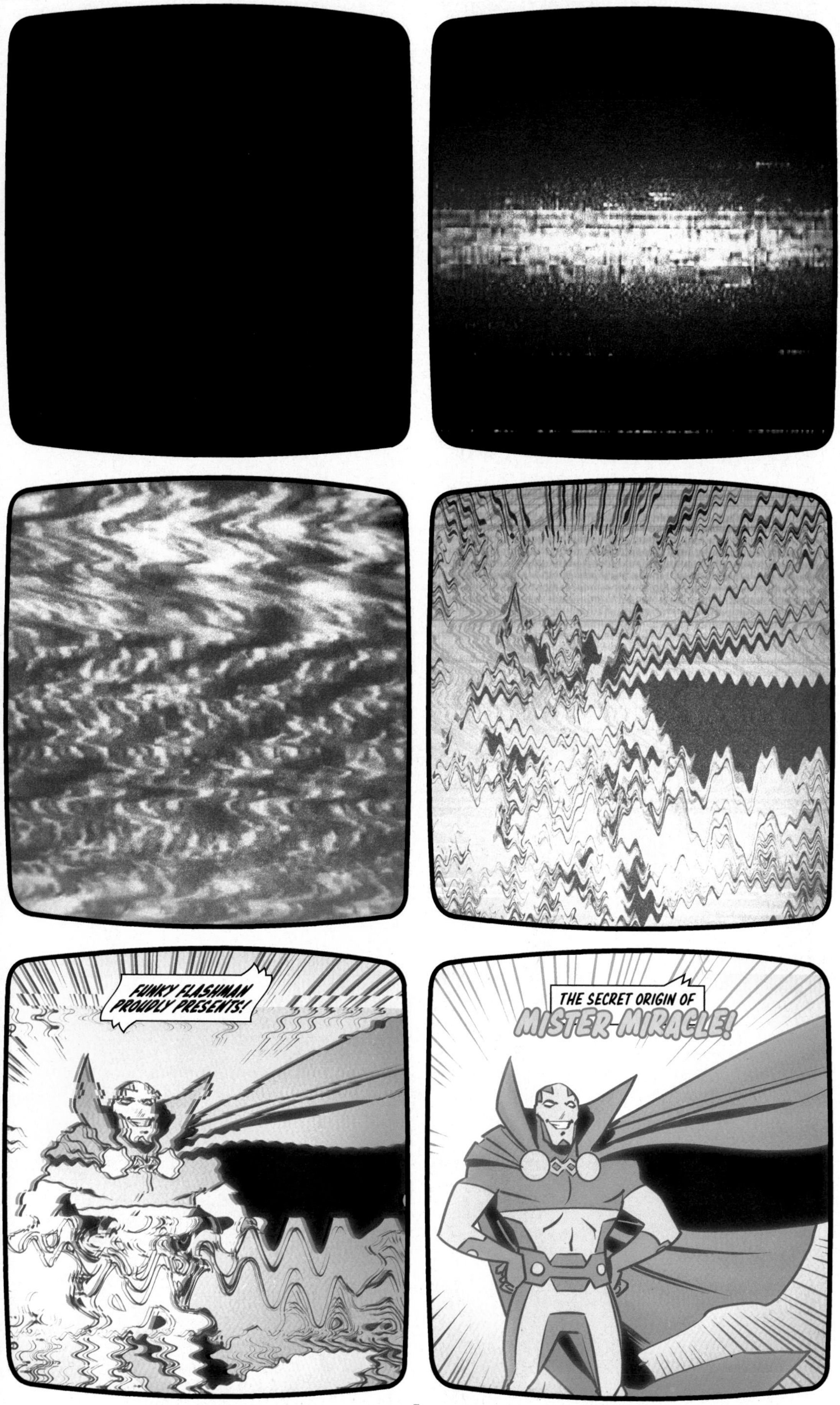
FUNKY FLASHMAN PROUDLY PRESENTS!
THE SECRET ORIGIN OF
MISTER MIRACLE!

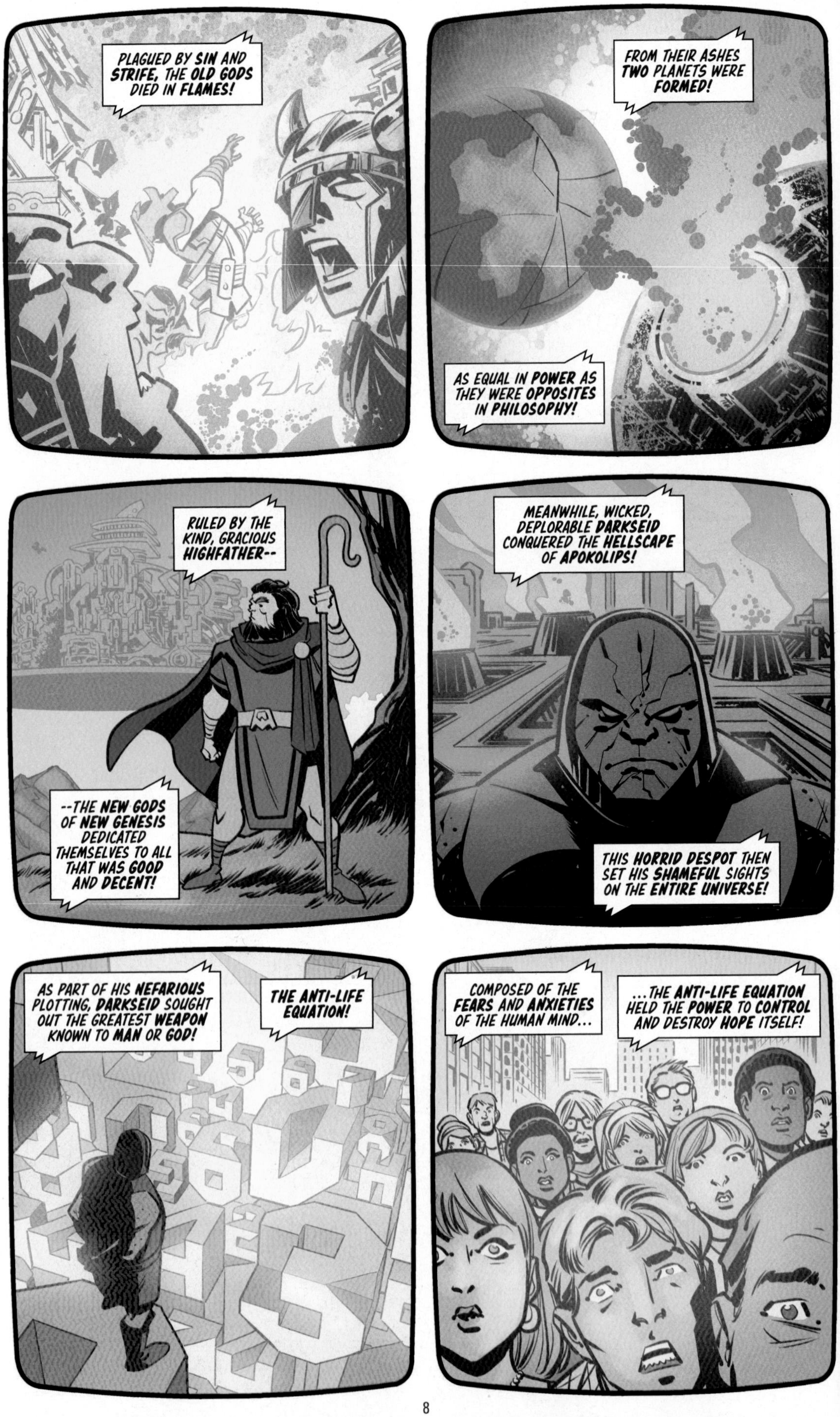
PLAGUED BY SIN AND STRIFE, THE OLD GODS DIED IN FLAMES!
FROM THEIR ASHES TWO PLANETS WERE FORMED!
AS EQUAL IN POWER AS THEY WERE OPPOSITES IN PHILOSOPHY!
RULED BY THE KIND, GRACIOUS HIGHFATHER--
--THE NEW GODS OF NEW GENESIS DEDICATED THEMSELVES TO ALL THAT WAS GOOD AND DECENT!
MEANWHILE, WICKED, DEPLORABLE DARKSEID CONQUERED THE HELLSCAPE OF APOKOLIPS!
THIS HORRID DESPOT THEN SET HIS SHAMEFUL SIGHTS ON THE ENTIRE UNIVERSE!
AS PART OF HIS NEFARIOUS PLOTTING, DARKSEID SOUGHT OUT THE GREATEST WEAPON KNOWN TO MAN OR GOD!
THE ANTI-LIFE EQUATION!
COMPOSED OF THE FEARS AND ANXIETIES OF THE HUMAN MIND...
...THE ANTI-LIFE EQUATION HELD THE POWER TO CONTROL AND DESTROY HOPE ITSELF!

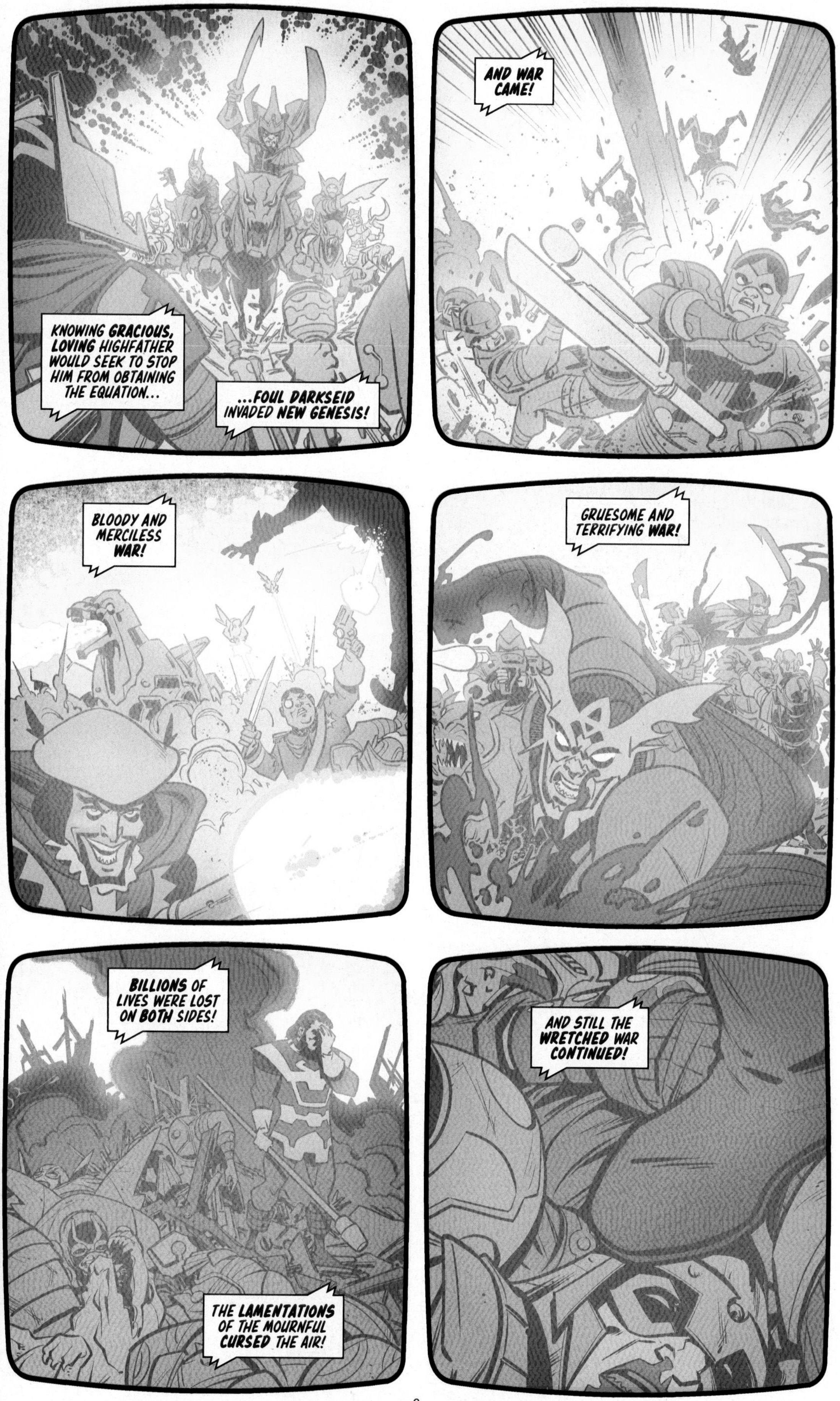
KNOWING GRACIOUS, LOVING HIGHFATHER WOULD SEEK TO STOP HIM FROM OBTAINING THE EQUATION...
...FOUL DARKSEID INVADED NEW GENESIS!
AND WAR CAME!
BLOODY AND MERCILESS WAR!
GRUESOME AND TERRIFYING WAR!
BILLIONS OF LIVES WERE LOST ON BOTH SIDES!
THE LAMENTATIONS OF THE MOURNFUL CURSED THE AIR!
AND STILL THE WRETCHED WAR CONTINUED!

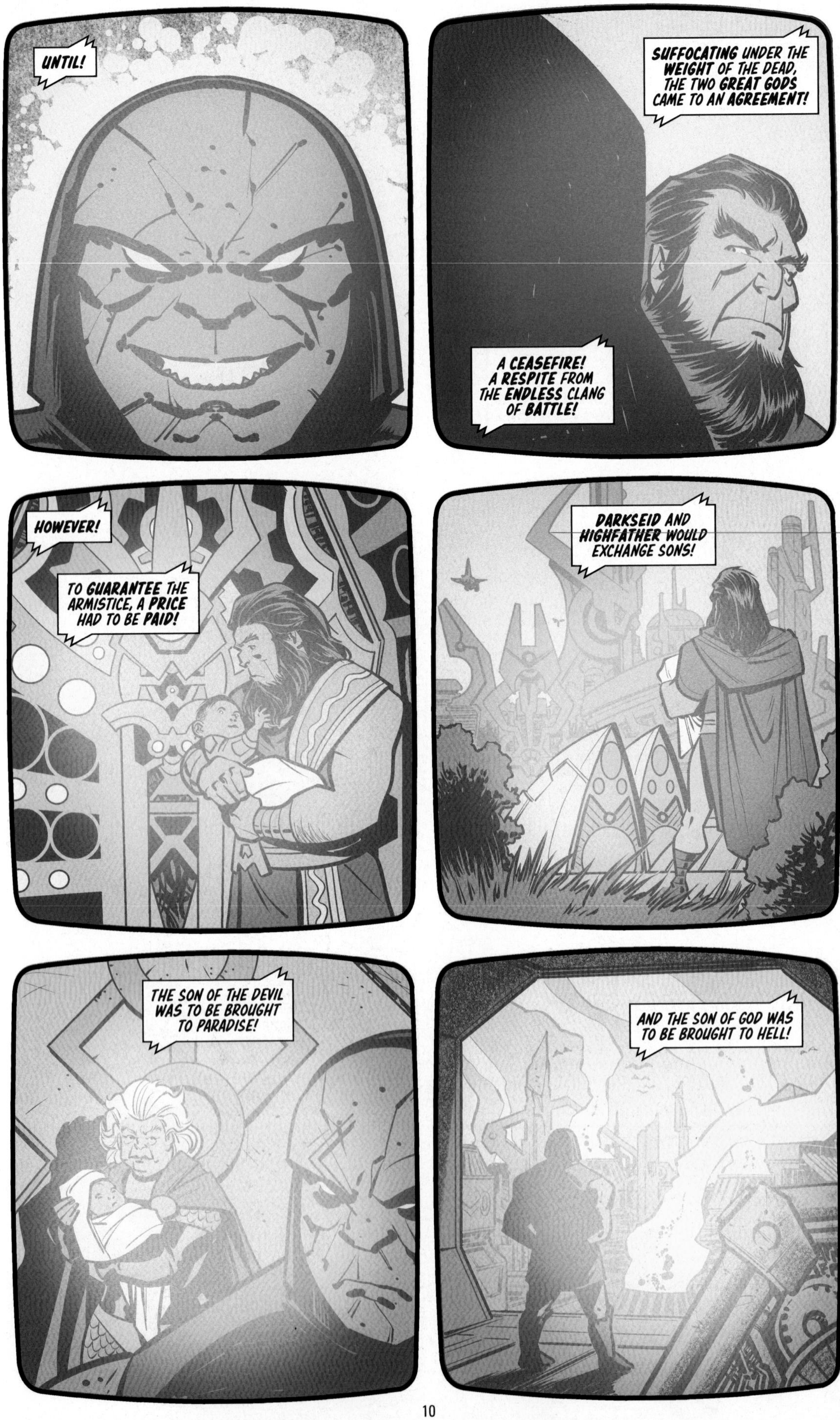

UNTIL!
SUFFOCATING UNDER THE WEIGHT OF THE DEAD, THE TWO GREAT GODS CAME TO AN AGREEMENT!
A CEASEFIRE! A RESPITE FROM THE ENDLESS CLANG OF BATTLE!
HOWEVER!
TO GUARANTEE THE ARMISTICE, A PRICE HAD TO BE PAID!
DARKSEID AND HIGHFATHER WOULD EXCHANGE SONS!
THE SON OF THE DEVIL WAS TO BE BROUGHT TO PARADISE!
AND THE SON OF GOD WAS TO BE BROUGHT TO HELL!

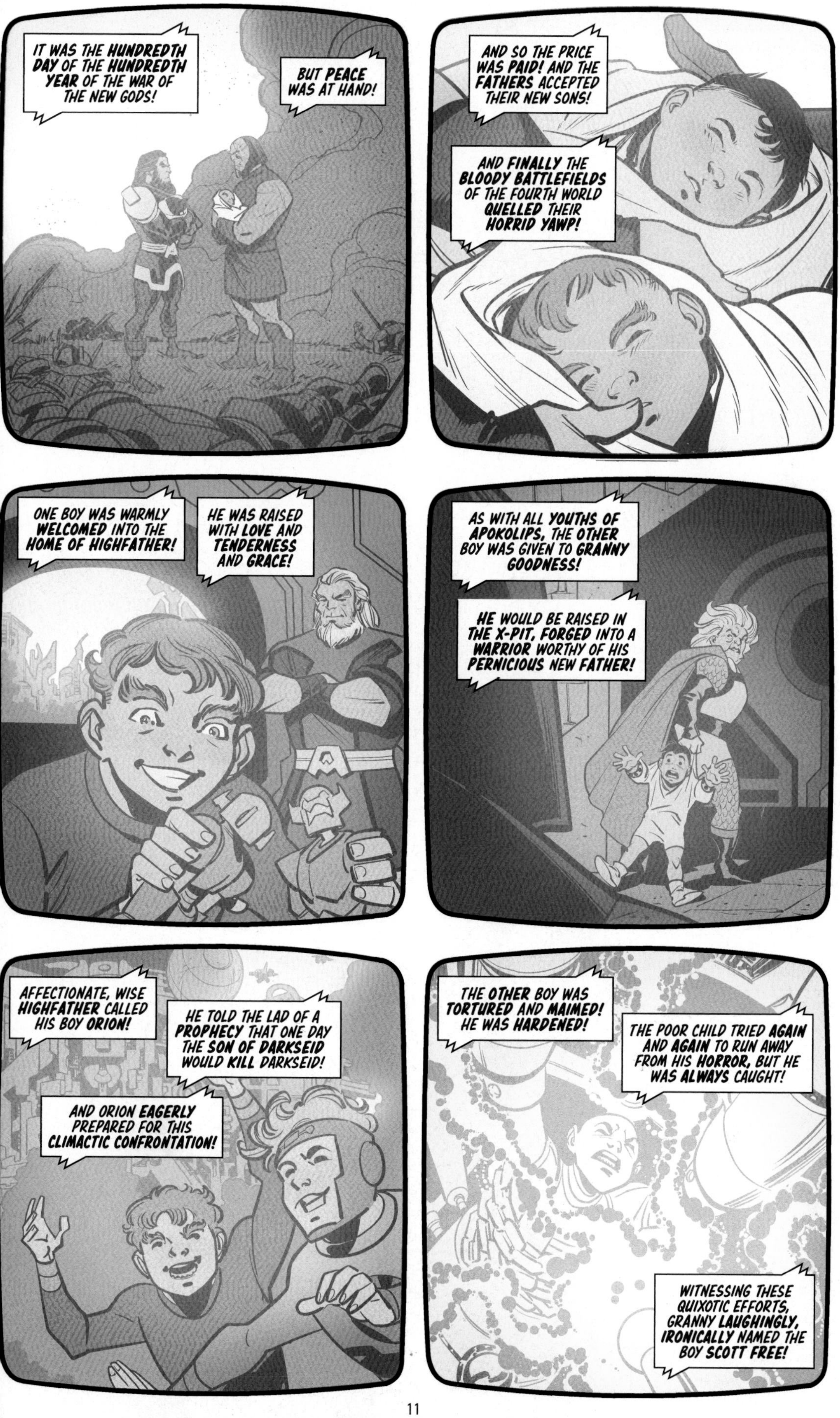
IT WAS THE HUNDREDTH DAY OF THE HUNDREDTH YEAR OF THE WAR OF THE NEW GODS!
BUT PEACE WAS AT HAND!
AND SO THE PRICE WAS PAID! AND THE FATHERS ACCEPTED THEIR NEW SONS!
AND FINALLY THE BLOODY BATTLEFIELDS OF THE FOURTH WORLD QUELLED THEIR HORRID YAWP!
ONE BOY WAS WARMLY WELCOMED INTO THE HOME OF HIGHFATHER!
HE WAS RAISED WITH LOVE AND TENDERNESS AND GRACE!
AS WITH ALL YOUTHS OF APOKOLIPS, THE OTHER BOY WAS GIVEN TO GRANNY GOODNESS!
HE WOULD BE RAISED IN THE X-PIT, FORGED INTO A WARRIOR WORTHY OF HIS PERNICIOUS NEW FATHER!
AFFECTIONATE, WISE HIGHFATHER CALLED HIS BOY ORION!
HE TOLD THE LAD OF A PROPHECY THAT ONE DAY THE SON OF DARKSEID WOULD KILL DARKSEID!
AND ORION EAGERLY PREPARED FOR THIS CLIMACTIC CONFRONTATION!
THE OTHER BOY WAS TORTURED AND MAIMED! HE WAS HARDENED!
THE POOR CHILD TRIED AGAIN AND AGAIN TO RUN AWAY FROM HIS HORROR, BUT HE WAS ALWAYS CAUGHT!
WITNESSING THESE QUIXOTIC EFFORTS, GRANNY LAUGHINGLY, IRONICALLY NAMED THE BOY SCOTT FREE!

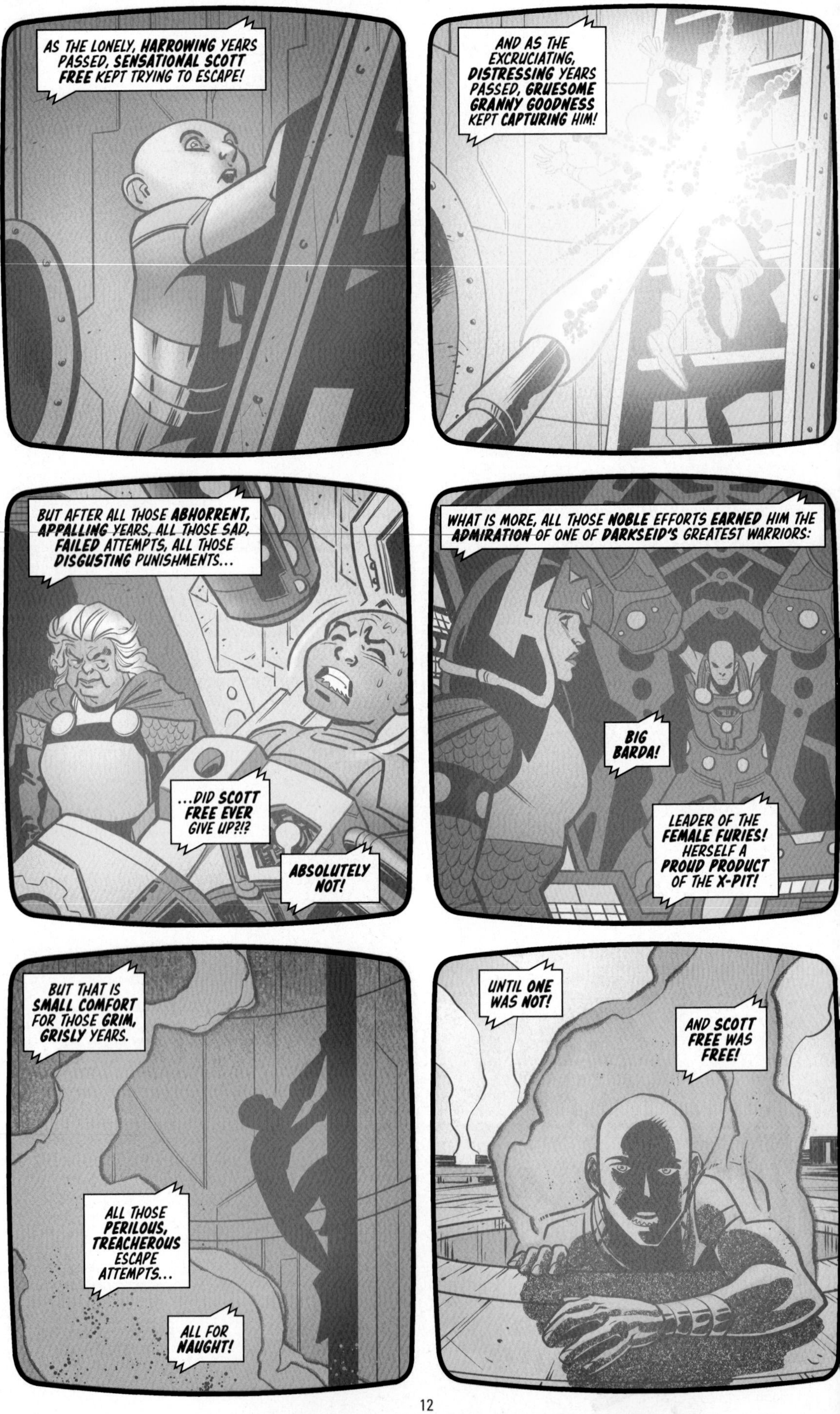
AS THE LONELY, HARROWING YEARS PASSED, SENSATIONAL SCOTT FREE KEPT TRYING TO ESCAPE!
AND AS THE EXCRUCIATING, DISTRESSING YEARS PASSED, GRUESOME GRANNY GOODNESS KEPT CAPTURING HIM!
BUT AFTER ALL THOSE ABHORRENT, APPALLING YEARS, ALL THOSE SAD, FAILED ATTEMPTS, ALL THOSE DISGUSTING PUNISHMENTS...
...DID SCOTT FREE EVER GIVE UP?!?
ABSOLUTELY NOT!
WHAT IS MORE, ALL THOSE NOBLE EFFORTS EARNED HIM THE ADMIRATION OF ONE OF DARKSEID'S GREATEST WARRIORS:
BIG BARDA!
LEADER OF THE FEMALE FURIES! HERSELF A PROUD PRODUCT OF THE X-PIT!
BUT THAT IS SMALL COMFORT FOR THOSE GRIM, GRISLY YEARS.
ALL THOSE PERILOUS, TREACHEROUS ESCAPE ATTEMPTS...
ALL FOR NAUGHT!
UNTIL ONE WAS NOT!
AND SCOTT FREE WAS FREE!

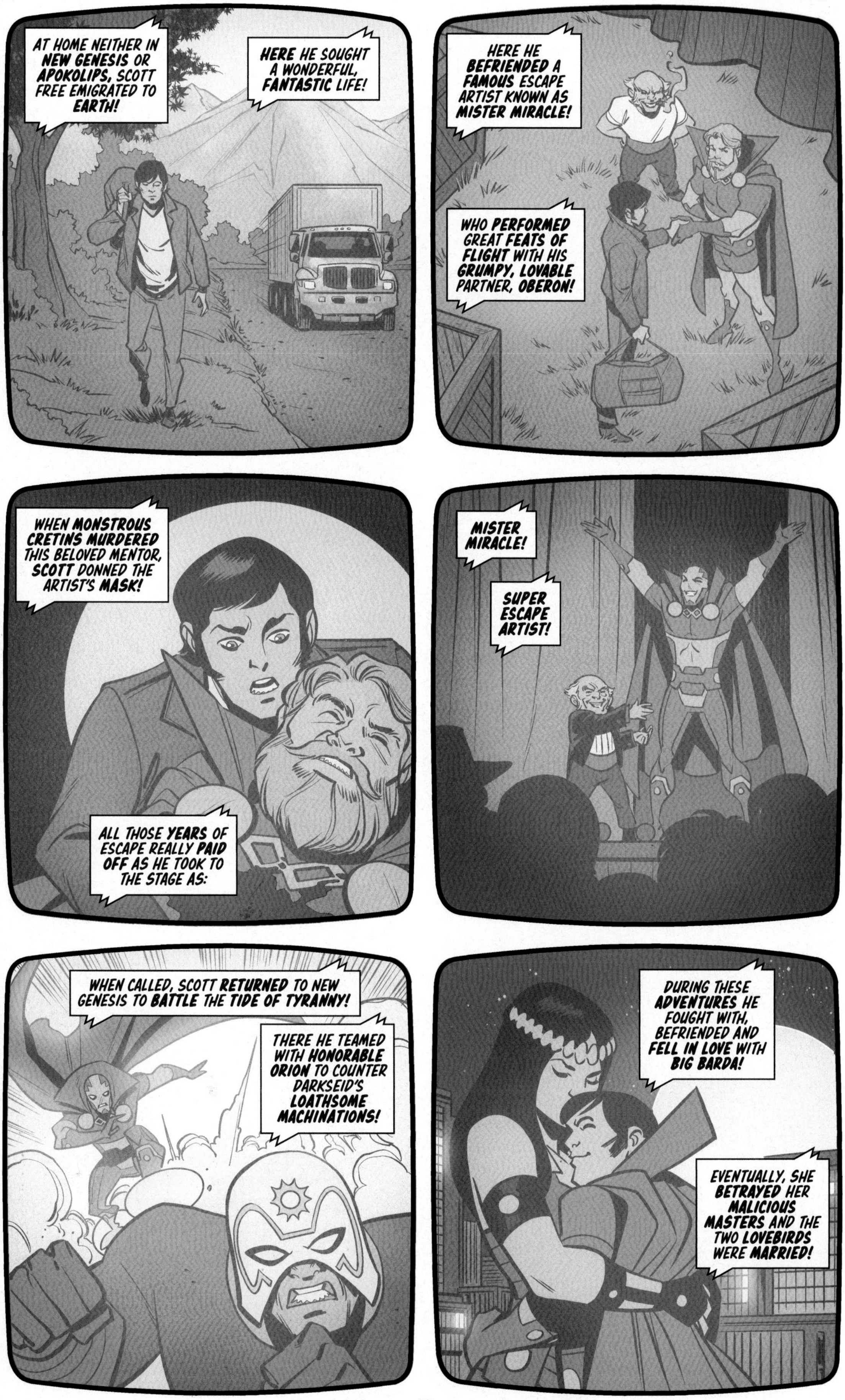

AT HOME NEITHER IN NEW GENESIS OR APOKOLIPS, SCOTT FREE EMIGRATED TO EARTH!
HERE HE SOUGHT A WONDERFUL, FANTASTIC LIFE!
HERE HE BEFRIENDED A FAMOUS ESCAPE ARTIST KNOWN AS MISTER MIRACLE!
WHO PERFORMED GREAT FEATS OF FLIGHT WITH HIS GRUMPY, LOVABLE PARTNER, OBERON!
WHEN MONSTROUS CRETINS MURDERED THIS BELOVED MENTOR, SCOTT DONNED THE ARTIST'S MASK!
ALL THOSE YEARS OF ESCAPE REALLY PAID OFF AS HE TOOK TO THE STAGE AS:
MISTER MIRACLE!
SUPER ESCAPE ARTIST!
WHEN CALLED, SCOTT RETURNED TO NEW GENESIS TO BATTLE THE TIDE OF TYRANNY!
THERE HE TEAMED WITH HONORABLE ORION TO COUNTER DARKSEID'S LOATHSOME MACHINATIONS!
DURING THESE ADVENTURES HE FOUGHT WITH, BEFRIENDED AND FELL IN LOVE WITH BIG BARDA!
EVENTUALLY, SHE BETRAYED HER MALICIOUS MASTERS AND THE TWO LOVEBIRDS WERE MARRIED!

AND SO FROM HIS *ROUGH* BEGINNINGS, SCOTT FREE *BUILT* A *NEW* FAMILY!

AND EMBRACED A *NEW DESTINY!*

I CAN ALWAYS ESCAPE!

BUT THOUGH OUR *GREAT* HERO NOW OCCUPIES A SEAT OF *COMFORT* AND *TRANQUILITY...*

...MISTER MIRACLE NEVER FORGETS THAT SOMEWHERE OUT THERE...

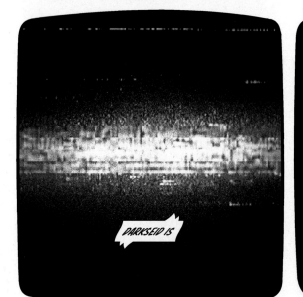

DARKSEID IS

TOM KING WRITER
MIKE NORTON ILLUSTRATOR
JORDIE BELLAIRE COLORS
CLAYTON COWLES LETTERER
BRITTANY HOLZHERR ASSOCIATE EDITOR
JAMIE S. RICH EDITOR

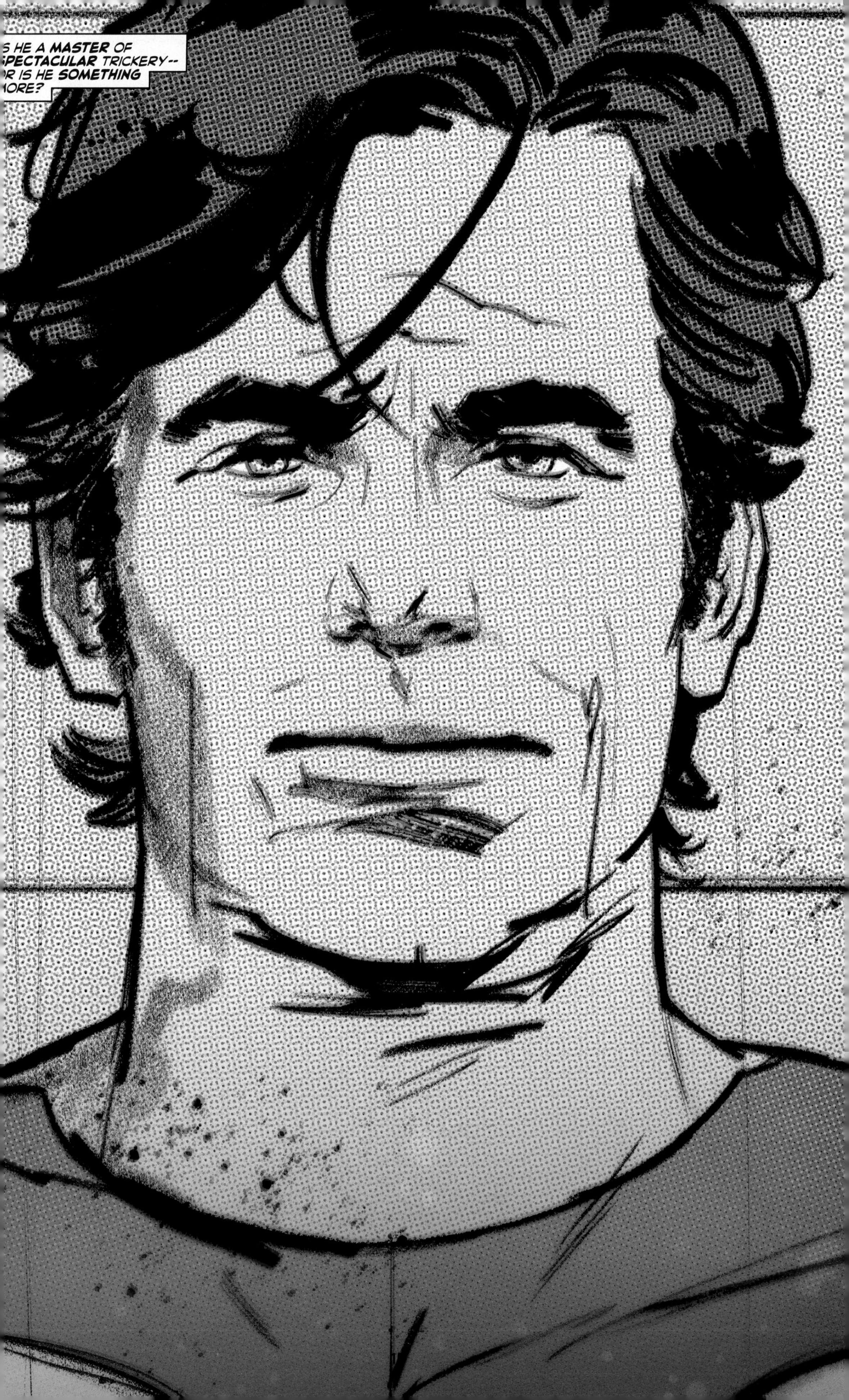
S HE A MASTER OF SPECTACULAR TRICKERY-- OR IS HE SOMETHING ORE?

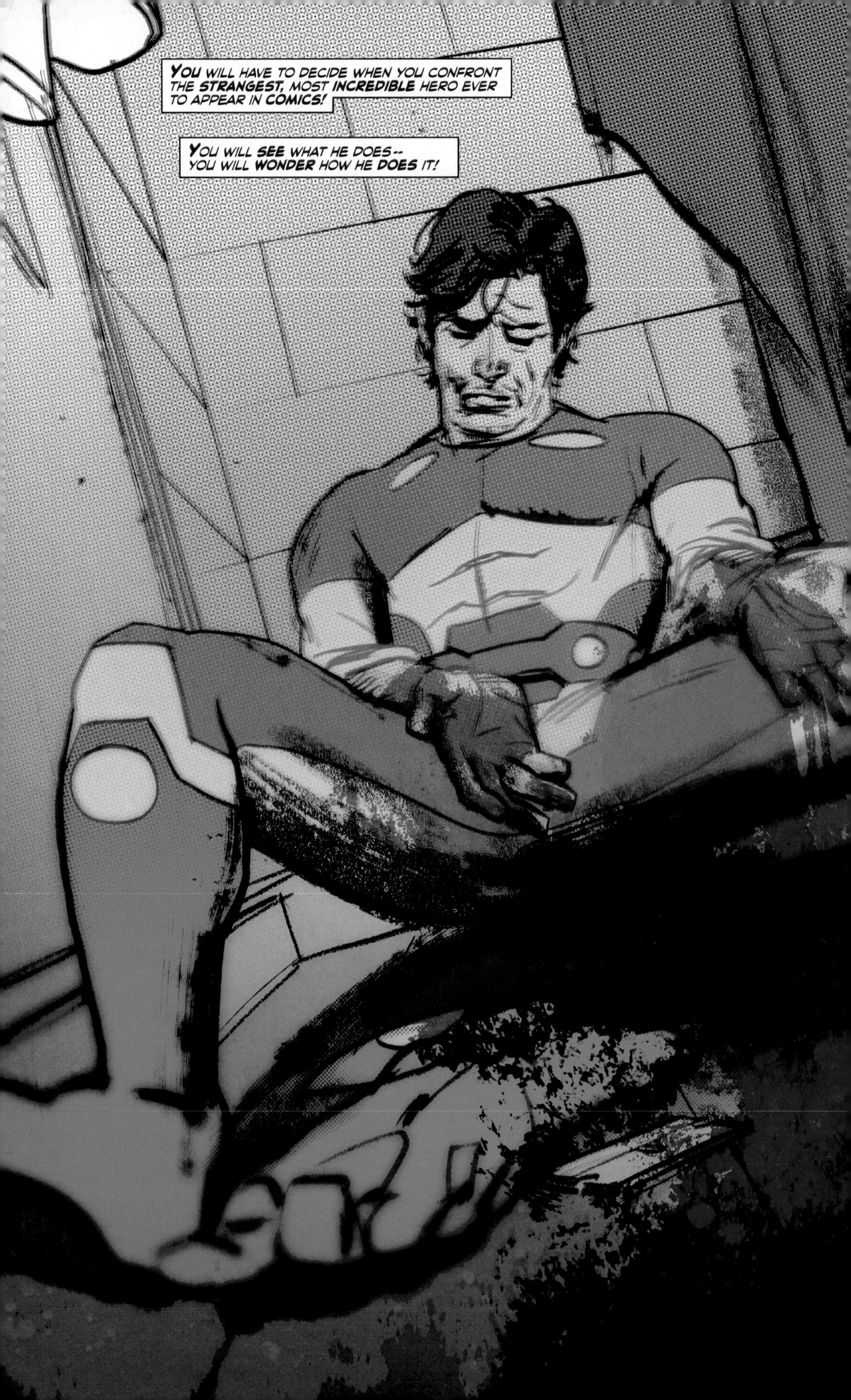
YOU WILL HAVE TO DECIDE WHEN YOU CONFRONT THE STRANGEST, MOST INCREDIBLE HERO EVER TO APPEAR IN COMICS!
YOU WILL SEE WHAT HE DOES-- YOU WILL WONDER HOW HE DOES IT!

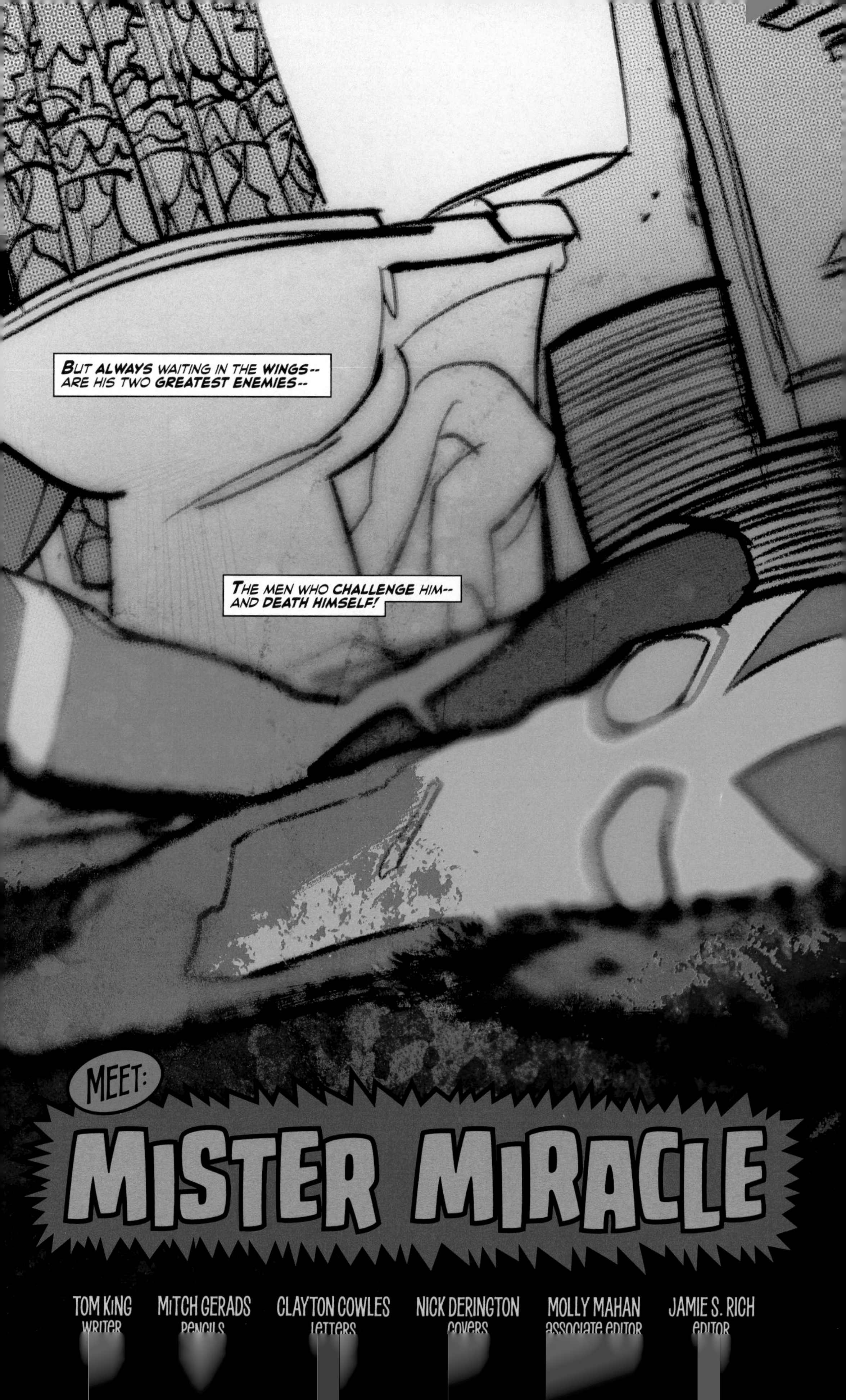

BUT ALWAYS WAITING IN THE WINGS--
ARE HIS TWO GREATEST ENEMIES--
THE MEN WHO CHALLENGE HIM--
AND DEATH HIMSELF!
MEET:
MISTER MIRACLE
TOM KING writer
MITCH GERADS pencils
CLAYTON COWLES letters
NICK DERINGTON covers
MOLLY MAHAN associate editor
JAMIE S. RICH editor

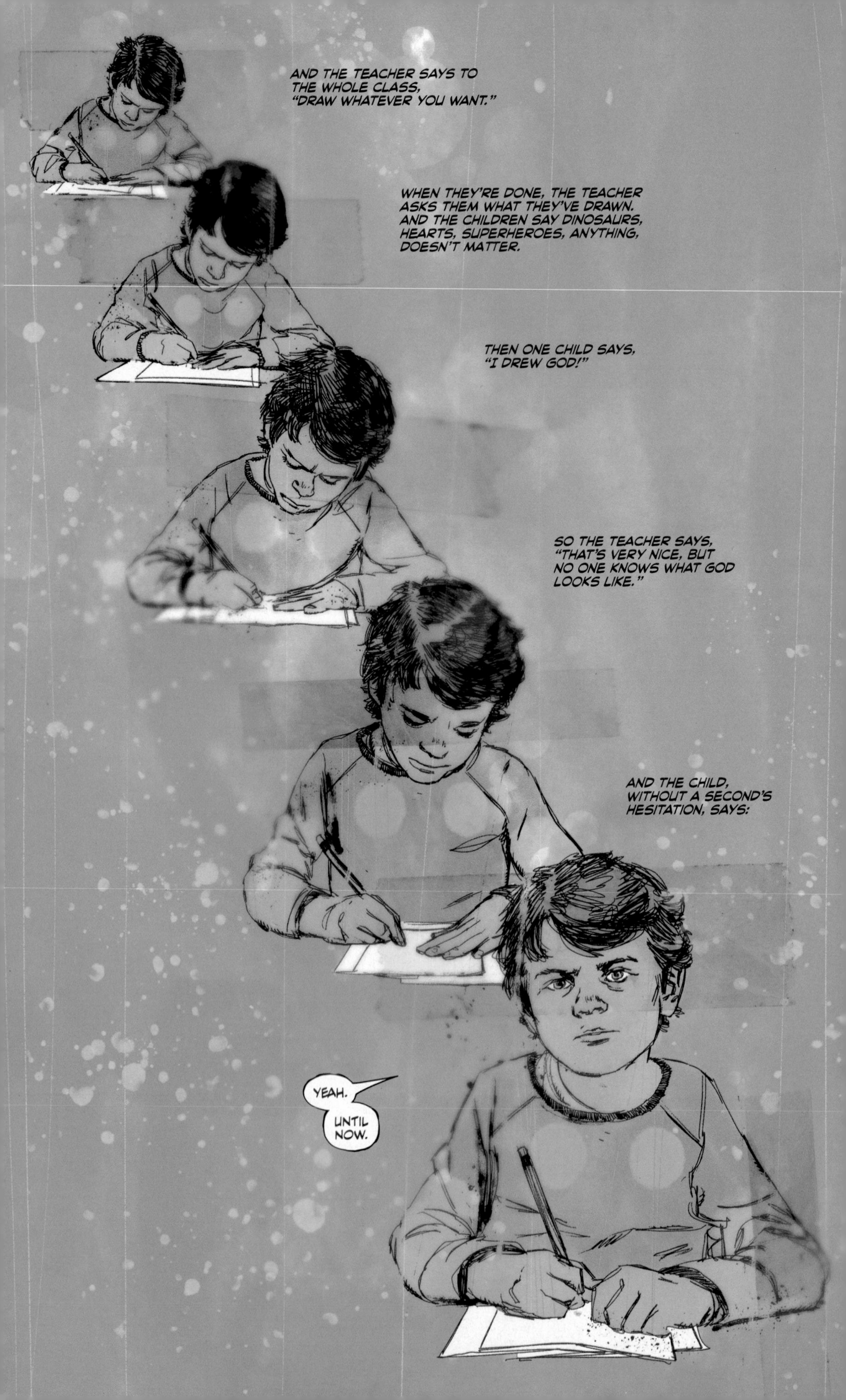
AND THE TEACHER SAYS TO THE WHOLE CLASS, "DRAW WHATEVER YOU WANT."
WHEN THEY'RE DONE, THE TEACHER ASKS THEM WHAT THEY'VE DRAWN. AND THE CHILDREN SAY DINOSAURS, HEARTS, SUPERHEROES, ANYTHING, DOESN'T MATTER.
THEN ONE CHILD SAYS, "I DREW GOD!"
SO THE TEACHER SAYS, "THAT'S VERY NICE, BUT NO ONE KNOWS WHAT GOD LOOKS LIKE."
AND THE CHILD, WITHOUT A SECOND'S HESITATION, SAYS:
YEAH.
UNTIL NOW.

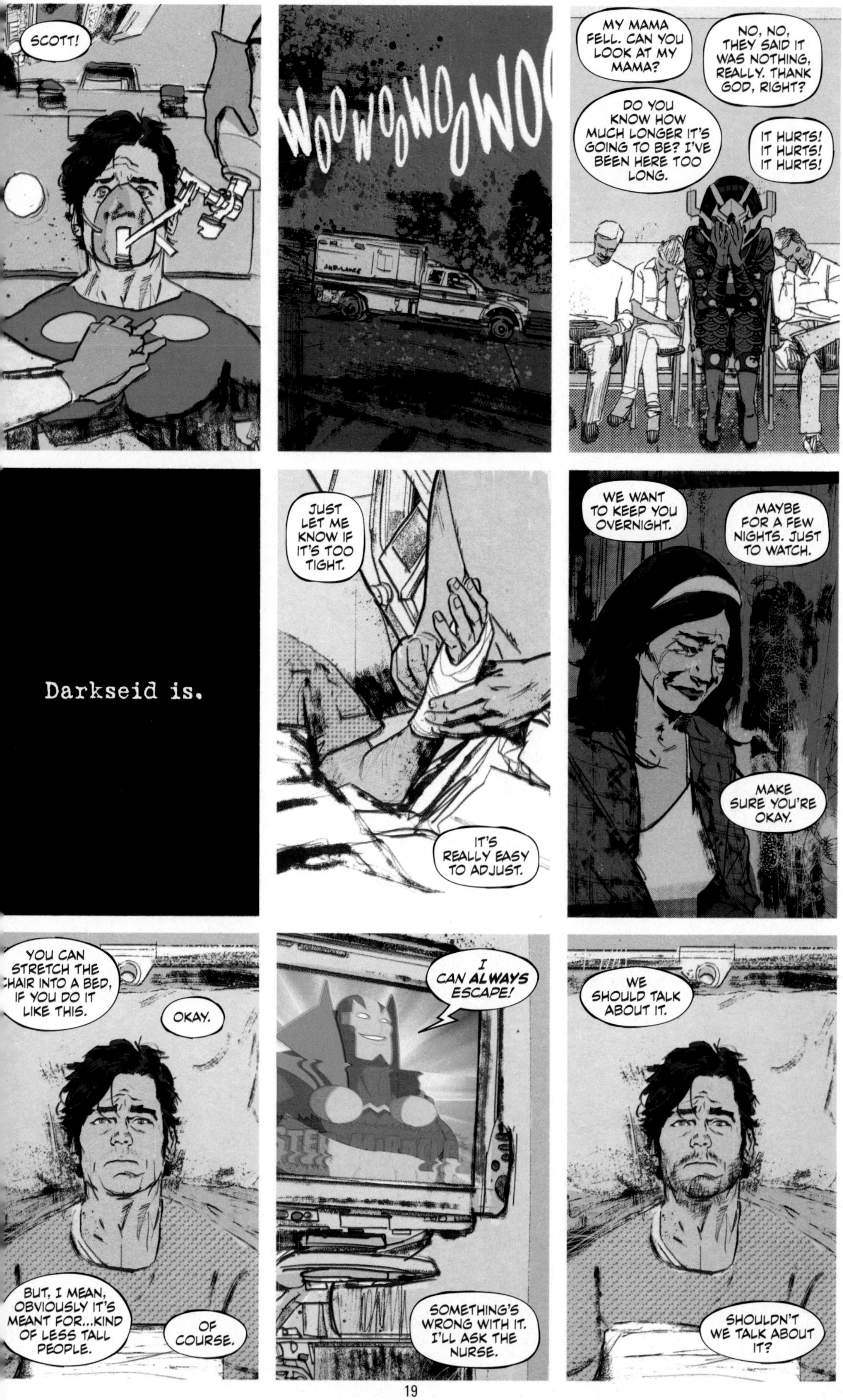

SCOTT!
WOOWOOWOOWOOWOO
MY MAMA FELL. CAN YOU LOOK AT MY MAMA?
NO, NO, THEY SAID IT WAS NOTHING, REALLY. THANK GOD, RIGHT?
DO YOU KNOW HOW MUCH LONGER IT'S GOING TO BE? I'VE BEEN HERE TOO LONG.
IT HURTS! IT HURTS! IT HURTS!
Darkseid is.
JUST LET ME KNOW IF IT'S TOO TIGHT.
IT'S REALLY EASY TO ADJUST.
WE WANT TO KEEP YOU OVERNIGHT.
MAYBE FOR A FEW NIGHTS. JUST TO WATCH.
MAKE SURE YOU'RE OKAY.
YOU CAN STRETCH THE CHAIR INTO A BED, IF YOU DO IT LIKE THIS.
OKAY.
BUT, I MEAN, OBVIOUSLY IT'S MEANT FOR...KIND OF LESS TALL PEOPLE.
OF COURSE.
I CAN **ALWAYS** ESCAPE!
SOMETHING'S WRONG WITH IT. I'LL ASK THE NURSE.
WE SHOULD TALK ABOUT IT.
SHOULDN'T WE TALK ABOUT IT?

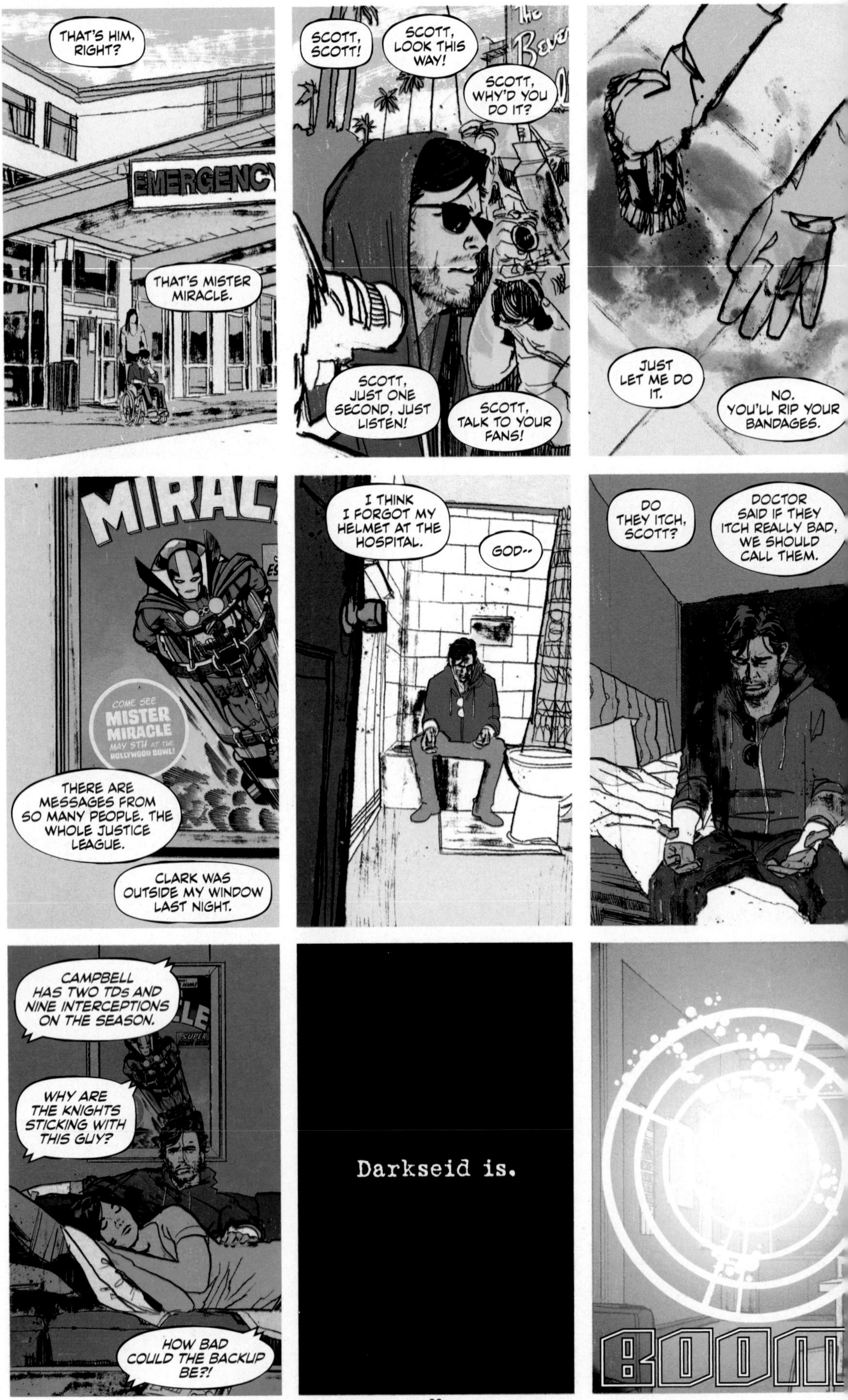
THAT'S HIM, RIGHT?
THAT'S MISTER MIRACLE.
EMERGENCY
SCOTT, SCOTT!
SCOTT, LOOK THIS WAY!
SCOTT, WHY'D YOU DO IT?
SCOTT, JUST ONE SECOND, JUST LISTEN!
SCOTT, TALK TO YOUR FANS!
JUST LET ME DO IT.
NO. YOU'LL RIP YOUR BANDAGES.
MIRAC
COME SEE MISTER MIRACLE MAY 5TH AT THE HOLLYWOOD BOWL!
THERE ARE MESSAGES FROM SO MANY PEOPLE. THE WHOLE JUSTICE LEAGUE.
CLARK WAS OUTSIDE MY WINDOW LAST NIGHT.
I THINK I FORGOT MY HELMET AT THE HOSPITAL.
GOD--
DO THEY ITCH, SCOTT?
DOCTOR SAID IF THEY ITCH REALLY BAD, WE SHOULD CALL THEM.
CAMPBELL HAS TWO TDs AND NINE INTERCEPTIONS ON THE SEASON.
WHY ARE THE KNIGHTS STICKING WITH THIS GUY?
HOW BAD COULD THE BACKUP BE?!
Darkseid is.
BOOM

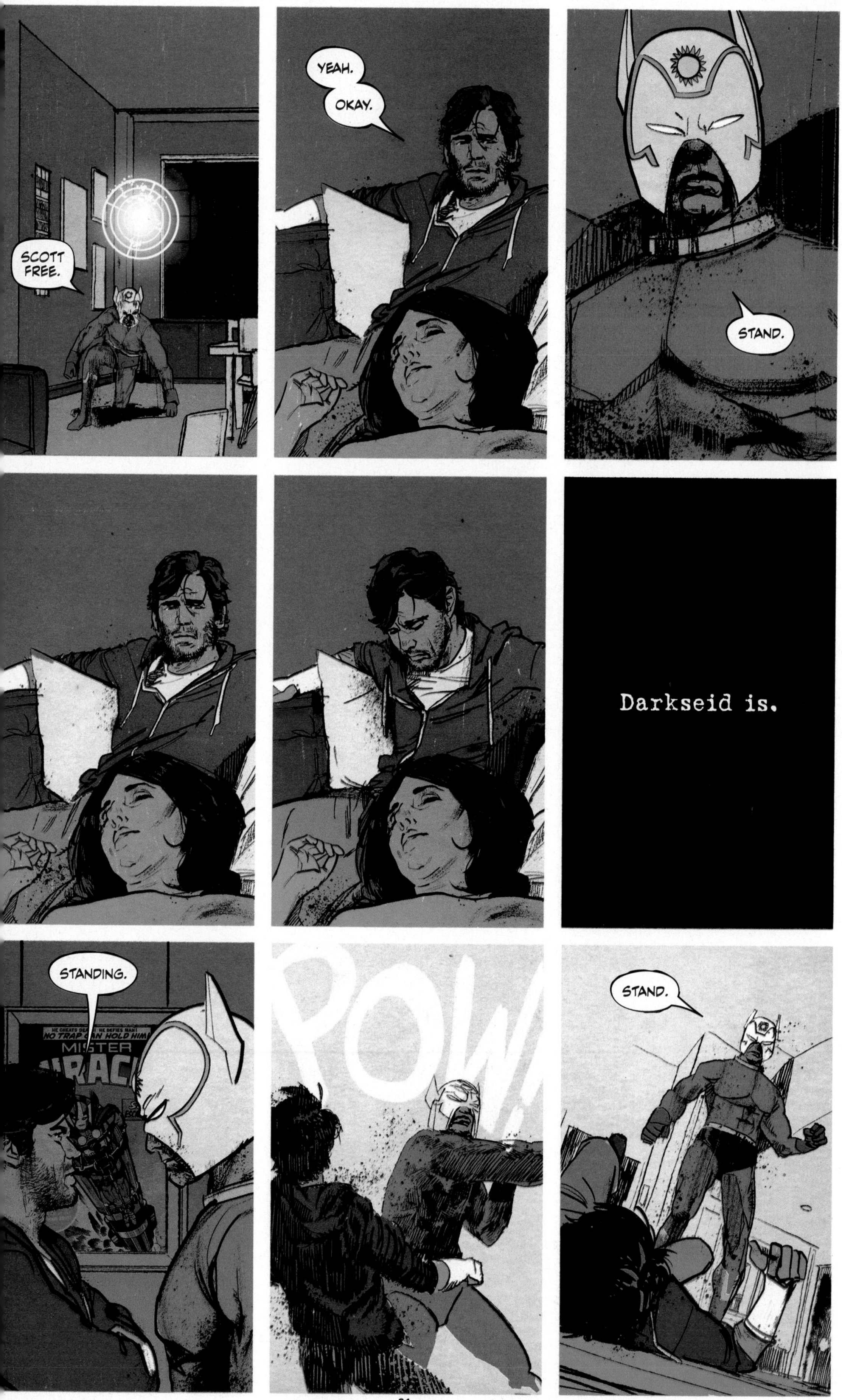
SCOTT FREE.
YEAH.
OKAY.
STAND.
Darkseid is.
STANDING.
NO TRAP CAN HOLD HIM!
MISTER
POW!
STAND.

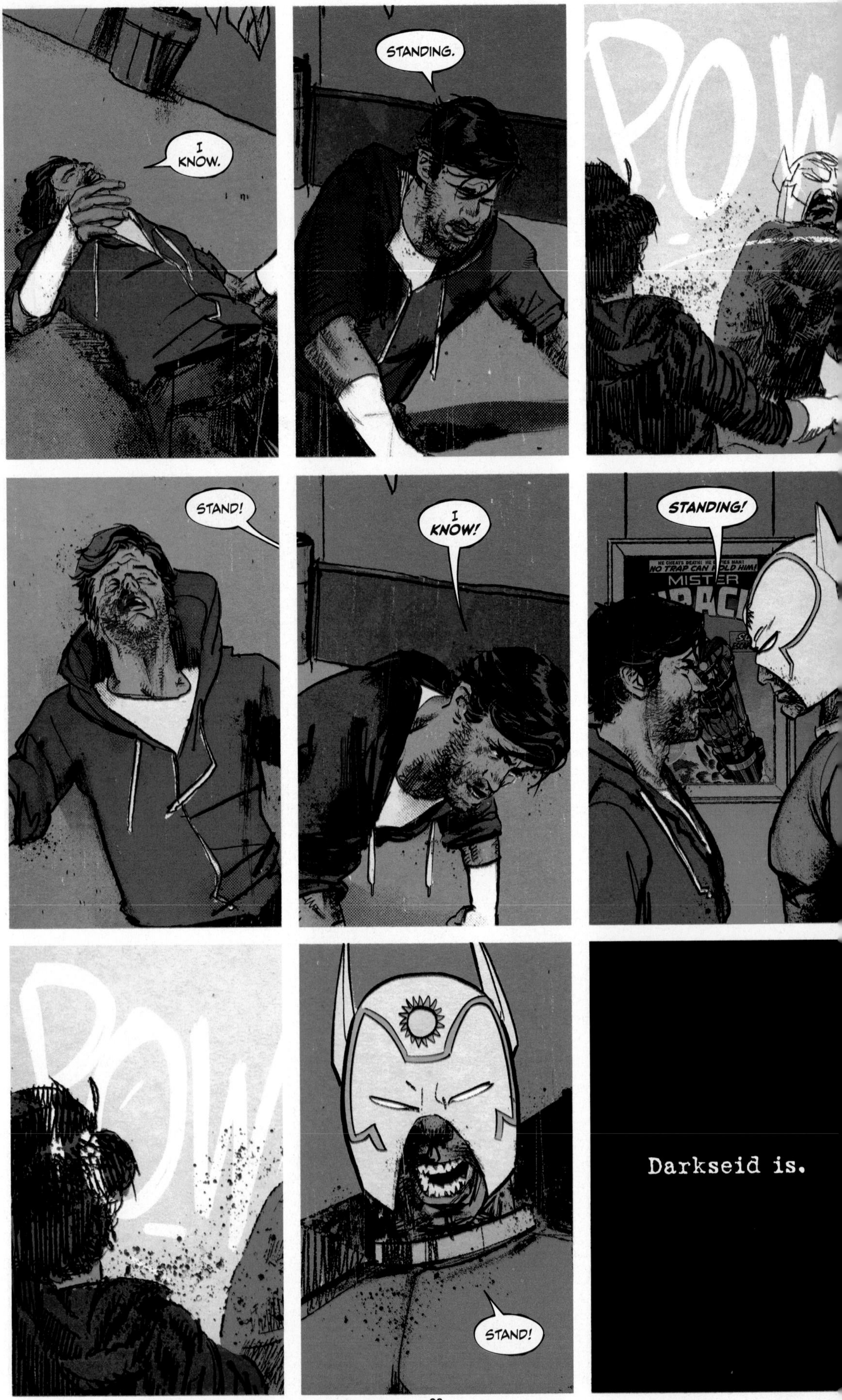
I KNOW.
STANDING.
POW
STAND!
I KNOW!
STANDING!
NO TRAP CAN HOLD HIM!
MISTER
POW
STAND!
Darkseid is.

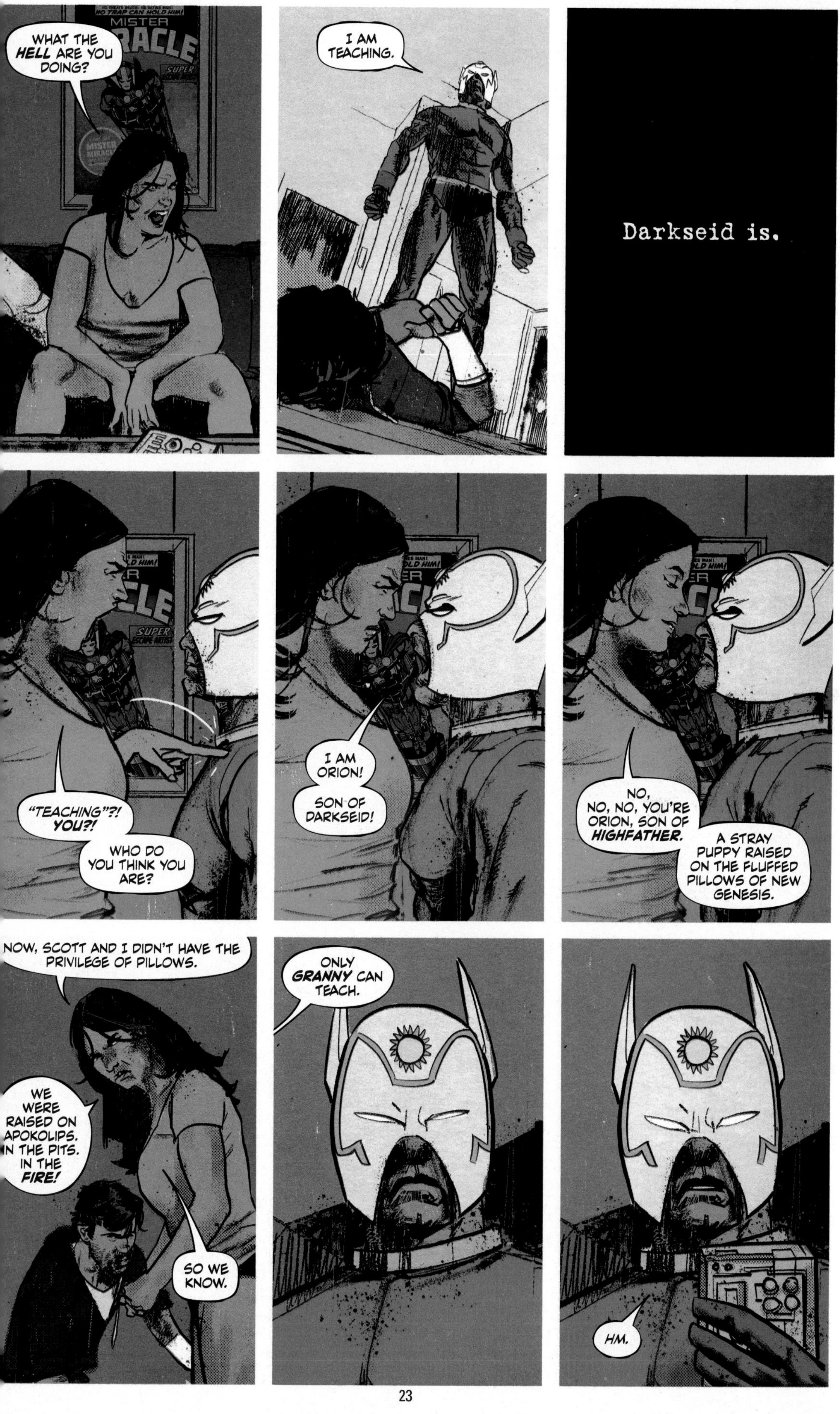
HE CHEATS DEATH! HE DEFIES MAN! NO TRAP CAN HOLD HIM!
MISTER MIRACLE
SUPER ESCAPE ARTIST
WHAT THE HELL ARE YOU DOING?
I AM TEACHING.
Darkseid is.
"TEACHING"?! YOU?!
WHO DO YOU THINK YOU ARE?
I AM ORION!
SON OF DARKSEID!
NO, NO, NO, YOU'RE ORION, SON OF HIGHFATHER.
A STRAY PUPPY RAISED ON THE FLUFFED PILLOWS OF NEW GENESIS.
NOW, SCOTT AND I DIDN'T HAVE THE PRIVILEGE OF PILLOWS.
WE WERE RAISED ON APOKOLIPS. IN THE PITS. IN THE FIRE!
SO WE KNOW.
ONLY GRANNY CAN TEACH.
HM.

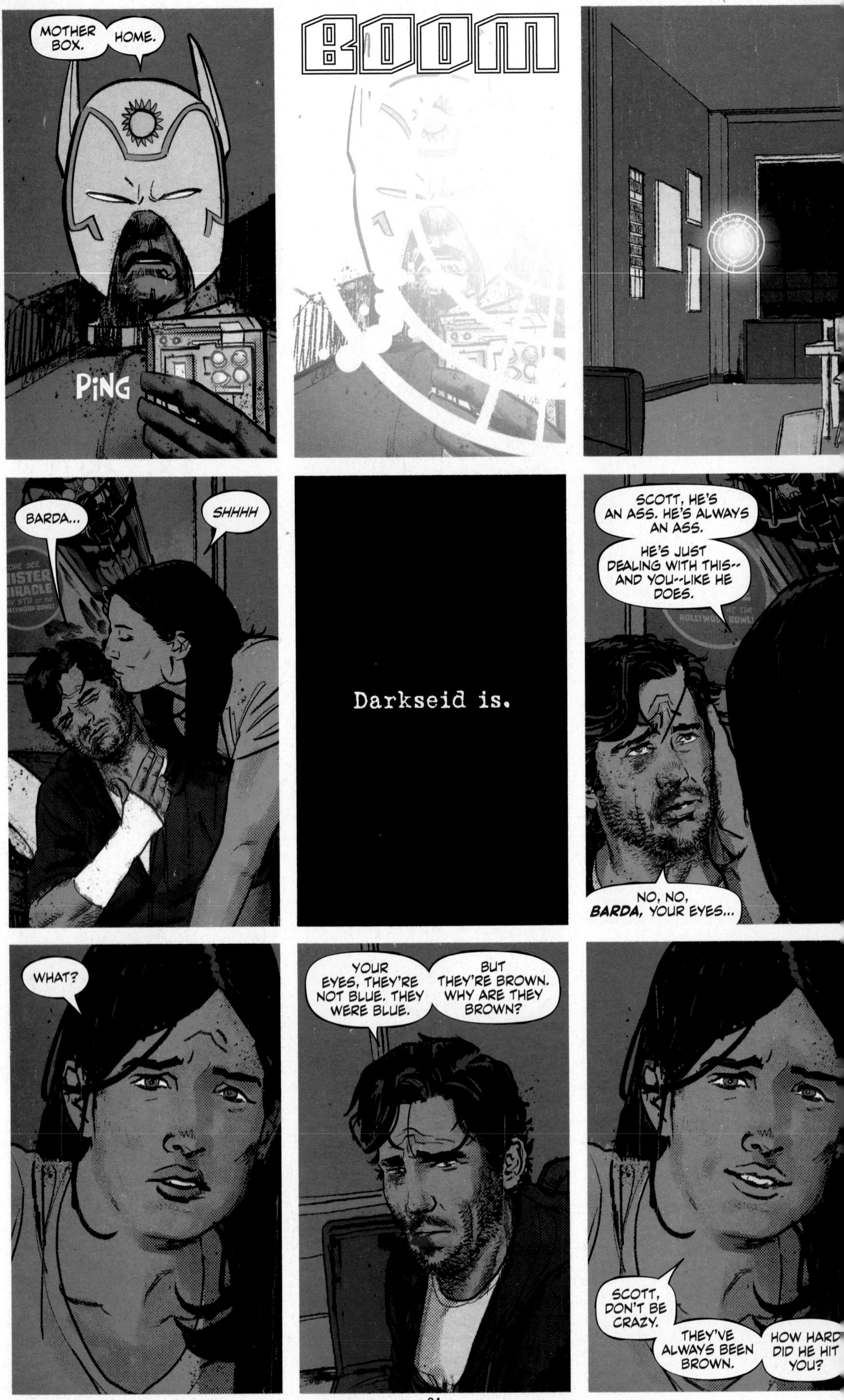
MOTHER BOX.
HOME.
PiNG
BOOM
BARDA...
SHHHH
COME SEE MISTER MIRACLE
Darkseid is.
SCOTT, HE'S AN ASS. HE'S ALWAYS AN ASS.
HE'S JUST DEALING WITH THIS--AND YOU--LIKE HE DOES.
NO, NO, BARDA, YOUR EYES...
WHAT?
YOUR EYES, THEY'RE NOT BLUE. THEY WERE BLUE.
BUT THEY'RE BROWN. WHY ARE THEY BROWN?
SCOTT, DON'T BE CRAZY.
THEY'VE ALWAYS BEEN BROWN.
HOW HARD DID HE HIT YOU?

Darkseid is.

OH MY GOD.

OH.

MY.

GOD.

JESUS.

OHMYGODOHMYGODOHMYGOD!

HOLY CHRIST.

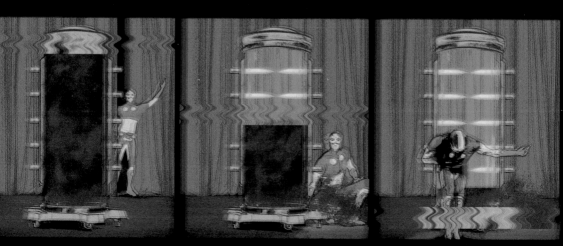

GOD DAMN!

GOD!

DAMN!

Clap Clap
Clap Clap Clap
Clap Clap

ONE MORE TIME,
EVERYONE!

MISTER MIRACLE!

NOW, NOW, MISTER MIRACLE. BEFORE WE GET
TO *EVERYTHING*, AND I MEAN EVERYTHING...

...WE ARE ALL, I THINK, ALL
WONDERING THE SAME THING.
THE SAME THING I'M WONDERING.

SOMETHING WE SHOULD...
PROBABLY...ADDRESS.

OF
COURSE.

ABOUT A MONTH BACK, IT WAS
REPORTED, WIDELY REPORTED,
THAT YOU--

--YOU TRIED TO...I *DON'T* KNOW THE RIGHT
WORDS...BUT *YOU* KNOW WHAT I'M SAYING.

YOU TRIED SOMETHING...
NEW.

YEAH, SOMETHING...
UHM...

...PRETTY
NEW.

Hahahaha

WELL, NOW WE'RE
HERE, WE'RE *ALL* HERE.

MAYBE, MISTER MIRACLE,
YOU'D LIKE TO TAKE A MOMENT
FOR YOUR FANS AND EXPLAIN.

OR IF YOU DON'T WANT TO...
WHATEVER YOU WANT.

Darkseid is.

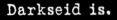

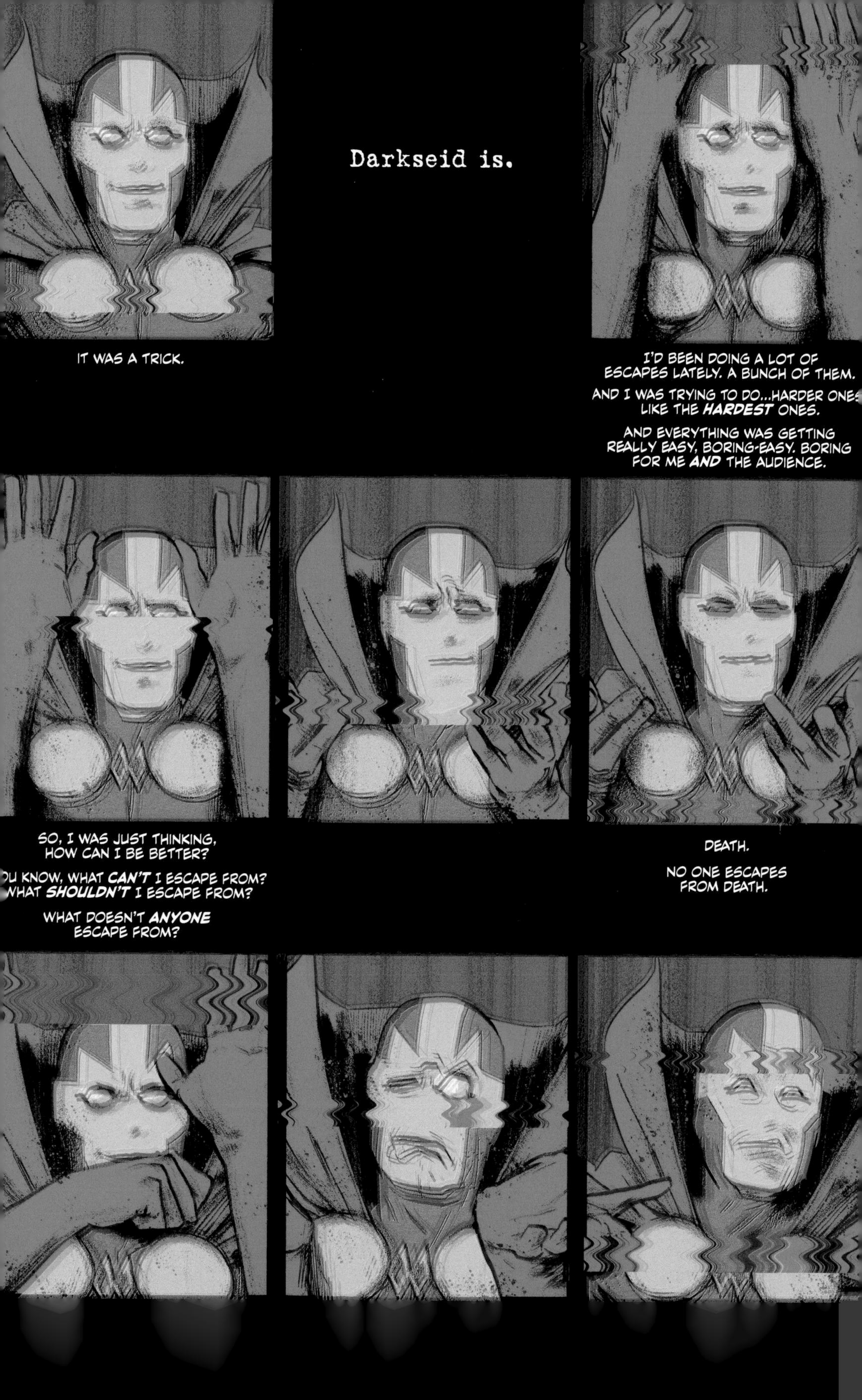
Darkseid is.
IT WAS A TRICK.
I'D BEEN DOING A LOT OF ESCAPES LATELY. A BUNCH OF THEM.
AND I WAS TRYING TO DO...HARDER ONE LIKE THE **HARDEST** ONES.
AND EVERYTHING WAS GETTING REALLY EASY, BORING-EASY. BORING FOR ME **AND** THE AUDIENCE.
SO, I WAS JUST THINKING, HOW CAN I BE BETTER?
U KNOW, WHAT **CAN'T** I ESCAPE FROM?
WHAT **SHOULDN'T** I ESCAPE FROM?
WHAT DOESN'T **ANYONE** ESCAPE FROM?
DEATH.
NO ONE ESCAPES FROM DEATH.

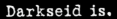
Darkseid is.

WHEN I WOKE UP, MY LOVELY WIFE, BARDA, WAS THERE. IN THE HOSPITAL.

SHE FOUND ME IN OUR APARTMENT, I GUESS, AND SHE TOOK ME TO THE HOSPITAL.

AND SO THAT'S...UH... THAT WAS ALL IT WAS.

GREAT. GREAT. JUST GREAT.

JUST AMAZING STUFF, REALLY.

BUUUUT...BUTBUTBUT-- I GUESS THAT DOES LEAVE **ONE** QUESTION UNANSWERED.

IT DOES, DOESN'T IT?

DID YOU ACTUALLY, REALLY **ESCAPE?**

I MEAN, DEATH, RIGHT?

DID YOU **ESCAPE** DEATH, MISTER MIRACLE?

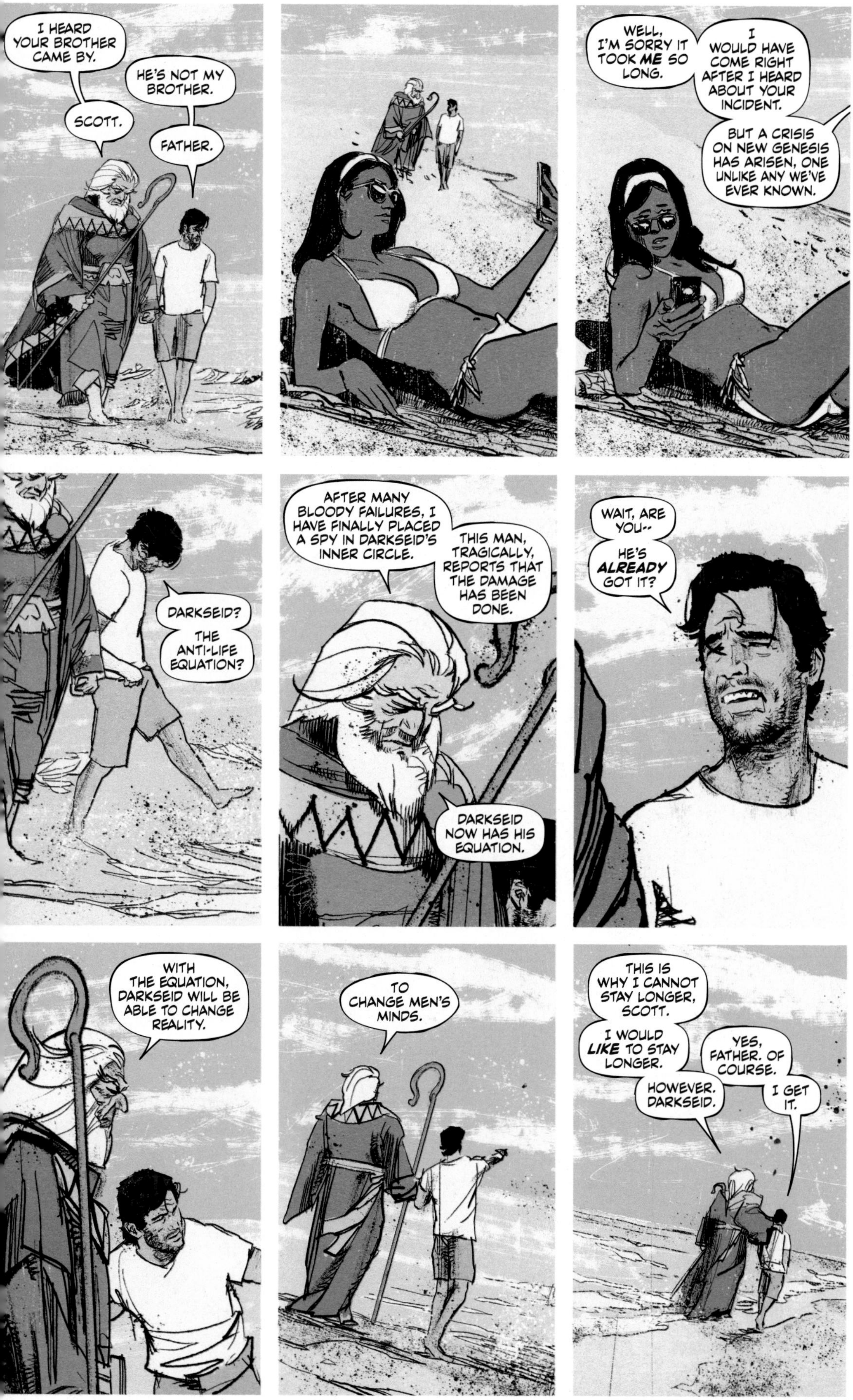
I HEARD YOUR BROTHER CAME BY.
SCOTT.
HE'S NOT MY BROTHER.
FATHER.
WELL, I'M SORRY IT TOOK ME SO LONG.
I WOULD HAVE COME RIGHT AFTER I HEARD ABOUT YOUR INCIDENT.
BUT A CRISIS ON NEW GENESIS HAS ARISEN, ONE UNLIKE ANY WE'VE EVER KNOWN.
DARKSEID?
THE ANTI-LIFE EQUATION?
AFTER MANY BLOODY FAILURES, I HAVE FINALLY PLACED A SPY IN DARKSEID'S INNER CIRCLE.
THIS MAN, TRAGICALLY, REPORTS THAT THE DAMAGE HAS BEEN DONE.
DARKSEID NOW HAS HIS EQUATION.
WAIT, ARE YOU--
HE'S ALREADY GOT IT?
WITH THE EQUATION, DARKSEID WILL BE ABLE TO CHANGE REALITY.
TO CHANGE MEN'S MINDS.
THIS IS WHY I CANNOT STAY LONGER, SCOTT.
I WOULD LIKE TO STAY LONGER.
HOWEVER. DARKSEID.
YES, FATHER. OF COURSE.
I GET IT.

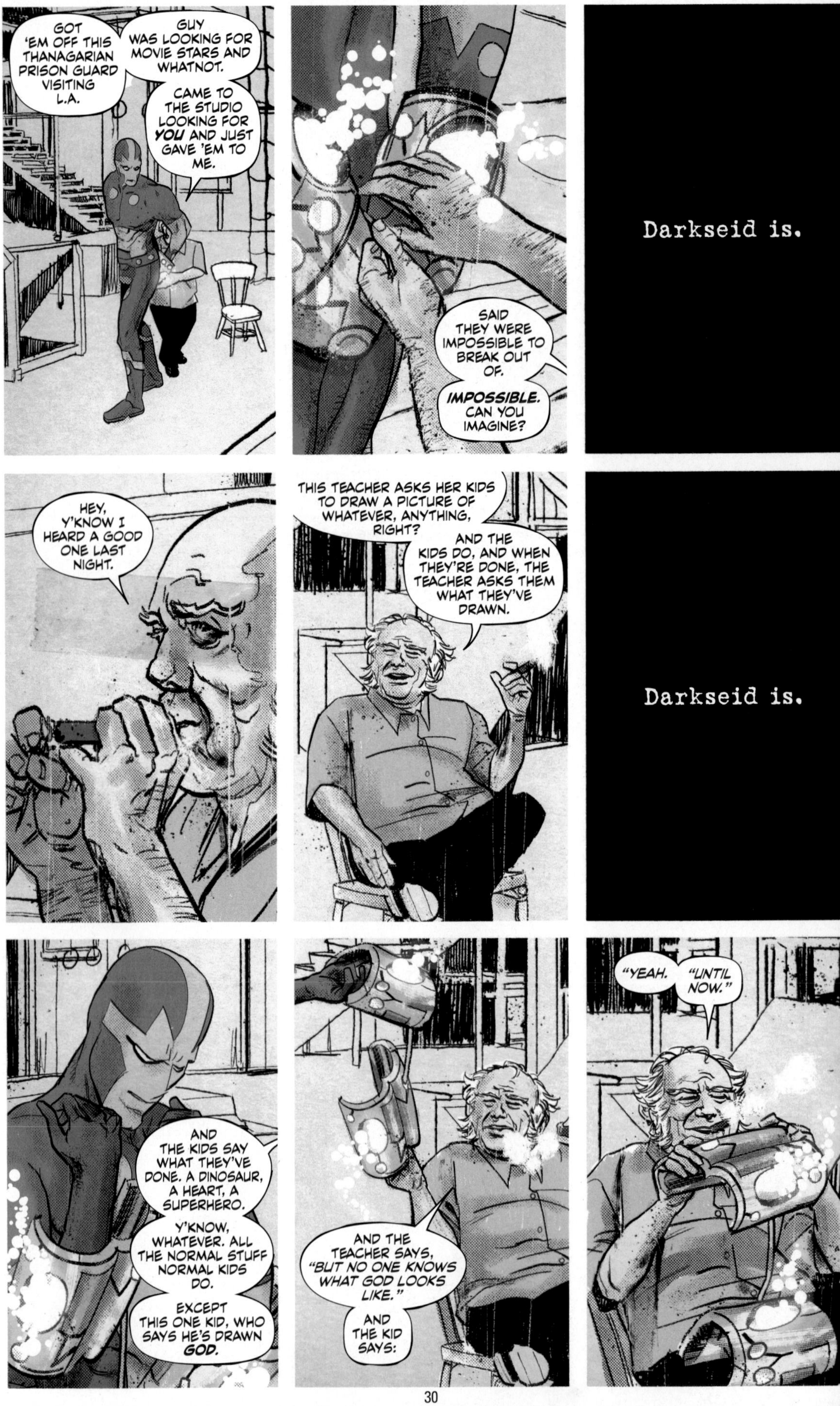
GOT 'EM OFF THIS THANAGARIAN PRISON GUARD VISITING L.A.
GUY WAS LOOKING FOR MOVIE STARS AND WHATNOT.
CAME TO THE STUDIO LOOKING FOR *YOU* AND JUST GAVE 'EM TO ME.
SAID THEY WERE IMPOSSIBLE TO BREAK OUT OF.
IMPOSSIBLE. CAN YOU IMAGINE?
Darkseid is.
HEY, Y'KNOW I HEARD A GOOD ONE LAST NIGHT.
THIS TEACHER ASKS HER KIDS TO DRAW A PICTURE OF WHATEVER, ANYTHING, RIGHT?
AND THE KIDS DO, AND WHEN THEY'RE DONE, THE TEACHER ASKS THEM WHAT THEY'VE DRAWN.
Darkseid is.
AND THE KIDS SAY WHAT THEY'VE DONE. A DINOSAUR, A HEART, A SUPERHERO.
Y'KNOW, WHATEVER. ALL THE NORMAL STUFF NORMAL KIDS DO.
EXCEPT THIS ONE KID, WHO SAYS HE'S DRAWN *GOD.*
AND THE TEACHER SAYS, *"BUT NO ONE KNOWS WHAT GOD LOOKS LIKE."*
AND THE KID SAYS:
"YEAH.
"UNTIL NOW."

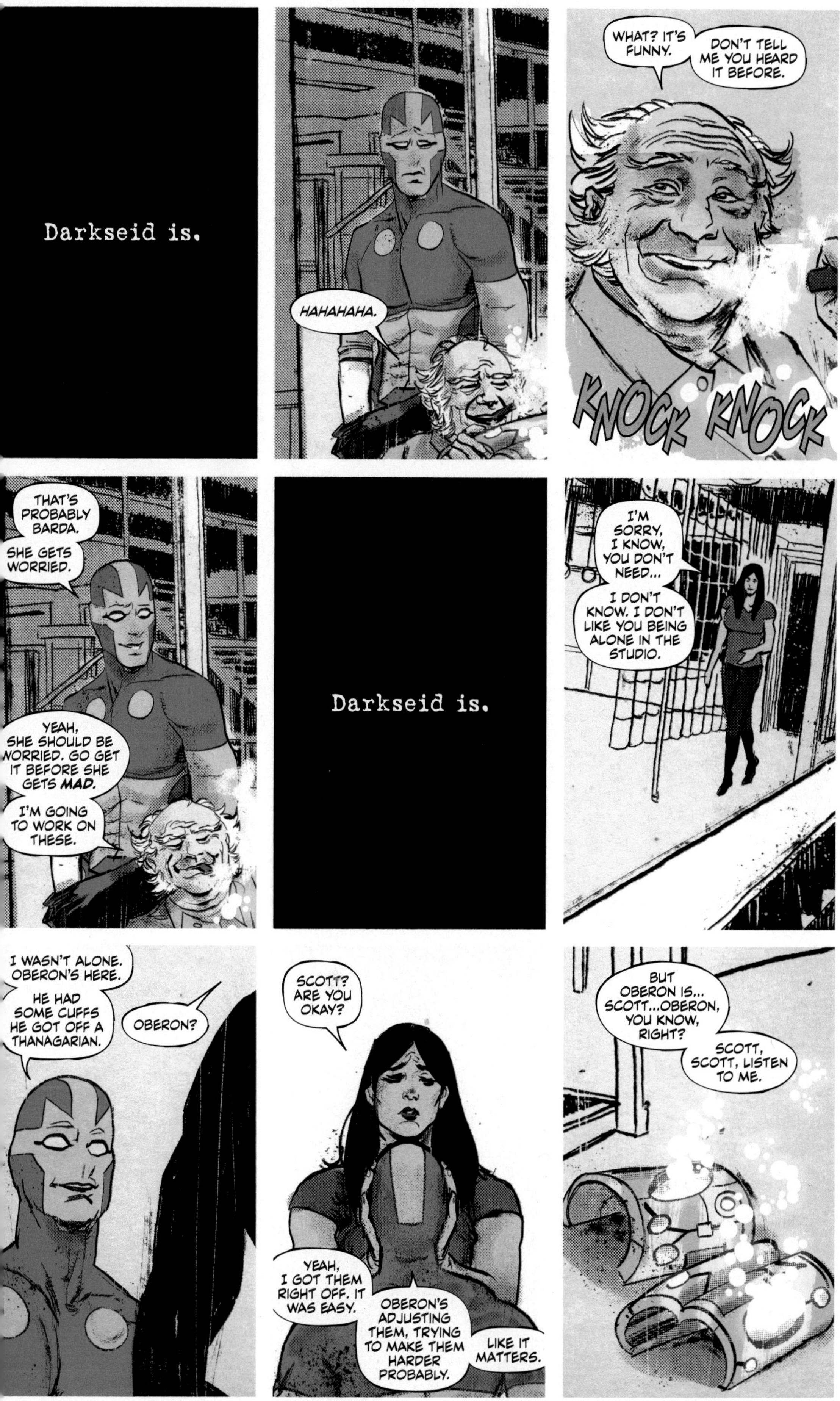
Darkseid is.
HAHAHAHA.
WHAT? IT'S FUNNY.
DON'T TELL ME YOU HEARD IT BEFORE.
KNOCK KNOCK
THAT'S PROBABLY BARDA.
SHE GETS WORRIED.
YEAH, SHE SHOULD BE WORRIED. GO GET IT BEFORE SHE GETS MAD.
I'M GOING TO WORK ON THESE.
Darkseid is.
I'M SORRY, I KNOW, YOU DON'T NEED...
I DON'T KNOW. I DON'T LIKE YOU BEING ALONE IN THE STUDIO.
I WASN'T ALONE. OBERON'S HERE.
HE HAD SOME CUFFS HE GOT OFF A THANAGARIAN.
OBERON?
SCOTT? ARE YOU OKAY?
YEAH, I GOT THEM RIGHT OFF. IT WAS EASY.
OBERON'S ADJUSTING THEM, TRYING TO MAKE THEM HARDER PROBABLY.
LIKE IT MATTERS.
BUT OBERON IS... SCOTT...OBERON, YOU KNOW, RIGHT?
SCOTT, SCOTT, LISTEN TO ME.

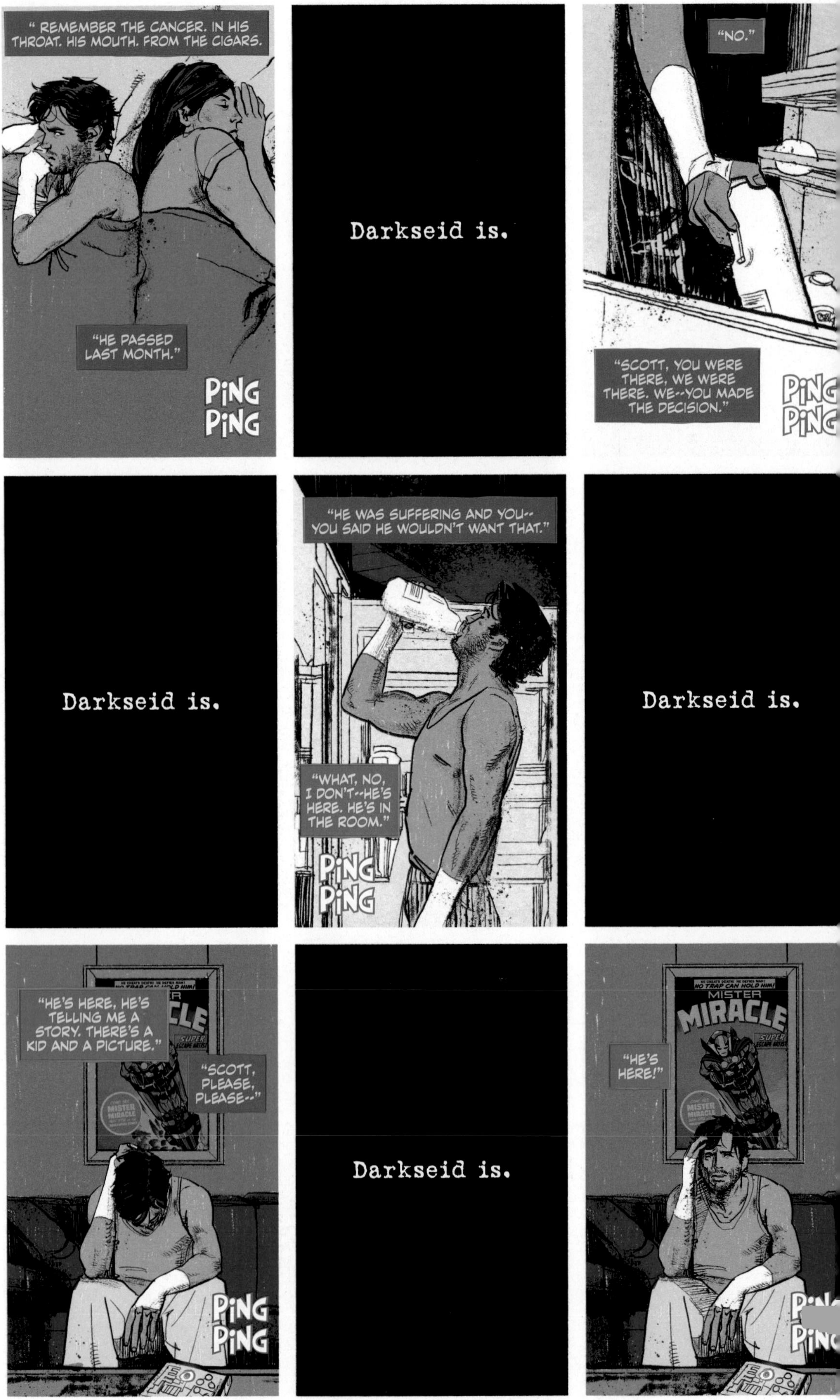
" REMEMBER THE CANCER. IN HIS THROAT. HIS MOUTH. FROM THE CIGARS.
"HE PASSED LAST MONTH."
PiNG PiNG
Darkseid is.
"NO."
"SCOTT, YOU WERE THERE, WE WERE THERE. WE--YOU MADE THE DECISION."
PiNG PiNG
Darkseid is.
"HE WAS SUFFERING AND YOU-- YOU SAID HE WOULDN'T WANT THAT."
"WHAT, NO, I DON'T--HE'S HERE. HE'S IN THE ROOM."
PiNG PiNG
Darkseid is.
"HE'S HERE, HE'S TELLING ME A STORY. THERE'S A KID AND A PICTURE."
"SCOTT, PLEASE, PLEASE--"
PiNG PiNG
Darkseid is.
NO TRAP CAN HOLD HIM!
MISTER MIRACLE
SUPER ESCAPE ARTIST
"HE'S HERE!"

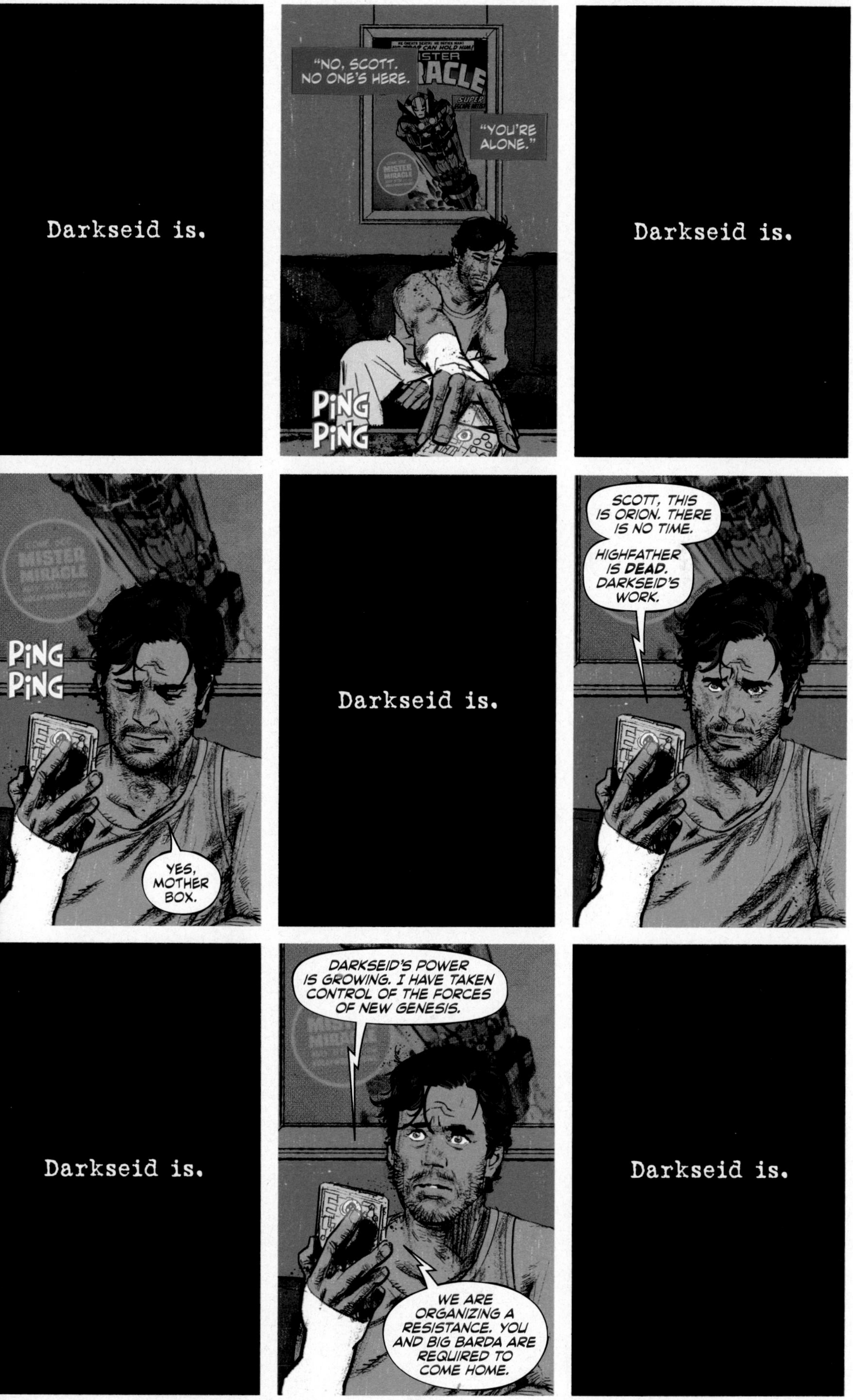
Darkseid is.
"NO, SCOTT. NO ONE'S HERE.
"YOU'RE ALONE."
PING PING
Darkseid is.
PING PING
YES, MOTHER BOX.
Darkseid is.
SCOTT, THIS IS ORION. THERE IS NO TIME.
HIGHFATHER IS DEAD. DARKSEID'S WORK.
Darkseid is.
DARKSEID'S POWER IS GROWING. I HAVE TAKEN CONTROL OF THE FORCES OF NEW GENESIS.
WE ARE ORGANIZING A RESISTANCE. YOU AND BIG BARDA ARE REQUIRED TO COME HOME.
Darkseid is.

Darkseid is.

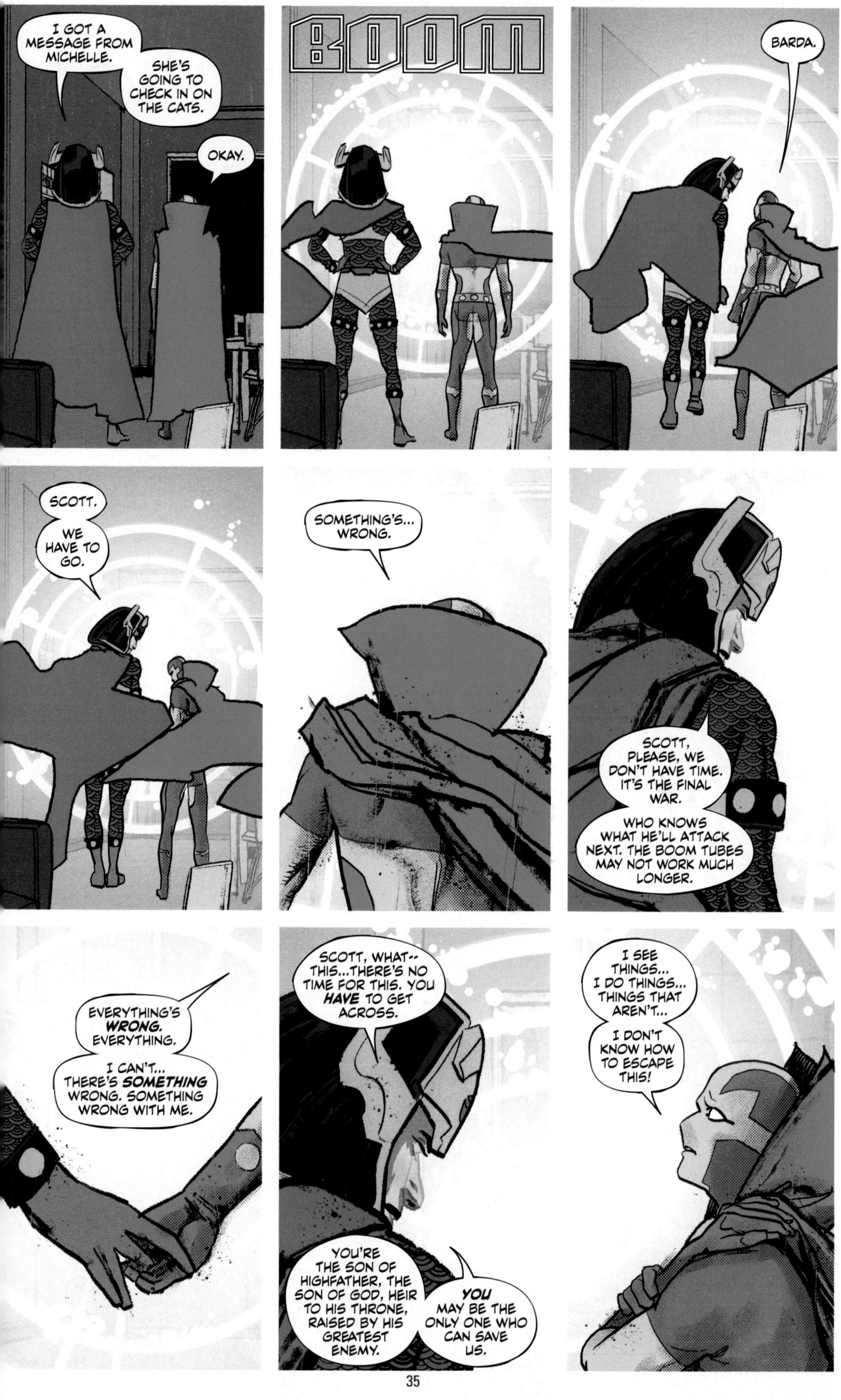
I GOT A MESSAGE FROM MICHELLE.
SHE'S GOING TO CHECK IN ON THE CATS.
OKAY.
BOOM
BARDA.
SCOTT.
WE HAVE TO GO.
SOMETHING'S... WRONG.
SCOTT, PLEASE, WE DON'T HAVE TIME. IT'S THE FINAL WAR.
WHO KNOWS WHAT HE'LL ATTACK NEXT. THE BOOM TUBES MAY NOT WORK MUCH LONGER.
EVERYTHING'S *WRONG.* EVERYTHING.
I CAN'T... THERE'S *SOMETHING* WRONG. SOMETHING WRONG WITH ME.
SCOTT, WHAT-- THIS...THERE'S NO TIME FOR THIS. YOU *HAVE* TO GET ACROSS.
YOU'RE THE SON OF HIGHFATHER, THE SON OF GOD, HEIR TO HIS THRONE, RAISED BY HIS GREATEST ENEMY.
YOU MAY BE THE ONLY ONE WHO CAN SAVE US.
I SEE THINGS... I DO THINGS... THINGS THAT AREN'T...
I DON'T KNOW HOW TO ESCAPE THIS!

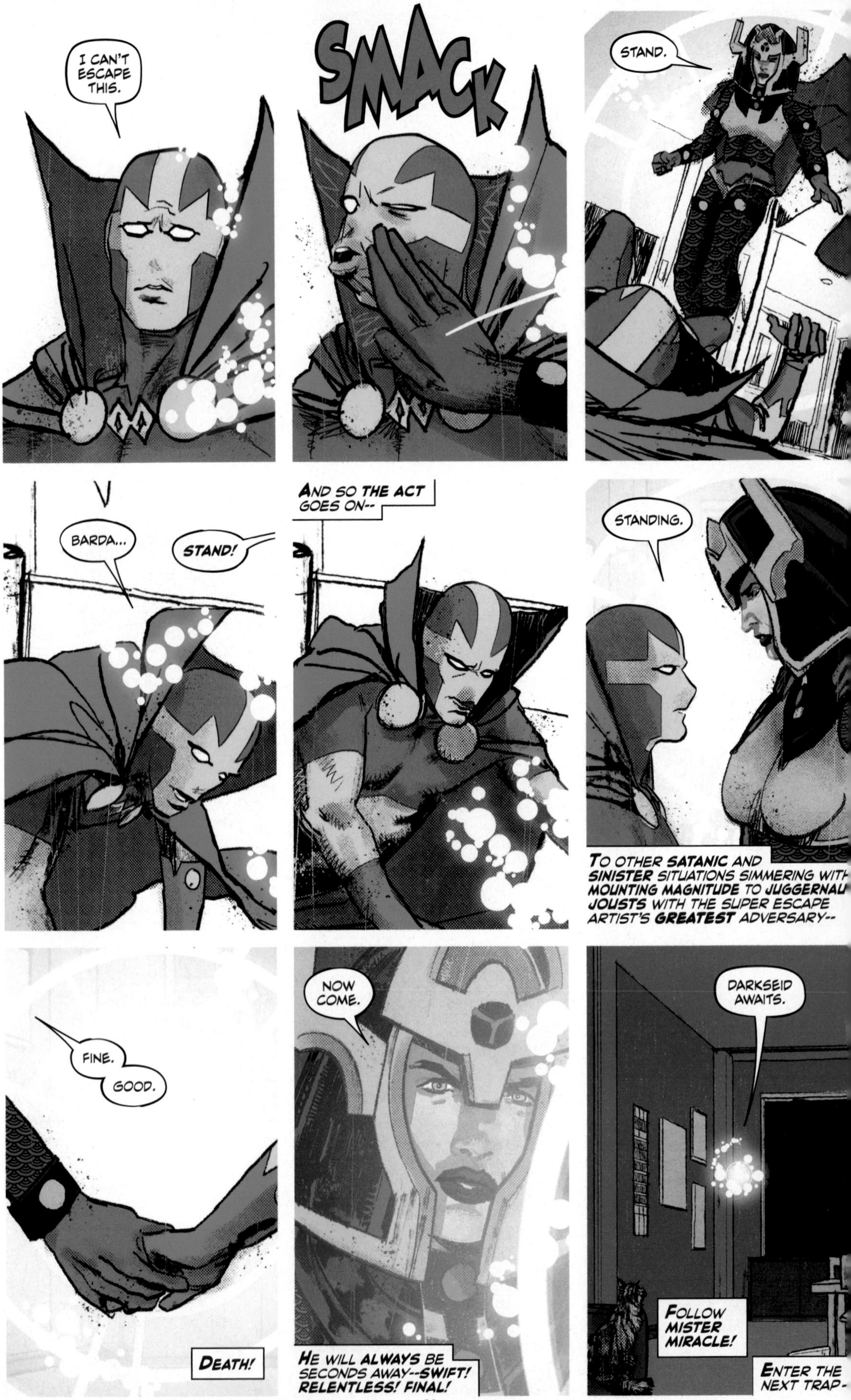
I CAN'T ESCAPE THIS.
SMACK
STAND.
BARDA...
STAND!
AND SO THE ACT GOES ON--
STANDING.
TO OTHER SATANIC AND SINISTER SITUATIONS SIMMERING WITH MOUNTING MAGNITUDE TO JUGGERNAU JOUSTS WITH THE SUPER ESCAPE ARTIST'S GREATEST ADVERSARY--
FINE.
GOOD.
DEATH!
NOW COME.
HE WILL ALWAYS BE SECONDS AWAY--SWIFT! RELENTLESS! FINAL!
DARKSEID AWAITS.
FOLLOW MISTER MIRACLE!
ENTER THE NEXT TRAP-

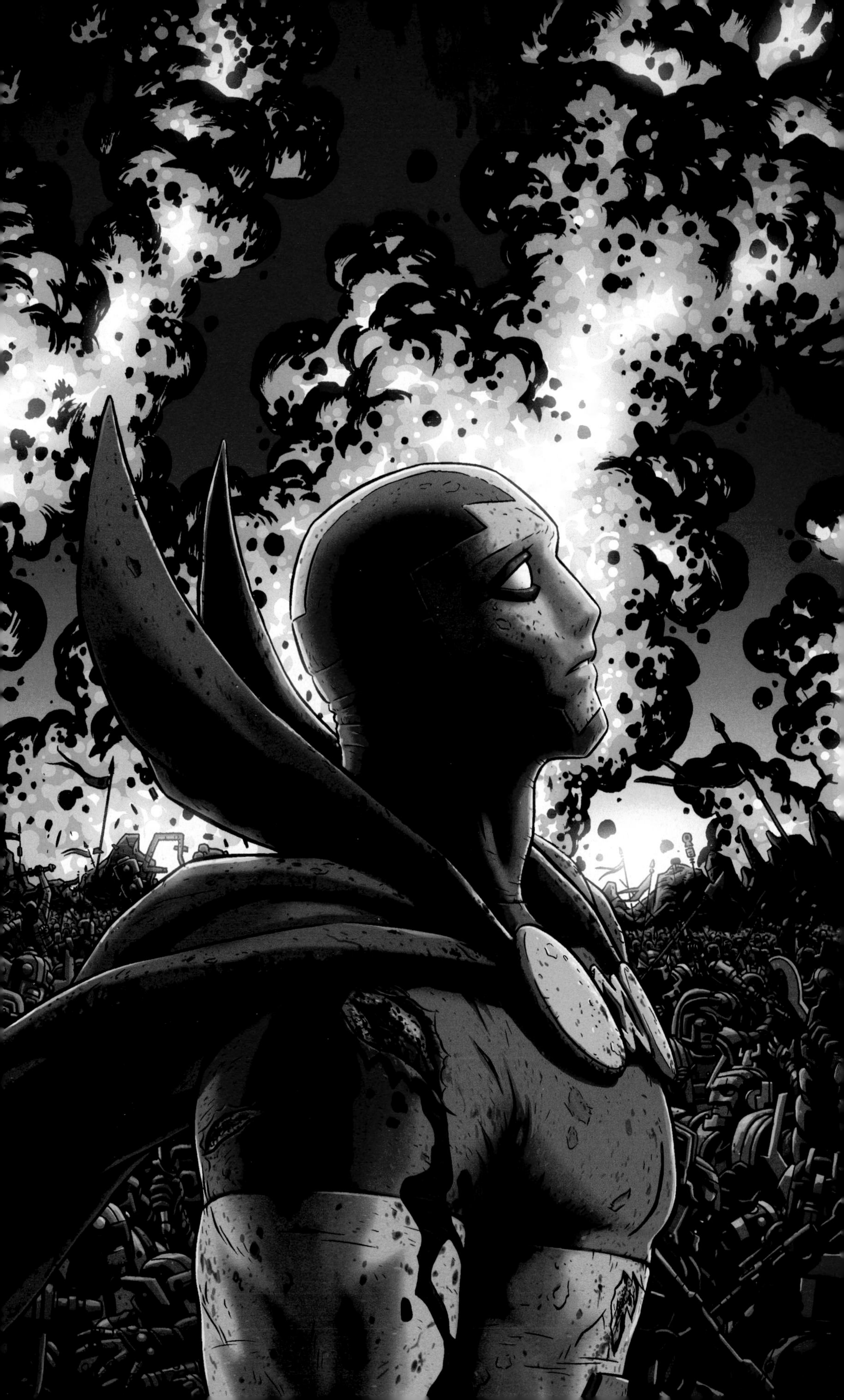

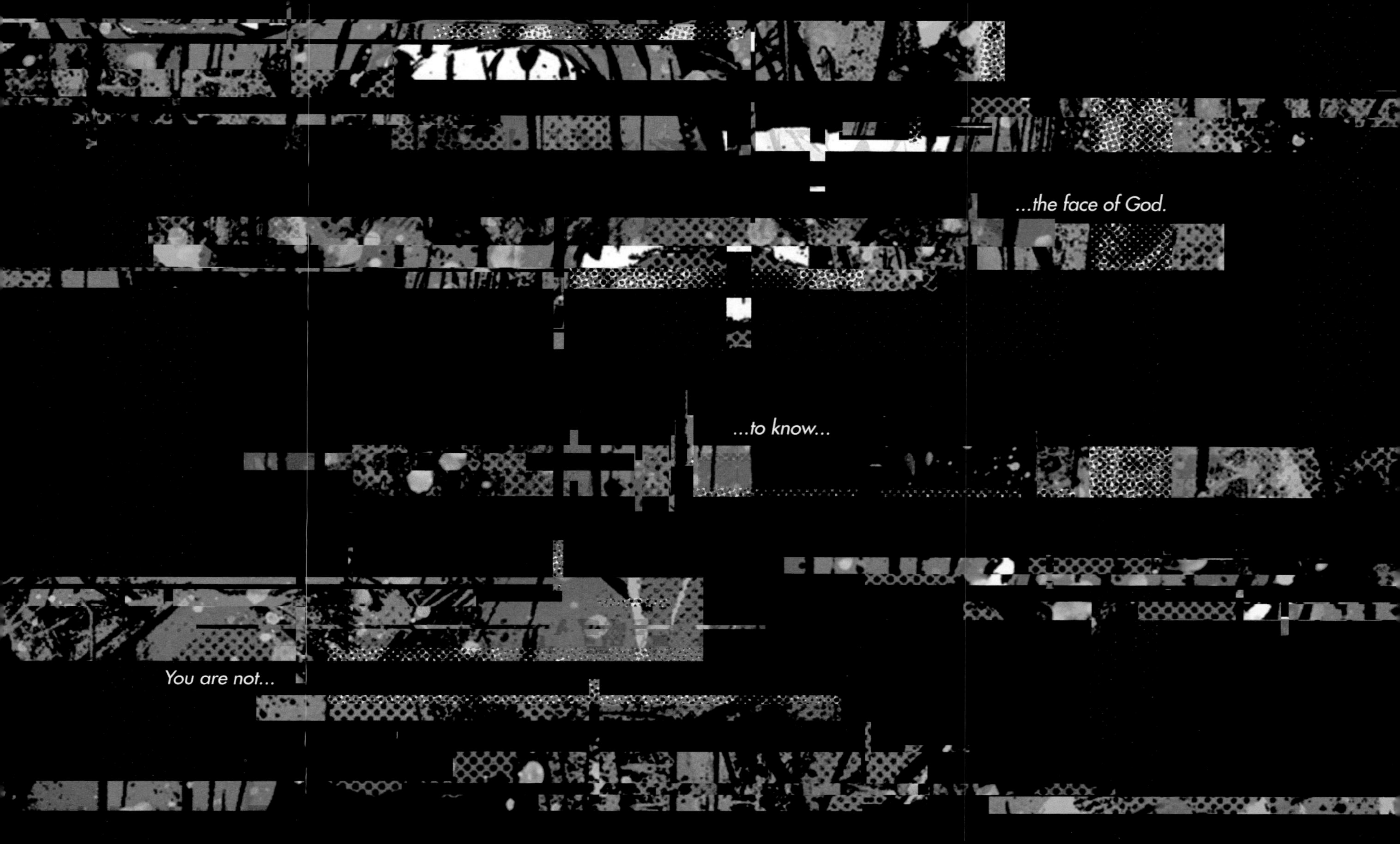
You are not...
...to know...
...the face of God.

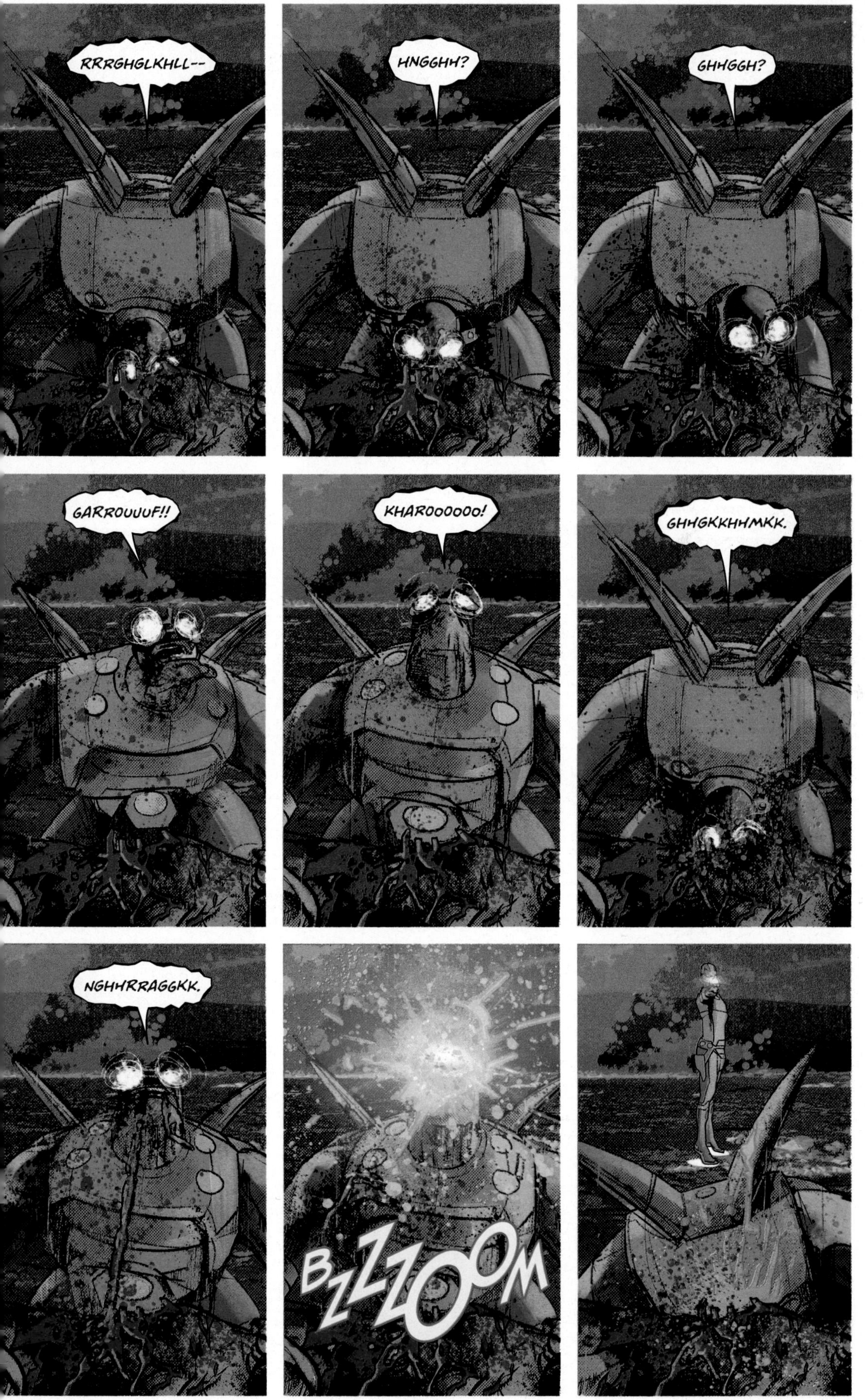
RRRGHGLKHLL--
HNGGHH?
GHHGGH?
GARROUUUF!!
KHAROOOOOO!
GHHGKKHHMKK.
NGHHRRAGGKK.
BZZZOOM

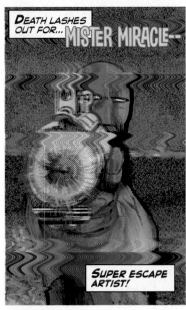

DEATH LASHES OUT FOR... MISTER MIRACLE--

SUPER ESCAPE ARTIST!

BUT IT IS NOT THE END, FRIEND!

WHAT LIES AHEAD IS EVEN MORE TO BE DREADED--

A TRAP SPRUNG BY A MIND NOT OF THIS EARTH--

THE TERRIBLE--

INESCAPABLE...

X-PIT!

ALSO--TO KNOW HER IS TO HATE HER--

GRANNY GOODNESS!

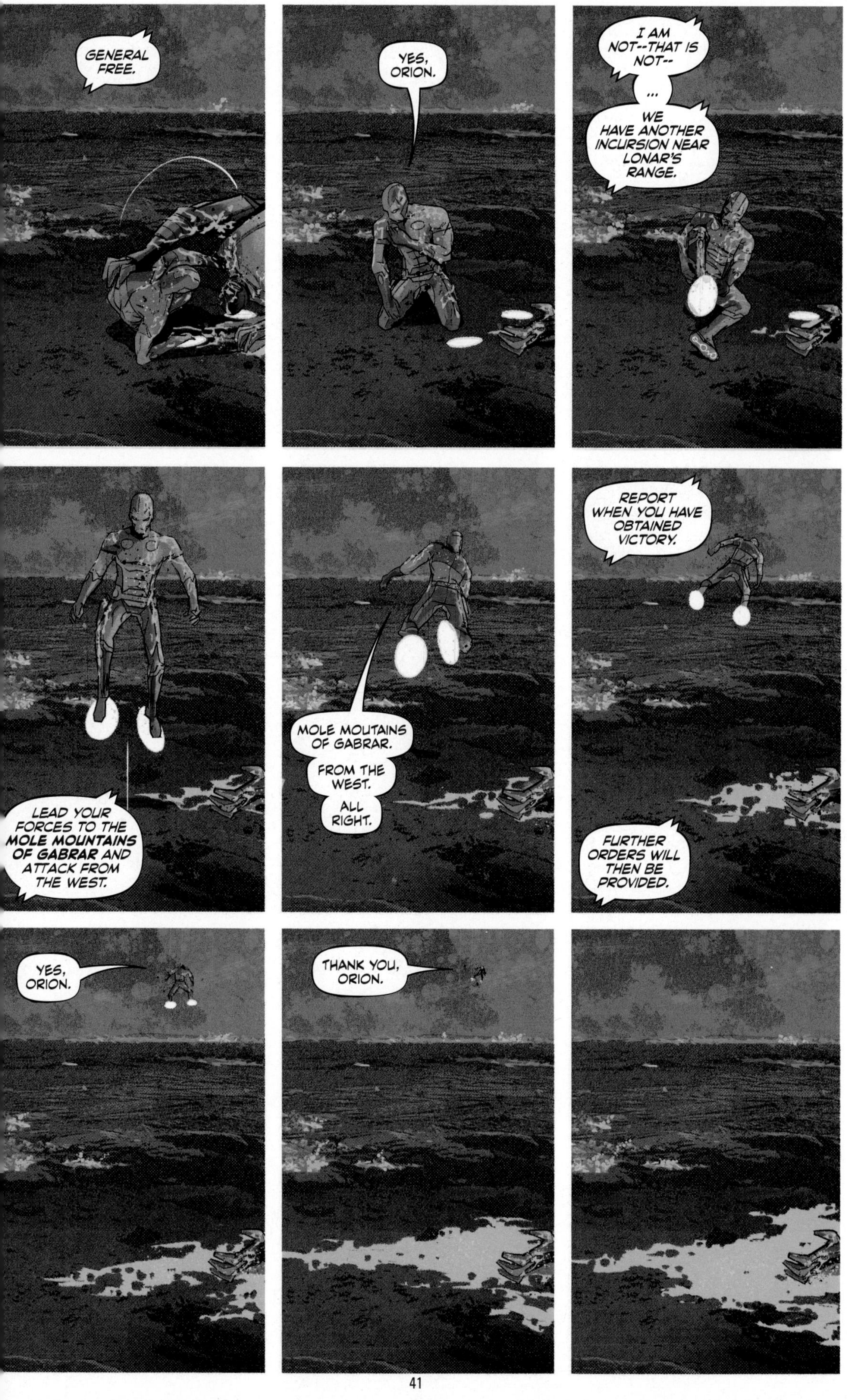
GENERAL FREE.
YES, ORION.
I AM NOT--THAT IS NOT--
...
WE HAVE ANOTHER INCURSION NEAR LONAR'S RANGE.
LEAD YOUR FORCES TO THE **MOLE MOUNTAINS OF GABRAR** AND ATTACK FROM THE WEST.
MOLE MOUTAINS OF GABRAR.
FROM THE WEST.
ALL RIGHT.
REPORT WHEN YOU HAVE OBTAINED VICTORY.
FURTHER ORDERS WILL THEN BE PROVIDED.
YES, ORION.
THANK YOU, ORION.

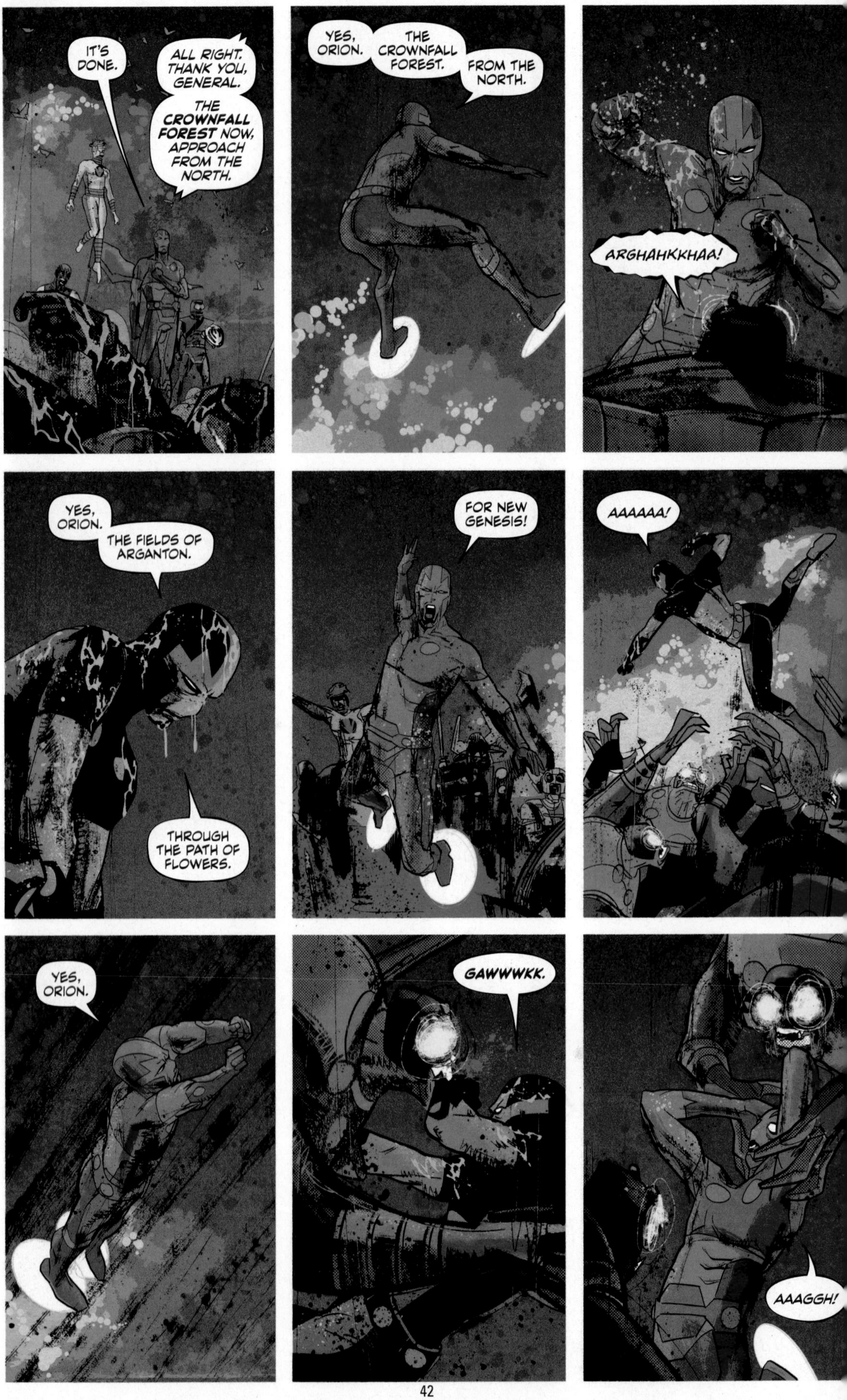
IT'S DONE.
ALL RIGHT. THANK YOU, GENERAL.
THE **CROWNFALL FOREST** NOW, APPROACH FROM THE NORTH.
YES, ORION.
THE CROWNFALL FOREST.
FROM THE NORTH.
ARGHAHKKHAA!
YES, ORION.
THE FIELDS OF ARGANTON.
THROUGH THE PATH OF FLOWERS.
FOR NEW GENESIS!
AAAAAA!
YES, ORION.
GAWWWKK.
AAAGGH!

A HUGE FORCE REPORTED AT THE MADALA SKYLINE.

I NEED YOU THERE NOW.

FOR NEW GENESIS!

FOR NEW GENESIS!

INVASION FORCES ON THE HIGH SEAS OF CUMARTRA.

APPROACH FROM THE SOUTHEAST.

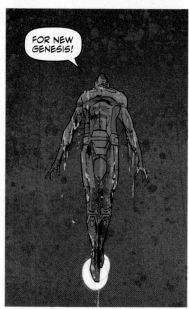

FOR NEW GENESIS!

YES, ORION.

THE FARSIDED RIDGES.

FOR NEW GENESIS!

FOR NEW GENESIS!

FOR NEW GENESIS!

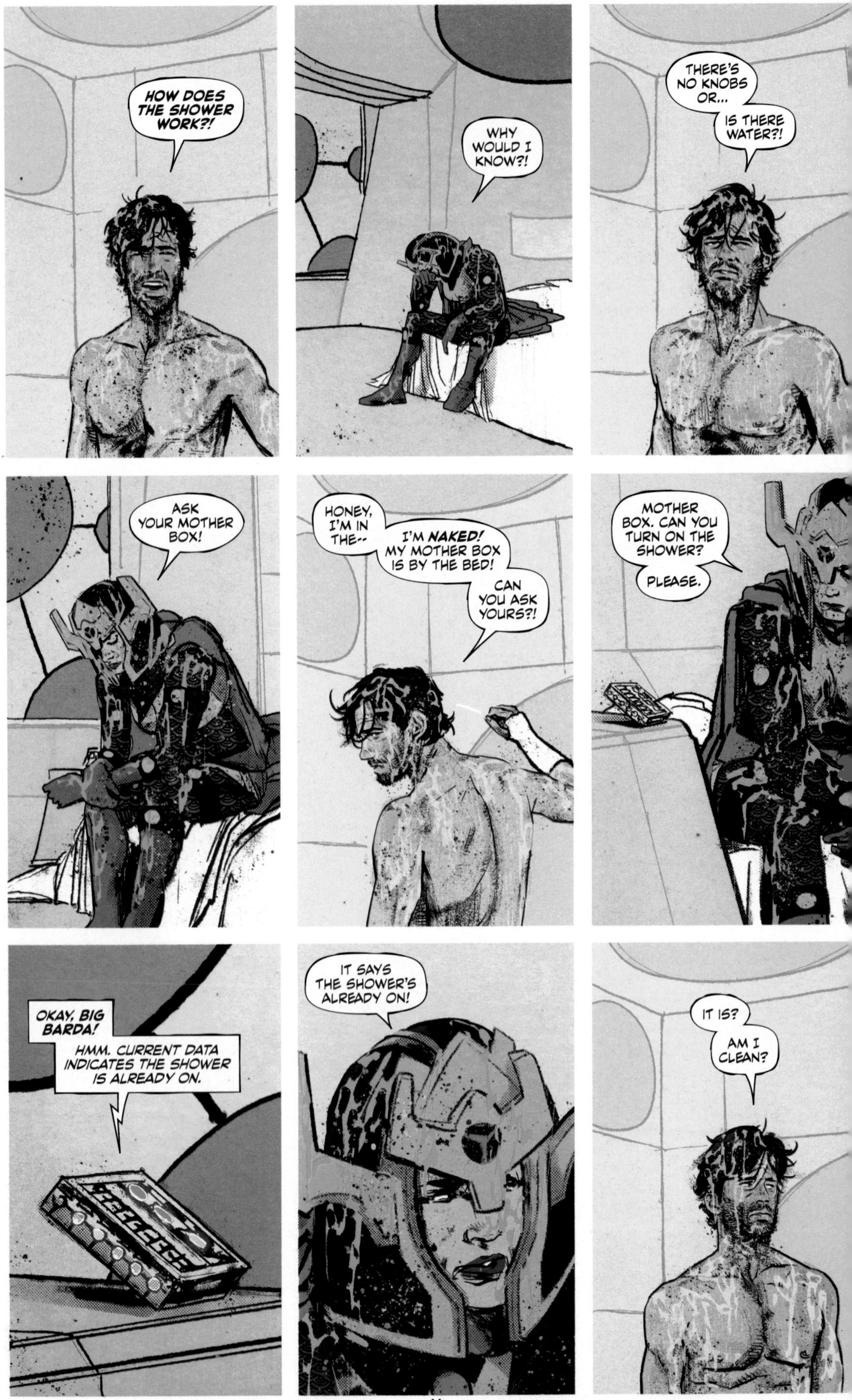

HOW DOES THE SHOWER WORK?!
WHY WOULD I KNOW?!
THERE'S NO KNOBS OR...
IS THERE WATER?!
ASK YOUR MOTHER BOX!
HONEY, I'M IN THE--
I'M NAKED! MY MOTHER BOX IS BY THE BED!
CAN YOU ASK YOURS?!
MOTHER BOX. CAN YOU TURN ON THE SHOWER?
PLEASE.
OKAY, BIG BARDA!
HMM. CURRENT DATA INDICATES THE SHOWER IS ALREADY ON.
IT SAYS THE SHOWER'S ALREADY ON!
IT IS?
AM I CLEAN?

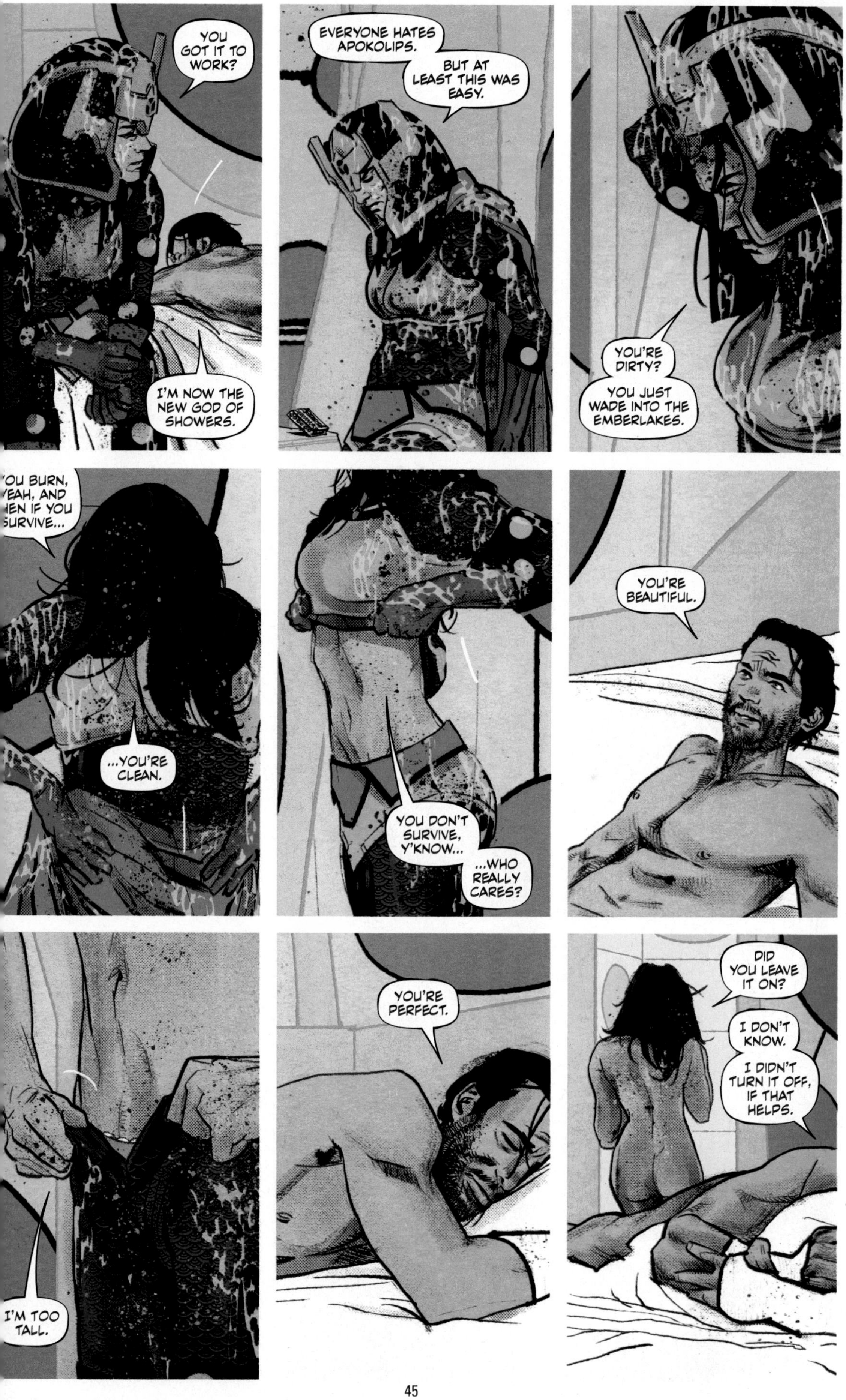
YOU GOT IT TO WORK?
I'M NOW THE NEW GOD OF SHOWERS.
EVERYONE HATES APOKOLIPS.
BUT AT LEAST THIS WAS EASY.
YOU'RE DIRTY?
YOU JUST WADE INTO THE EMBERLAKES.
OU BURN, EAH, AND HEN IF YOU SURVIVE...
...YOU'RE CLEAN.
YOU DON'T SURVIVE, Y'KNOW...
...WHO REALLY CARES?
YOU'RE BEAUTIFUL.
I'M TOO TALL.
YOU'RE PERFECT.
DID YOU LEAVE IT ON?
I DON'T KNOW.
I DIDN'T TURN IT OFF, IF THAT HELPS.

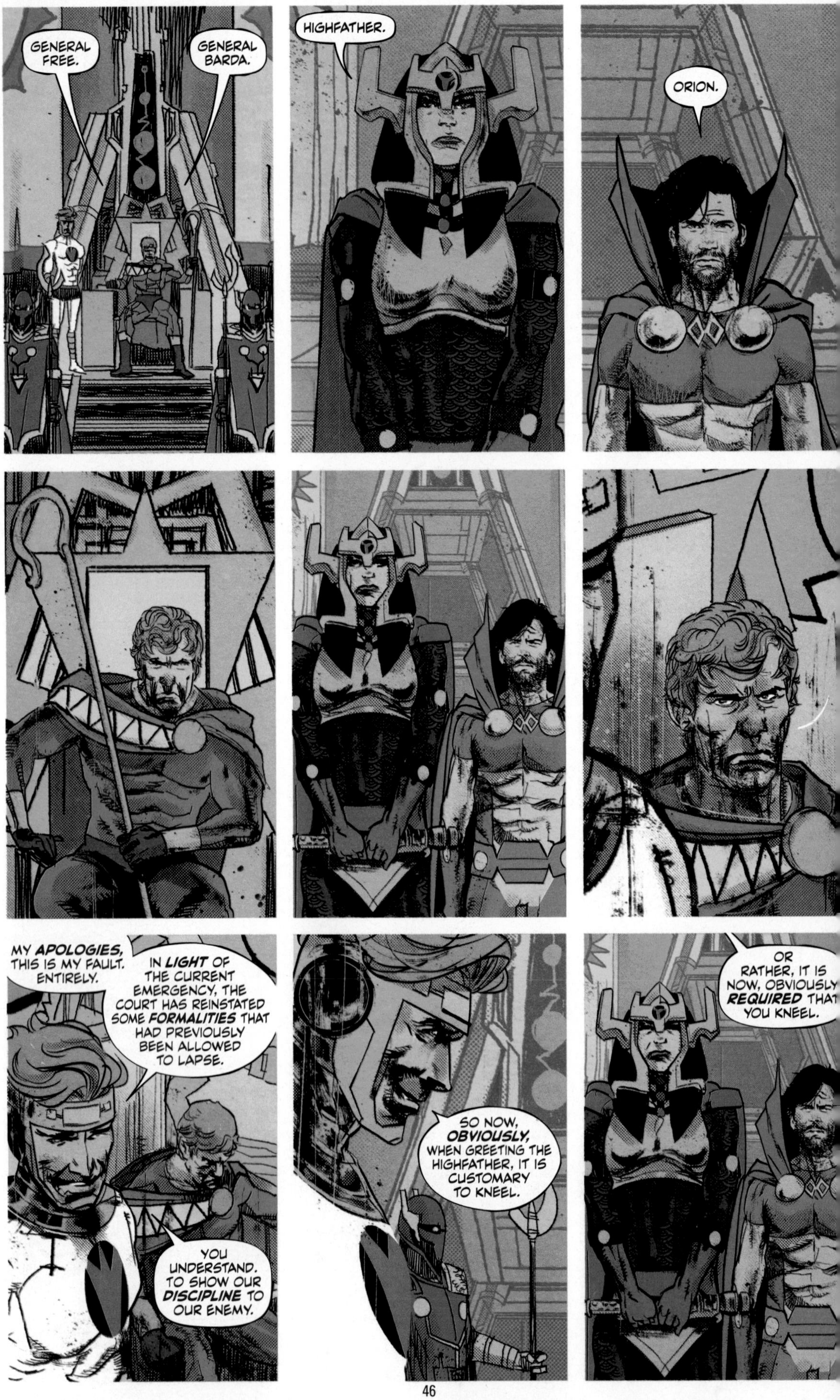
GENERAL FREE.
GENERAL BARDA.
HIGHFATHER.
ORION.
MY APOLOGIES, THIS IS MY FAULT. ENTIRELY.
IN LIGHT OF THE CURRENT EMERGENCY, THE COURT HAS REINSTATED SOME FORMALITIES THAT HAD PREVIOUSLY BEEN ALLOWED TO LAPSE.
YOU UNDERSTAND. TO SHOW OUR DISCIPLINE TO OUR ENEMY.
SO NOW, OBVIOUSLY, WHEN GREETING THE HIGHFATHER, IT IS CUSTOMARY TO KNEEL.
OR RATHER, IT IS NOW, OBVIOUSLY REQUIRED THAT YOU KNEEL.

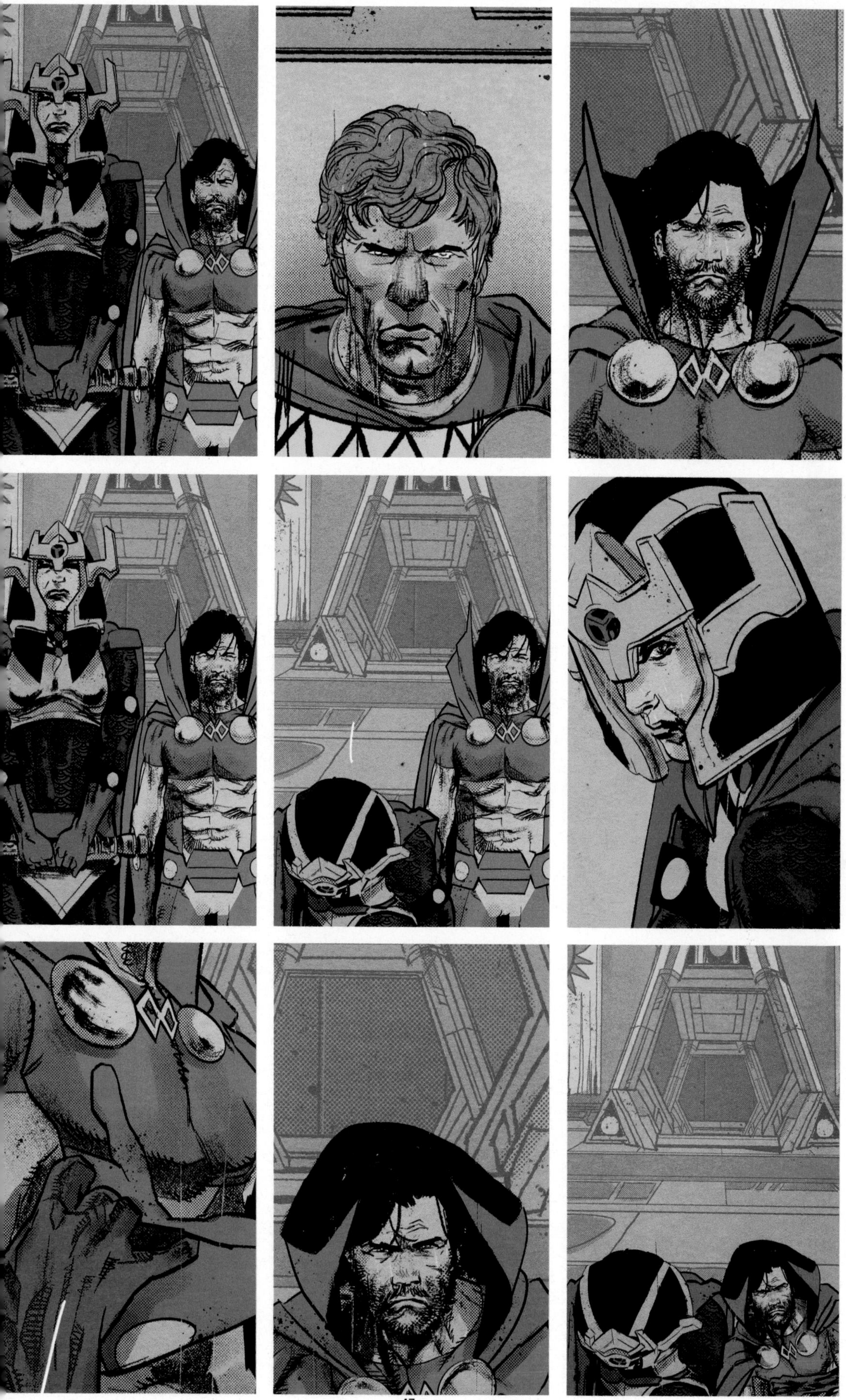

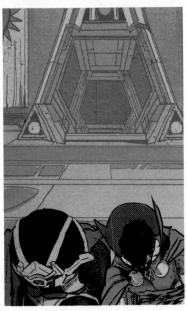

IT IS A BLESSING WORTHY OF THE OLD GODS THAT YOU TWO HAVE COME NOW TO NEW GENESIS.

THIS IS OUR TIME OF NEED, AND WE *NEED* YOU.

AS *HIGHFATHER OF NEW GENESIS*, PLEASE ACCEPT MY GRATITUDE FOR YOUR SERVICE.

YES, HIGHFATHER.

THAT'S *FINE.* YOU DID GREAT. *REALLY.*

YOU CAN STAND NOW.

OKAY.

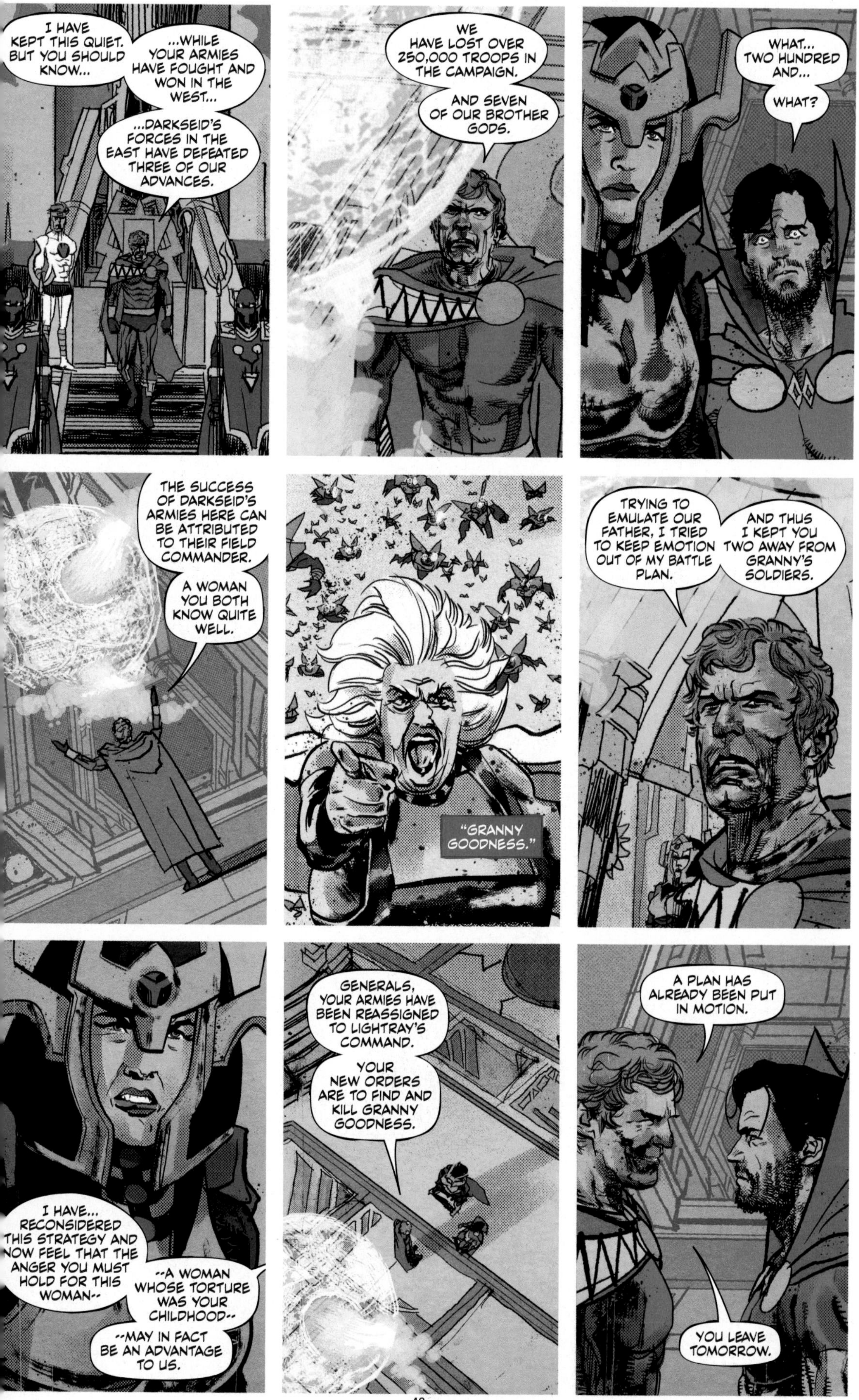
I HAVE KEPT THIS QUIET. BUT YOU SHOULD KNOW...
...WHILE YOUR ARMIES HAVE FOUGHT AND WON IN THE WEST...
...DARKSEID'S FORCES IN THE EAST HAVE DEFEATED THREE OF OUR ADVANCES.
WE HAVE LOST OVER 250,000 TROOPS IN THE CAMPAIGN.
AND SEVEN OF OUR BROTHER GODS.
WHAT... TWO HUNDRED AND...
WHAT?
THE SUCCESS OF DARKSEID'S ARMIES HERE CAN BE ATTRIBUTED TO THEIR FIELD COMMANDER.
A WOMAN YOU BOTH KNOW QUITE WELL.
"GRANNY GOODNESS."
TRYING TO EMULATE OUR FATHER, I TRIED TO KEEP EMOTION OUT OF MY BATTLE PLAN.
AND THUS I KEPT YOU TWO AWAY FROM GRANNY'S SOLDIERS.
I HAVE... RECONSIDERED THIS STRATEGY AND NOW FEEL THAT THE ANGER YOU MUST HOLD FOR THIS WOMAN--
--A WOMAN WHOSE TORTURE WAS YOUR CHILDHOOD--
--MAY IN FACT BE AN ADVANTAGE TO US.
GENERALS, YOUR ARMIES HAVE BEEN REASSIGNED TO LIGHTRAY'S COMMAND.
YOUR NEW ORDERS ARE TO FIND AND KILL GRANNY GOODNESS.
A PLAN HAS ALREADY BEEN PUT IN MOTION.
YOU LEAVE TOMORROW.

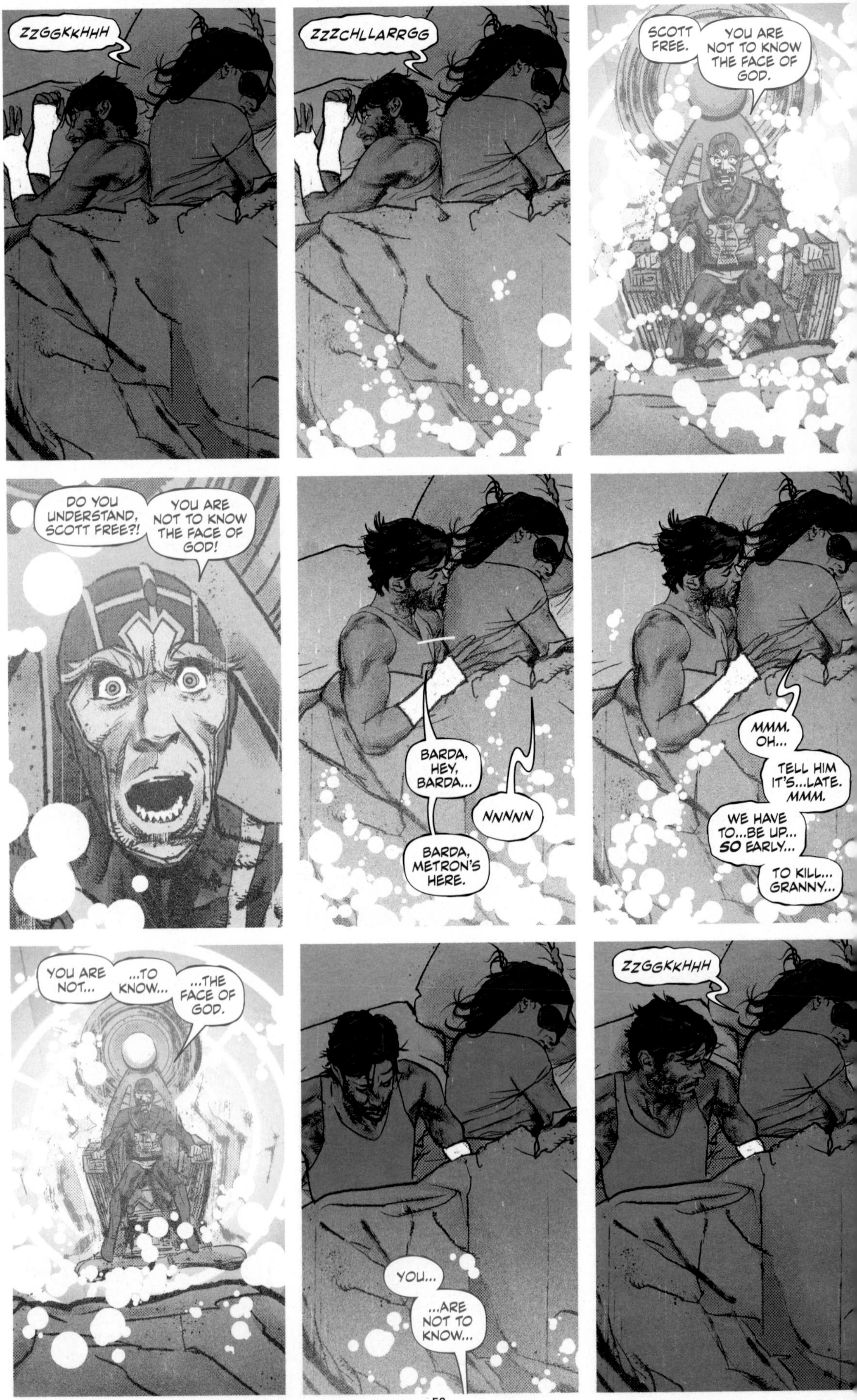
ZZGGKKHHH
ZZZCHLLARRGG
SCOTT FREE.
YOU ARE NOT TO KNOW THE FACE OF GOD.
DO YOU UNDERSTAND, SCOTT FREE?!
YOU ARE NOT TO KNOW THE FACE OF GOD!
BARDA, HEY, BARDA...
NNNNN
BARDA, METRON'S HERE.
MMM. OH...
TELL HIM IT'S...LATE. MMM.
WE HAVE TO...BE UP... SO EARLY...
TO KILL... GRANNY...
YOU ARE NOT...
...TO KNOW...
...THE FACE OF GOD.
YOU...
...ARE NOT TO KNOW...
ZZGGKKHHH

MOTHER BOX, A BOOM TUBE TO GRANNY GOODNESS, PLEASE.

OKAY, BIG BARDA! I WILL HAVE THAT FOR YOU IN .4 SECONDS!

BOOM

BARDA, ALL THOSE YEARS IN THE...I DON'T KNOW. THE HURT OF IT. I KNOW.

I MEAN, DID YOU EVER LIKE HER?

ONCE, I REMEMBER, I MEAN--IN THE X-PIT, I WAS IN THE JUDAS CRADLE.

HANGING FOR DAYS. I'D SPILLED MY MILK AT BREAKFAST OR WHATEVER--

BUT THEN SHE CAME--I WAS SUPPOSED TO BE IN LONGER. MORE DAYS.

AND SHE CAME AND SHE--SHE CAME EARLY.

SHE TOOK ME DOWN.

SHE... I WAS DOWN AND SHE...

...HELD ME. I GUESS.

SHE HELD ME. I DON'T KNOW.

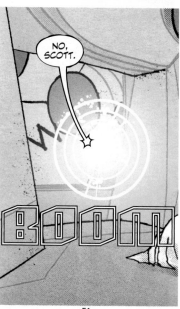

NO, SCOTT.

BOOM

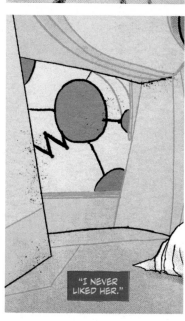

"I NEVER LIKED HER."

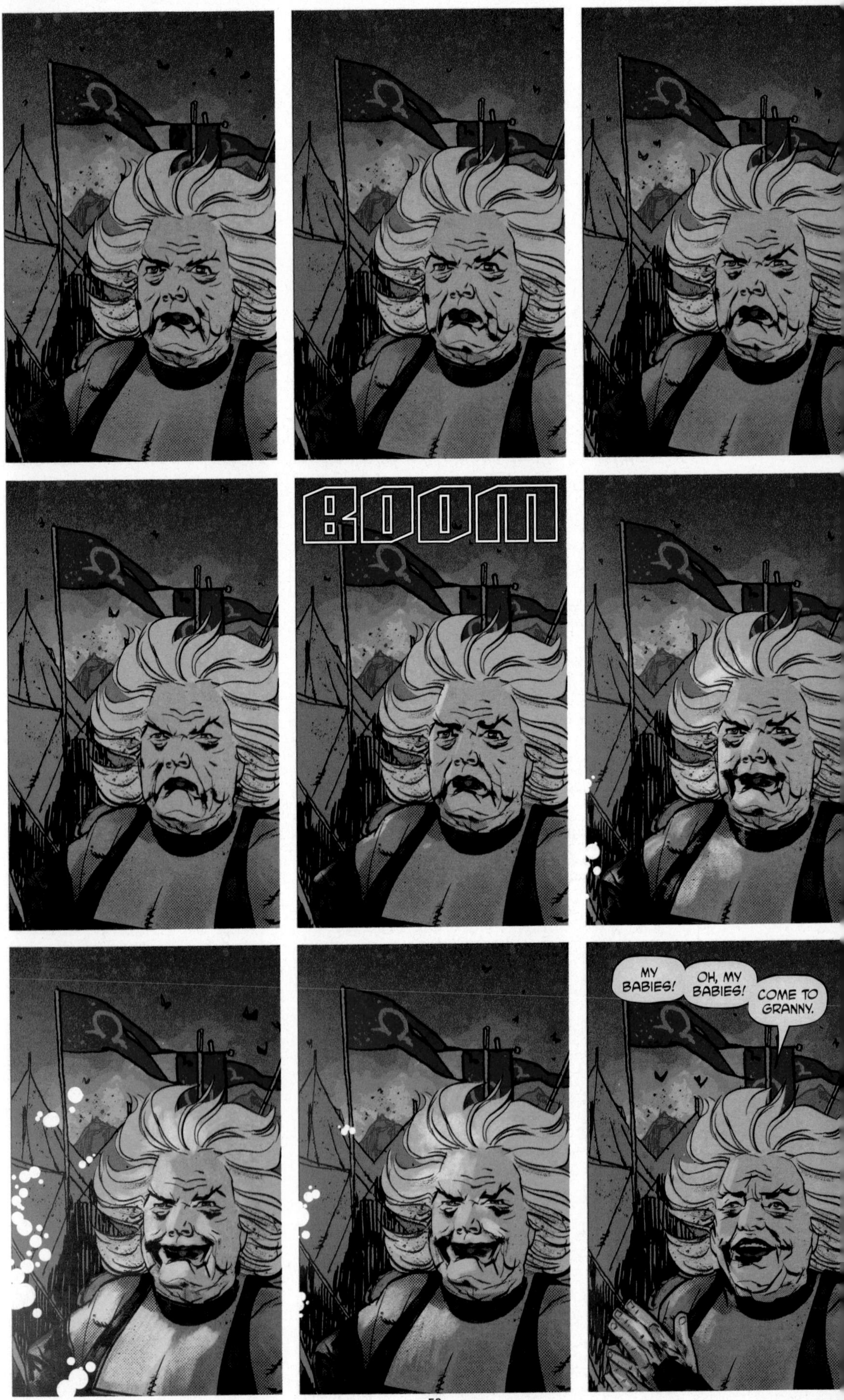
BOOM
MY BABIES!
OH, MY BABIES!
COME TO GRANNY.

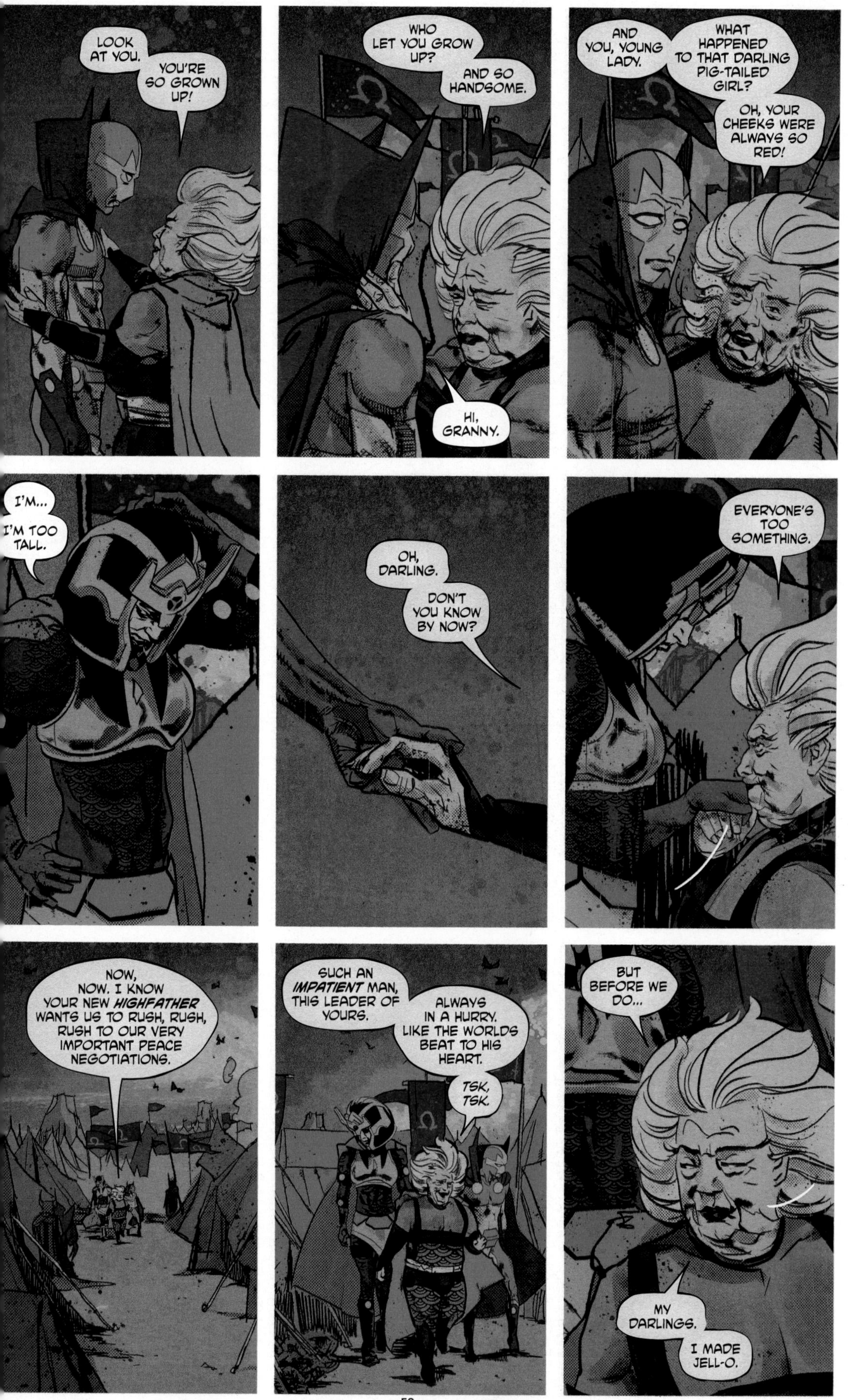
LOOK AT YOU.
YOU'RE SO GROWN UP!
WHO LET YOU GROW UP?
AND SO HANDSOME.
HI, GRANNY.
AND YOU, YOUNG LADY.
WHAT HAPPENED TO THAT DARLING PIG-TAILED GIRL?
OH, YOUR CHEEKS WERE ALWAYS SO RED!
I'M... I'M TOO TALL.
OH, DARLING.
DON'T YOU KNOW BY NOW?
EVERYONE'S TOO SOMETHING.
NOW, NOW. I KNOW YOUR NEW *HIGHFATHER* WANTS US TO RUSH, RUSH, RUSH TO OUR VERY IMPORTANT PEACE NEGOTIATIONS.
SUCH AN *IMPATIENT* MAN, THIS LEADER OF YOURS.
ALWAYS IN A HURRY. LIKE THE WORLDS BEAT TO HIS HEART.
TSK, TSK.
BUT BEFORE WE DO...
MY DARLINGS.
I MADE JELL-O.

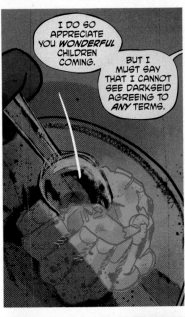

I DO SO APPRECIATE YOU *WONDERFUL* CHILDREN COMING.

BUT I MUST SAY THAT I CANNOT SEE DARKSEID AGREEING TO *ANY* TERMS.

EXCEPT, OF COURSE, UNCONDITIONAL SURRENDER.

AND THE DELIVERY OF ORION'S HEAD.

IN A BASKET. OR MAYBE A BUCKET.

WHATEVER YOU HAVE ON HAND.

NNNN

IT DOESN'T HAVE TO BE SOMETHING SPECIAL.

THAT'S... *STORMFORGE?*

HE WAS...IS THAT HIM?

YES, DEAR, HE LED ONE OF YOUR ARMIES AGAINST ME. I'M STARVING HIM TO DEATH.

BUT I LIKE TO HAVE HIM WATCH OTHERS EAT. IT'S SO SILLY.

OH MY, I HOPE THAT DOESN'T BOTHER YOU. DOES IT?

I'M NOT BOTHERED, GRANNY.

I'M JUST HUNGRY.

REMEMBER THAT TIME I DIDN'T LET YOU HAVE WATER FOR TWO WEEKS, BARDA?

GOODNESS, YOU SCREAMED AND CRIED. LIKE A CHILD. BUT YOU WERE ALREADY *FOUR!*

"GRANNY, *GRANNY, PLEASE,*" YOU WERE ADORABLE! "*PLEASE, PLEASE, PLEASE.*" HA!

HOW THE TIME GOES BY.

IT'S TRUE WHAT THEY SAY ABOUT RAISING CHILDREN.

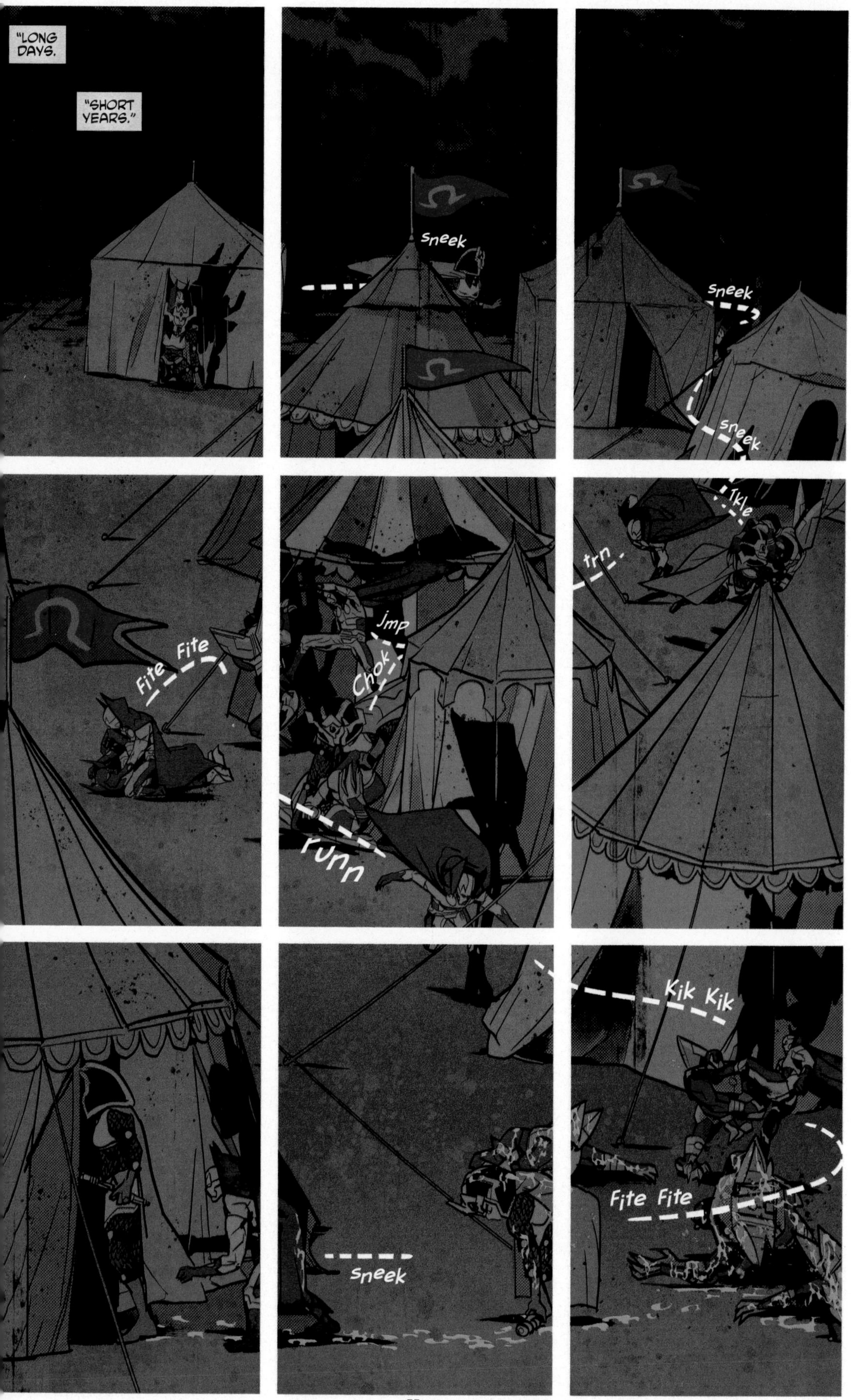
"LONG DAYS.
"SHORT YEARS."
sneek
sneek
sneek
Fite Fite
jmp
Chok
runn
trn
Tkle
sneek
Kik Kik
Fite Fite

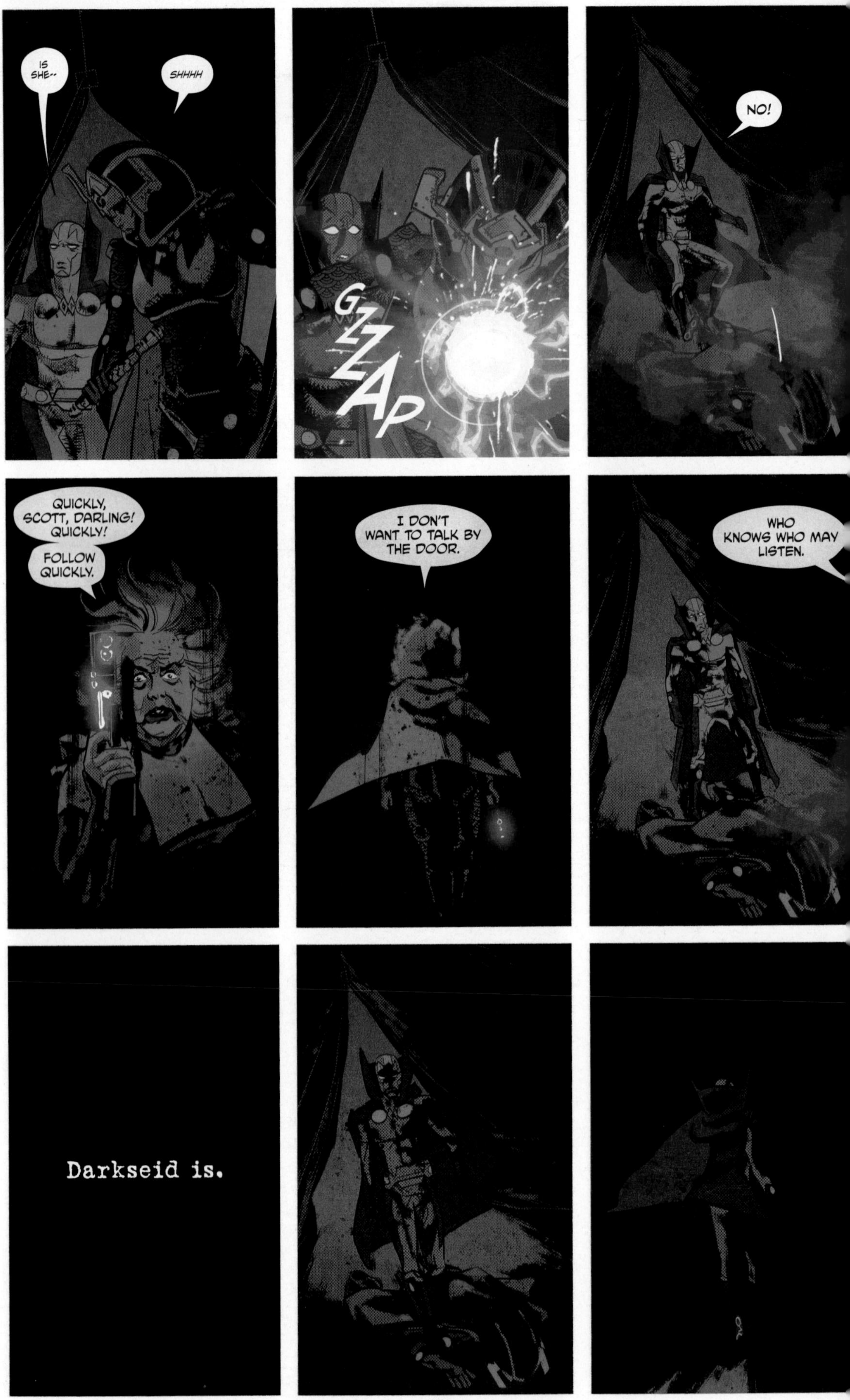
IS SHE--
SHHHH
GZZAP
NO!
QUICKLY, SCOTT, DARLING! QUICKLY!
FOLLOW QUICKLY.
I DON'T WANT TO TALK BY THE DOOR.
WHO KNOWS WHO MAY LISTEN.
Darkseid is.

I'M SO SORRY, MY POOR, DEAR LITTLE BOY.

FOR SO MUCH.

I DON'T... UNDERSTAND.

THERE'S NO TIME TO UNDERSTAND, SCOTT!

JUST LISTEN!

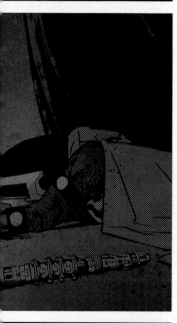

DID METRON VISIT YOU LAST NIGHT?

NO. I MEAN--

YES, BUT I THOUGHT IT WAS A DREAM.

GOOD, GOOD.

THERE'S SO MUCH YOU NEED TO KNOW.

NNN.

"ORION CONTACTED ME THIS MORNING."

I **HAD** TO WARN YOU. I CAN'T RISK WHAT MIGHT COME.

I SADLY BELIEVE SCOTT AND BARDA INTEND TO **BREAK THE PEACE** AT OUR CONFERENCE.

THEY CANNOT FORGIVE WHAT THEY PERCEIVE TO BE **YOUR**... PAST SINS.

BE ALERT, **ORION** SAID. THEY'LL DO ANYTHING, HE SAID.

AND IF THEY DID ANYTHING, HE SAID...

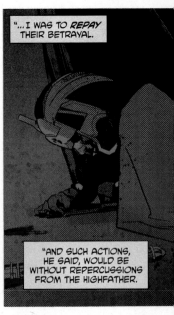

"... I WAS TO **REPAY** THEIR BETRAYAL.

"AND SUCH ACTIONS, HE SAID, WOULD BE WITHOUT REPERCUSSIONS FROM THE HIGHFATHER.

HE WANTED ME TO **KILL** YOU, SCOTT.

MY OWN SWEET BOY!

"WHAT HE DOESN'T KNOW, THOUGH...

"IS THAT I HAVE BEEN A LOYAL FRIEND TO THE HIGHFATHER, THE **REAL** HIGHFATHER.

"THE HIGHFATHER WHO MEANT FOR YOU, MY OWN CHILD, TO HAVE HIS THRONE.

"IT WAS ME!"

"**I** WAS THE ONE WHO TOLD HIM THAT DARKSEID HAS THE ANTI-LIFE EQUATION!

"I DID IT! I TRIED TO SAVE **YOU**."

ME?

YOU, SCOTT! YOU! **MY** BOY!

I COULDN'T LET DARKSEID HURT MY OWN PRECIOUS BOY.

"I DON'T KNOW--ORION NOW, I DON'T KNOW, I DON'T KNOW. HIS POWER IS SO GREAT.

"WHO IS TRUE TO US? WHO IS TRUE AT ALL?

"EVEN BARDA. DOES SHE KNOW? DOES SHE UNDERSTAND THEIR **NEED**, SCOTT?

THE **PROPHECY**, SCOTT. IT'S THE PROPHECY THAT COMPELS THEM.

DARKSEID CAN ONLY DIE BY THE HANDS OF HIS OWN SON.

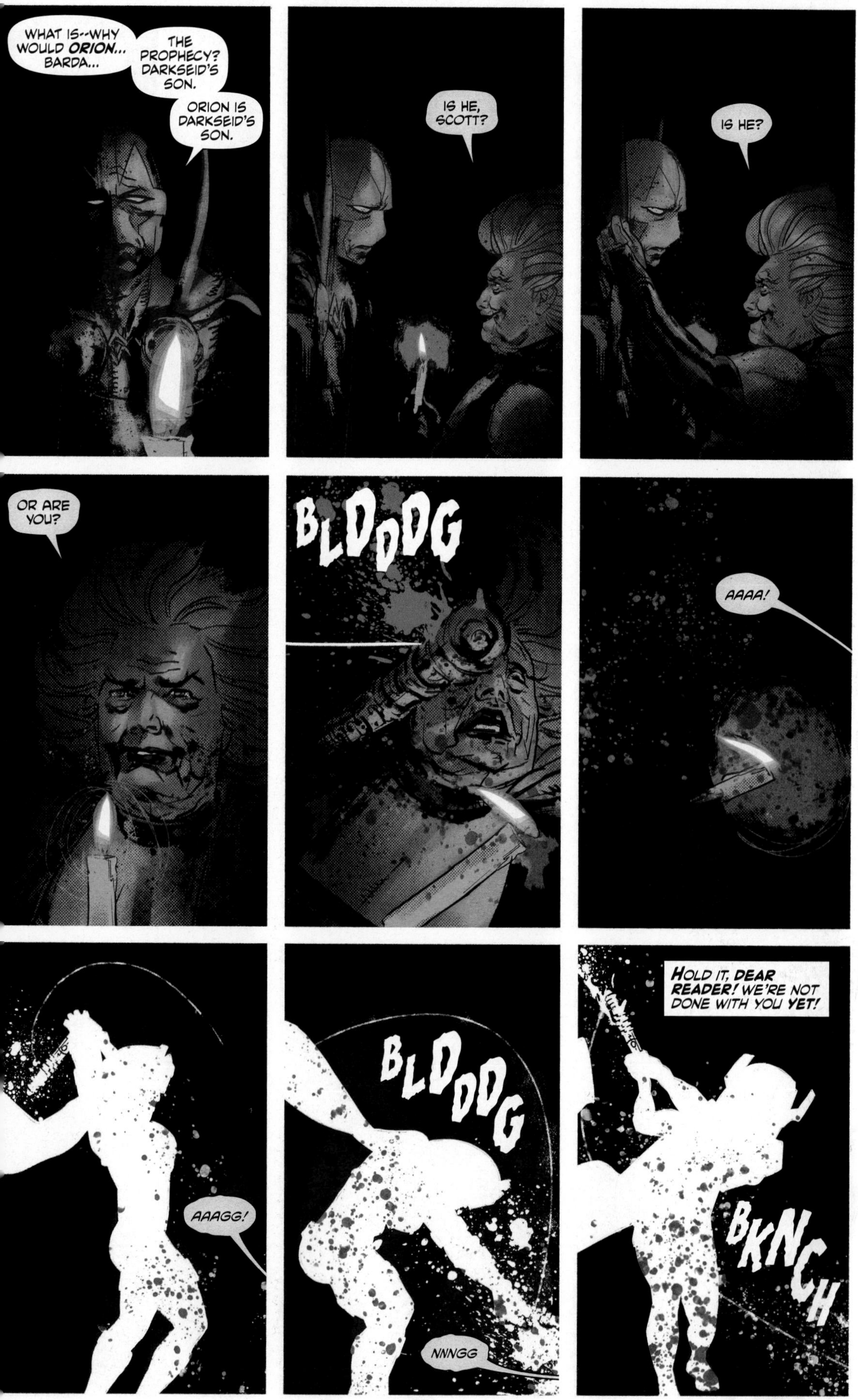
WHAT IS--WHY WOULD ORION... BARDA...
THE PROPHECY? DARKSEID'S SON.
ORION IS DARKSEID'S SON.
IS HE, SCOTT?
IS HE?
OR ARE YOU?
BLDDDG
AAAA!
AAAGG!
BLDDDG
NNNGG
HOLD IT, DEAR READER! WE'RE NOT DONE WITH YOU YET!
BKNCH

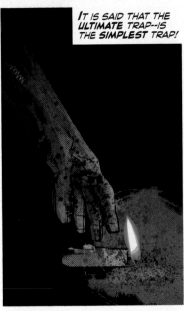

IT IS SAID THAT THE **ULTIMATE TRAP**--IS THE **SIMPLEST TRAP!**

MOTHER BOX.

WE NEED A **BOOM TUBE** TO NEW GENESIS.

AND **WHAT** COULD BE MORE **SIMPLE**--

OKAY, BIG **BARDA!**

IT WILL BE AVAILABLE IN **.4 SECONDS.**

-- THAN **ENTERING** AN LEAVING A BUILDING?

BOOM

FOR MISTER MIRACLE, THIS COULD MEAN **DEFEAT** AND **DEATH!**

YOU'LL BE **MAD** ABOUT HIS NEW EXPLOIT--

IF YOU SWALLOW

"THE **PARANOID PILL!**"

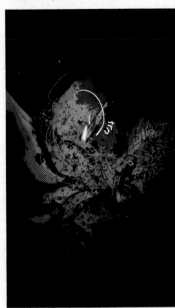

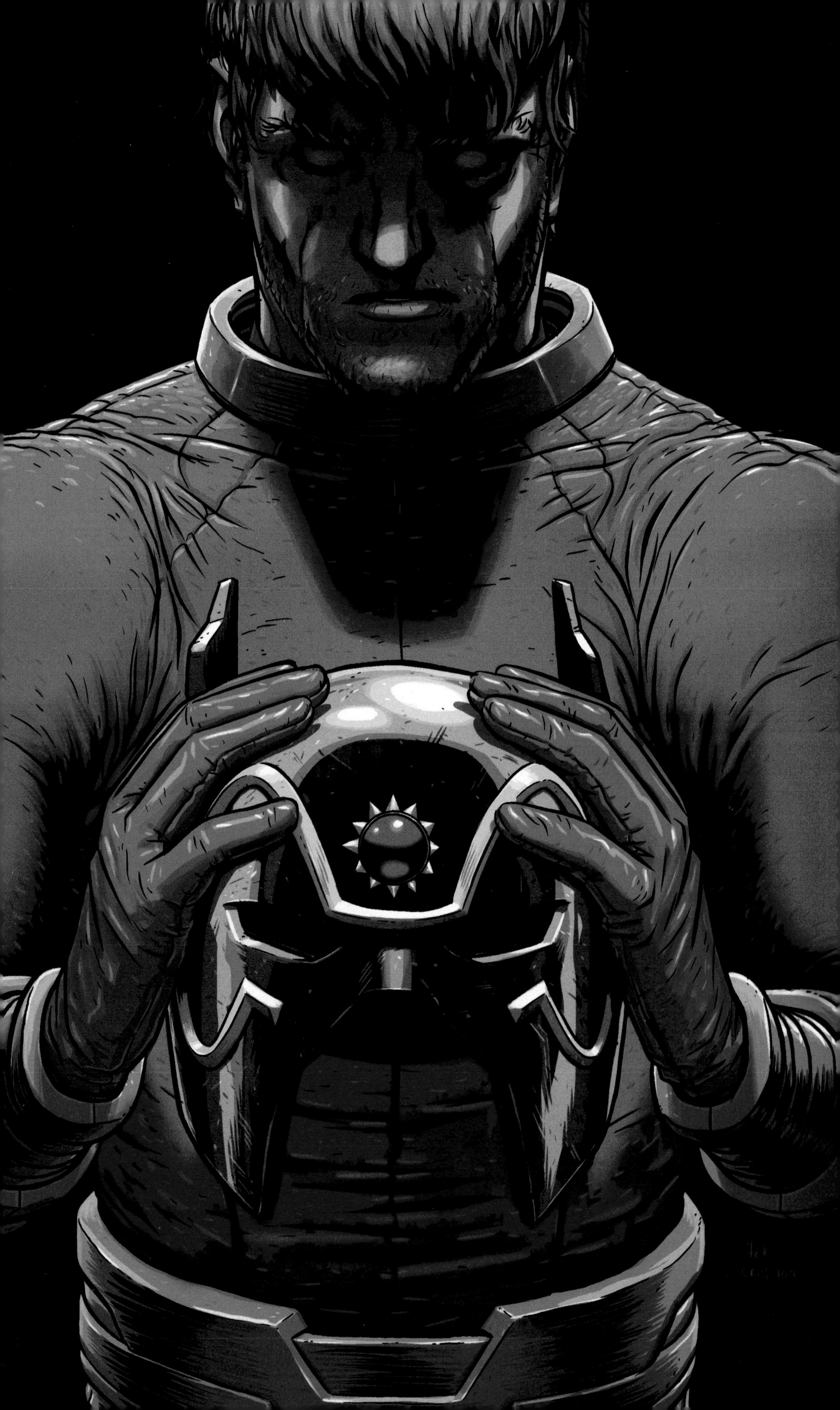

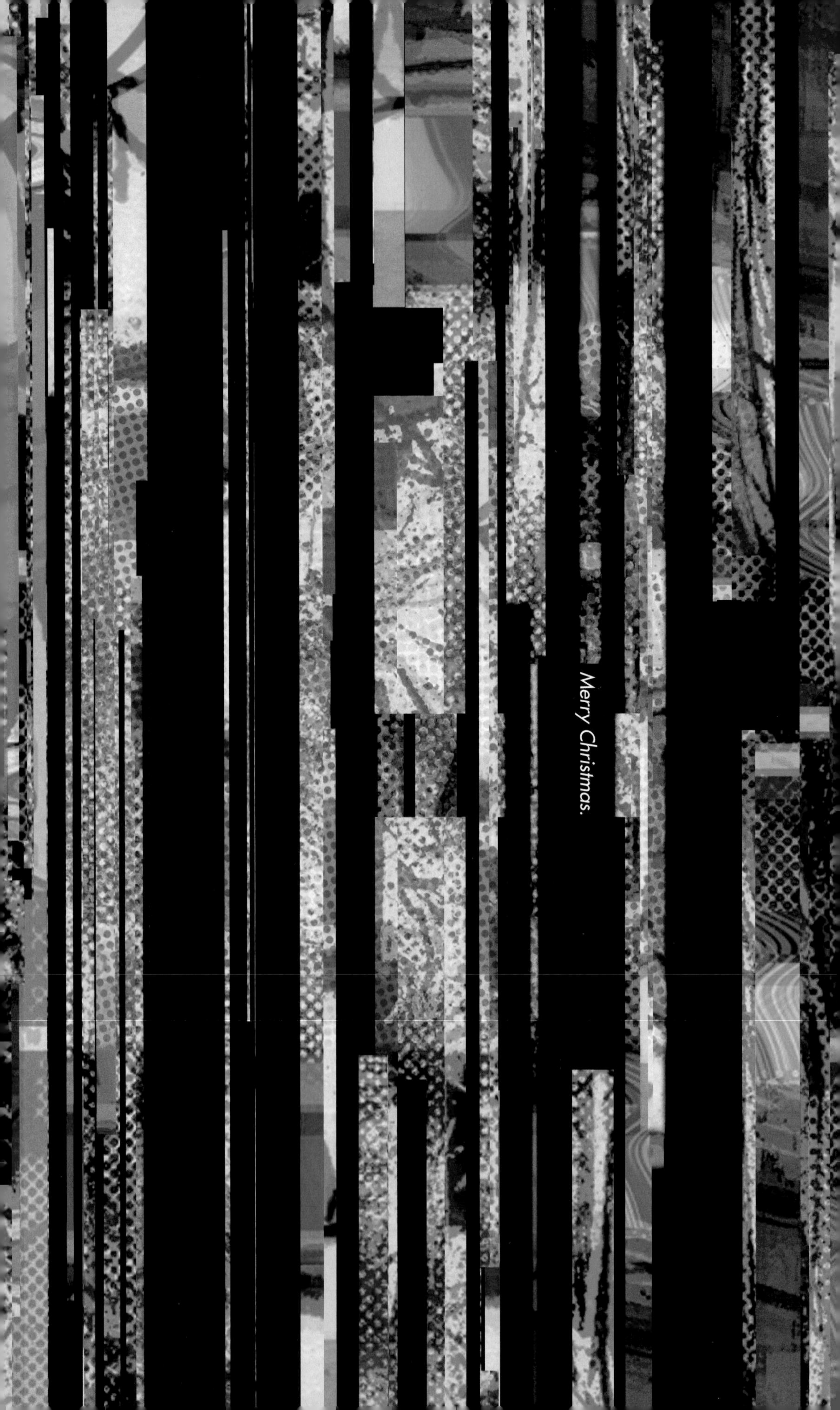
Merry Christmas.

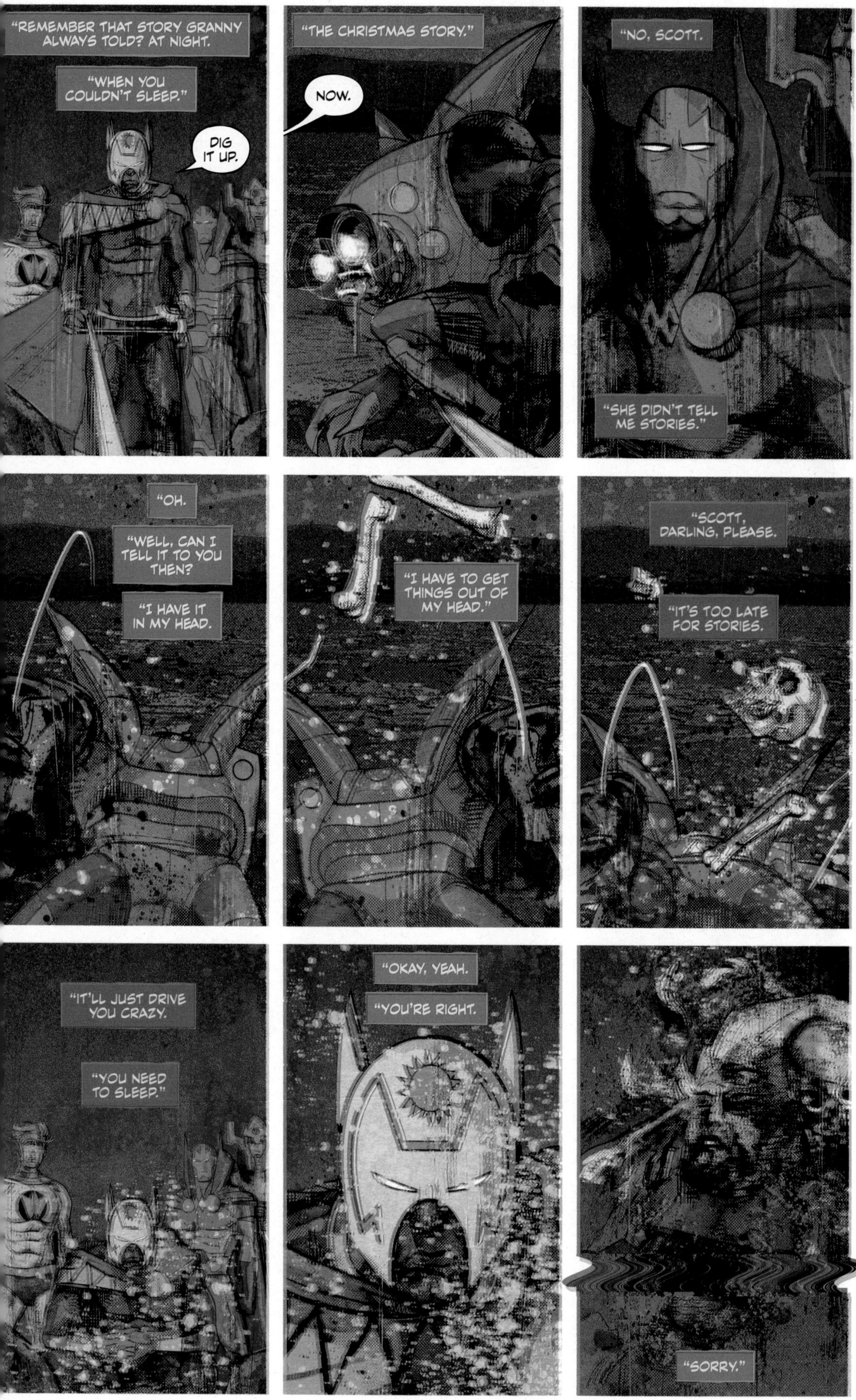
"REMEMBER THAT STORY GRANNY ALWAYS TOLD? AT NIGHT.
"WHEN YOU COULDN'T SLEEP."
DIG IT UP.
"THE CHRISTMAS STORY."
NOW.
"NO, SCOTT.
"SHE DIDN'T TELL ME STORIES."
"OH.
"WELL, CAN I TELL IT TO YOU THEN?
"I HAVE IT IN MY HEAD.
"I HAVE TO GET THINGS OUT OF MY HEAD."
"SCOTT, DARLING, PLEASE.
"IT'S TOO LATE FOR STORIES.
"IT'LL JUST DRIVE YOU CRAZY.
"YOU NEED TO SLEEP."
"OKAY, YEAH.
"YOU'RE RIGHT.
"SORRY."

"THIS IS ON EARTH. BEFORE CHRISTMAS. IN THE NETHERLANDS.

"IN 1942 OR SOMETHING. WHEN THE GERMANS HAD IT.

"A LITTLE BOY, I DON'T KNOW, CALL HIM WHATEVER.

"SVEN.

"SVEN'S IN SCHOOL. A CHRISTIAN SCHOOL. OR CATHOLIC. WHATEVER.

"WITH NUNS AND THE WHOLE THING.

"AND IT'S RIGHT BEFORE CHRISTMAS, AND THE TEACHER'S TELLING THEM ABOUT JESUS.

"AND SHE'S TALKING ABOUT MARY AND JOSEPH AND THE MANGER.

"HOW THEY COULDN'T FIND ANYWHERE SAFE. TO HAVE THE BABY.

"AND SHE MENTIONS THAT MARY AND JOSEPH WERE JEWS.

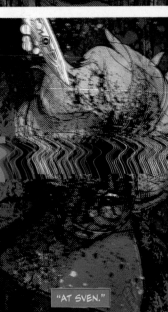

"AND SVEN, THE KID, HE STARTS TALKING. HE'S, Y'KNOW, FIVE OR WHATEVER.

"AND HE SAYS, 'THEY COULD COME TO OUR BASEMENT!'

"AND THE NUN WHO'S TEACHING JUST STOPS.

"JUST FROZEN. HEARING THIS. LOOKING AT THIS KID.

"AT SVEN."

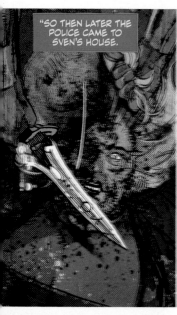

"SO THEN LATER THE POLICE CAME TO SVEN'S HOUSE.

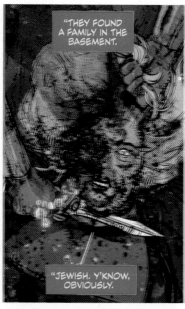

"THEY FOUND A FAMILY IN THE BASEMENT.

"JEWISH. Y'KNOW, OBVIOUSLY.

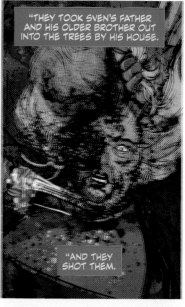

"THEY TOOK SVEN'S FATHER AND HIS OLDER BROTHER OUT INTO THE TREES BY HIS HOUSE.

"AND THEY SHOT THEM.

"SVEN AND HIS MOM AND HIS THREE SISTERS ENDED UP IN A WORK CAMP.

"FOR A WHILE. ONE OF HIS SISTERS DIED THERE.

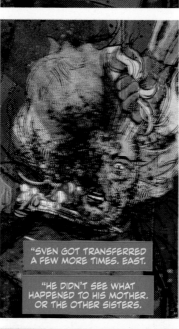

"SVEN GOT TRANSFERRED A FEW MORE TIMES. EAST.

"HE DIDN'T SEE WHAT HAPPENED TO HIS MOTHER. OR THE OTHER SISTERS.

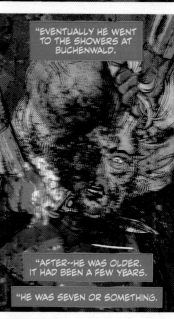

"EVENTUALLY HE WENT TO THE SHOWERS AT BUCHENWALD.

"AFTER--HE WAS OLDER. IT HAD BEEN A FEW YEARS.

"HE WAS SEVEN OR SOMETHING.

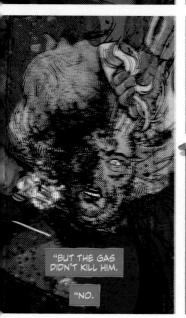

"BUT THE GAS DIDN'T KILL HIM.

"NO.

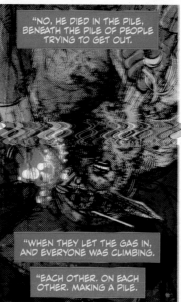

"NO, HE DIED IN THE PILE, BENEATH THE PILE OF PEOPLE TRYING TO GET OUT.

"WHEN THEY LET THE GAS IN, AND EVERYONE WAS CLIMBING.

"EACH OTHER. ON EACH OTHER. MAKING A PILE.

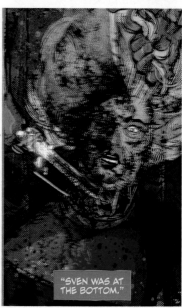

"SVEN WAS AT THE BOTTOM."

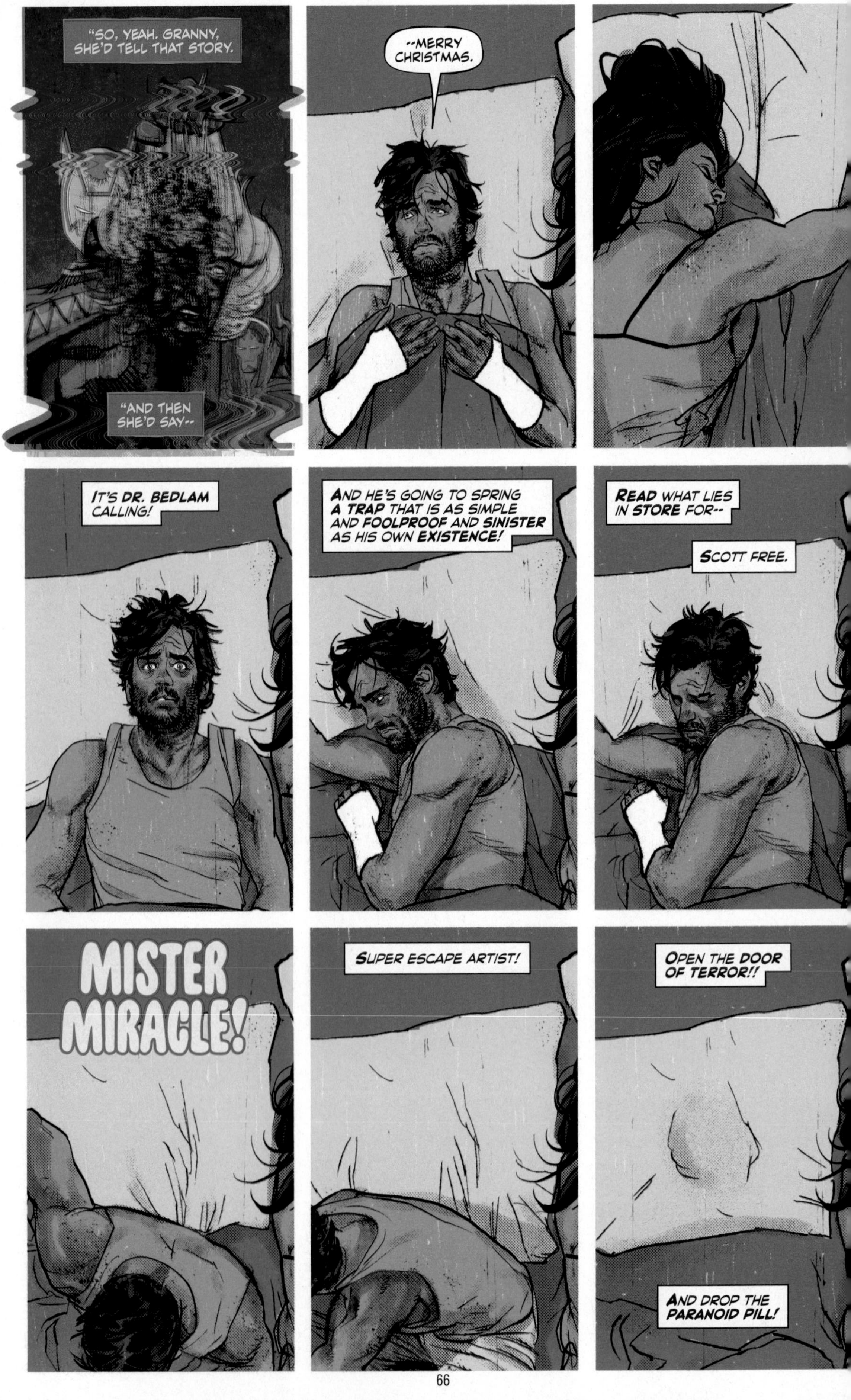
"SO, YEAH. GRANNY, SHE'D TELL THAT STORY.
"AND THEN SHE'D SAY--
--MERRY CHRISTMAS.
IT'S DR. BEDLAM CALLING!
AND HE'S GOING TO SPRING A TRAP THAT IS AS SIMPLE AND FOOLPROOF AND SINISTER AS HIS OWN EXISTENCE!
READ WHAT LIES IN STORE FOR--
SCOTT FREE.
MISTER MIRACLE!
SUPER ESCAPE ARTIST!
OPEN THE DOOR OF TERROR!!
AND DROP THE PARANOID PILL!

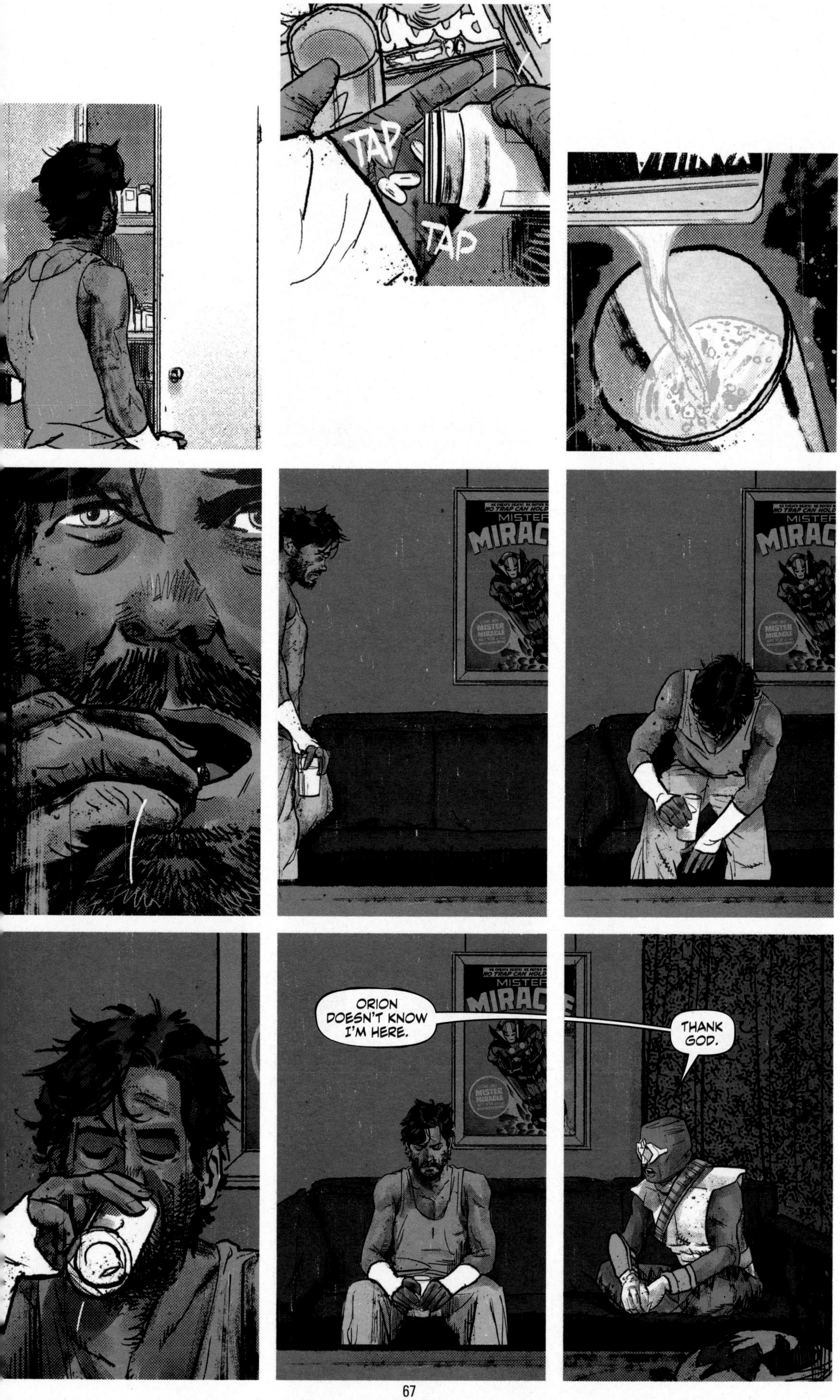
TAP
TAP
WE CHEATS DEATH! WE DEFIES MAN! NO TRAP CAN HOLD
MISTER MIRACLE
MISTER MIRACLE
ORION DOESN'T KNOW I'M HERE.
THANK GOD.

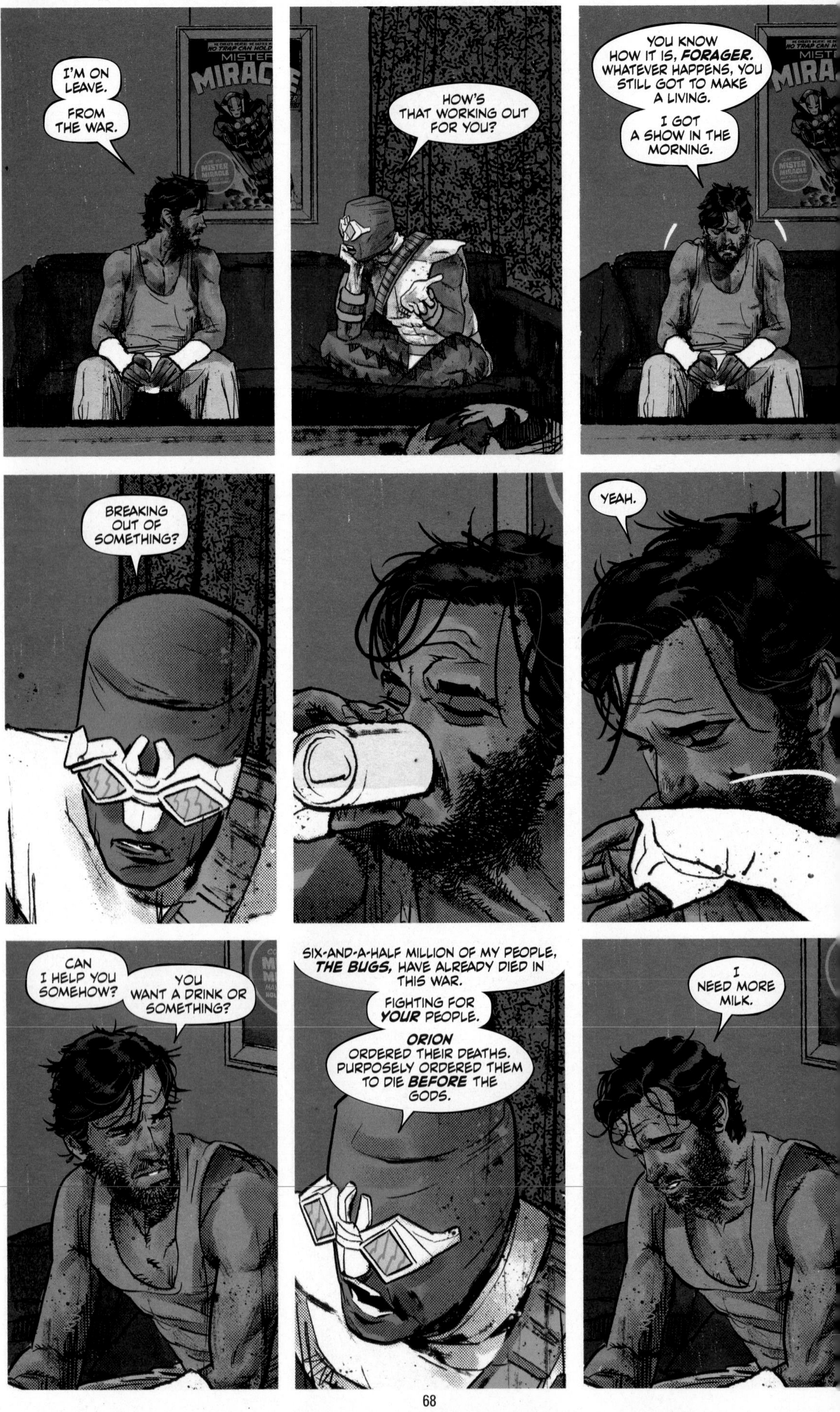
I'M ON LEAVE.
FROM THE WAR.
HOW'S THAT WORKING OUT FOR YOU?
YOU KNOW HOW IT IS, *FORAGER.* WHATEVER HAPPENS, YOU STILL GOT TO MAKE A LIVING.
I GOT A SHOW IN THE MORNING.
BREAKING OUT OF SOMETHING?
YEAH.
CAN I HELP YOU SOMEHOW?
YOU WANT A DRINK OR SOMETHING?
SIX-AND-A-HALF MILLION OF MY PEOPLE, *THE BUGS,* HAVE ALREADY DIED IN THIS WAR.
FIGHTING FOR *YOUR* PEOPLE.
ORION ORDERED THEIR DEATHS. PURPOSELY ORDERED THEM TO DIE *BEFORE* THE GODS.
I NEED MORE MILK.

NOW THAT **GRANNY'S** BEEN DEFEATED, ORION WANTS TO LEAD US TO APOKOLIPS.

GO ON THE **OFFENSIVE.** TAKE OUT DARKSEID. RIGHT.

AND, OF COURSE, THE BUGS WILL BE UP FRONT AGAIN--**CANNON FODDER** FOR THE GODS.

AND THAT'LL BE **TRIPLE** THE NUMBER WE'VE **ALREADY** SACRIFICED.

AND WHAT, WHAT DO WE GET? AT SOME POINT IT'S **YOUR** VICTORY, **OUR** BLOOD.

I'M NOT SAYING WE DON'T GO AFTER DARKSEID. DARKSEID IS.

BUT THERE'S **A LIMIT** TO WHAT THIS POPULATION CAN TAKE RIGHT NOW.

AND **ORION.** HE DOESN'T UNDERSTAND-- SEEM TO UNDERSTAND **LIMITS.**

I DON'T KNOW, FORAGER--

--HAVE YOU TALKED TO HIM?

WE... WE SENT OUR QUEEN.

MAY SHE EVER BREED.

AND E HAD HER...

SHE WAS EXECUTED. HE **EXECUTED** HER. FOR TREASON.

HER HEAD HANGS WITH GRANNY.

NO.

I WOULD'VE HEARD.

SOMEONE WOULD HAVE TOLD ME.

COME SEE MISTE MIRAC MAY 5TH HOLLYWOOD B

I'M TELLING YOU.

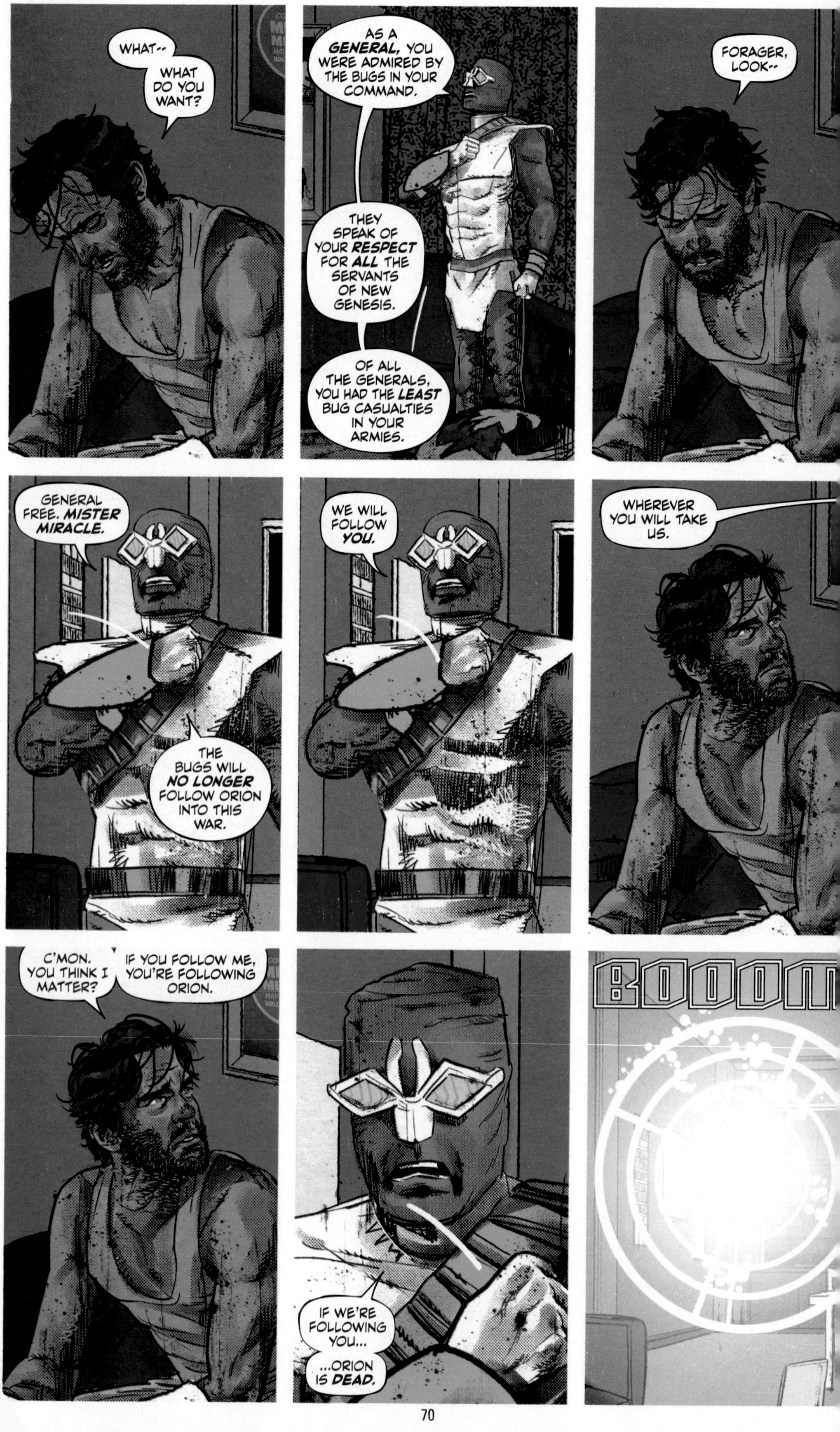
WHAT--
WHAT DO YOU WANT?
AS A **GENERAL,** YOU WERE ADMIRED BY THE BUGS IN YOUR COMMAND.
THEY SPEAK OF YOUR **RESPECT** FOR **ALL** THE SERVANTS OF NEW GENESIS.
OF ALL THE GENERALS, YOU HAD THE **LEAST** BUG CASUALTIES IN YOUR ARMIES.
FORAGER, LOOK--
GENERAL FREE. **MISTER MIRACLE.**
THE BUGS WILL **NO LONGER** FOLLOW ORION INTO THIS WAR.
WE WILL FOLLOW **YOU.**
WHEREVER YOU WILL TAKE US.
C'MON. YOU THINK I MATTER?
IF YOU FOLLOW ME, YOU'RE FOLLOWING ORION.
IF WE'RE FOLLOWING YOU...
...ORION IS **DEAD.**
BOOOM

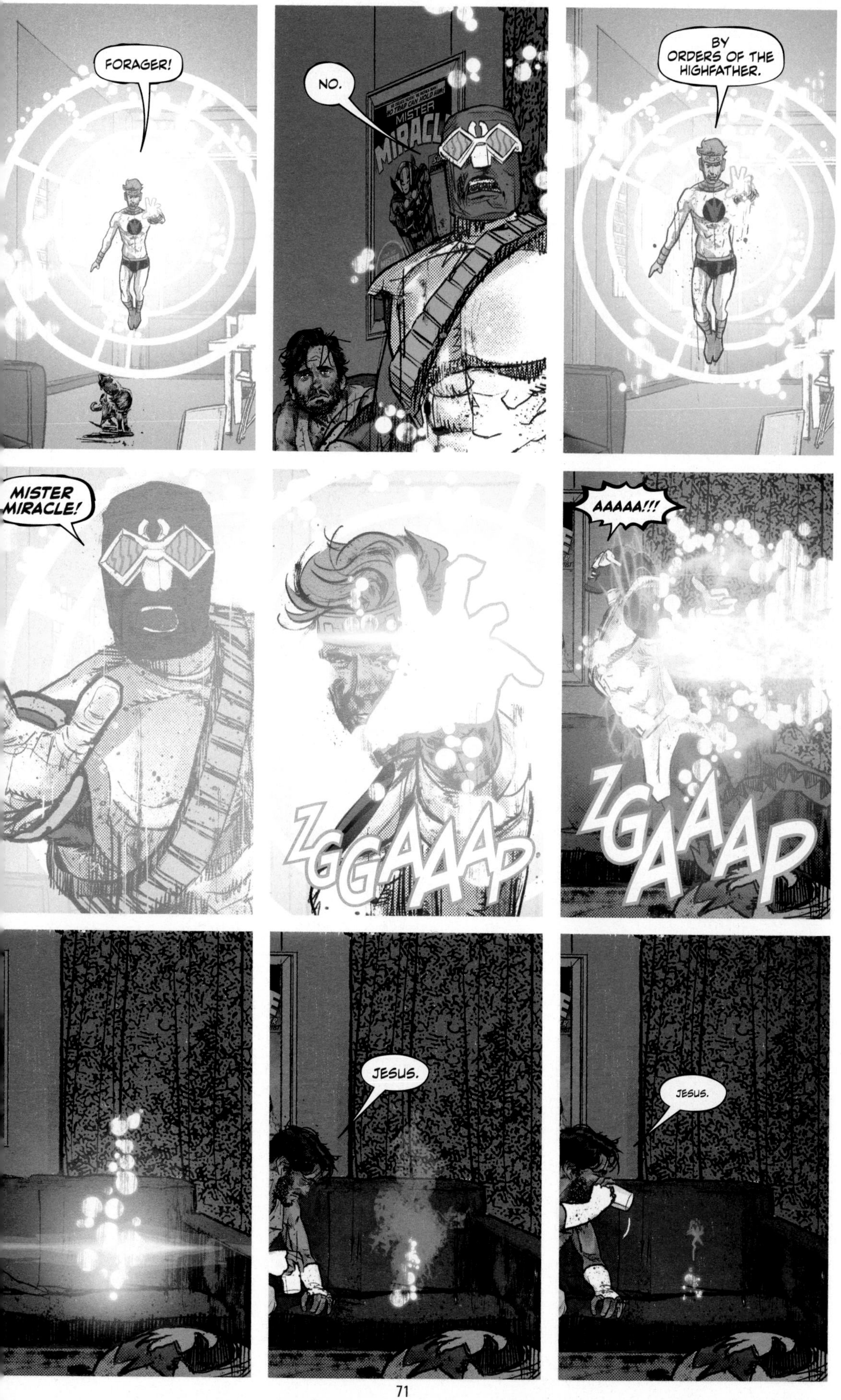
FORAGER!
NO.
BY ORDERS OF THE HIGHFATHER.
MISTER MIRACLE!
ZGGAAAP
AAAAA!!!
ZGAAAAP
JESUS.
JESUS.

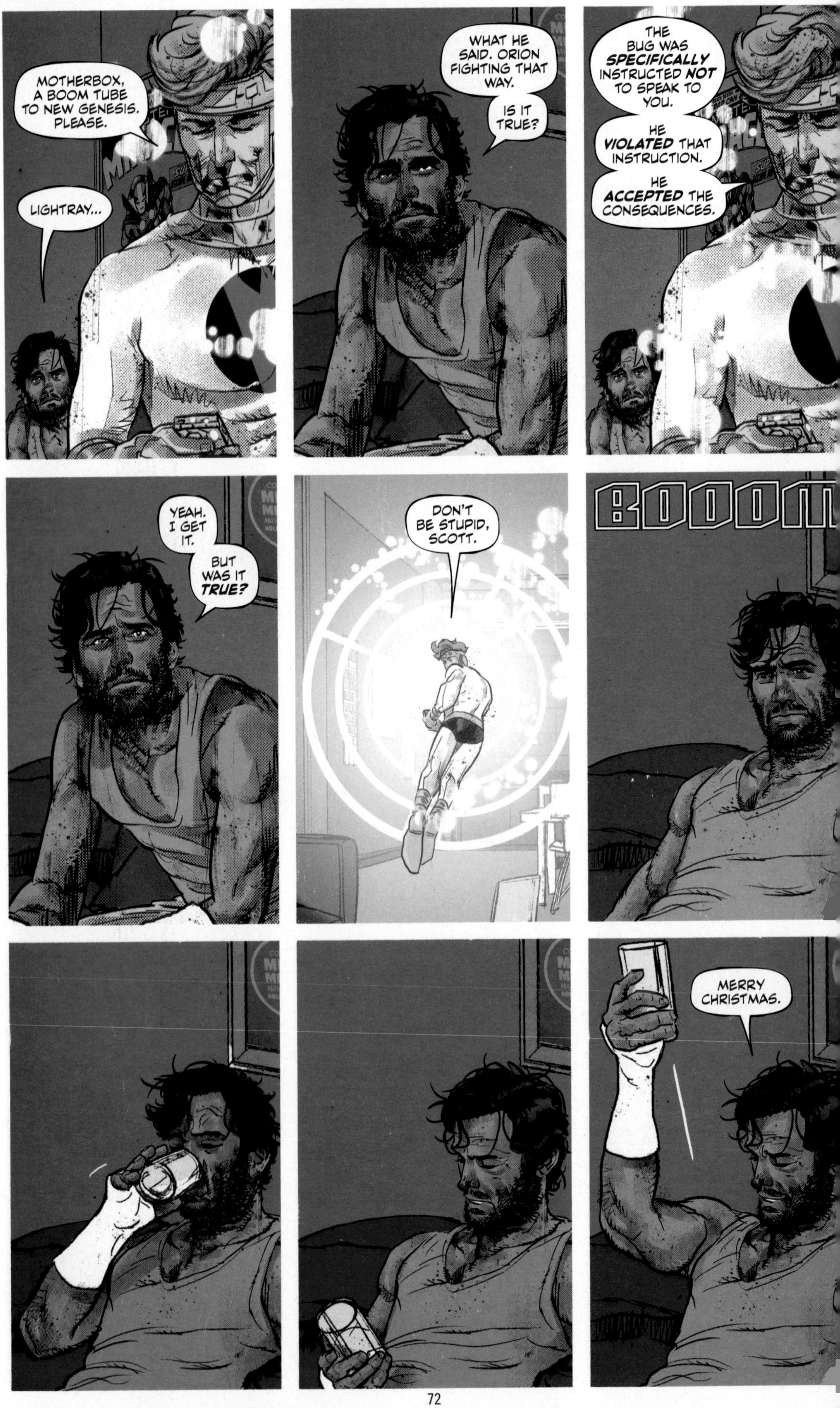

MOTHERBOX, A BOOM TUBE TO NEW GENESIS. PLEASE.
LIGHTRAY...
WHAT HE SAID. ORION FIGHTING THAT WAY.
IS IT TRUE?
THE BUG WAS **SPECIFICALLY** INSTRUCTED **NOT** TO SPEAK TO YOU.
HE **VIOLATED** THAT INSTRUCTION.
HE **ACCEPTED** THE CONSEQUENCES.
YEAH. I GET IT.
BUT WAS IT **TRUE?**
DON'T BE STUPID, SCOTT.
BOOOM
MERRY CHRISTMAS.

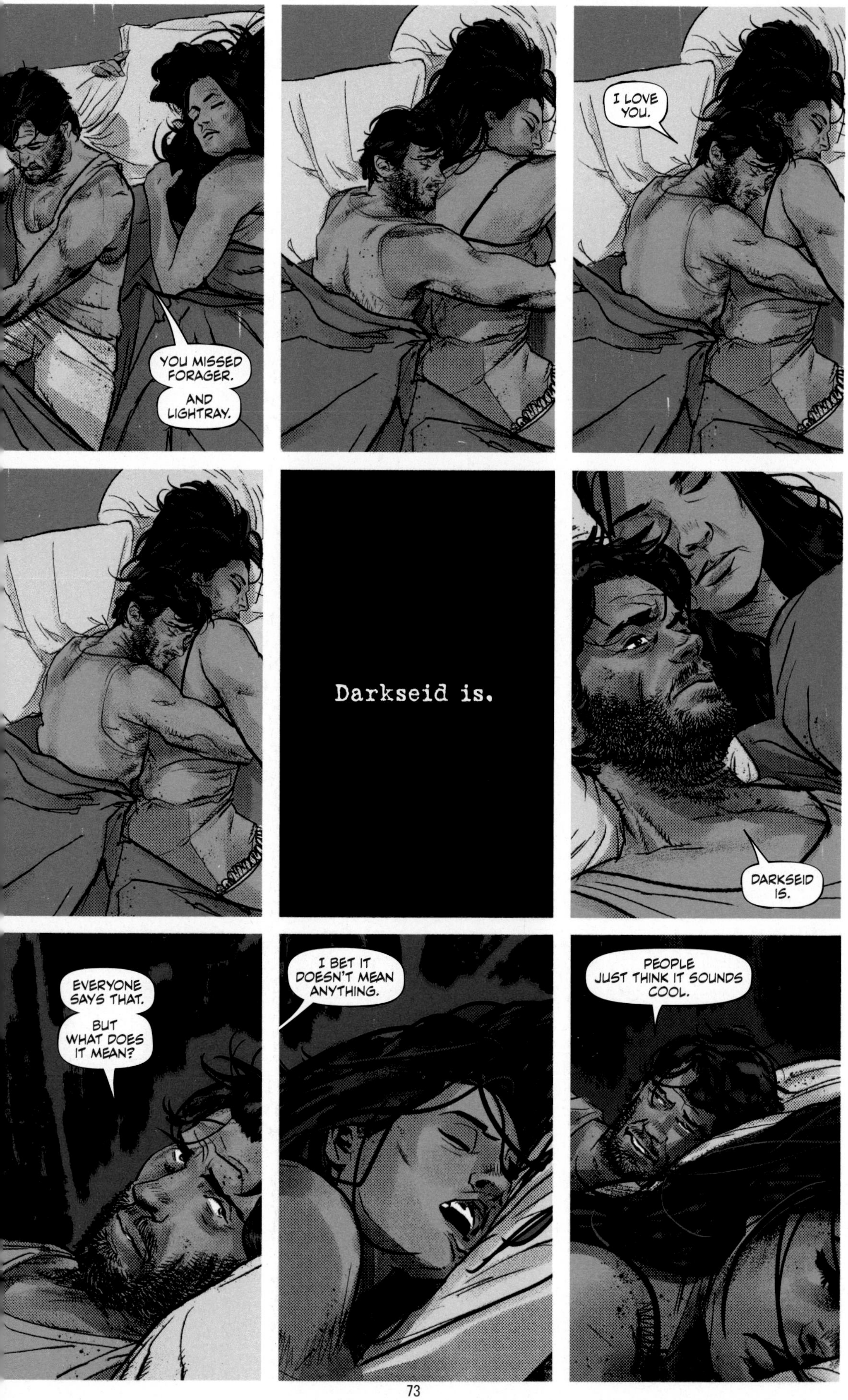
YOU MISSED FORAGER.
AND LIGHTRAY.
I LOVE YOU.
Darkseid is.
DARKSEID IS.
EVERYONE SAYS THAT.
BUT WHAT DOES IT MEAN?
I BET IT DOESN'T MEAN ANYTHING.
PEOPLE JUST THINK IT SOUNDS COOL.

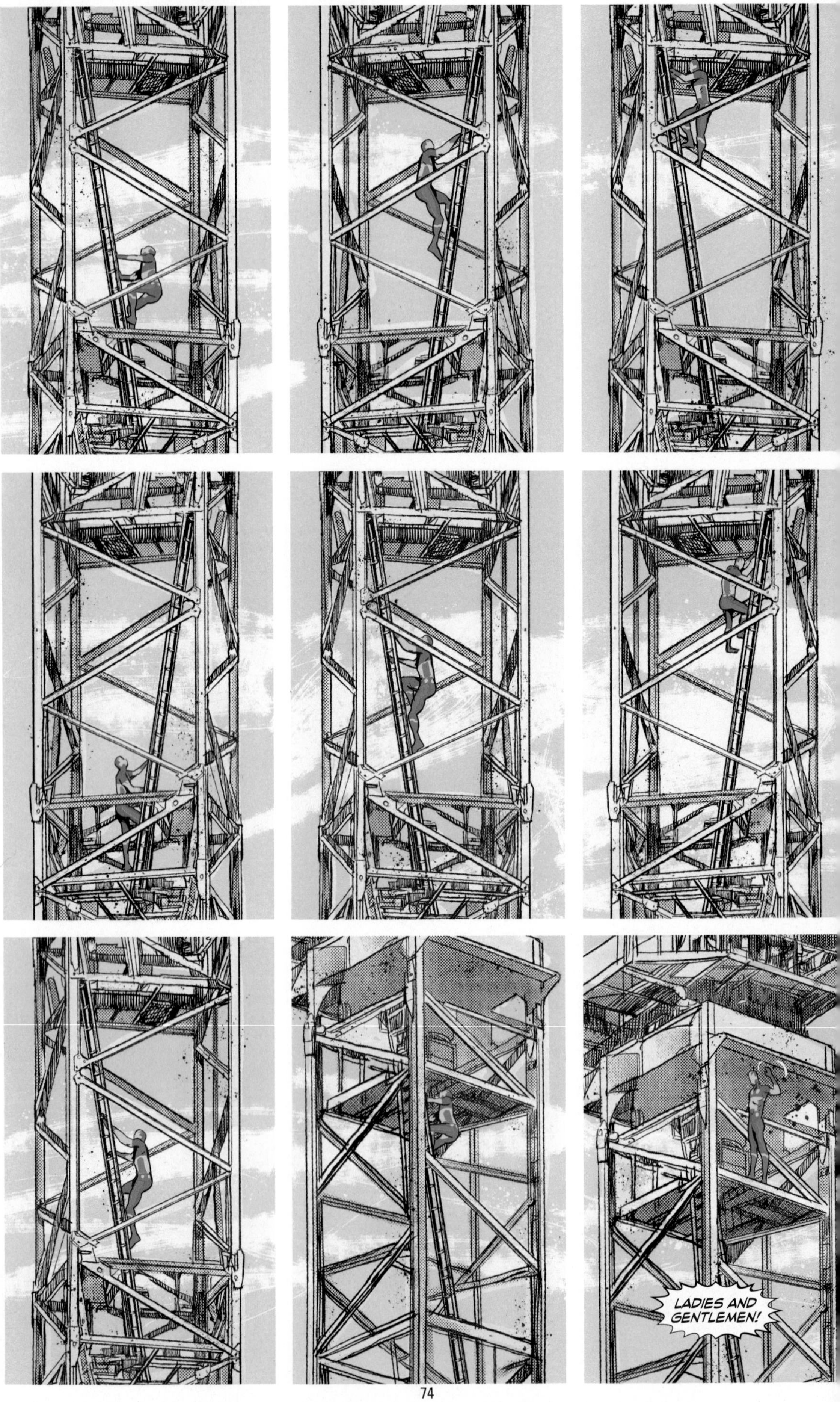
LADIES AND GENTLEMEN!

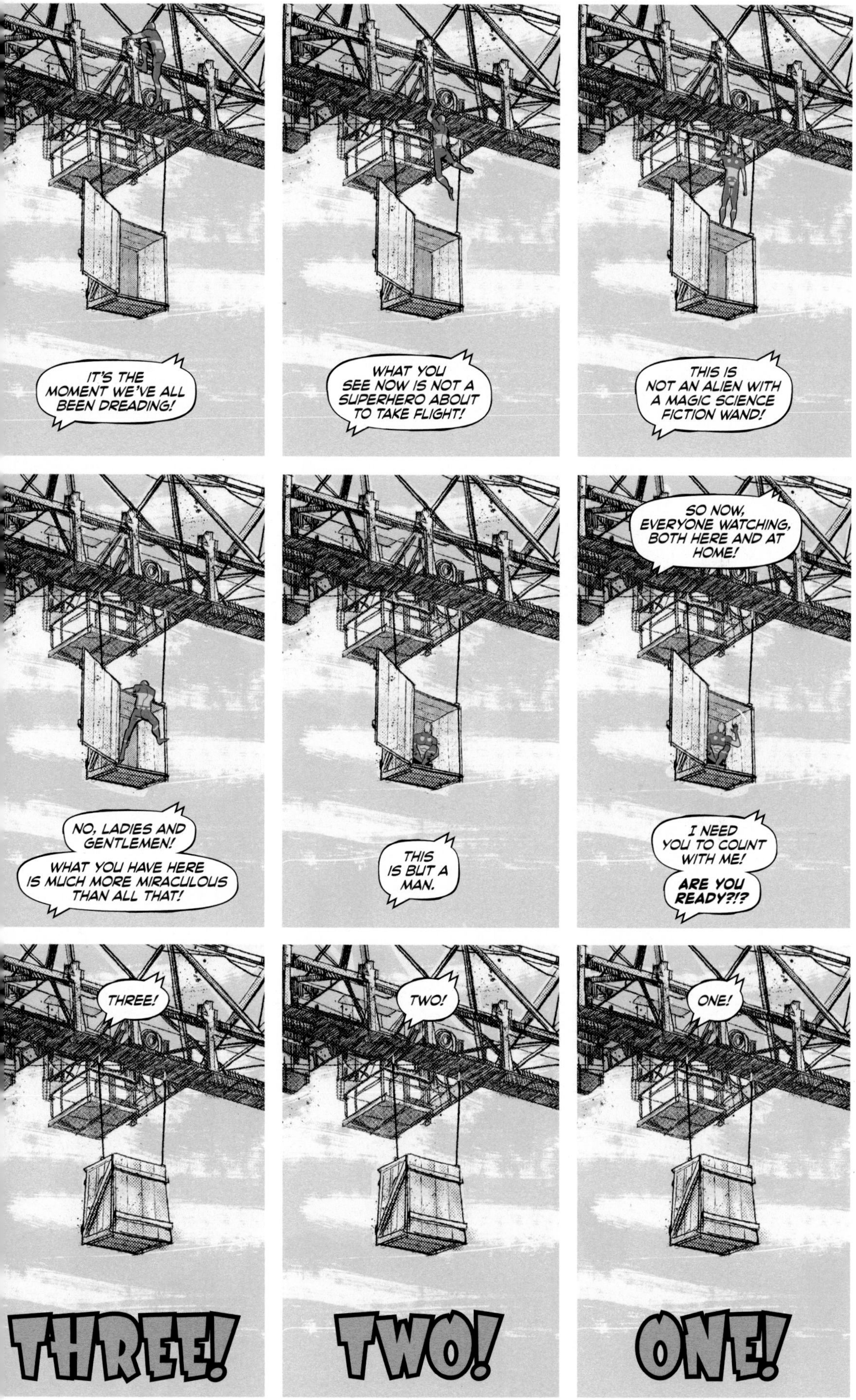
IT'S THE MOMENT WE'VE ALL BEEN DREADING!
WHAT YOU SEE NOW IS NOT A SUPERHERO ABOUT TO TAKE FLIGHT!
THIS IS NOT AN ALIEN WITH A MAGIC SCIENCE FICTION WAND!
NO, LADIES AND GENTLEMEN!
WHAT YOU HAVE HERE IS MUCH MORE MIRACULOUS THAN ALL THAT!
THIS IS BUT A MAN.
SO NOW, EVERYONE WATCHING, BOTH HERE AND AT HOME!
I NEED YOU TO COUNT WITH ME!
ARE YOU READY?!?
THREE!
THREE!
TWO!
TWO!
ONE!
ONE!

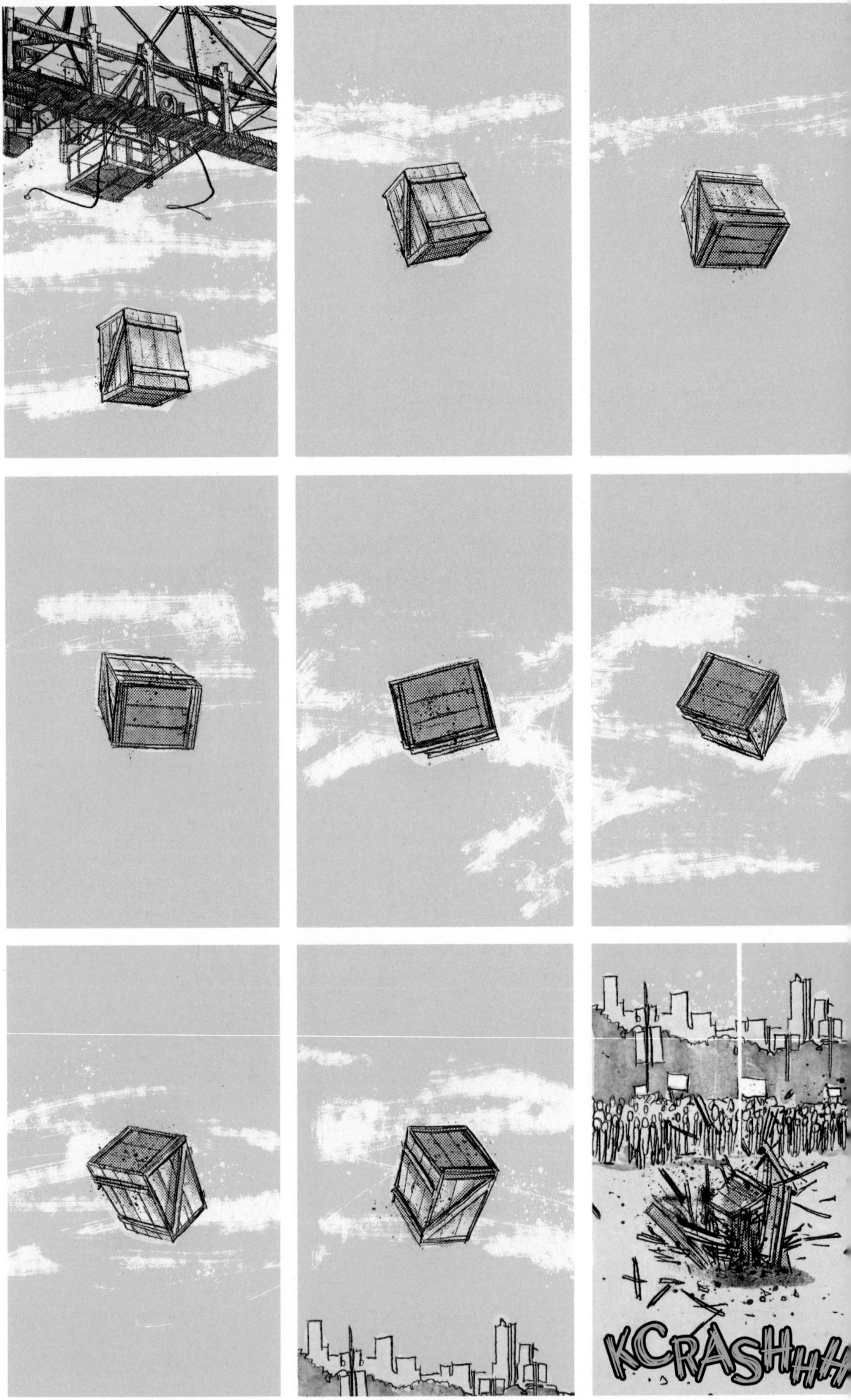
KCRASHHH

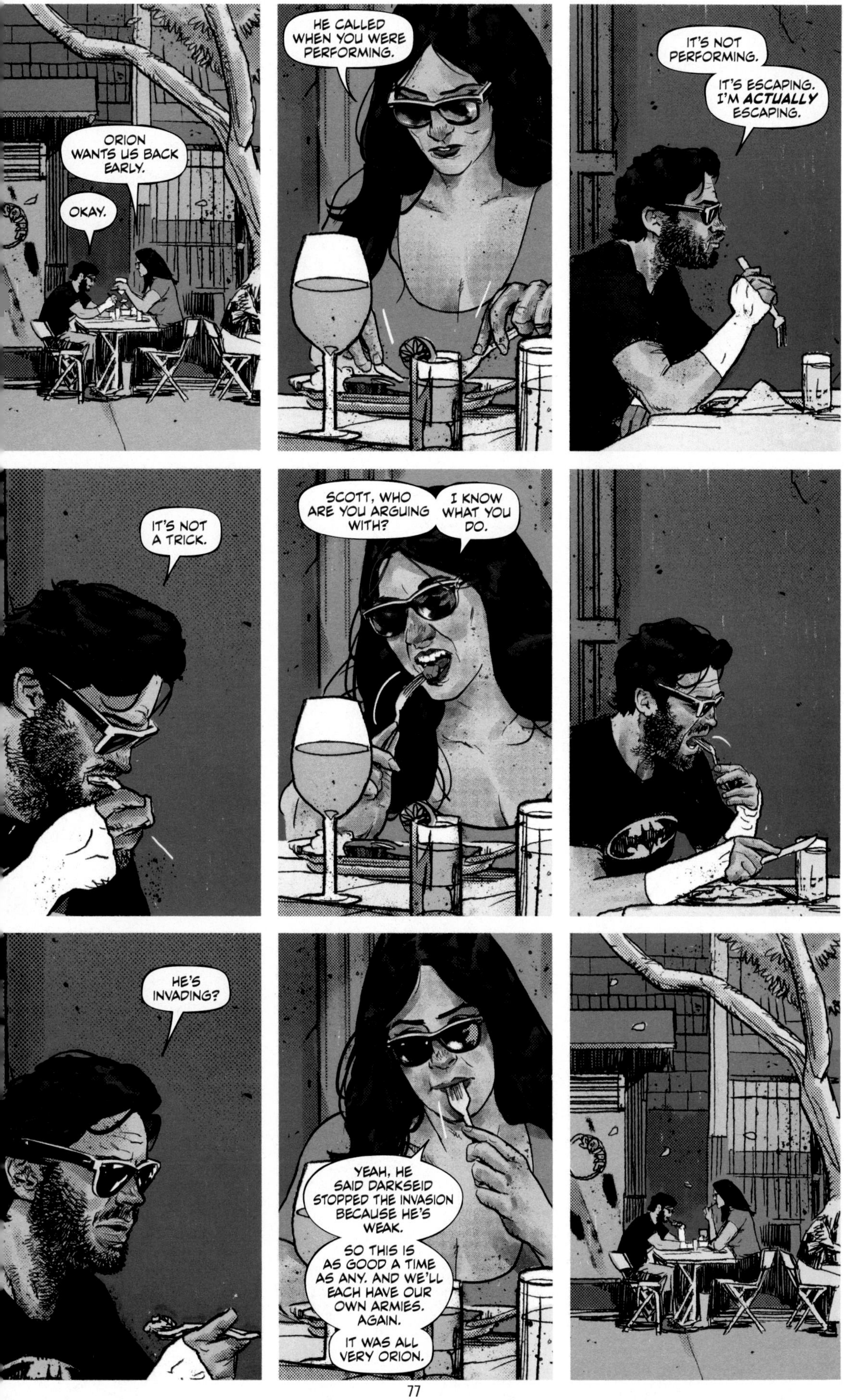
ORION WANTS US BACK EARLY.
OKAY.
HE CALLED WHEN YOU WERE PERFORMING.
IT'S NOT PERFORMING.
IT'S ESCAPING. I'M *ACTUALLY* ESCAPING.
IT'S NOT A TRICK.
SCOTT, WHO ARE YOU ARGUING WITH?
I KNOW WHAT YOU DO.
HE'S INVADING?
YEAH, HE SAID DARKSEID STOPPED THE INVASION BECAUSE HE'S WEAK.
SO THIS IS AS GOOD A TIME AS ANY. AND WE'LL EACH HAVE OUR OWN ARMIES. AGAIN.
IT WAS ALL VERY ORION.

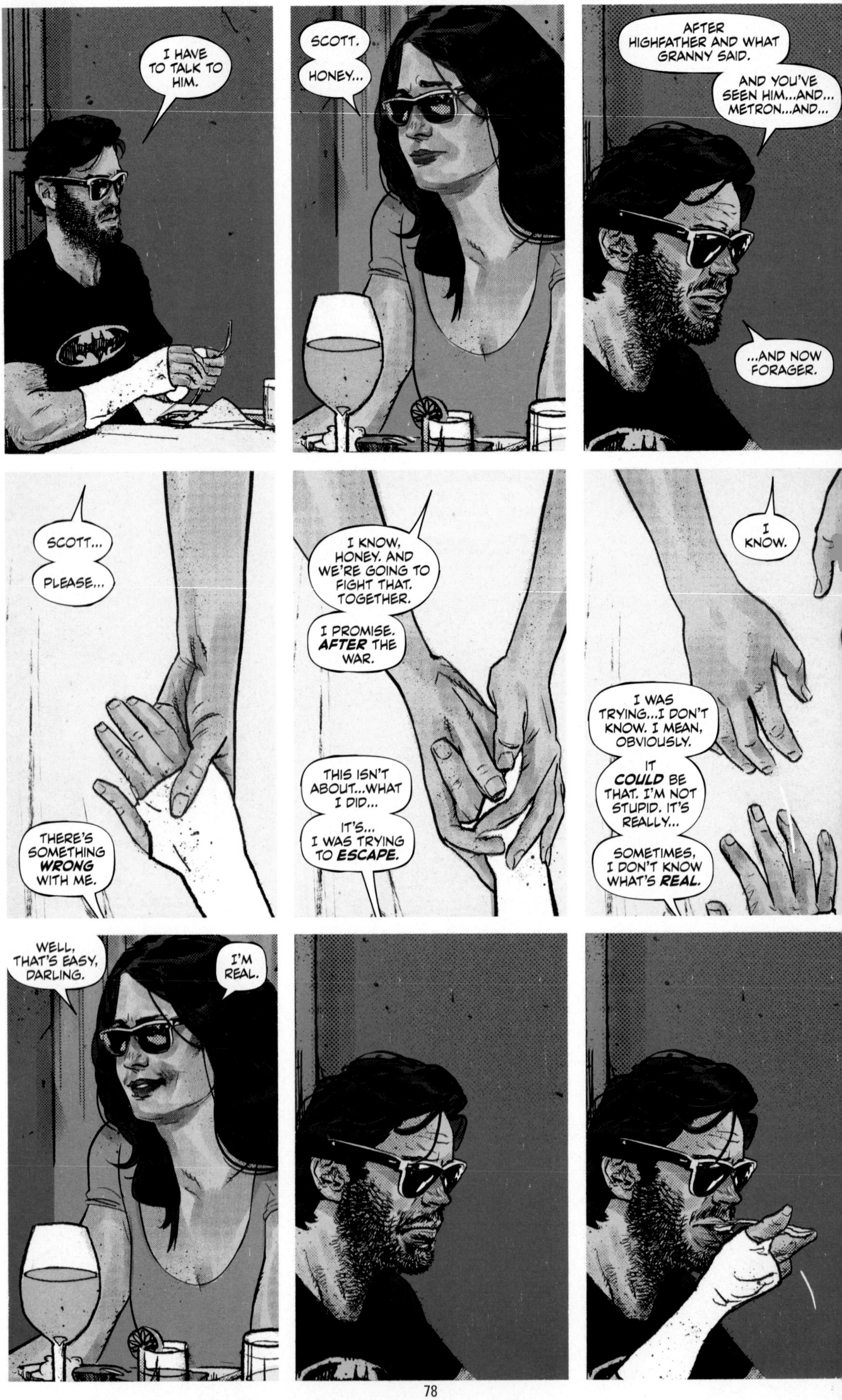
I HAVE TO TALK TO HIM.
SCOTT.
HONEY...
AFTER HIGHFATHER AND WHAT GRANNY SAID.
AND YOU'VE SEEN HIM...AND... METRON...AND...
...AND NOW FORAGER.
SCOTT...
PLEASE...
THERE'S SOMETHING **WRONG** WITH ME.
I KNOW, HONEY. AND WE'RE GOING TO FIGHT THAT. TOGETHER.
I PROMISE. **AFTER** THE WAR.
THIS ISN'T ABOUT...WHAT I DID...
IT'S... I WAS TRYING TO **ESCAPE.**
I KNOW.
I WAS TRYING...I DON'T KNOW. I MEAN, OBVIOUSLY.
IT **COULD** BE THAT. I'M NOT STUPID. IT'S REALLY...
SOMETIMES, I DON'T KNOW WHAT'S **REAL.**
WELL, THAT'S EASY, DARLING.
I'M REAL.

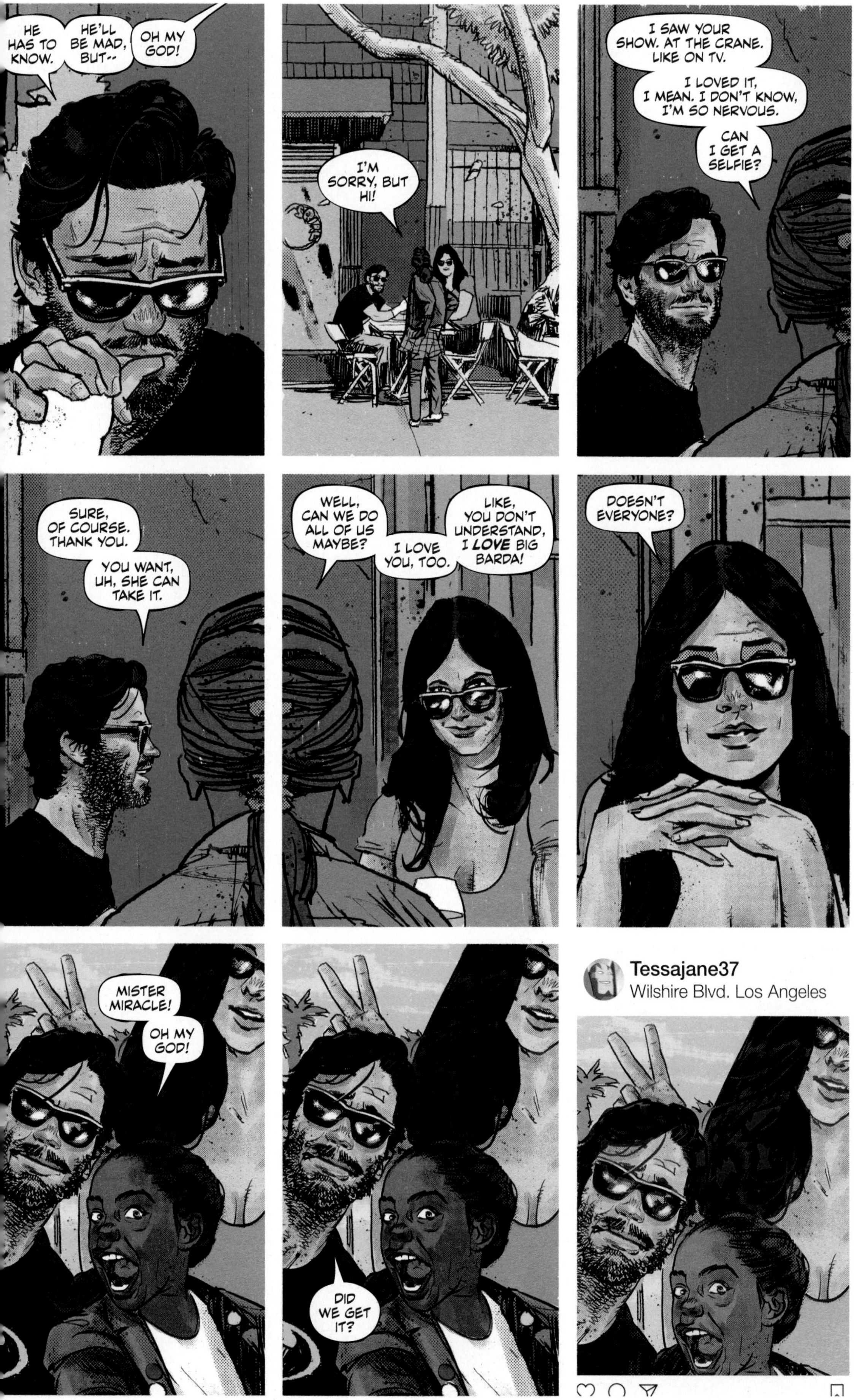
HE HAS TO KNOW.
HE'LL BE MAD, BUT--
OH MY GOD!
I'M SORRY, BUT HI!
I SAW YOUR SHOW. AT THE CRANE. LIKE ON TV.
I LOVED IT, I MEAN. I DON'T KNOW, I'M SO NERVOUS.
CAN I GET A SELFIE?
SURE, OF COURSE. THANK YOU.
YOU WANT, UH, SHE CAN TAKE IT.
WELL, CAN WE DO ALL OF US MAYBE?
I LOVE YOU, TOO.
LIKE, YOU DON'T UNDERSTAND, I LOVE BIG BARDA!
DOESN'T EVERYONE?
MISTER MIRACLE!
OH MY GOD!
DID WE GET IT?
Tessajane37
Wilshire Blvd. Los Angeles

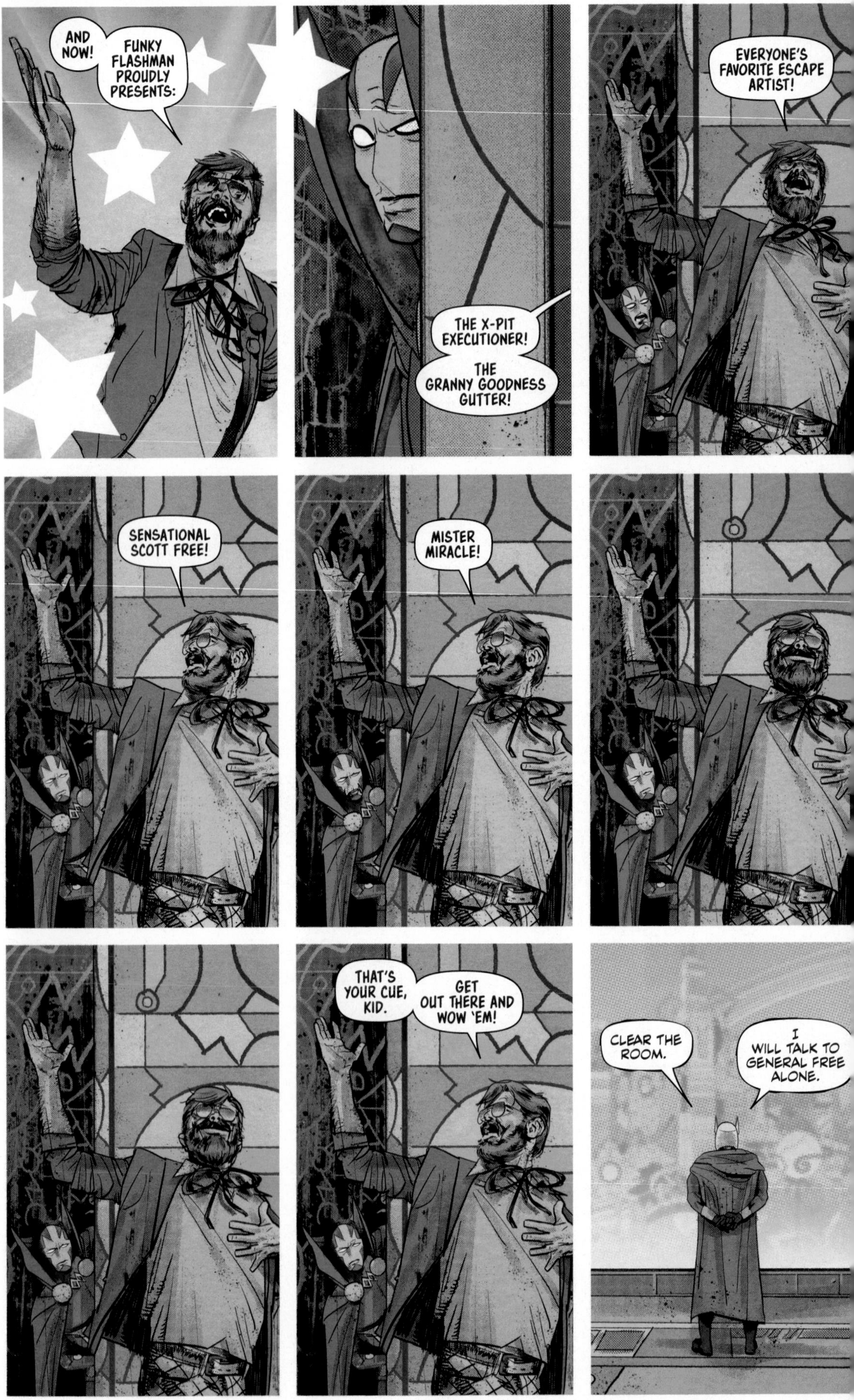
AND NOW!
FUNKY FLASHMAN PROUDLY PRESENTS:
THE X-PIT EXECUTIONER!
THE GRANNY GOODNESS GUTTER!
EVERYONE'S FAVORITE ESCAPE ARTIST!
SENSATIONAL SCOTT FREE!
MISTER MIRACLE!
THAT'S YOUR CUE, KID.
GET OUT THERE AND WOW 'EM!
CLEAR THE ROOM.
I WILL TALK TO GENERAL FREE ALONE.

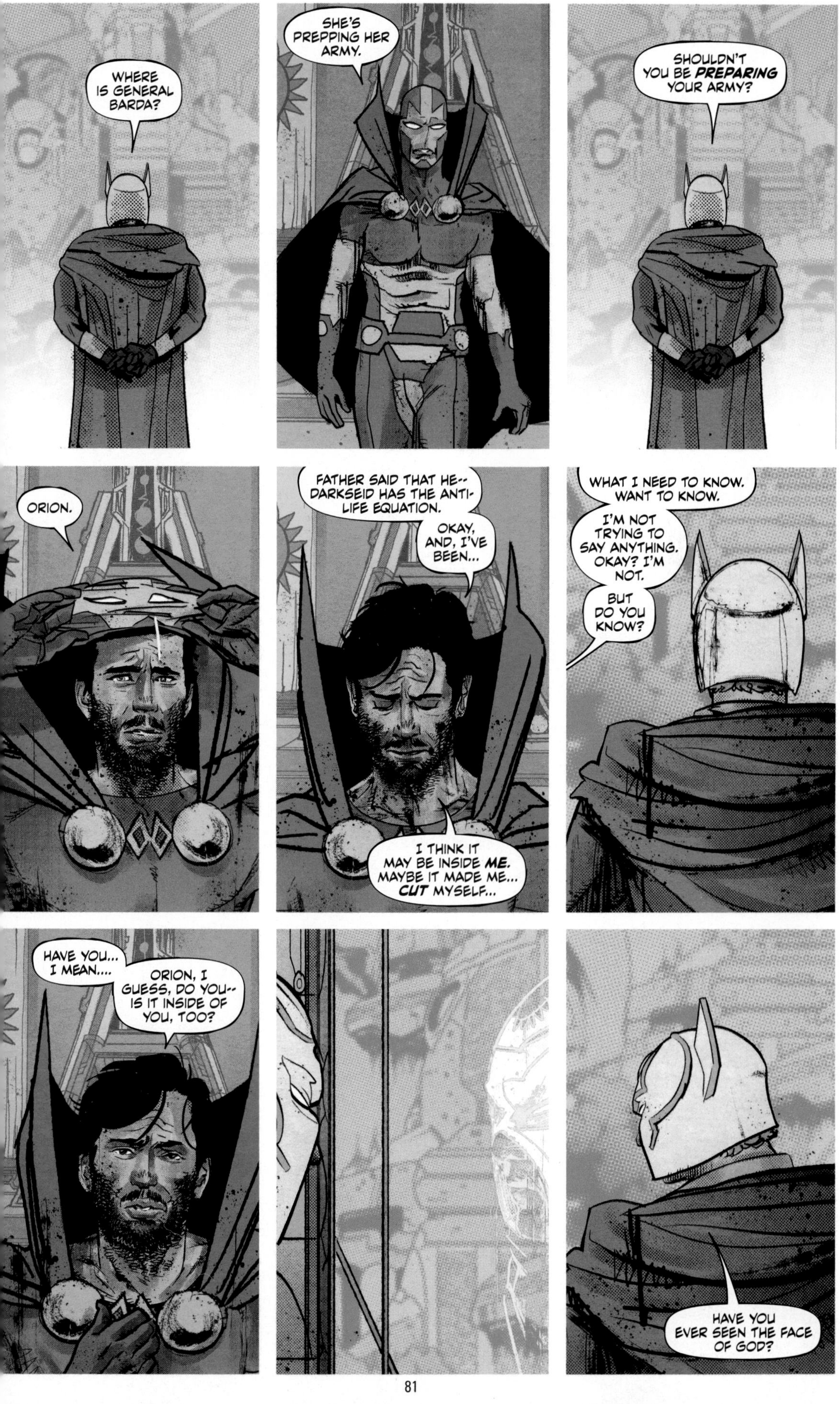

WHERE IS GENERAL BARDA?
SHE'S PREPPING HER ARMY.
SHOULDN'T YOU BE PREPARING YOUR ARMY?
ORION.
FATHER SAID THAT HE-- DARKSEID HAS THE ANTI-LIFE EQUATION.
OKAY, AND, I'VE BEEN...
I THINK IT MAY BE INSIDE ME. MAYBE IT MADE ME... CUT MYSELF...
WHAT I NEED TO KNOW. WANT TO KNOW.
I'M NOT TRYING TO SAY ANYTHING. OKAY? I'M NOT.
BUT DO YOU KNOW?
HAVE YOU... I MEAN....
ORION, I GUESS, DO YOU-- IS IT INSIDE OF YOU, TOO?
HAVE YOU EVER SEEN THE FACE OF GOD?

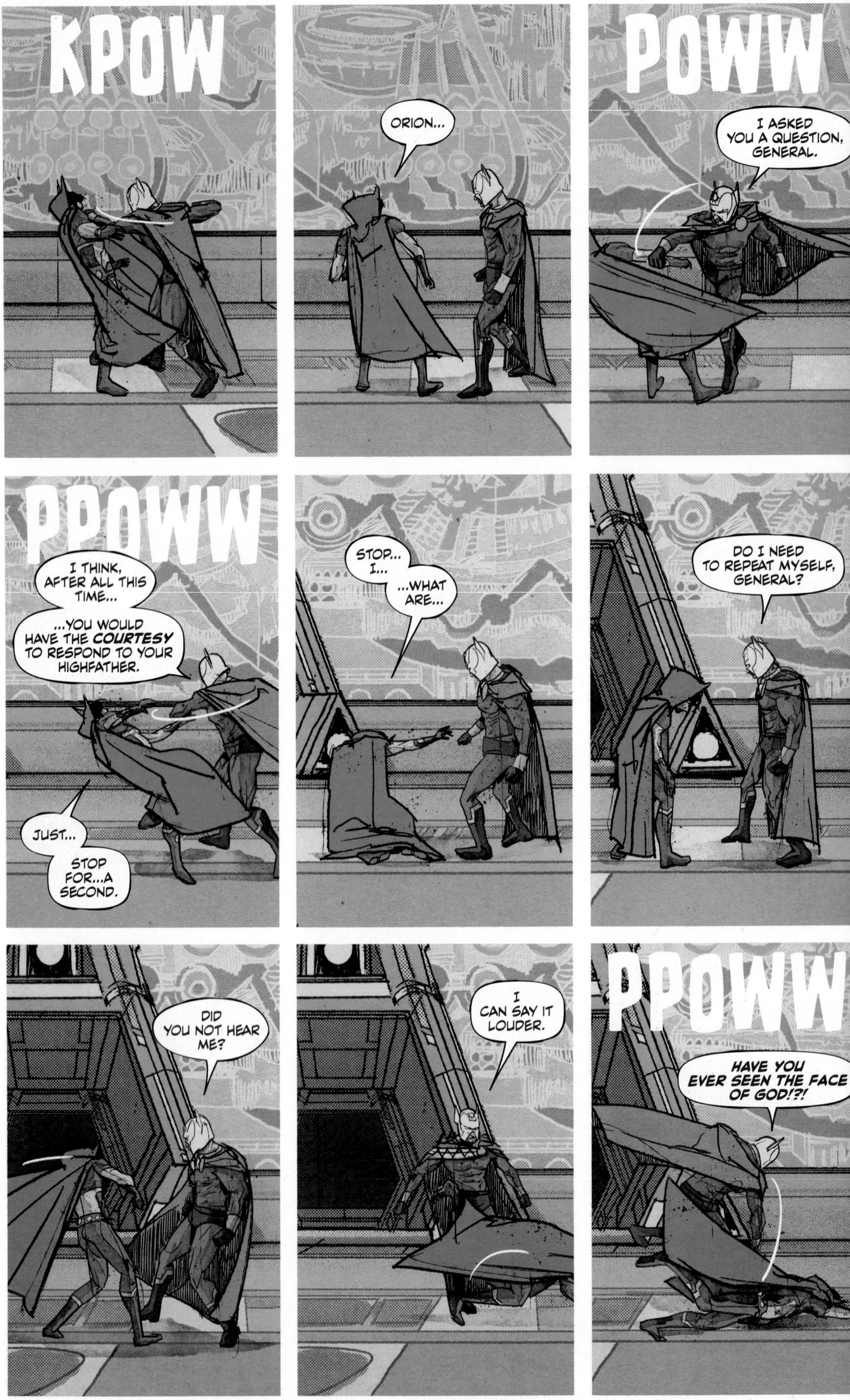
KPOW
ORION...
POWW
I ASKED YOU A QUESTION, GENERAL.
PPOWW
I THINK, AFTER ALL THIS TIME...
...YOU WOULD HAVE THE COURTESY TO RESPOND TO YOUR HIGHFATHER.
JUST... STOP FOR...A SECOND.
STOP... I...
...WHAT ARE...
DO I NEED TO REPEAT MYSELF, GENERAL?
DID YOU NOT HEAR ME?
I CAN SAY IT LOUDER.
PPOWW
HAVE YOU EVER SEEN THE FACE OF GOD!?!

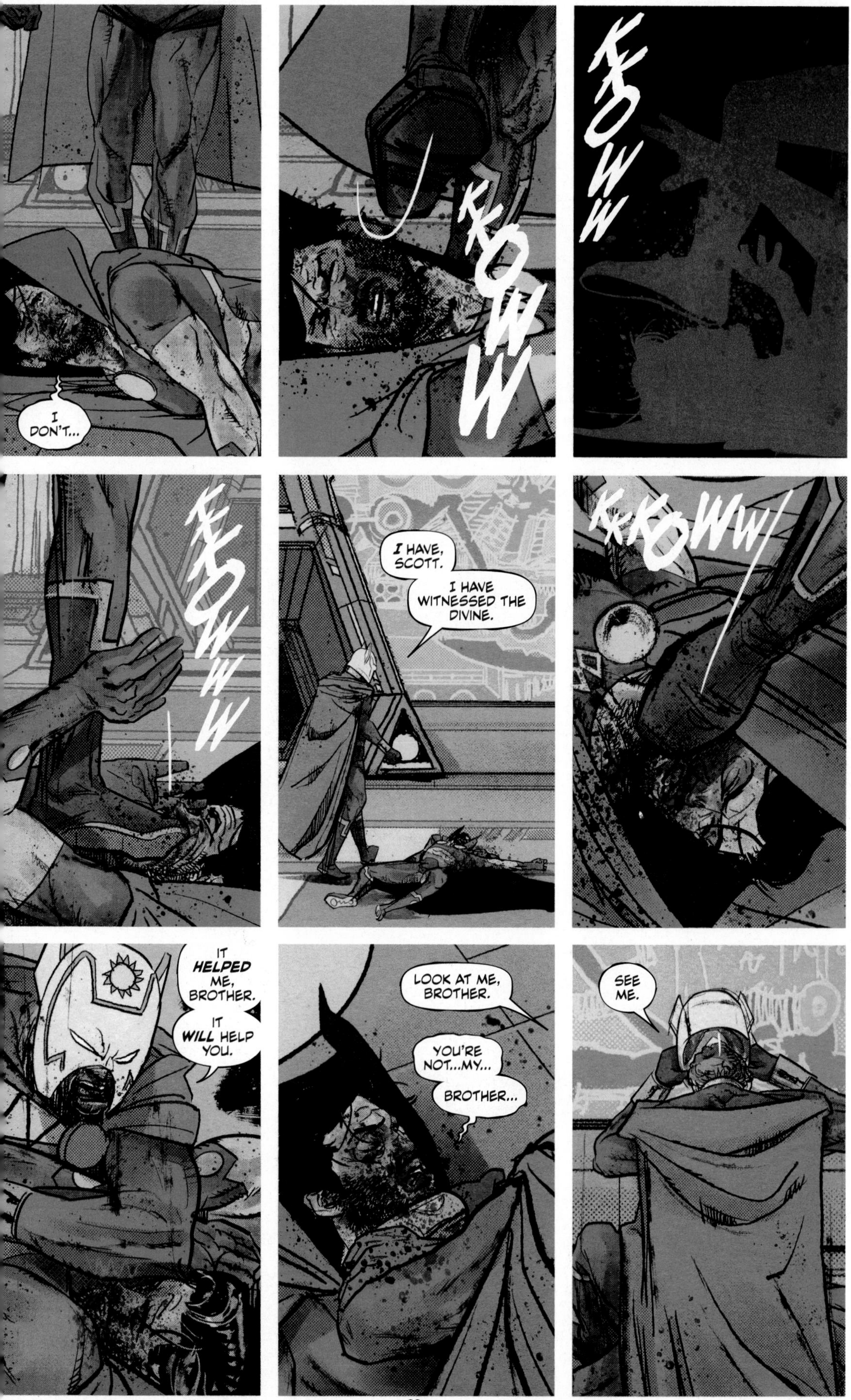
I DON'T...
KKOWW
KKOWWW
KKOWWWW
I HAVE, SCOTT.
I HAVE WITNESSED THE DIVINE.
KKKOWWW
IT ***HELPED*** ME, BROTHER.
IT ***WILL*** HELP YOU.
LOOK AT ME, BROTHER.
YOU'RE NOT...MY...
BROTHER...
SEE ME.

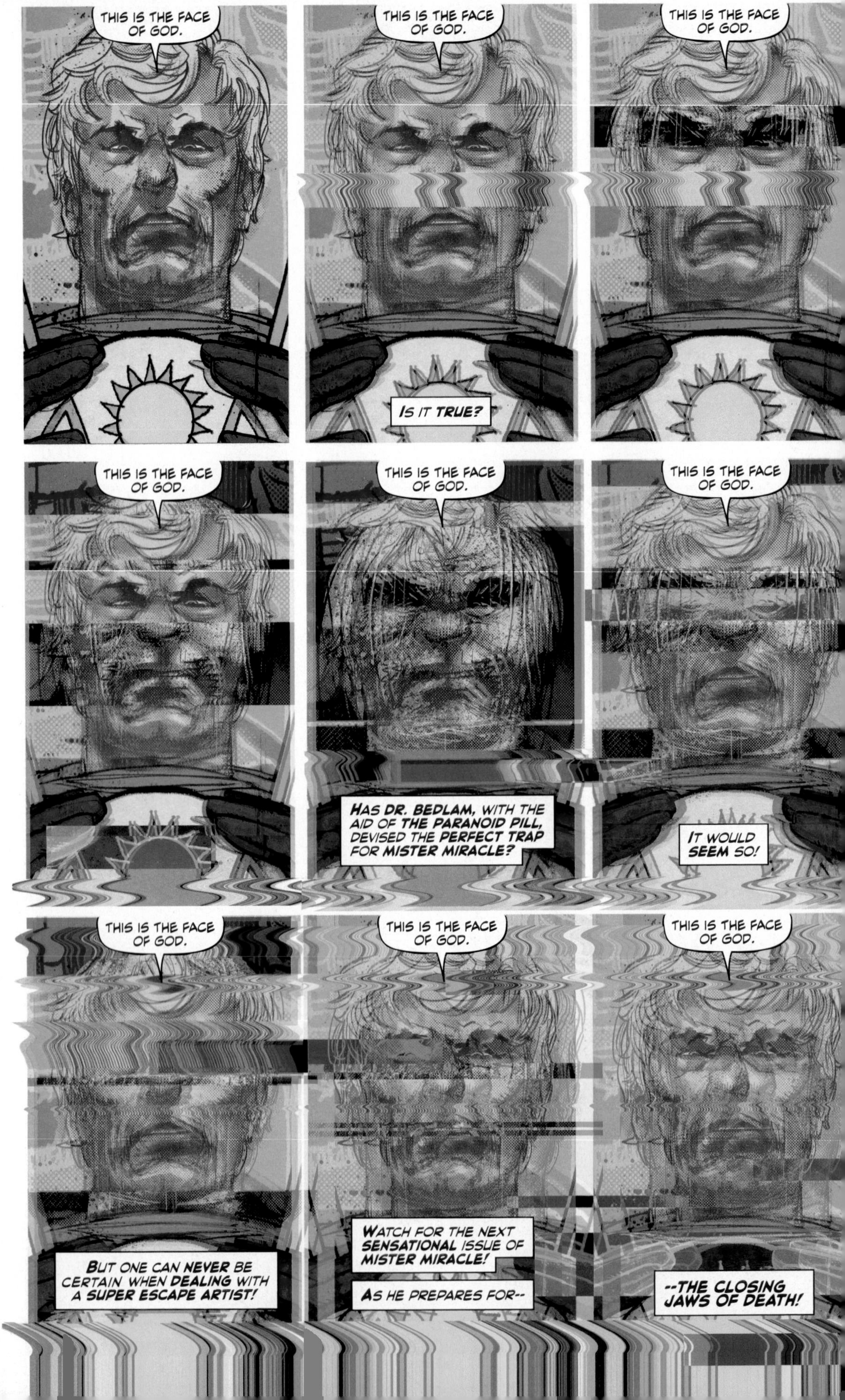

THIS IS THE FACE OF GOD.
THIS IS THE FACE OF GOD.
IS IT TRUE?
THIS IS THE FACE OF GOD.
THIS IS THE FACE OF GOD.
THIS IS THE FACE OF GOD.
HAS DR. BEDLAM, WITH THE AID OF THE PARANOID PILL, DEVISED THE PERFECT TRAP FOR MISTER MIRACLE?
THIS IS THE FACE OF GOD.
IT WOULD SEEM SO!
THIS IS THE FACE OF GOD.
BUT ONE CAN NEVER BE CERTAIN WHEN DEALING WITH A SUPER ESCAPE ARTIST!
THIS IS THE FACE OF GOD.
WATCH FOR THE NEXT SENSATIONAL ISSUE OF MISTER MIRACLE!
AS HE PREPARES FOR--
THIS IS THE FACE OF GOD.
--THE CLOSING JAWS OF DEATH!

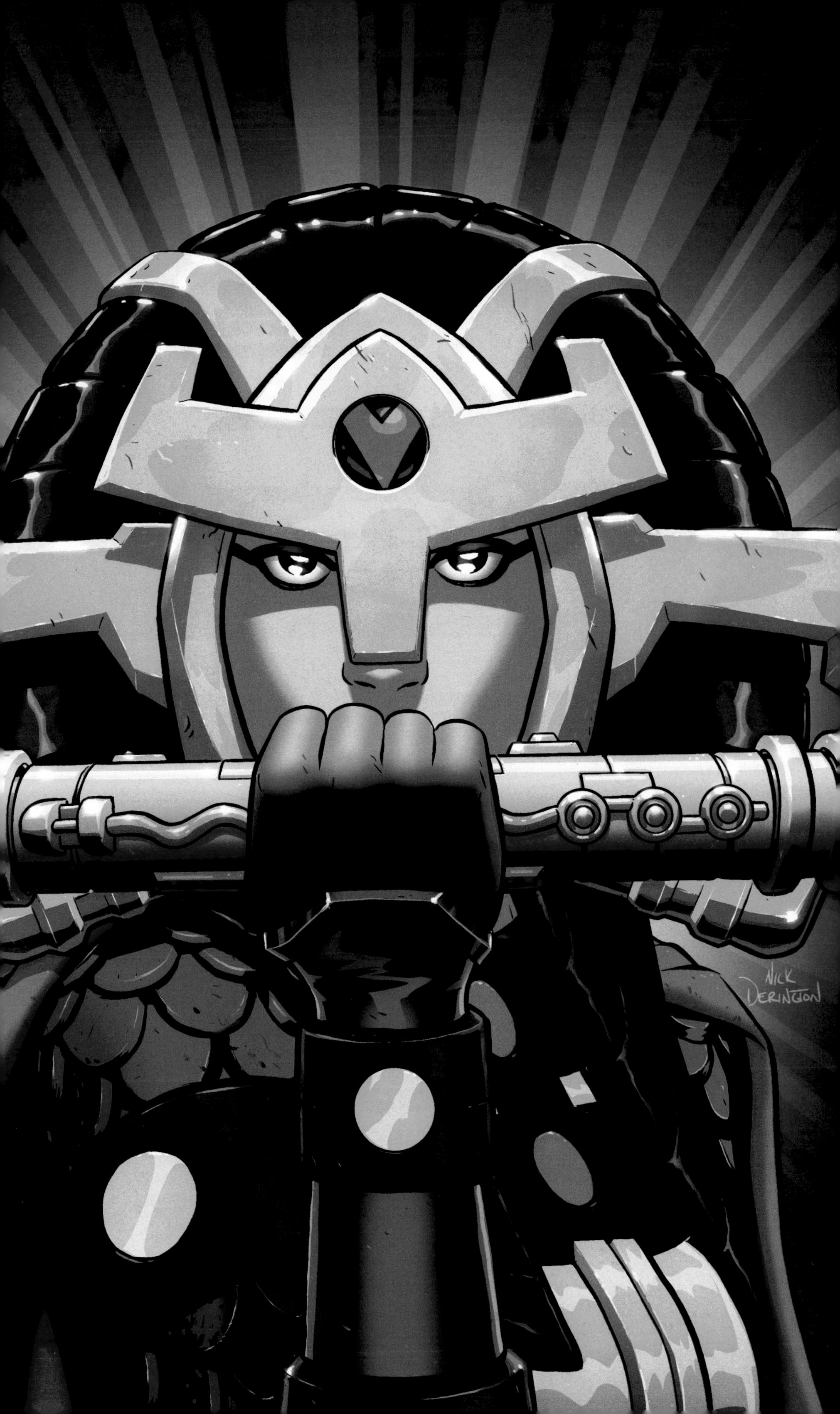
NICK DERINGTON

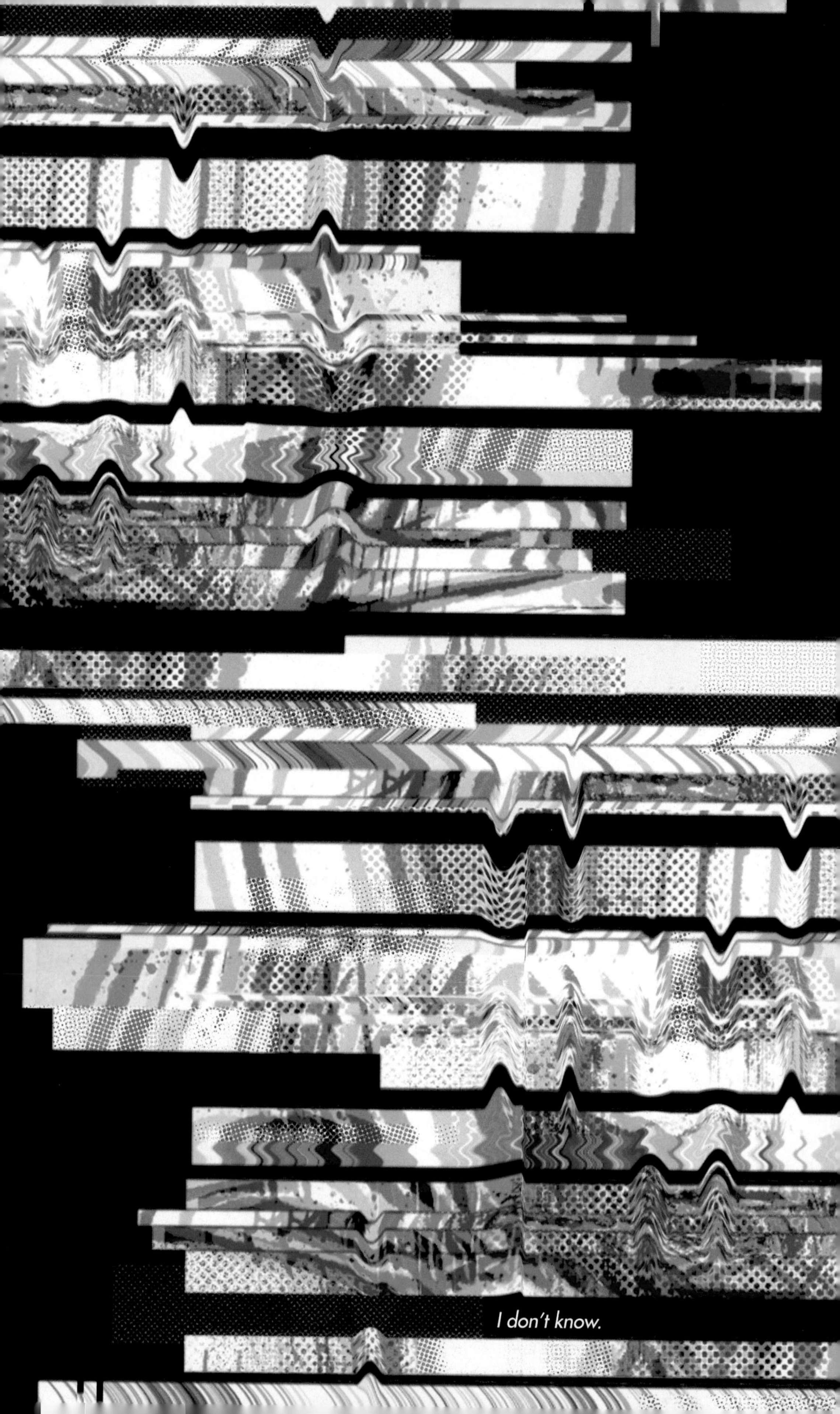
I don't know.

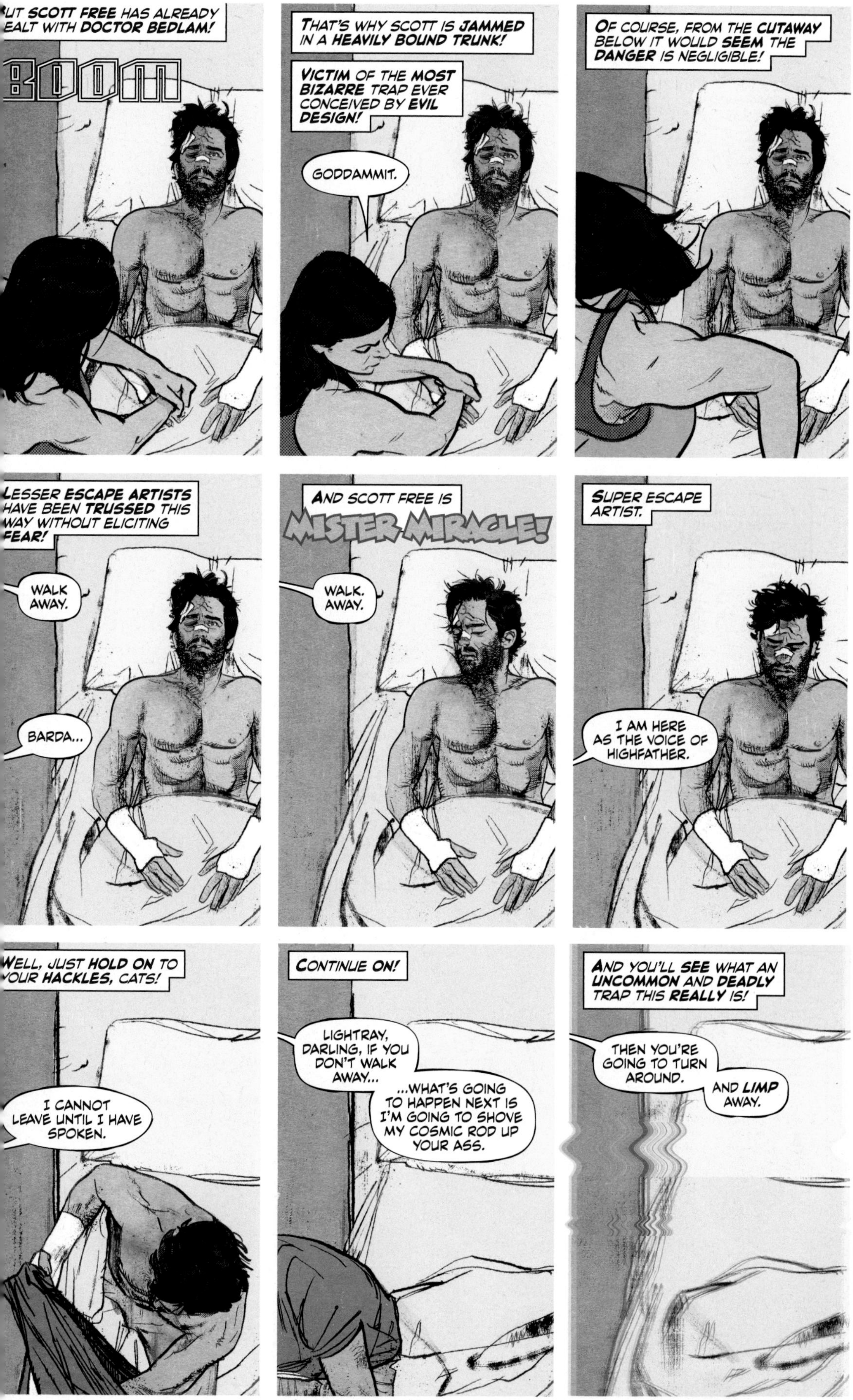

UT SCOTT FREE HAS ALREADY EALT WITH DOCTOR BEDLAM!
BOOM
THAT'S WHY SCOTT IS JAMMED IN A HEAVILY BOUND TRUNK!
VICTIM OF THE MOST BIZARRE TRAP EVER CONCEIVED BY EVIL DESIGN!
GODDAMMIT.
OF COURSE, FROM THE CUTAWAY BELOW IT WOULD SEEM THE DANGER IS NEGLIGIBLE!
LESSER ESCAPE ARTISTS HAVE BEEN TRUSSED THIS WAY WITHOUT ELICITING FEAR!
WALK AWAY.
BARDA...
AND SCOTT FREE IS
MISTER MIRACLE!
WALK. AWAY.
SUPER ESCAPE ARTIST.
I AM HERE AS THE VOICE OF HIGHFATHER.
WELL, JUST HOLD ON TO YOUR HACKLES, CATS!
I CANNOT LEAVE UNTIL I HAVE SPOKEN.
CONTINUE ON!
LIGHTRAY, DARLING, IF YOU DON'T WALK AWAY...
...WHAT'S GOING TO HAPPEN NEXT IS I'M GOING TO SHOVE MY COSMIC ROD UP YOUR ASS.
AND YOU'LL SEE WHAT AN UNCOMMON AND DEADLY TRAP THIS REALLY IS!
THEN YOU'RE GOING TO TURN AROUND.
AND LIMP AWAY.

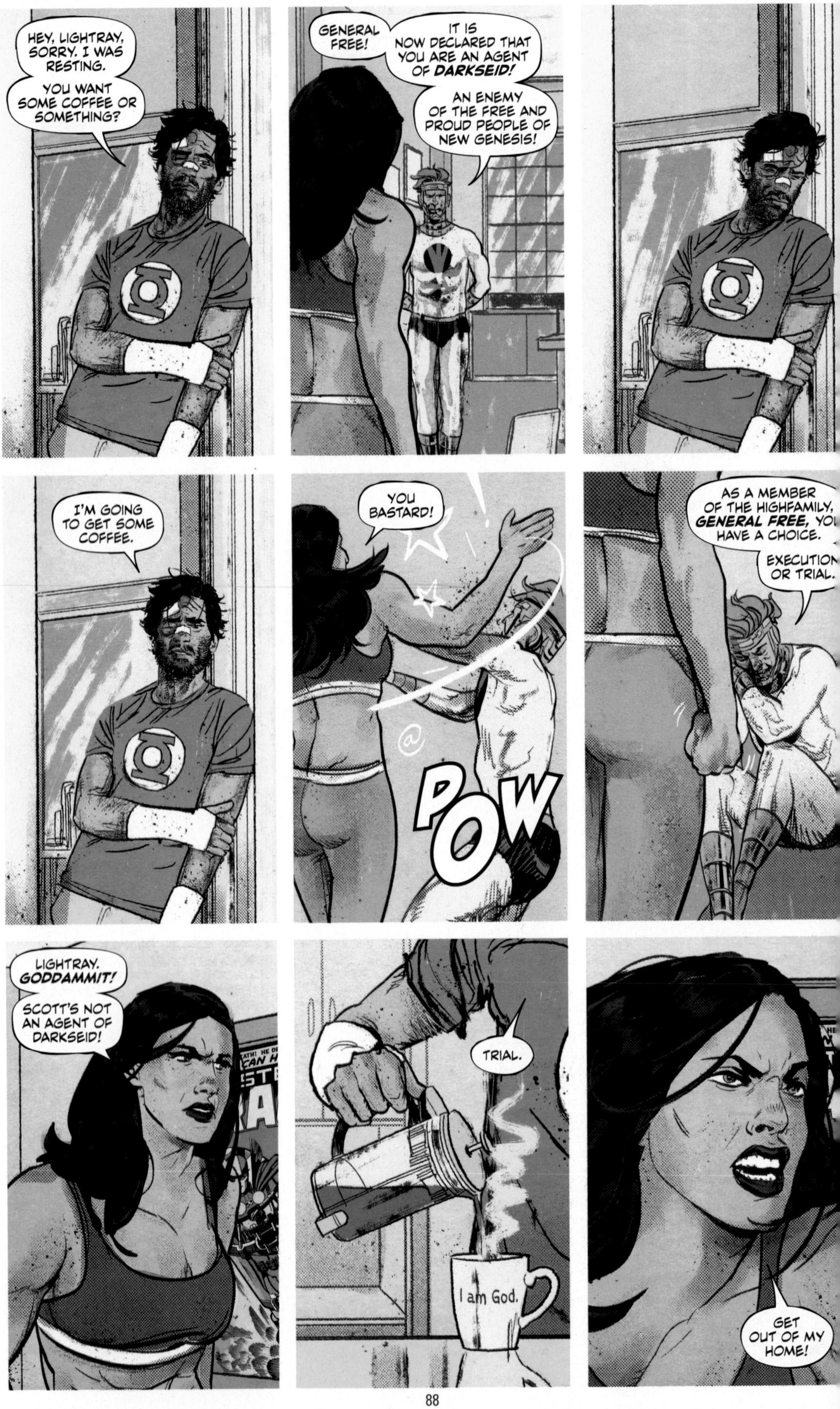
HEY, LIGHTRAY, SORRY. I WAS RESTING.
YOU WANT SOME COFFEE OR SOMETHING?
GENERAL FREE!
IT IS NOW DECLARED THAT YOU ARE AN AGENT OF DARKSEID!
AN ENEMY OF THE FREE AND PROUD PEOPLE OF NEW GENESIS!
I'M GOING TO GET SOME COFFEE.
YOU BASTARD!
POW
AS A MEMBER OF THE HIGHFAMILY, GENERAL FREE, YOU HAVE A CHOICE.
EXECUTION OR TRIAL.
LIGHTRAY. GODDAMMIT!
SCOTT'S NOT AN AGENT OF DARKSEID!
TRIAL.
I am God.
GET OUT OF MY HOME!

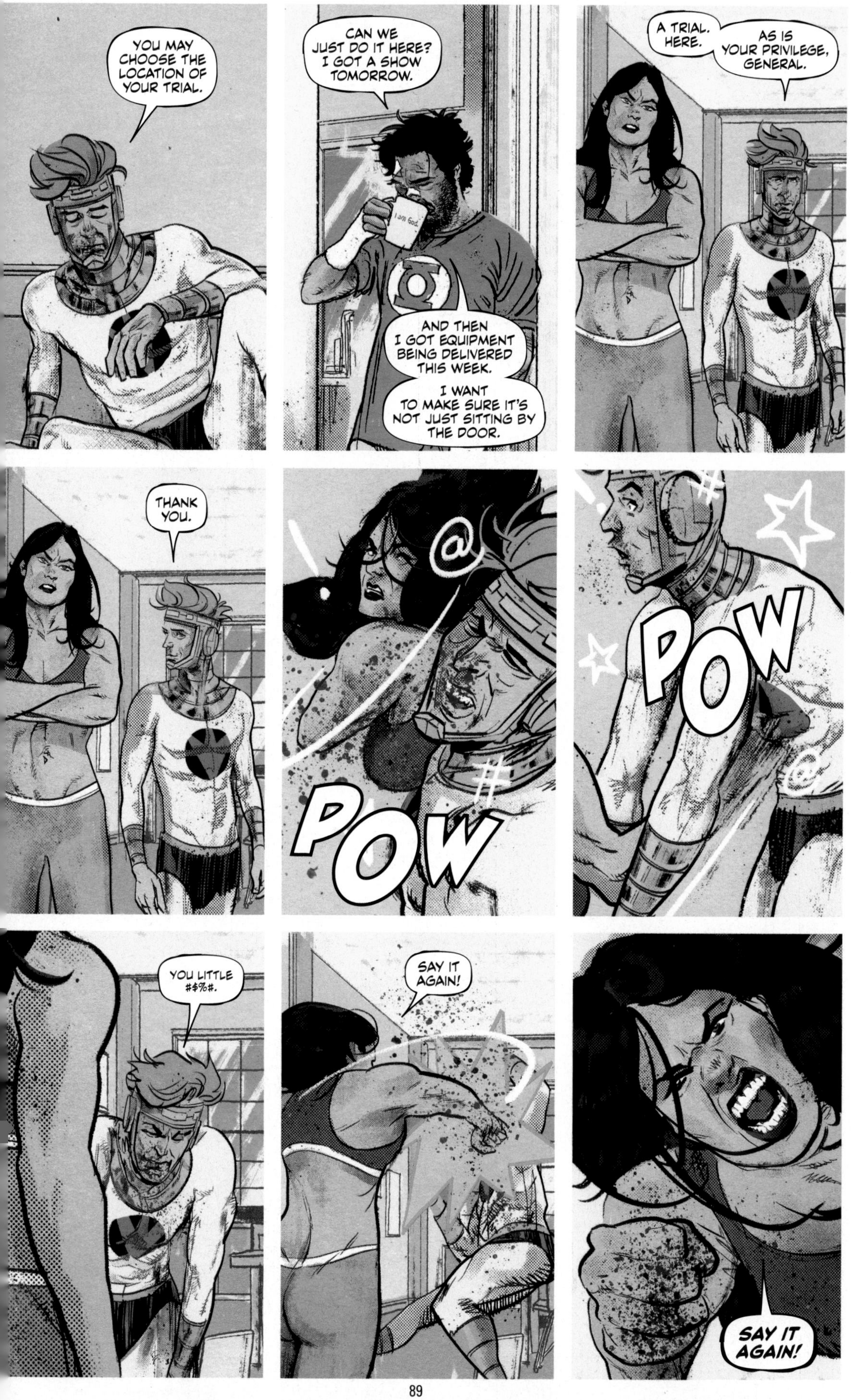

YOU MAY CHOOSE THE LOCATION OF YOUR TRIAL.
CAN WE JUST DO IT HERE? I GOT A SHOW TOMORROW.
AND THEN I GOT EQUIPMENT BEING DELIVERED THIS WEEK.
I WANT TO MAKE SURE IT'S NOT JUST SITTING BY THE DOOR.
A TRIAL. HERE.
AS IS YOUR PRIVILEGE, GENERAL.
THANK YOU.
POW
POW
YOU LITTLE #$%#.
SAY IT AGAIN!
SAY IT AGAIN!

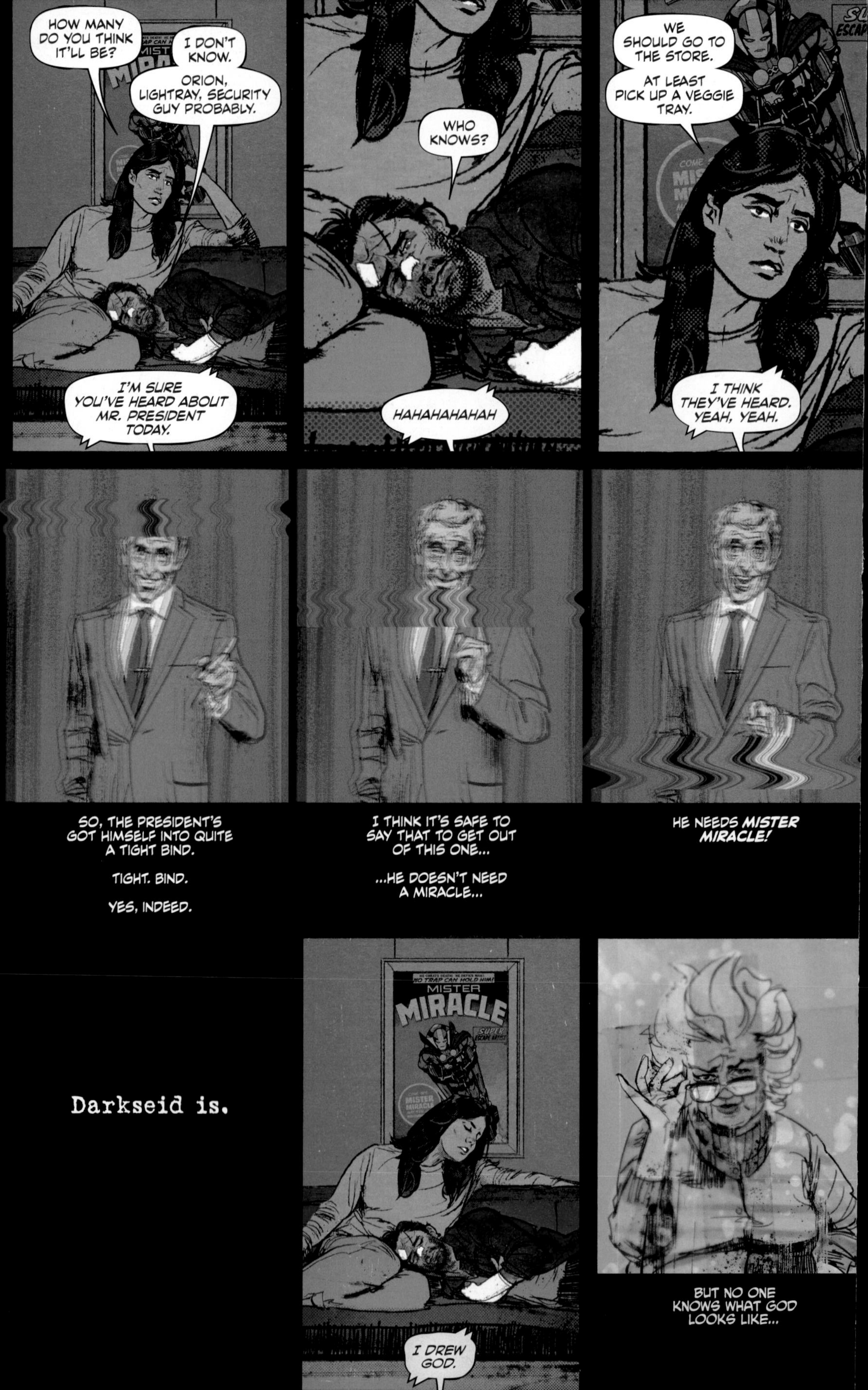

HOW MANY DO YOU THINK IT'LL BE?
I DON'T KNOW.
ORION, LIGHTRAY, SECURITY GUY PROBABLY.
I'M SURE YOU'VE HEARD ABOUT MR. PRESIDENT TODAY.
WHO KNOWS?
HAHAHAHAHAH
WE SHOULD GO TO THE STORE.
AT LEAST PICK UP A VEGGIE TRAY.
I THINK THEY'VE HEARD. YEAH, YEAH.
SO, THE PRESIDENT'S GOT HIMSELF INTO QUITE A TIGHT BIND.
TIGHT. BIND.
YES, INDEED.
I THINK IT'S SAFE TO SAY THAT TO GET OUT OF THIS ONE...
...HE DOESN'T NEED A MIRACLE...
HE NEEDS *MISTER MIRACLE!*
Darkseid is.
NO TRAP CAN HOLD HIM!
MISTER MIRACLE
SUPER ESCAPE ARTIST
I DREW GOD.
BUT NO ONE KNOWS WHAT GOD LOOKS LIKE...

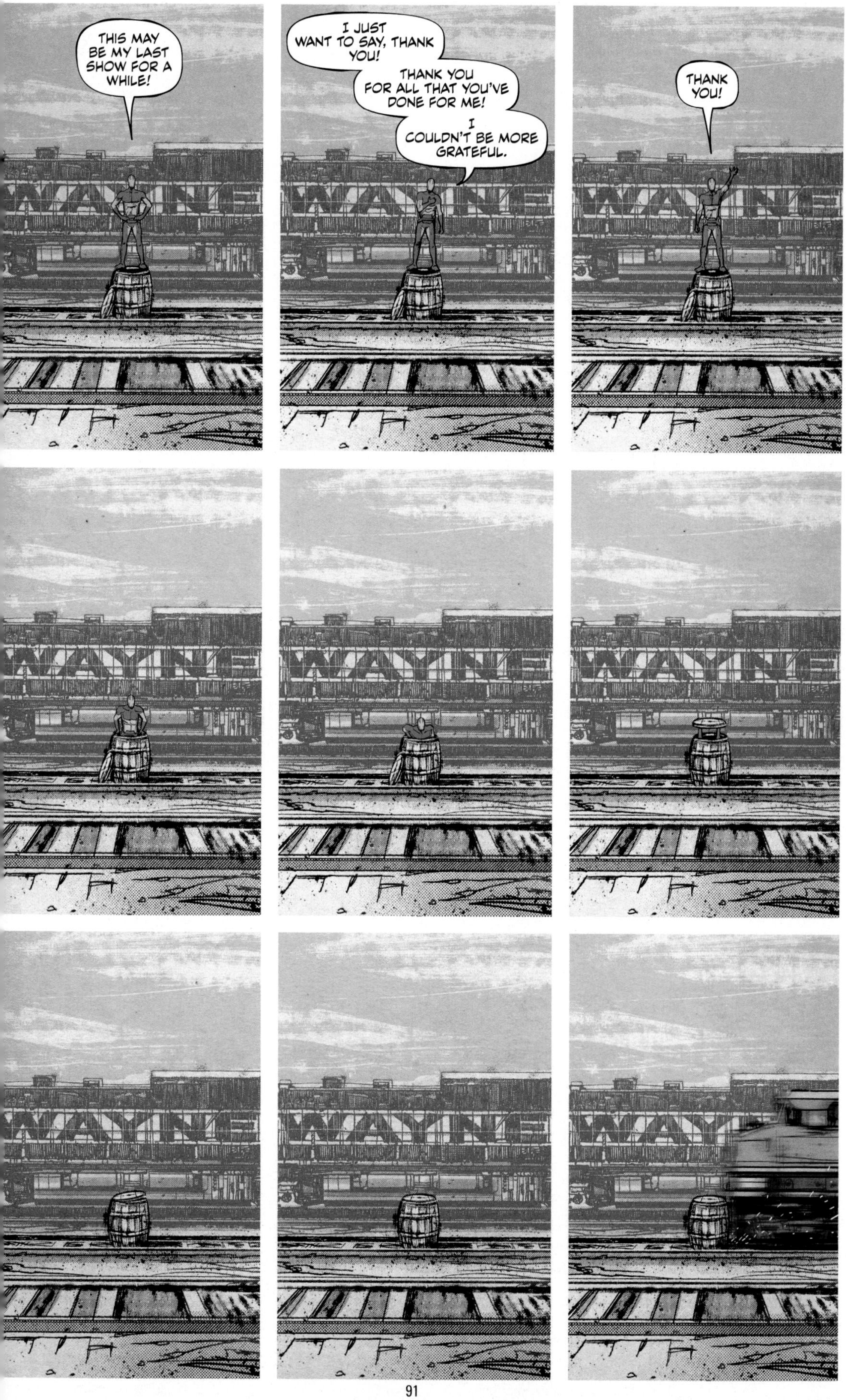

THIS MAY BE MY LAST SHOW FOR A WHILE!
I JUST WANT TO SAY, THANK YOU!
THANK YOU FOR ALL THAT YOU'VE DONE FOR ME!
I COULDN'T BE MORE GRATEFUL.
THANK YOU!

WE GOT A VEGGIE TRAY.

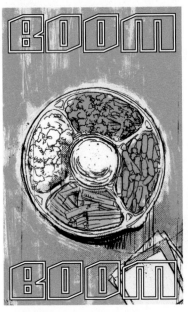

SHOULD I SIT OR STAND?

SIT.

SITTING.

GOOD.

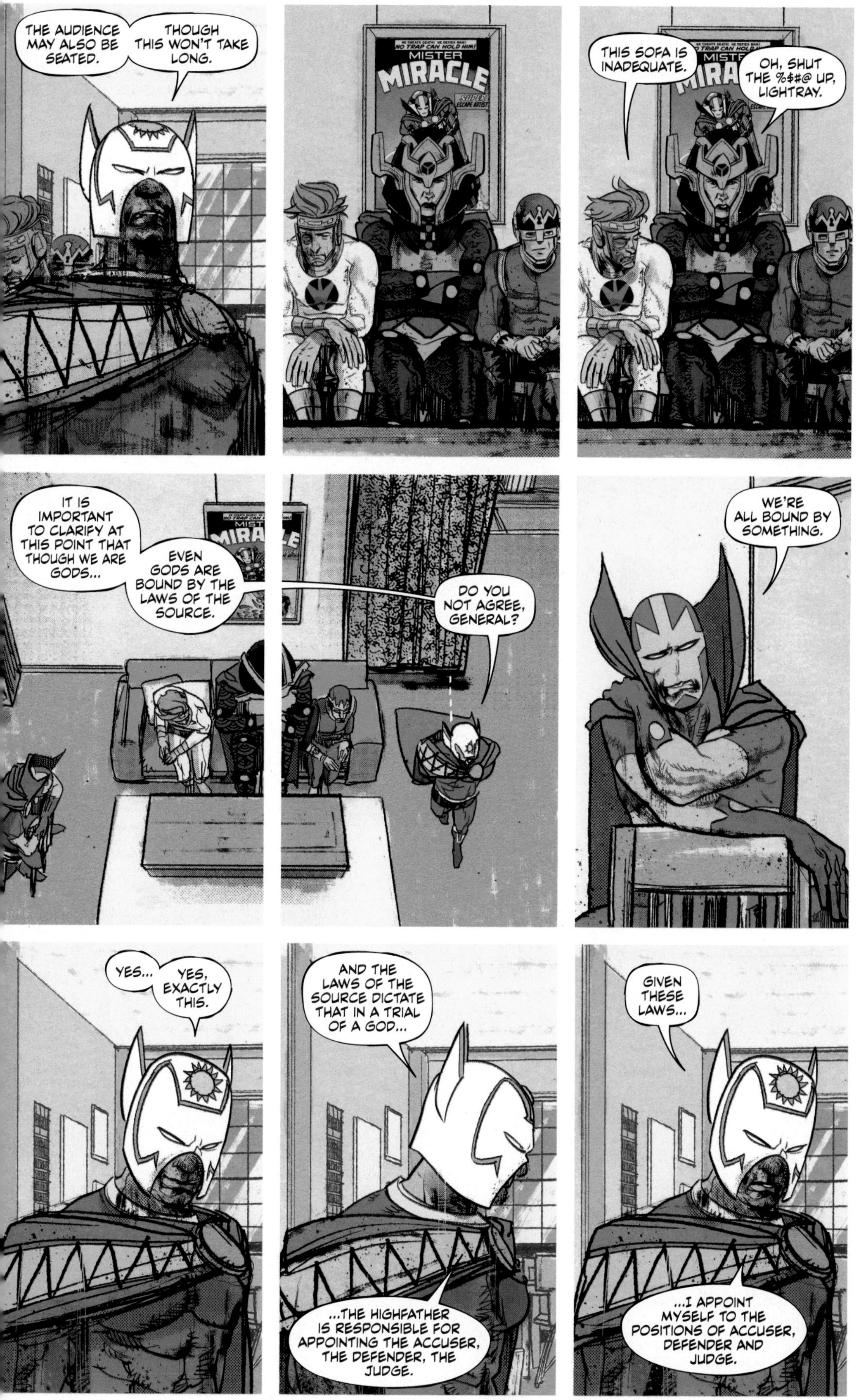
THE AUDIENCE MAY ALSO BE SEATED.
THOUGH THIS WON'T TAKE LONG.
HE CHEATS DEATH! HE DEFIES MAN! NO TRAP CAN HOLD HIM!
MISTER MIRACLE
SUPER ESCAPE ARTIST
THIS SOFA IS INADEQUATE.
OH, SHUT THE %$#@ UP, LIGHTRAY.
IT IS IMPORTANT TO CLARIFY AT THIS POINT THAT THOUGH WE ARE GODS...
EVEN GODS ARE BOUND BY THE LAWS OF THE SOURCE.
DO YOU NOT AGREE, GENERAL?
WE'RE ALL BOUND BY SOMETHING.
YES...
YES, EXACTLY THIS.
AND THE LAWS OF THE SOURCE DICTATE THAT IN A TRIAL OF A GOD...
...THE HIGHFATHER IS RESPONSIBLE FOR APPOINTING THE ACCUSER, THE DEFENDER, THE JUDGE.
GIVEN THESE LAWS...
...I APPOINT MYSELF TO THE POSITIONS OF ACCUSER, DEFENDER AND JUDGE.

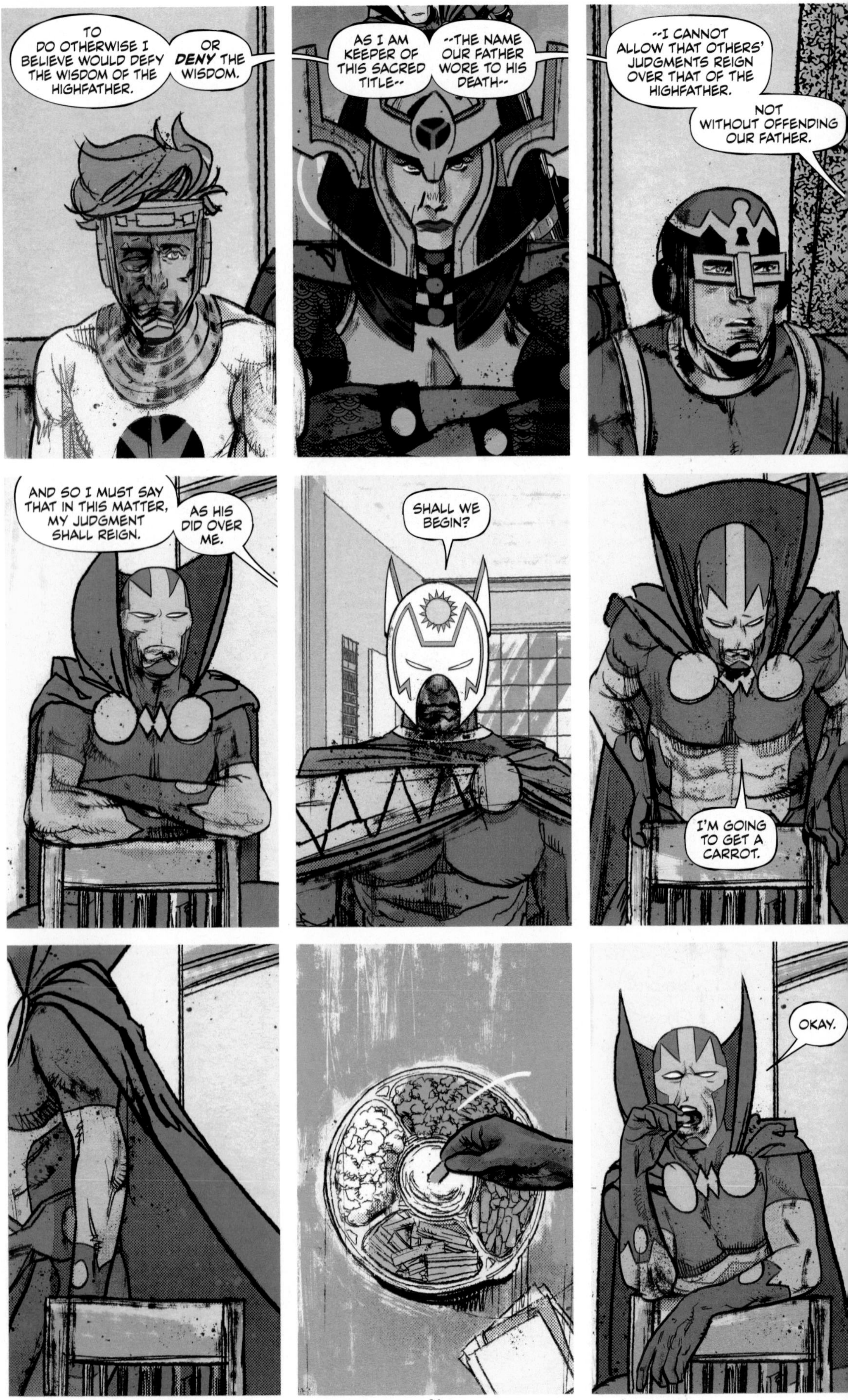
TO DO OTHERWISE I BELIEVE WOULD DEFY THE WISDOM OF THE HIGHFATHER.
OR DENY THE WISDOM.
AS I AM KEEPER OF THIS SACRED TITLE--
--THE NAME OUR FATHER WORE TO HIS DEATH--
--I CANNOT ALLOW THAT OTHERS' JUDGMENTS REIGN OVER THAT OF THE HIGHFATHER.
NOT WITHOUT OFFENDING OUR FATHER.
AND SO I MUST SAY THAT IN THIS MATTER, MY JUDGMENT SHALL REIGN.
AS HIS DID OVER ME.
SHALL WE BEGIN?
I'M GOING TO GET A CARROT.
OKAY.

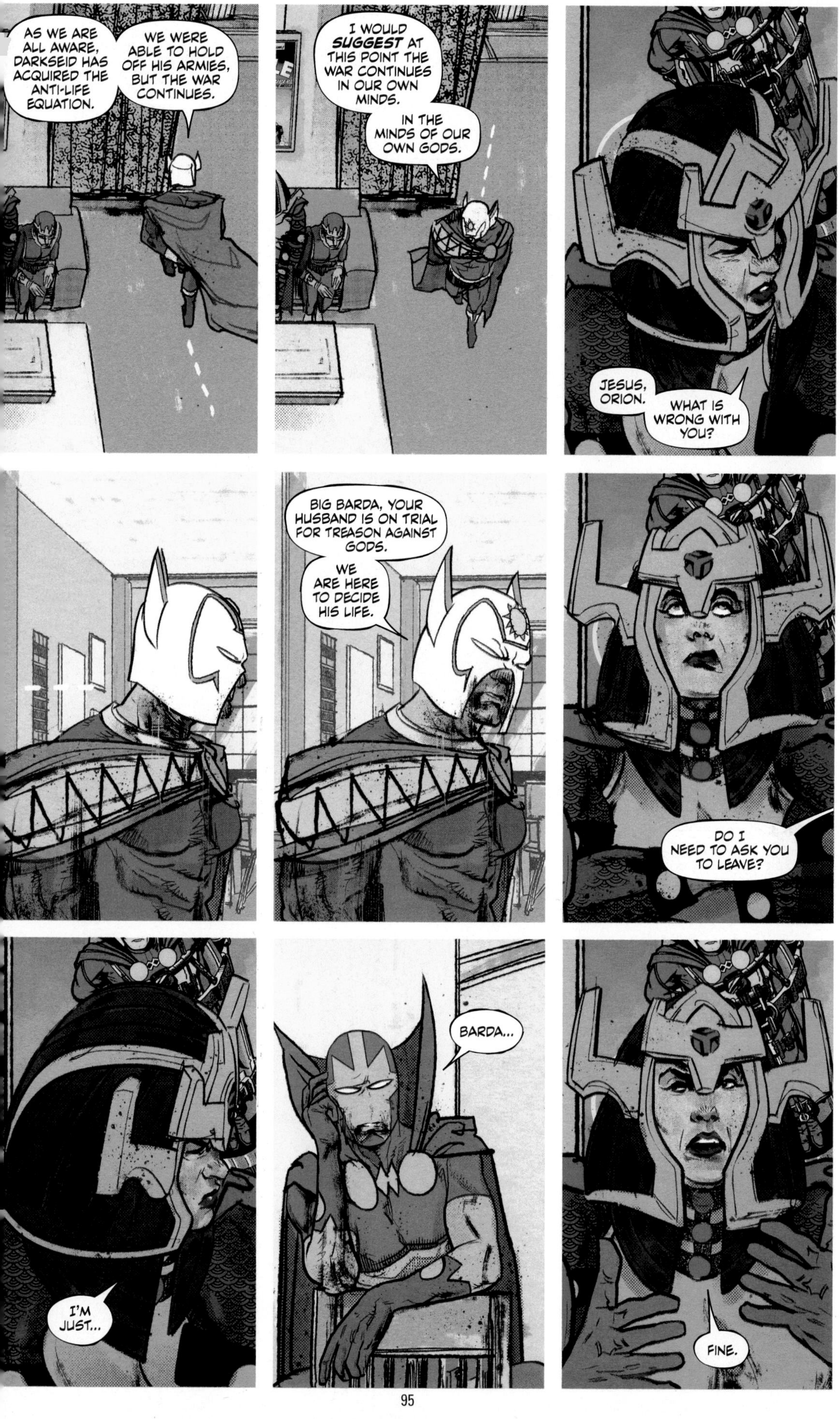
AS WE ARE ALL AWARE, DARKSEID HAS ACQUIRED THE ANTI-LIFE EQUATION.
WE WERE ABLE TO HOLD OFF HIS ARMIES, BUT THE WAR CONTINUES.
I WOULD *SUGGEST* AT THIS POINT THE WAR CONTINUES IN OUR OWN MINDS.
IN THE MINDS OF OUR OWN GODS.
JESUS, ORION.
WHAT IS WRONG WITH YOU?
BIG BARDA, YOUR HUSBAND IS ON TRIAL FOR TREASON AGAINST GODS.
WE ARE HERE TO DECIDE HIS LIFE.
DO I NEED TO ASK YOU TO LEAVE?
I'M JUST...
BARDA...
FINE.

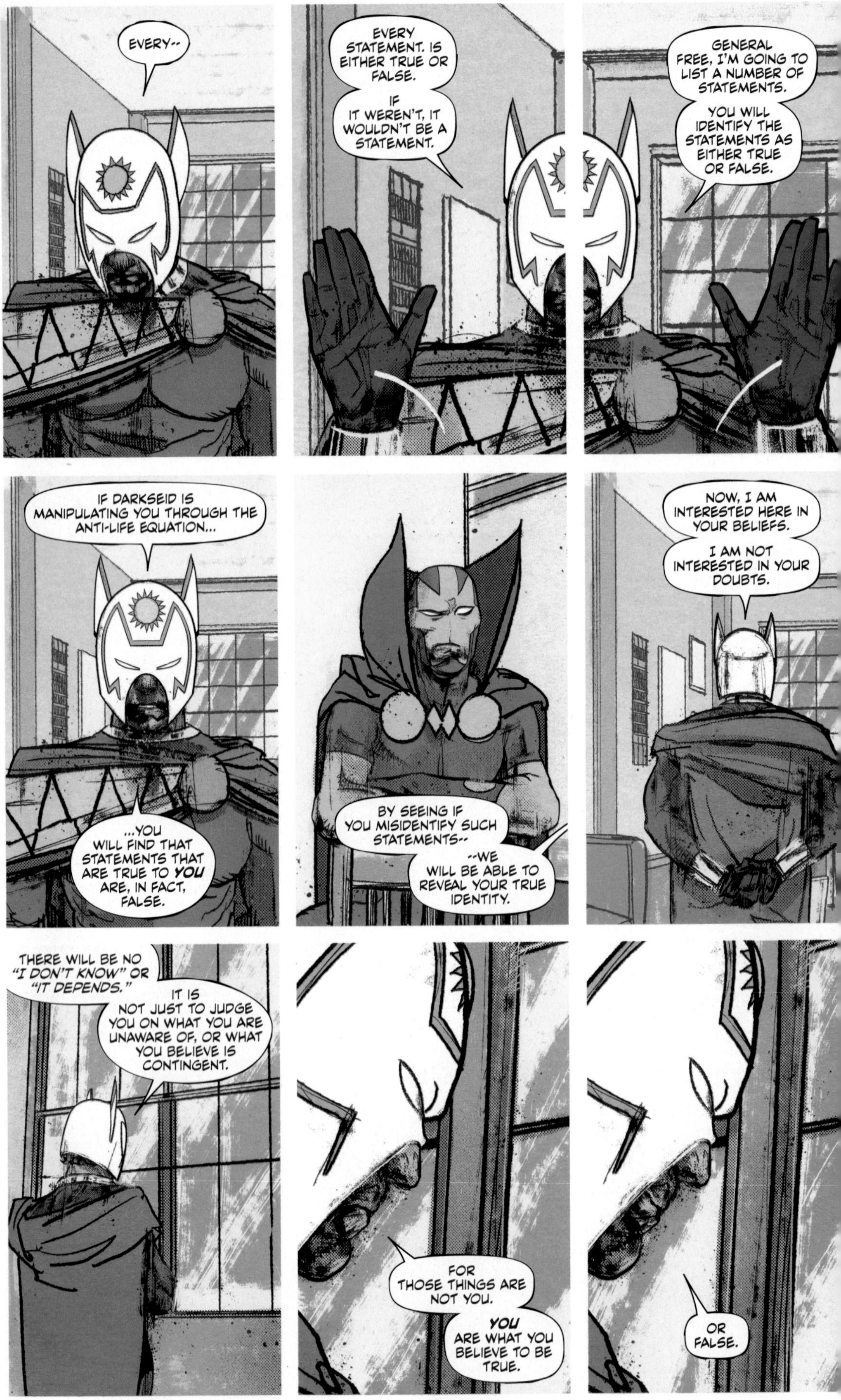
EVERY--
EVERY STATEMENT. IS EITHER TRUE OR FALSE.
IF IT WEREN'T, IT WOULDN'T BE A STATEMENT.
GENERAL FREE, I'M GOING TO LIST A NUMBER OF STATEMENTS.
YOU WILL IDENTIFY THE STATEMENTS AS EITHER TRUE OR FALSE.
IF DARKSEID IS MANIPULATING YOU THROUGH THE ANTI-LIFE EQUATION...
...YOU WILL FIND THAT STATEMENTS THAT ARE TRUE TO *YOU* ARE, IN FACT, FALSE.
BY SEEING IF YOU MISIDENTIFY SUCH STATEMENTS--
--WE WILL BE ABLE TO REVEAL YOUR TRUE IDENTITY.
NOW, I AM INTERESTED HERE IN YOUR BELIEFS.
I AM NOT INTERESTED IN YOUR DOUBTS.
THERE WILL BE NO *"I DON'T KNOW"* OR *"IT DEPENDS."*
IT IS NOT JUST TO JUDGE YOU ON WHAT YOU ARE UNAWARE OF, OR WHAT YOU BELIEVE IS CONTINGENT.
FOR THOSE THINGS ARE NOT YOU.
YOU ARE WHAT YOU BELIEVE TO BE TRUE.
OR FALSE.

WE BEGIN.

YOU CONFESSED YOU BELIEVED DARKSEID HAD INFECTED YOU WITH THE ANTI-LIFE EQUATION.

TRUE OR FALSE?

TRUE.

YOU THEN ACCUSED THE HIGHFATHER OF BEING SIMILARLY INFECTED.

TRUE OR FALSE?

TRUE.

THE HIGHFATHER IS AN AGENT OF DARKSEID.

TRUE OR FALSE?

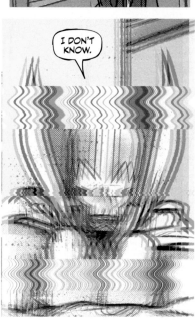

I DON'T KNOW.

AGAIN, YOUR LACK OF KNOWLEDGE WILL NOT SAVE OR CONDEMN YOU.

ONLY YOUR BELIEFS CAN.

WHAT...

ORION, C'MON, HOW AM I SUPPOSED TO KNOW?

GENERAL, YOU KNOW WHAT YOU BELIEVE.

TRUE OR FALSE?

I... DON'T...

YEAH, FINE, I KNOW WHAT I BELIEVE. WHATEVER. TRUE.

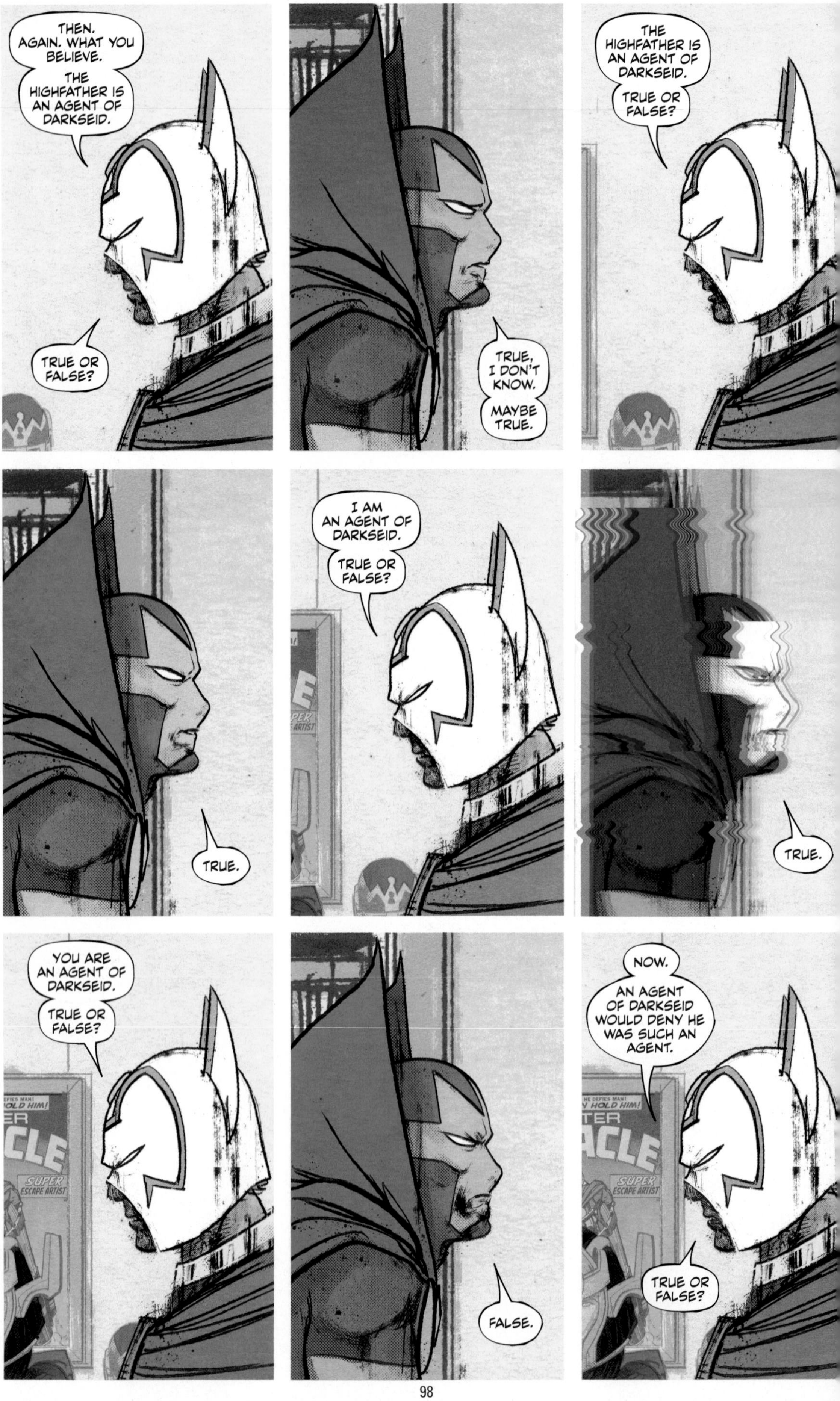
THEN. AGAIN. WHAT YOU BELIEVE.
THE HIGHFATHER IS AN AGENT OF DARKSEID.
TRUE OR FALSE?
TRUE, I DON'T KNOW.
MAYBE TRUE.
THE HIGHFATHER IS AN AGENT OF DARKSEID.
TRUE OR FALSE?
TRUE.
I AM AN AGENT OF DARKSEID.
TRUE OR FALSE?
TRUE.
YOU ARE AN AGENT OF DARKSEID.
TRUE OR FALSE?
FALSE.
NOW.
AN AGENT OF DARKSEID WOULD DENY HE WAS SUCH AN AGENT.
TRUE OR FALSE?

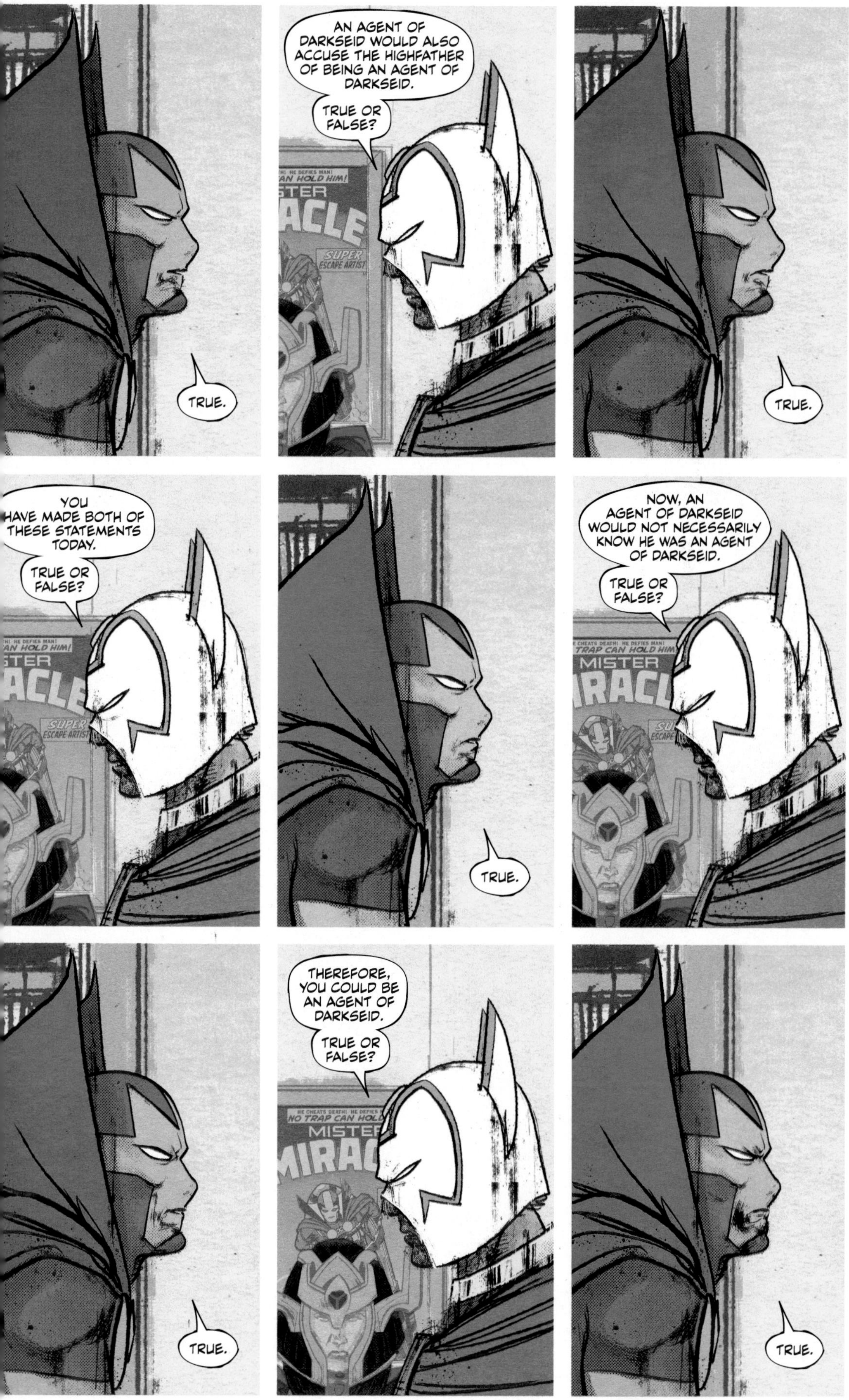
TRUE.
AN AGENT OF DARKSEID WOULD ALSO ACCUSE THE HIGHFATHER OF BEING AN AGENT OF DARKSEID.
TRUE OR FALSE?
TRUE.
YOU HAVE MADE BOTH OF THESE STATEMENTS TODAY.
TRUE OR FALSE?
TRUE.
NOW, AN AGENT OF DARKSEID WOULD NOT NECESSARILY KNOW HE WAS AN AGENT OF DARKSEID.
TRUE OR FALSE?
TRUE.
THEREFORE, YOU COULD BE AN AGENT OF DARKSEID.
TRUE OR FALSE?
TRUE.

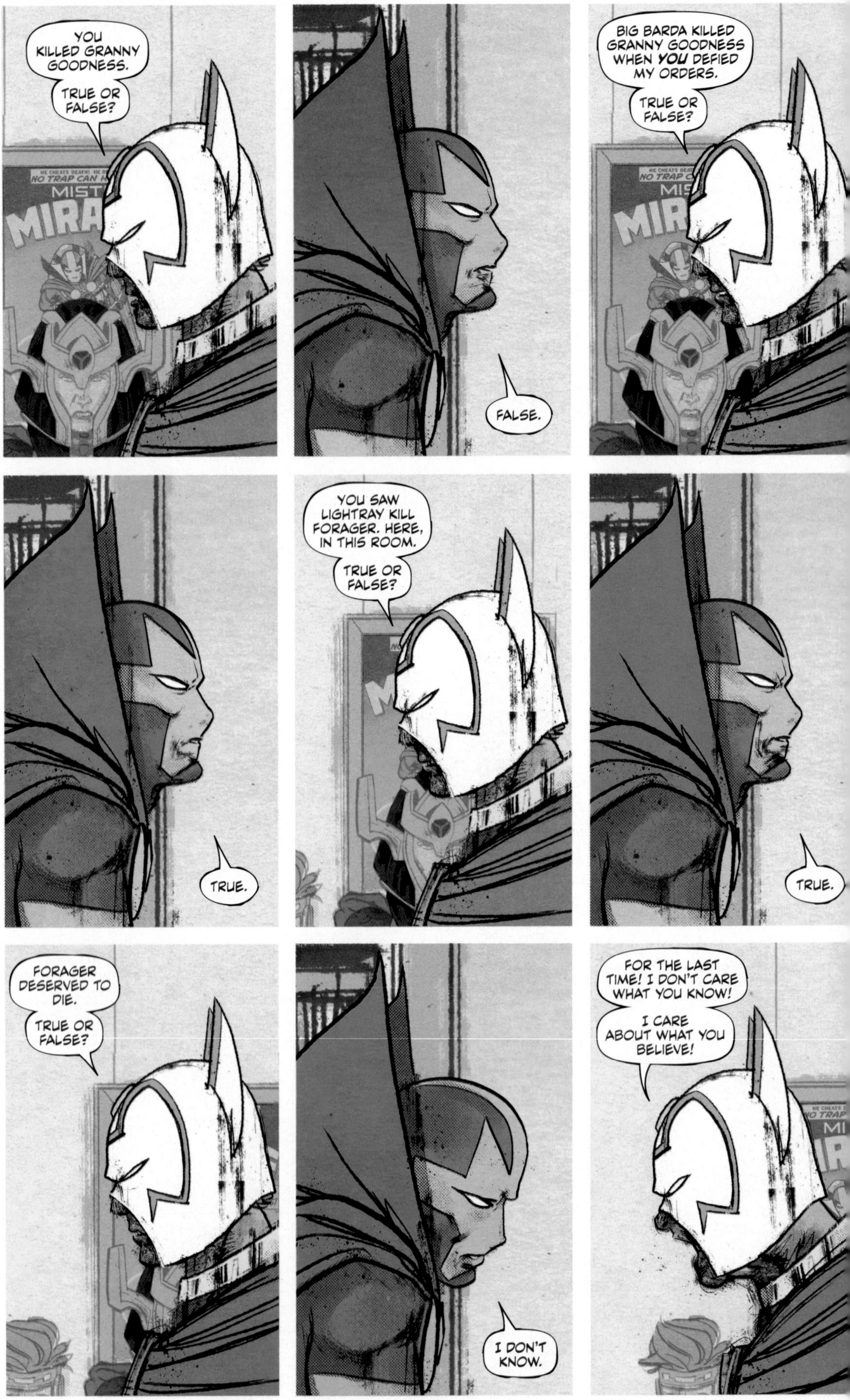
YOU KILLED GRANNY GOODNESS.
TRUE OR FALSE?
FALSE.
BIG BARDA KILLED GRANNY GOODNESS WHEN YOU DEFIED MY ORDERS.
TRUE OR FALSE?
TRUE.
YOU SAW LIGHTRAY KILL FORAGER. HERE, IN THIS ROOM.
TRUE OR FALSE?
TRUE.
FORAGER DESERVED TO DIE.
TRUE OR FALSE?
I DON'T KNOW.
FOR THE LAST TIME! I DON'T CARE WHAT YOU KNOW!
I CARE ABOUT WHAT YOU BELIEVE!

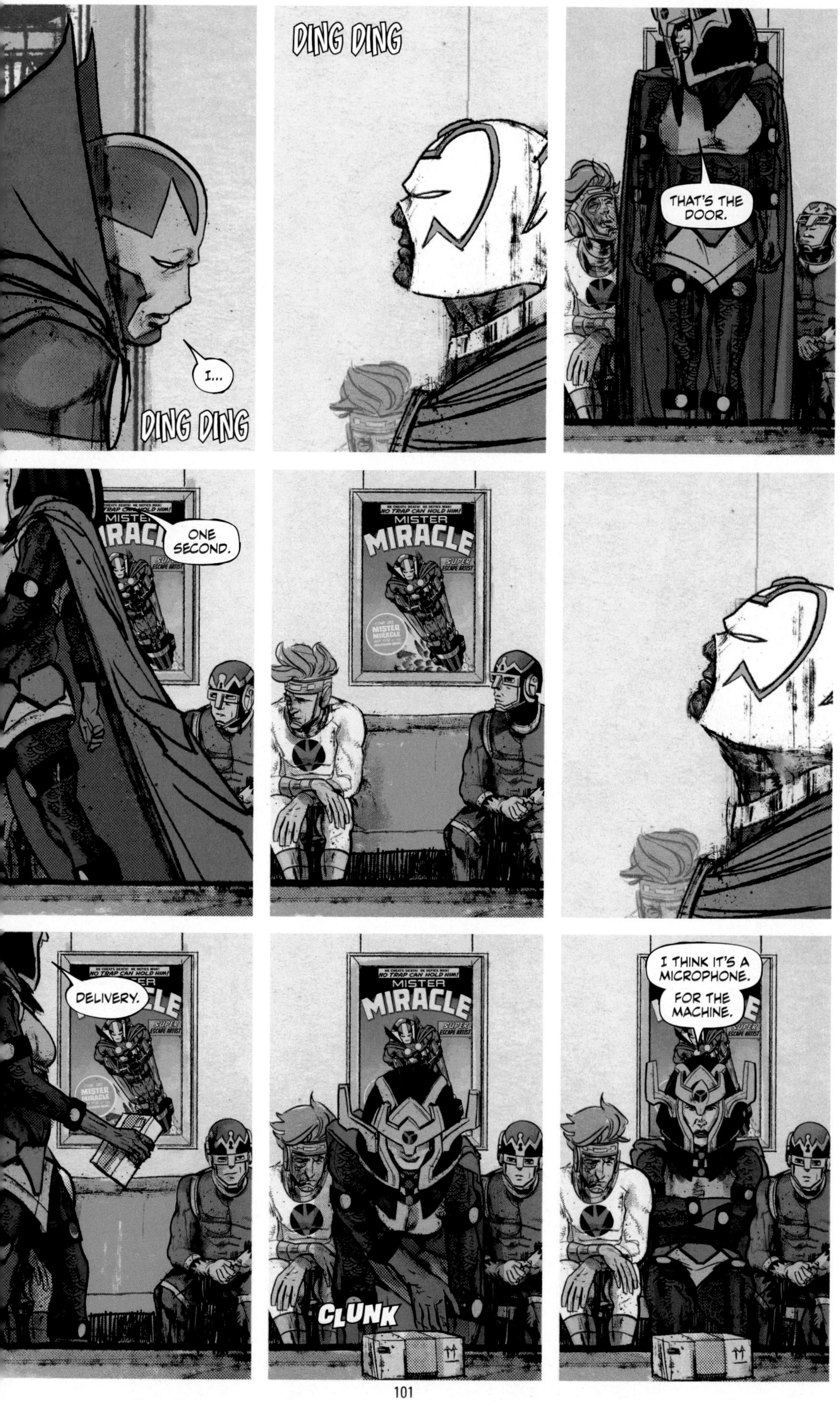
I...
DING DING
DING DING
THAT'S THE DOOR.
ONE SECOND.
HE CHEATS DEATH! HE DEFIES MAN!
NO TRAP CAN HOLD HIM!
MISTER MIRACLE
SUPER ESCAPE ARTIST
DELIVERY.
CLUNK
I THINK IT'S A MICROPHONE.
FOR THE MACHINE.

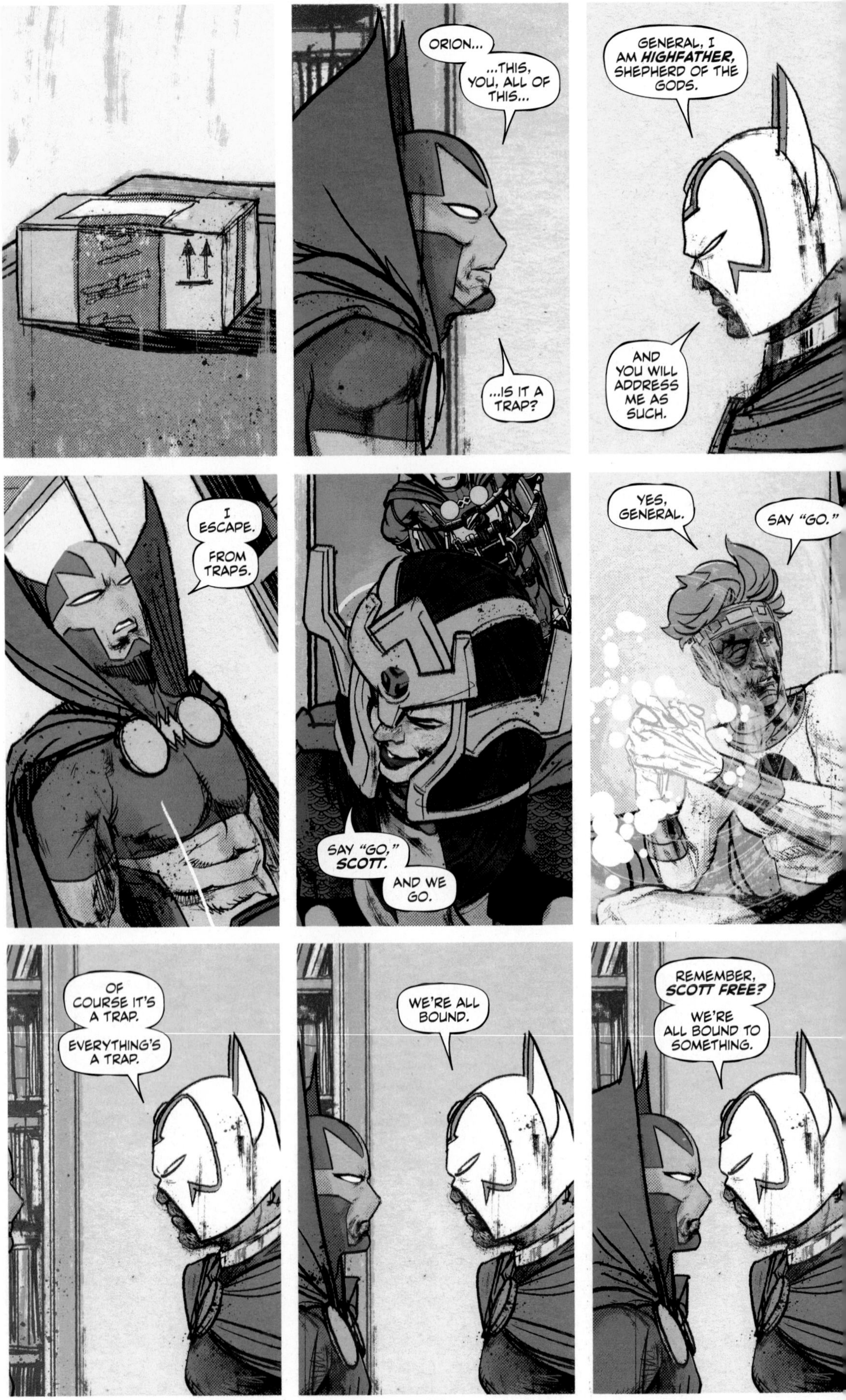
ORION...
...THIS, YOU, ALL OF THIS...
...IS IT A TRAP?
GENERAL, I AM **HIGHFATHER,** SHEPHERD OF THE GODS.
AND YOU WILL ADDRESS ME AS SUCH.
I ESCAPE.
FROM TRAPS.
SAY "GO," **SCOTT.**
AND WE GO.
YES, GENERAL.
SAY "GO."
OF COURSE IT'S A TRAP.
EVERYTHING'S A TRAP.
WE'RE ALL BOUND.
REMEMBER, **SCOTT FREE?**
WE'RE ALL BOUND TO SOMETHING.

SCOTT--

MY NAME IS NOT SCOTT FREE.

THAT'S JUST WHAT GRANNY CALLED ME. WHEN I WAS LITTLE.

'CAUSE I KEPT GETTING OUT AND RUNNING WHEN SHE...AFTER SHE'D HURT ME.

SHE'D CAPTURE ME AGAIN AND SHE'D LAUGH AND CALL ME "SCOTT FREE."

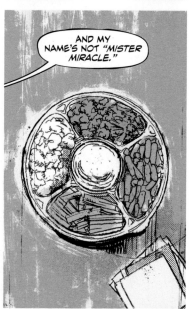

AND MY NAME'S NOT "MISTER MIRACLE."

THAT'S THE NAME OF A PERFORMER, A GUY I MET HERE. ON EARTH.

WHEN HE DIED, I TOOK HIS UNIFORM, HIS GIG. HIS NAME.

EVEN OBERON. OBERON WAS JUST FROM THAT GUY.

MY REAL NAME...I... I DON'T KNOW. I SHOULD'VE ASKED FATHER.

I WAS YOUNG WHEN HE GAVE ME TO DARKSEID.

BUT I WAS BORN HERE. I MUST HAVE HAD A NAME.

BUT I DIDN'T ASK HIM.

I DON'T KNOW WHY.

AND NOW HE'S...

WHY DIDN'T HE JUST...

...HE COULD'VE GIVEN ME A NAME.

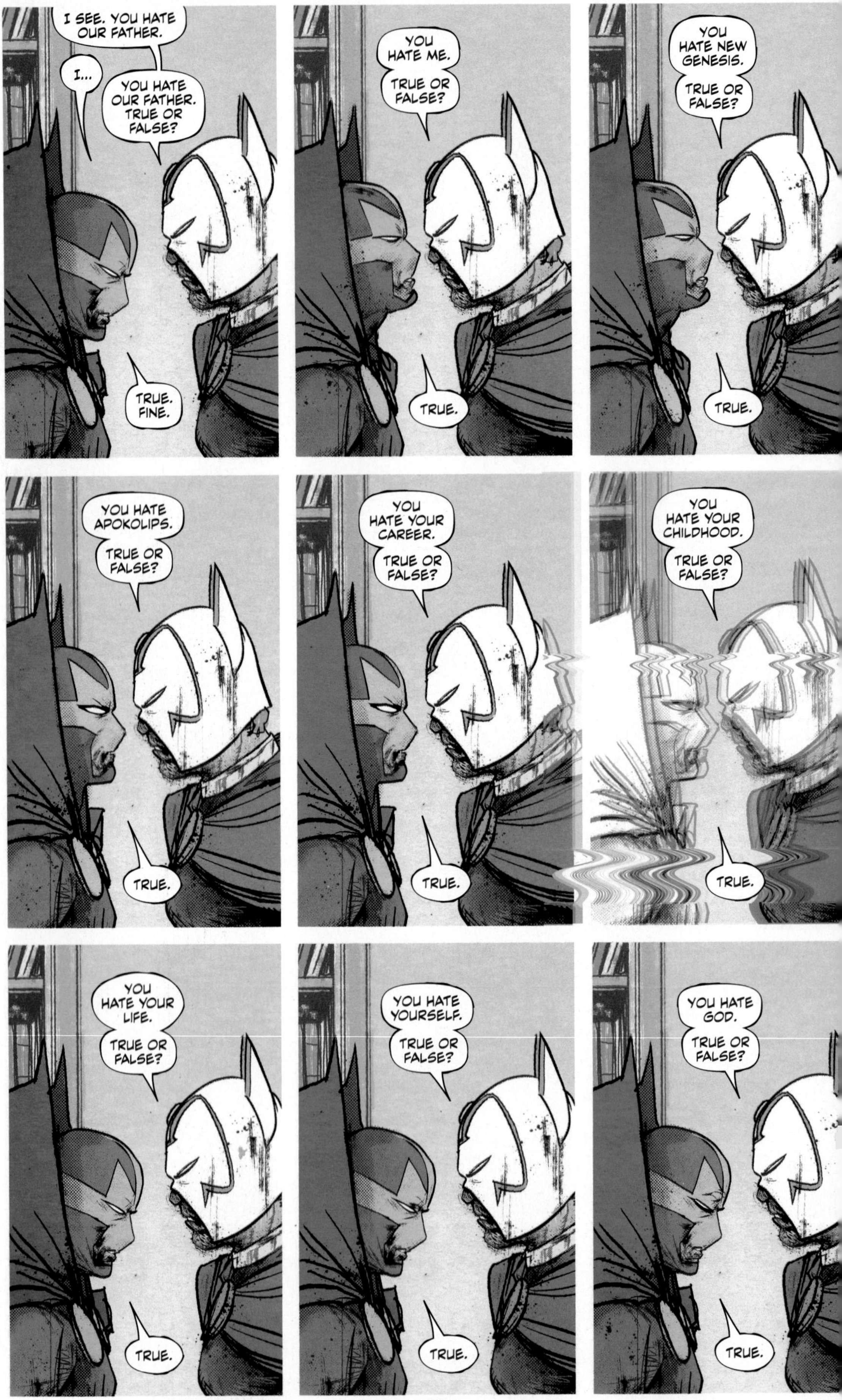

I SEE. YOU HATE OUR FATHER.
I...
YOU HATE OUR FATHER. TRUE OR FALSE?
TRUE. FINE.
YOU HATE ME.
TRUE OR FALSE?
TRUE.
YOU HATE NEW GENESIS.
TRUE OR FALSE?
TRUE.
YOU HATE APOKOLIPS.
TRUE OR FALSE?
TRUE.
YOU HATE YOUR CAREER.
TRUE OR FALSE?
TRUE.
YOU HATE YOUR CHILDHOOD.
TRUE OR FALSE?
TRUE.
YOU HATE YOUR LIFE.
TRUE OR FALSE?
TRUE.
YOU HATE YOURSELF.
TRUE OR FALSE?
TRUE.
YOU HATE GOD.
TRUE OR FALSE?
TRUE.

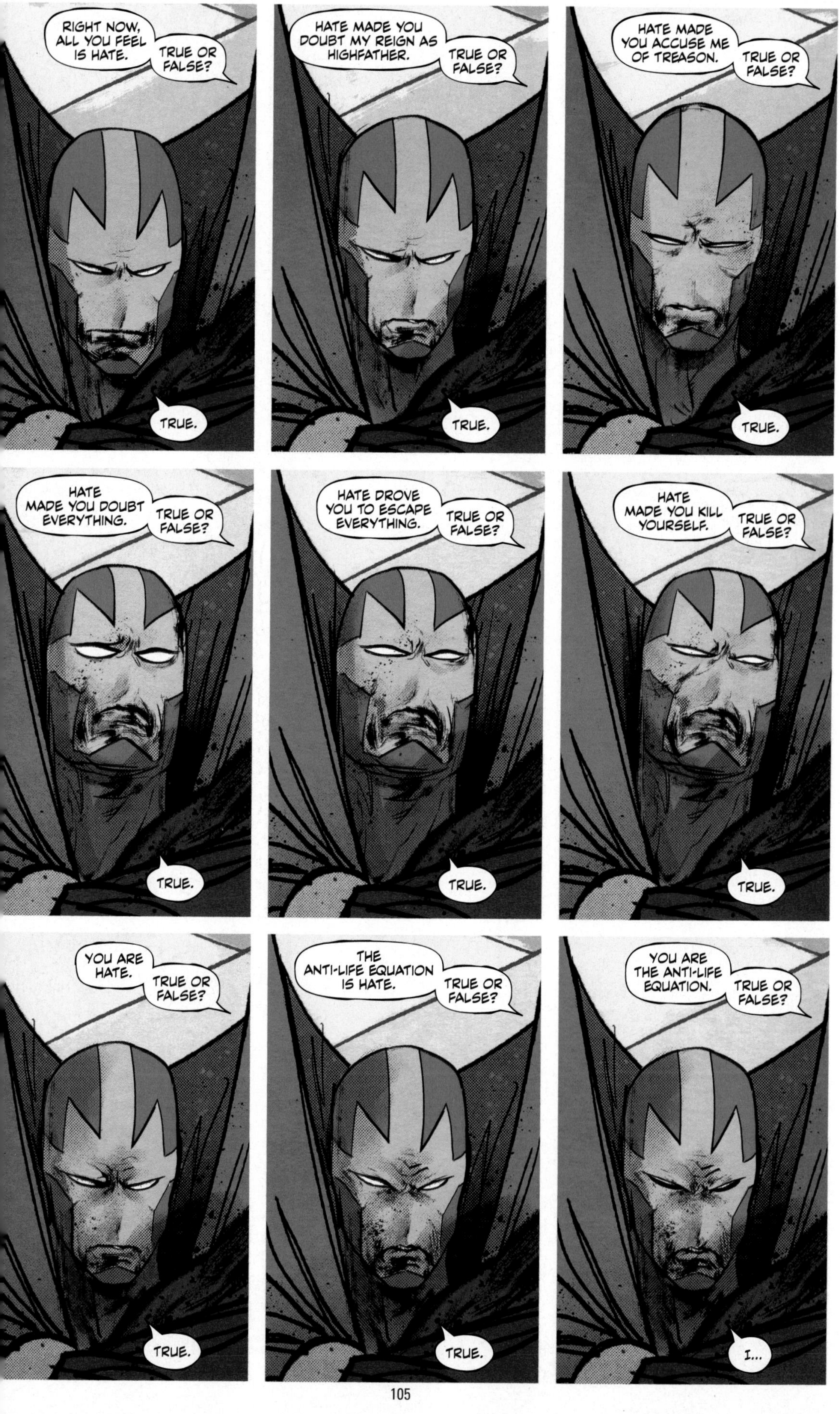
RIGHT NOW, ALL YOU FEEL IS HATE.
TRUE OR FALSE?
TRUE.
HATE MADE YOU DOUBT MY REIGN AS HIGHFATHER.
TRUE OR FALSE?
TRUE.
HATE MADE YOU ACCUSE ME OF TREASON.
TRUE OR FALSE?
TRUE.
HATE MADE YOU DOUBT EVERYTHING.
TRUE OR FALSE?
TRUE.
HATE DROVE YOU TO ESCAPE EVERYTHING.
TRUE OR FALSE?
TRUE.
HATE MADE YOU KILL YOURSELF.
TRUE OR FALSE?
TRUE.
YOU ARE HATE.
TRUE OR FALSE?
TRUE.
THE ANTI-LIFE EQUATION IS HATE.
TRUE OR FALSE?
TRUE.
YOU ARE THE ANTI-LIFE EQUATION.
TRUE OR FALSE?
I...

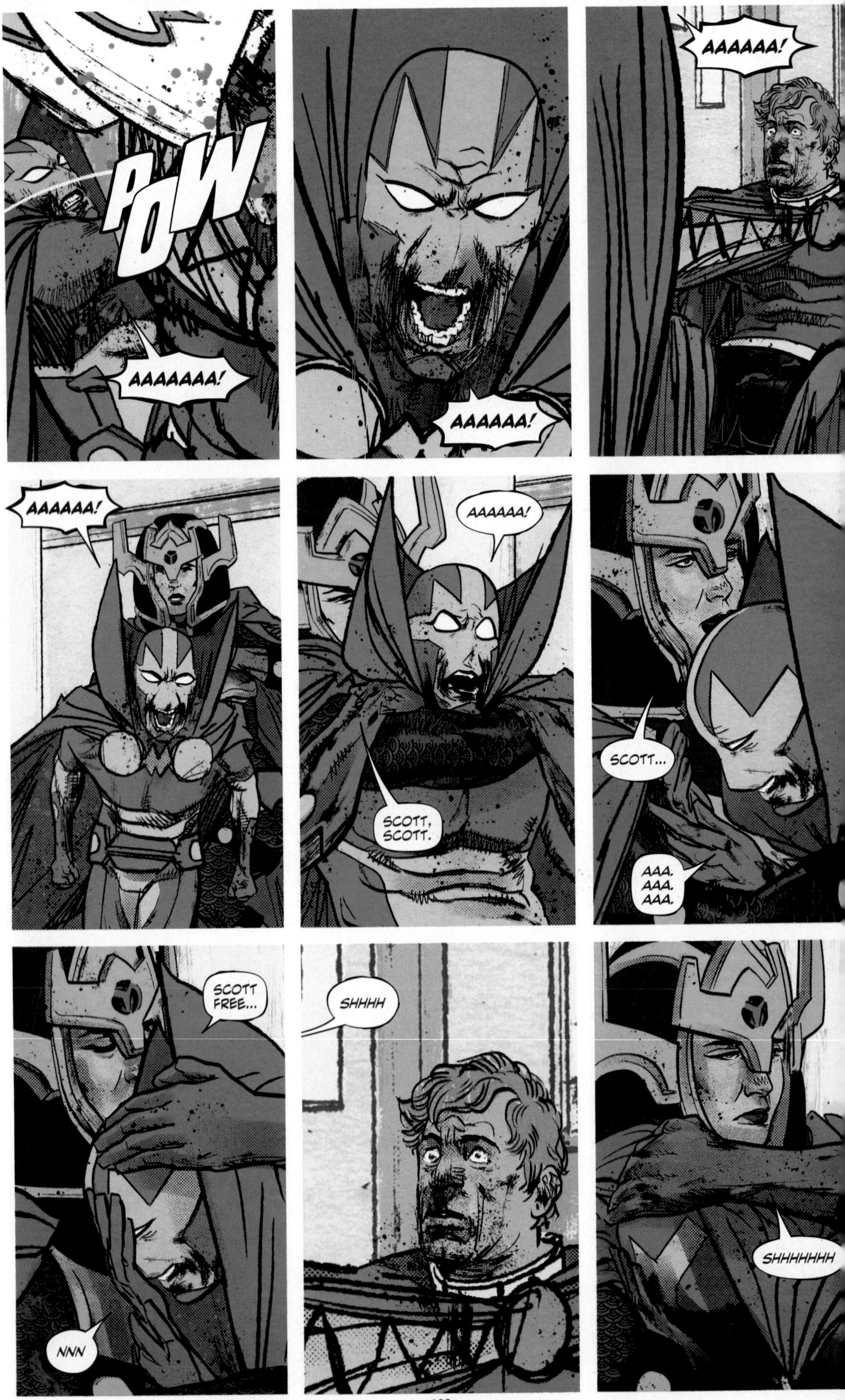
POW
AAAAAAA!
AAAAAA!
AAAAAA!
AAAAAA!
AAAAAA!
SCOTT, SCOTT.
SCOTT...
AAA. AAA. AAA.
SCOTT FREE...
NNN
SHHHH
SHHHHHHH

JESUS.

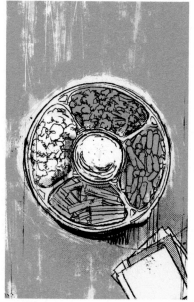

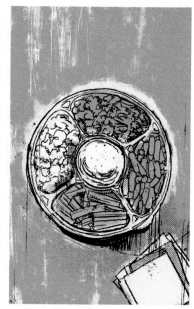

GUILTY. YOU ARE *JUDGED* GUILTY.

AS I CANNOT CONTAIN YOU, *MISTER MIRACLE...*

YOU WILL REPORT TO MY THRONE IN THREE DAYS.

WHERE I WILL PERFORM YOUR EXECUTION.

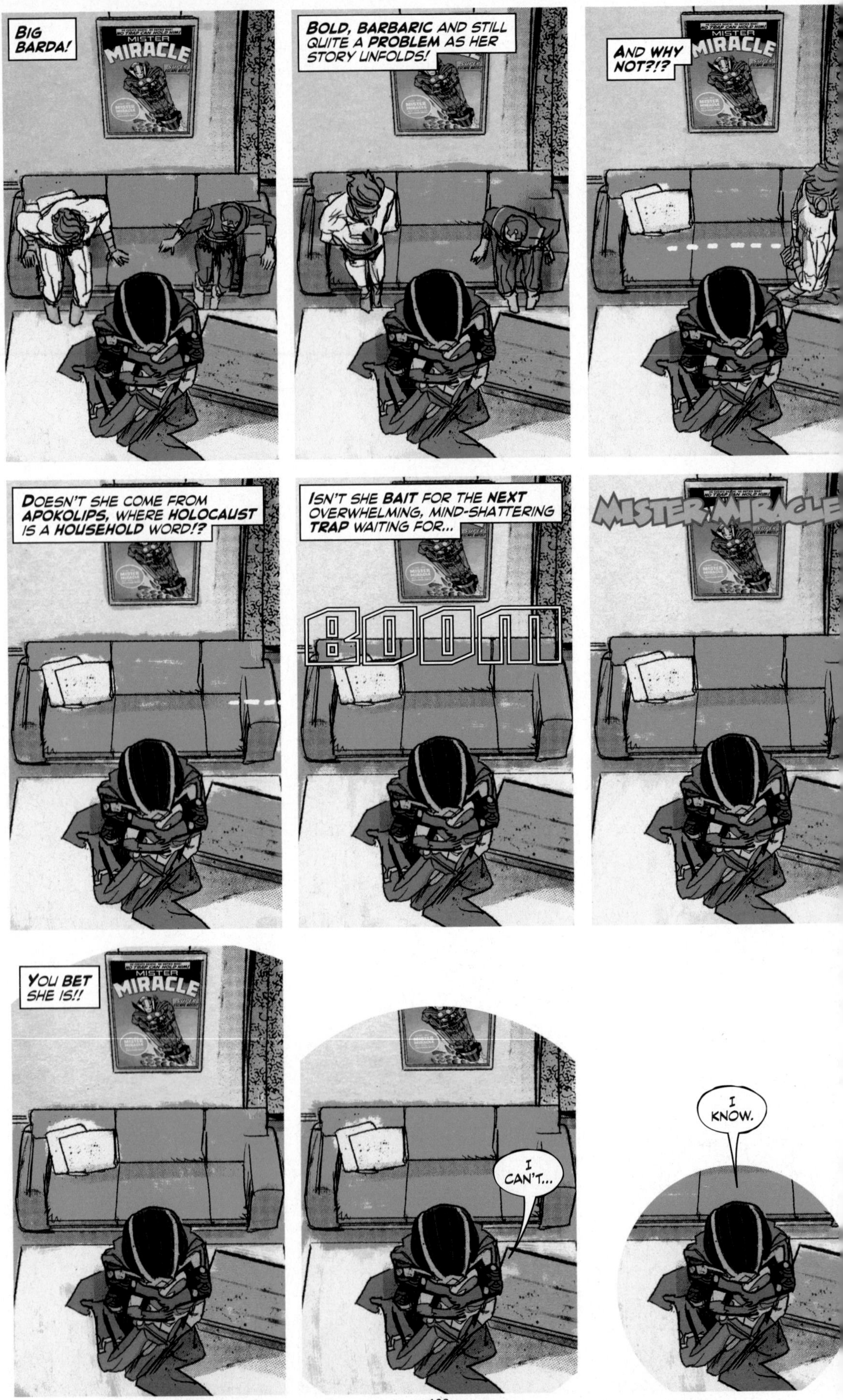
BIG BARDA!
BOLD, BARBARIC AND STILL QUITE A PROBLEM AS HER STORY UNFOLDS!
AND WHY NOT?!?
DOESN'T SHE COME FROM APOKOLIPS, WHERE HOLOCAUST IS A HOUSEHOLD WORD!?
ISN'T SHE BAIT FOR THE NEXT OVERWHELMING, MIND-SHATTERING TRAP WAITING FOR...
BOOM
MISTER MIRACLE
YOU BET SHE IS!!
I CAN'T...
I KNOW.

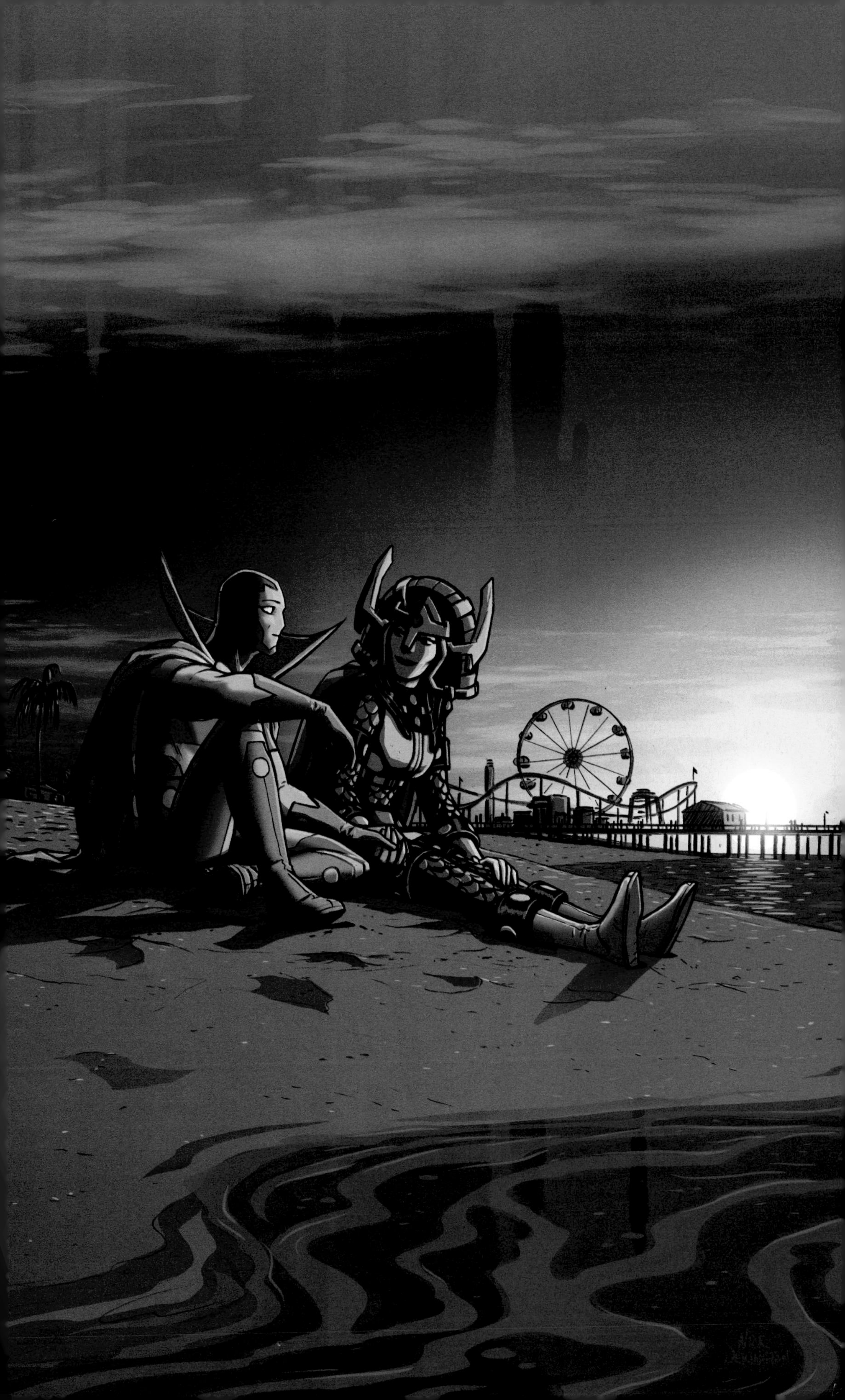

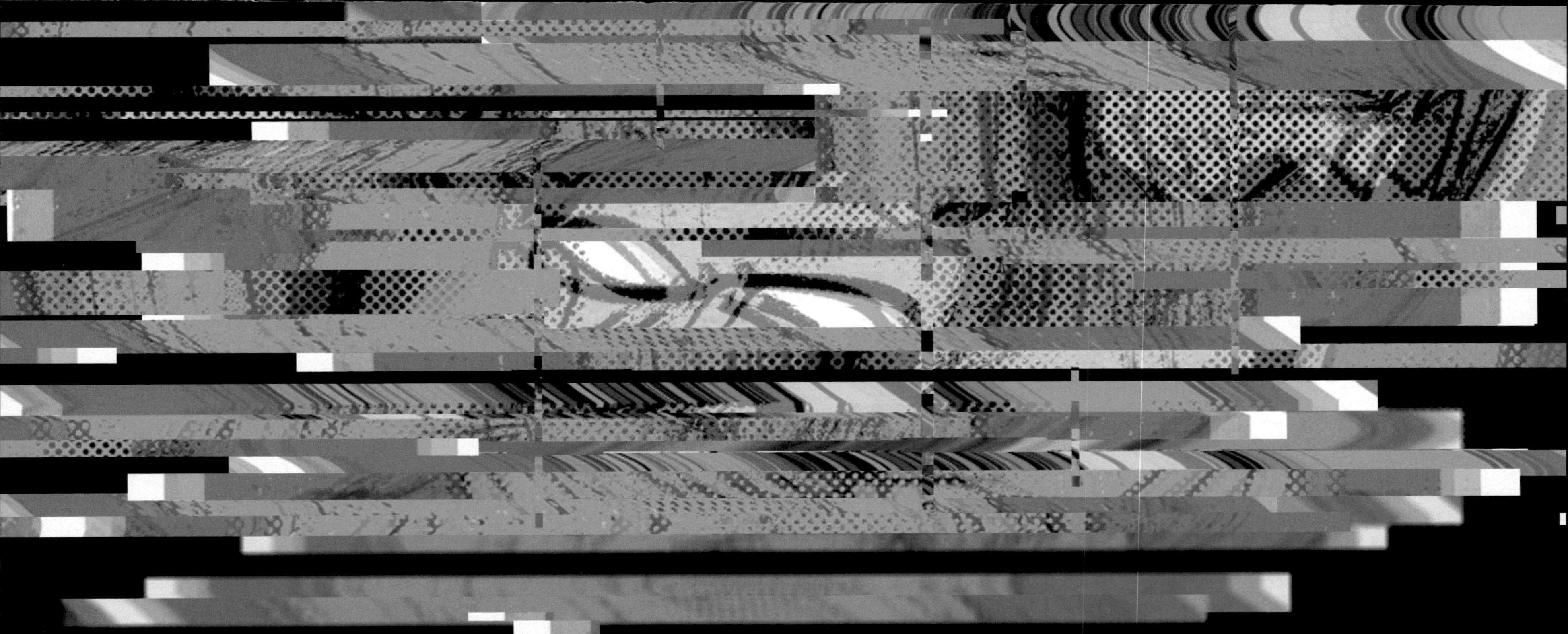
You said you can escape anything.

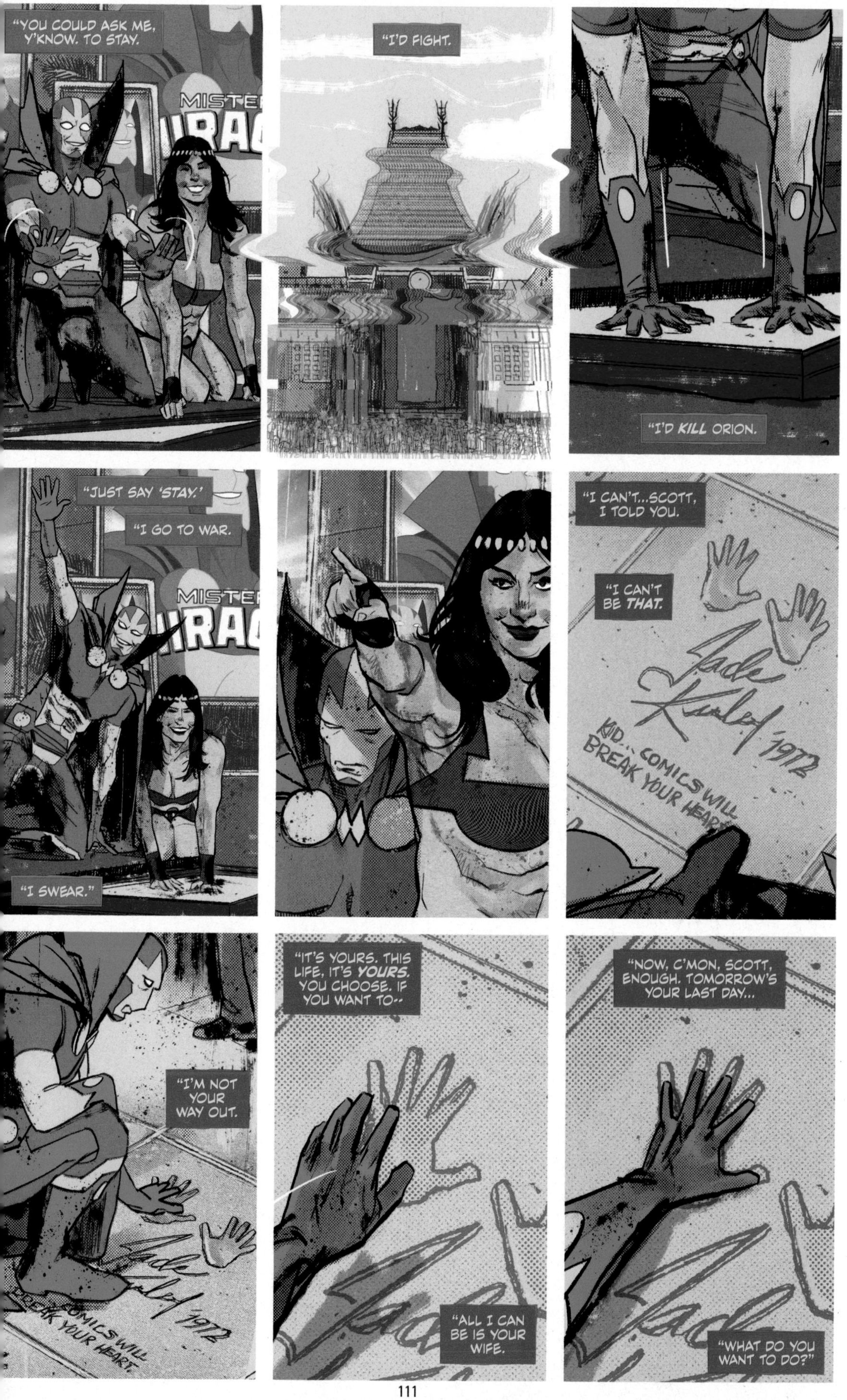
"YOU COULD ASK ME, Y'KNOW. TO STAY.
MISTER MIRAC
"I'D FIGHT.
"I'D KILL ORION.
"JUST SAY 'STAY.'
"I GO TO WAR.
MISTER MIRAC
"I SWEAR."
"I CAN'T...SCOTT, I TOLD YOU.
"I CAN'T BE THAT.
Jade Kurley 1972
KID... COMICS WILL BREAK YOUR HEART
"I'M NOT YOUR WAY OUT.
"IT'S YOURS. THIS LIFE, IT'S YOURS. YOU CHOOSE. IF YOU WANT TO--
"ALL I CAN BE IS YOUR WIFE.
"NOW, C'MON, SCOTT, ENOUGH. TOMORROW'S YOUR LAST DAY...
"WHAT DO YOU WANT TO DO?"

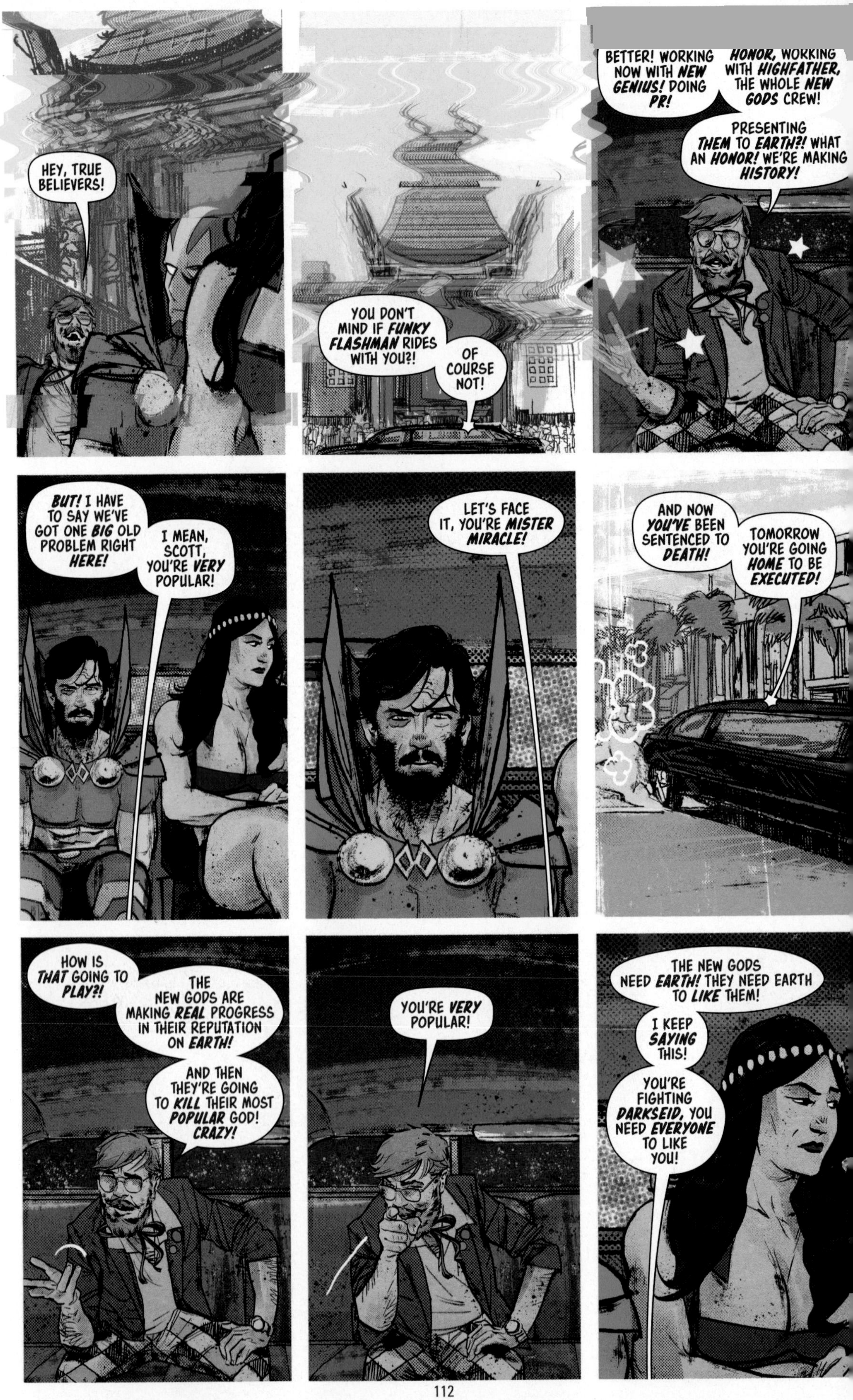
HEY, TRUE BELIEVERS!
YOU DON'T MIND IF FUNKY FLASHMAN RIDES WITH YOU?!
OF COURSE NOT!
BETTER! WORKING NOW WITH NEW GENIUS! DOING PR!
HONOR, WORKING WITH HIGHFATHER, THE WHOLE NEW GODS CREW!
PRESENTING THEM TO EARTH?! WHAT AN HONOR! WE'RE MAKING HISTORY!
BUT! I HAVE TO SAY WE'VE GOT ONE BIG OLD PROBLEM RIGHT HERE!
I MEAN, SCOTT, YOU'RE VERY POPULAR!
LET'S FACE IT, YOU'RE MISTER MIRACLE!
AND NOW YOU'VE BEEN SENTENCED TO DEATH!
TOMORROW YOU'RE GOING HOME TO BE EXECUTED!
HOW IS THAT GOING TO PLAY?!
THE NEW GODS ARE MAKING REAL PROGRESS IN THEIR REPUTATION ON EARTH!
AND THEN THEY'RE GOING TO KILL THEIR MOST POPULAR GOD! CRAZY!
YOU'RE VERY POPULAR!
THE NEW GODS NEED EARTH! THEY NEED EARTH TO LIKE THEM!
I KEEP SAYING THIS!
YOU'RE FIGHTING DARKSEID, YOU NEED EVERYONE TO LIKE YOU!

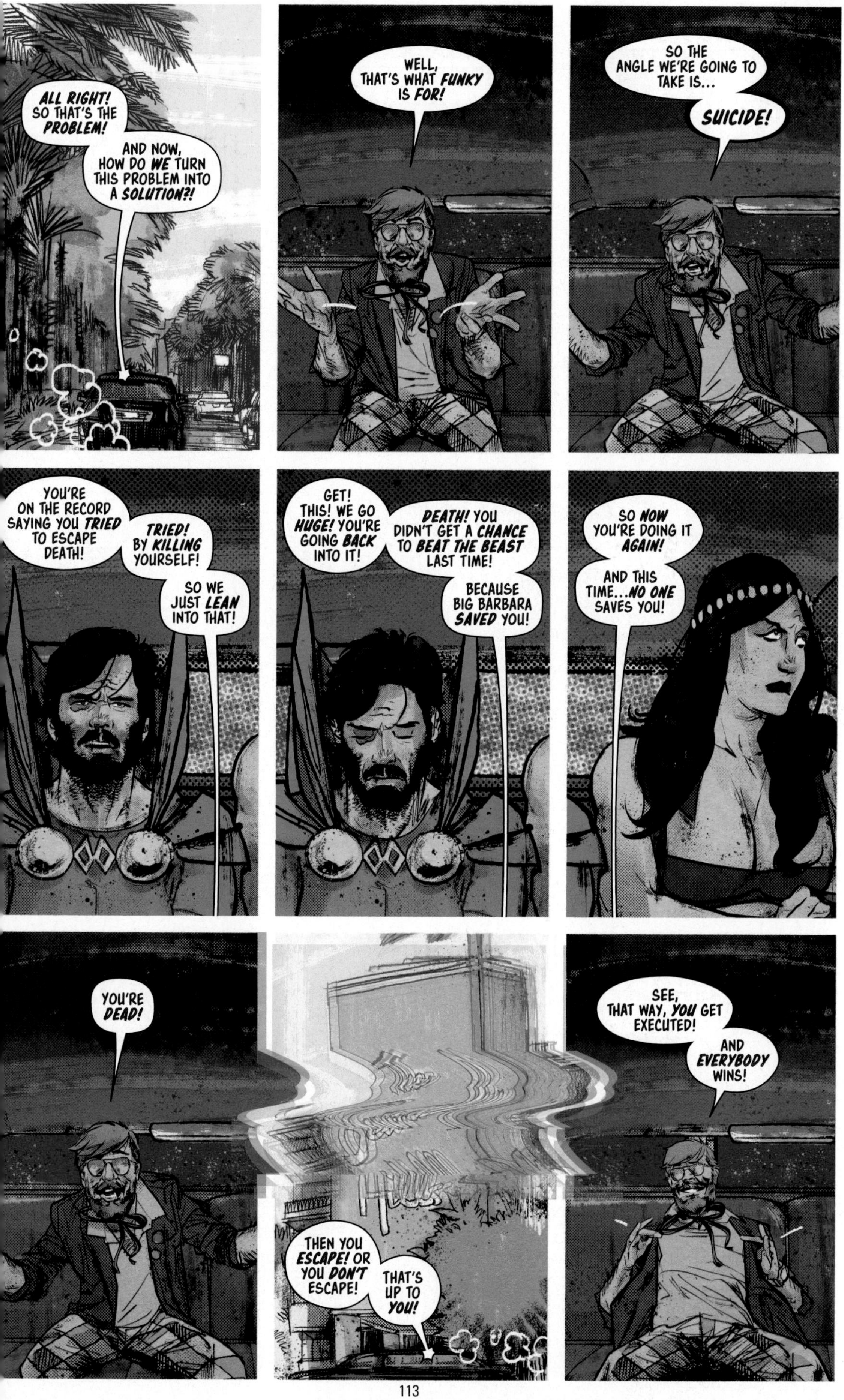
ALL RIGHT! SO THAT'S THE PROBLEM!
AND NOW, HOW DO WE TURN THIS PROBLEM INTO A SOLUTION?!
WELL, THAT'S WHAT FUNKY IS FOR!
SO THE ANGLE WE'RE GOING TO TAKE IS...
SUICIDE!
YOU'RE ON THE RECORD SAYING YOU TRIED TO ESCAPE DEATH!
TRIED! BY KILLING YOURSELF!
SO WE JUST LEAN INTO THAT!
GET! THIS! WE GO HUGE! YOU'RE GOING BACK INTO IT!
DEATH! YOU DIDN'T GET A CHANCE TO BEAT THE BEAST LAST TIME!
BECAUSE BIG BARBARA SAVED YOU!
SO NOW YOU'RE DOING IT AGAIN!
AND THIS TIME...NO ONE SAVES YOU!
YOU'RE DEAD!
THEN YOU ESCAPE! OR YOU DON'T ESCAPE!
THAT'S UP TO YOU!
SEE, THAT WAY, YOU GET EXECUTED!
AND EVERYBODY WINS!

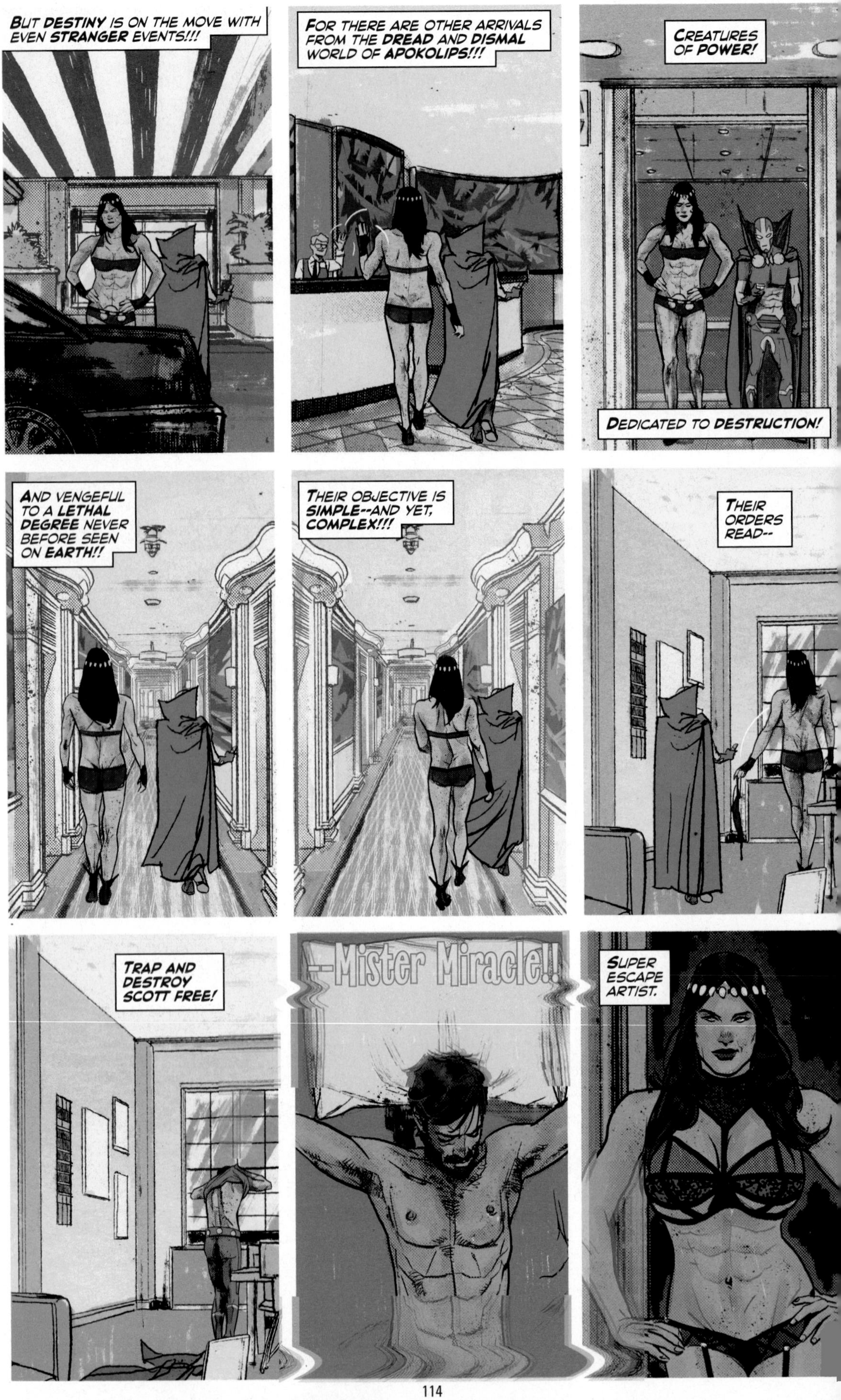
BUT DESTINY IS ON THE MOVE WITH EVEN STRANGER EVENTS!!!
FOR THERE ARE OTHER ARRIVALS FROM THE DREAD AND DISMAL WORLD OF APOKOLIPS!!!
CREATURES OF POWER!
DEDICATED TO DESTRUCTION!
AND VENGEFUL TO A LETHAL DEGREE NEVER BEFORE SEEN ON EARTH!!
THEIR OBJECTIVE IS SIMPLE--AND YET, COMPLEX!!!
THEIR ORDERS READ--
TRAP AND DESTROY SCOTT FREE!
--Mister Miracle!!
SUPER ESCAPE ARTIST.

I CAN ALWAYS ESCAPE.

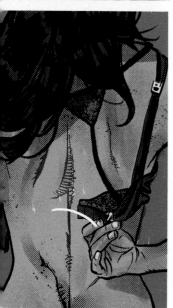

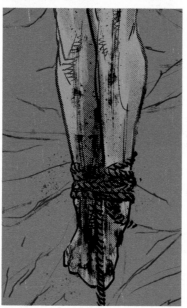

CAN YOU NOW?

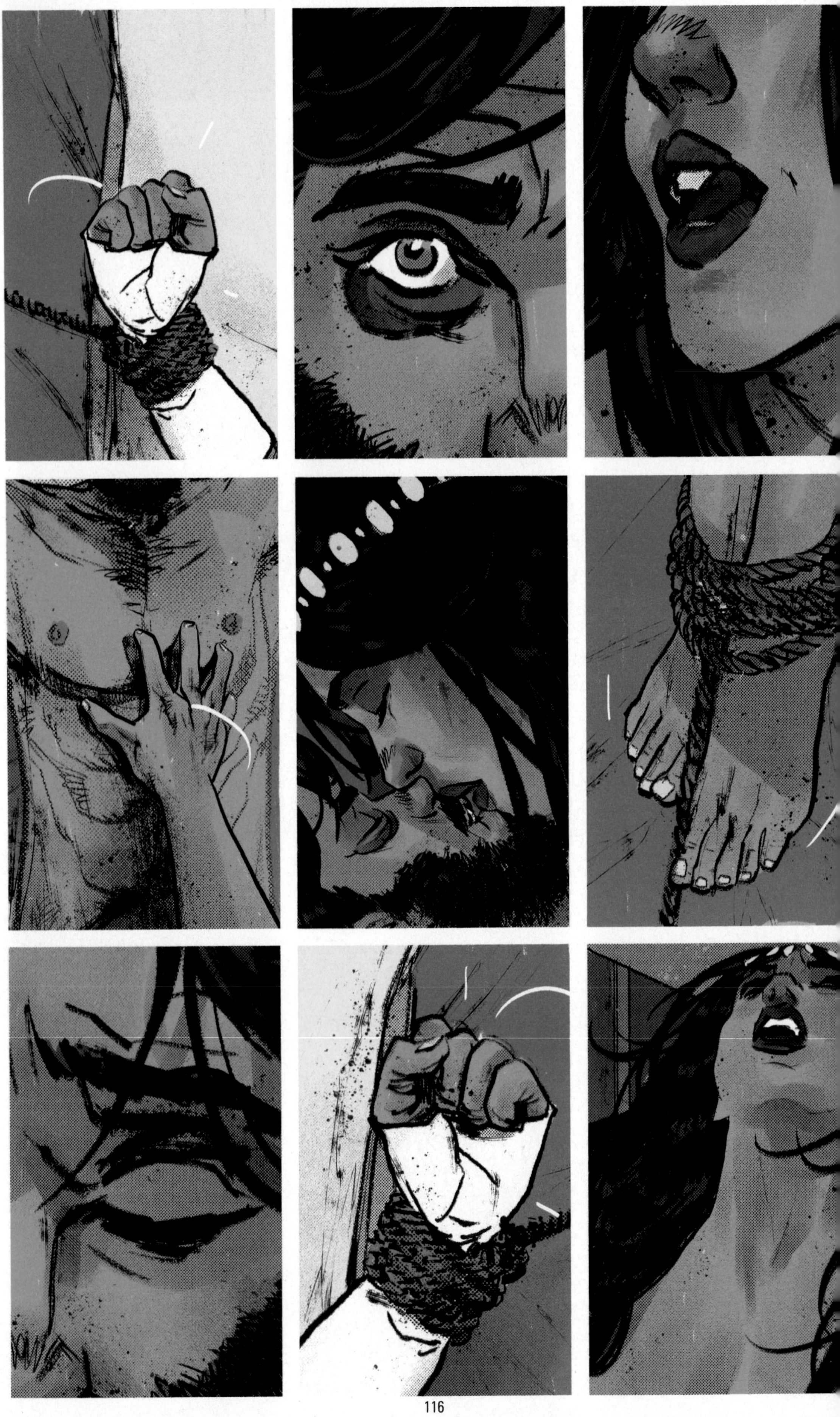

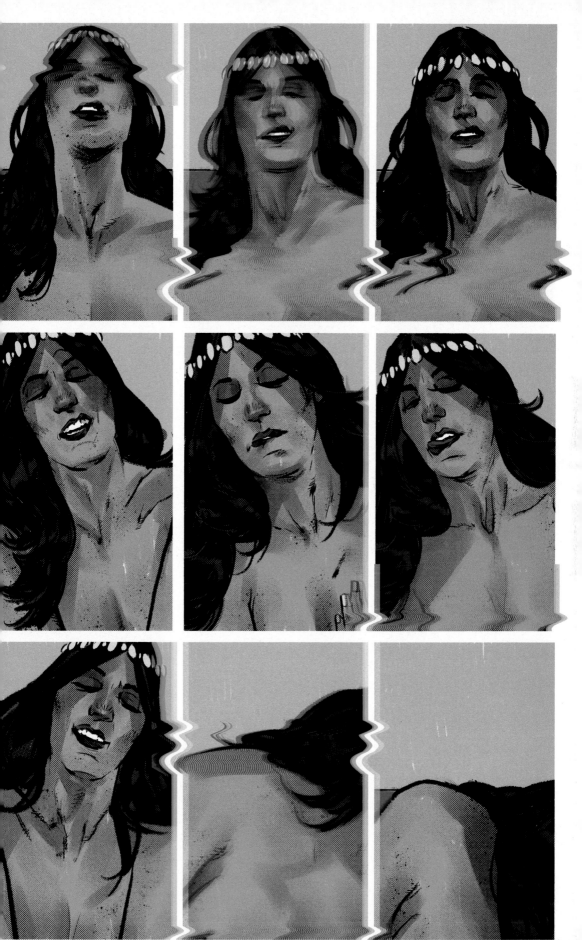

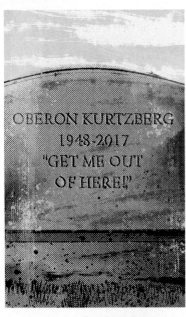

OBERON KURTZBERG
1948-2017
"GET ME OUT
OF HERE!"

IT'S
IMPOSSIBLE.

IT'S NOT
RUSH HOUR
YET.

WE'LL BE
OKAY.

MOTHER BOX, ON
THE 101, HOW
LONG IS IT TO
DOWNTOWN?

FROM
HERE, IF WE
LEAVE NOW.

SEVENTY-THREE
MINUTES.

GOOD-BYE,
OLD PAL.

SEE YOU
SOON.

EVERYTHING
IS RUSH
HOUR.

MOTHER BOX,
IF WE JUST BOOM-
TUBED THERE?

HOW
MUCH DAMAGE
WOULD THAT
CAUSE?

EARTH-TO-EARTH BOOM
TUBE TRAVEL HOLDS THE
POSSIBILITY OF SHEARING
THE FABRIC OF SPACE TIME.

POSSIBLY CRITICALLY
WOUNDING YOUR
CURRENT REALITY.

SEVENTY-THREE
MINUTES.

MIGHT
BE WORTH
IT.

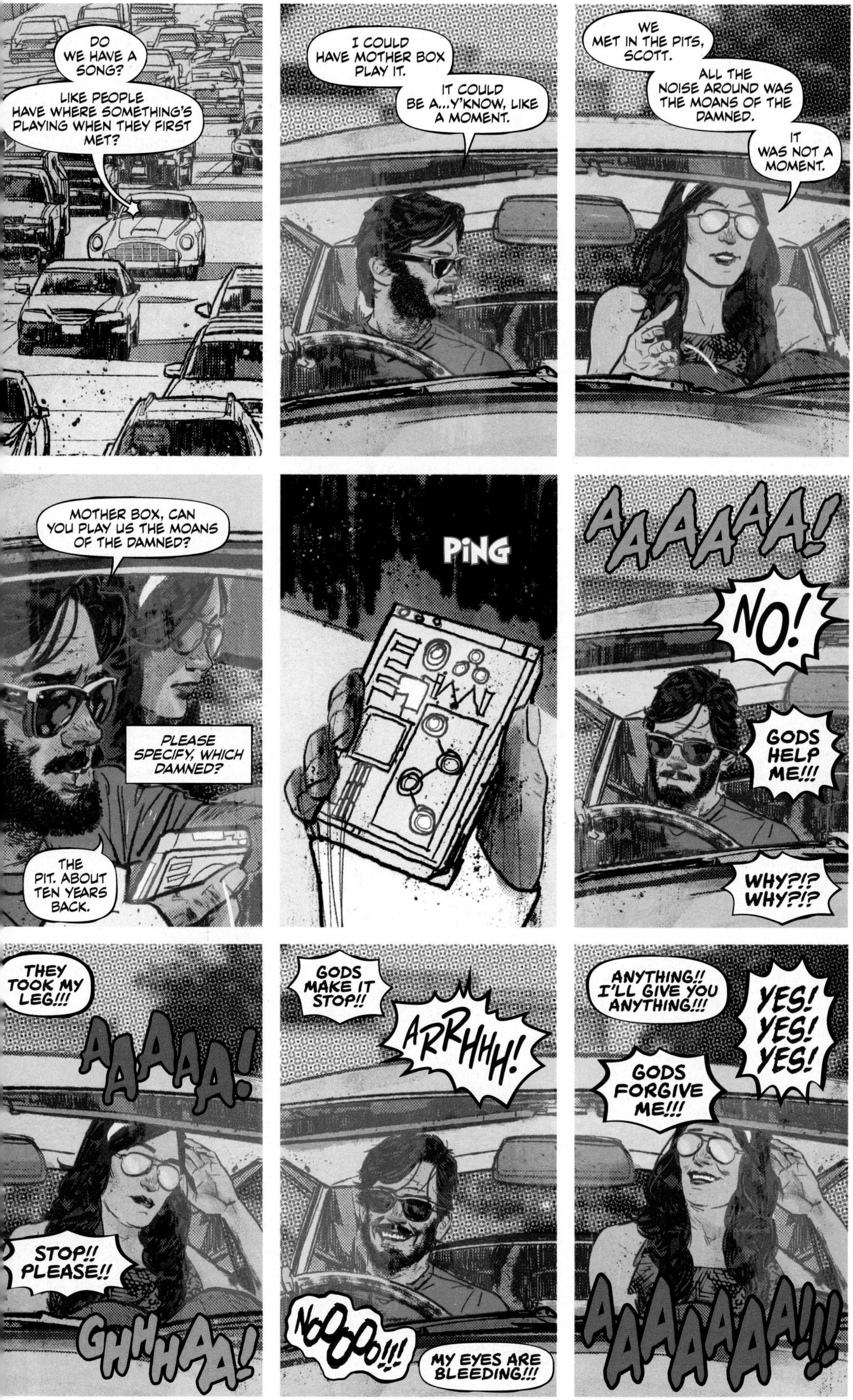
DO WE HAVE A SONG?
LIKE PEOPLE HAVE WHERE SOMETHING'S PLAYING WHEN THEY FIRST MET?
I COULD HAVE MOTHER BOX PLAY IT.
IT COULD BE A...Y'KNOW, LIKE A MOMENT.
WE MET IN THE PITS, SCOTT.
ALL THE NOISE AROUND WAS THE MOANS OF THE DAMNED.
IT WAS NOT A MOMENT.
MOTHER BOX, CAN YOU PLAY US THE MOANS OF THE DAMNED?
PLEASE SPECIFY, WHICH DAMNED?
THE PIT. ABOUT TEN YEARS BACK.
PiNG
AAAAAA!
NO!
GODS HELP ME!!!
WHY?!? WHY?!?
THEY TOOK MY LEG!!!
AAAAAA!
STOP!! PLEASE!!
GHHHAAA!
GODS MAKE IT STOP!!
ARRHHH!
NOOOOO!!!
MY EYES ARE BLEEDING!!!
ANYTHING!! I'LL GIVE YOU ANYTHING!!!
YES! YES! YES!
GODS FORGIVE ME!!!
AAAAAAA!!!

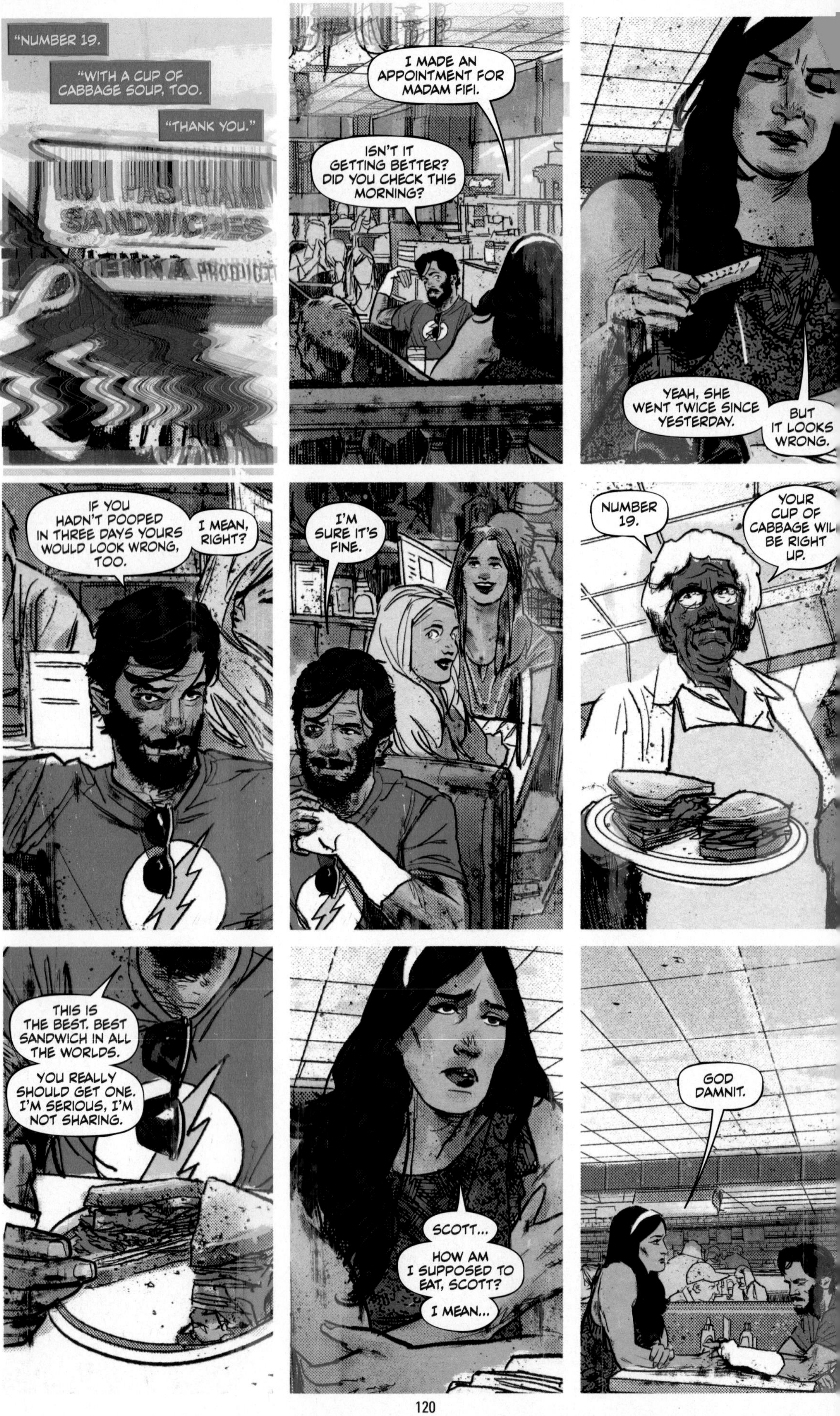
"NUMBER 19.
"WITH A CUP OF CABBAGE SOUP, TOO.
"THANK YOU."
HOT PASTRAMI SANDWICHES
I MADE AN APPOINTMENT FOR MADAM FIFI.
ISN'T IT GETTING BETTER? DID YOU CHECK THIS MORNING?
YEAH, SHE WENT TWICE SINCE YESTERDAY.
BUT IT LOOKS WRONG.
IF YOU HADN'T POOPED IN THREE DAYS YOURS WOULD LOOK WRONG, TOO.
I MEAN, RIGHT?
I'M SURE IT'S FINE.
NUMBER 19.
YOUR CUP OF CABBAGE WIL BE RIGHT UP.
THIS IS THE BEST. BEST SANDWICH IN ALL THE WORLDS.
YOU REALLY SHOULD GET ONE. I'M SERIOUS, I'M NOT SHARING.
SCOTT...
HOW AM I SUPPOSED TO EAT, SCOTT?
I MEAN...
GOD DAMNIT.

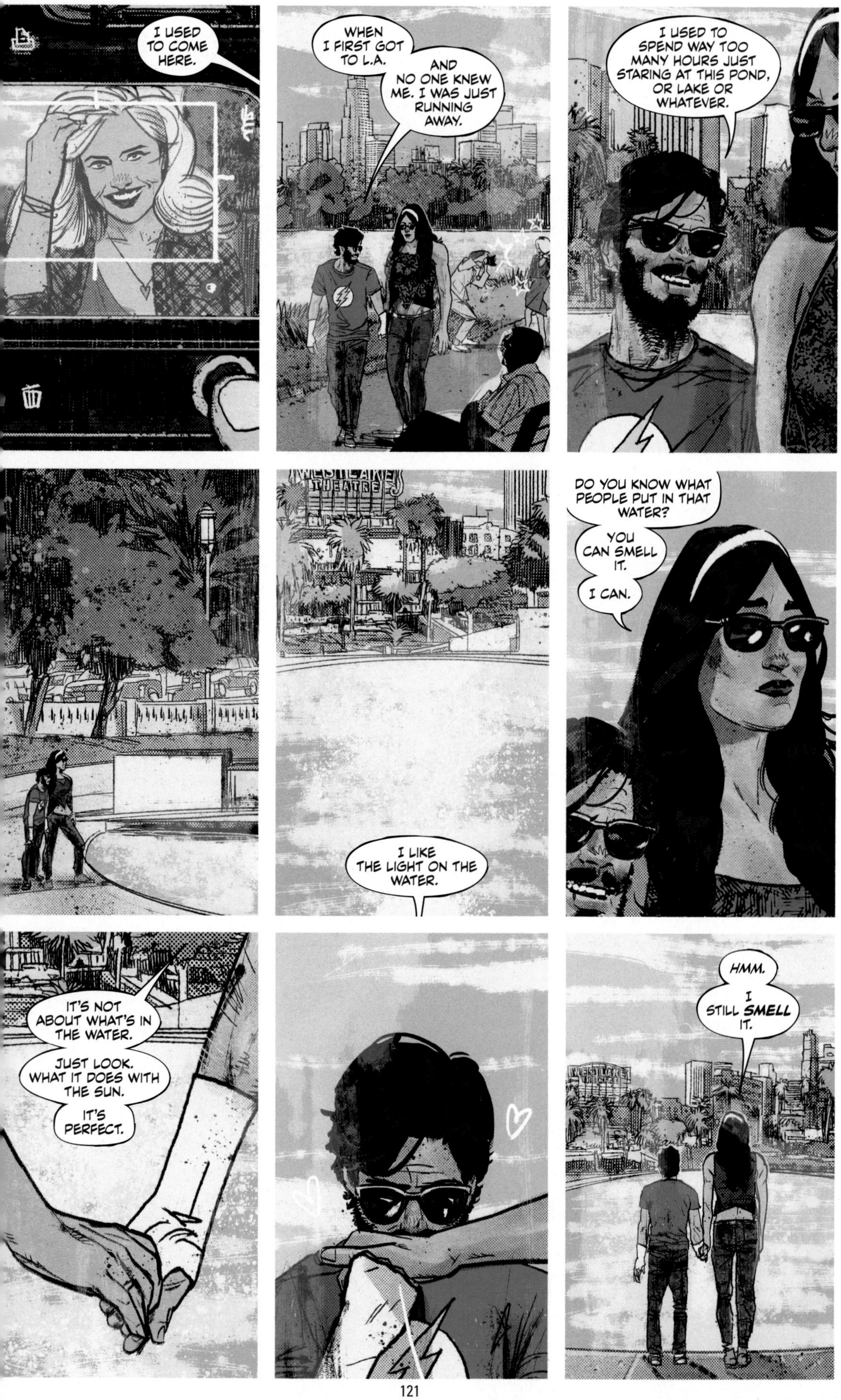
I USED TO COME HERE.
WHEN I FIRST GOT TO L.A.
AND NO ONE KNEW ME. I WAS JUST RUNNING AWAY.
I USED TO SPEND WAY TOO MANY HOURS JUST STARING AT THIS POND, OR LAKE OR WHATEVER.
I LIKE THE LIGHT ON THE WATER.
DO YOU KNOW WHAT PEOPLE PUT IN THAT WATER?
YOU CAN SMELL IT.
I CAN.
IT'S NOT ABOUT WHAT'S IN THE WATER.
JUST LOOK. WHAT IT DOES WITH THE SUN.
IT'S PERFECT.
HMM.
I STILL SMELL IT.

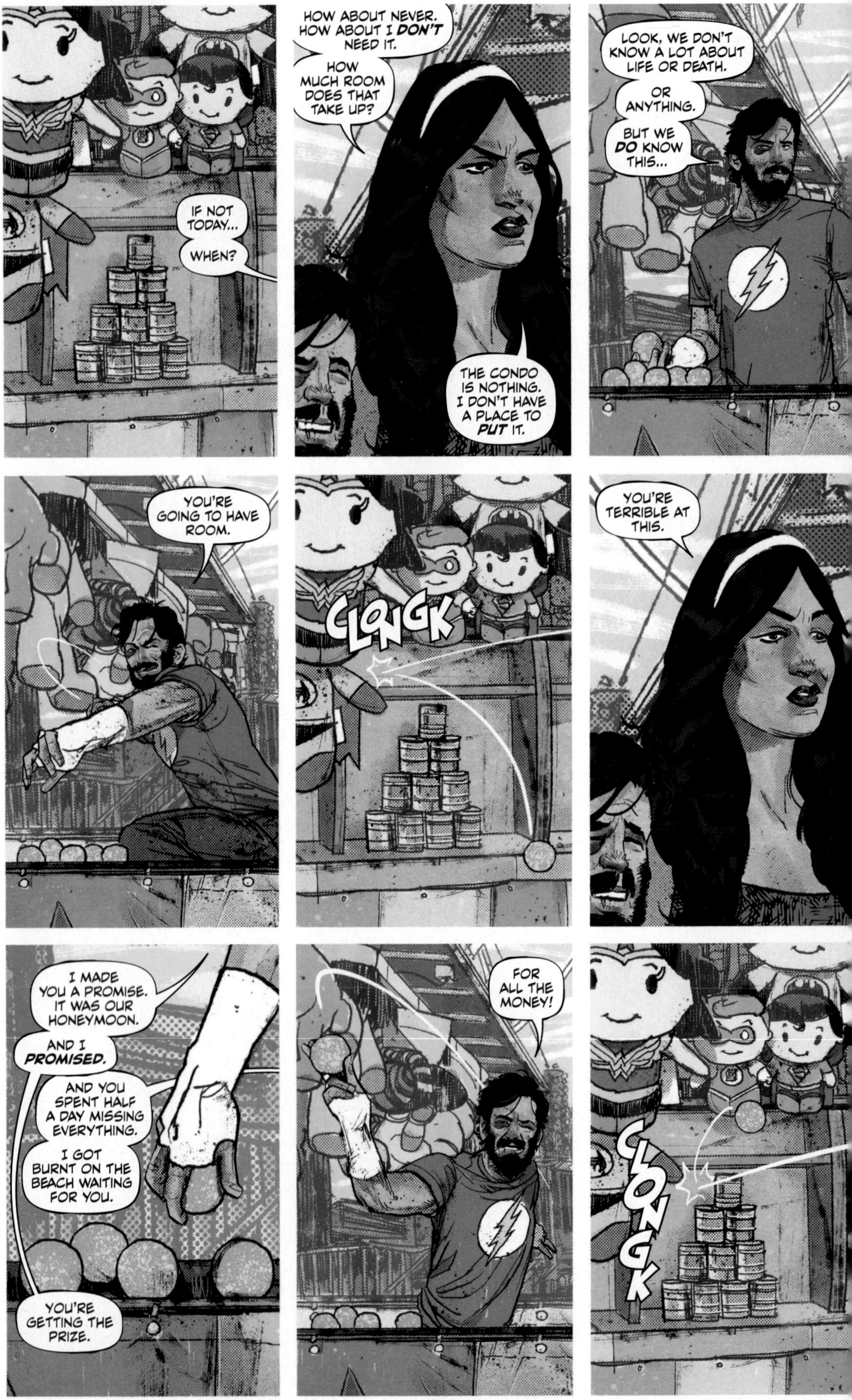
IF NOT TODAY...
WHEN?
HOW ABOUT NEVER. HOW ABOUT I DON'T NEED IT.
HOW MUCH ROOM DOES THAT TAKE UP?
THE CONDO IS NOTHING. I DON'T HAVE A PLACE TO PUT IT.
LOOK, WE DON'T KNOW A LOT ABOUT LIFE OR DEATH.
OR ANYTHING.
BUT WE DO KNOW THIS...
YOU'RE GOING TO HAVE ROOM.
CLONGK
YOU'RE TERRIBLE AT THIS.
I MADE YOU A PROMISE. IT WAS OUR HONEYMOON.
AND I PROMISED.
AND YOU SPENT HALF A DAY MISSING EVERYTHING.
I GOT BURNT ON THE BEACH WAITING FOR YOU.
YOU'RE GETTING THE PRIZE.
FOR ALL THE MONEY!
CLONGK

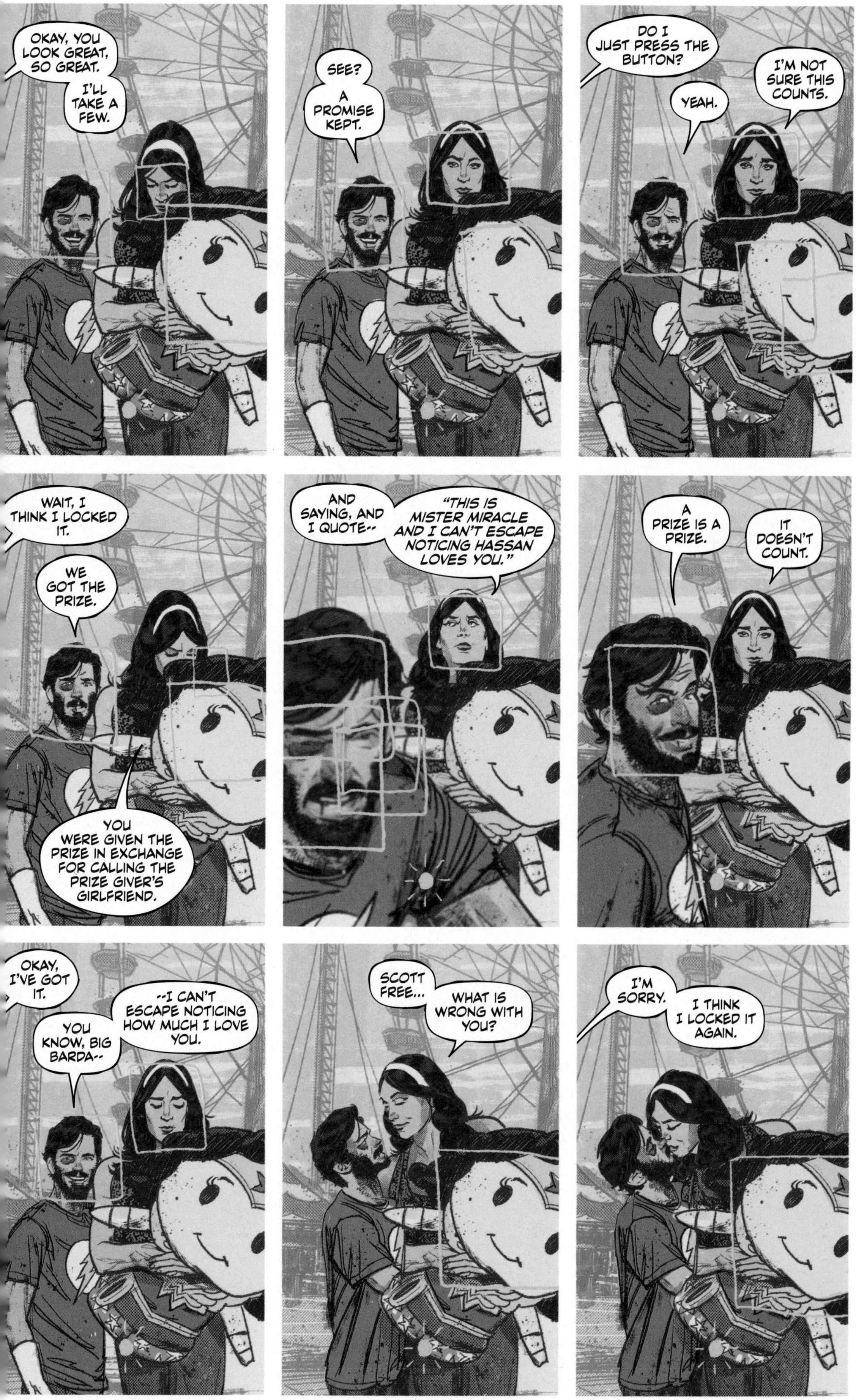
OKAY, YOU LOOK GREAT, SO GREAT.
I'LL TAKE A FEW.
SEE? A PROMISE KEPT.
DO I JUST PRESS THE BUTTON?
YEAH.
I'M NOT SURE THIS COUNTS.
WAIT, I THINK I LOCKED IT.
WE GOT THE PRIZE.
YOU WERE GIVEN THE PRIZE IN EXCHANGE FOR CALLING THE PRIZE GIVER'S GIRLFRIEND.
AND SAYING, AND I QUOTE--
"THIS IS MISTER MIRACLE AND I CAN'T ESCAPE NOTICING HASSAN LOVES YOU."
A PRIZE IS A PRIZE.
IT DOESN'T COUNT.
OKAY, I'VE GOT IT.
YOU KNOW, BIG BARDA--
--I CAN'T ESCAPE NOTICING HOW MUCH I LOVE YOU.
SCOTT FREE...
WHAT IS WRONG WITH YOU?
I'M SORRY.
I THINK I LOCKED IT AGAIN.

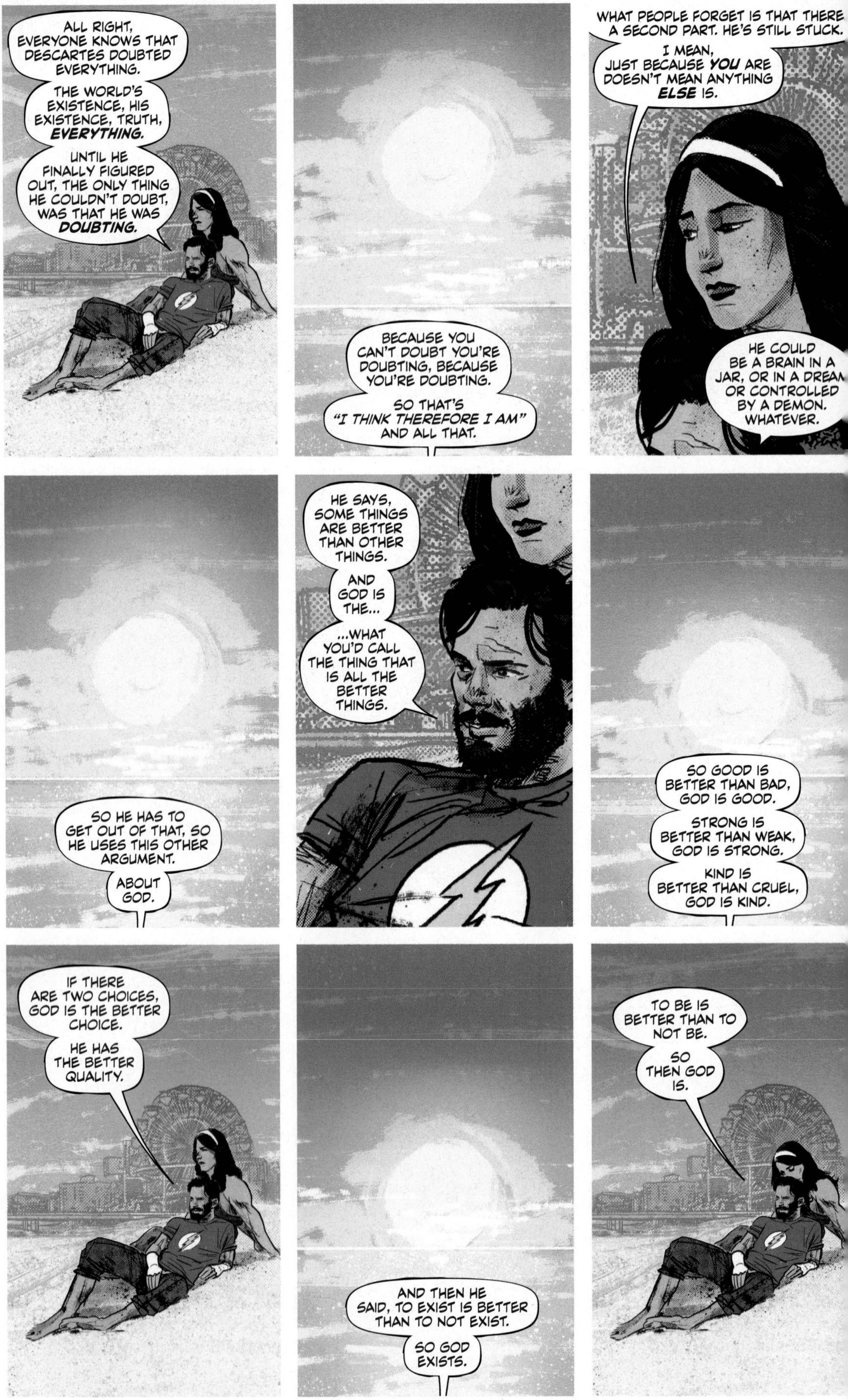
ALL RIGHT, EVERYONE KNOWS THAT DESCARTES DOUBTED EVERYTHING.
THE WORLD'S EXISTENCE, HIS EXISTENCE, TRUTH, **EVERYTHING.**
UNTIL HE FINALLY FIGURED OUT, THE ONLY THING HE COULDN'T DOUBT, WAS THAT HE WAS **DOUBTING.**
BECAUSE YOU CAN'T DOUBT YOU'RE DOUBTING, BECAUSE YOU'RE DOUBTING.
SO THAT'S *"I THINK THEREFORE I AM"* AND ALL THAT.
WHAT PEOPLE FORGET IS THAT THERE A SECOND PART. HE'S STILL STUCK.
I MEAN, JUST BECAUSE ***YOU*** ARE DOESN'T MEAN ANYTHING ***ELSE*** IS.
HE COULD BE A BRAIN IN A JAR, OR IN A DREAM OR CONTROLLED BY A DEMON. WHATEVER.
SO HE HAS TO GET OUT OF THAT, SO HE USES THIS OTHER ARGUMENT.
ABOUT GOD.
HE SAYS, SOME THINGS ARE BETTER THAN OTHER THINGS.
AND GOD IS THE...
...WHAT YOU'D CALL THE THING THAT IS ALL THE BETTER THINGS.
SO GOOD IS BETTER THAN BAD, GOD IS GOOD.
STRONG IS BETTER THAN WEAK, GOD IS STRONG.
KIND IS BETTER THAN CRUEL, GOD IS KIND.
IF THERE ARE TWO CHOICES, GOD IS THE BETTER CHOICE.
HE HAS THE BETTER QUALITY.
AND THEN HE SAID, TO EXIST IS BETTER THAN TO NOT EXIST.
SO GOD EXISTS.
TO BE IS BETTER THAN TO NOT BE.
SO THEN GOD IS.

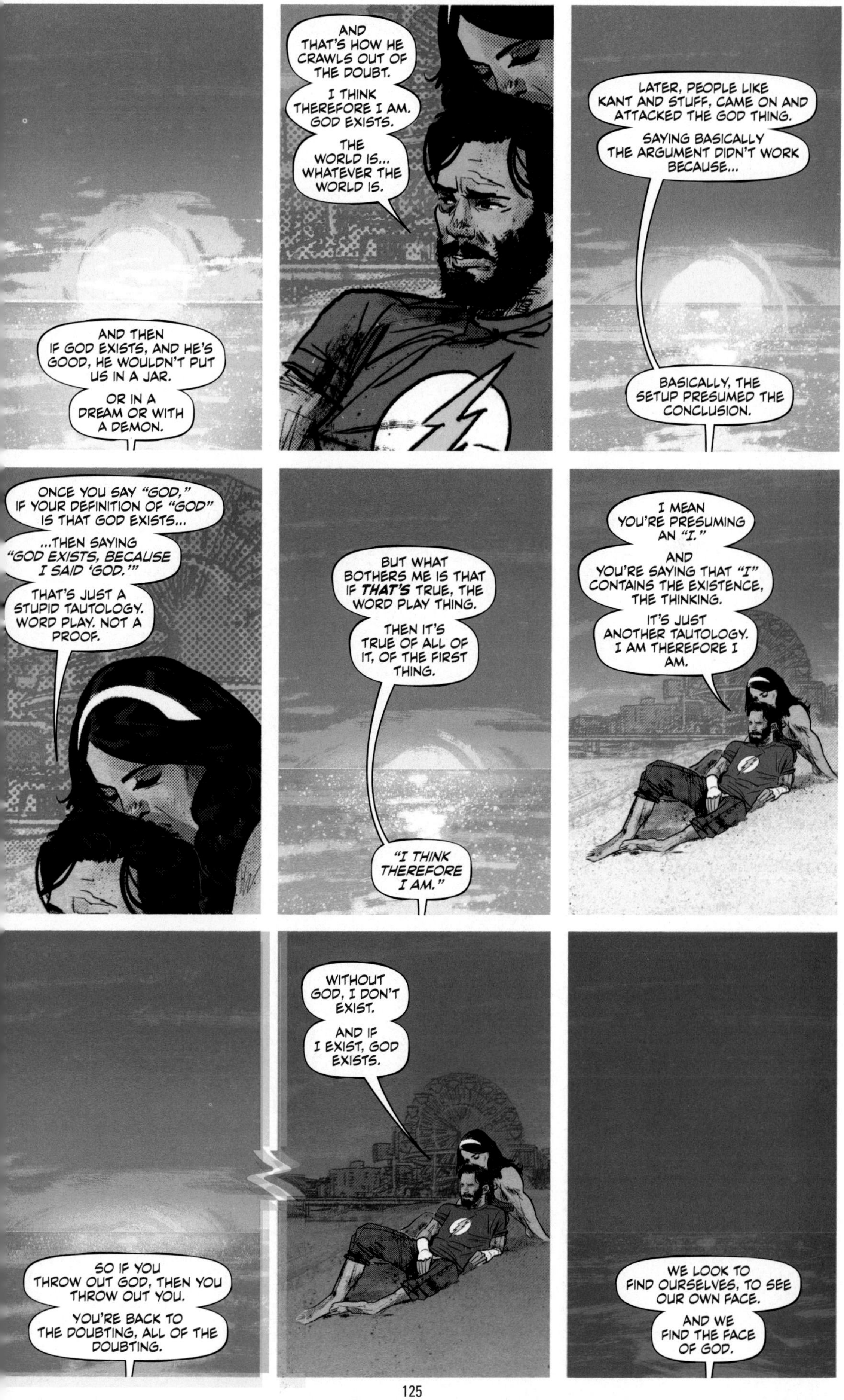
AND THEN IF GOD EXISTS, AND HE'S GOOD, HE WOULDN'T PUT US IN A JAR.
OR IN A DREAM OR WITH A DEMON.
AND THAT'S HOW HE CRAWLS OUT OF THE DOUBT.
I THINK THEREFORE I AM. GOD EXISTS.
THE WORLD IS... WHATEVER THE WORLD IS.
LATER, PEOPLE LIKE KANT AND STUFF, CAME ON AND ATTACKED THE GOD THING.
SAYING BASICALLY THE ARGUMENT DIDN'T WORK BECAUSE...
BASICALLY, THE SETUP PRESUMED THE CONCLUSION.
ONCE YOU SAY "GOD," IF YOUR DEFINITION OF "GOD" IS THAT GOD EXISTS...
...THEN SAYING *"GOD EXISTS, BECAUSE I SAID 'GOD.'"*
THAT'S JUST A STUPID TAUTOLOGY. WORD PLAY. NOT A PROOF.
BUT WHAT BOTHERS ME IS THAT IF ***THAT'S*** TRUE, THE WORD PLAY THING.
THEN IT'S TRUE OF ALL OF IT, OF THE FIRST THING.
"I THINK THEREFORE I AM."
I MEAN YOU'RE PRESUMING AN *"I."*
AND YOU'RE SAYING THAT *"I"* CONTAINS THE EXISTENCE, THE THINKING.
IT'S JUST ANOTHER TAUTOLOGY. I AM THEREFORE I AM.
SO IF YOU THROW OUT GOD, THEN YOU THROW OUT YOU.
YOU'RE BACK TO THE DOUBTING, ALL OF THE DOUBTING.
WITHOUT GOD, I DON'T EXIST.
AND IF I EXIST, GOD EXISTS.
WE LOOK TO FIND OURSELVES, TO SEE OUR OWN FACE.
AND WE FIND THE FACE OF GOD.

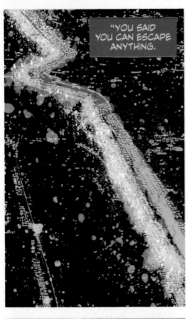

"YOU SAID YOU CAN ESCAPE ANYTHING.

ESCAPE THIS.

OUR LAST DAY.

ON THIS OR ON ANY PLANET.

AND WE'RE STUCK ON THE 10.

MAYBE WE SHOULD TAKE SANTA MONICA.

IT'S TOO MANY LIGHTS.

ONCE WE GET TO THE 405 IT'LL BE BETTER.

NO, IT WON'T.

THIS IS IT. THE LAST MEMORY YOU'LL GET OF THE WORLD THAT LOVED YOU.

RED LIGHTS. ENDLESS.

JESUS.

AT LEAST IT'S PRETTY.

IT'S ALMOST PRETTY.

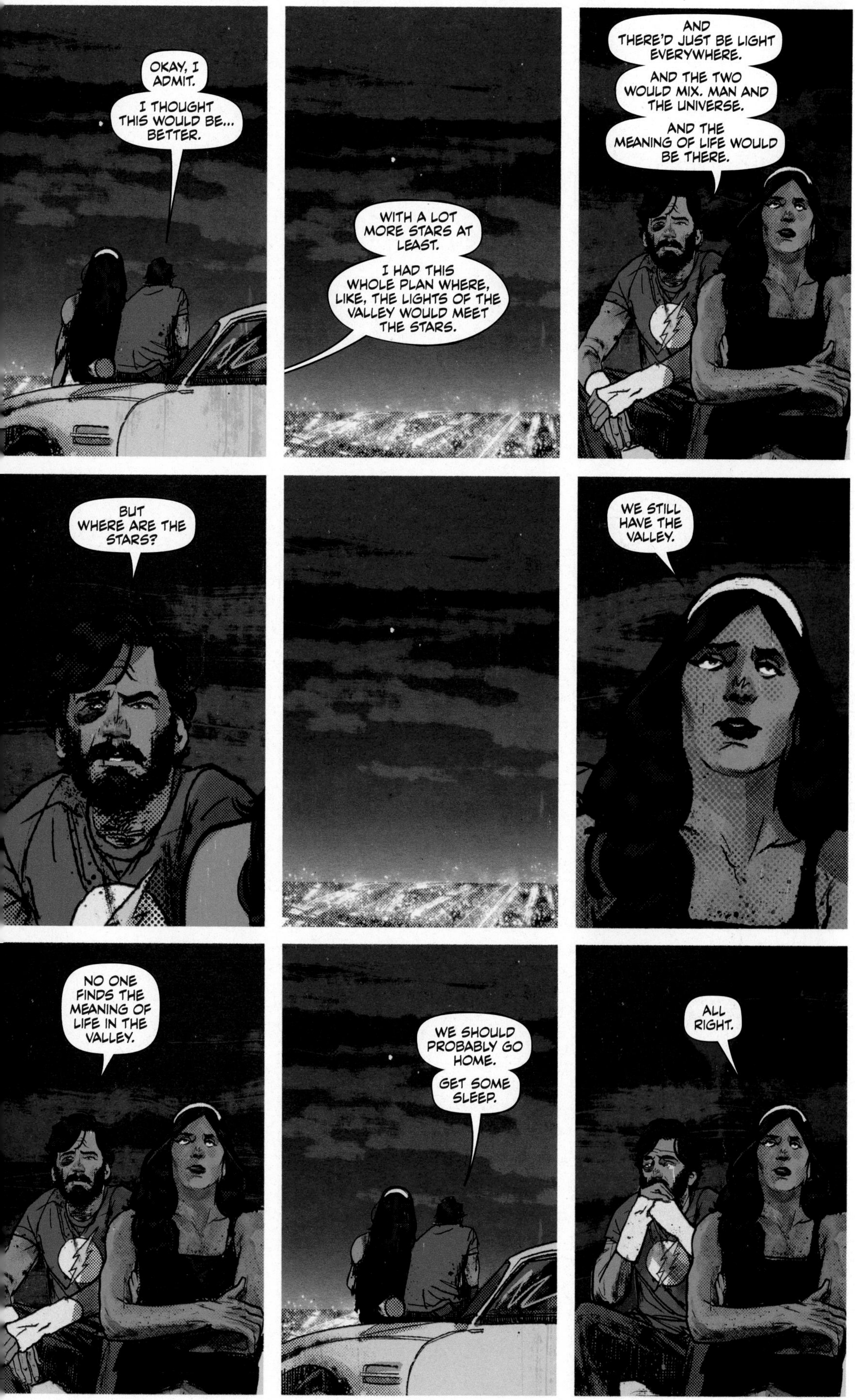

OKAY, I ADMIT.
I THOUGHT THIS WOULD BE... BETTER.
WITH A LOT MORE STARS AT LEAST.
I HAD THIS WHOLE PLAN WHERE, LIKE, THE LIGHTS OF THE VALLEY WOULD MEET THE STARS.
AND THERE'D JUST BE LIGHT EVERYWHERE.
AND THE TWO WOULD MIX. MAN AND THE UNIVERSE.
AND THE MEANING OF LIFE WOULD BE THERE.
BUT WHERE ARE THE STARS?
WE STILL HAVE THE VALLEY.
NO ONE FINDS THE MEANING OF LIFE IN THE VALLEY.
WE SHOULD PROBABLY GO HOME.
GET SOME SLEEP.
ALL RIGHT.

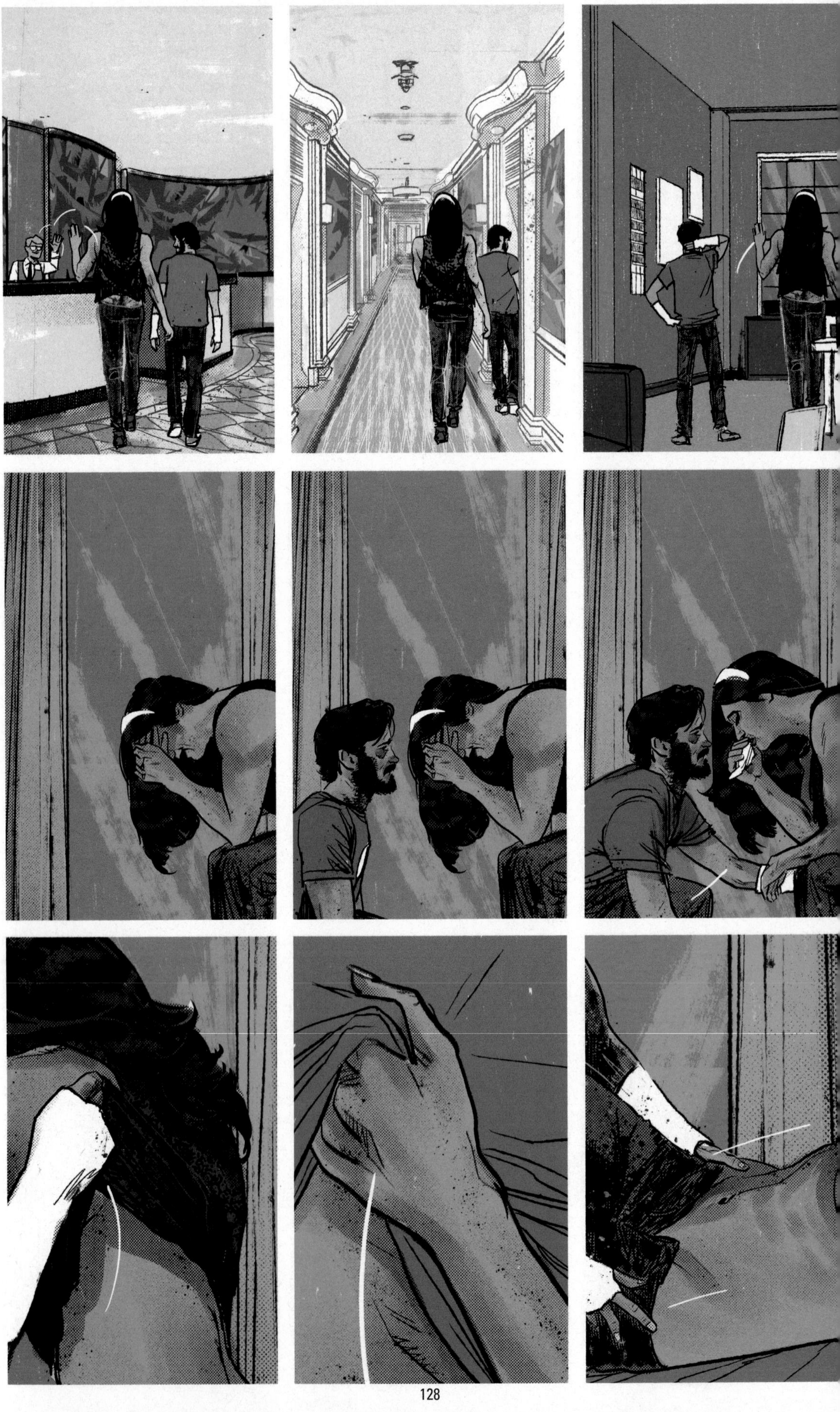

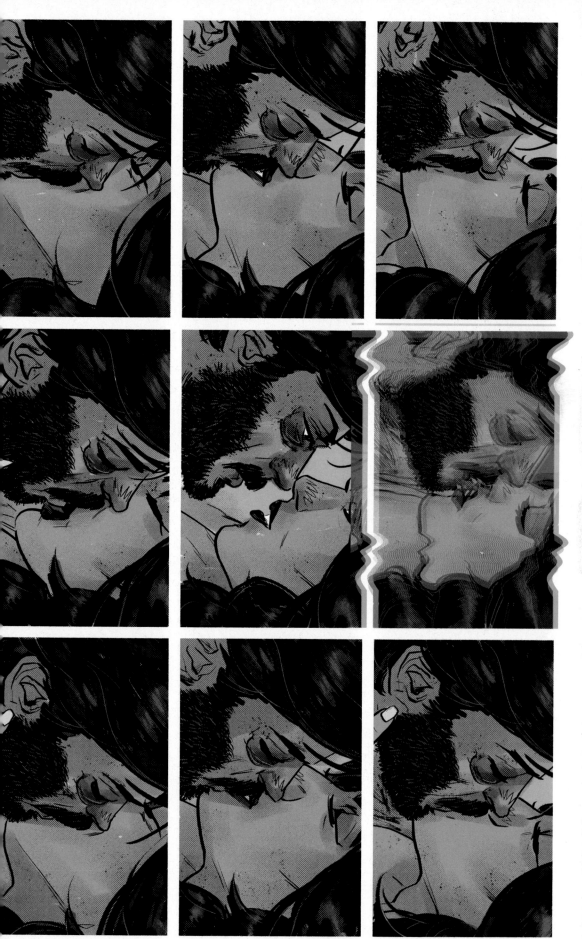

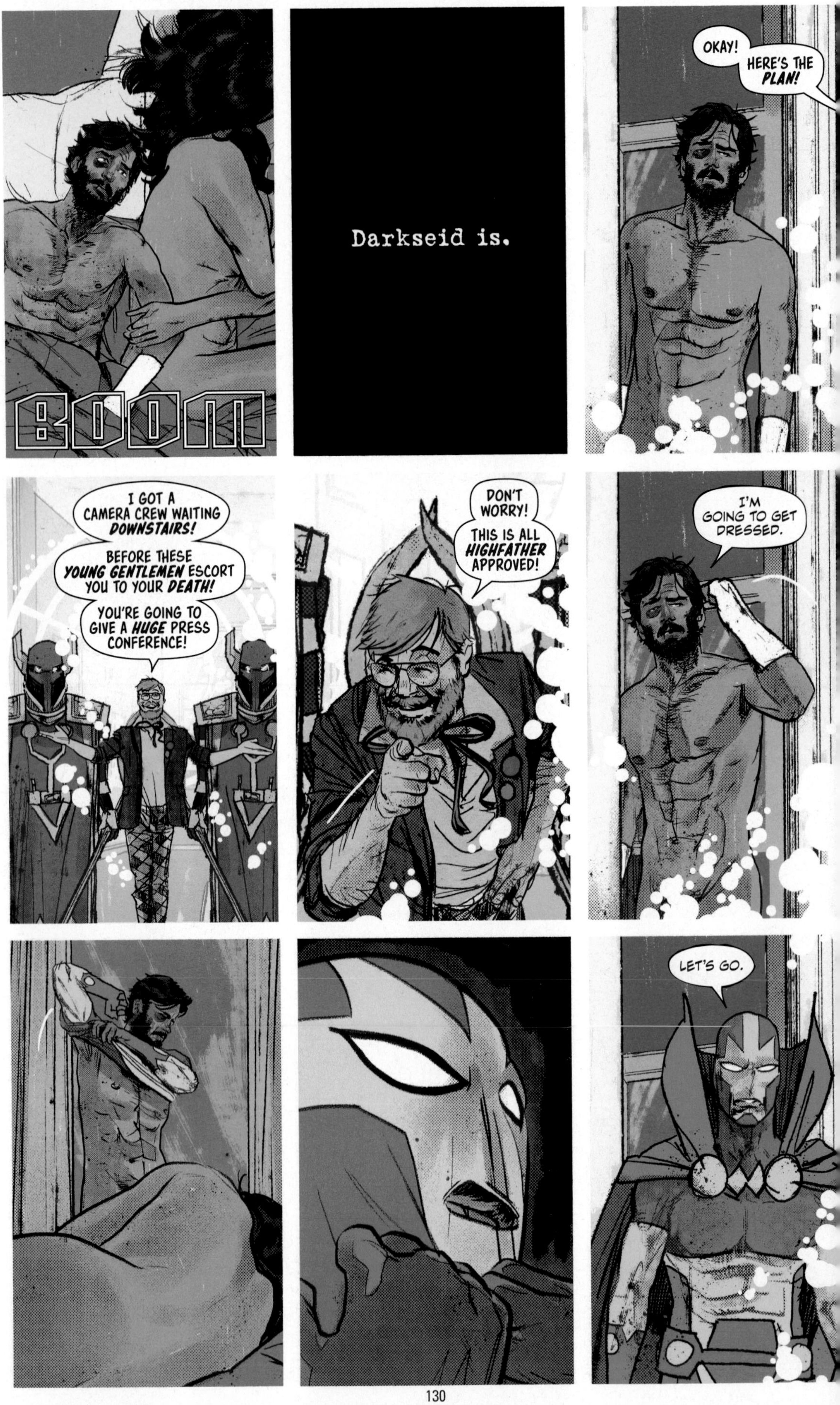
BOOM
Darkseid is.
OKAY!
HERE'S THE PLAN!
I GOT A CAMERA CREW WAITING DOWNSTAIRS!
BEFORE THESE YOUNG GENTLEMEN ESCORT YOU TO YOUR DEATH!
YOU'RE GOING TO GIVE A HUGE PRESS CONFERENCE!
DON'T WORRY!
THIS IS ALL HIGHFATHER APPROVED!
I'M GOING TO GET DRESSED.
LET'S GO.

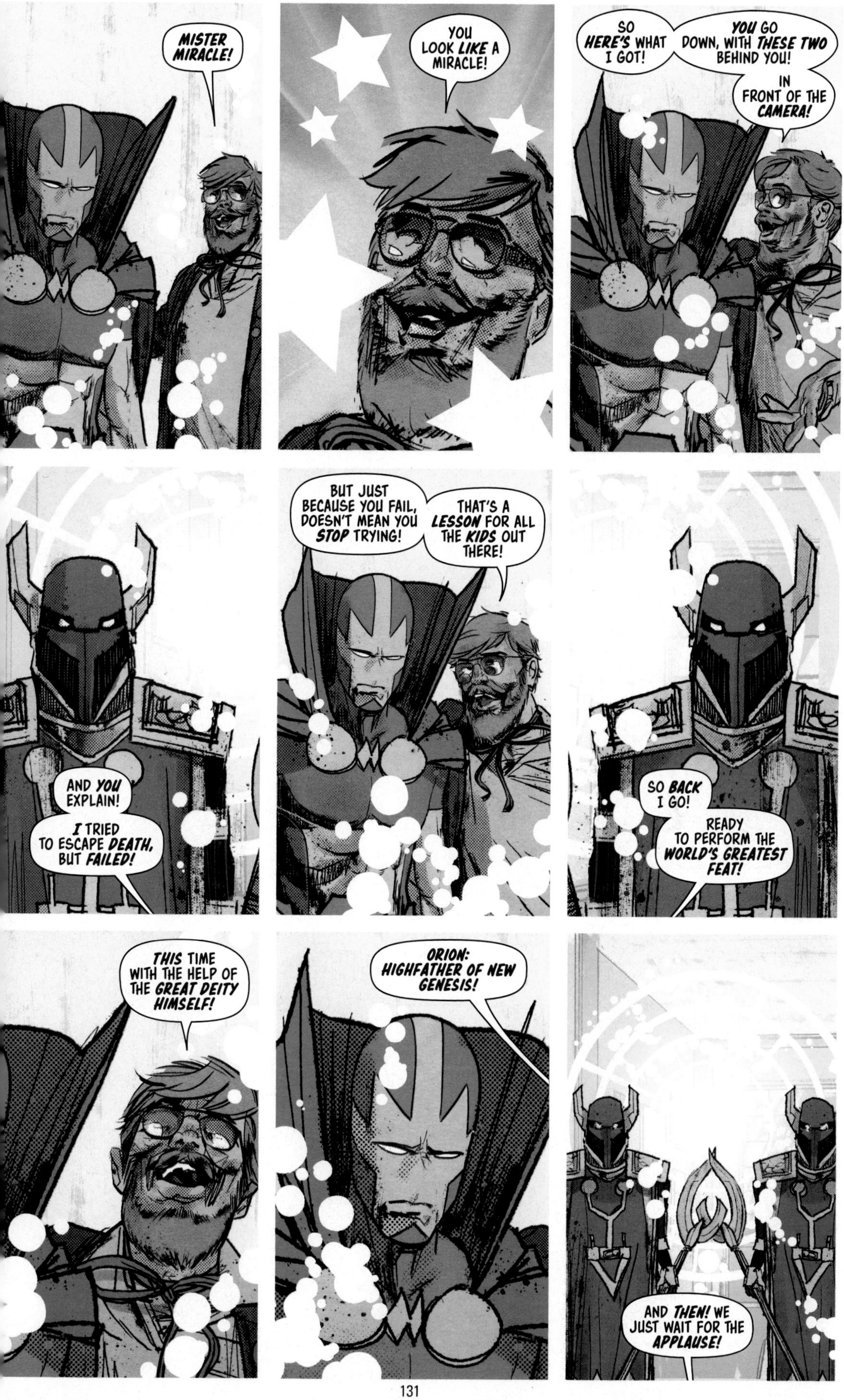
MISTER MIRACLE!
YOU LOOK LIKE A MIRACLE!
SO HERE'S WHAT I GOT!
YOU GO DOWN, WITH THESE TWO BEHIND YOU!
IN FRONT OF THE CAMERA!
AND YOU EXPLAIN!
I TRIED TO ESCAPE DEATH, BUT FAILED!
BUT JUST BECAUSE YOU FAIL, DOESN'T MEAN YOU STOP TRYING!
THAT'S A LESSON FOR ALL THE KIDS OUT THERE!
SO BACK I GO!
READY TO PERFORM THE WORLD'S GREATEST FEAT!
THIS TIME WITH THE HELP OF THE GREAT DEITY HIMSELF!
ORION: HIGHFATHER OF NEW GENESIS!
AND THEN! WE JUST WAIT FOR THE APPLAUSE!

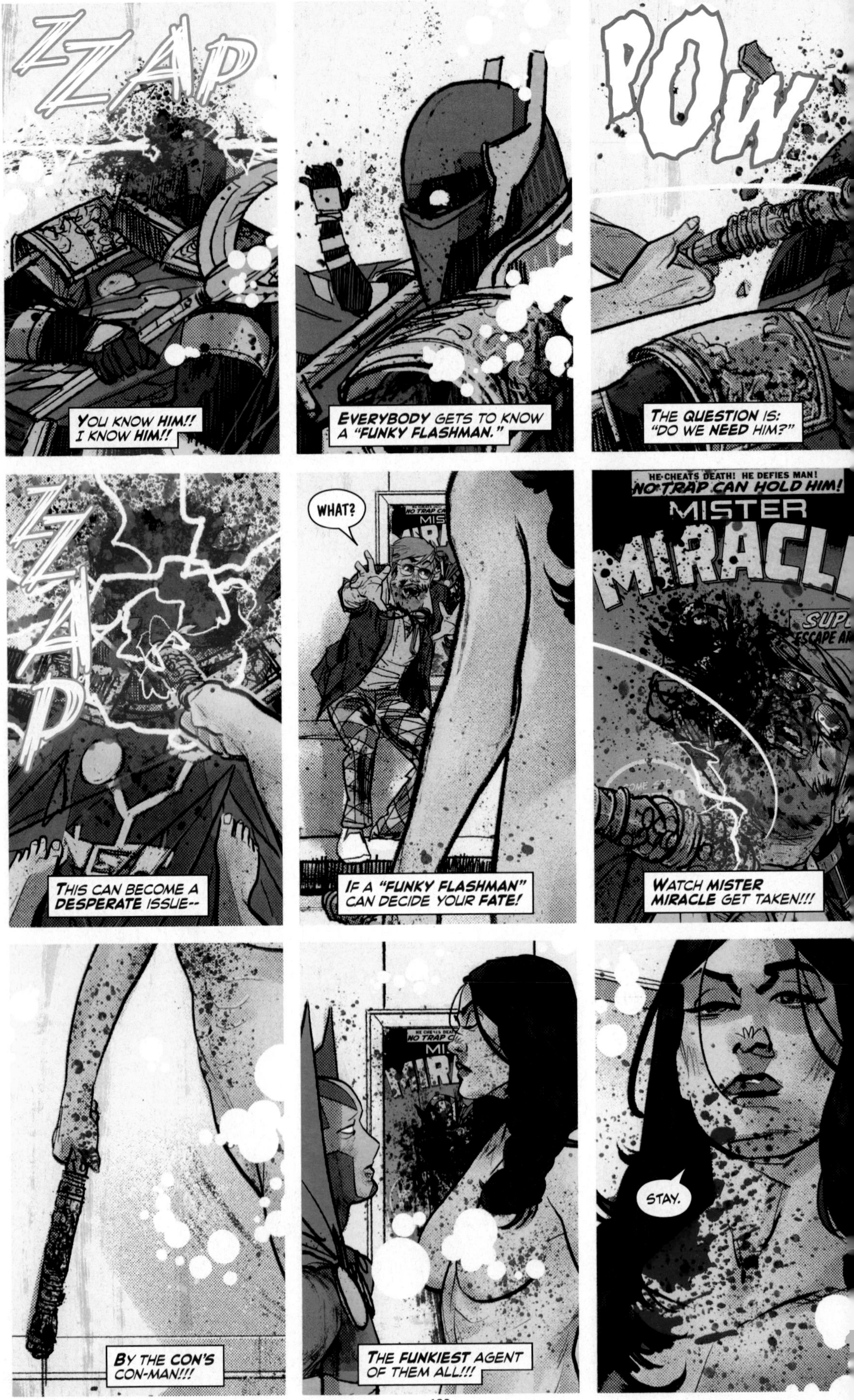
ZZAP
YOU KNOW HIM!! I KNOW HIM!!
EVERYBODY GETS TO KNOW A "FUNKY FLASHMAN."
POW
THE QUESTION IS: "DO WE NEED HIM?"
ZZAP
THIS CAN BECOME A DESPERATE ISSUE--
WHAT?
IF A "FUNKY FLASHMAN" CAN DECIDE YOUR FATE!
HE-CHEATS DEATH! HE DEFIES MAN!
NO TRAP CAN HOLD HIM!
MISTER
WATCH MISTER MIRACLE GET TAKEN!!!
BY THE CON'S CON-MAN!!!
THE FUNKIEST AGENT OF THEM ALL!!!
STAY.

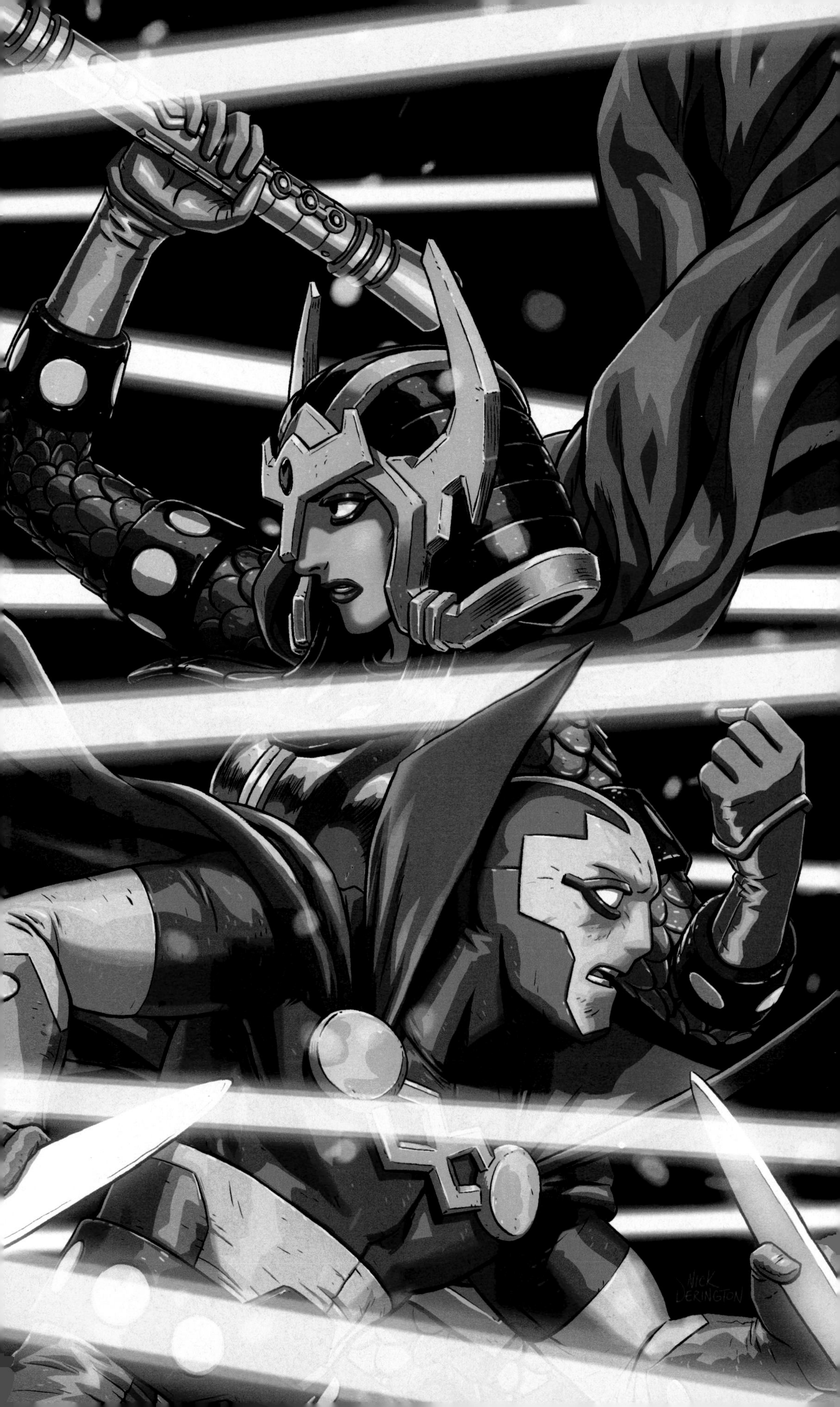
NICK DERINGTON

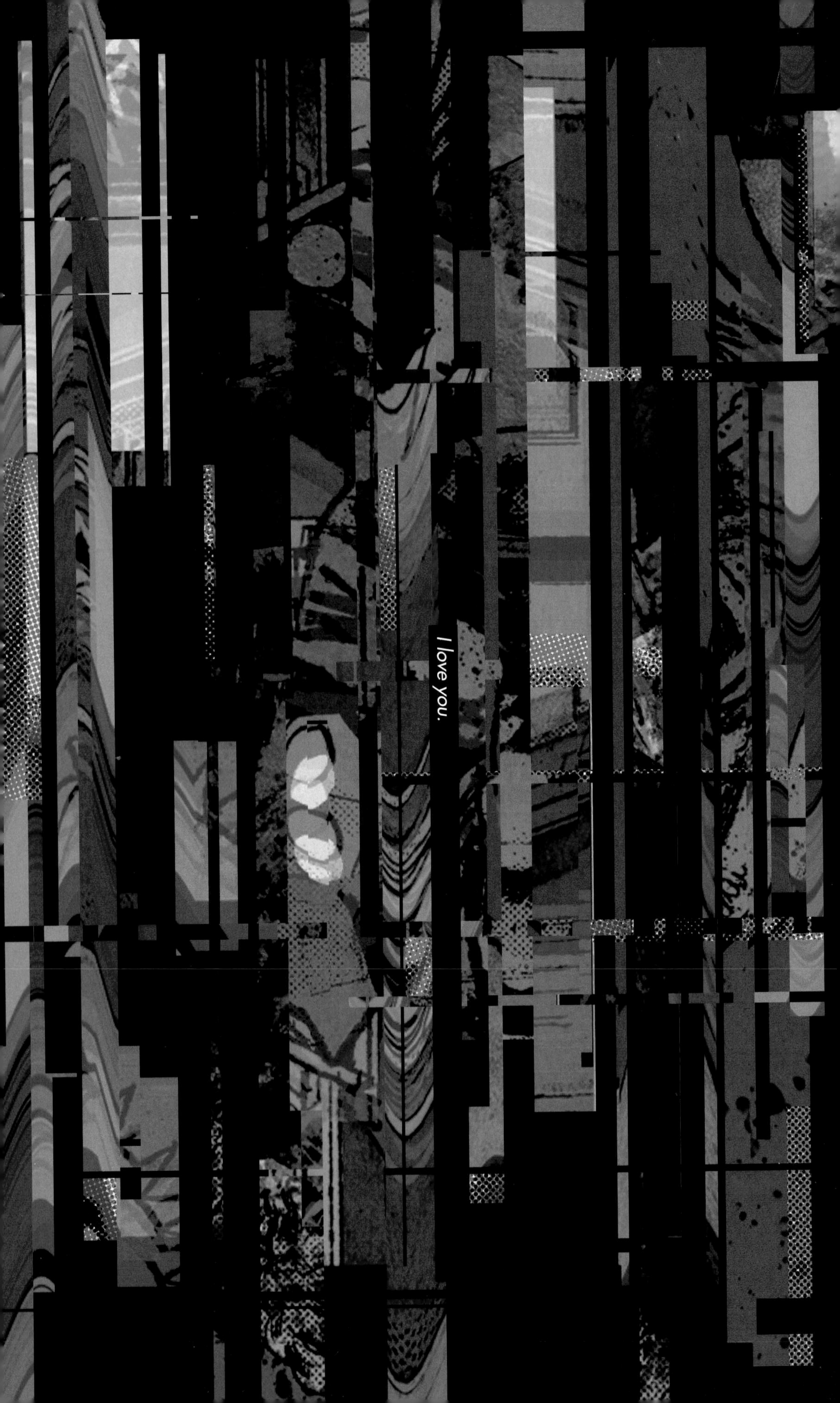
I love you.

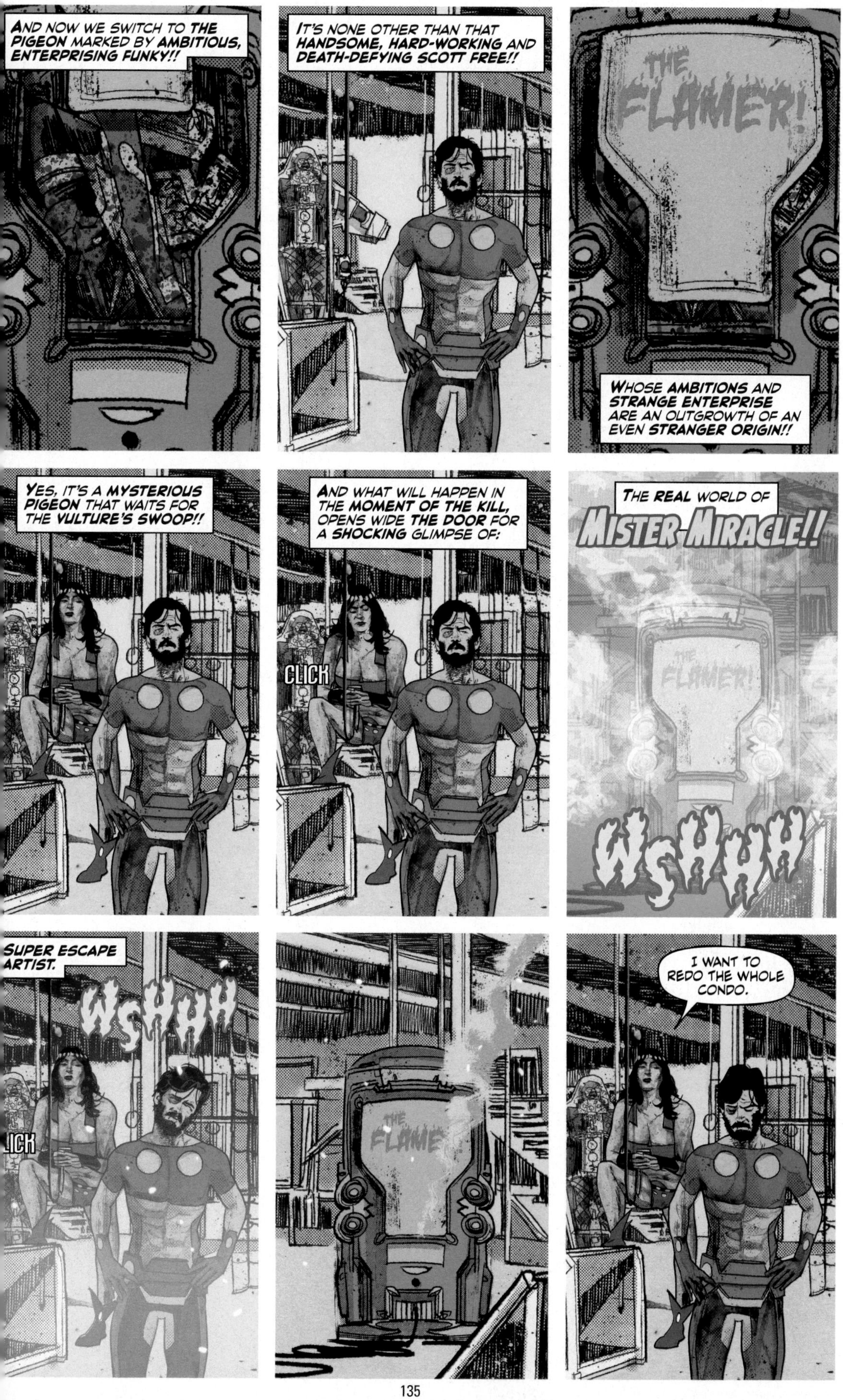
AND NOW WE SWITCH TO THE PIGEON MARKED BY AMBITIOUS, ENTERPRISING FUNKY!!
IT'S NONE OTHER THAN THAT HANDSOME, HARD-WORKING AND DEATH-DEFYING SCOTT FREE!!
THE FLAMER!
WHOSE AMBITIONS AND STRANGE ENTERPRISE ARE AN OUTGROWTH OF AN EVEN STRANGER ORIGIN!!
YES, IT'S A MYSTERIOUS PIGEON THAT WAITS FOR THE VULTURE'S SWOOP!!
AND WHAT WILL HAPPEN IN THE MOMENT OF THE KILL, OPENS WIDE THE DOOR FOR A SHOCKING GLIMPSE OF:
CLICK
THE REAL WORLD OF
MISTER-MIRACLE!!
THE FLAMER!
WSHUH
SUPER ESCAPE ARTIST.
WSHUH
LICK
THE FLAME
I WANT TO REDO THE WHOLE CONDO.

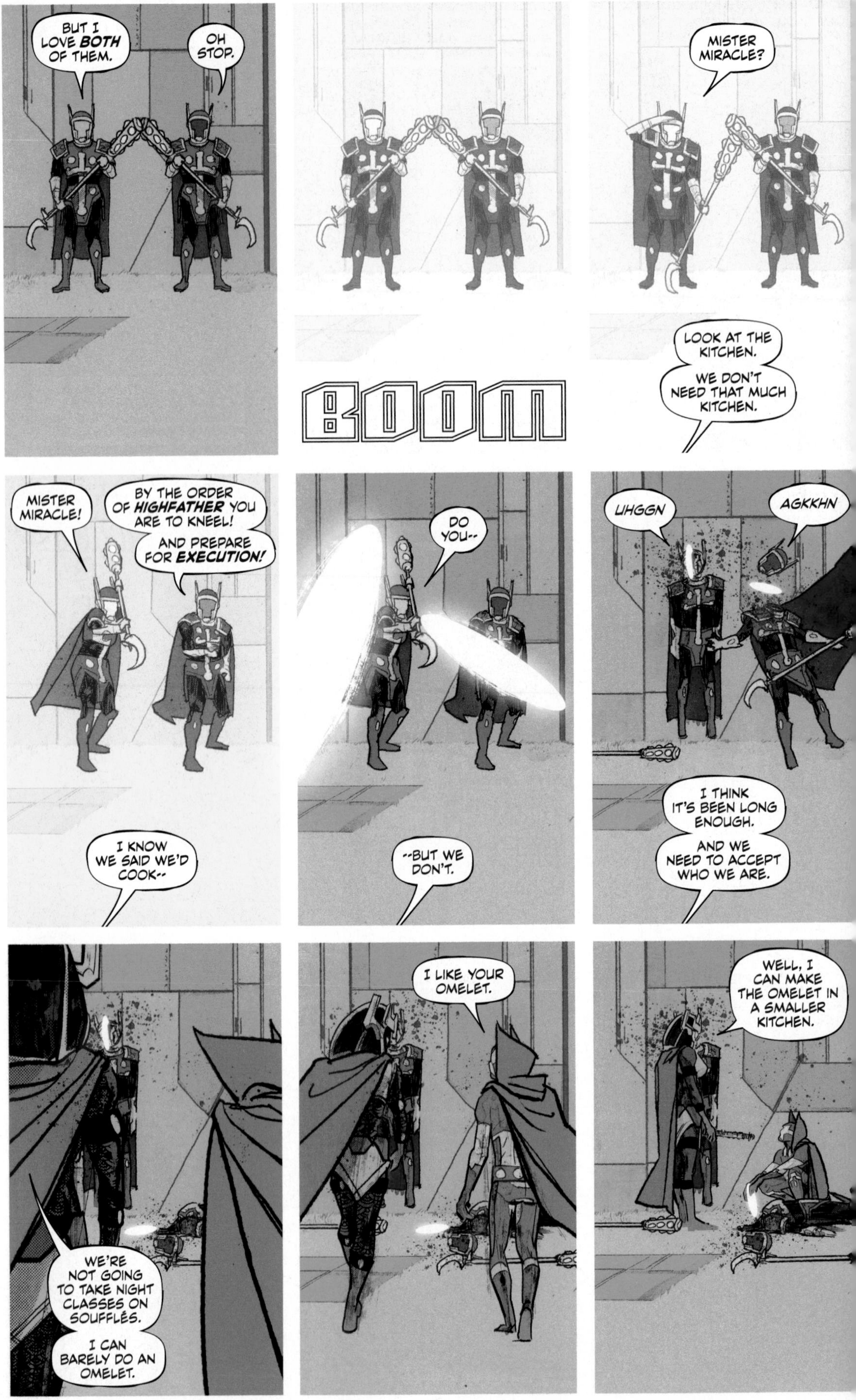

BUT I LOVE **BOTH** OF THEM.
OH STOP.
BOOM
MISTER MIRACLE?
LOOK AT THE KITCHEN.
WE DON'T NEED THAT MUCH KITCHEN.
MISTER MIRACLE!
BY THE ORDER OF **HIGHFATHER** YOU ARE TO KNEEL!
AND PREPARE FOR **EXECUTION!**
I KNOW WE SAID WE'D COOK--
DO YOU--
--BUT WE DON'T.
UHGGN
AGKKHN
I THINK IT'S BEEN LONG ENOUGH.
AND WE NEED TO ACCEPT WHO WE ARE.
WE'RE NOT GOING TO TAKE NIGHT CLASSES ON SOUFFLÉS.
I CAN BARELY DO AN OMELET.
I LIKE YOUR OMELET.
WELL, I CAN MAKE THE OMELET IN A SMALLER KITCHEN.

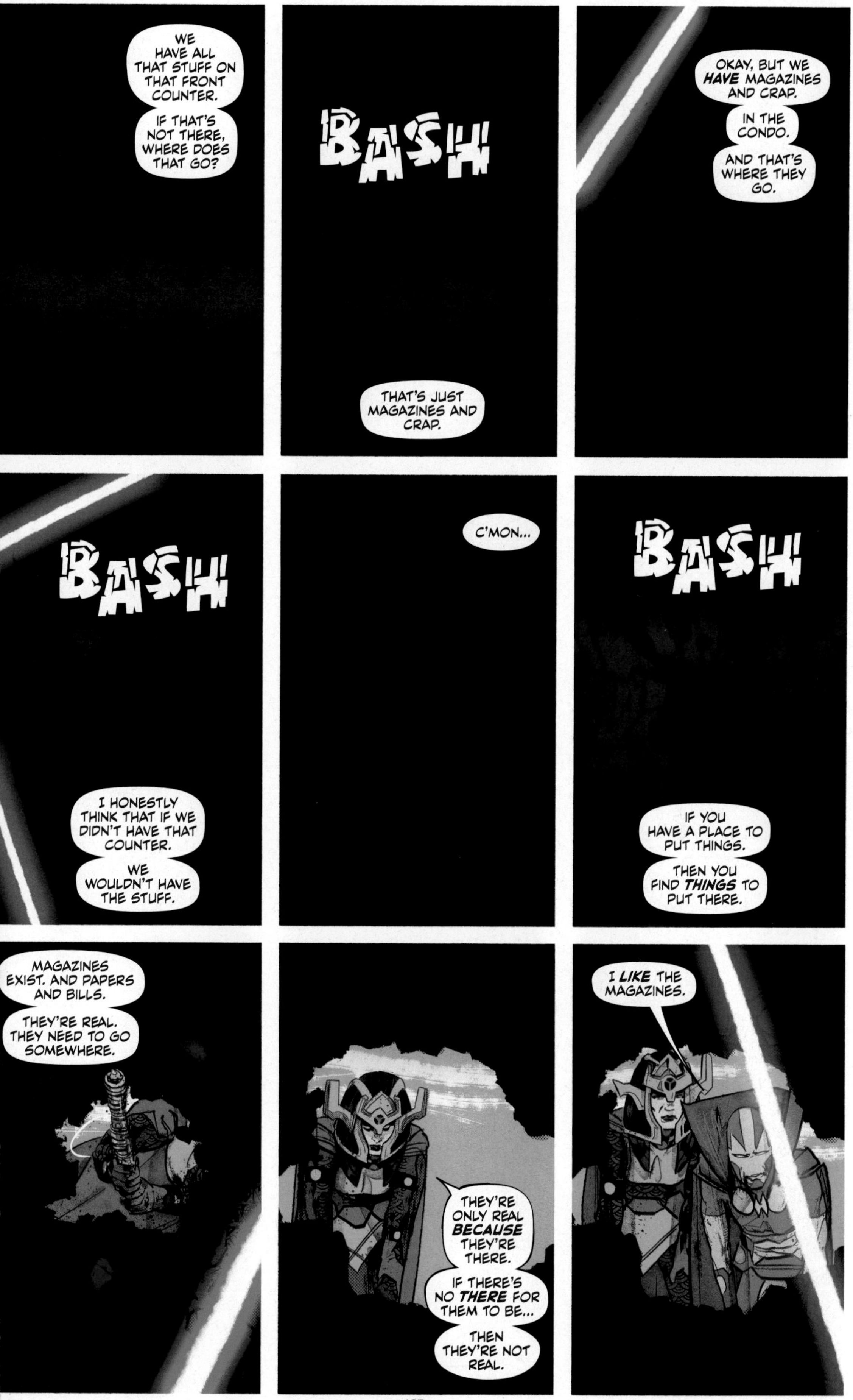

WE HAVE ALL THAT STUFF ON THAT FRONT COUNTER.
IF THAT'S NOT THERE, WHERE DOES THAT GO?
BASH
THAT'S JUST MAGAZINES AND CRAP.
OKAY, BUT WE HAVE MAGAZINES AND CRAP.
IN THE CONDO.
AND THAT'S WHERE THEY GO.
BASH
I HONESTLY THINK THAT IF WE DIDN'T HAVE THAT COUNTER.
WE WOULDN'T HAVE THE STUFF.
C'MON...
BASH
IF YOU HAVE A PLACE TO PUT THINGS.
THEN YOU FIND THINGS TO PUT THERE.
MAGAZINES EXIST. AND PAPERS AND BILLS.
THEY'RE REAL. THEY NEED TO GO SOMEWHERE.
THEY'RE ONLY REAL BECAUSE THEY'RE THERE.
IF THERE'S NO THERE FOR THEM TO BE...
THEN THEY'RE NOT REAL.
I LIKE THE MAGAZINES.

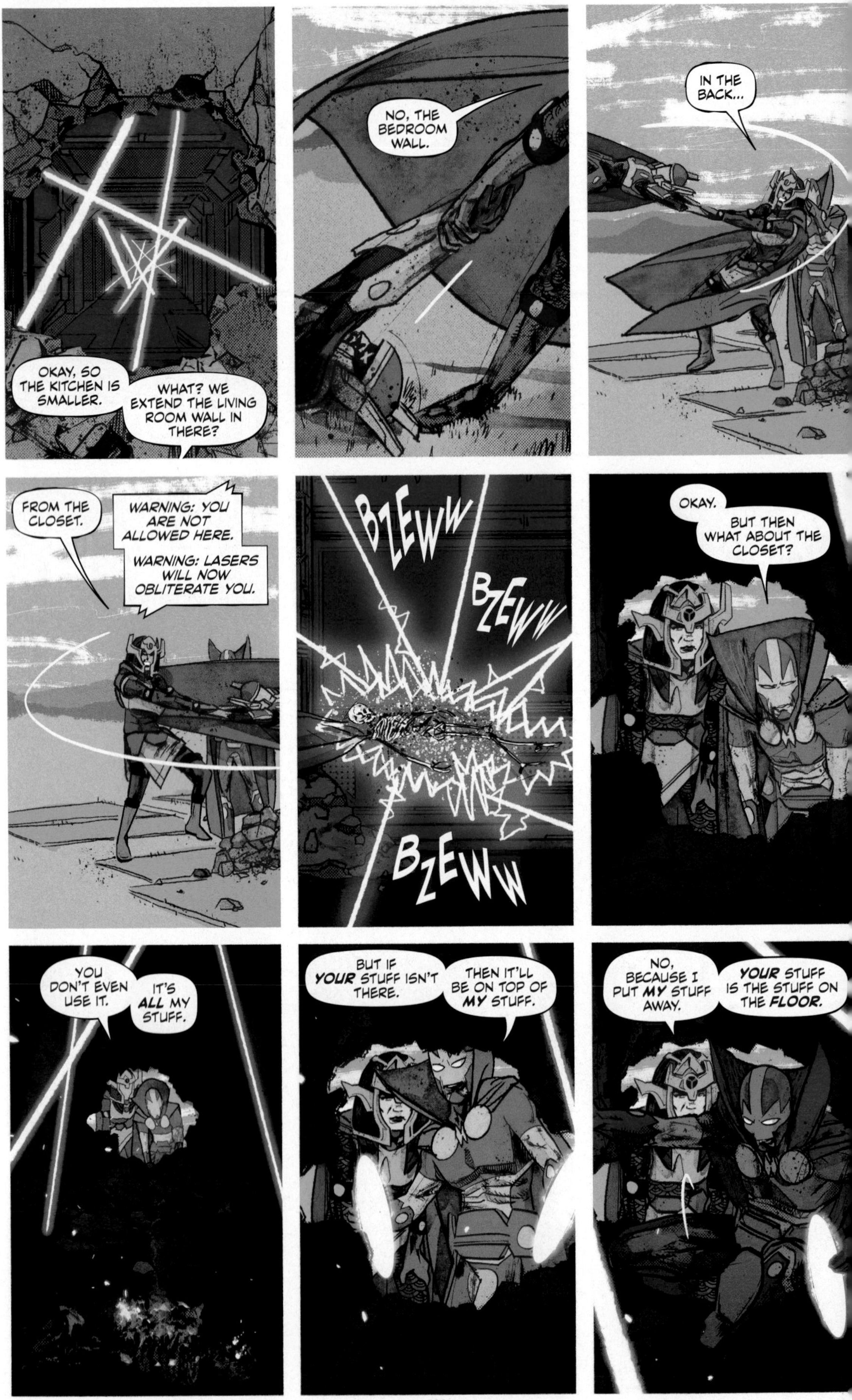
OKAY, SO THE KITCHEN IS SMALLER.
WHAT? WE EXTEND THE LIVING ROOM WALL IN THERE?
NO, THE BEDROOM WALL.
IN THE BACK...
FROM THE CLOSET.
WARNING: YOU ARE NOT ALLOWED HERE.
WARNING: LASERS WILL NOW OBLITERATE YOU.
BZEWW
BZEWW
BZEWW
OKAY.
BUT THEN WHAT ABOUT THE CLOSET?
YOU DON'T EVEN USE IT.
IT'S ALL MY STUFF.
BUT IF YOUR STUFF ISN'T THERE.
THEN IT'LL BE ON TOP OF MY STUFF.
NO, BECAUSE I PUT MY STUFF AWAY.
YOUR STUFF IS THE STUFF ON THE FLOOR.

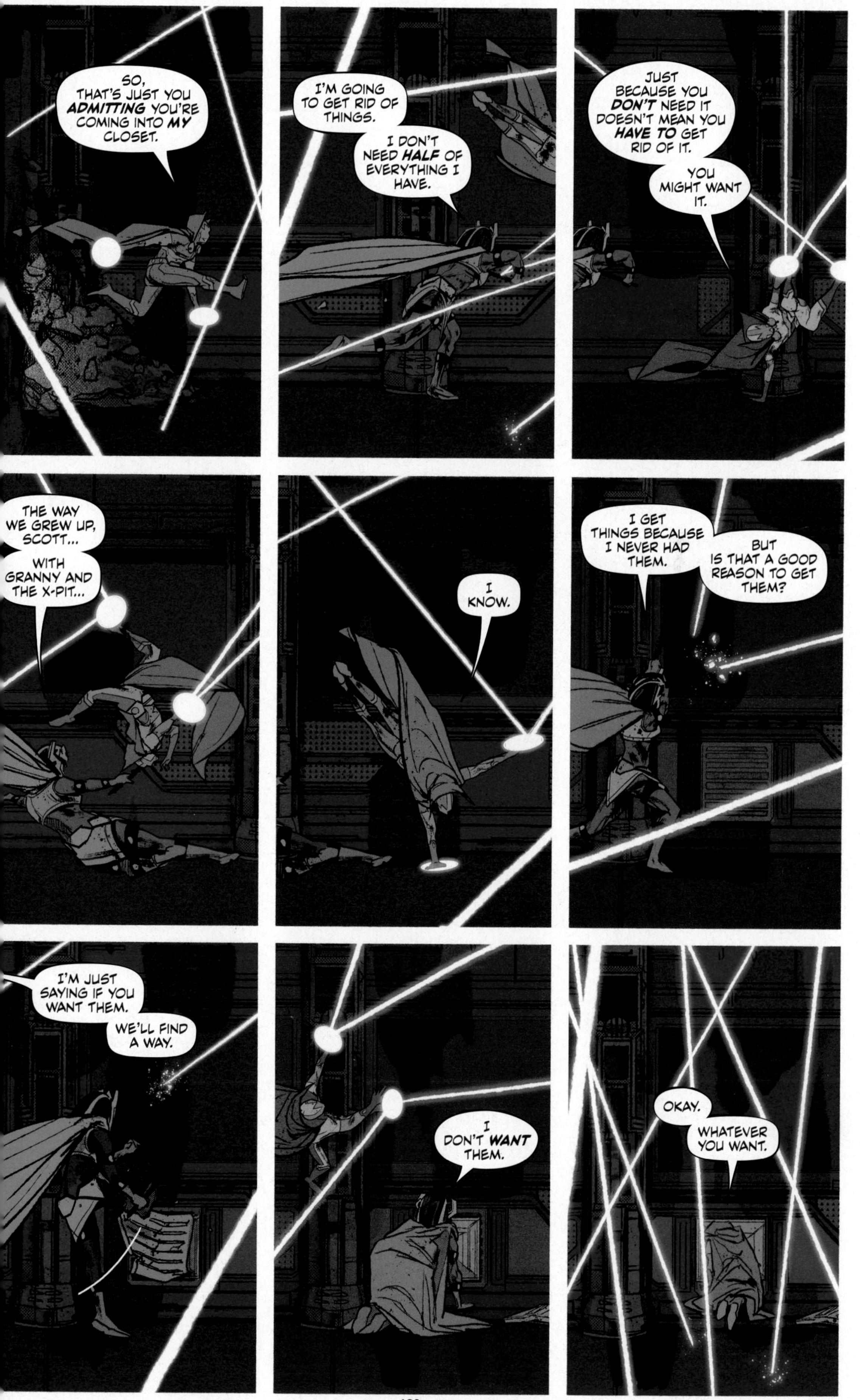
SO, THAT'S JUST YOU ADMITTING YOU'RE COMING INTO MY CLOSET.
I'M GOING TO GET RID OF THINGS.
I DON'T NEED HALF OF EVERYTHING I HAVE.
JUST BECAUSE YOU DON'T NEED IT DOESN'T MEAN YOU HAVE TO GET RID OF IT.
YOU MIGHT WANT IT.
THE WAY WE GREW UP, SCOTT...
WITH GRANNY AND THE X-PIT...
I KNOW.
I GET THINGS BECAUSE I NEVER HAD THEM.
BUT IS THAT A GOOD REASON TO GET THEM?
I'M JUST SAYING IF YOU WANT THEM.
WE'LL FIND A WAY.
I DON'T WANT THEM.
OKAY.
WHATEVER YOU WANT.

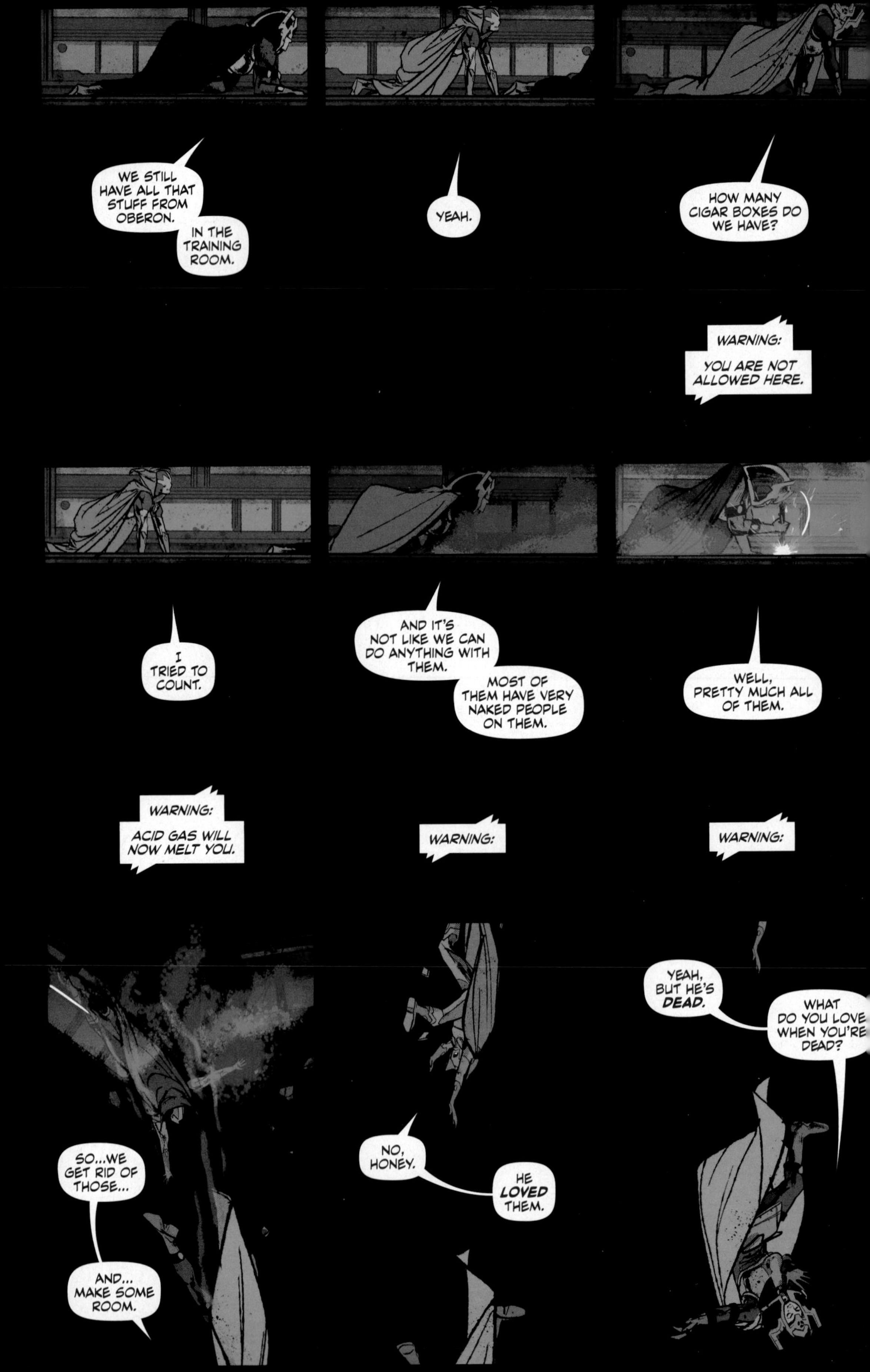
WE STILL HAVE ALL THAT STUFF FROM OBERON.
IN THE TRAINING ROOM.
YEAH.
HOW MANY CIGAR BOXES DO WE HAVE?
WARNING:
YOU ARE NOT ALLOWED HERE.
I TRIED TO COUNT.
AND IT'S NOT LIKE WE CAN DO ANYTHING WITH THEM.
MOST OF THEM HAVE VERY NAKED PEOPLE ON THEM.
WELL, PRETTY MUCH ALL OF THEM.
WARNING:
ACID GAS WILL NOW MELT YOU.
WARNING:
WARNING:
SO...WE GET RID OF THOSE...
AND... MAKE SOME ROOM.
NO, HONEY.
HE *LOVED* THEM.
YEAH, BUT HE'S *DEAD*.
WHAT DO YOU LOVE WHEN YOU'RE DEAD?

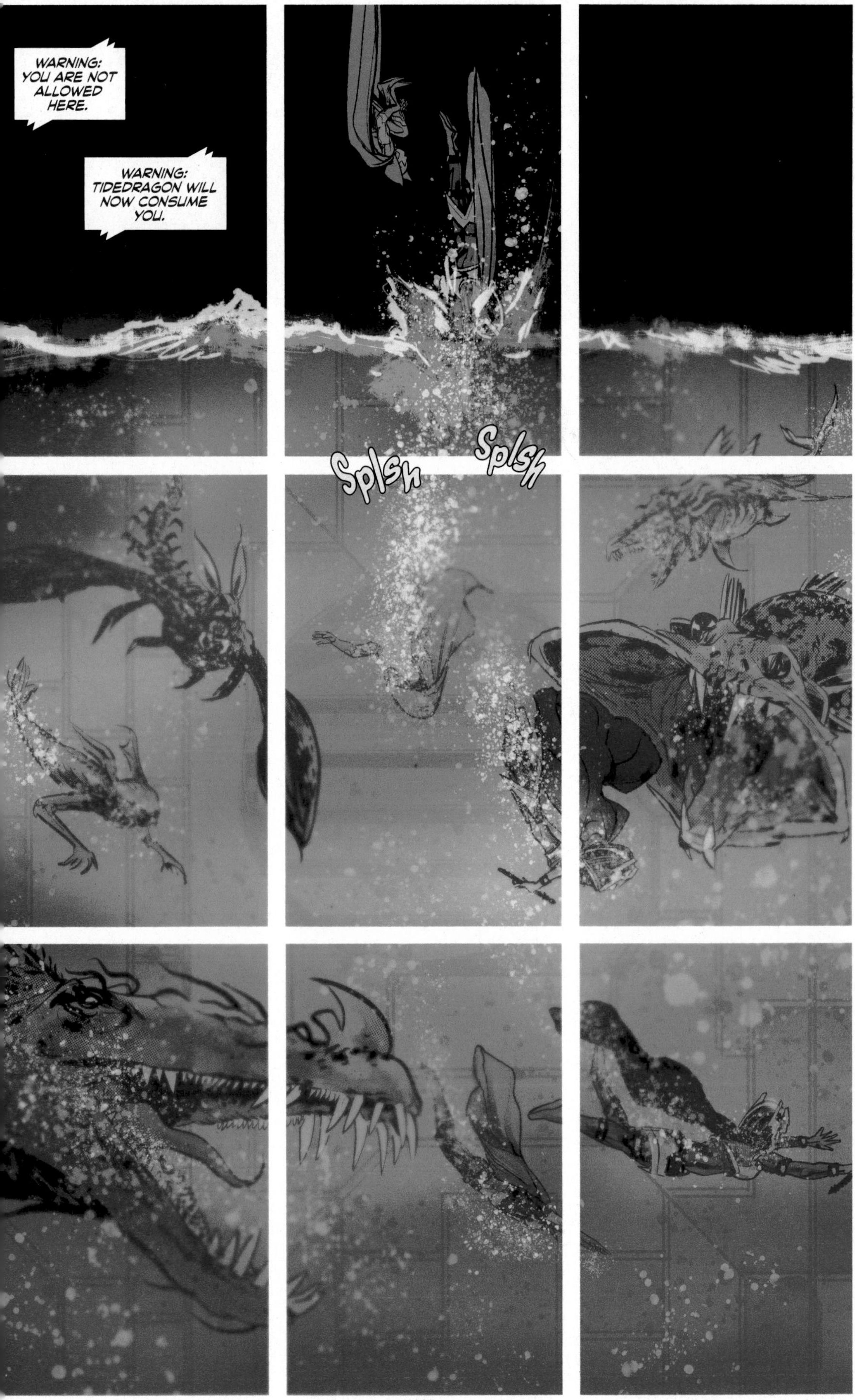
WARNING: YOU ARE NOT ALLOWED HERE.
WARNING: TIDEDRAGON WILL NOW CONSUME YOU.
Splsh
Splsh

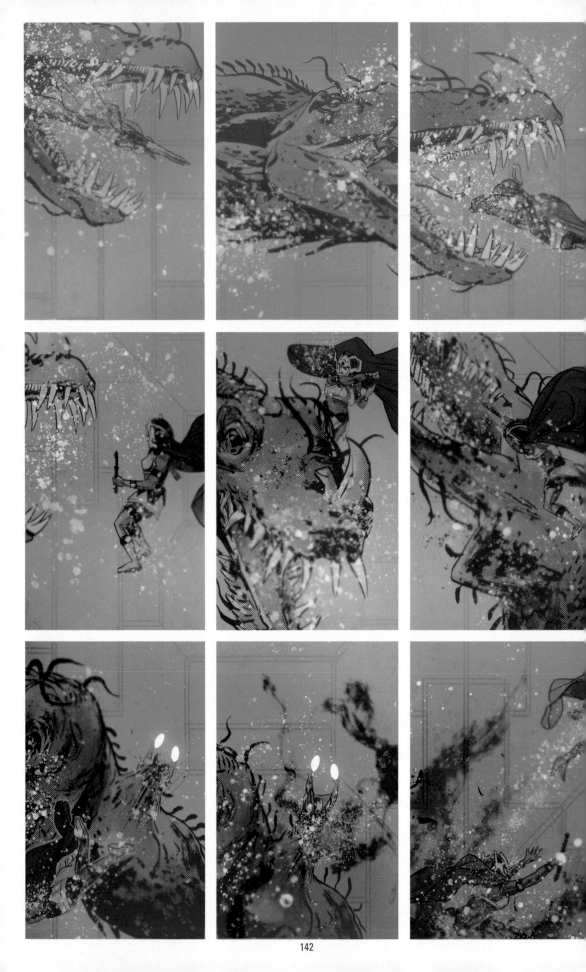

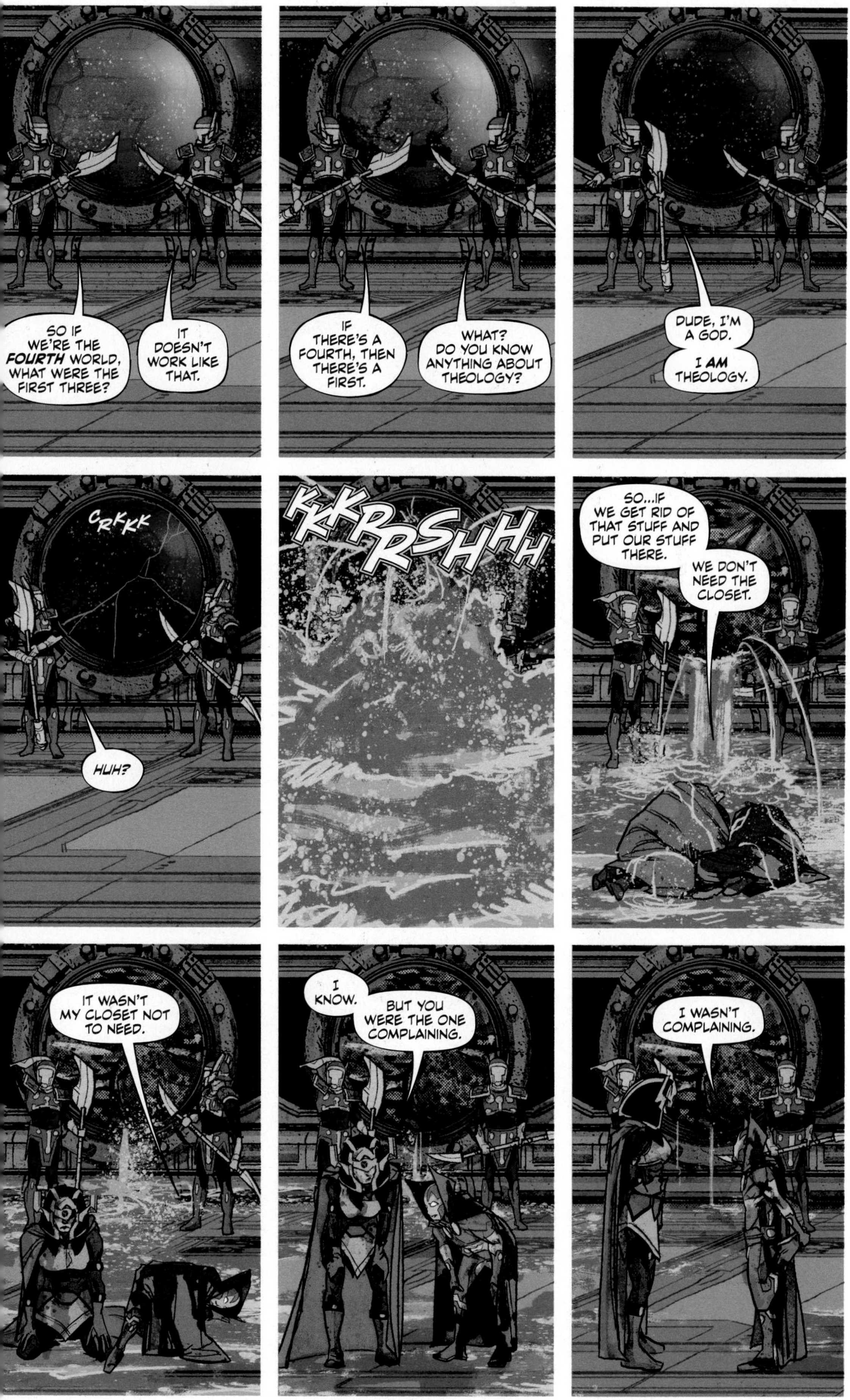
SO IF WE'RE THE FOURTH WORLD, WHAT WERE THE FIRST THREE?
IT DOESN'T WORK LIKE THAT.
IF THERE'S A FOURTH, THEN THERE'S A FIRST.
WHAT? DO YOU KNOW ANYTHING ABOUT THEOLOGY?
DUDE, I'M A GOD.
I AM THEOLOGY.
CRKKK
HUH?
KKKRRSHHHH
SO...IF WE GET RID OF THAT STUFF AND PUT OUR STUFF THERE.
WE DON'T NEED THE CLOSET.
IT WASN'T MY CLOSET NOT TO NEED.
I KNOW.
BUT YOU WERE THE ONE COMPLAINING.
I WASN'T COMPLAINING.

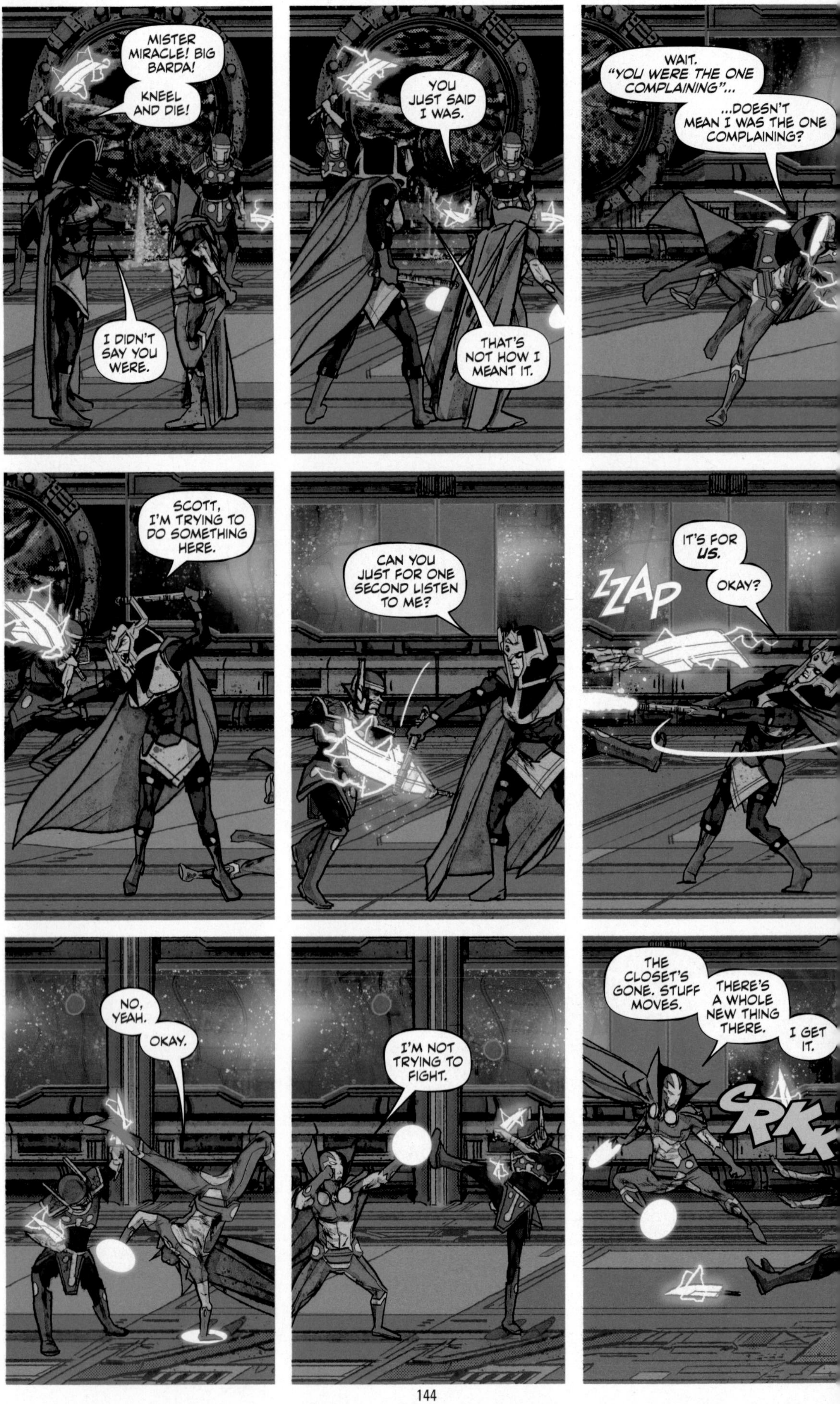

MISTER MIRACLE! BIG BARDA!
KNEEL AND DIE!
I DIDN'T SAY YOU WERE.
YOU JUST SAID I WAS.
THAT'S NOT HOW I MEANT IT.
WAIT. "YOU WERE THE ONE COMPLAINING"...
...DOESN'T MEAN I WAS THE ONE COMPLAINING?
SCOTT, I'M TRYING TO DO SOMETHING HERE.
CAN YOU JUST FOR ONE SECOND LISTEN TO ME?
ZZAP
IT'S FOR US.
OKAY?
NO, YEAH.
OKAY.
I'M NOT TRYING TO FIGHT.
THE CLOSET'S GONE. STUFF MOVES.
THERE'S A WHOLE NEW THING THERE.
I GET IT.
SRKK

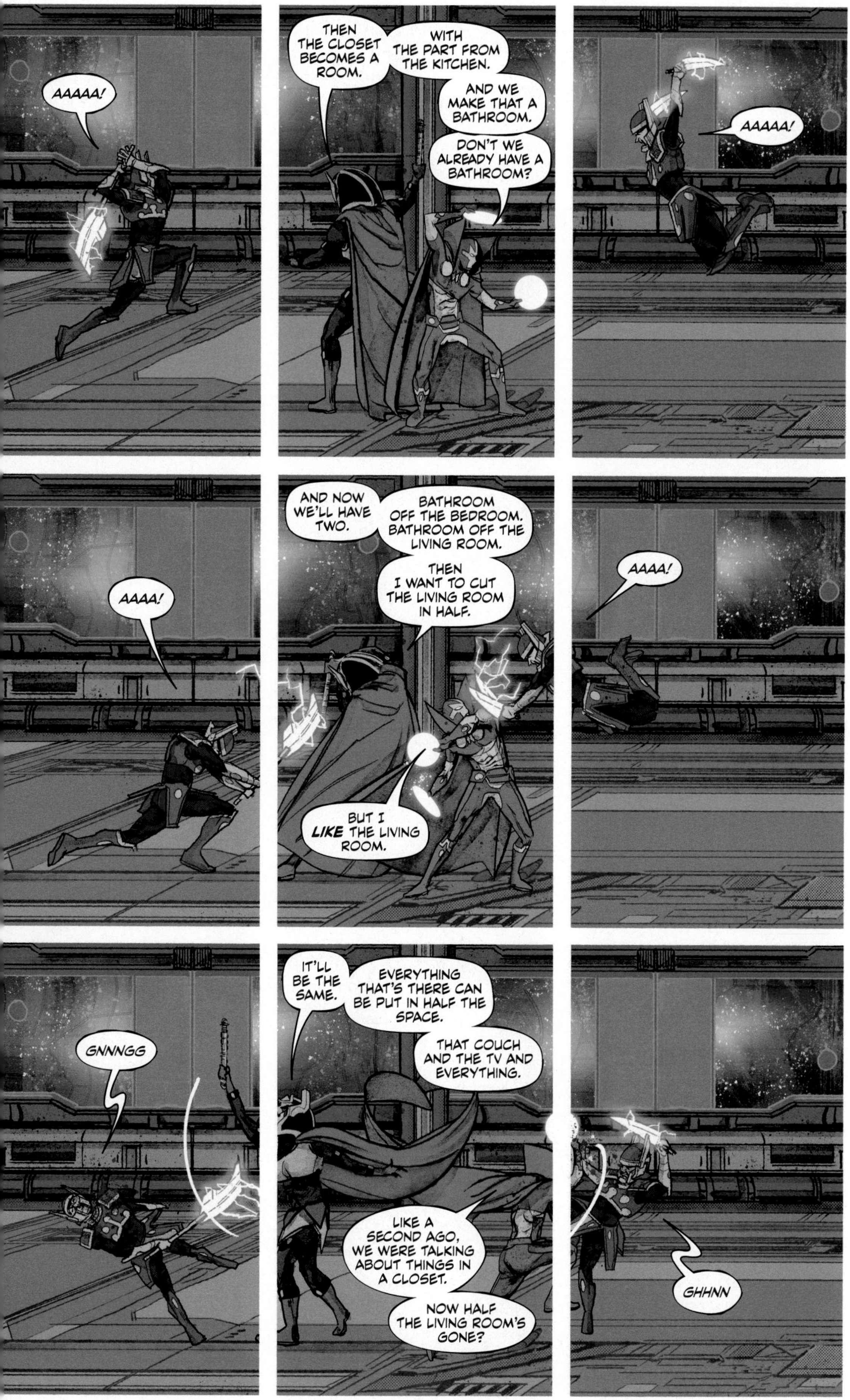
AAAAA!
THEN THE CLOSET BECOMES A ROOM.
WITH THE PART FROM THE KITCHEN.
AND WE MAKE THAT A BATHROOM.
DON'T WE ALREADY HAVE A BATHROOM?
AAAAA!
AAAA!
AND NOW WE'LL HAVE TWO.
BATHROOM OFF THE BEDROOM. BATHROOM OFF THE LIVING ROOM.
THEN I WANT TO CUT THE LIVING ROOM IN HALF.
BUT I LIKE THE LIVING ROOM.
AAAA!
GNNNGG
IT'LL BE THE SAME.
EVERYTHING THAT'S THERE CAN BE PUT IN HALF THE SPACE.
THAT COUCH AND THE TV AND EVERYTHING.
LIKE A SECOND AGO, WE WERE TALKING ABOUT THINGS IN A CLOSET.
NOW HALF THE LIVING ROOM'S GONE?
GHHNN

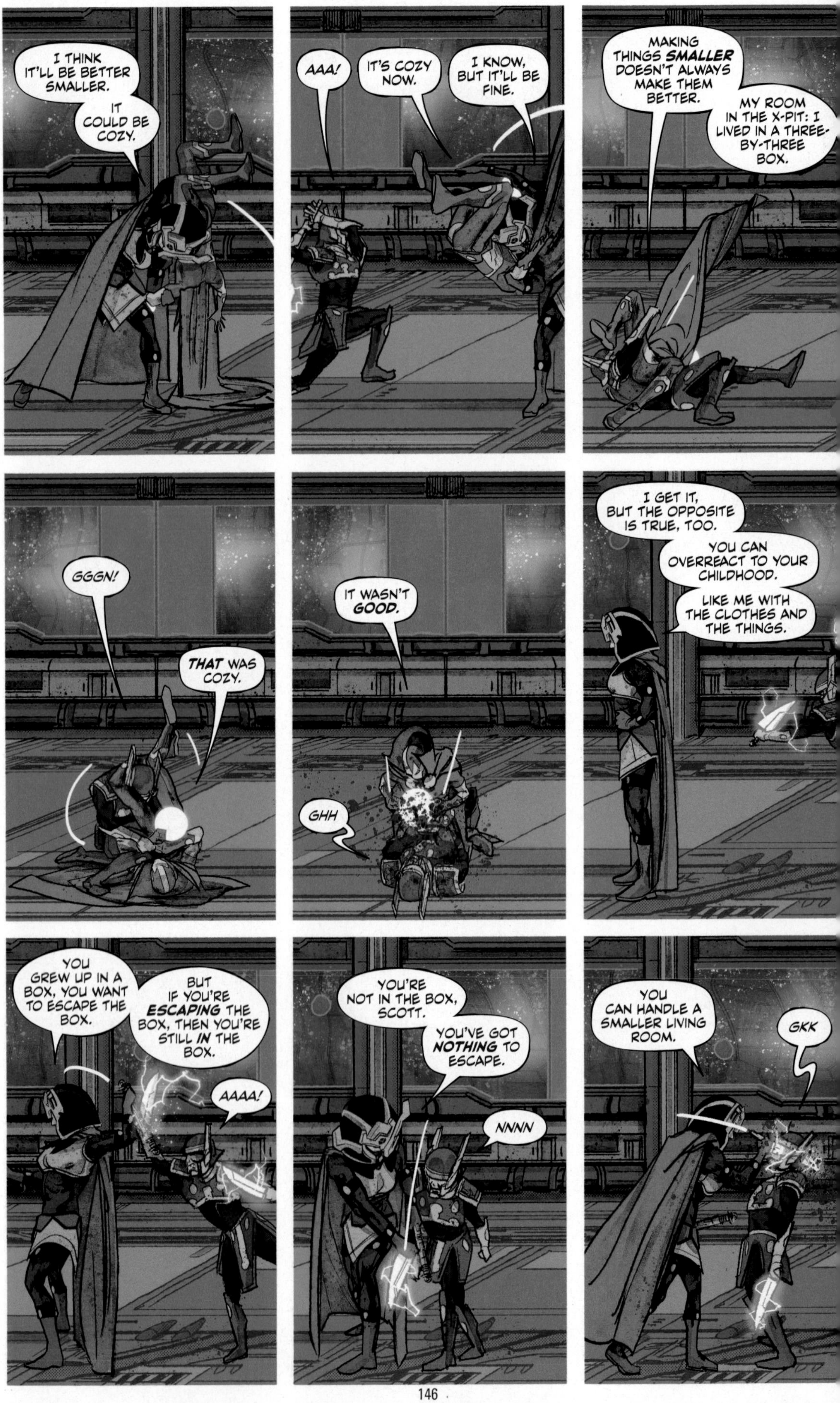
I THINK IT'LL BE BETTER SMALLER.
IT COULD BE COZY.
AAA!
IT'S COZY NOW.
I KNOW, BUT IT'LL BE FINE.
MAKING THINGS SMALLER DOESN'T ALWAYS MAKE THEM BETTER.
MY ROOM IN THE X-PIT: I LIVED IN A THREE-BY-THREE BOX.
GGGN!
THAT WAS COZY.
IT WASN'T GOOD.
GHH
I GET IT, BUT THE OPPOSITE IS TRUE, TOO.
YOU CAN OVERREACT TO YOUR CHILDHOOD.
LIKE ME WITH THE CLOTHES AND THE THINGS.
YOU GREW UP IN A BOX, YOU WANT TO ESCAPE THE BOX.
BUT IF YOU'RE ESCAPING THE BOX, THEN YOU'RE STILL IN THE BOX.
AAAA!
YOU'RE NOT IN THE BOX, SCOTT.
YOU'VE GOT NOTHING TO ESCAPE.
NNNN
YOU CAN HANDLE A SMALLER LIVING ROOM.
GKK

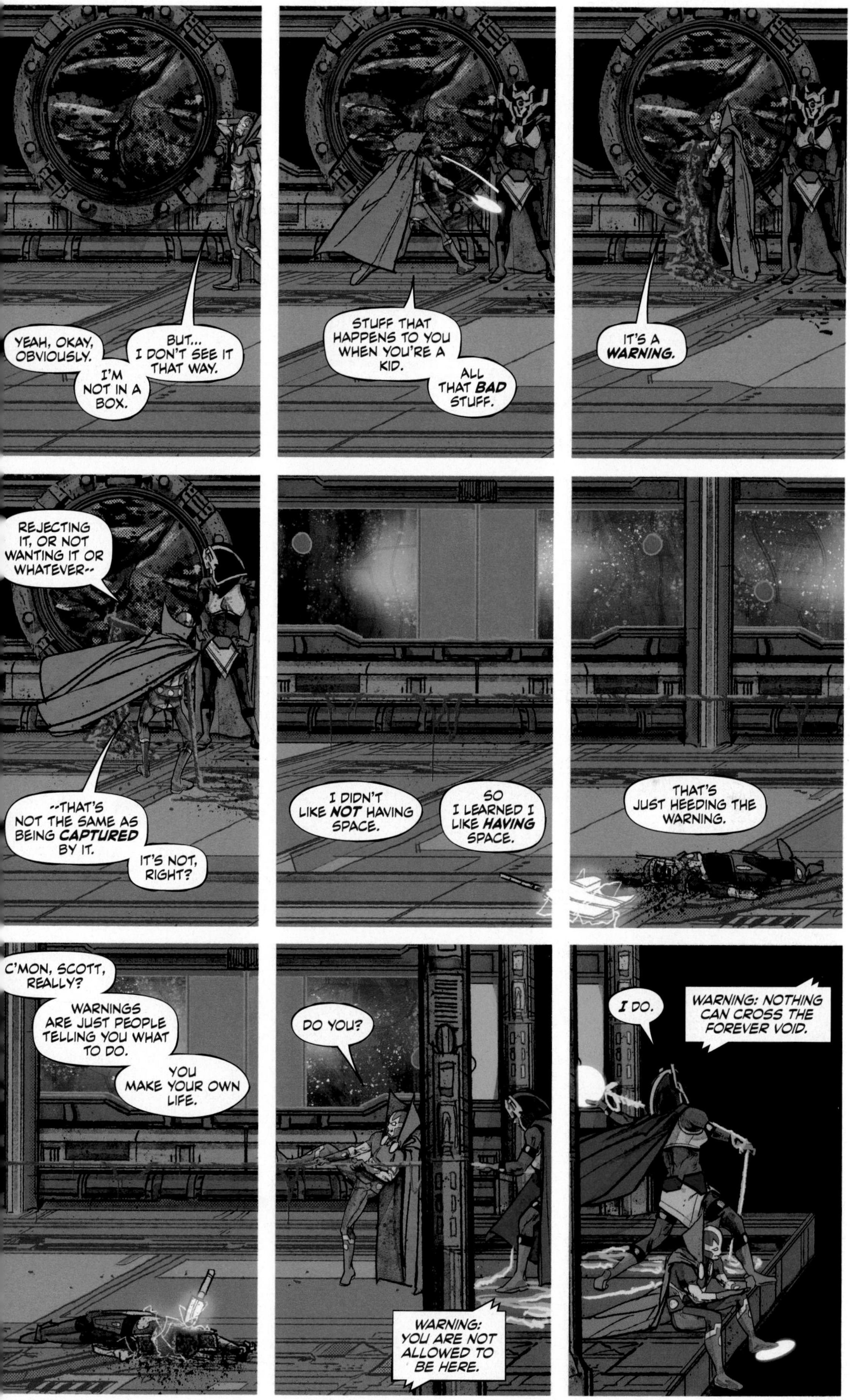

YEAH, OKAY, OBVIOUSLY.
I'M NOT IN A BOX.
BUT... I DON'T SEE IT THAT WAY.
STUFF THAT HAPPENS TO YOU WHEN YOU'RE A KID.
ALL THAT BAD STUFF.
IT'S A WARNING.
REJECTING IT, OR NOT WANTING IT OR WHATEVER--
--THAT'S NOT THE SAME AS BEING CAPTURED BY IT.
IT'S NOT, RIGHT?
I DIDN'T LIKE NOT HAVING SPACE.
SO I LEARNED I LIKE HAVING SPACE.
THAT'S JUST HEEDING THE WARNING.
C'MON, SCOTT, REALLY?
WARNINGS ARE JUST PEOPLE TELLING YOU WHAT TO DO.
YOU MAKE YOUR OWN LIFE.
DO YOU?
WARNING: YOU ARE NOT ALLOWED TO BE HERE.
I DO.
WARNING: NOTHING CAN CROSS THE FOREVER VOID.

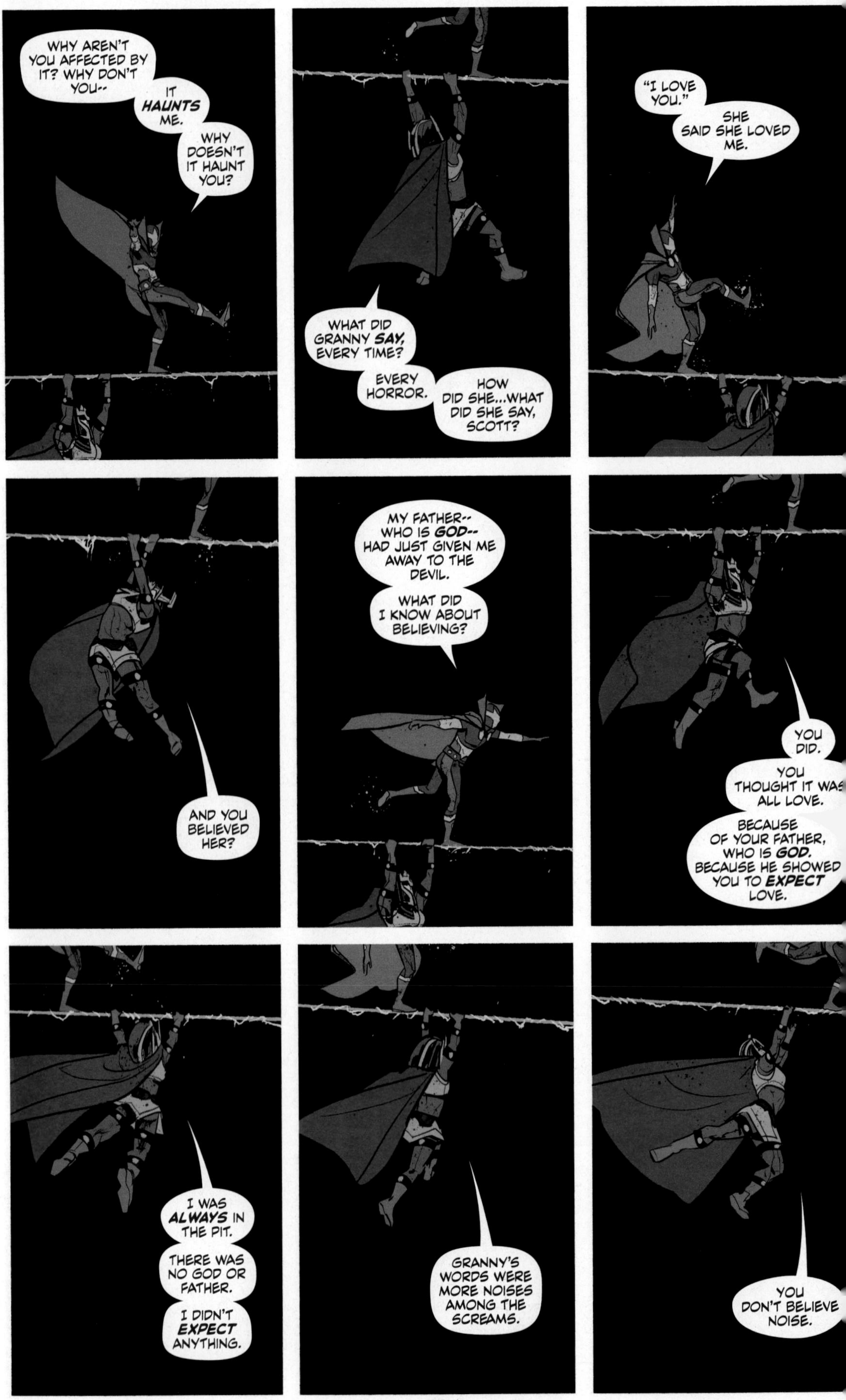
WHY AREN'T YOU AFFECTED BY IT? WHY DON'T YOU--
IT HAUNTS ME.
WHY DOESN'T IT HAUNT YOU?
WHAT DID GRANNY SAY, EVERY TIME?
EVERY HORROR.
HOW DID SHE...WHAT DID SHE SAY, SCOTT?
"I LOVE YOU."
SHE SAID SHE LOVED ME.
AND YOU BELIEVED HER?
MY FATHER-- WHO IS GOD-- HAD JUST GIVEN ME AWAY TO THE DEVIL.
WHAT DID I KNOW ABOUT BELIEVING?
YOU DID.
YOU THOUGHT IT WAS ALL LOVE.
BECAUSE OF YOUR FATHER, WHO IS GOD. BECAUSE HE SHOWED YOU TO EXPECT LOVE.
I WAS ALWAYS IN THE PIT.
THERE WAS NO GOD OR FATHER.
I DIDN'T EXPECT ANYTHING.
GRANNY'S WORDS WERE MORE NOISES AMONG THE SCREAMS.
YOU DON'T BELIEVE NOISE.

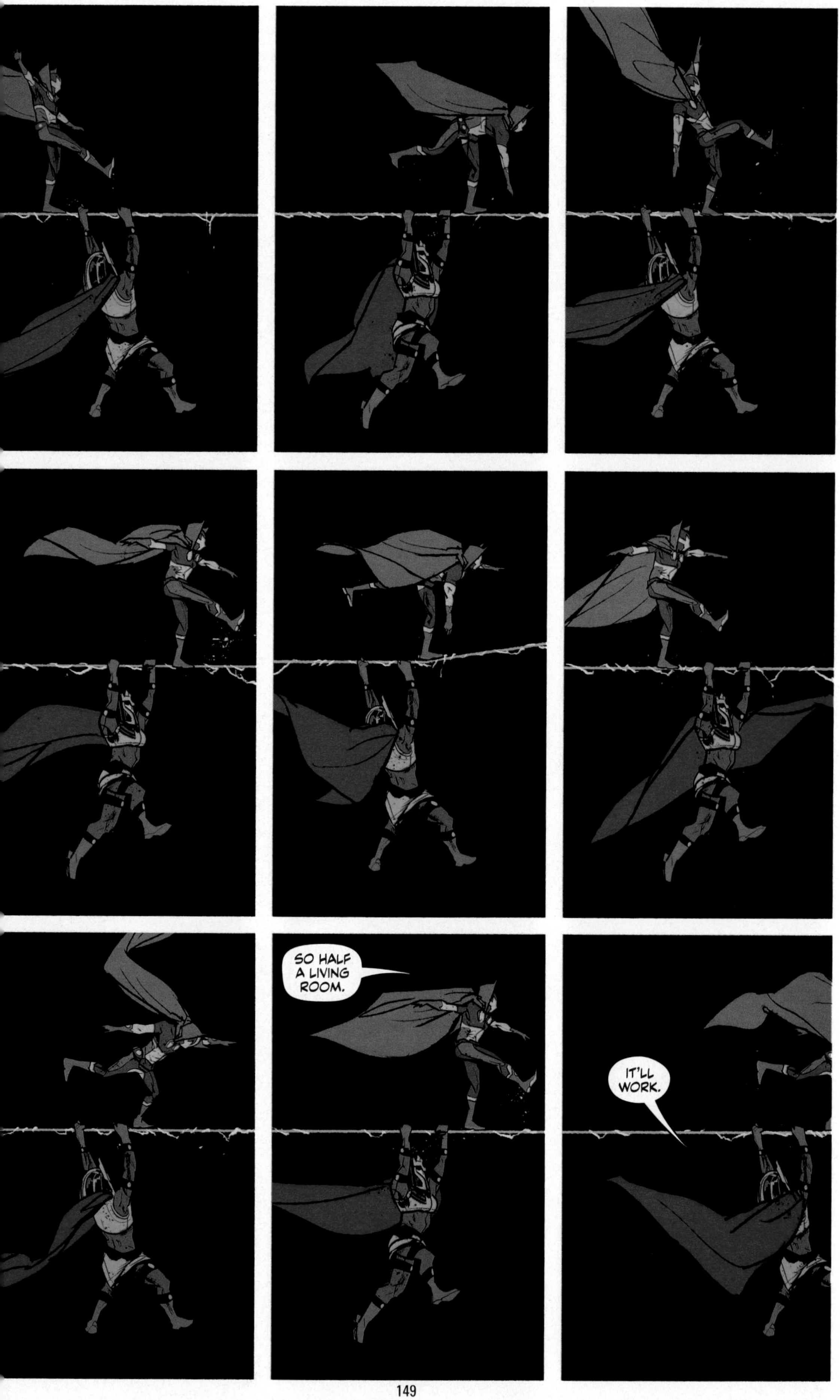
SO HALF A LIVING ROOM.
IT'LL WORK.

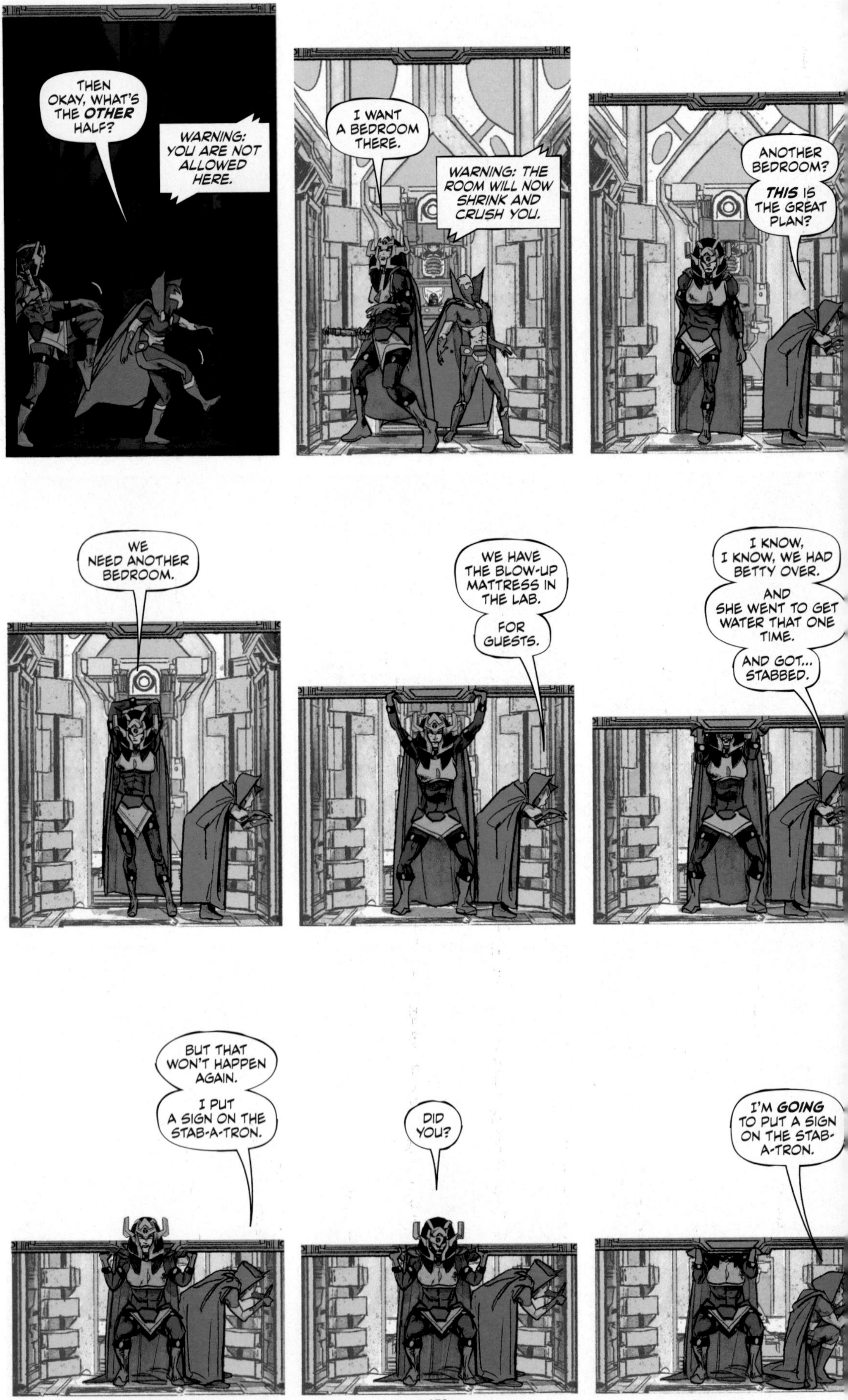
THEN OKAY, WHAT'S THE **OTHER** HALF?
WARNING: YOU ARE NOT ALLOWED HERE.
I WANT A BEDROOM THERE.
WARNING: THE ROOM WILL NOW SHRINK AND CRUSH YOU.
ANOTHER BEDROOM?
THIS IS THE GREAT PLAN?
WE NEED ANOTHER BEDROOM.
WE HAVE THE BLOW-UP MATTRESS IN THE LAB.
FOR GUESTS.
I KNOW, I KNOW, WE HAD BETTY OVER.
AND SHE WENT TO GET WATER THAT ONE TIME.
AND GOT... STABBED.
BUT THAT WON'T HAPPEN AGAIN.
I PUT A SIGN ON THE STAB-A-TRON.
DID YOU?
I'M **GOING** TO PUT A SIGN ON THE STAB-A-TRON.

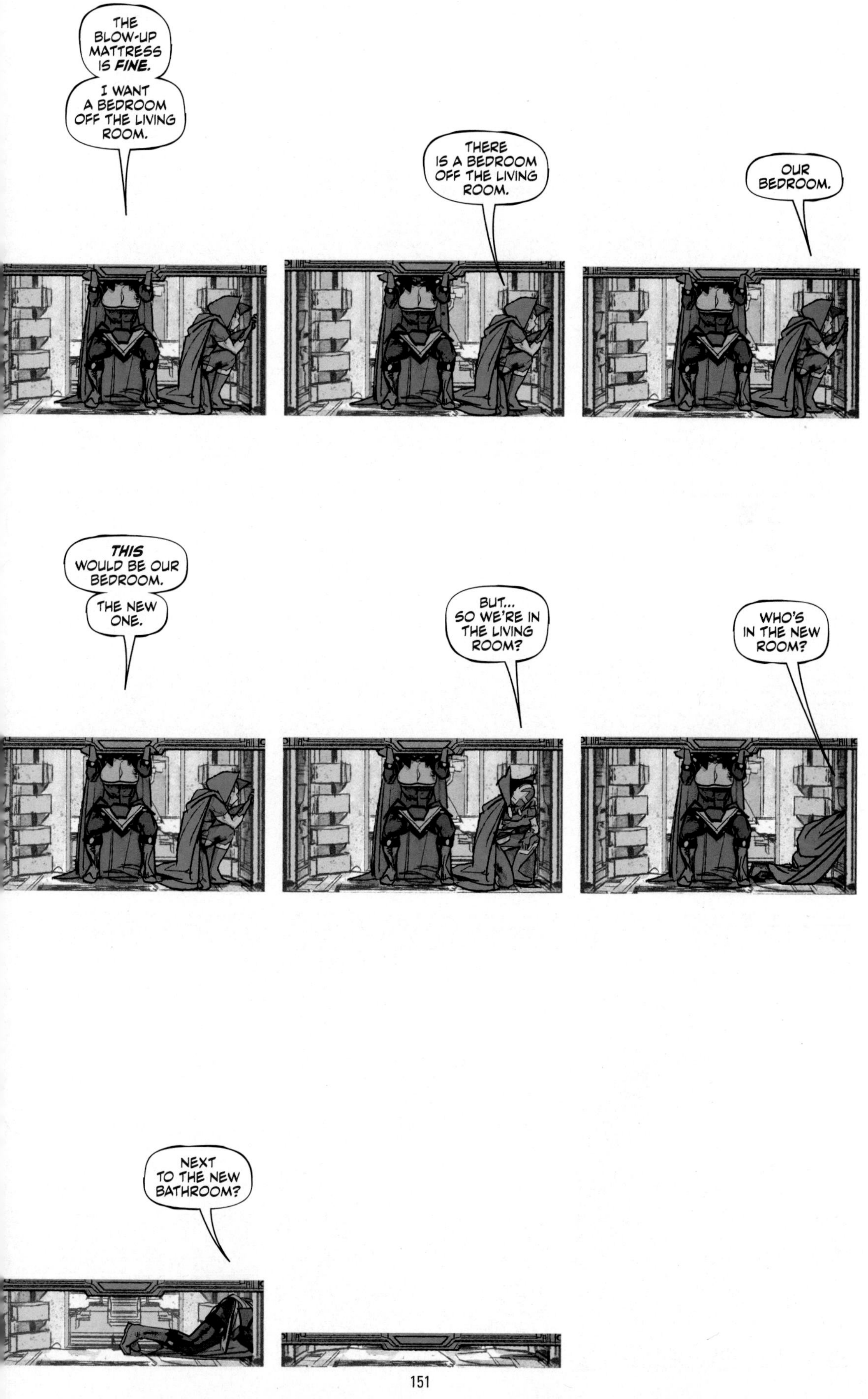
THE BLOW-UP MATTRESS IS FINE.
I WANT A BEDROOM OFF THE LIVING ROOM.
THERE IS A BEDROOM OFF THE LIVING ROOM.
OUR BEDROOM.
THIS WOULD BE OUR BEDROOM.
THE NEW ONE.
BUT... SO WE'RE IN THE LIVING ROOM?
WHO'S IN THE NEW ROOM?
NEXT TO THE NEW BATHROOM?

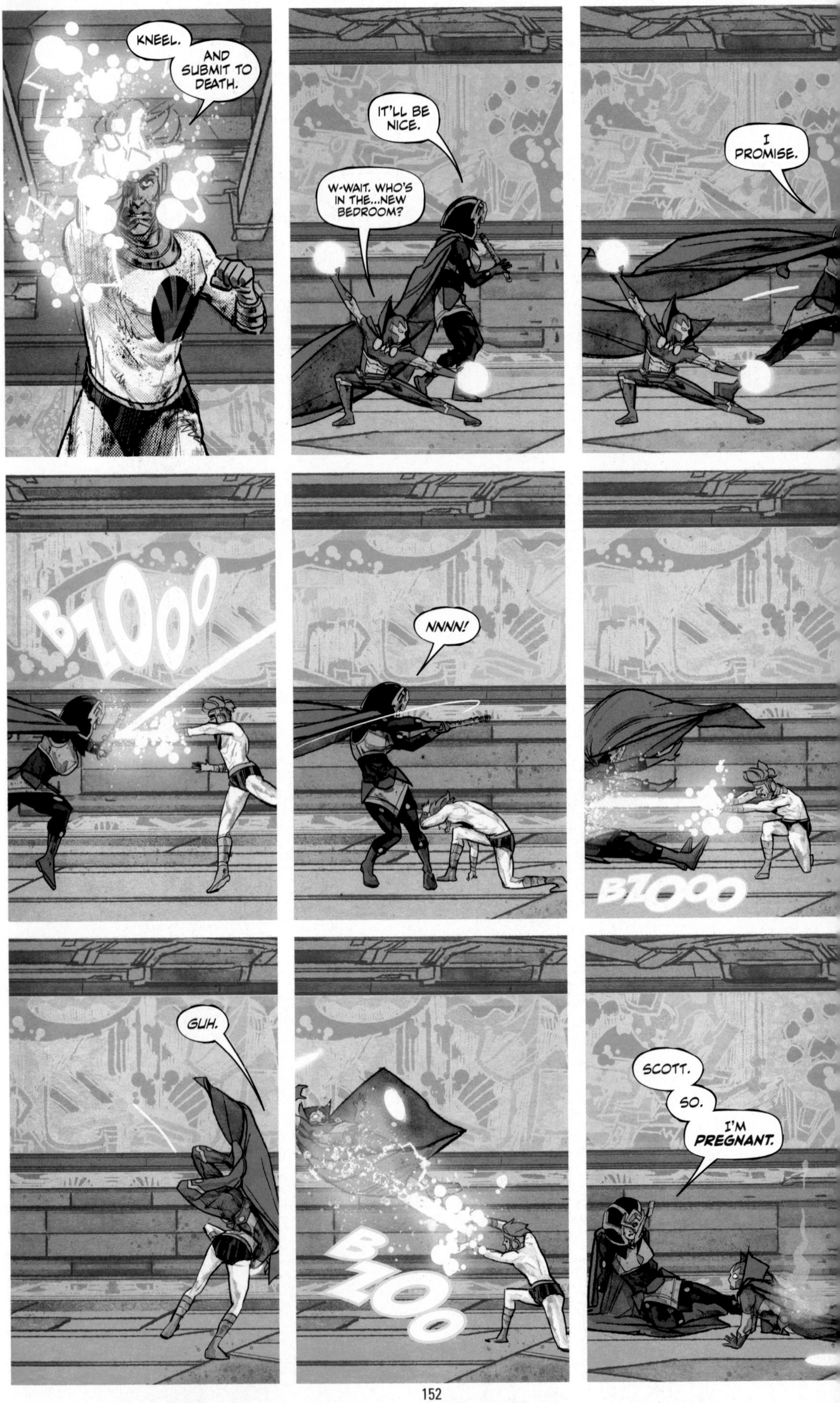
KNEEL.
AND SUBMIT TO DEATH.
IT'LL BE NICE.
W-WAIT. WHO'S IN THE...NEW BEDROOM?
I PROMISE.
BZOOO
NNNN!
BZOOO
GUH.
BZOO
SCOTT.
SO.
I'M PREGNANT.

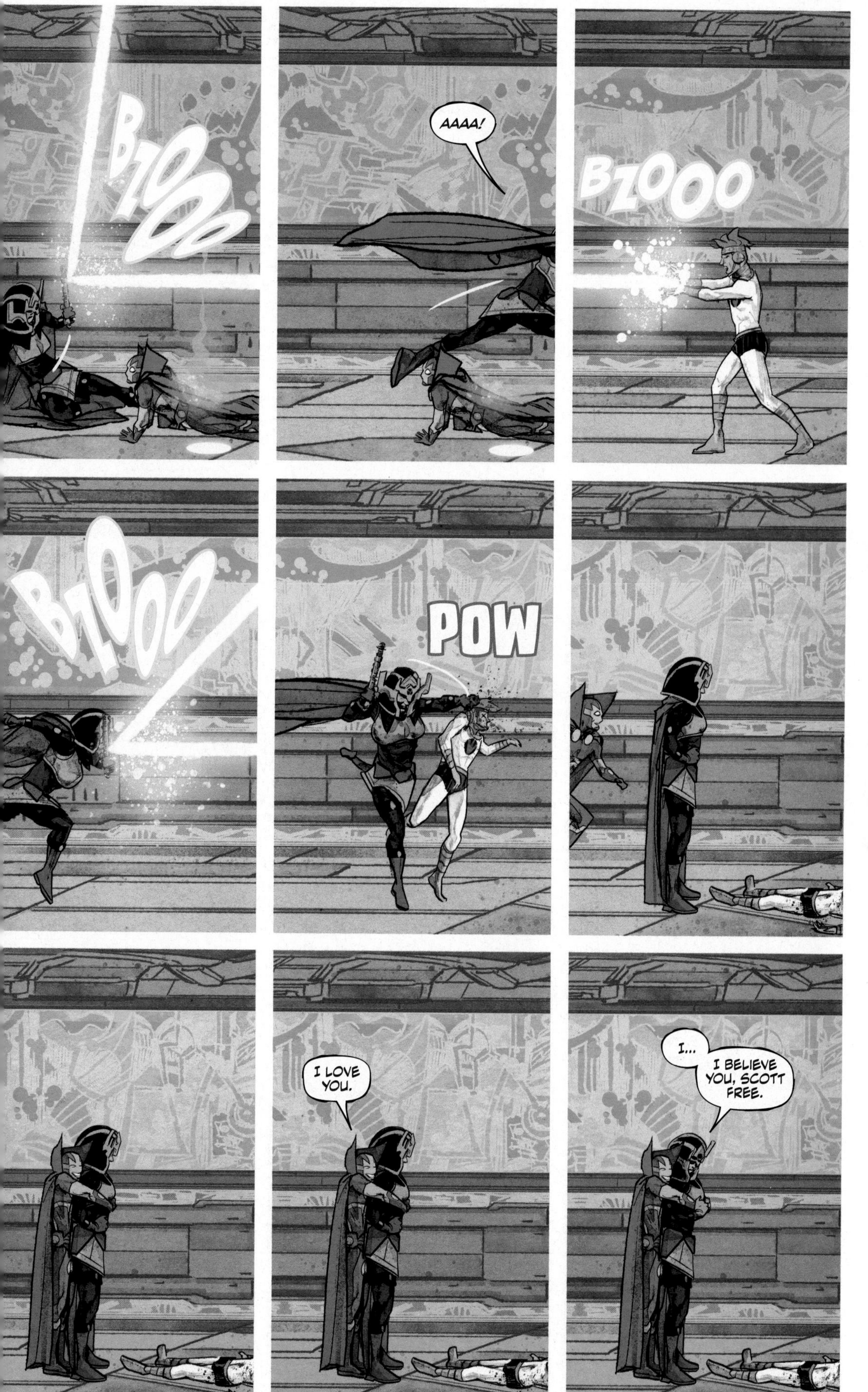
BZOOO
AAAA!
BZOOO
BZOOO
POW
I LOVE YOU.
I...
I BELIEVE YOU, SCOTT FREE.

WHAT DO I DO?

WARNING: YOU ARE NOT ALLOWED HERE.

ORION WILL NOW KILL YOU.

HE'S YOUR BROTHER.

TALK TO HIM.

HE'S NOT MY BROTHER.

AND HE DOESN'T... *TALK.*

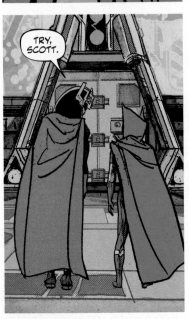

TRY, SCOTT.

AND IF YOU TRY, *SINCERELY,* AND HE *STILL* WON'T TALK...

Y'KNOW...

CUT HIS #$^@ING #$^@$ OFF.

HEY, I'LL GET RID OF THE CIGAR BOXES WHEN WE GET BACK.

SOUNDS GOOD.

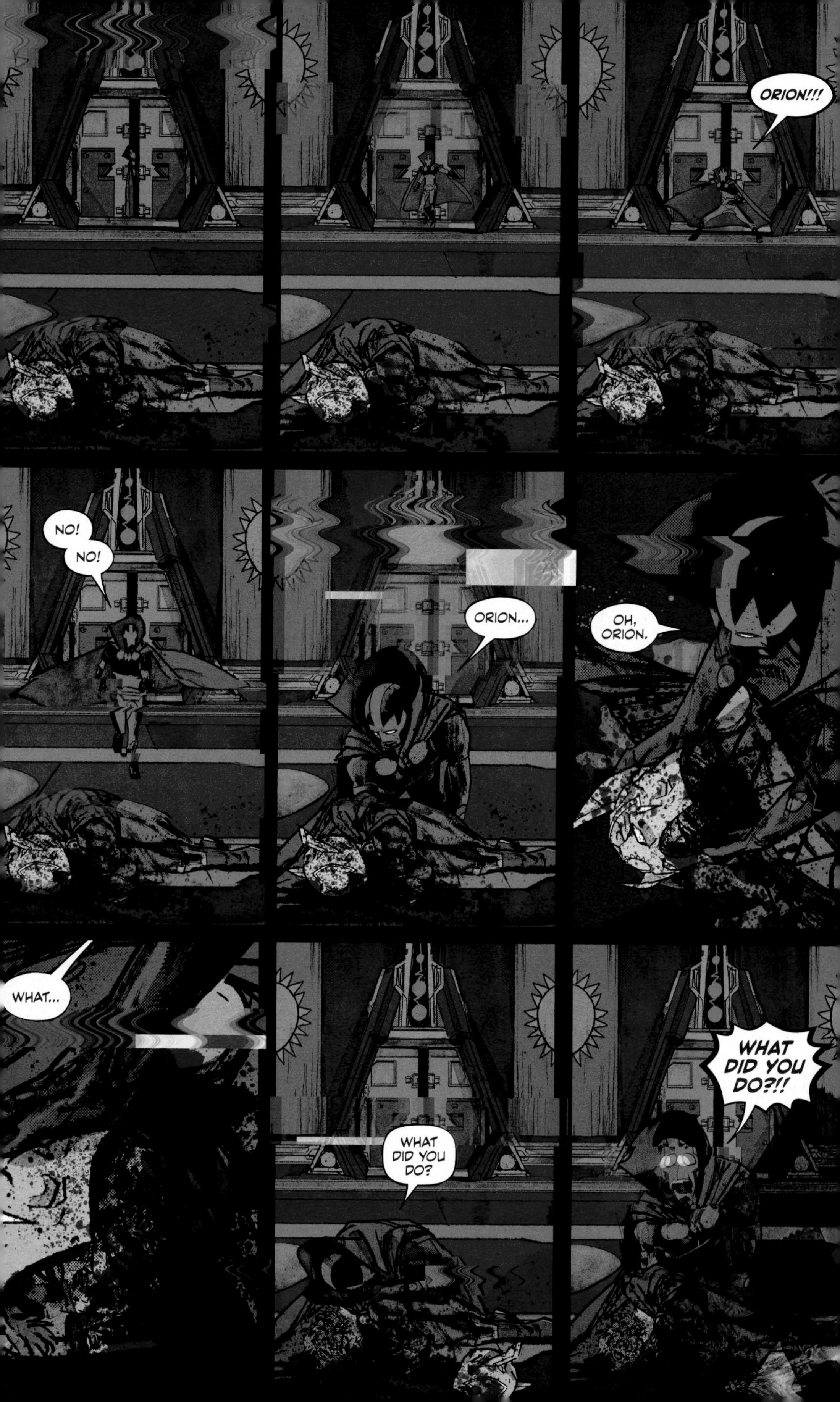
ORION!!!
NO!
NO!
ORION...
OH, ORION.
WHAT...
WHAT DID YOU DO?
WHAT DID YOU DO?!!

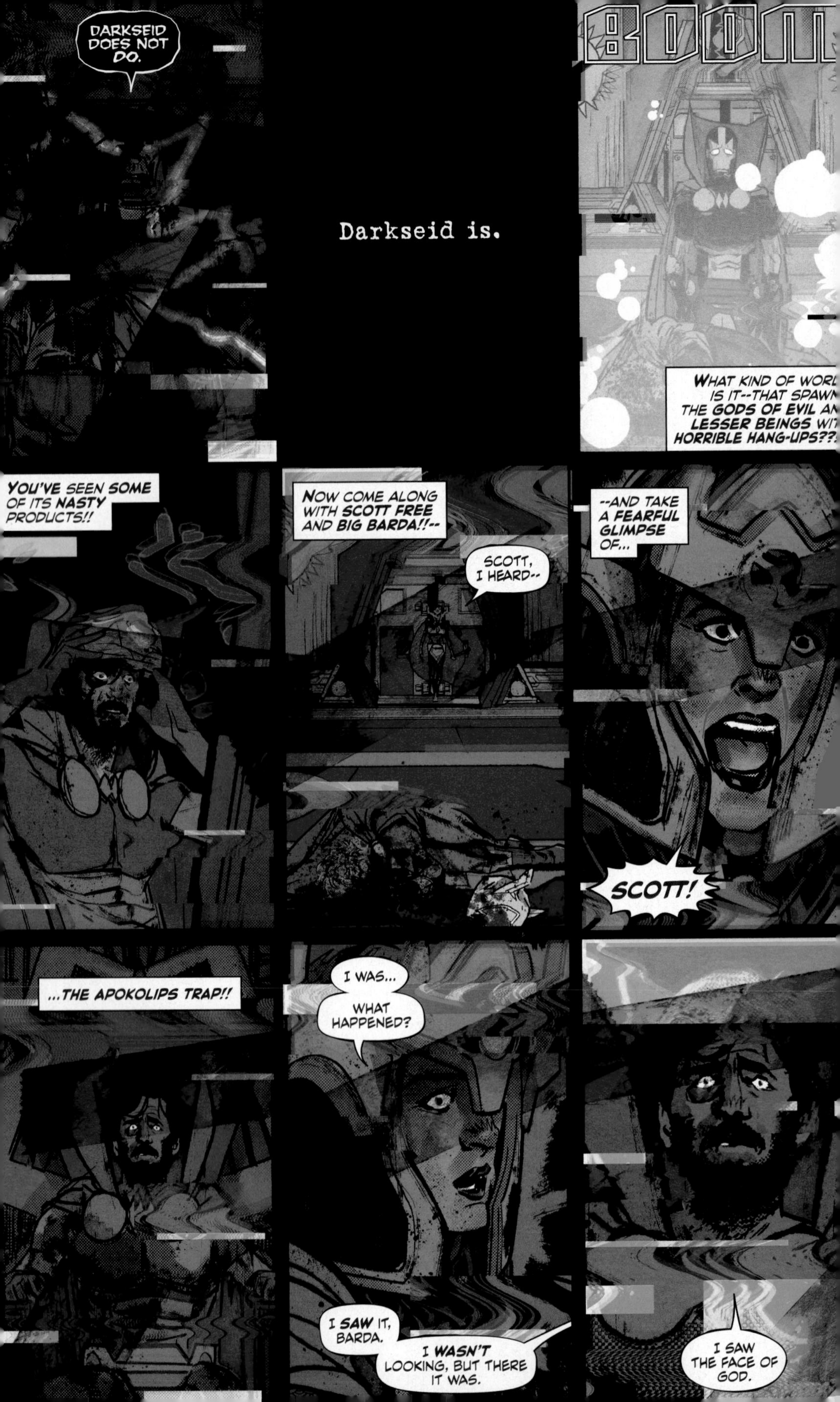

DARKSEID DOES NOT DO.
Darkseid is.
BOOM
WHAT KIND OF WORL
IS IT--THAT SPAWN
THE GODS OF EVIL AN
LESSER BEINGS WIT
HORRIBLE HANG-UPS??
YOU'VE SEEN SOME OF ITS NASTY PRODUCTS!!
NOW COME ALONG WITH SCOTT FREE AND BIG BARDA!!--
SCOTT, I HEARD--
--AND TAKE A FEARFUL GLIMPSE OF...
SCOTT!
...THE APOKOLIPS TRAP!!
I WAS...
WHAT HAPPENED?
I SAW IT, BARDA.
I WASN'T LOOKING, BUT THERE IT WAS.
I SAW THE FACE OF GOD.

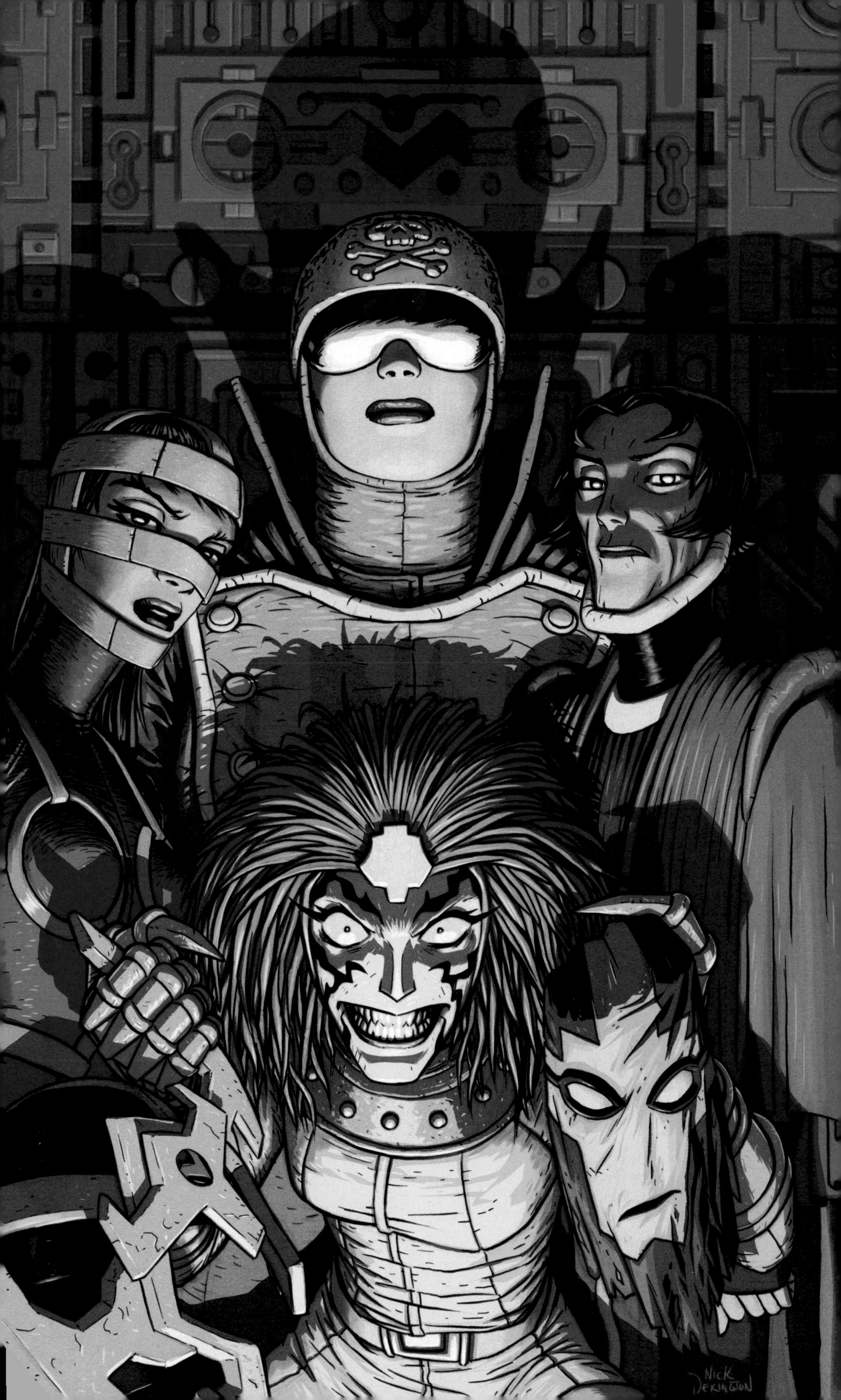
NICK DERINGTON

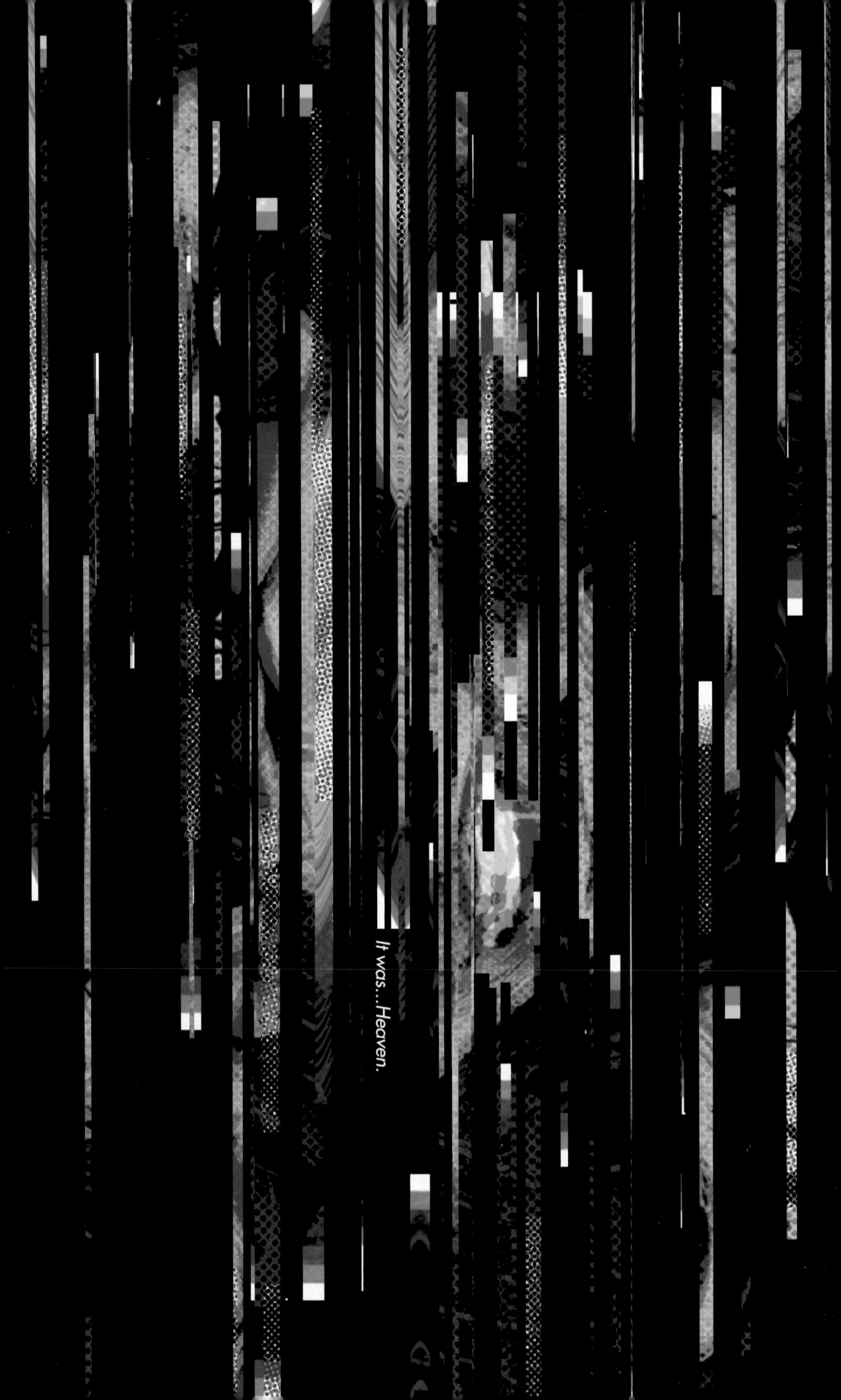
It was...Heaven.

WOULD **SCOTT FREE** BE SO FOOLHARDY AS TO RETURN TO THE **NIGHTMARE** WORLD FROM WHICH HE **ESCAPED??**

YES, GOOD FRIENDS!

IT **STILL** HAS **ROOTS** THAT **MUST** BE CUT!

ROOTS THAT COULD **REACH** TO EARTH AND **DESTROY** ALL THAT SCOTT HAS LEARNED TO **LOVE**--

HIS FRIENDS!

HIS CRAFT!

HIS NEW LIFE!

AND BESIDES--**DEATH** HAS THE **SAME** FACE--

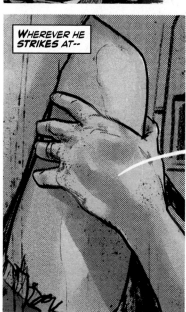

WHEREVER HE STRIKES AT--

MISTER MIRACLE!!

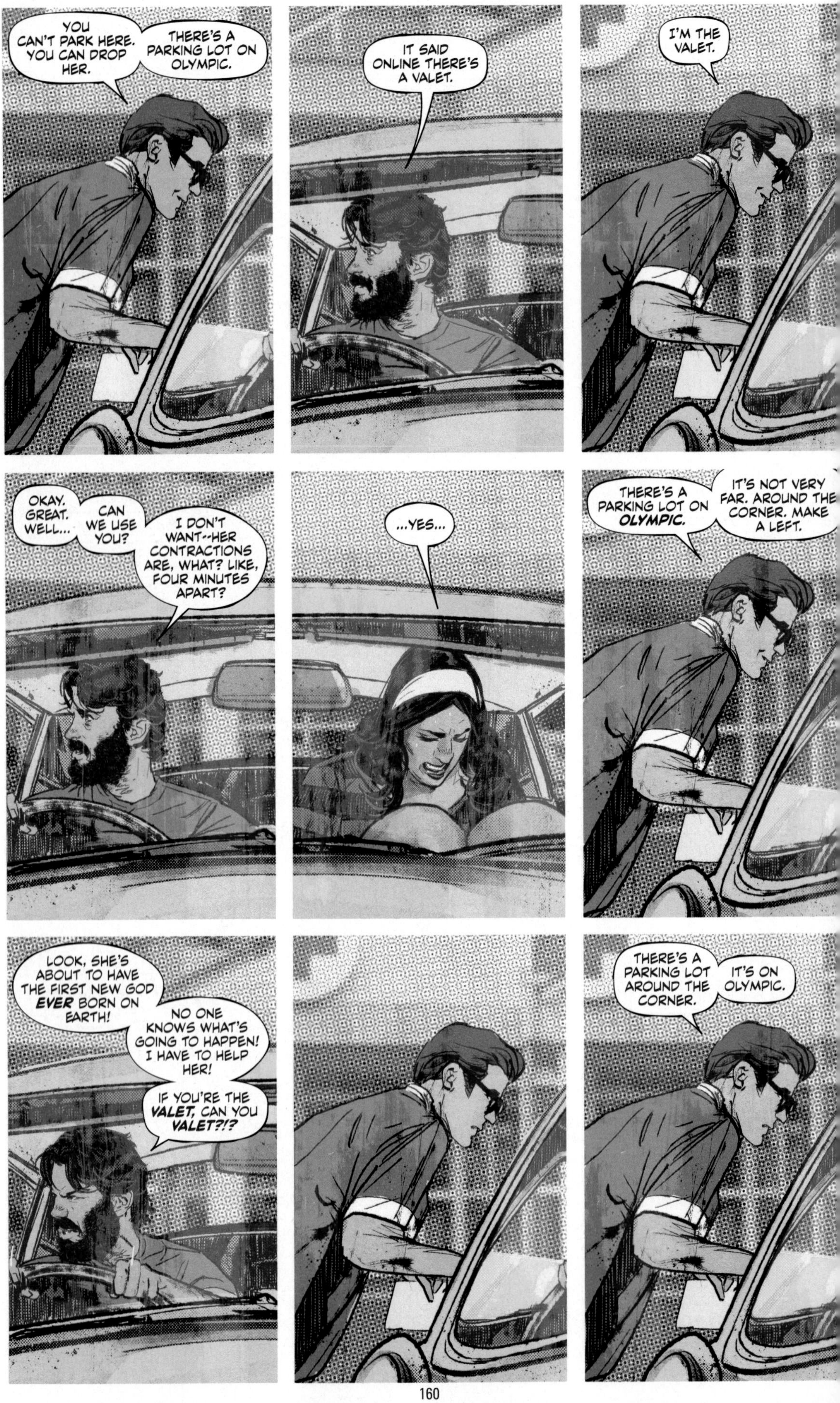

YOU CAN'T PARK HERE. YOU CAN DROP HER.
THERE'S A PARKING LOT ON OLYMPIC.
IT SAID ONLINE THERE'S A VALET.
I'M THE VALET.
OKAY. GREAT. WELL...
CAN WE USE YOU?
I DON'T WANT--HER CONTRACTIONS ARE, WHAT? LIKE, FOUR MINUTES APART?
...YES...
THERE'S A PARKING LOT ON OLYMPIC.
IT'S NOT VERY FAR. AROUND THE CORNER. MAKE A LEFT.
LOOK, SHE'S ABOUT TO HAVE THE FIRST NEW GOD EVER BORN ON EARTH!
NO ONE KNOWS WHAT'S GOING TO HAPPEN! I HAVE TO HELP HER!
IF YOU'RE THE VALET, CAN YOU VALET?!?
THERE'S A PARKING LOT AROUND THE CORNER.
IT'S ON OLYMPIC.

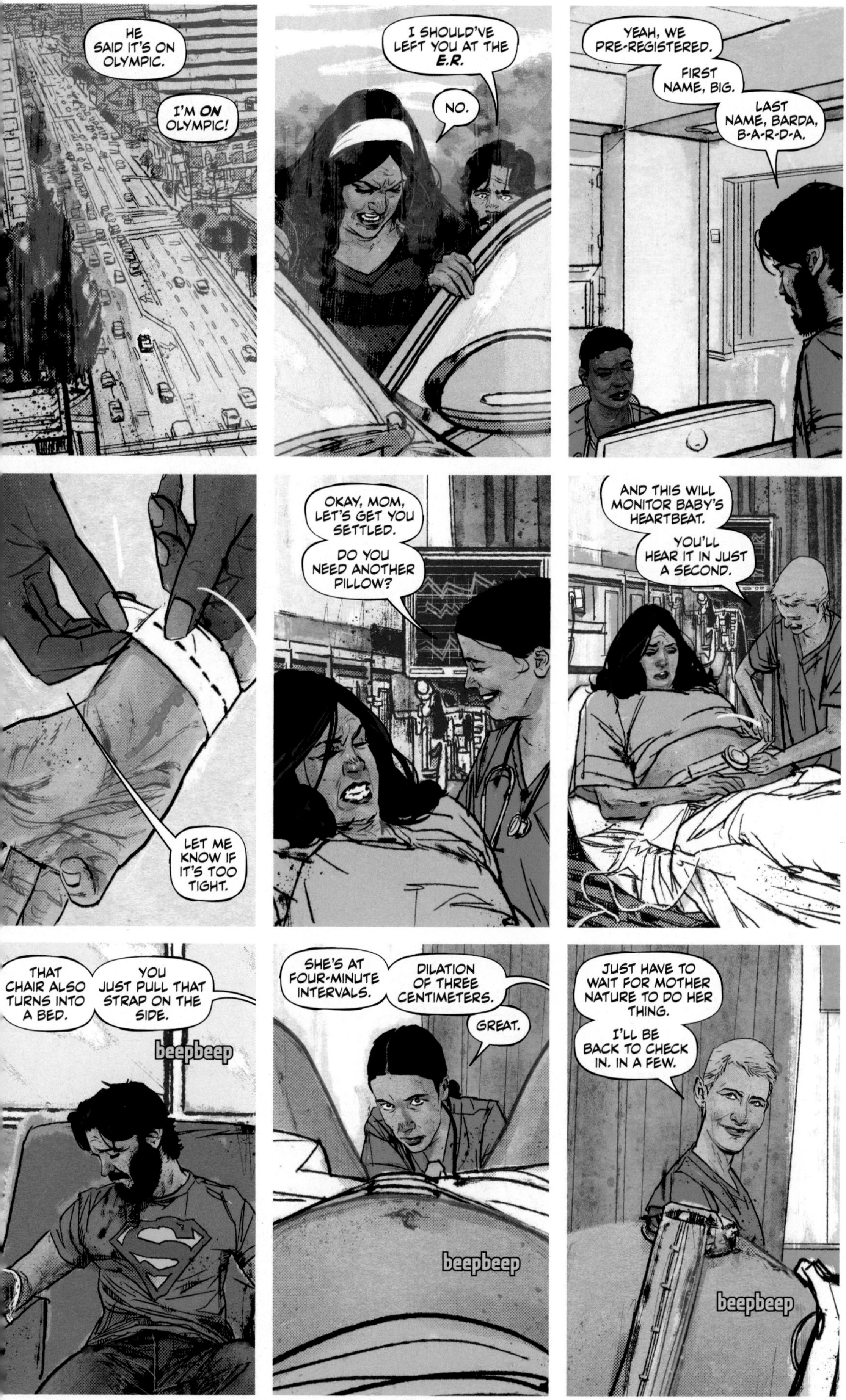
HE SAID IT'S ON OLYMPIC.
I'M ON OLYMPIC!
I SHOULD'VE LEFT YOU AT THE E.R.
NO.
YEAH, WE PRE-REGISTERED.
FIRST NAME, BIG.
LAST NAME, BARDA, B-A-R-D-A.
LET ME KNOW IF IT'S TOO TIGHT.
OKAY, MOM, LET'S GET YOU SETTLED.
DO YOU NEED ANOTHER PILLOW?
AND THIS WILL MONITOR BABY'S HEARTBEAT.
YOU'LL HEAR IT IN JUST A SECOND.
THAT CHAIR ALSO TURNS INTO A BED.
YOU JUST PULL THAT STRAP ON THE SIDE.
beepbeep
SHE'S AT FOUR-MINUTE INTERVALS.
DILATION OF THREE CENTIMETERS.
GREAT.
beepbeep
JUST HAVE TO WAIT FOR MOTHER NATURE TO DO HER THING.
I'LL BE BACK TO CHECK IN. IN A FEW.
beepbeep

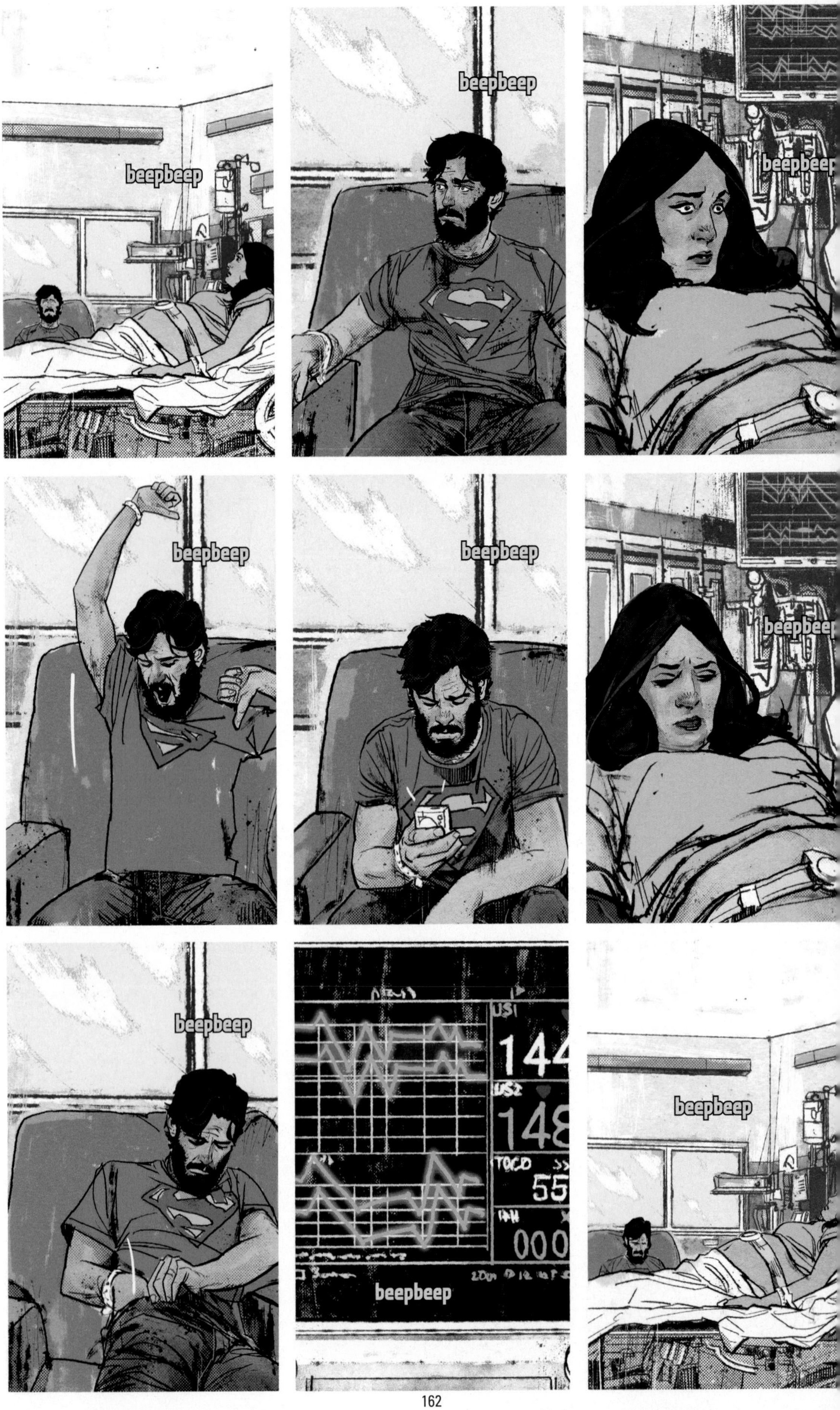
beepbeep
beepbeep
beepbeep
beepbeep
beepbeep
beepbee
beepbeep
US1
144
US2
148
TOCO
55
000
beepbeep
beepbeep

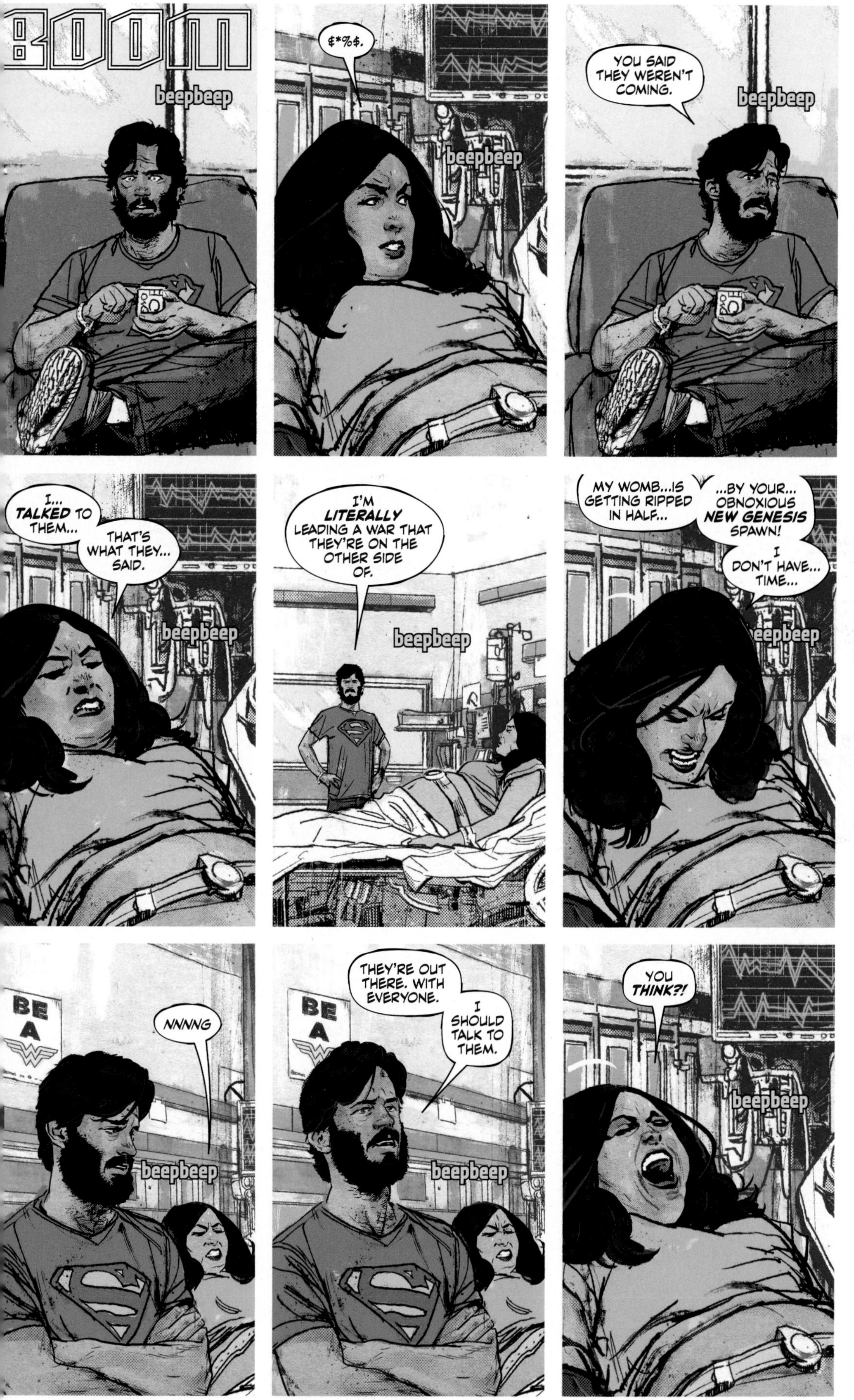
BOOM
beepbeep
$*%$.
beepbeep
YOU SAID THEY WEREN'T COMING.
beepbeep
I... TALKED TO THEM...
THAT'S WHAT THEY... SAID.
beepbeep
I'M LITERALLY LEADING A WAR THAT THEY'RE ON THE OTHER SIDE OF.
beepbeep
MY WOMB...IS GETTING RIPPED IN HALF...
...BY YOUR... OBNOXIOUS NEW GENESIS SPAWN!
I DON'T HAVE... TIME...
eepbeep
BE A
NNNNG
beepbeep
THEY'RE OUT THERE. WITH EVERYONE.
I SHOULD TALK TO THEM.
beepbeep
YOU THINK?!
beepbeep

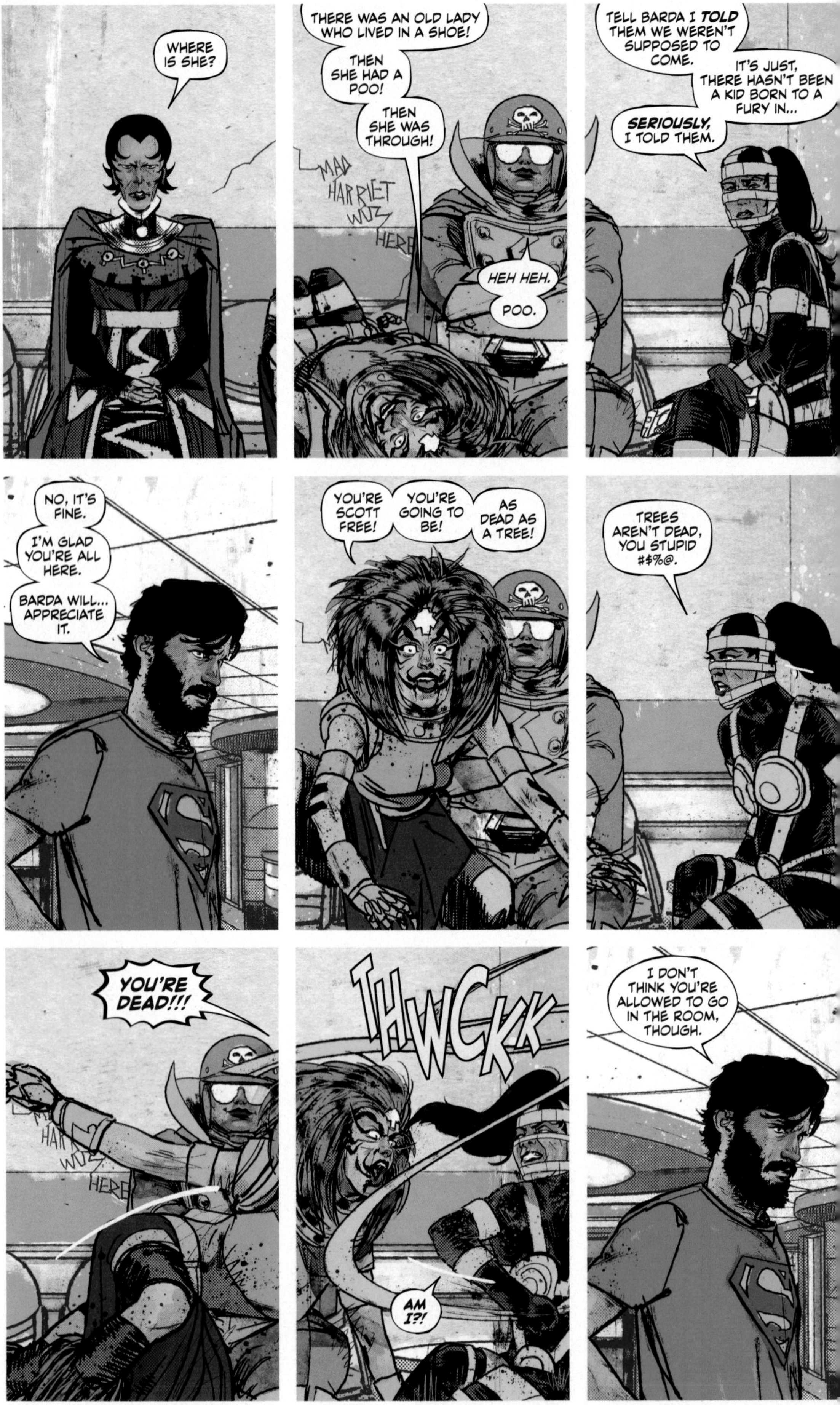
WHERE IS SHE?
THERE WAS AN OLD LADY WHO LIVED IN A SHOE!
THEN SHE HAD A POO!
THEN SHE WAS THROUGH!
MAD HARRIET WUZ HERE
HEH HEH.
POO.
TELL BARDA I TOLD THEM WE WEREN'T SUPPOSED TO COME.
IT'S JUST, THERE HASN'T BEEN A KID BORN TO A FURY IN...
SERIOUSLY, I TOLD THEM.
NO, IT'S FINE.
I'M GLAD YOU'RE ALL HERE.
BARDA WILL... APPRECIATE IT.
YOU'RE SCOTT FREE!
YOU'RE GOING TO BE!
AS DEAD AS A TREE!
TREES AREN'T DEAD, YOU STUPID #$%@.
YOU'RE DEAD!!!
THWCKK
AM I?!
I DON'T THINK YOU'RE ALLOWED TO GO IN THE ROOM, THOUGH.

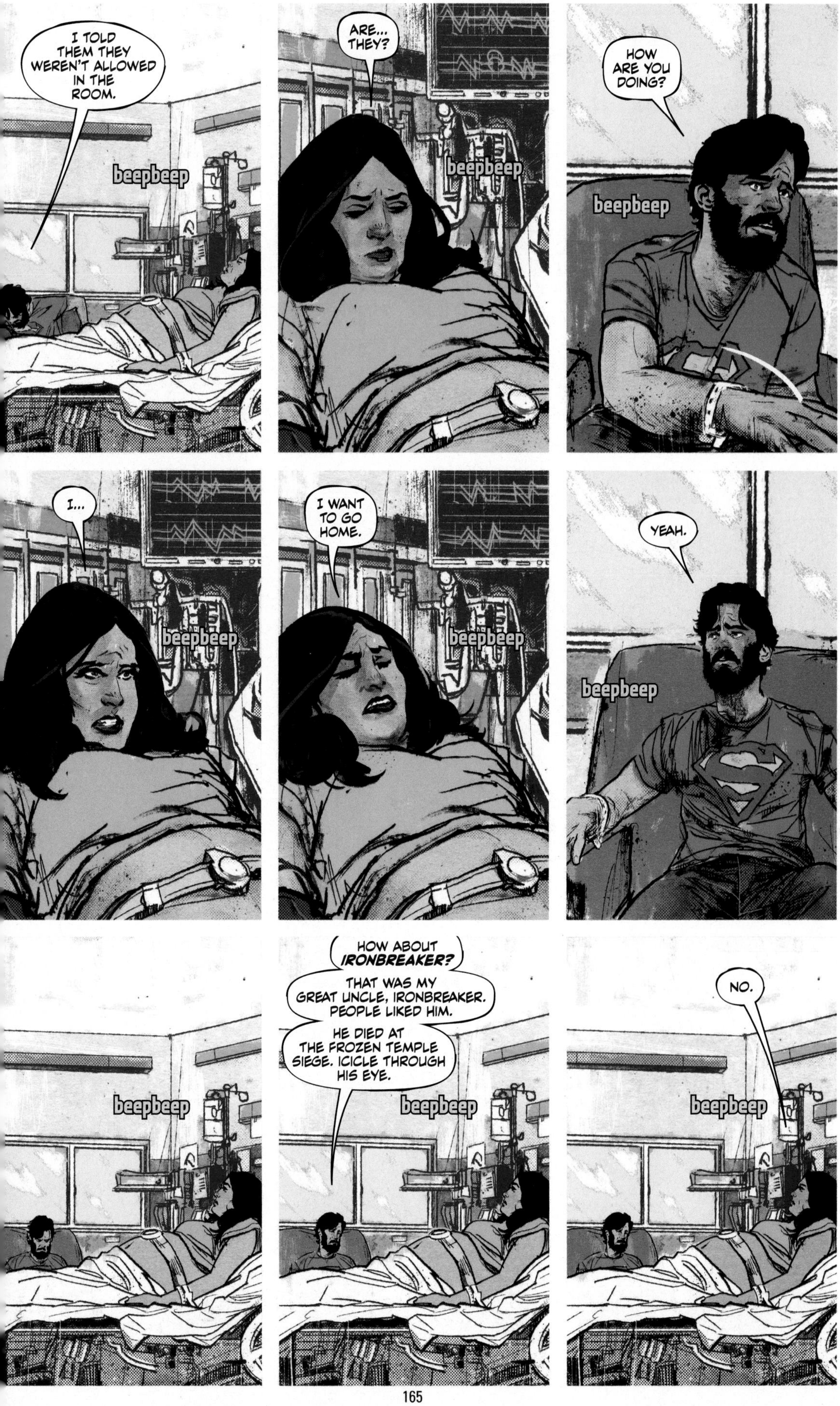
I TOLD THEM THEY WEREN'T ALLOWED IN THE ROOM.
beepbeep
ARE... THEY?
beepbeep
HOW ARE YOU DOING?
beepbeep
I...
beepbeep
I WANT TO GO HOME.
beepbeep
YEAH.
beepbeep
beepbeep
HOW ABOUT IRONBREAKER?
THAT WAS MY GREAT UNCLE, IRONBREAKER. PEOPLE LIKED HIM.
HE DIED AT THE FROZEN TEMPLE SIEGE. ICICLE THROUGH HIS EYE.
beepbeep
NO.
beepbeep

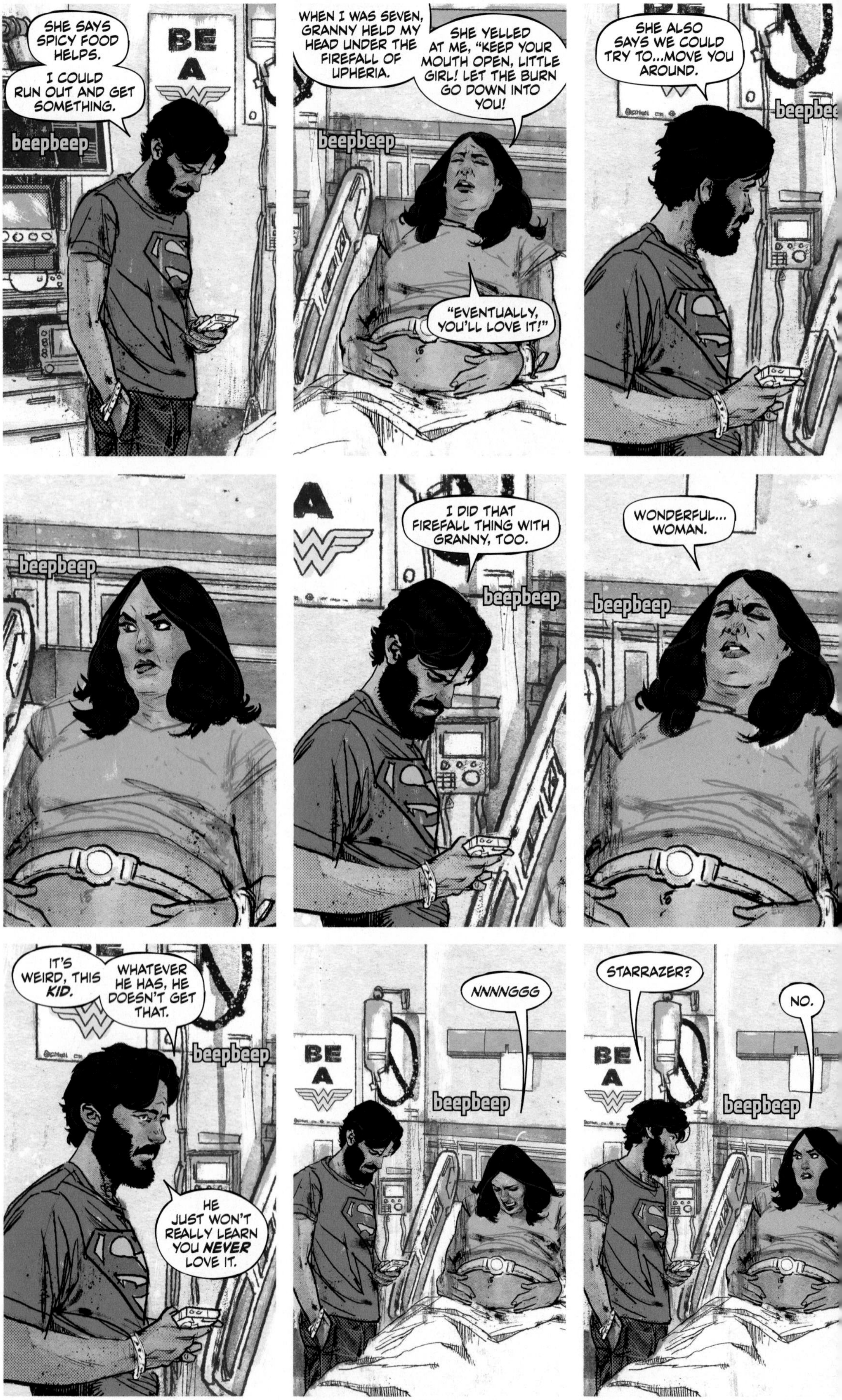
SHE SAYS SPICY FOOD HELPS.
I COULD RUN OUT AND GET SOMETHING.
beepbeep
BE A
WHEN I WAS SEVEN, GRANNY HELD MY HEAD UNDER THE FIREFALL OF UPHERIA.
SHE YELLED AT ME, "KEEP YOUR MOUTH OPEN, LITTLE GIRL! LET THE BURN GO DOWN INTO YOU!
beepbeep
"EVENTUALLY, YOU'LL LOVE IT!"
SHE ALSO SAYS WE COULD TRY TO...MOVE YOU AROUND.
beepbeep
I DID THAT FIREFALL THING WITH GRANNY, TOO.
beepbeep
WONDERFUL... WOMAN.
beepbeep
IT'S WEIRD, THIS **KID.**
WHATEVER HE HAS, HE DOESN'T GET THAT.
beepbeep
HE JUST WON'T REALLY LEARN YOU **NEVER** LOVE IT.
NNNNGGG
BE A
beepbeep
STARRAZER?
NO.
BE A
beepbeep

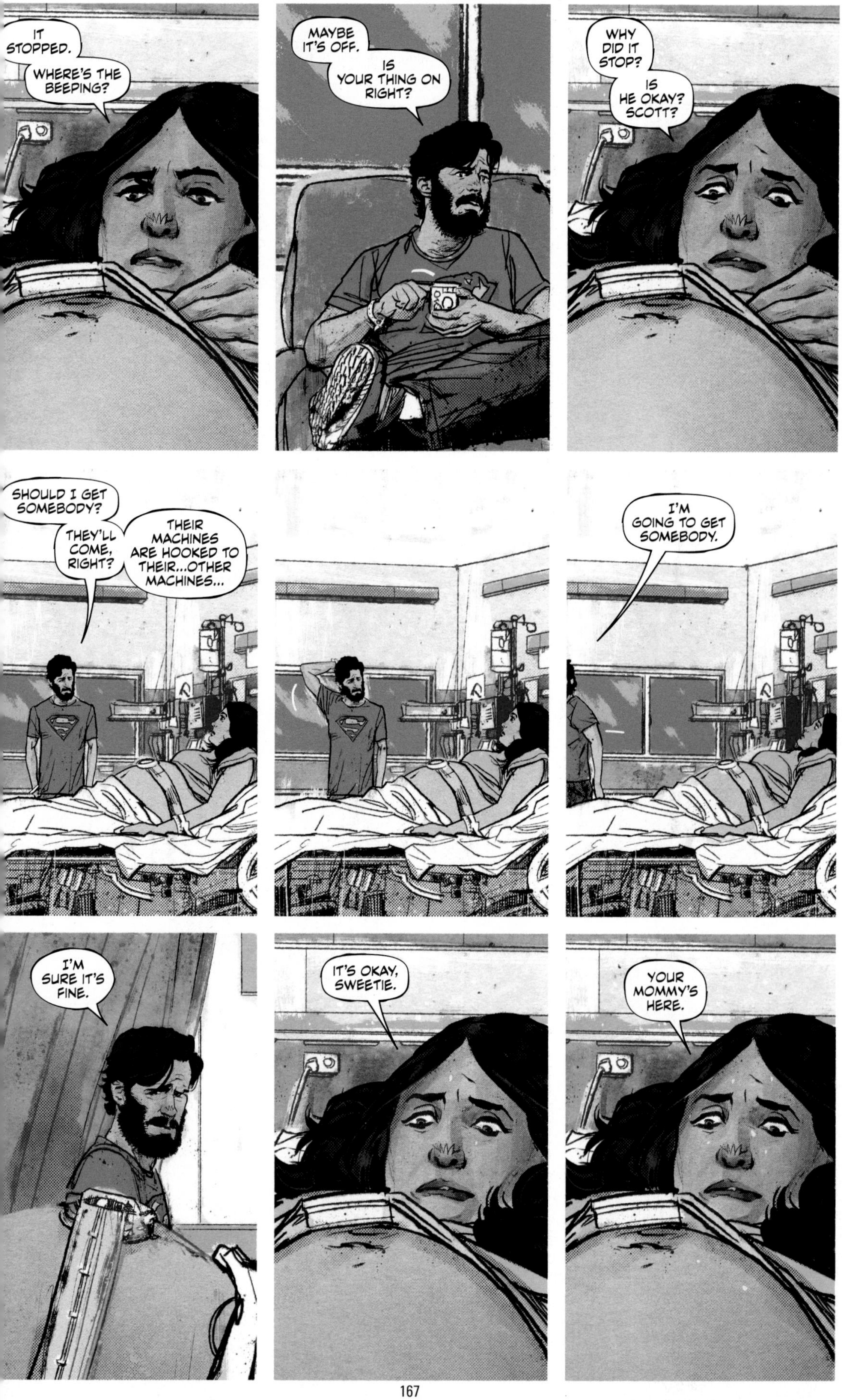
IT STOPPED.
WHERE'S THE BEEPING?
MAYBE IT'S OFF.
IS YOUR THING ON RIGHT?
WHY DID IT STOP?
IS HE OKAY? SCOTT?
SHOULD I GET SOMEBODY?
THEY'LL COME, RIGHT?
THEIR MACHINES ARE HOOKED TO THEIR...OTHER MACHINES...
I'M GOING TO GET SOMEBODY.
I'M SURE IT'S FINE.
IT'S OKAY, SWEETIE.
YOUR MOMMY'S HERE.

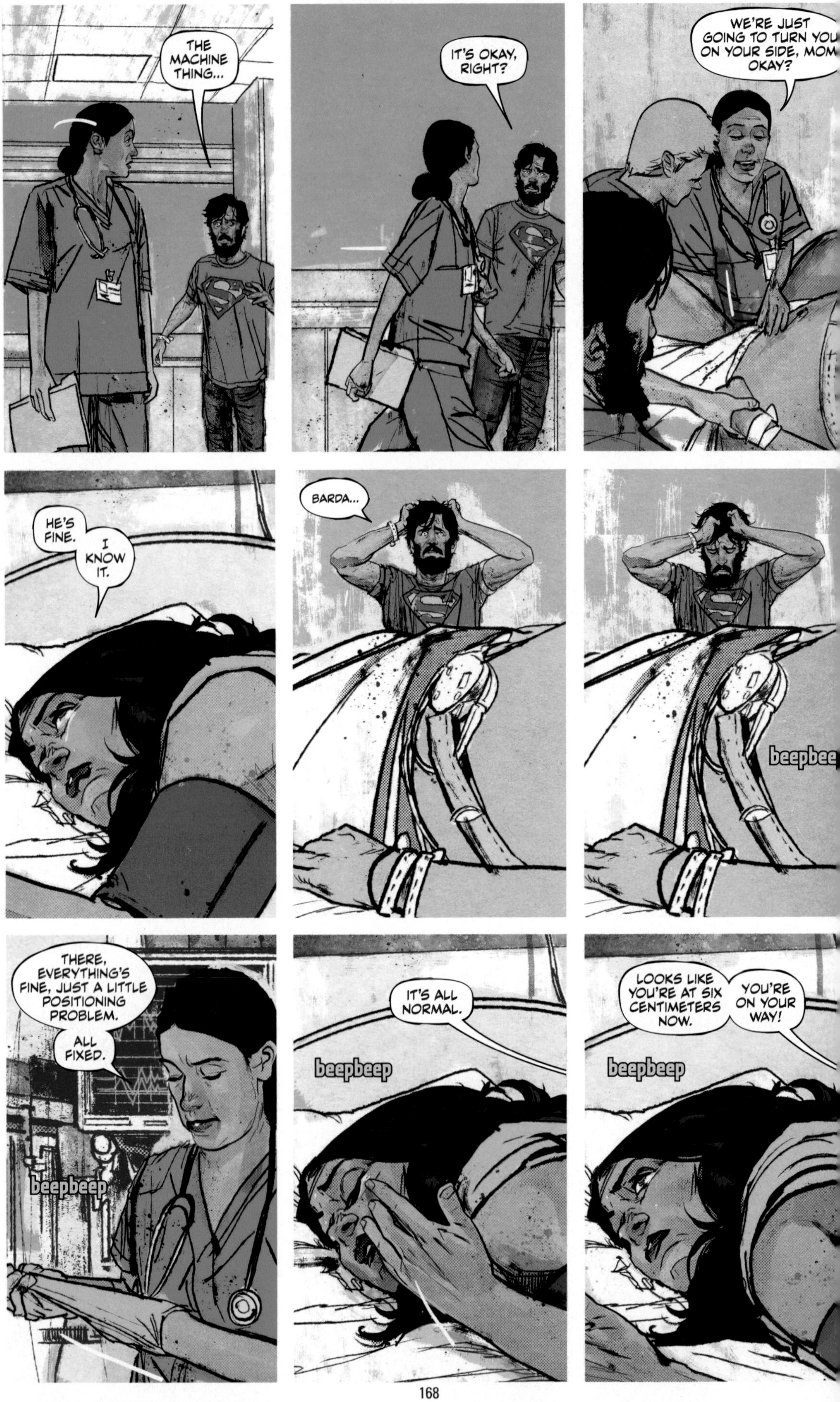

THE MACHINE THING...
IT'S OKAY, RIGHT?
WE'RE JUST GOING TO TURN YOU ON YOUR SIDE, MOM OKAY?
HE'S FINE.
I KNOW IT.
BARDA...
THERE, EVERYTHING'S FINE, JUST A LITTLE POSITIONING PROBLEM.
ALL FIXED.
beepbeep
IT'S ALL NORMAL.
beepbeep
LOOKS LIKE YOU'RE AT SIX CENTIMETERS NOW.
YOU'RE ON YOUR WAY!
beepbeep

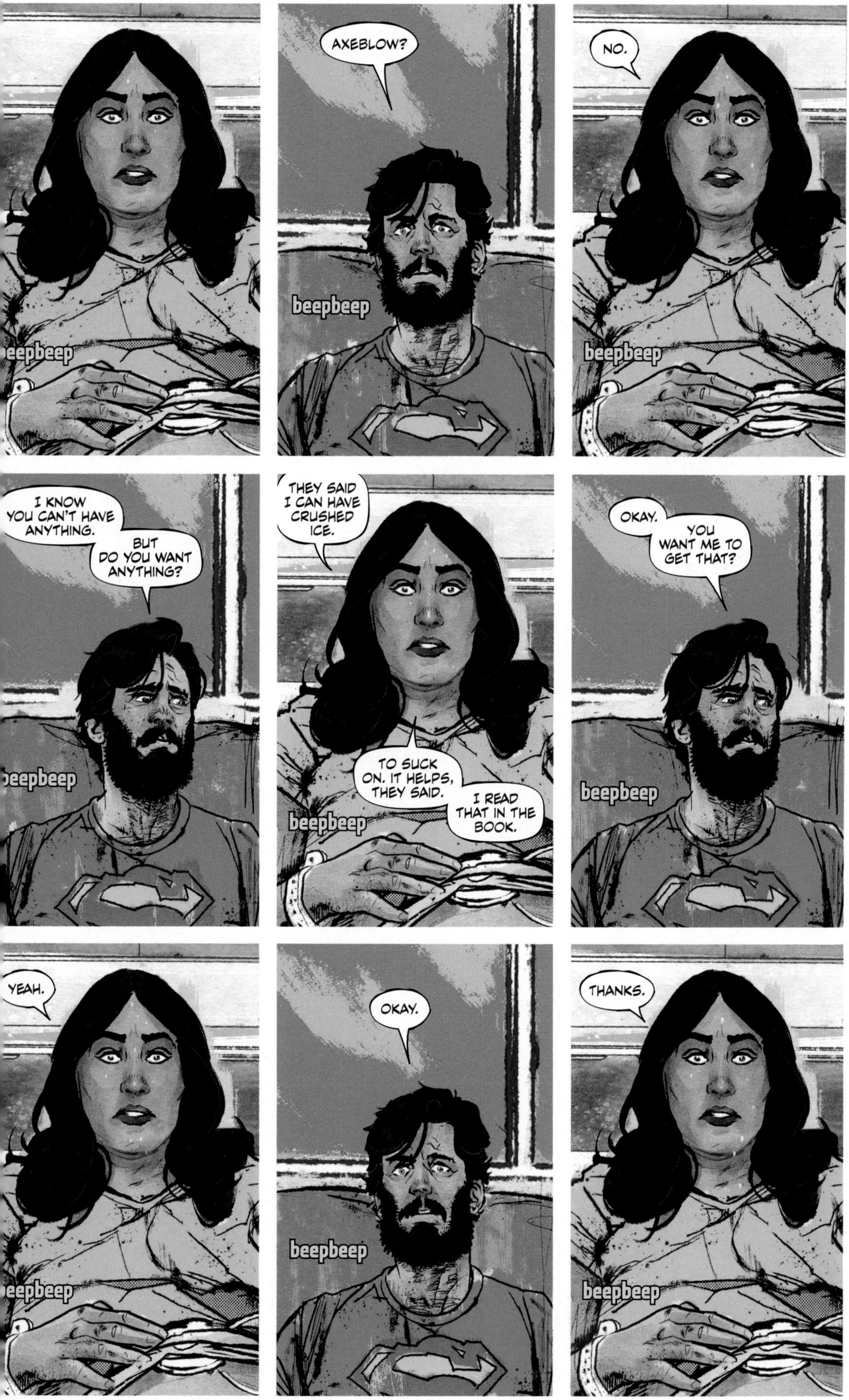
beepbeep
AXEBLOW?
beepbeep
NO.
beepbeep
I KNOW YOU CAN'T HAVE ANYTHING.
BUT DO YOU WANT ANYTHING?
beepbeep
THEY SAID I CAN HAVE CRUSHED ICE.
TO SUCK ON. IT HELPS, THEY SAID.
I READ THAT IN THE BOOK.
beepbeep
OKAY.
YOU WANT ME TO GET THAT?
beepbeep
YEAH.
beepbeep
OKAY.
beepbeep
THANKS.
beepbeep

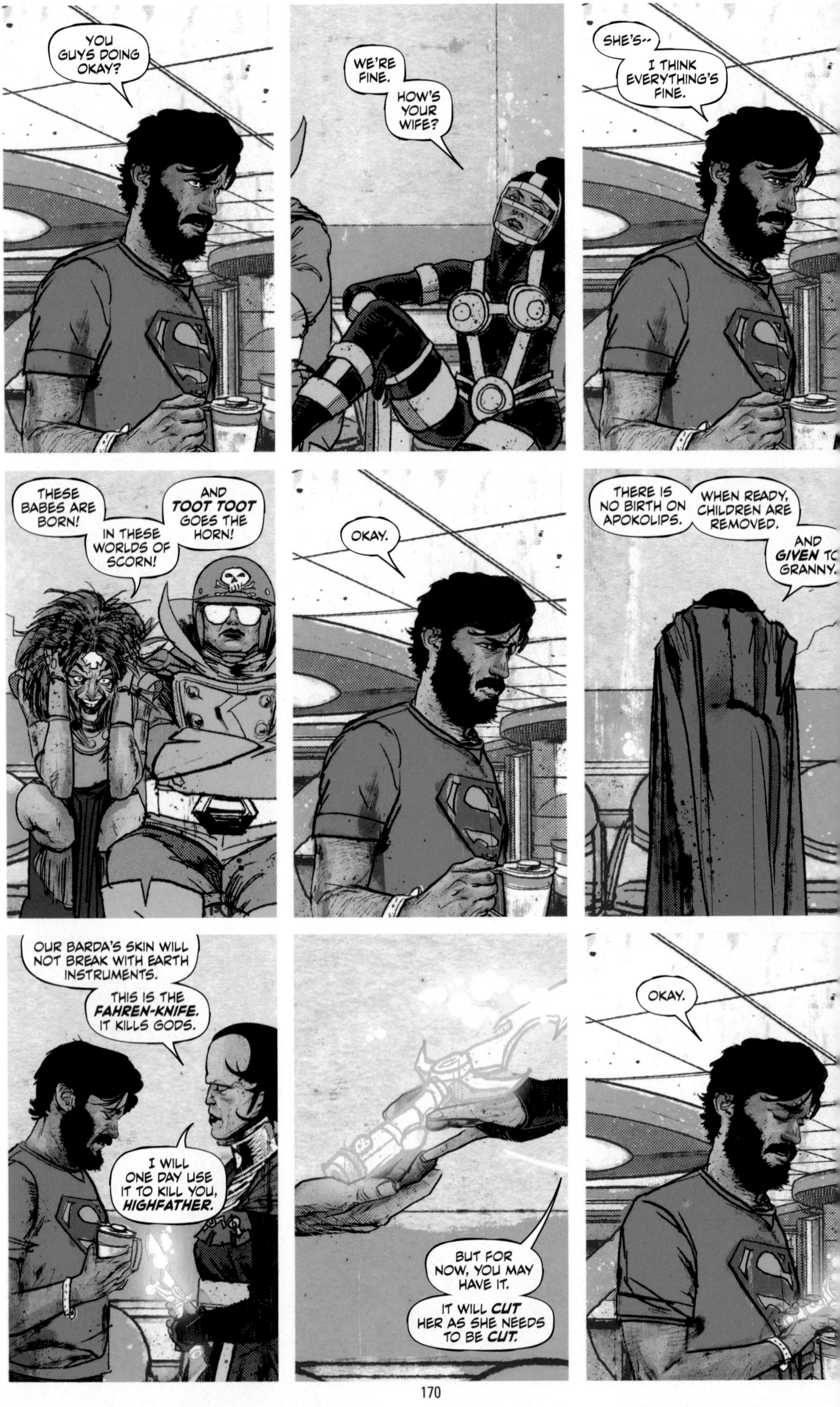

YOU GUYS DOING OKAY?
WE'RE FINE.
HOW'S YOUR WIFE?
SHE'S--
I THINK EVERYTHING'S FINE.
THESE BABES ARE BORN!
IN THESE WORLDS OF SCORN!
AND TOOT TOOT GOES THE HORN!
OKAY.
THERE IS NO BIRTH ON APOKOLIPS.
WHEN READY, CHILDREN ARE REMOVED.
AND GIVEN TO GRANNY.
OUR BARDA'S SKIN WILL NOT BREAK WITH EARTH INSTRUMENTS.
THIS IS THE FAHREN-KNIFE. IT KILLS GODS.
I WILL ONE DAY USE IT TO KILL YOU, HIGHFATHER.
BUT FOR NOW, YOU MAY HAVE IT.
IT WILL CUT HER AS SHE NEEDS TO BE CUT.
OKAY.

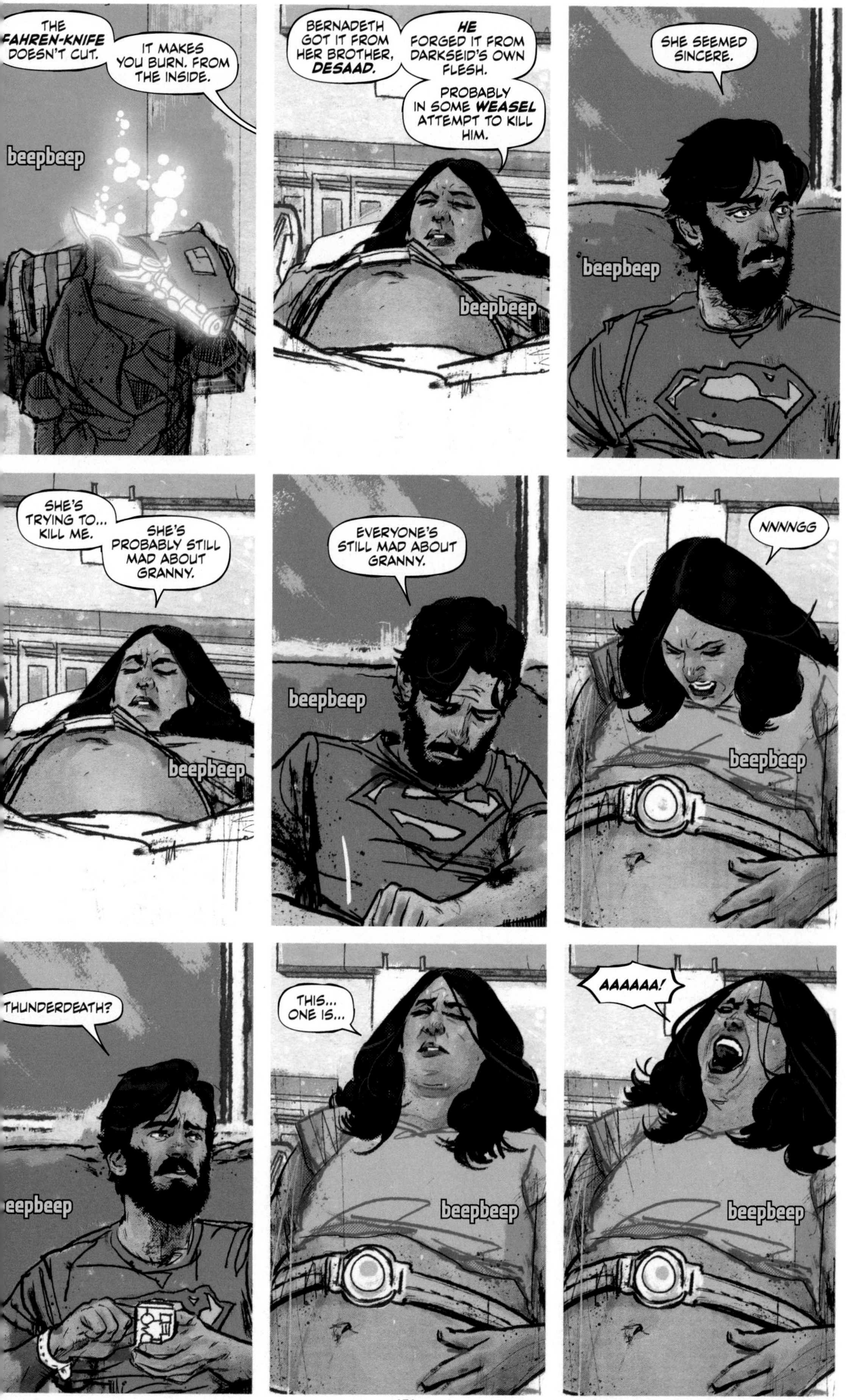
THE FAHREN-KNIFE DOESN'T CUT.
IT MAKES YOU BURN. FROM THE INSIDE.
beepbeep
BERNADETH GOT IT FROM HER BROTHER, DESAAD.
HE FORGED IT FROM DARKSEID'S OWN FLESH.
PROBABLY IN SOME WEASEL ATTEMPT TO KILL HIM.
beepbeep
SHE SEEMED SINCERE.
beepbeep
SHE'S TRYING TO... KILL ME.
SHE'S PROBABLY STILL MAD ABOUT GRANNY.
beepbeep
EVERYONE'S STILL MAD ABOUT GRANNY.
beepbeep
NNNNGG
beepbeep
THUNDERDEATH?
eepbeep
THIS... ONE IS...
beepbeep
AAAAAA!
beepbeep

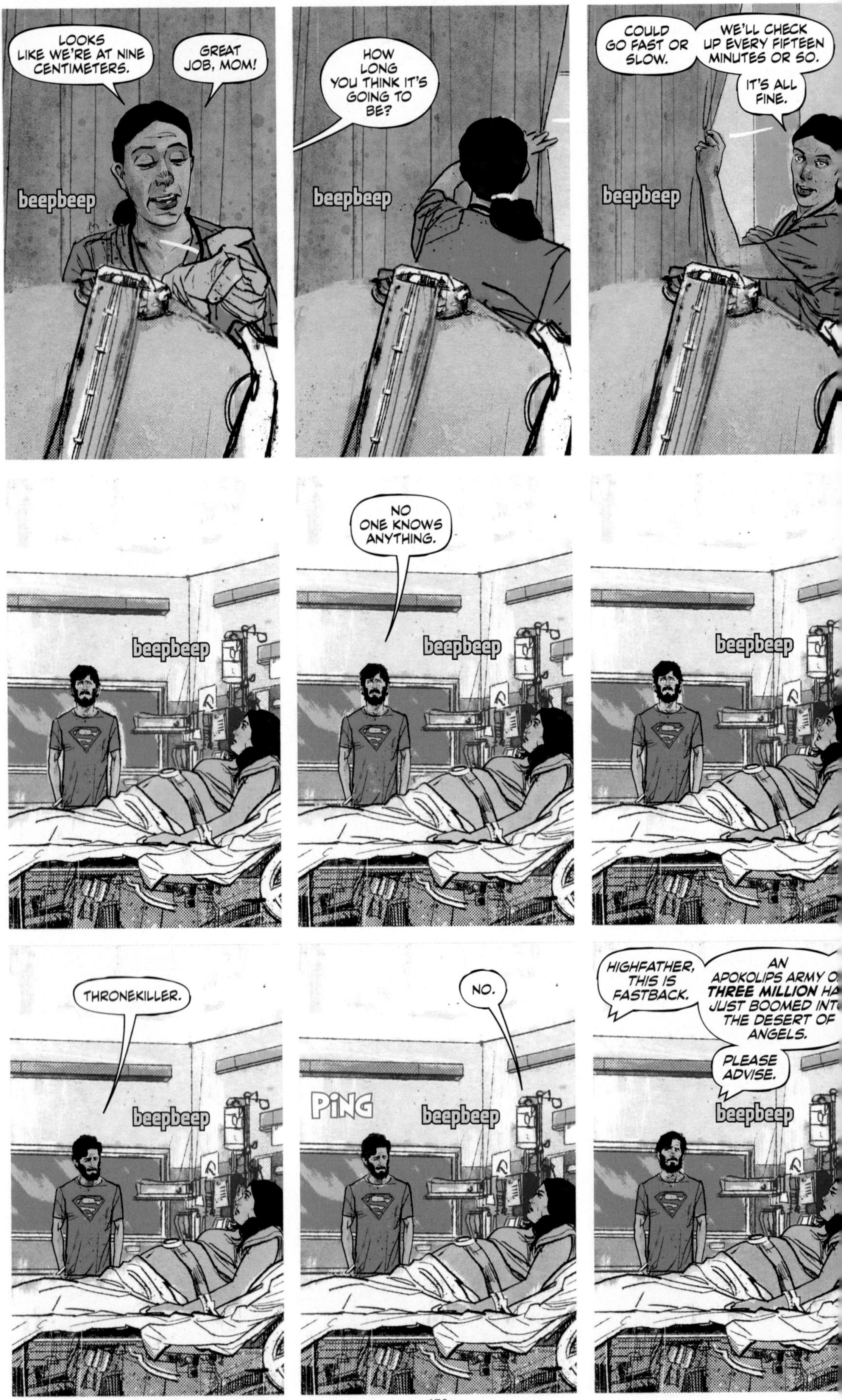

LOOKS LIKE WE'RE AT NINE CENTIMETERS.
GREAT JOB, MOM!
beepbeep
HOW LONG YOU THINK IT'S GOING TO BE?
beepbeep
COULD GO FAST OR SLOW.
WE'LL CHECK UP EVERY FIFTEEN MINUTES OR SO.
IT'S ALL FINE.
beepbeep
beepbeep
NO ONE KNOWS ANYTHING.
beepbeep
beepbeep
THRONEKILLER.
beepbeep
NO.
PING
beepbeep
HIGHFATHER, THIS IS FASTBACK.
AN APOKOLIPS ARMY O
THREE MILLION HA
JUST BOOMED INT
THE DESERT OF ANGELS.
PLEASE ADVISE.
beepbeep

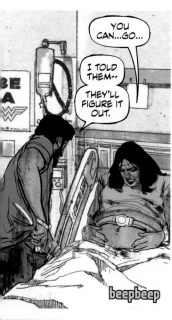

YOU CAN...GO...

I TOLD THEM--

THEY'LL FIGURE IT OUT.

beepbeep

NNNNNGGG

beepbeep

AAANNNGGG

beepbeep

MOTHER¢*$@#!

beepbeep

*¢%#@.

beepbeep

DO YOU REMEMBER... JACOB'S LADDER...

beepbeep

YEAH, OF COURSE.

ONLY WAY OUT OF THE X-PIT.

USED TO STARE AT IT.

beepbeep

THE BOOK SAID YOU'RE SUPPOSED TO THINK OF SOMETHING CALM.

I THINK OF...JACOB'S LADDER...

beepbeep

THAT'S GOOD.

beepbeep

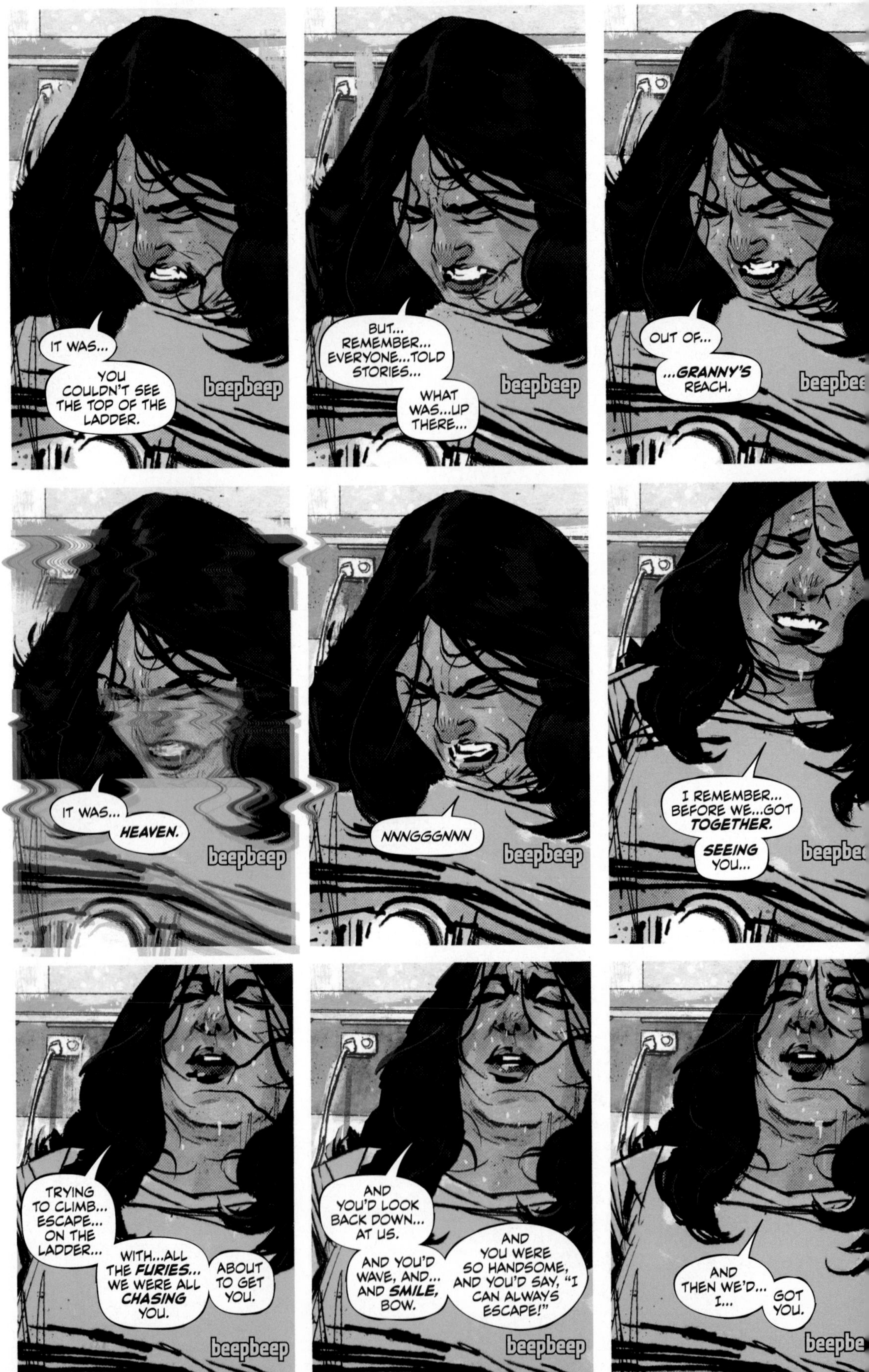
IT WAS...
YOU COULDN'T SEE THE TOP OF THE LADDER.
beepbeep
BUT... REMEMBER... EVERYONE...TOLD STORIES...
WHAT WAS...UP THERE...
beepbeep
OUT OF...
...GRANNY'S REACH.
IT WAS...
HEAVEN.
beepbeep
NNNGGGNNN
beepbeep
I REMEMBER... BEFORE WE...GOT TOGETHER.
SEEING YOU...
TRYING TO CLIMB... ESCAPE... ON THE LADDER...
WITH...ALL THE FURIES... WE WERE ALL CHASING YOU.
ABOUT TO GET YOU.
beepbeep
AND YOU'D LOOK BACK DOWN... AT US.
AND YOU'D WAVE, AND... AND SMILE, BOW.
AND YOU WERE SO HANDSOME, AND YOU'D SAY, "I CAN ALWAYS ESCAPE!"
beepbeep
AND THEN WE'D... I...
GOT YOU.

YOU'RE DOING GREAT, MOM!
WE'RE ALMOST READY TO PUSH.
beepbeep
I WANT YOU TO HOLD ONE OF HER LEGS BACK LIKE THIS.
beepbeep
CAN I PUSH NOW?
I REALLY WANT TO PUSH.
beepbeep
YOU'RE DOING GREAT, HONEY!
beepbeep
OKAY, HERE WE GO, MS. BARDA.
WE'RE ALMOST READY HERE.
beepbeep
I LOVE YOU.
beepbeep
NNNGGGG
beepbeep
OKAY, MOM, LET'S DO A PUSH NOW.
BREATHE IN, *FFFT FFFT FFFT,* THEN PUSH OUT.
beepbeep
GRRRRNNNAAA!
beepbeep

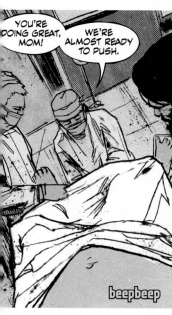

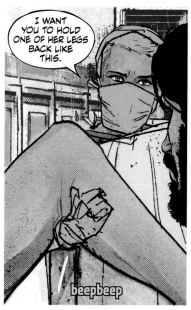

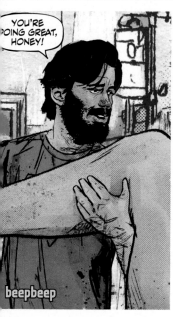

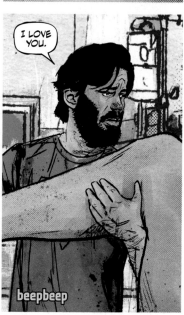

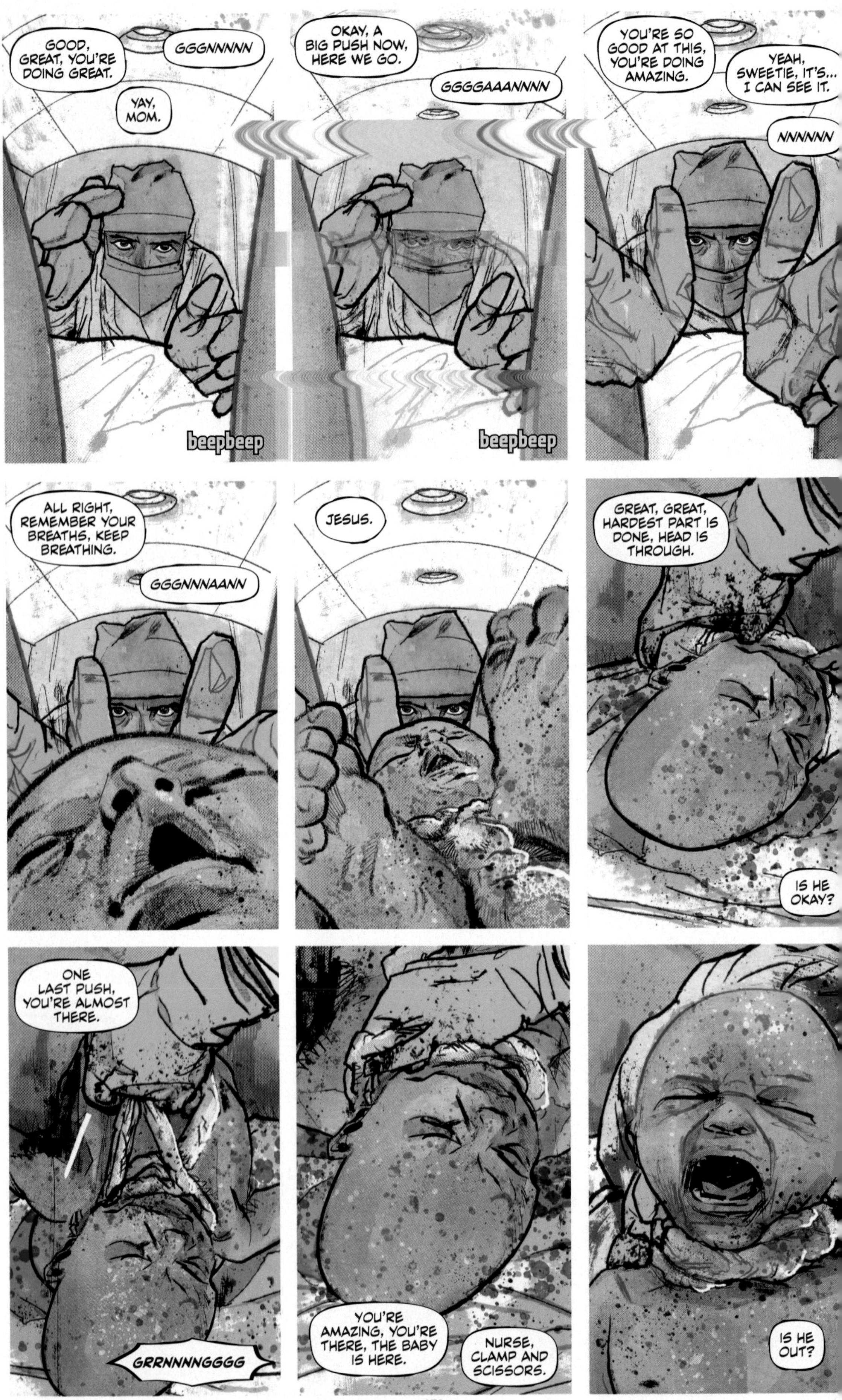
GOOD, GREAT, YOU'RE DOING GREAT.
GGGNNNNN
YAY, MOM.
beepbeep
OKAY, A BIG PUSH NOW, HERE WE GO.
GGGGAAANNNN
beepbeep
YOU'RE SO GOOD AT THIS, YOU'RE DOING AMAZING.
YEAH, SWEETIE, IT'S... I CAN SEE IT.
NNNNNN
ALL RIGHT, REMEMBER YOUR BREATHS, KEEP BREATHING.
GGGNNNAANN
JESUS.
GREAT, GREAT, HARDEST PART IS DONE, HEAD IS THROUGH.
IS HE OKAY?
ONE LAST PUSH, YOU'RE ALMOST THERE.
GRRNNNNGGGG
YOU'RE AMAZING, YOU'RE THERE, THE BABY IS HERE.
NURSE, CLAMP AND SCISSORS.
IS HE OUT?

WHAT'S...
WRONG...?

SHOULDN'T
HE...CRY?

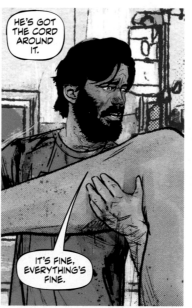

HE'S GOT
THE CORD
AROUND
IT.

IT'S FINE,
EVERYTHING'S
FINE.

IT CAN'T
GET THROUGH! IT'S
LIKE STEEL!

DO WE
HAVE ANYTHING
SHARPER?!

PAGE
SURGICAL,
SEE WHAT
THEY
HAVE!

I'M NOT
MAKING ANY
PROGRESS
HERE!

WE
DON'T HAVE
TIME!

Darkseid is.

TELL FRANCIS
WE NEED THE BONE
CUTTER!

WITH
THE DIAMOND
BLADE!

TELL
HIM WE NEED
IT *NOW!*

NOW!

THIS'LL...
WORK.

WHERE...

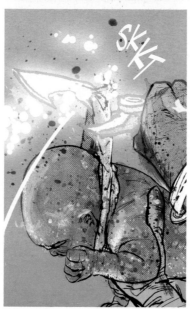

SK/KT

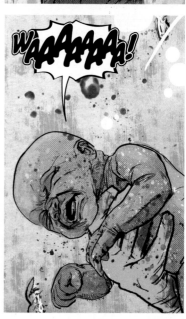

WAAAAAAA!

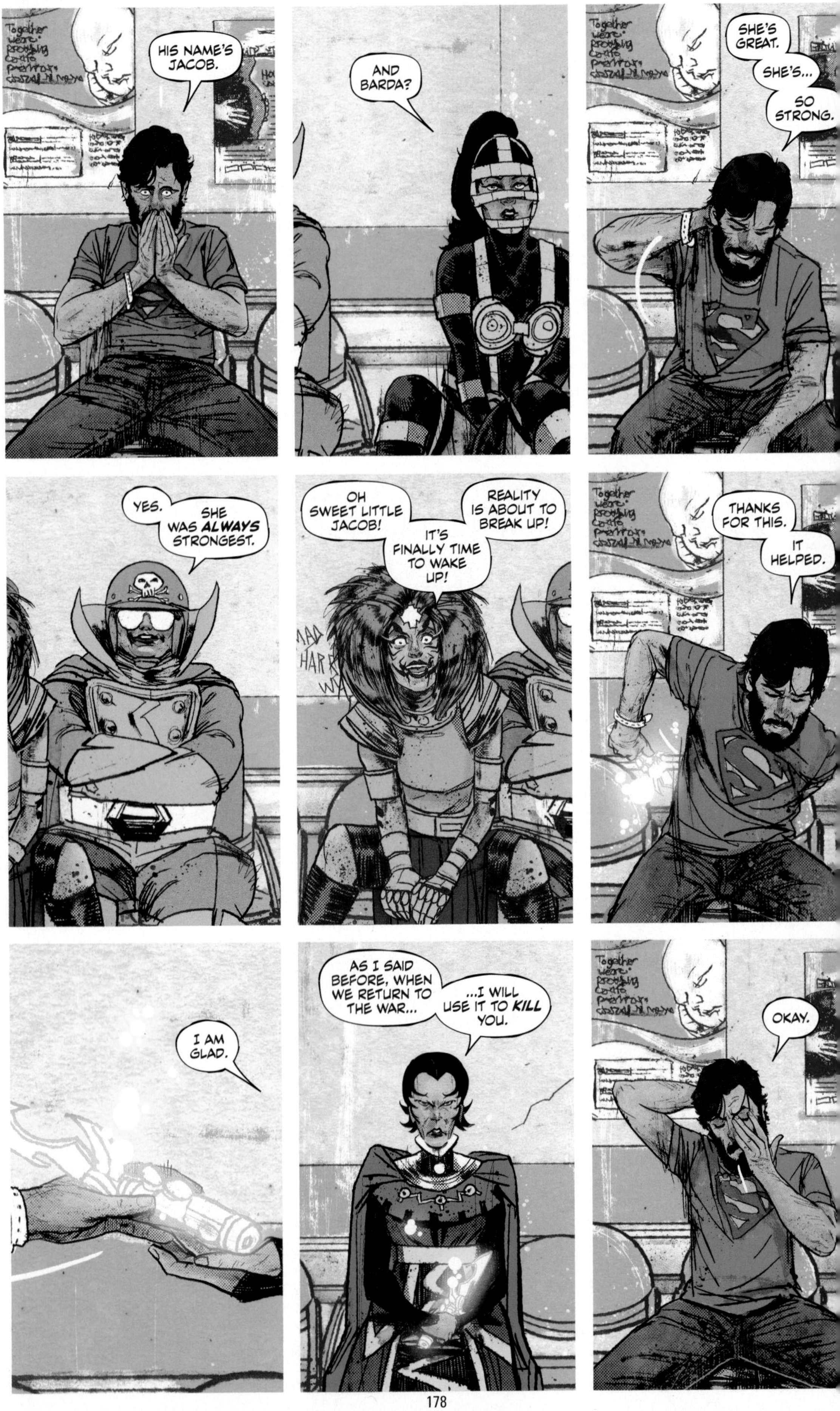
HIS NAME'S JACOB.
AND BARDA?
SHE'S GREAT.
SHE'S...
SO STRONG.
YES.
SHE WAS ALWAYS STRONGEST.
OH SWEET LITTLE JACOB!
IT'S FINALLY TIME TO WAKE UP!
REALITY IS ABOUT TO BREAK UP!
THANKS FOR THIS.
IT HELPED.
I AM GLAD.
AS I SAID BEFORE, WHEN WE RETURN TO THE WAR...
...I WILL USE IT TO KILL YOU.
OKAY.

I LIKE HIM.

I THINK WE SHOULD KEEP HIM.

GRANDSON OF DARKSEID.

SON OF HIGHFATHER.

THE FIRST CHILD BORN OF APOKOLIPS AND NEW GENESIS.

A NEW GOD.

A LITTLE MIRACLE.

I DON'T KNOW...

HE LOOKS MORE LIKE A...

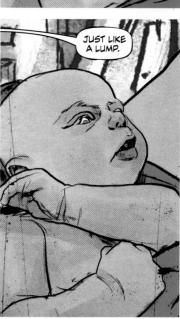

JUST LIKE A LUMP.

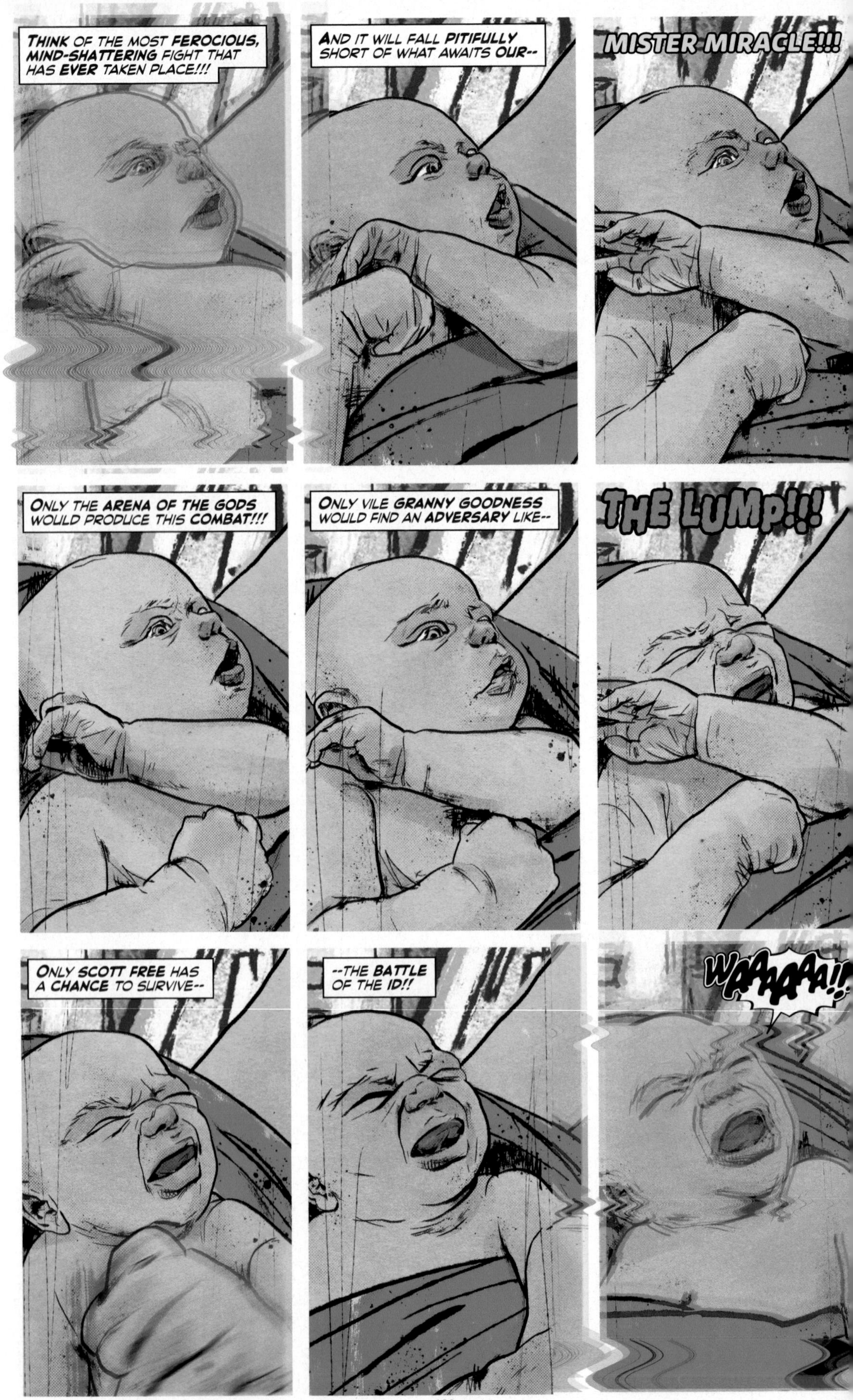
THINK OF THE MOST FEROCIOUS, MIND-SHATTERING FIGHT THAT HAS EVER TAKEN PLACE!!!
AND IT WILL FALL PITIFULLY SHORT OF WHAT AWAITS OUR--
MISTER MIRACLE!!!
ONLY THE ARENA OF THE GODS WOULD PRODUCE THIS COMBAT!!!
ONLY VILE GRANNY GOODNESS WOULD FIND AN ADVERSARY LIKE--
THE LUMP!!!
ONLY SCOTT FREE HAS A CHANCE TO SURVIVE--
--THE BATTLE OF THE ID!!
WAAAAAA!!

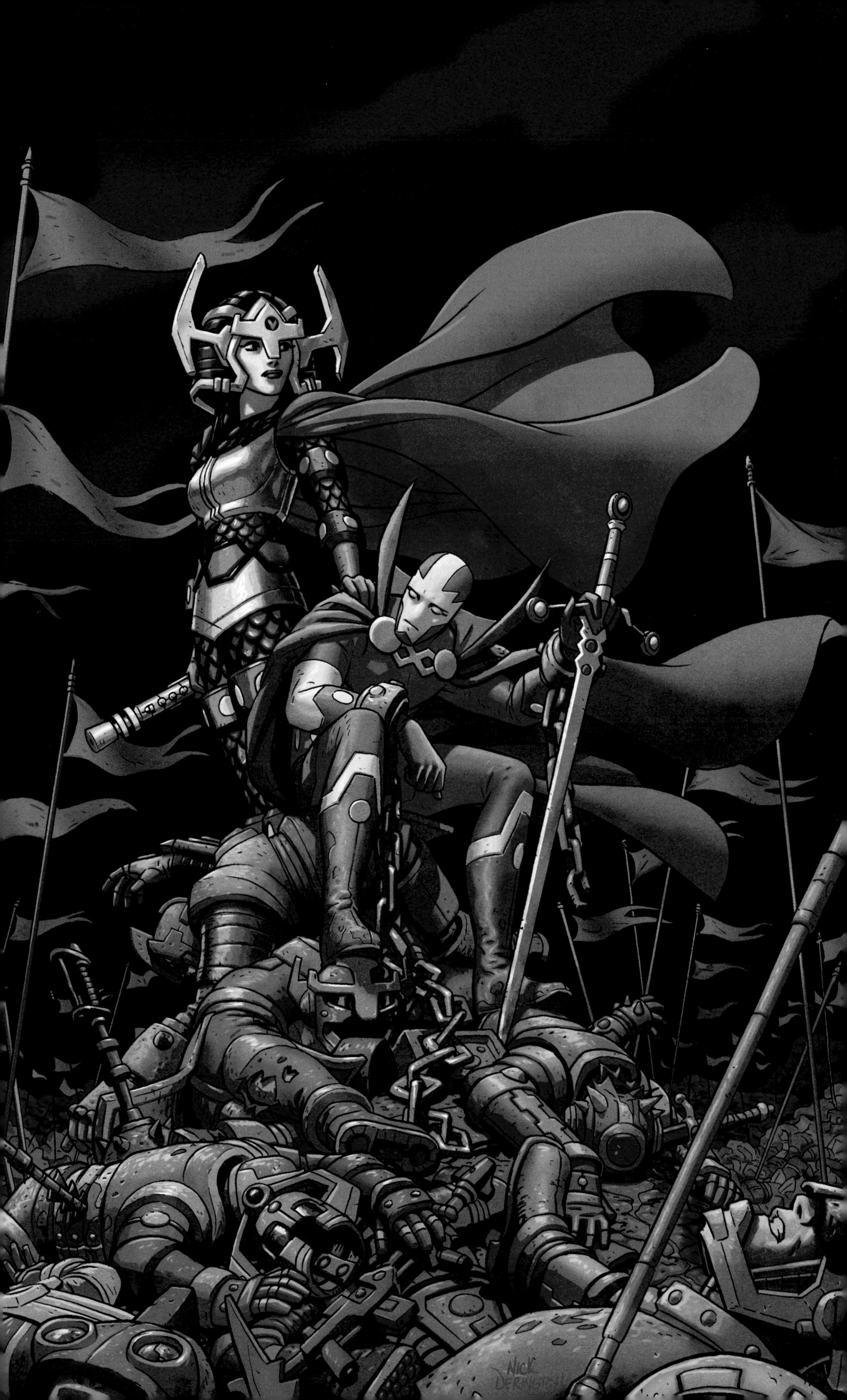

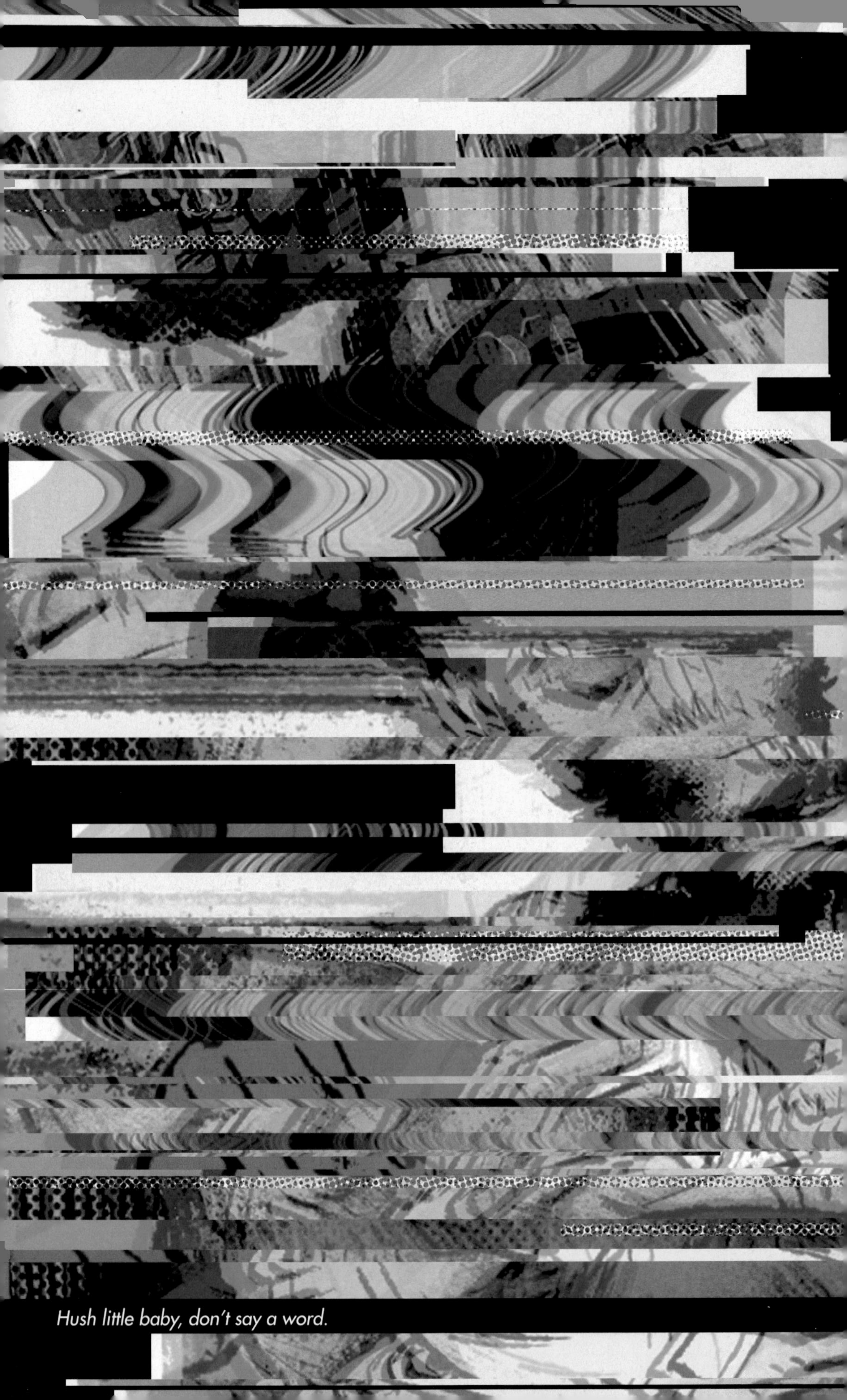

Hush little baby, don't say a word.

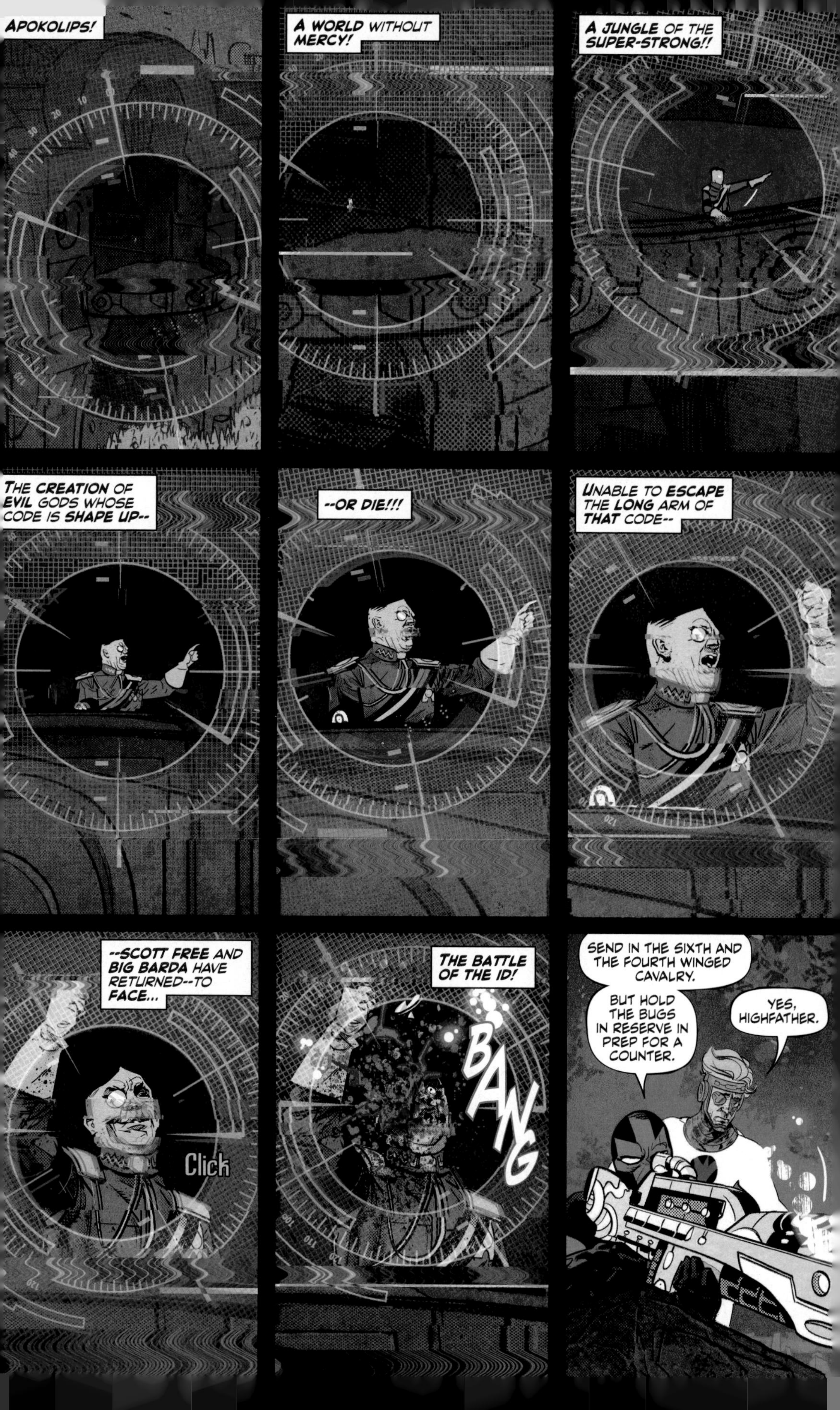
APOKOLIPS!
A WORLD WITHOUT MERCY!
A JUNGLE OF THE SUPER-STRONG!!
THE CREATION OF EVIL GODS WHOSE CODE IS SHAPE UP--
--OR DIE!!!
UNABLE TO ESCAPE THE LONG ARM OF THAT CODE--
--SCOTT FREE AND BIG BARDA HAVE RETURNED--TO FACE...
Click
THE BATTLE OF THE ID!
BANG
SEND IN THE SIXTH AND THE FOURTH WINGED CAVALRY.
BUT HOLD THE BUGS IN RESERVE IN PREP FOR A COUNTER.
YES, HIGHFATHER.

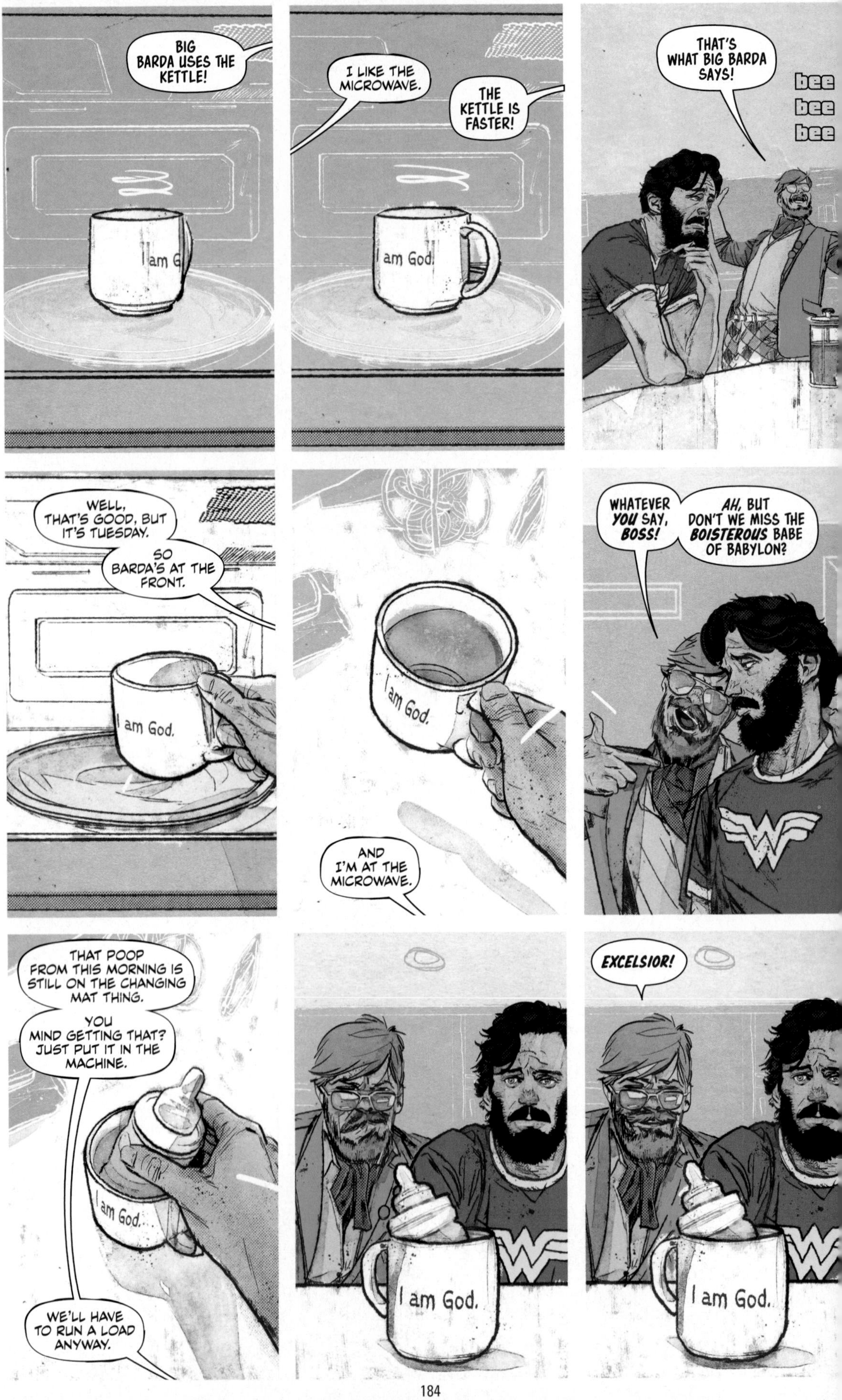
BIG BARDA USES THE KETTLE!
I am G
I LIKE THE MICROWAVE.
THE KETTLE IS FASTER!
I am God.
THAT'S WHAT BIG BARDA SAYS!
bee bee bee
WELL, THAT'S GOOD, BUT IT'S TUESDAY.
SO BARDA'S AT THE FRONT.
I am God.
I am God.
AND I'M AT THE MICROWAVE.
WHATEVER YOU SAY, BOSS!
AH, BUT DON'T WE MISS THE BOISTEROUS BABE OF BABYLON?
THAT POOP FROM THIS MORNING IS STILL ON THE CHANGING MAT THING.
YOU MIND GETTING THAT? JUST PUT IT IN THE MACHINE.
I am God.
WE'LL HAVE TO RUN A LOAD ANYWAY.
I am God.
EXCELSIOR!
I am God.

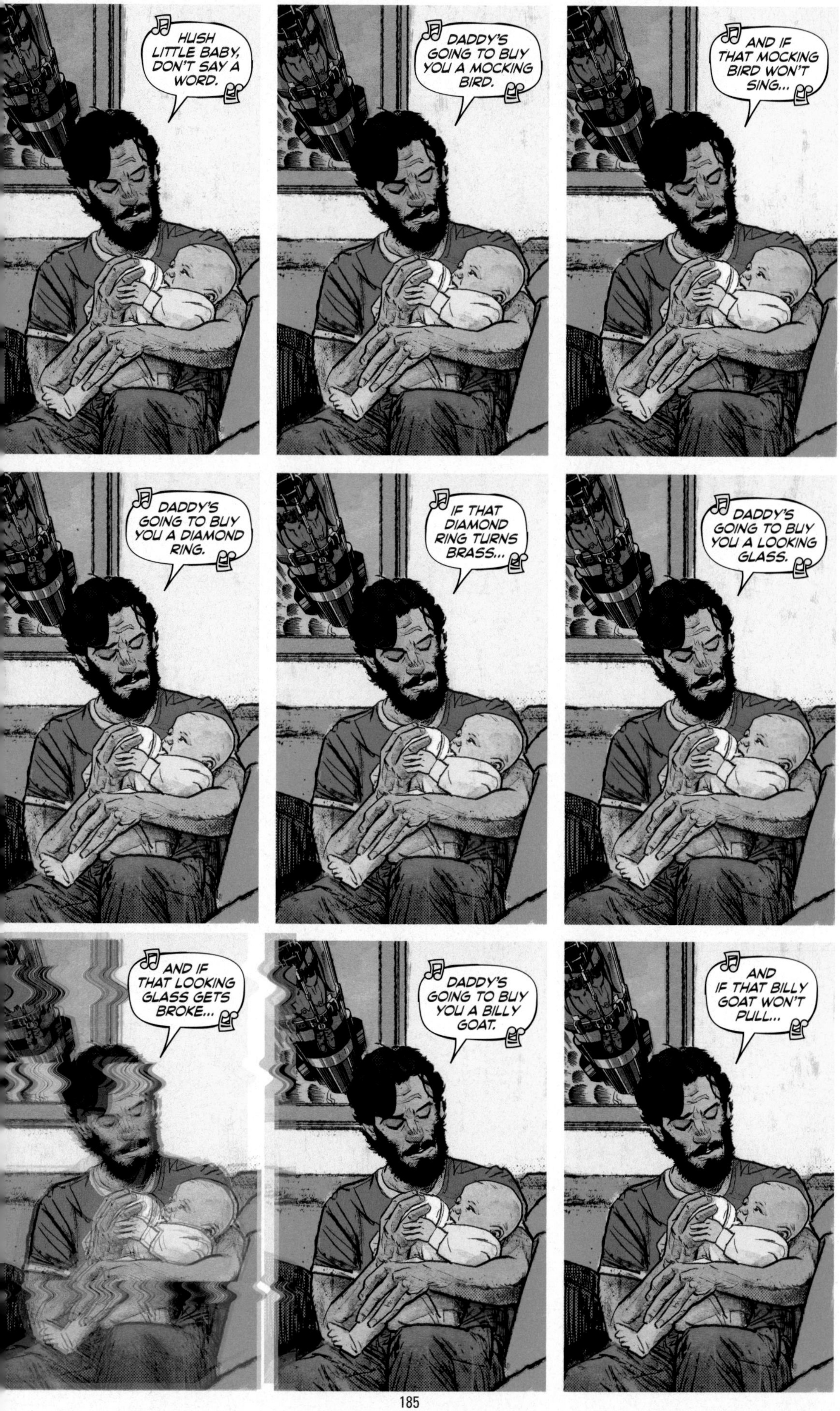
HUSH LITTLE BABY, DON'T SAY A WORD.
DADDY'S GOING TO BUY YOU A MOCKING BIRD.
AND IF THAT MOCKING BIRD WON'T SING...
DADDY'S GOING TO BUY YOU A DIAMOND RING.
IF THAT DIAMOND RING TURNS BRASS...
DADDY'S GOING TO BUY YOU A LOOKING GLASS.
AND IF THAT LOOKING GLASS GETS BROKE...
DADDY'S GOING TO BUY YOU A BILLY GOAT.
AND IF THAT BILLY GOAT WON'T PULL...

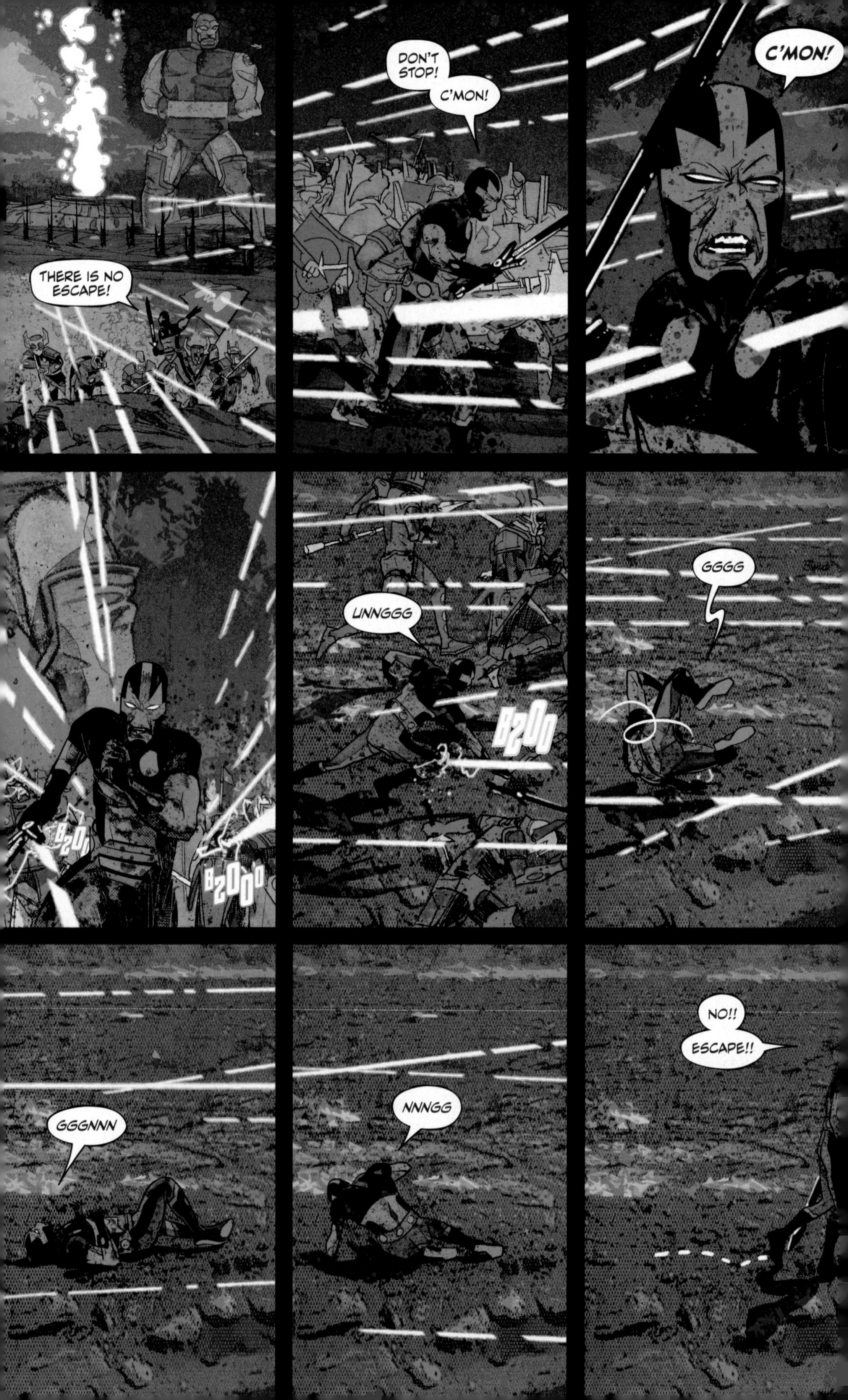
THERE IS NO ESCAPE!
DON'T STOP!
C'MON!
C'MON!
BZOO
BZOOO
UNNGGG
BZOO
GGGG
GGGNNN
NNNGG
NO!!
ESCAPE!!

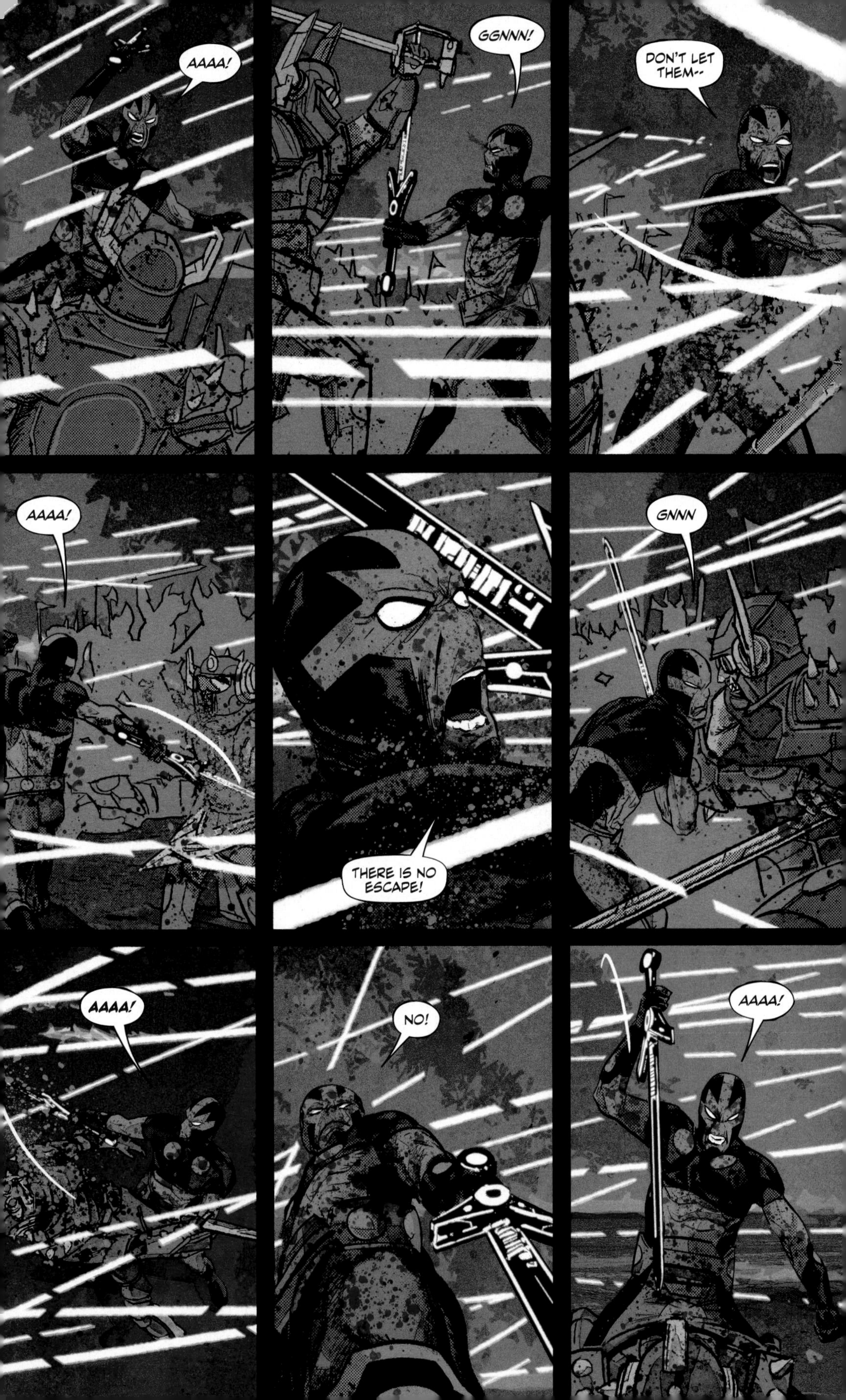
AAAA!
GGNNN!
DON'T LET THEM--
AAAA!
THERE IS NO ESCAPE!
GNNN
AAAA!
NO!
AAAA!

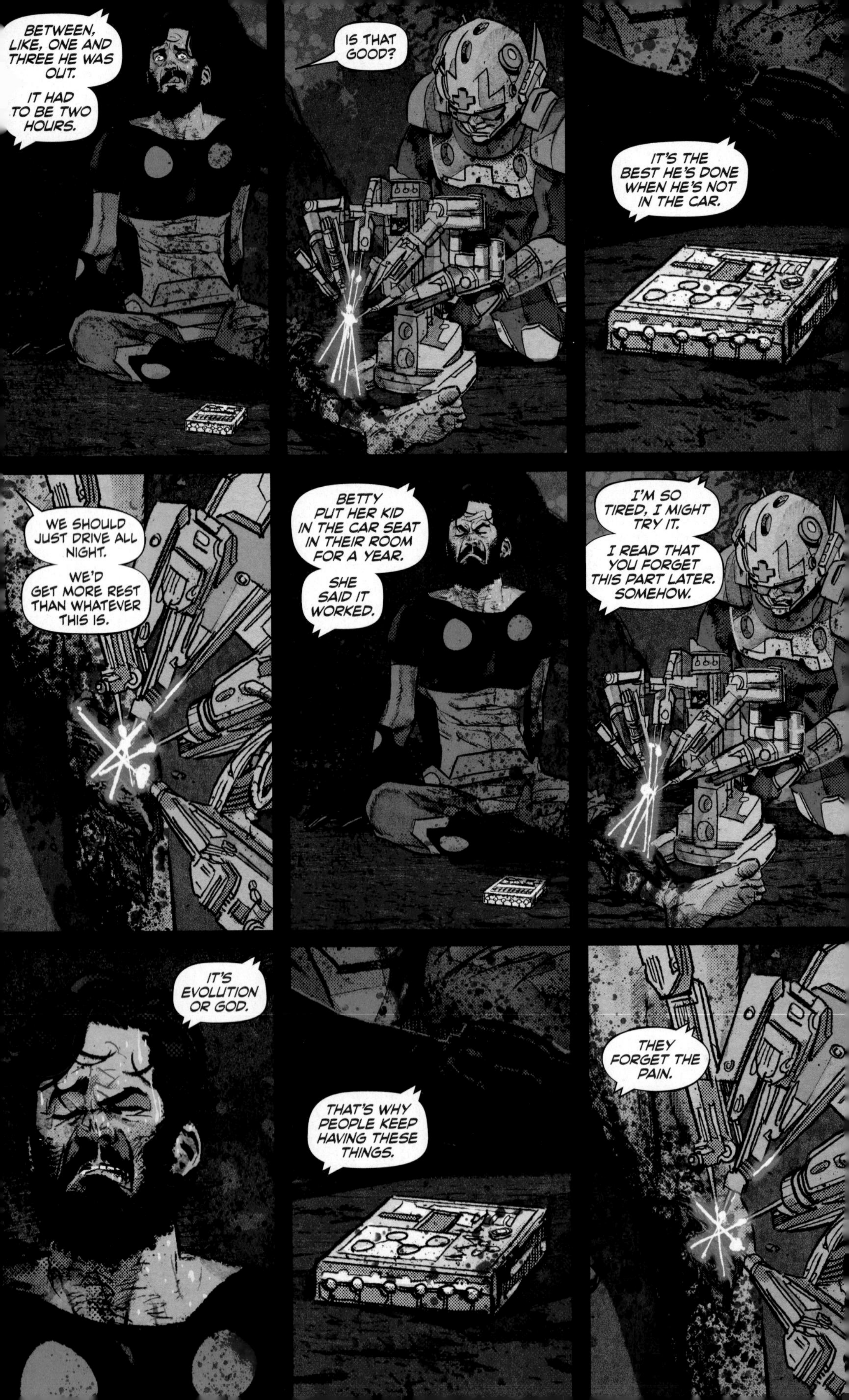
BETWEEN, LIKE, ONE AND THREE HE WAS OUT.
IT HAD TO BE TWO HOURS.
IS THAT GOOD?
IT'S THE BEST HE'S DONE WHEN HE'S NOT IN THE CAR.
WE SHOULD JUST DRIVE ALL NIGHT.
WE'D GET MORE REST THAN WHATEVER THIS IS.
BETTY PUT HER KID IN THE CAR SEAT IN THEIR ROOM FOR A YEAR.
SHE SAID IT WORKED.
I'M SO TIRED, I MIGHT TRY IT.
I READ THAT YOU FORGET THIS PART LATER. SOMEHOW.
IT'S EVOLUTION OR GOD.
THAT'S WHY PEOPLE KEEP HAVING THESE THINGS.
THEY FORGET THE PAIN.

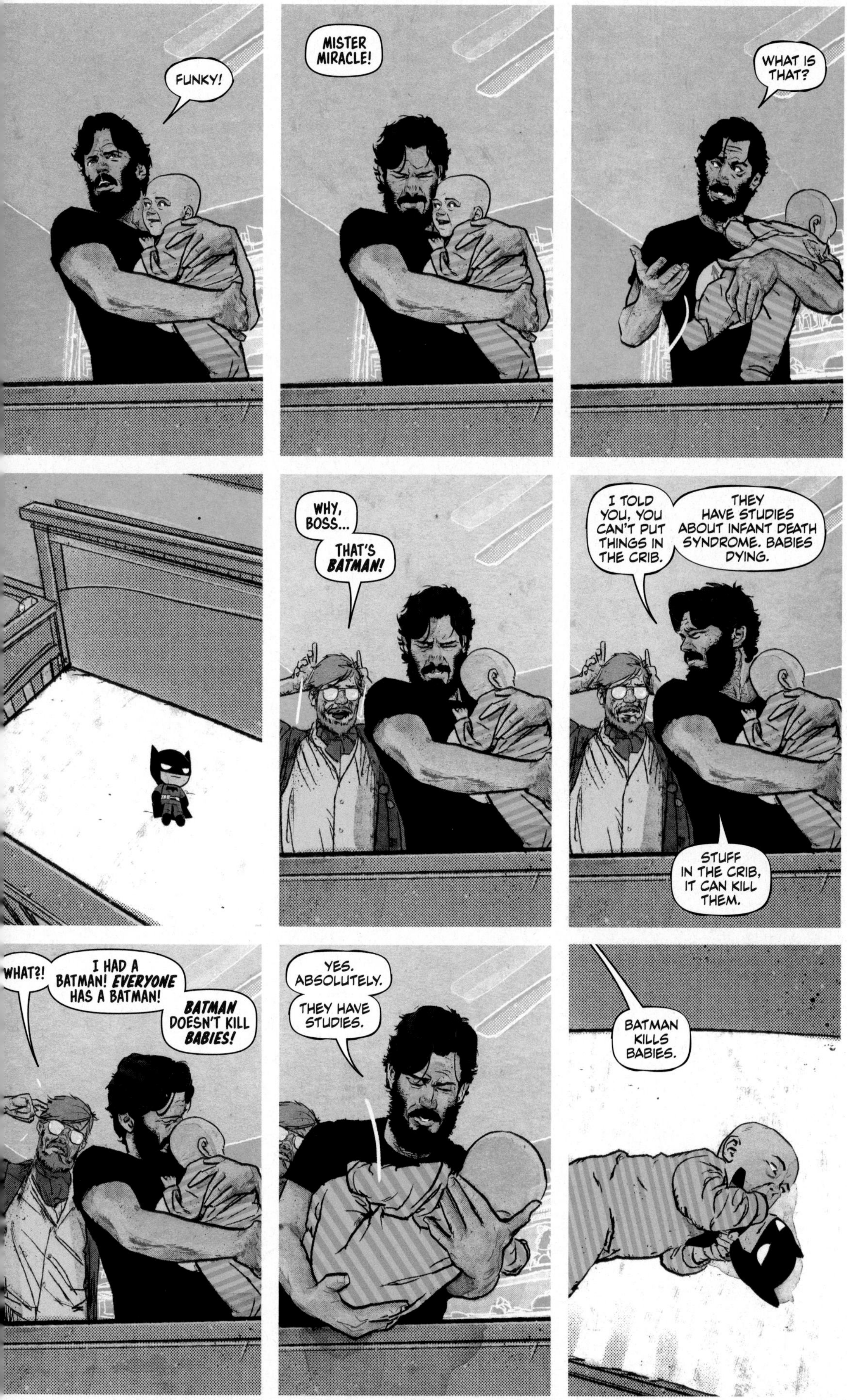

FUNKY!
MISTER MIRACLE!
WHAT IS THAT?
WHY, BOSS...
THAT'S *BATMAN!*
I TOLD YOU, YOU CAN'T PUT THINGS IN THE CRIB.
THEY HAVE STUDIES ABOUT INFANT DEATH SYNDROME. BABIES DYING.
STUFF IN THE CRIB, IT CAN KILL THEM.
WHAT?!
I HAD A BATMAN! *EVERYONE* HAS A BATMAN!
BATMAN DOESN'T KILL *BABIES!*
YES. ABSOLUTELY.
THEY HAVE STUDIES.
BATMAN KILLS BABIES.

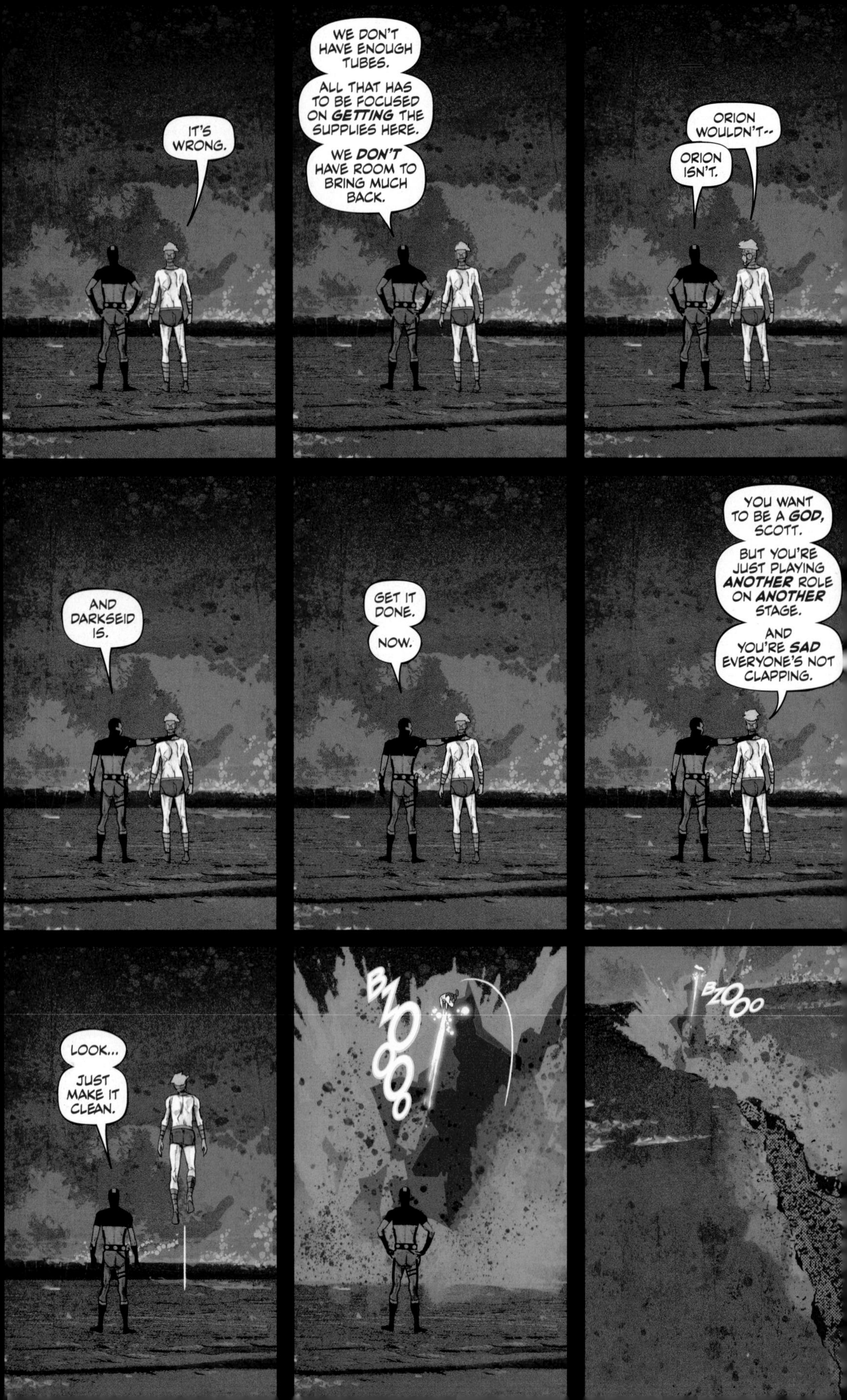
IT'S WRONG.
WE DON'T HAVE ENOUGH TUBES.
ALL THAT HAS TO BE FOCUSED ON GETTING THE SUPPLIES HERE.
WE DON'T HAVE ROOM TO BRING MUCH BACK.
ORION WOULDN'T--
ORION ISN'T.
AND DARKSEID IS.
GET IT DONE.
NOW.
YOU WANT TO BE A GOD, SCOTT.
BUT YOU'RE JUST PLAYING ANOTHER ROLE ON ANOTHER STAGE.
AND YOU'RE SAD EVERYONE'S NOT CLAPPING.
LOOK...
JUST MAKE IT CLEAN.
BZOOOOO
BZOOO

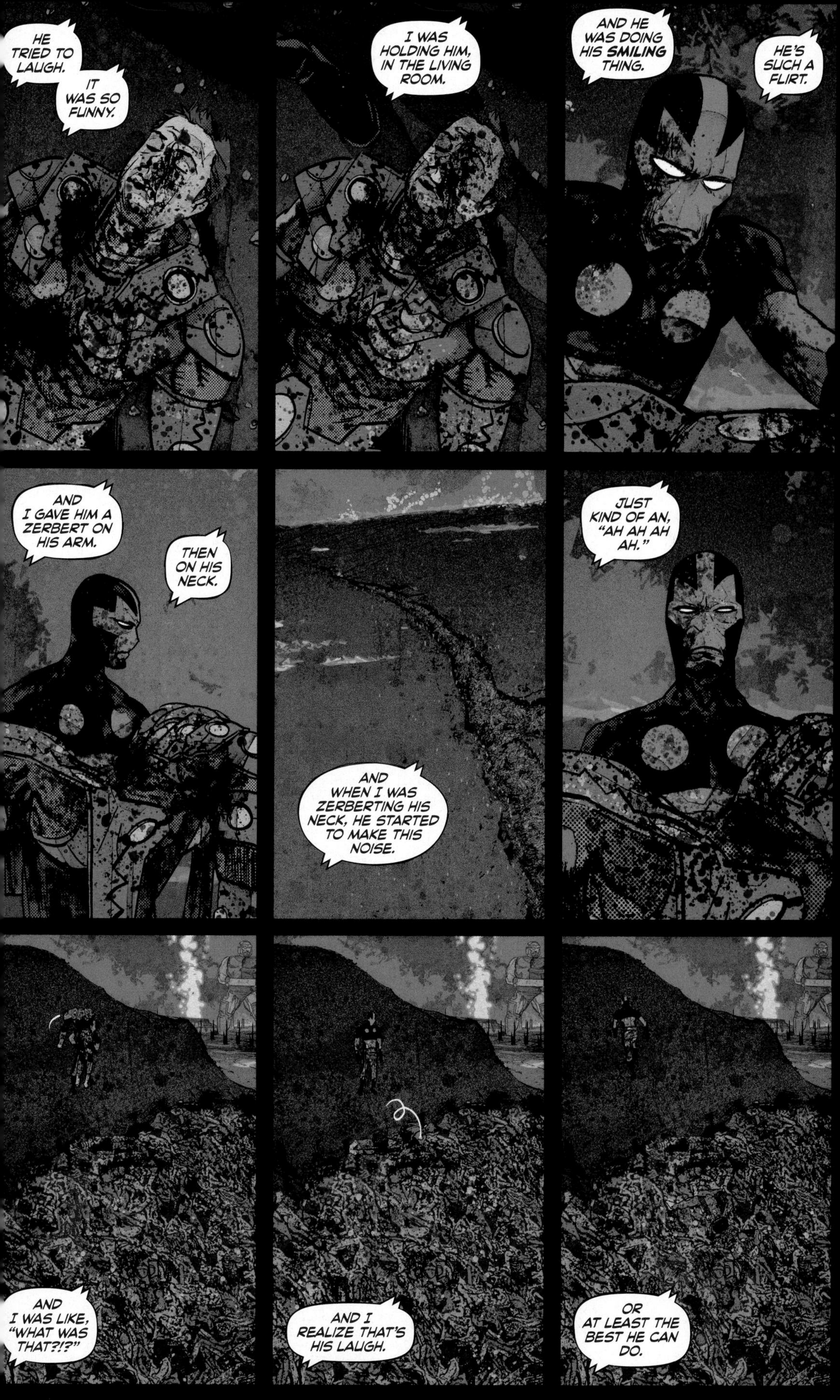
HE TRIED TO LAUGH.
IT WAS SO FUNNY.
I WAS HOLDING HIM, IN THE LIVING ROOM.
AND HE WAS DOING HIS SMILING THING.
HE'S SUCH A FLIRT.
AND I GAVE HIM A ZERBERT ON HIS ARM.
THEN ON HIS NECK.
AND WHEN I WAS ZERBERTING HIS NECK, HE STARTED TO MAKE THIS NOISE.
JUST KIND OF AN, "AH AH AH AH."
AND I WAS LIKE, "WHAT WAS THAT?!?"
AND I REALIZE THAT'S HIS LAUGH.
OR AT LEAST THE BEST HE CAN DO.

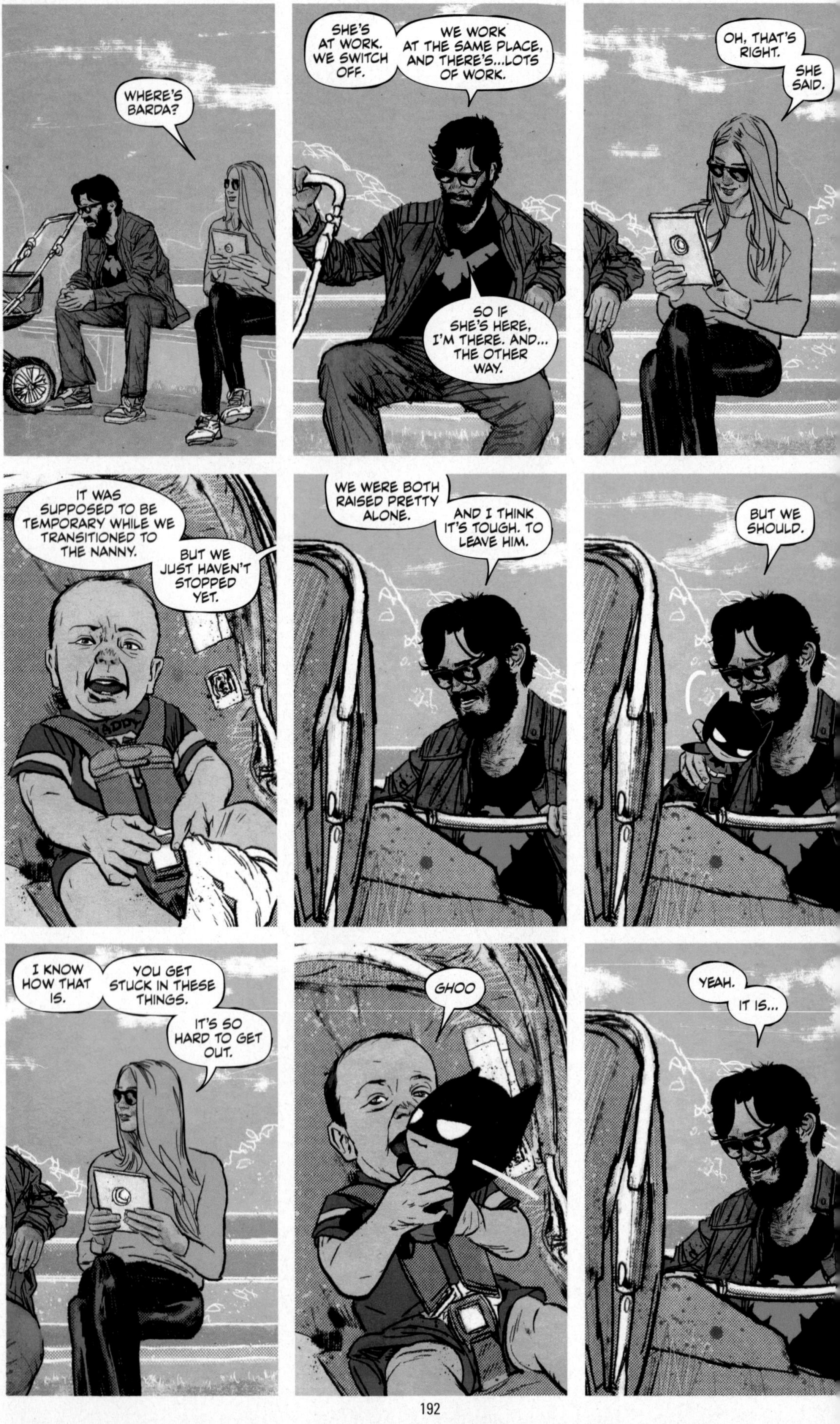
WHERE'S BARDA?
SHE'S AT WORK. WE SWITCH OFF.
WE WORK AT THE SAME PLACE, AND THERE'S...LOTS OF WORK.
SO IF SHE'S HERE, I'M THERE. AND... THE OTHER WAY.
OH, THAT'S RIGHT.
SHE SAID.
IT WAS SUPPOSED TO BE TEMPORARY WHILE WE TRANSITIONED TO THE NANNY.
BUT WE JUST HAVEN'T STOPPED YET.
WE WERE BOTH RAISED PRETTY ALONE.
AND I THINK IT'S TOUGH. TO LEAVE HIM.
BUT WE SHOULD.
I KNOW HOW THAT IS.
YOU GET STUCK IN THESE THINGS.
IT'S SO HARD TO GET OUT.
GHOO
YEAH.
IT IS...

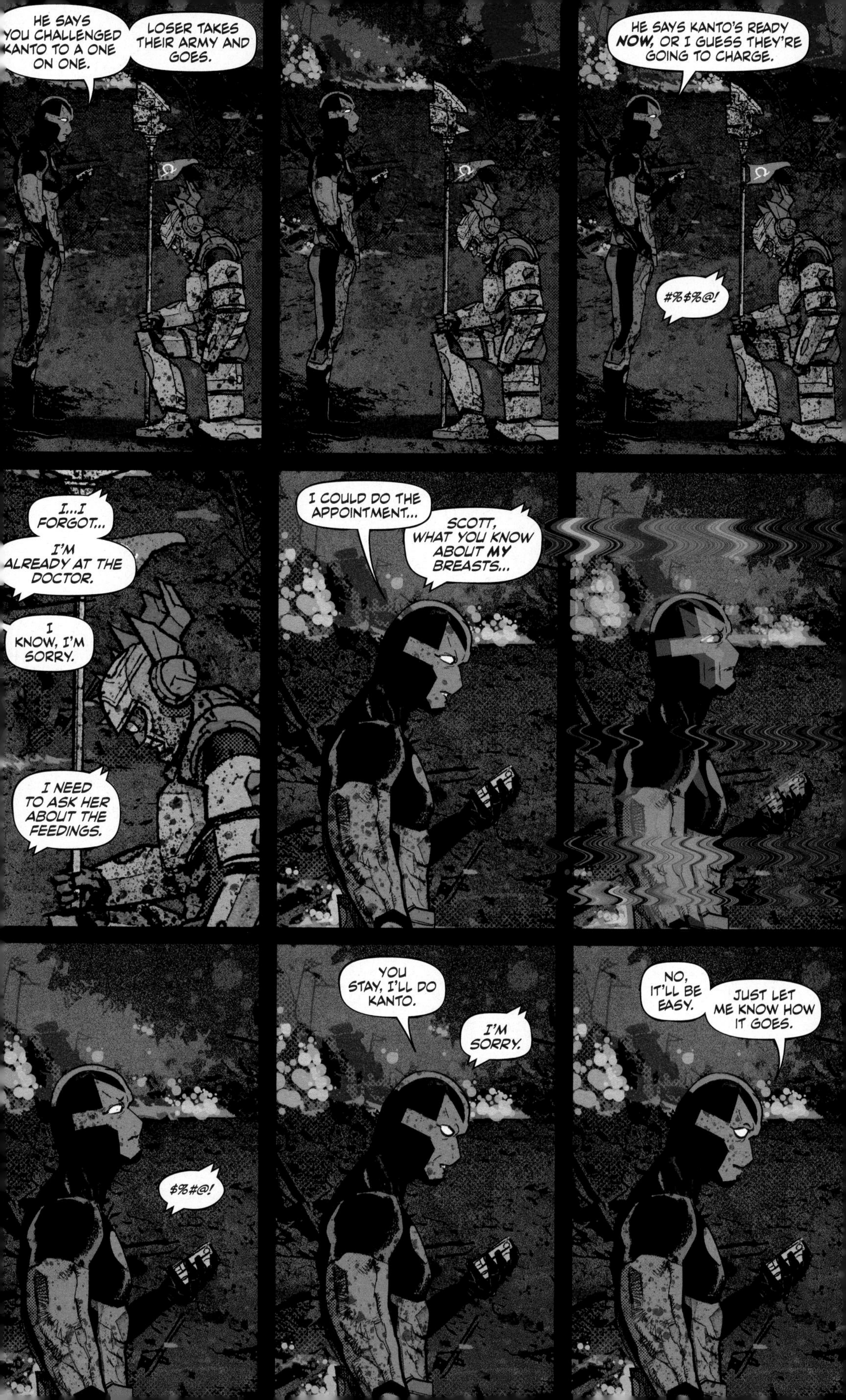
HE SAYS YOU CHALLENGED KANTO TO A ONE ON ONE.
LOSER TAKES THEIR ARMY AND GOES.
HE SAYS KANTO'S READY **NOW,** OR I GUESS THEY'RE GOING TO CHARGE.
#%$%@!
I...I FORGOT...
I'M ALREADY AT THE DOCTOR.
I KNOW, I'M SORRY.
I NEED TO ASK HER ABOUT THE FEEDINGS.
I COULD DO THE APPOINTMENT...
SCOTT, WHAT YOU KNOW ABOUT **MY** BREASTS...
$%#@!
YOU STAY, I'LL DO KANTO.
I'M SORRY.
NO, IT'LL BE EASY.
JUST LET ME KNOW HOW IT GOES.

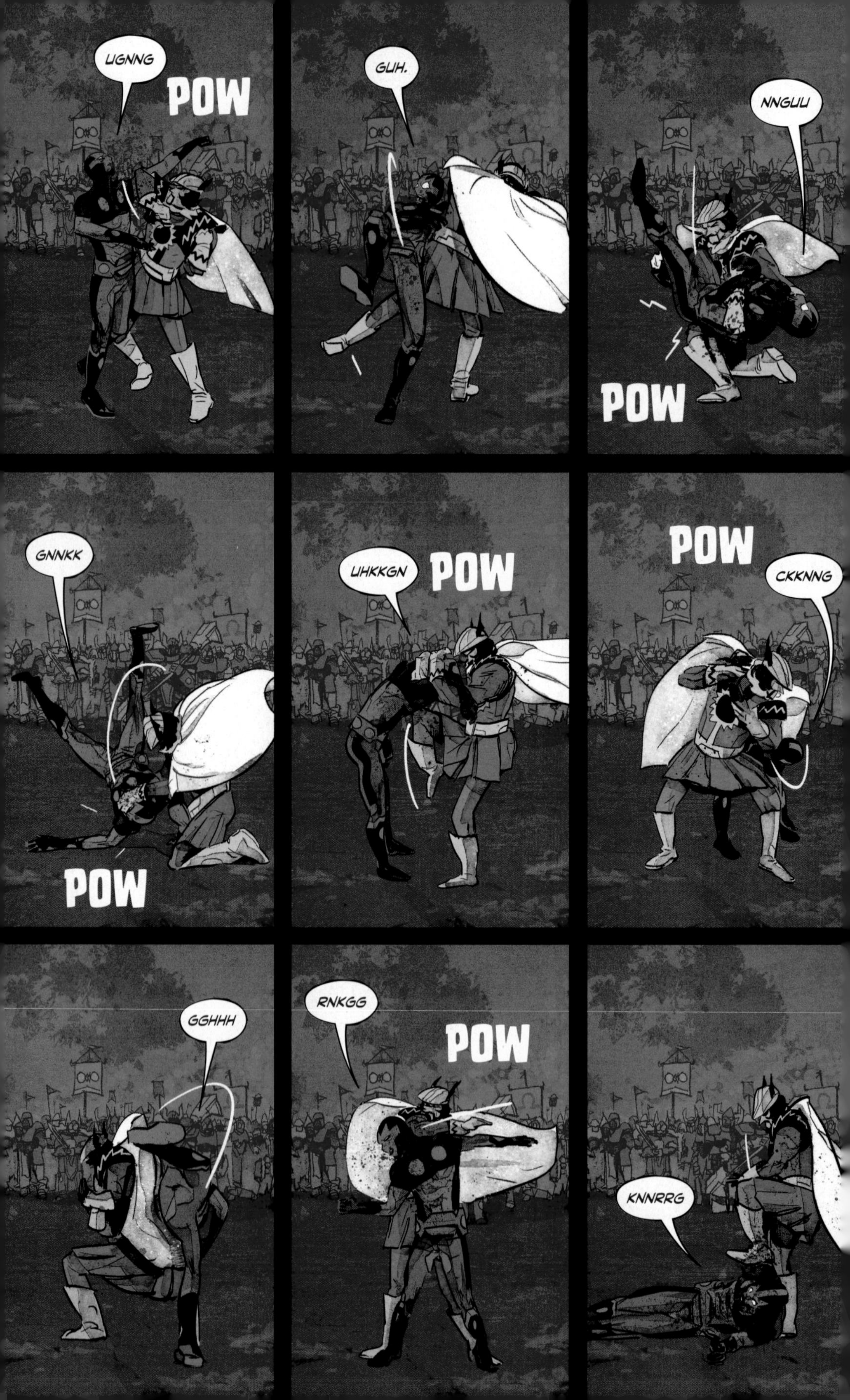
UGNNG
POW
GUH.
NNGUU
POW
GNNKK
POW
UHKKGN
POW
POW
CKKNNG
GGHHH
RNKGG
POW
KNNRRG

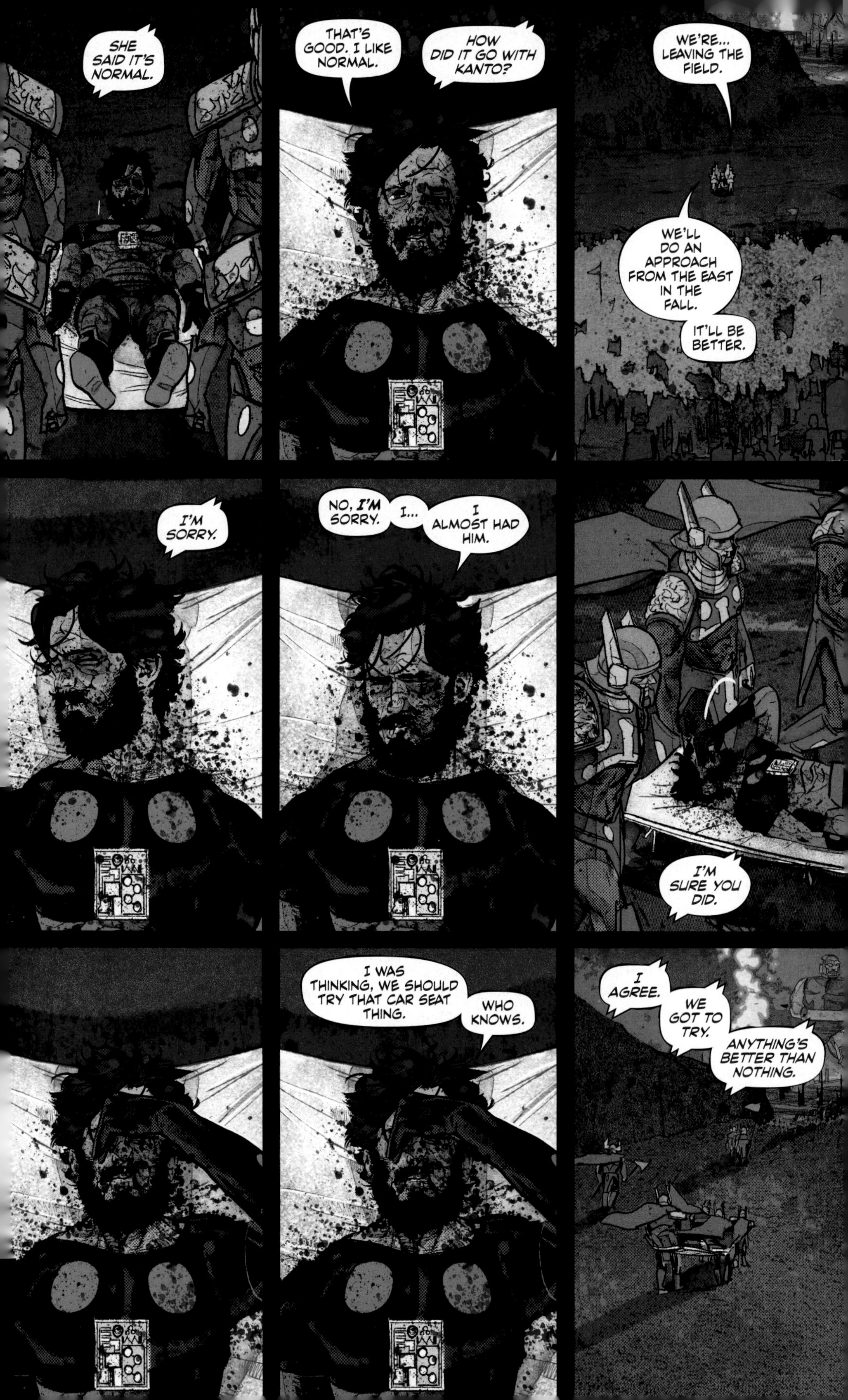
SHE SAID IT'S NORMAL.
THAT'S GOOD. I LIKE NORMAL.
HOW DID IT GO WITH KANTO?
WE'RE... LEAVING THE FIELD.
WE'LL DO AN APPROACH FROM THE EAST IN THE FALL.
IT'LL BE BETTER.
I'M SORRY.
NO, I'M SORRY.
I...
I ALMOST HAD HIM.
I'M SURE YOU DID.
I WAS THINKING, WE SHOULD TRY THAT CAR SEAT THING.
WHO KNOWS.
I AGREE.
WE GOT TO TRY.
ANYTHING'S BETTER THAN NOTHING.

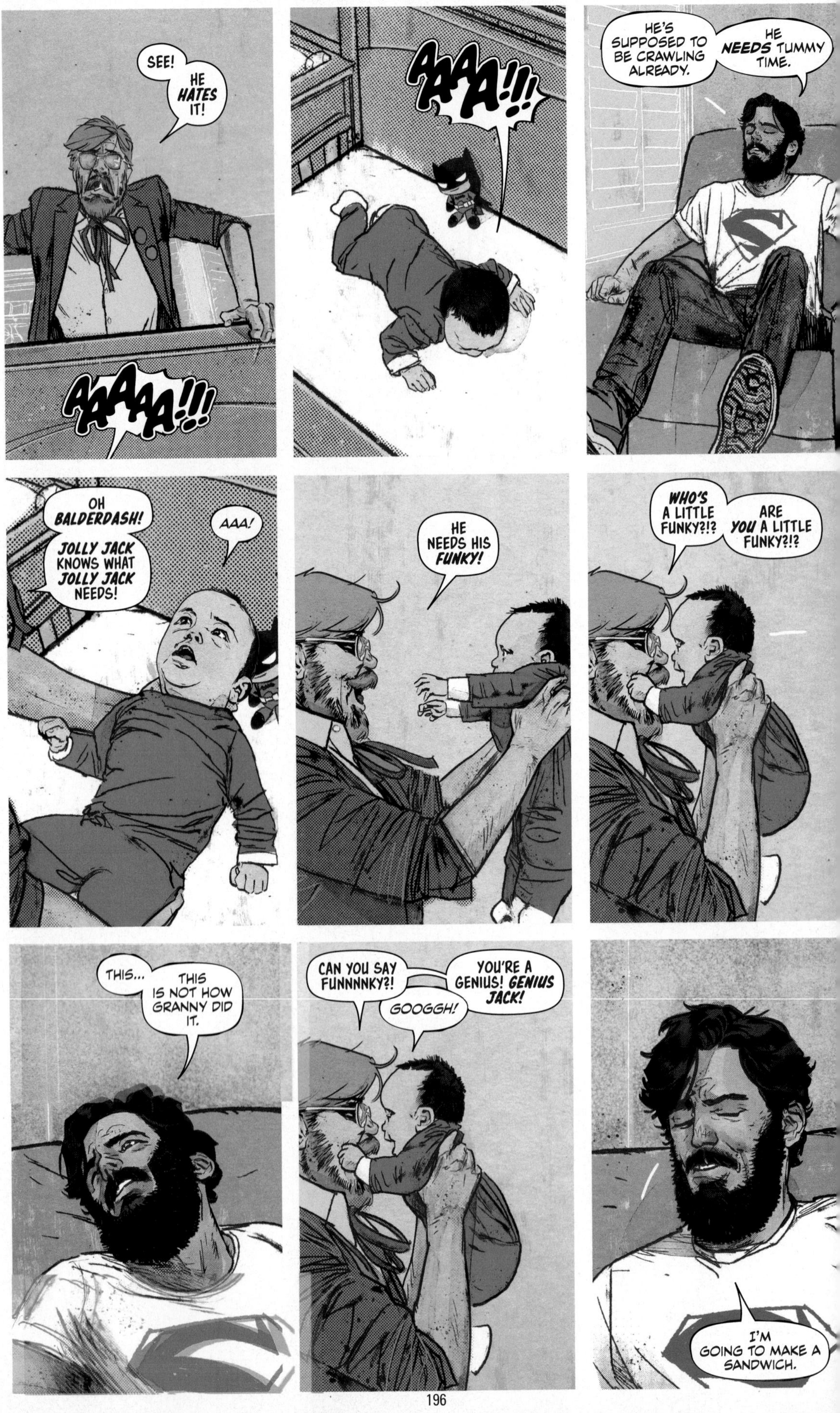
SEE!
HE HATES IT!
AAAAA!!!
AAAA!!!
HE'S SUPPOSED TO BE CRAWLING ALREADY.
HE NEEDS TUMMY TIME.
OH BALDERDASH!
JOLLY JACK KNOWS WHAT JOLLY JACK NEEDS!
AAA!
HE NEEDS HIS FUNKY!
WHO'S A LITTLE FUNKY?!?
ARE YOU A LITTLE FUNKY?!?
THIS...
THIS IS NOT HOW GRANNY DID IT.
CAN YOU SAY FUNNNNKY?!
YOU'RE A GENIUS! GENIUS JACK!
GOOGGH!
I'M GOING TO MAKE A SANDWICH.

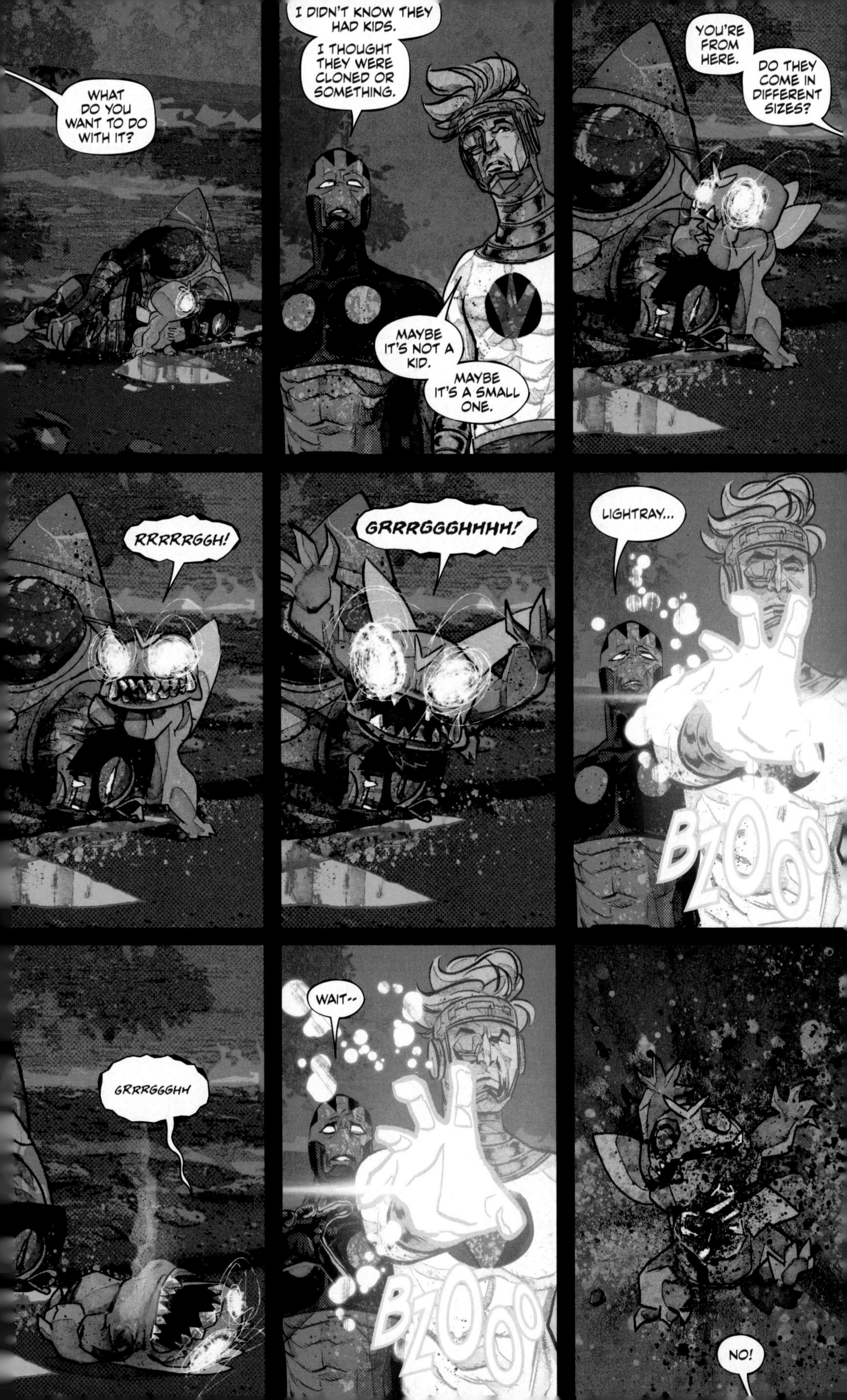
WHAT DO YOU WANT TO DO WITH IT?
I DIDN'T KNOW THEY HAD KIDS.
I THOUGHT THEY WERE CLONED OR SOMETHING.
MAYBE IT'S NOT A KID.
MAYBE IT'S A SMALL ONE.
YOU'RE FROM HERE.
DO THEY COME IN DIFFERENT SIZES?
RRRRRGGH!
GRRRGGGHHHH!
LIGHTRAY...
BZOOO
GRRRGGGHH
WAIT--
BZOOO
NO!

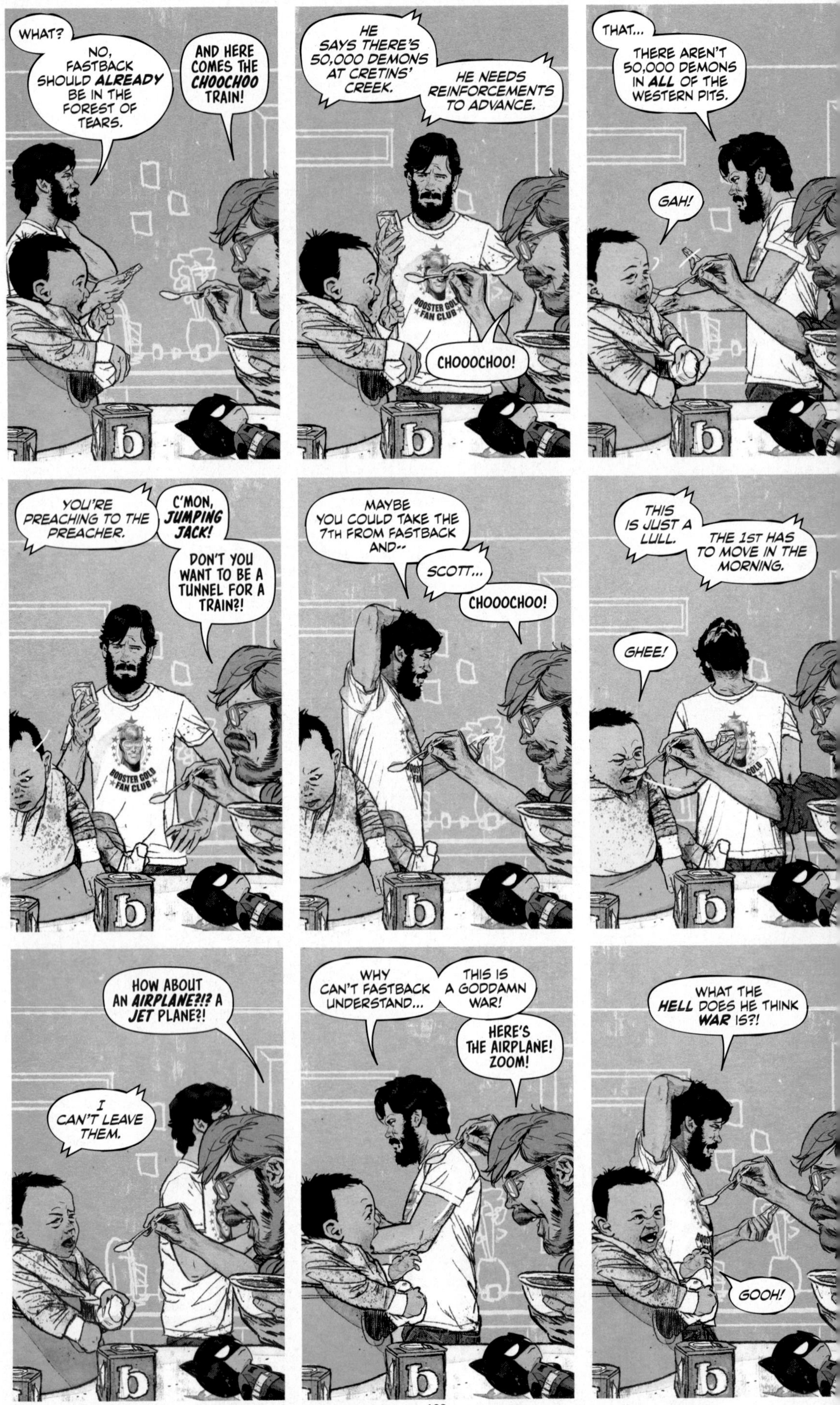

WHAT?
NO, FASTBACK SHOULD ALREADY BE IN THE FOREST OF TEARS.
AND HERE COMES THE CHOOCHOO TRAIN!
HE SAYS THERE'S 50,000 DEMONS AT CRETINS' CREEK.
HE NEEDS REINFORCEMENTS TO ADVANCE.
BOOSTER GOLD FAN CLUB
CHOOOCHOO!
THAT...
THERE AREN'T 50,000 DEMONS IN ALL OF THE WESTERN PITS.
GAH!
YOU'RE PREACHING TO THE PREACHER.
C'MON, JUMPING JACK!
DON'T YOU WANT TO BE A TUNNEL FOR A TRAIN?!
BOOSTER GOLD FAN CLUB
MAYBE YOU COULD TAKE THE 7TH FROM FASTBACK AND--
SCOTT...
CHOOOCHOO!
THIS IS JUST A LULL.
THE 1ST HAS TO MOVE IN THE MORNING.
GHEE!
HOW ABOUT AN AIRPLANE?!? A JET PLANE?!
I CAN'T LEAVE THEM.
WHY CAN'T FASTBACK UNDERSTAND...
THIS IS A GODDAMN WAR!
HERE'S THE AIRPLANE! ZOOM!
WHAT THE HELL DOES HE THINK WAR IS?!
GOOH!

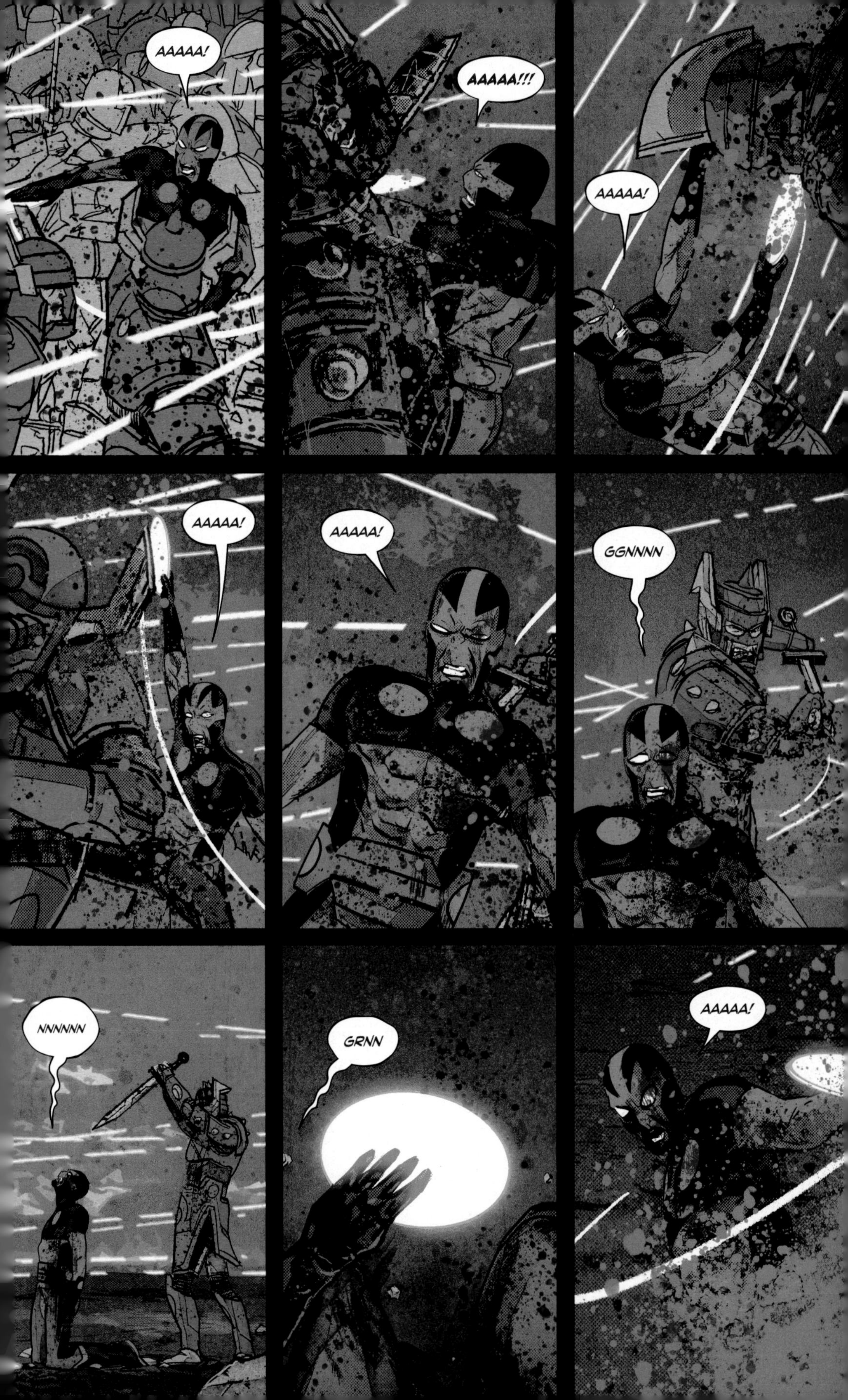
AAAAA!
AAAAA!!!
AAAAA!
AAAAA!
AAAAA!
GGNNNN
NNNNNN
GRNN
AAAAA!

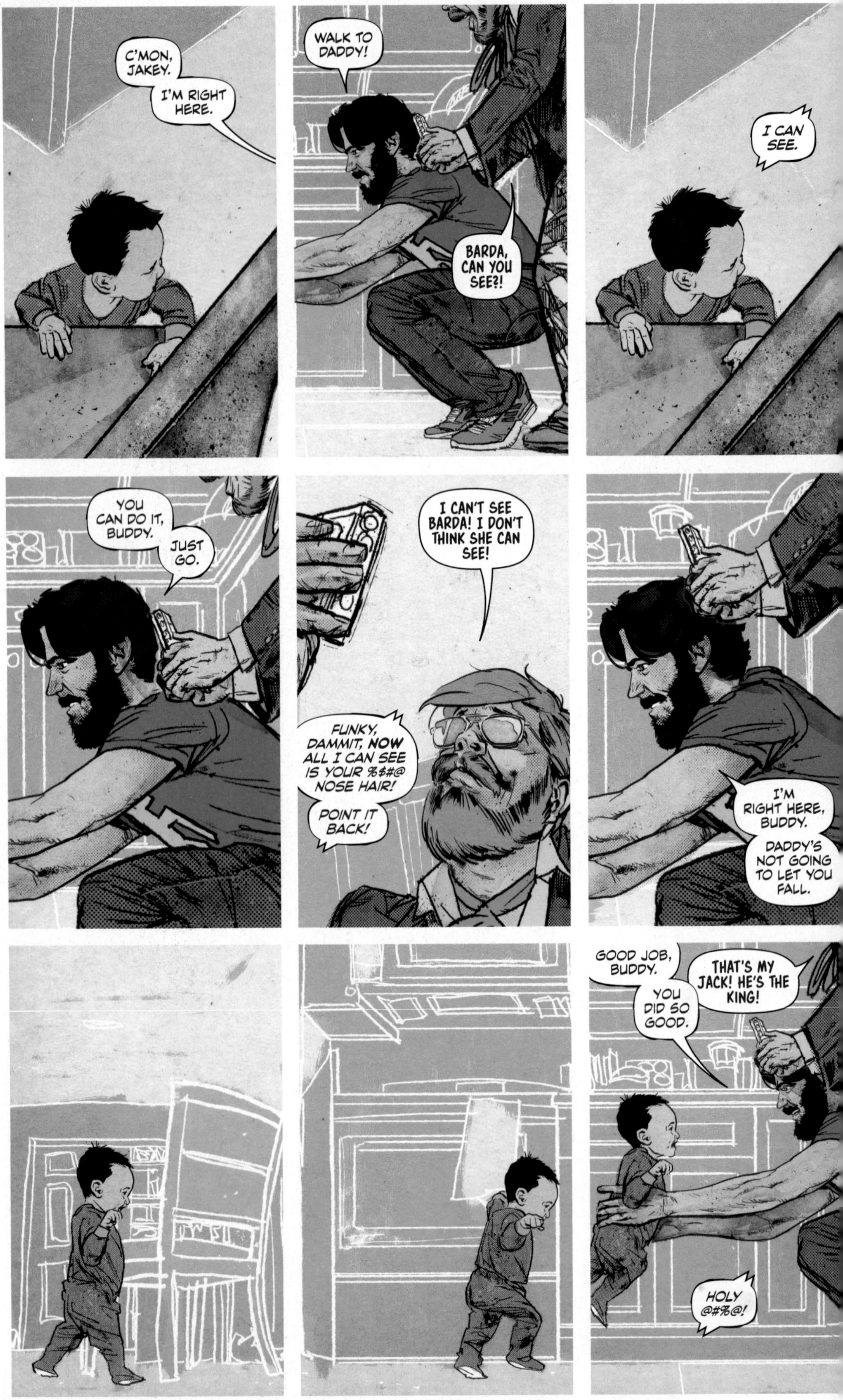
C'MON, JAKEY.
I'M RIGHT HERE.
WALK TO DADDY!
BARDA, CAN YOU SEE?!
I CAN SEE.
YOU CAN DO IT, BUDDY.
JUST GO.
I CAN'T SEE BARDA! I DON'T THINK SHE CAN SEE!
FUNKY, DAMMIT, NOW ALL I CAN SEE IS YOUR %$#@ NOSE HAIR!
POINT IT BACK!
I'M RIGHT HERE, BUDDY.
DADDY'S NOT GOING TO LET YOU FALL.
GOOD JOB, BUDDY.
YOU DID SO GOOD.
THAT'S MY JACK! HE'S THE KING!
HOLY @#%@!

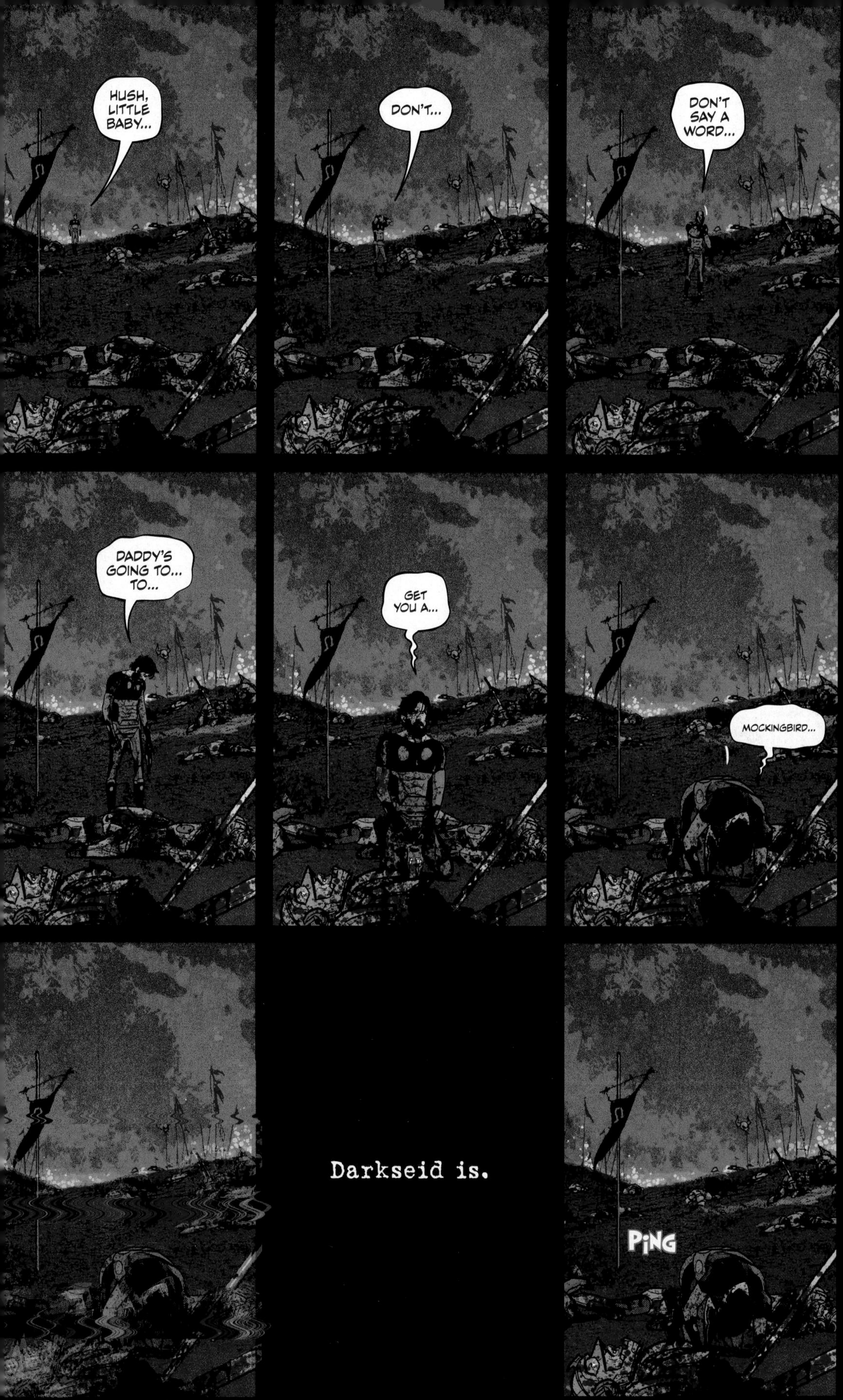
HUSH, LITTLE BABY...
DON'T...
DON'T SAY A WORD...
DADDY'S GOING TO... TO...
GET YOU A...
MOCKINGBIRD...
Darkseid is.
PiNG

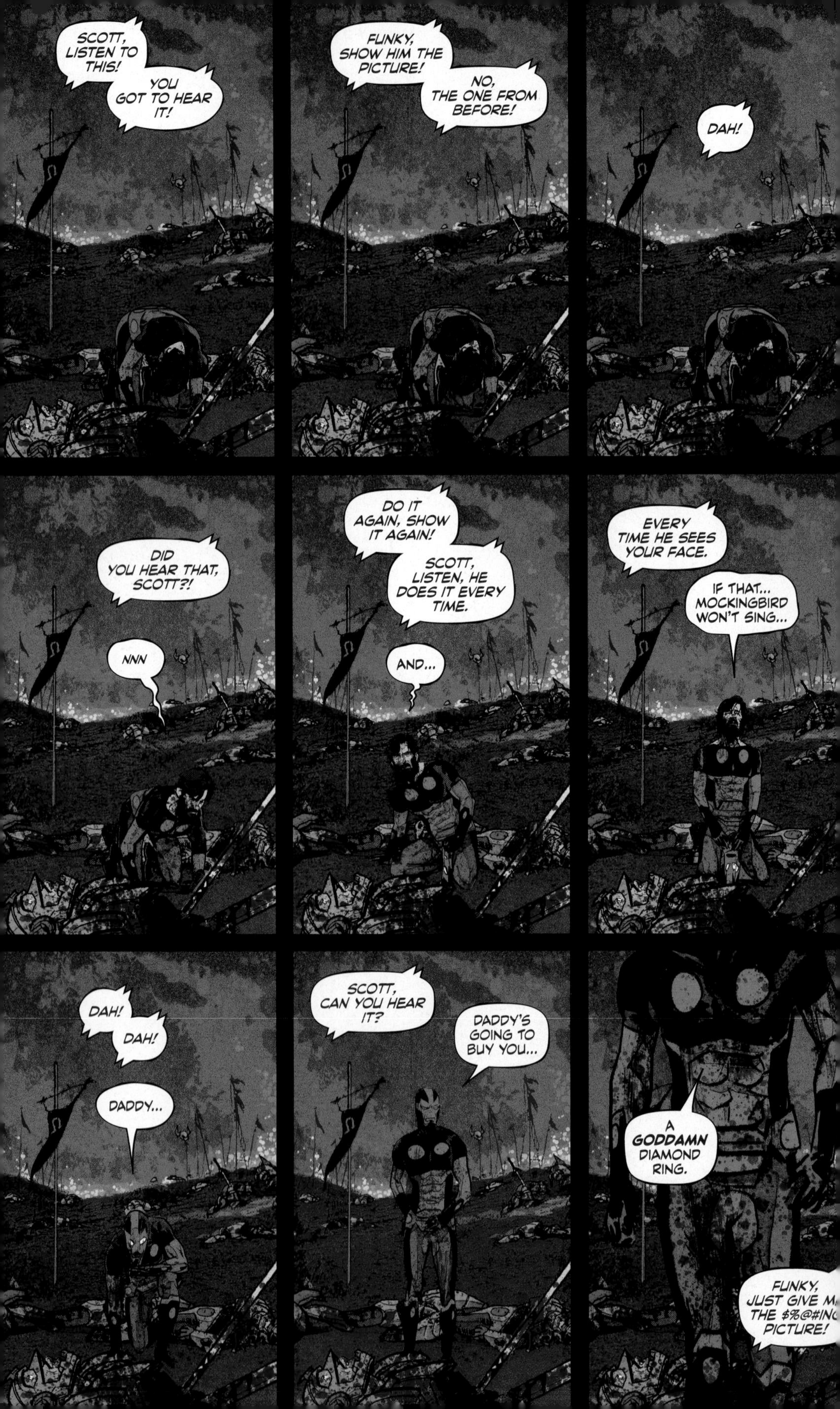

SCOTT, LISTEN TO THIS!
YOU GOT TO HEAR IT!
FUNKY, SHOW HIM THE PICTURE!
NO, THE ONE FROM BEFORE!
DAH!
DID YOU HEAR THAT, SCOTT?!
NNN
DO IT AGAIN, SHOW IT AGAIN!
SCOTT, LISTEN, HE DOES IT EVERY TIME.
AND...
EVERY TIME HE SEES YOUR FACE.
IF THAT... MOCKINGBIRD WON'T SING...
DAH!
DAH!
DADDY...
SCOTT, CAN YOU HEAR IT?
DADDY'S GOING TO BUY YOU...
A **GODDAMN** DIAMOND RING.
FUNKY, JUST GIVE M THE $%@#IN PICTURE!

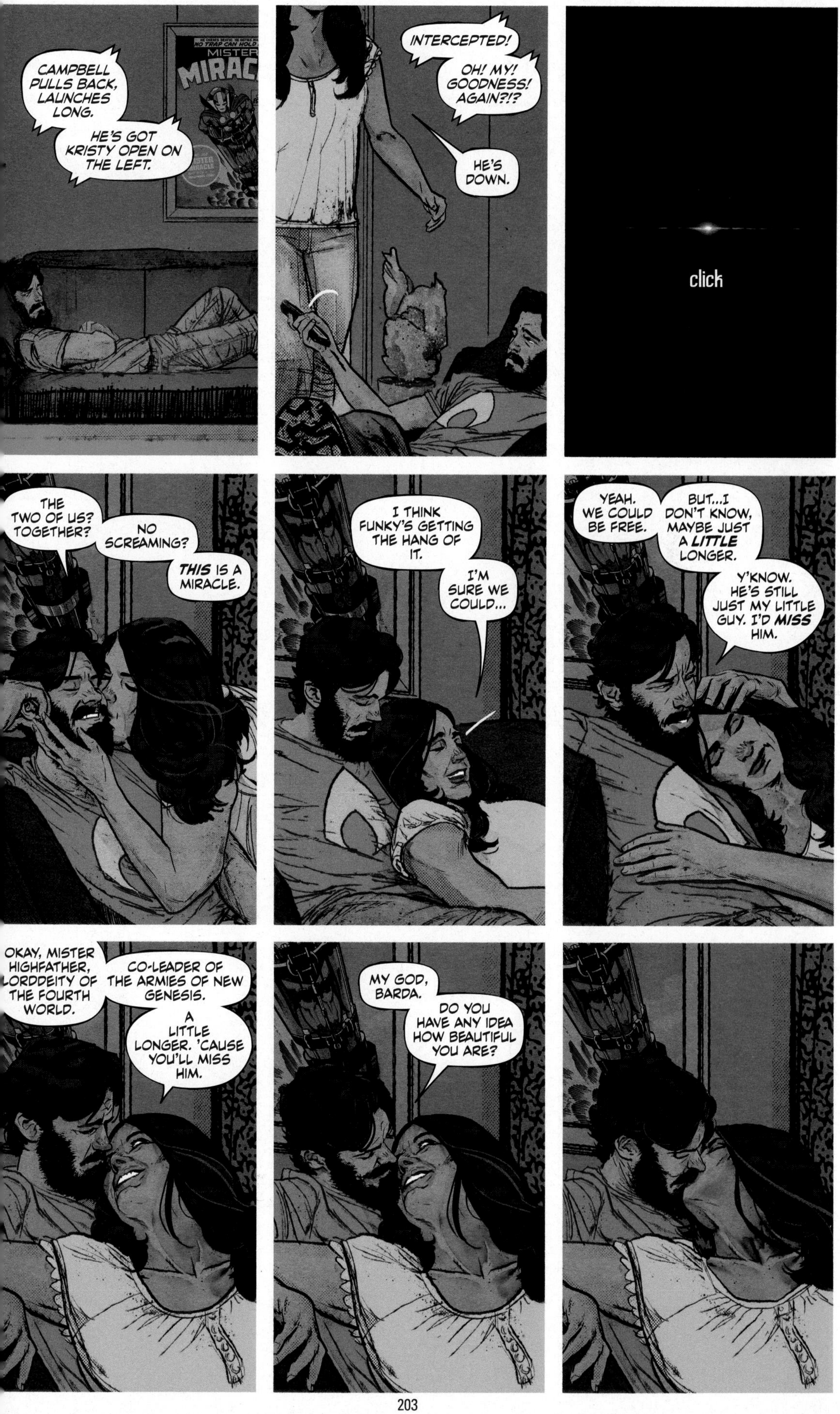

MISTER MIRACLE
NO TRAP CAN HOLD
CAMPBELL PULLS BACK, LAUNCHES LONG.
HE'S GOT KRISTY OPEN ON THE LEFT.
INTERCEPTED!
OH! MY! GOODNESS! AGAIN?!?
HE'S DOWN.
click
THE TWO OF US? TOGETHER?
NO SCREAMING?
THIS IS A MIRACLE.
I THINK FUNKY'S GETTING THE HANG OF IT.
I'M SURE WE COULD...
YEAH. WE COULD BE FREE.
BUT...I DON'T KNOW, MAYBE JUST A LITTLE LONGER.
Y'KNOW. HE'S STILL JUST MY LITTLE GUY. I'D MISS HIM.
OKAY, MISTER HIGHFATHER, LORDDEITY OF THE FOURTH WORLD.
CO-LEADER OF THE ARMIES OF NEW GENESIS.
A LITTLE LONGER. 'CAUSE YOU'LL MISS HIM.
MY GOD, BARDA.
DO YOU HAVE ANY IDEA HOW BEAUTIFUL YOU ARE?

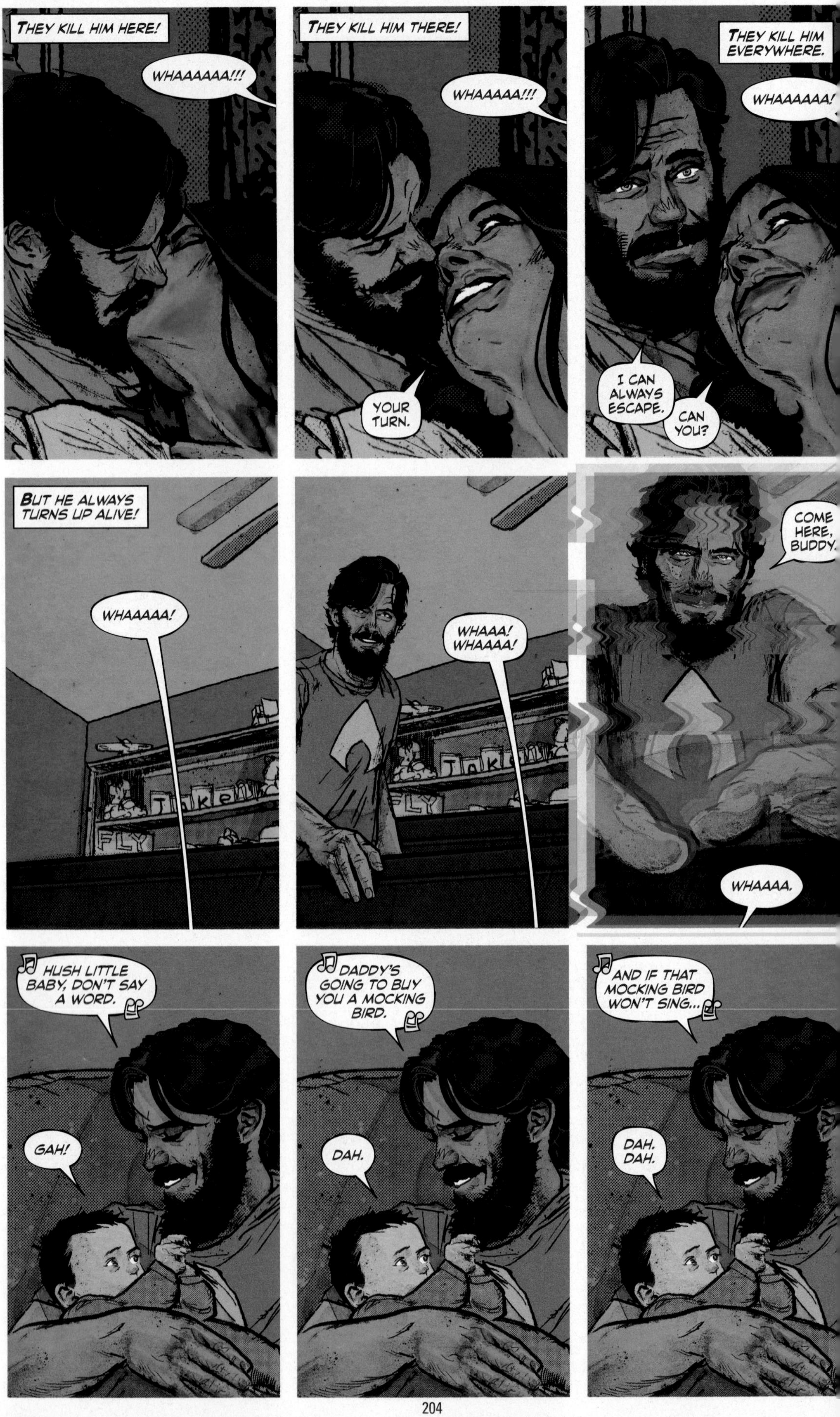

THEY KILL HIM HERE!
WHAAAAAA!!!
THEY KILL HIM THERE!
WHAAAAAA!!!
YOUR TURN.
THEY KILL HIM EVERYWHERE.
WHAAAAAAA!
I CAN ALWAYS ESCAPE.
CAN YOU?
BUT HE ALWAYS TURNS UP ALIVE!
WHAAAAAA!
WHAAA! WHAAAA!
COME HERE, BUDDY.
WHAAAA.
HUSH LITTLE BABY, DON'T SAY A WORD.
GAH!
DADDY'S GOING TO BUY YOU A MOCKING BIRD.
DAH.
AND IF THAT MOCKING BIRD WON'T SING...
DAH. DAH.

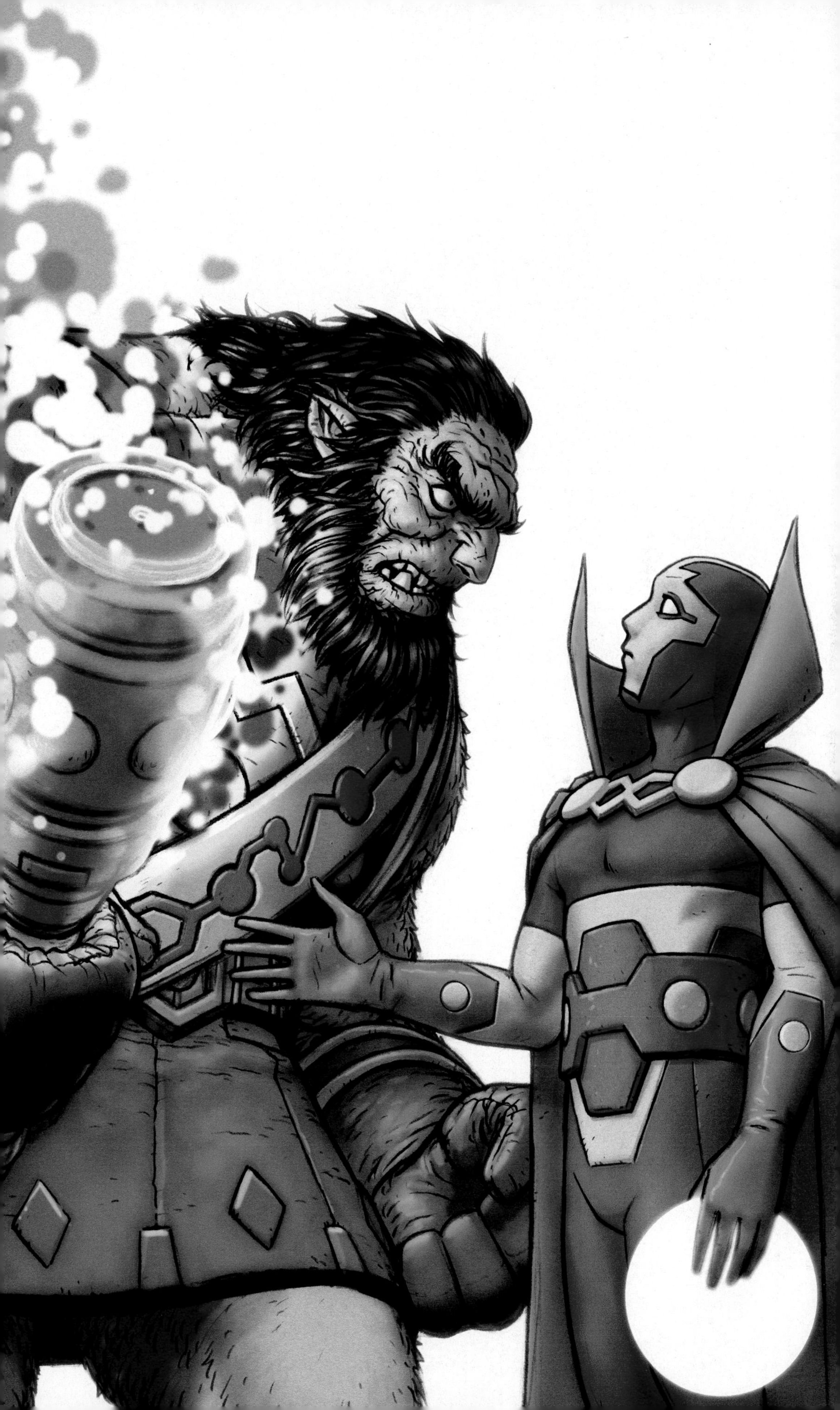

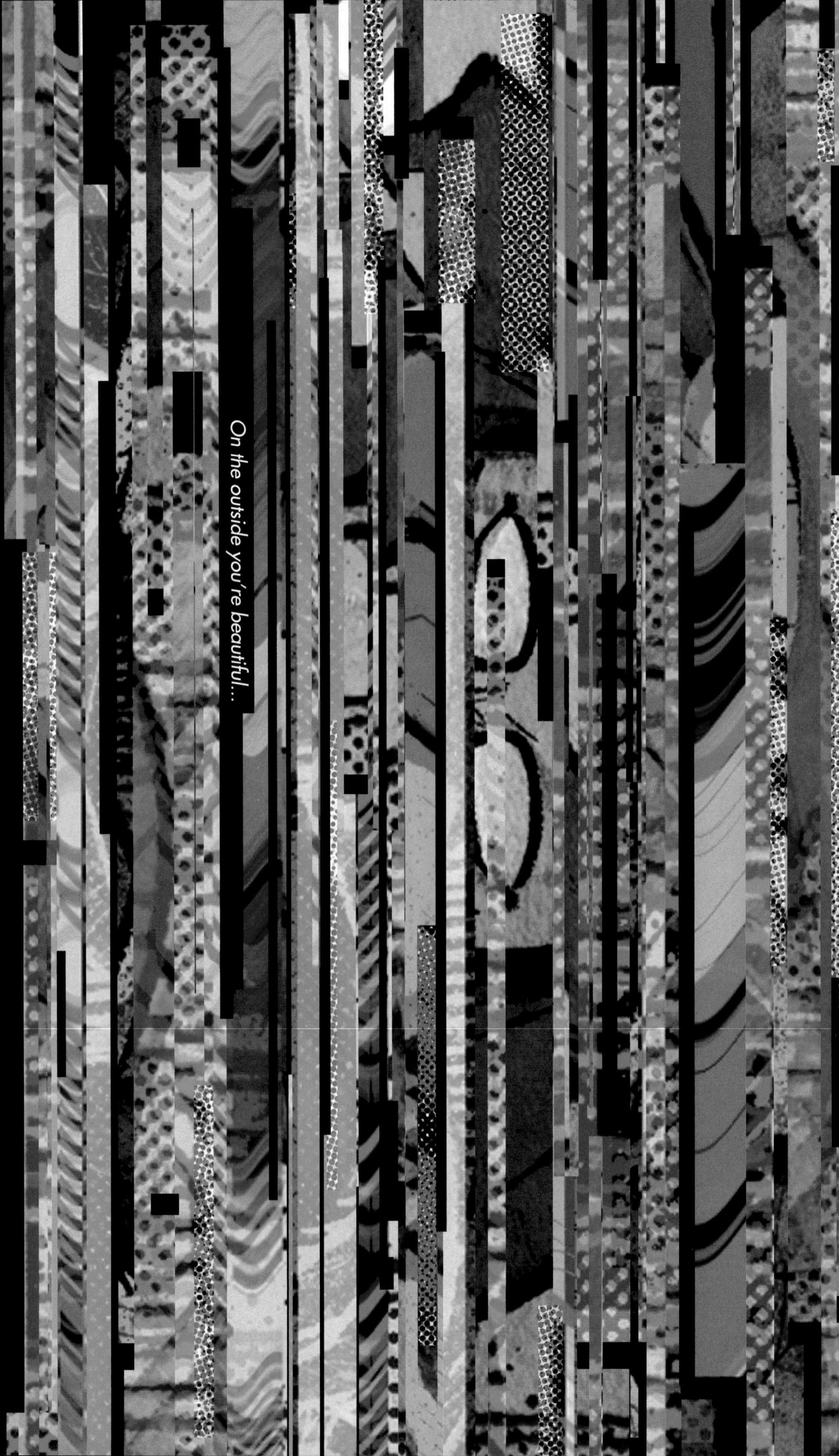
On the outside you're beautiful...

AY 1.

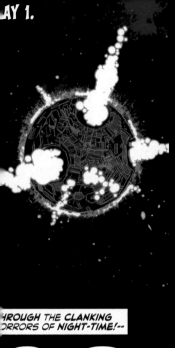

THE HEART OF APOKOLIPS LIES BEYOND THE GREYBORDERS--

ACROSS THE DARKENING ROAD TO LONGSHADOW!--

HROUGH THE CLANKING ORRORS OF NIGHT-TIME!--

COME AND STAY.

COME AND PLAY.

NEVER EVER GO AWAY.

AND RISES WHITE HOT--

AAAAAAA!!!

AT THE RAGING, HISSING INFERNOS OF THE PLANETARY FIRE-PITS!

HE RAW AND DIRTY EDGE FROM HICH GREAT DARKSEID DRAWS MAMMOTH POWER!

--AND FEEDS UPON A MIGHTY FEAR.

IS THERE A RESTROOM?

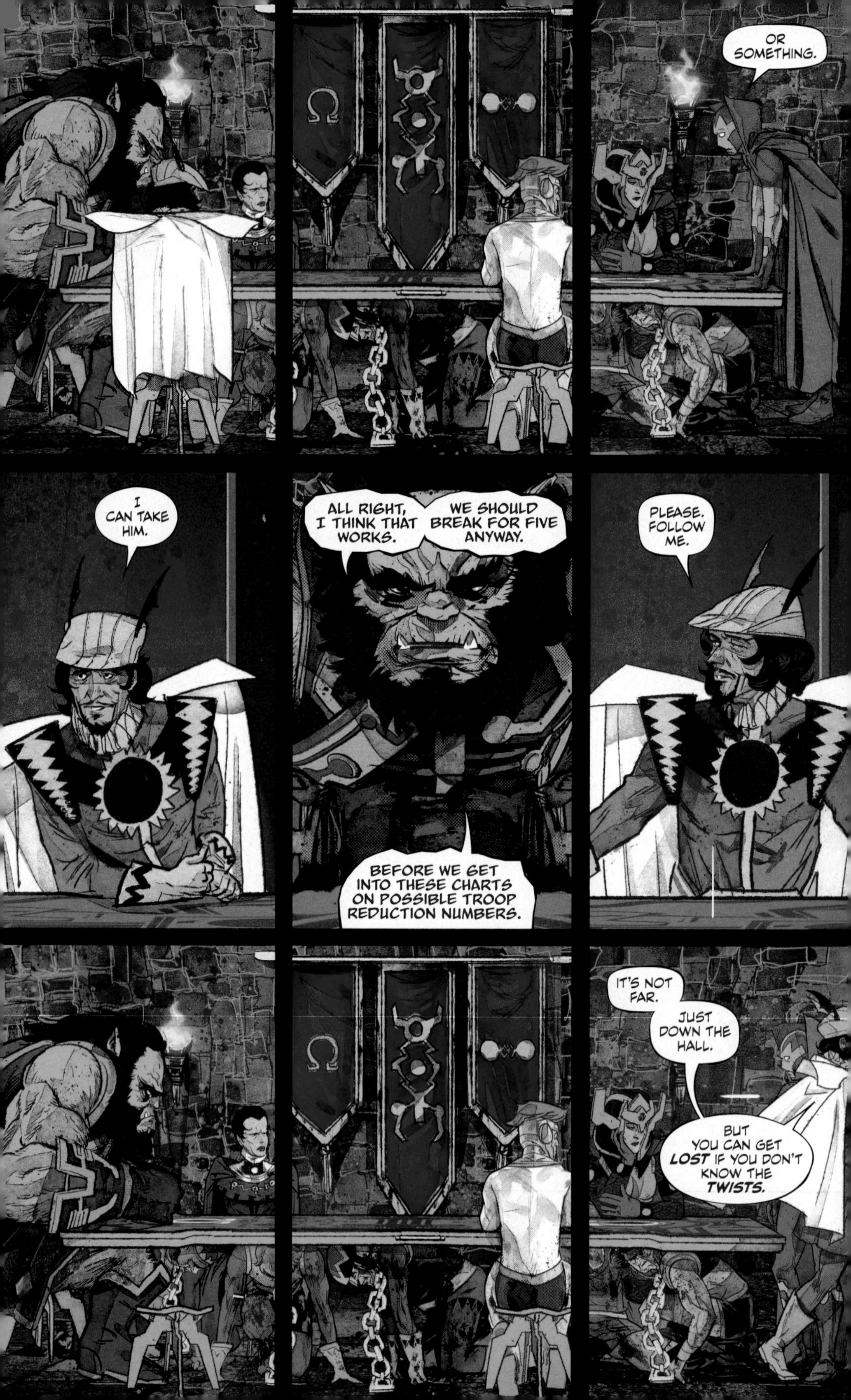
OR SOMETHING.
I CAN TAKE HIM.
ALL RIGHT, I THINK THAT WORKS.
WE SHOULD BREAK FOR FIVE ANYWAY.
BEFORE WE GET INTO THESE CHARTS ON POSSIBLE TROOP REDUCTION NUMBERS.
PLEASE. FOLLOW ME.
IT'S NOT FAR.
JUST DOWN THE HALL.
BUT YOU CAN GET LOST IF YOU DON'T KNOW THE TWISTS.

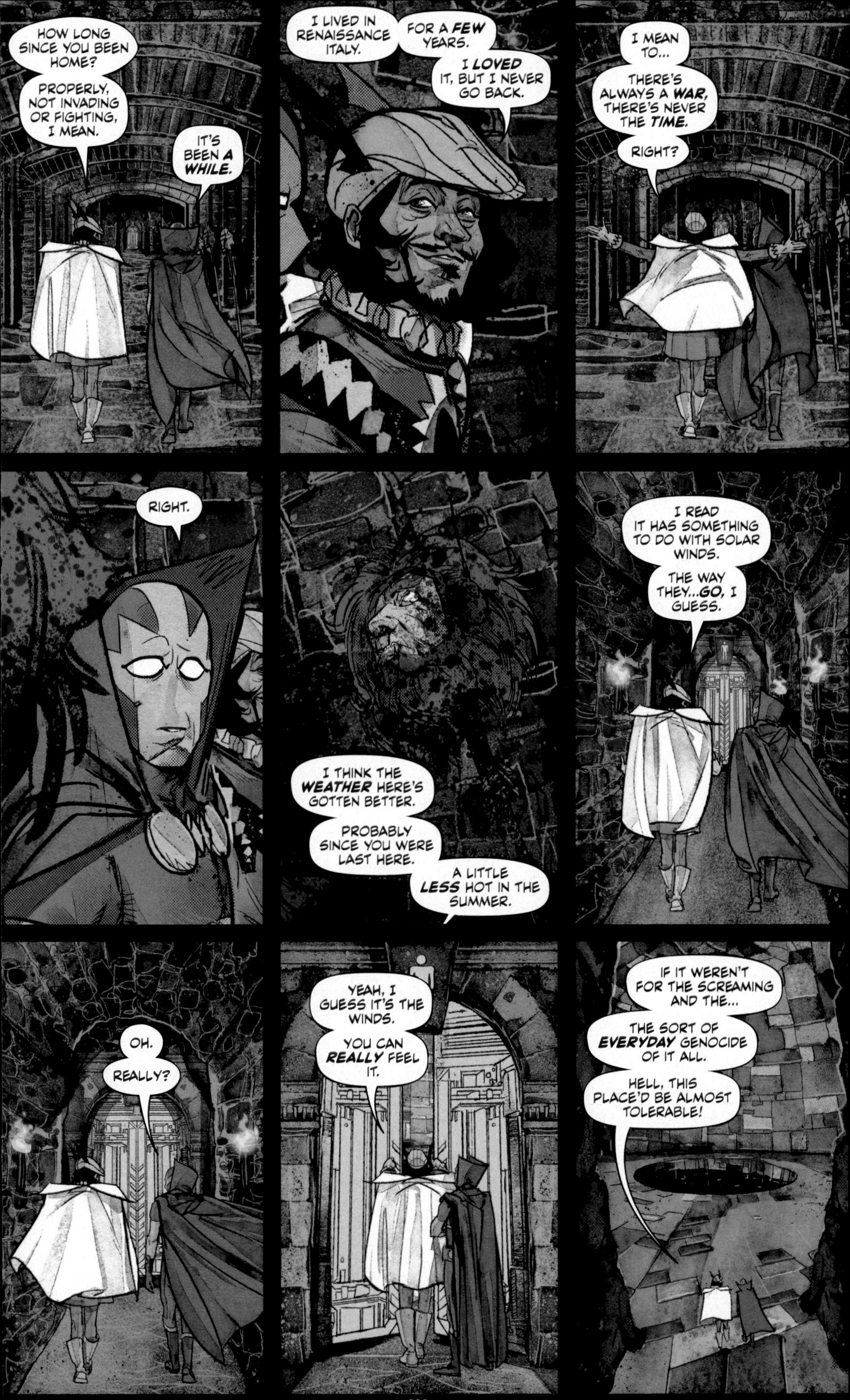

HOW LONG SINCE YOU BEEN HOME?
PROPERLY, NOT INVADING OR FIGHTING, I MEAN.
IT'S BEEN A WHILE.
I LIVED IN RENAISSANCE ITALY.
FOR A FEW YEARS.
I LOVED IT, BUT I NEVER GO BACK.
I MEAN TO...
THERE'S ALWAYS A WAR, THERE'S NEVER THE TIME.
RIGHT?
RIGHT.
I THINK THE WEATHER HERE'S GOTTEN BETTER.
PROBABLY SINCE YOU WERE LAST HERE.
A LITTLE LESS HOT IN THE SUMMER.
I READ IT HAS SOMETHING TO DO WITH SOLAR WINDS.
THE WAY THEY...GO, I GUESS.
OH.
REALLY?
YEAH, I GUESS IT'S THE WINDS.
YOU CAN REALLY FEEL IT.
IF IT WEREN'T FOR THE SCREAMING AND THE...
THE SORT OF EVERYDAY GENOCIDE OF IT ALL.
HELL, THIS PLACE'D BE ALMOST TOLERABLE!

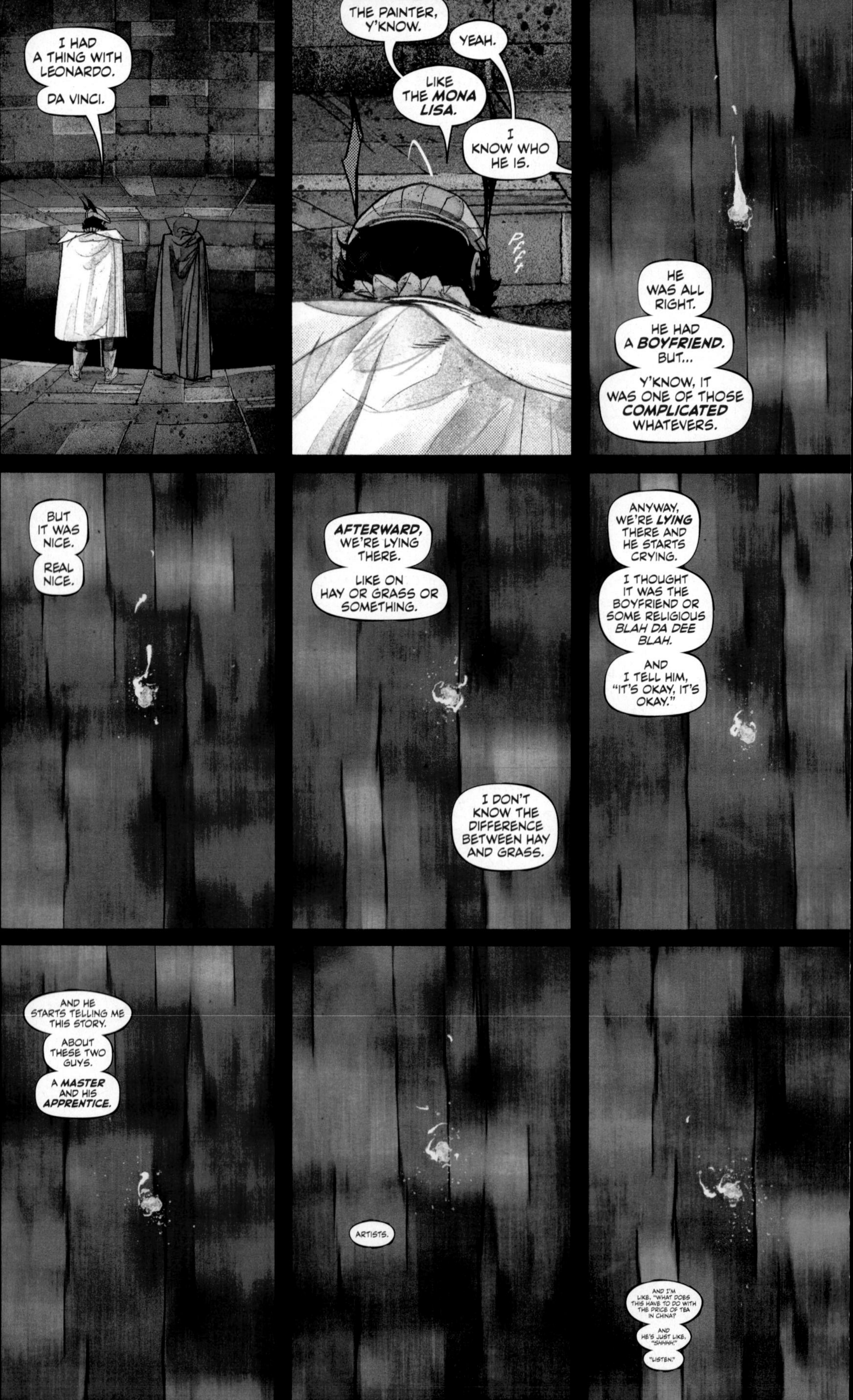
I HAD A THING WITH LEONARDO.
DA VINCI.
THE PAINTER, Y'KNOW.
YEAH.
LIKE THE MONA LISA.
I KNOW WHO HE IS.
Pfft
HE WAS ALL RIGHT.
HE HAD A BOYFRIEND. BUT...
Y'KNOW, IT WAS ONE OF THOSE COMPLICATED WHATEVERS.
BUT IT WAS NICE.
REAL NICE.
AFTERWARD, WE'RE LYING THERE.
LIKE ON HAY OR GRASS OR SOMETHING.
I DON'T KNOW THE DIFFERENCE BETWEEN HAY AND GRASS.
ANYWAY, WE'RE LYING THERE AND HE STARTS CRYING.
I THOUGHT IT WAS THE BOYFRIEND OR SOME RELIGIOUS BLAH DA DEE BLAH.
AND I TELL HIM, "IT'S OKAY, IT'S OKAY."
AND HE STARTS TELLING ME THIS STORY.
ABOUT THESE TWO GUYS.
A MASTER AND HIS APPRENTICE.
ARTISTS.
AND I'M LIKE, "WHAT DOES THIS HAVE TO DO WITH THE PRICE OF TEA IN CHINA?
AND HE'S JUST LIKE, "SHHHH."
"LISTEN."

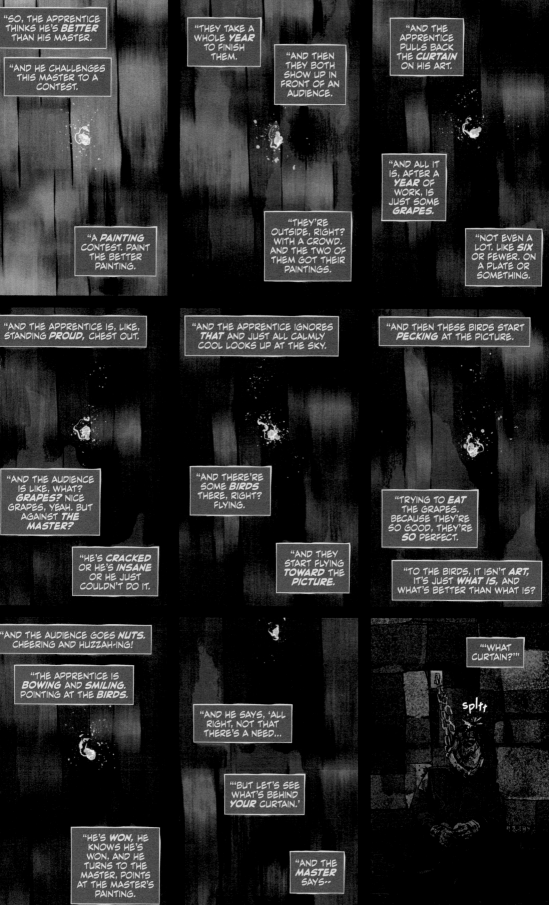

"SO, THE APPRENTICE THINKS HE'S *BETTER* THAN HIS MASTER.

"AND HE CHALLENGES THIS MASTER TO A CONTEST.

"A *PAINTING* CONTEST. PAINT THE BETTER PAINTING.

"THEY TAKE A WHOLE *YEAR* TO FINISH THEM.

"AND THEN THEY BOTH SHOW UP IN FRONT OF AN AUDIENCE.

"THEY'RE OUTSIDE, RIGHT? WITH A CROWD. AND THE TWO OF THEM GOT THEIR PAINTINGS.

"AND THE APPRENTICE PULLS BACK THE *CURTAIN* ON HIS ART.

"AND ALL IT IS, AFTER A *YEAR* OF WORK, IS JUST SOME *GRAPES.*

"NOT EVEN A LOT. LIKE *SIX* OR FEWER. ON A PLATE OR SOMETHING.

"AND THE APPRENTICE IS, LIKE, STANDING *PROUD,* CHEST OUT.

"AND THE AUDIENCE IS LIKE, WHAT? *GRAPES?* NICE GRAPES, YEAH. BUT AGAINST *THE MASTER?*

"HE'S *CRACKED* OR HE'S *INSANE* OR HE JUST COULDN'T DO IT.

"AND THE APPRENTICE IGNORES *THAT* AND JUST ALL CALMLY COOL LOOKS UP AT THE SKY.

"AND THERE'RE SOME *BIRDS* THERE, RIGHT? FLYING.

"AND THEY START FLYING *TOWARD* THE PICTURE.

"AND THEN THESE BIRDS START *PECKING* AT THE PICTURE.

"TRYING TO *EAT* THE GRAPES. BECAUSE THEY'RE SO GOOD, THEY'RE *SO* PERFECT.

"TO THE BIRDS, IT ISN'T *ART,* IT'S JUST *WHAT IS,* AND WHAT'S BETTER THAN WHAT IS?

"AND THE AUDIENCE GOES *NUTS.* CHEERING AND HUZZAH-ING!

"THE APPRENTICE IS *BOWING* AND *SMILING.* POINTING AT THE *BIRDS.*

"HE'S *WON,* HE KNOWS HE'S WON, AND HE TURNS TO THE MASTER, POINTS AT THE MASTER'S PAINTING.

"AND HE SAYS, 'ALL RIGHT, NOT THAT THERE'S A NEED...

"'BUT LET'S SEE WHAT'S BEHIND *YOUR* CURTAIN.'

"AND THE *MASTER* SAYS--

"'WHAT CURTAIN?'"

spltt

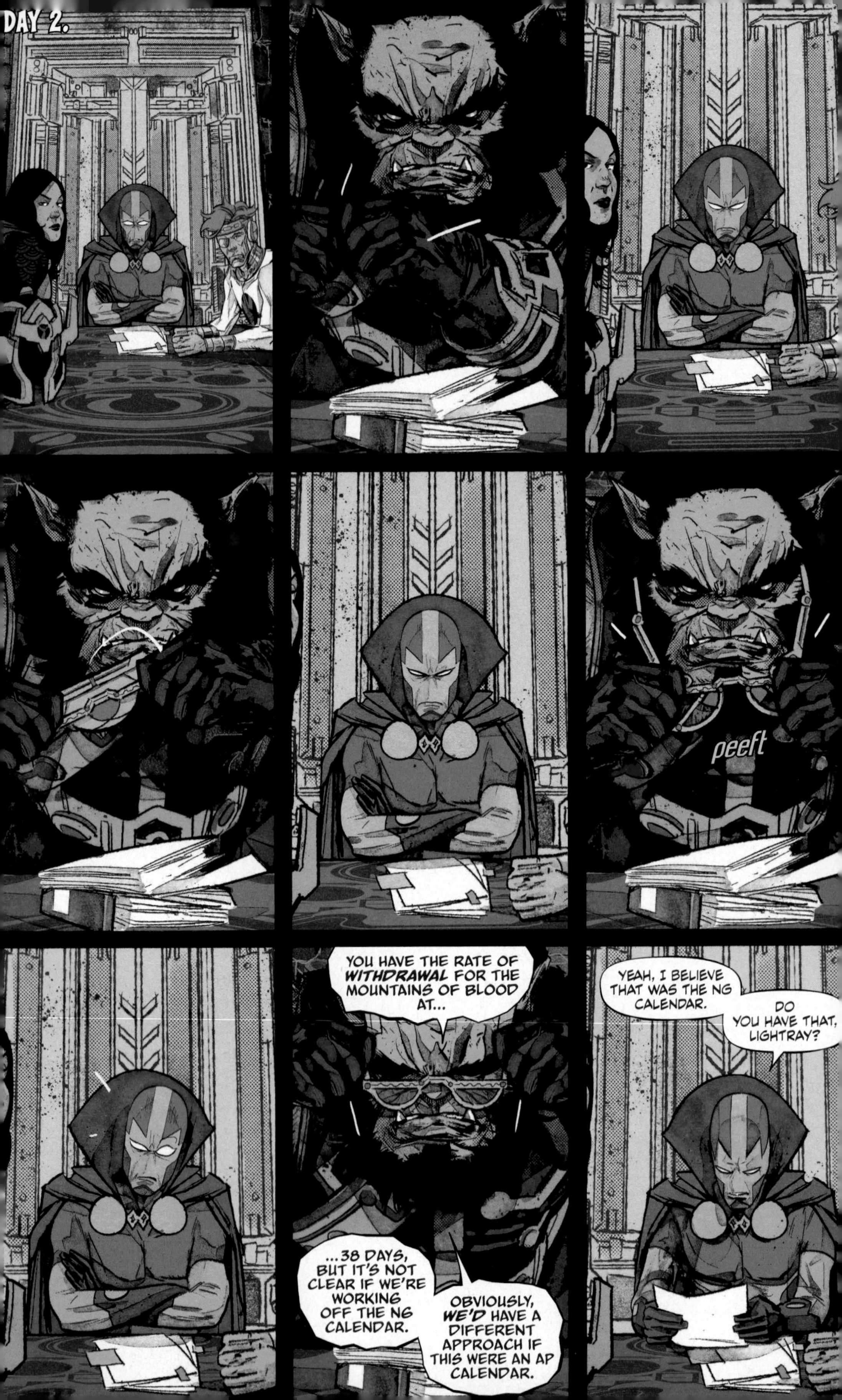
DAY 2.
peeft
YOU HAVE THE RATE OF WITHDRAWAL FOR THE MOUNTAINS OF BLOOD AT...
...38 DAYS, BUT IT'S NOT CLEAR IF WE'RE WORKING OFF THE NG CALENDAR.
OBVIOUSLY, WE'D HAVE A DIFFERENT APPROACH IF THIS WERE AN AP CALENDAR.
YEAH, I BELIEVE THAT WAS THE NG CALENDAR.
DO YOU HAVE THAT, LIGHTRAY?

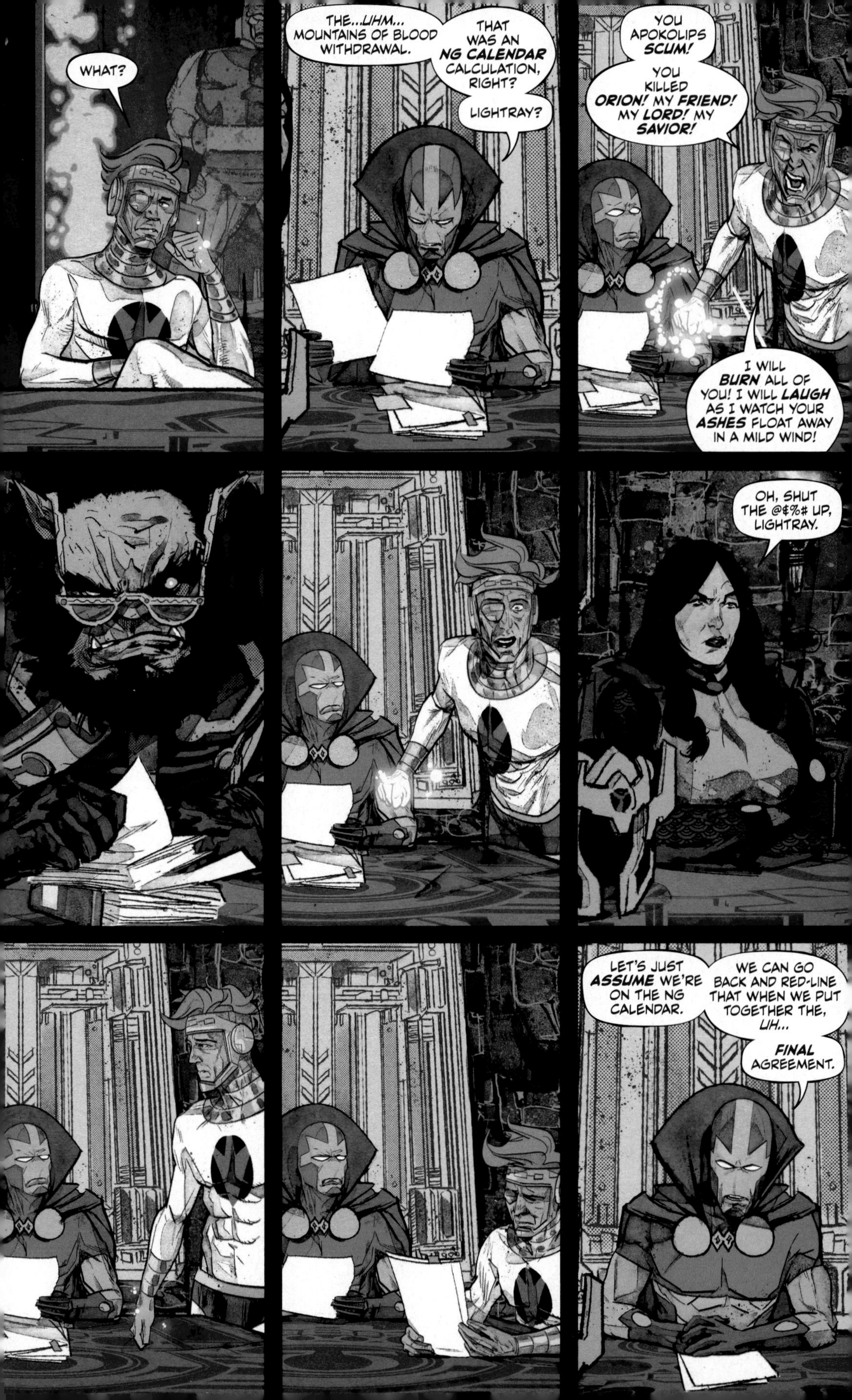
WHAT?
THE...UHM... MOUNTAINS OF BLOOD WITHDRAWAL.
THAT WAS AN NG CALENDAR CALCULATION, RIGHT?
LIGHTRAY?
YOU APOKOLIPS SCUM!
YOU KILLED ORION! MY FRIEND! MY LORD! MY SAVIOR!
I WILL BURN ALL OF YOU! I WILL LAUGH AS I WATCH YOUR ASHES FLOAT AWAY IN A MILD WIND!
OH, SHUT THE @¢%# UP, LIGHTRAY.
LET'S JUST ASSUME WE'RE ON THE NG CALENDAR.
WE CAN GO BACK AND RED-LINE THAT WHEN WE PUT TOGETHER THE, UH...
FINAL AGREEMENT.

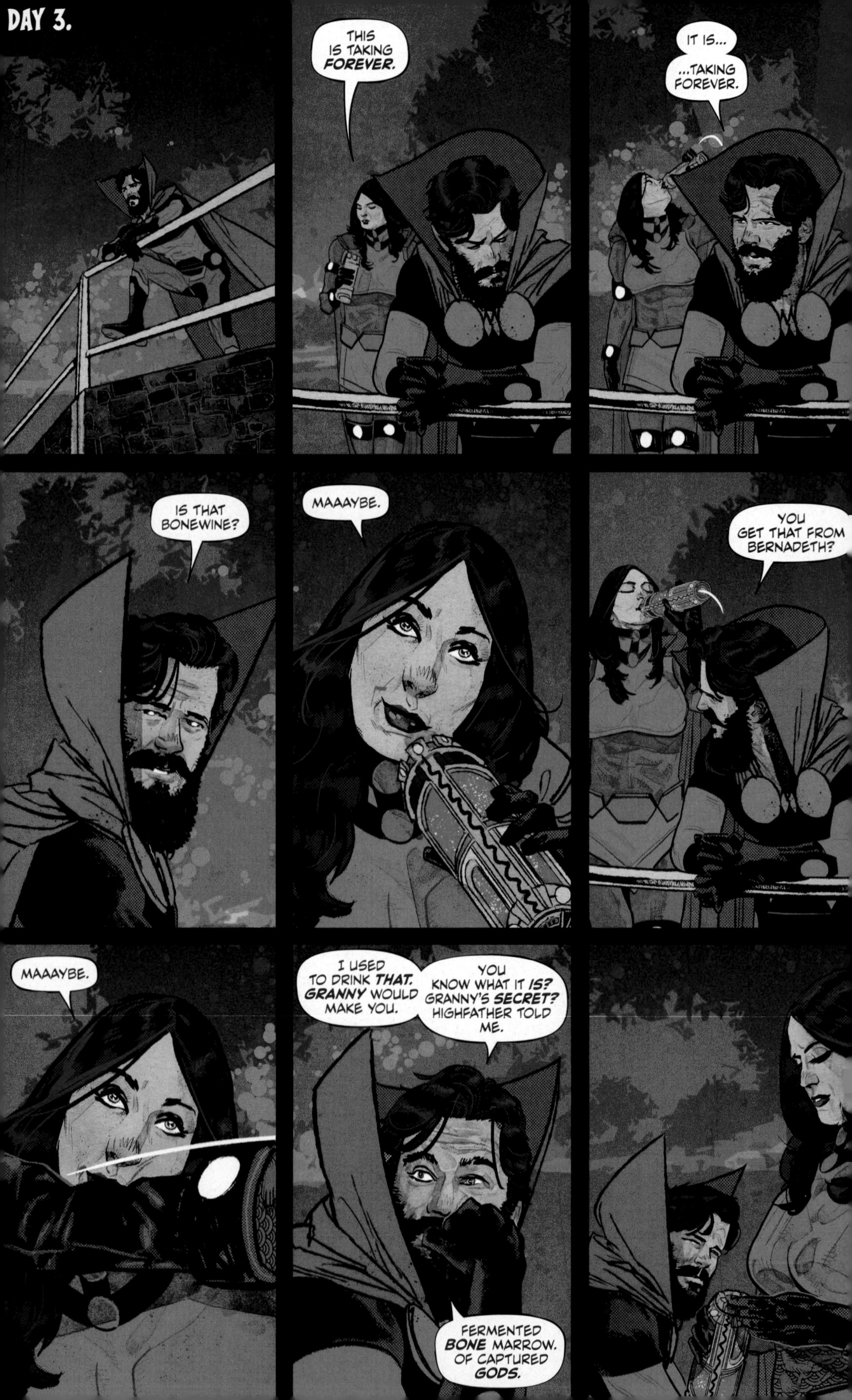
DAY 3.
THIS IS TAKING FOREVER.
IT IS...
...TAKING FOREVER.
IS THAT BONEWINE?
MAAAYBE.
YOU GET THAT FROM BERNADETH?
MAAAYBE.
I USED TO DRINK THAT. GRANNY WOULD MAKE YOU.
YOU KNOW WHAT IT IS? GRANNY'S SECRET? HIGHFATHER TOLD ME.
FERMENTED BONE MARROW. OF CAPTURED GODS.

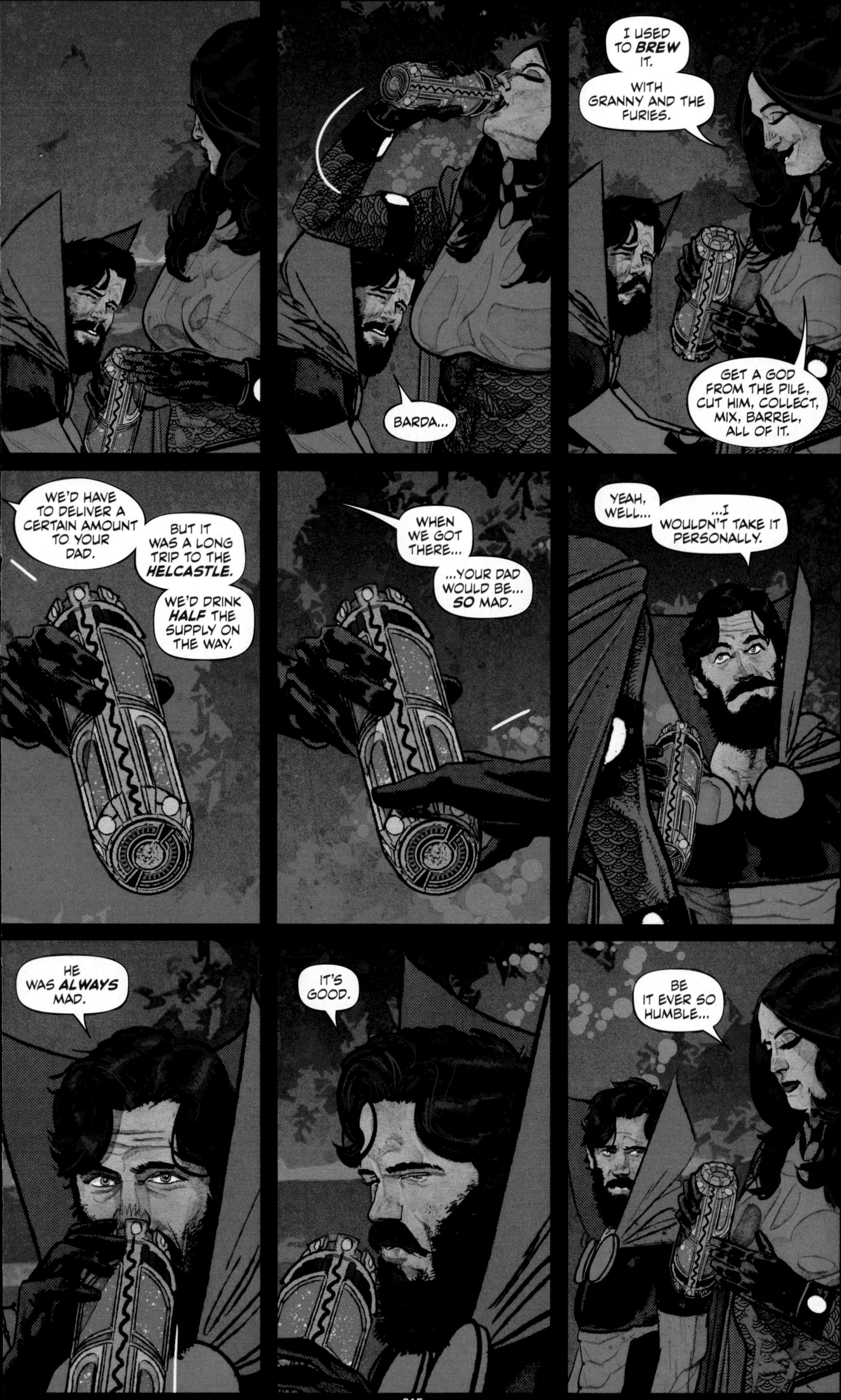
BARDA...
I USED TO BREW IT.
WITH GRANNY AND THE FURIES.
GET A GOD FROM THE PILE, CUT HIM, COLLECT, MIX, BARREL, ALL OF IT.
WE'D HAVE TO DELIVER A CERTAIN AMOUNT TO YOUR DAD.
BUT IT WAS A LONG TRIP TO THE HELCASTLE.
WE'D DRINK HALF THE SUPPLY ON THE WAY.
WHEN WE GOT THERE...
...YOUR DAD WOULD BE... SO MAD.
YEAH, WELL...
...I WOULDN'T TAKE IT PERSONALLY.
HE WAS ALWAYS MAD.
IT'S GOOD.
BE IT EVER SO HUMBLE...

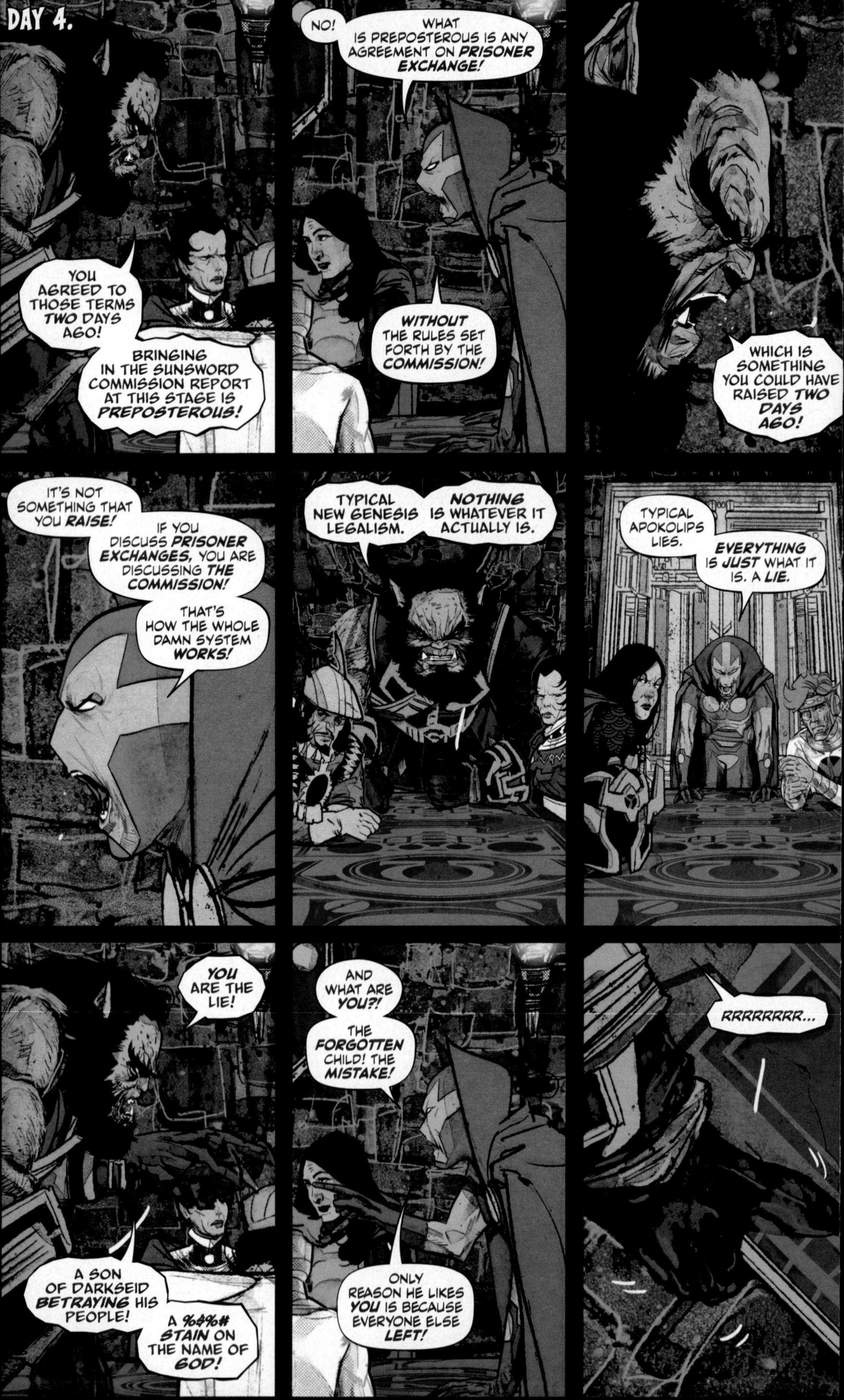
DAY 4.
YOU AGREED TO THOSE TERMS TWO DAYS AGO!
BRINGING IN THE SUNSWORD COMMISSION REPORT AT THIS STAGE IS PREPOSTEROUS!
NO!
WHAT IS PREPOSTEROUS IS ANY AGREEMENT ON PRISONER EXCHANGE!
WITHOUT THE RULES SET FORTH BY THE COMMISSION!
WHICH IS SOMETHING YOU COULD HAVE RAISED TWO DAYS AGO!
IT'S NOT SOMETHING THAT YOU RAISE!
IF YOU DISCUSS PRISONER EXCHANGES, YOU ARE DISCUSSING THE COMMISSION!
THAT'S HOW THE WHOLE DAMN SYSTEM WORKS!
TYPICAL NEW GENESIS LEGALISM.
NOTHING IS WHATEVER IT ACTUALLY IS.
TYPICAL APOKOLIPS LIES.
EVERYTHING IS JUST WHAT IT IS. A LIE.
YOU ARE THE LIE!
A SON OF DARKSEID BETRAYING HIS PEOPLE!
A %$%# STAIN ON THE NAME OF GOD!
AND WHAT ARE YOU?!
THE FORGOTTEN CHILD! THE MISTAKE!
ONLY REASON HE LIKES YOU IS BECAUSE EVERYONE ELSE LEFT!
RRRRRRRR...

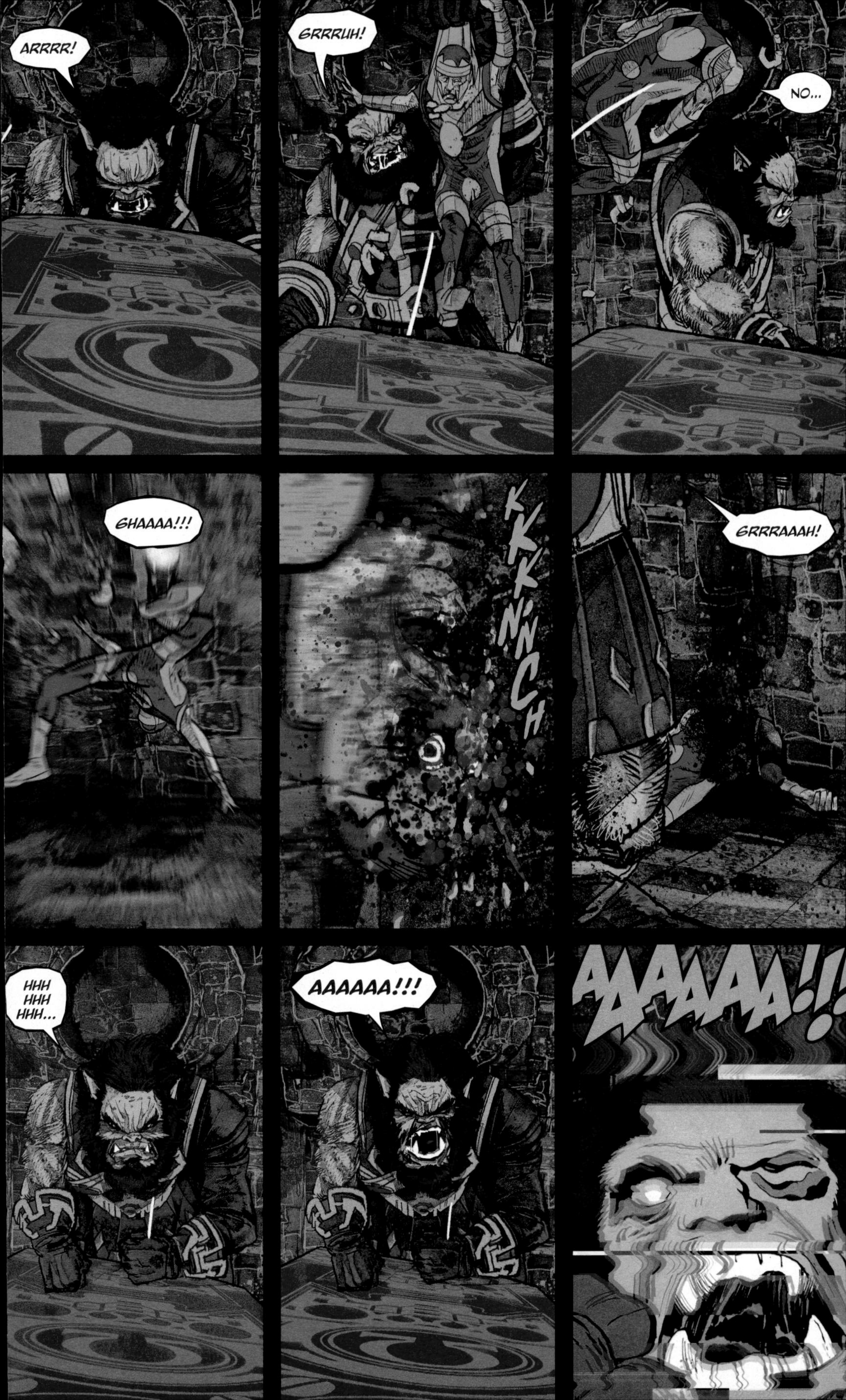
ARRRR!
GRRRUH!
NO...
GHAAAA!!!
KKKNNCH
GRRRAAAH!
HHH HHH HHH...
AAAAAA!!!
AAAAAA!!!

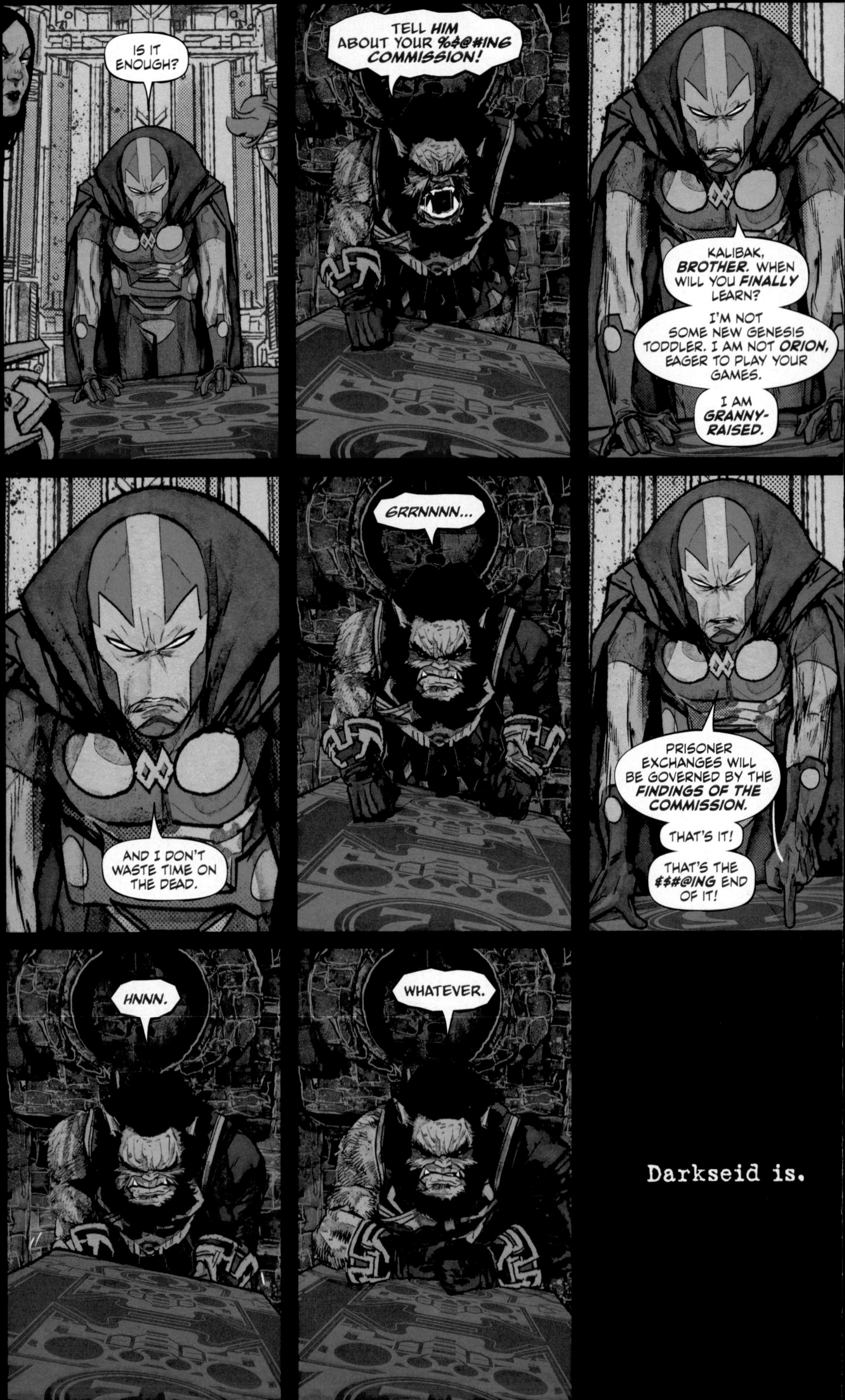
IS IT ENOUGH?
TELL HIM ABOUT YOUR %$@#ING COMMISSION!
KALIBAK, BROTHER. WHEN WILL YOU FINALLY LEARN?
I'M NOT SOME NEW GENESIS TODDLER. I AM NOT ORION, EAGER TO PLAY YOUR GAMES.
I AM GRANNY-RAISED.
AND I DON'T WASTE TIME ON THE DEAD.
GRRNNNN...
PRISONER EXCHANGES WILL BE GOVERNED BY THE FINDINGS OF THE COMMISSION.
THAT'S IT!
THAT'S THE $$#@ING END OF IT!
HNNN.
WHATEVER.
Darkseid is.

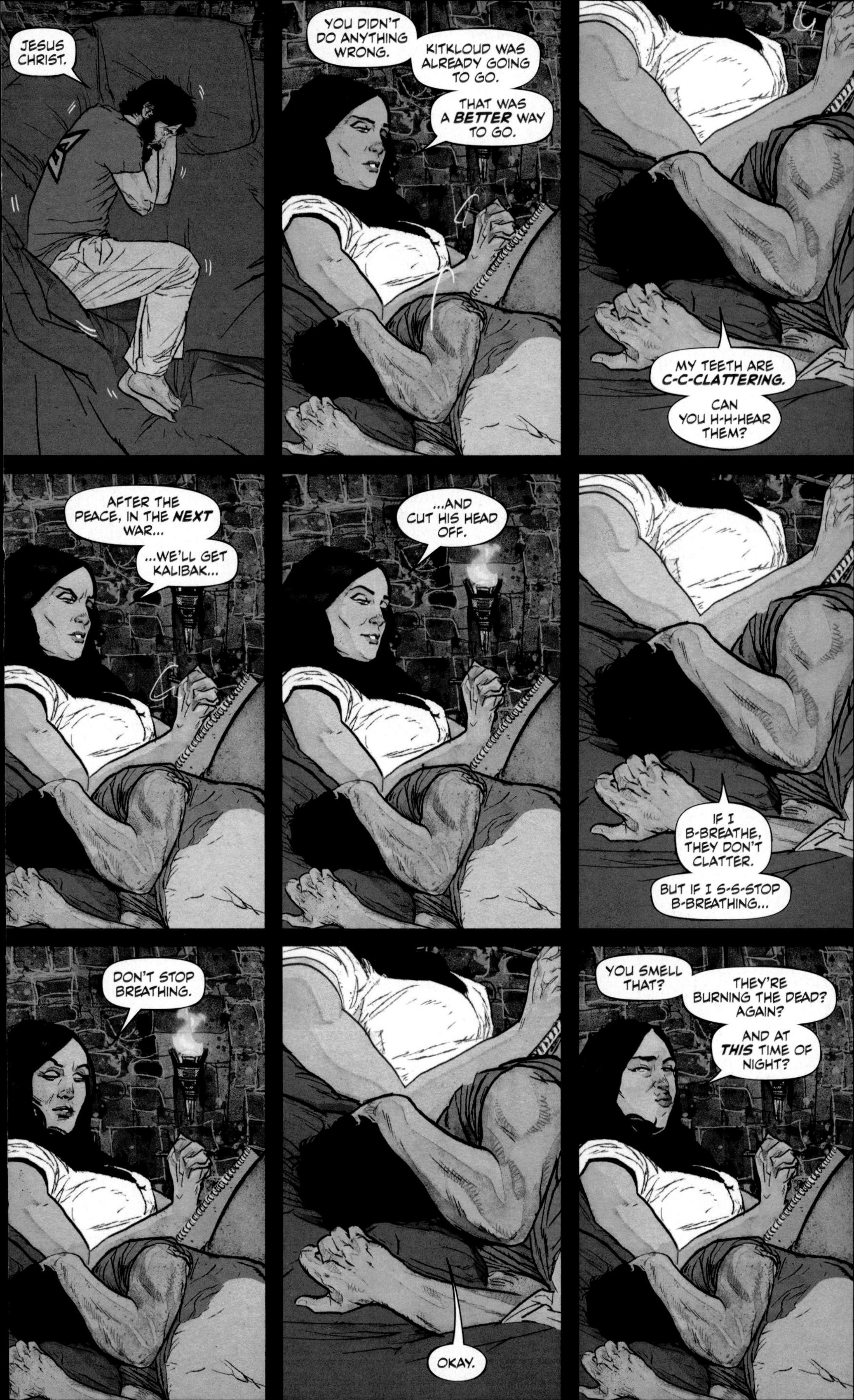

JESUS CHRIST.
YOU DIDN'T DO ANYTHING WRONG.
KITKLOUD WAS ALREADY GOING TO GO.
THAT WAS A BETTER WAY TO GO.
MY TEETH ARE C-C-CLATTERING.
CAN YOU H-H-HEAR THEM?
AFTER THE PEACE, IN THE NEXT WAR...
...WE'LL GET KALIBAK...
...AND CUT HIS HEAD OFF.
IF I B-BREATHE, THEY DON'T CLATTER.
BUT IF I S-S-STOP B-BREATHING...
DON'T STOP BREATHING.
OKAY.
YOU SMELL THAT?
THEY'RE BURNING THE DEAD? AGAIN?
AND AT THIS TIME OF NIGHT?

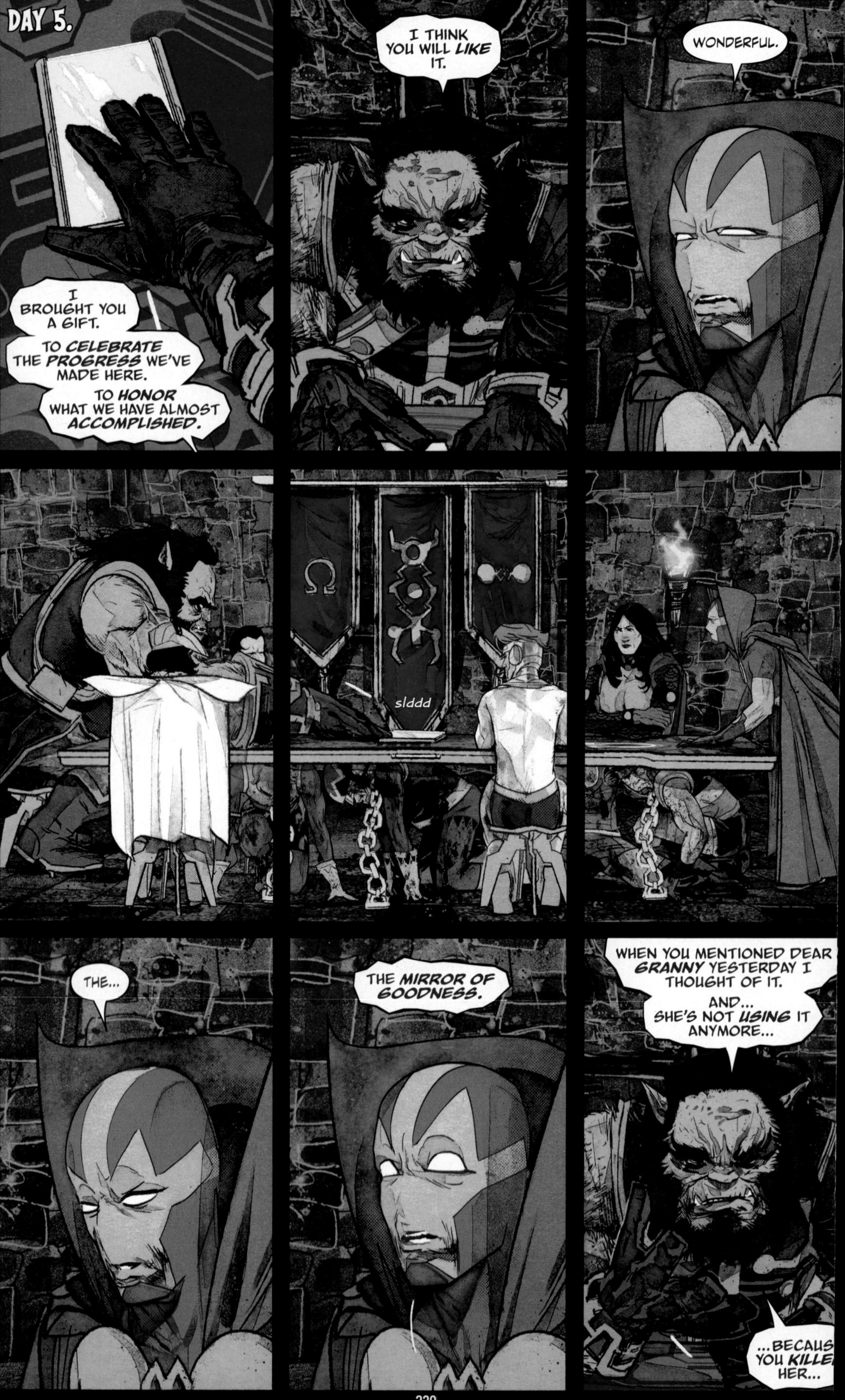
DAY 5.
I BROUGHT YOU A GIFT.
TO CELEBRATE THE PROGRESS WE'VE MADE HERE.
TO HONOR WHAT WE HAVE ALMOST ACCOMPLISHED.
I THINK YOU WILL LIKE IT.
WONDERFUL.
slddd
THE...
THE MIRROR OF GOODNESS.
WHEN YOU MENTIONED DEAR GRANNY YESTERDAY I THOUGHT OF IT.
AND... SHE'S NOT USING IT ANYMORE...
...BECAUS YOU KILLE HER...

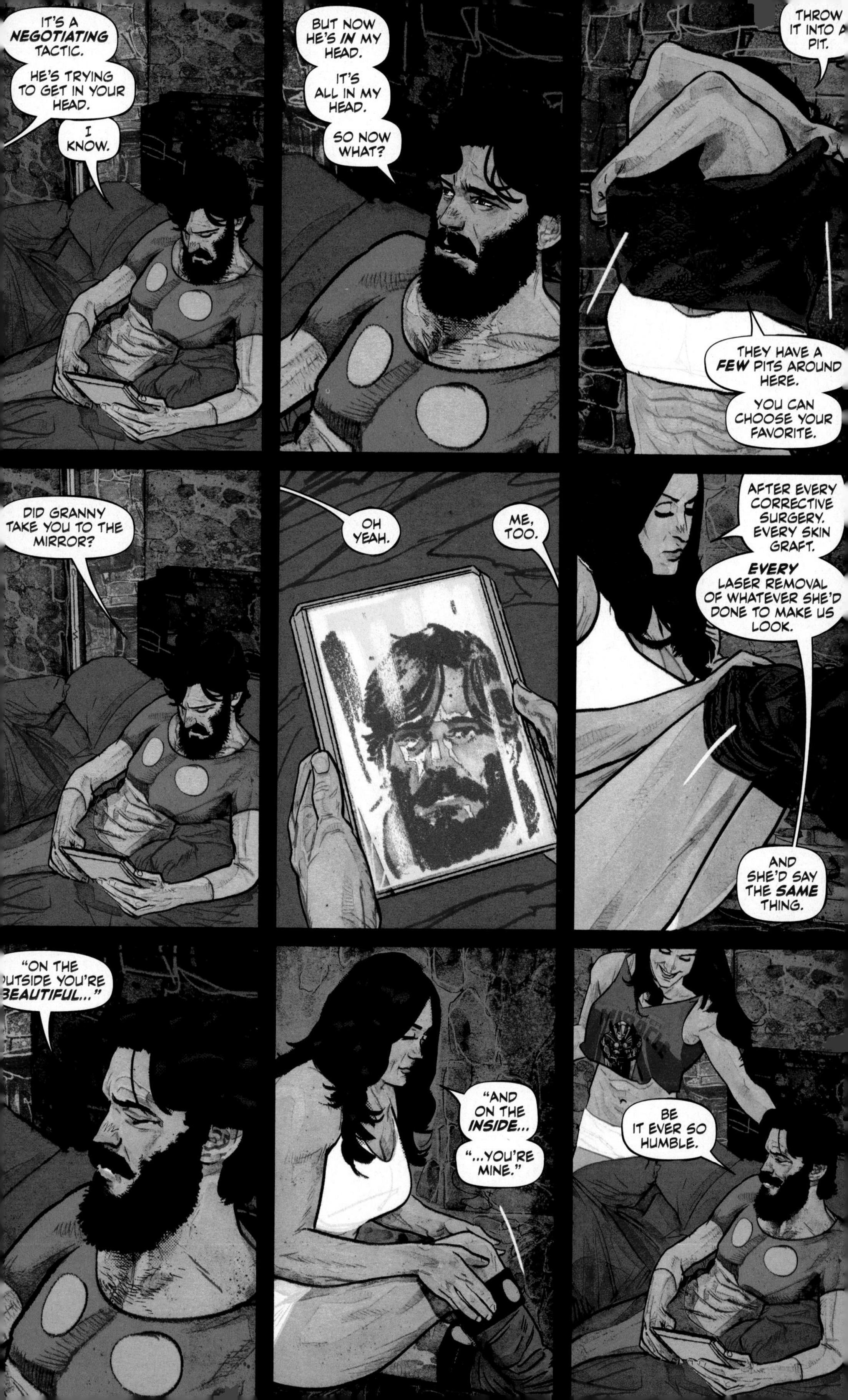
IT'S A NEGOTIATING TACTIC.
HE'S TRYING TO GET IN YOUR HEAD.
I KNOW.
BUT NOW HE'S IN MY HEAD.
IT'S ALL IN MY HEAD.
SO NOW WHAT?
THROW IT INTO A PIT.
THEY HAVE A FEW PITS AROUND HERE.
YOU CAN CHOOSE YOUR FAVORITE.
DID GRANNY TAKE YOU TO THE MIRROR?
OH YEAH.
ME, TOO.
AFTER EVERY CORRECTIVE SURGERY. EVERY SKIN GRAFT.
EVERY LASER REMOVAL OF WHATEVER SHE'D DONE TO MAKE US LOOK.
AND SHE'D SAY THE SAME THING.
"ON THE OUTSIDE YOU'RE BEAUTIFUL..."
"AND ON THE INSIDE...
"...YOU'RE MINE."
BE IT EVER SO HUMBLE.

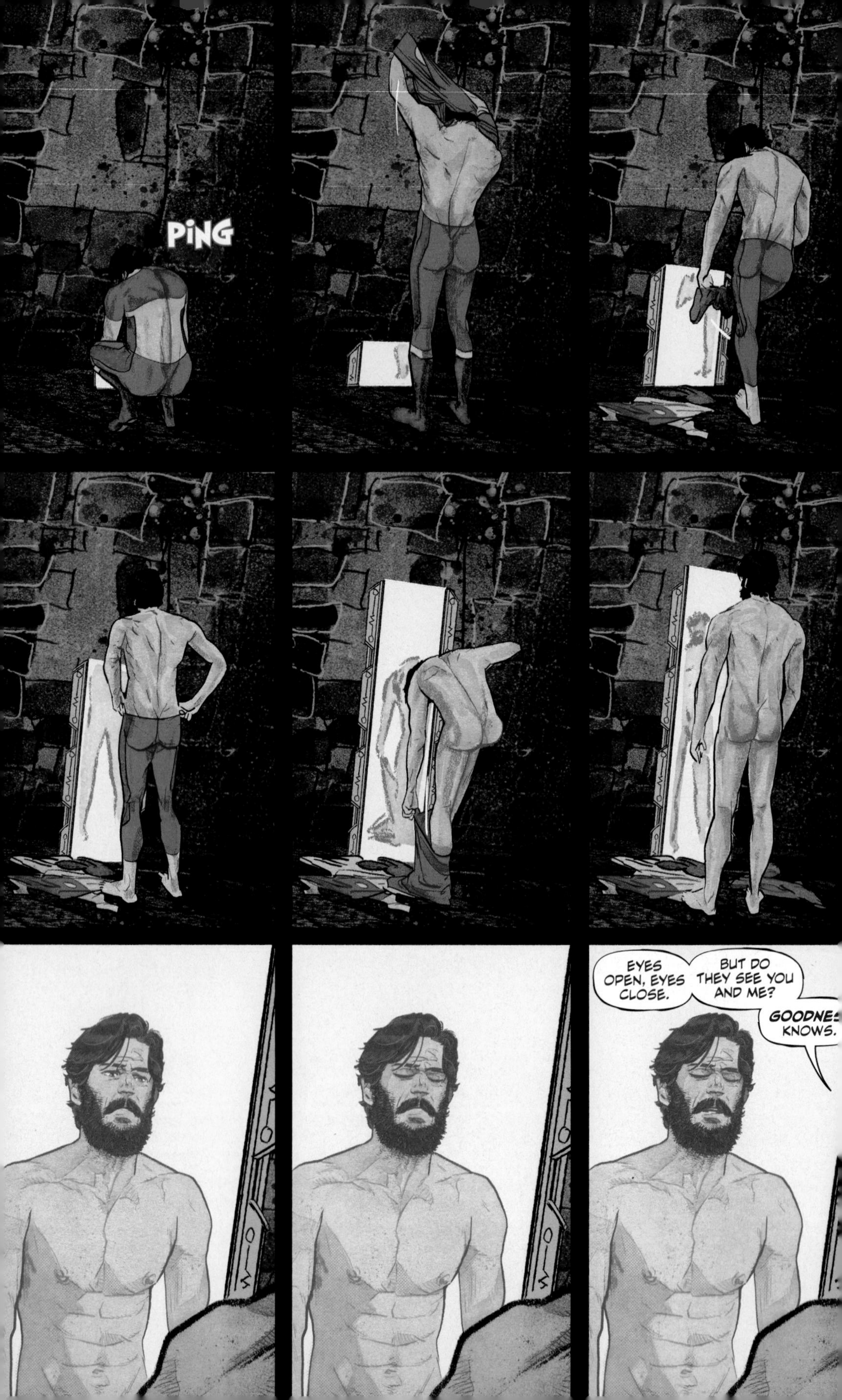
PING
EYES OPEN, EYES CLOSE.
BUT DO THEY SEE YOU AND ME?
GOODNE KNOWS.

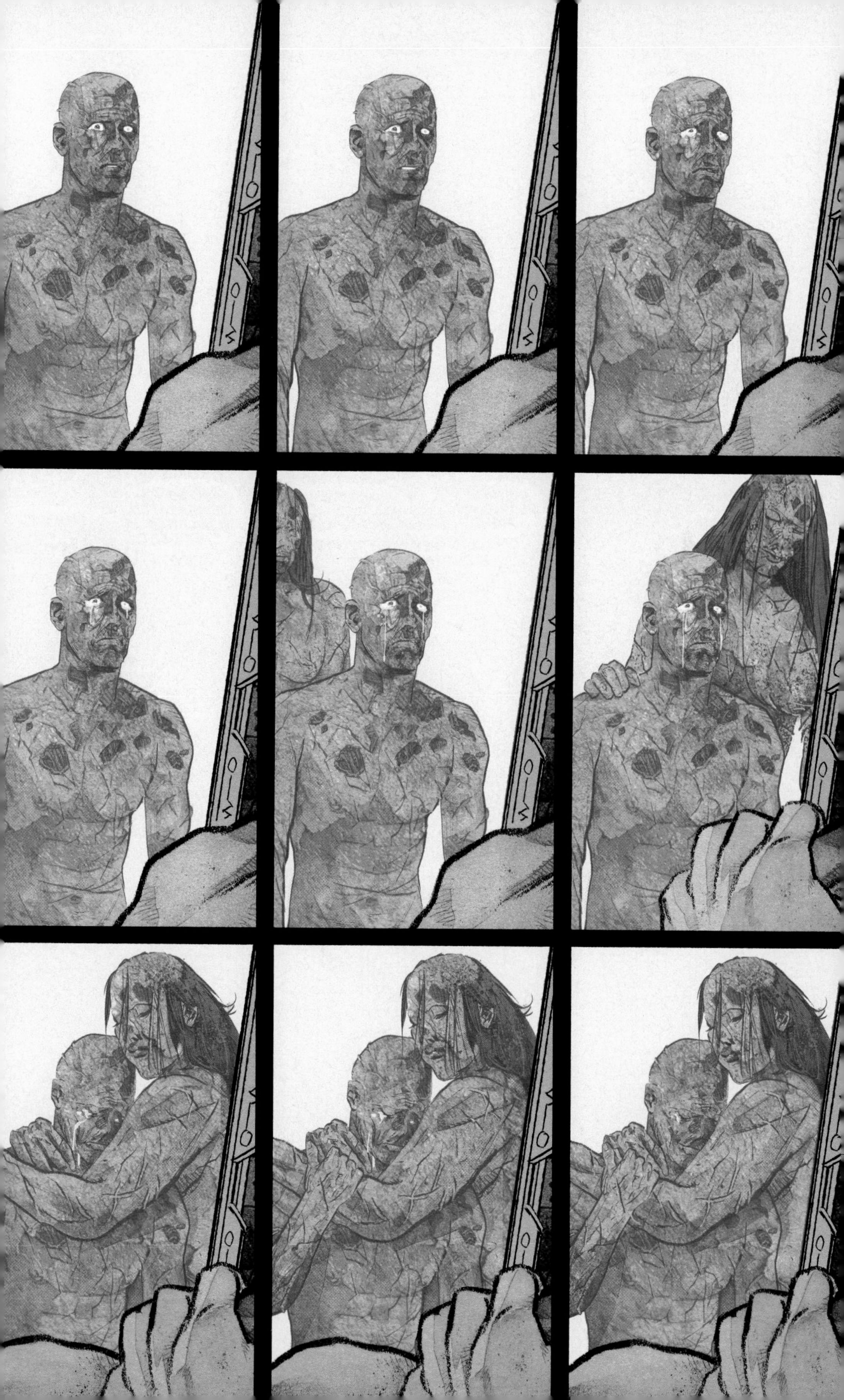

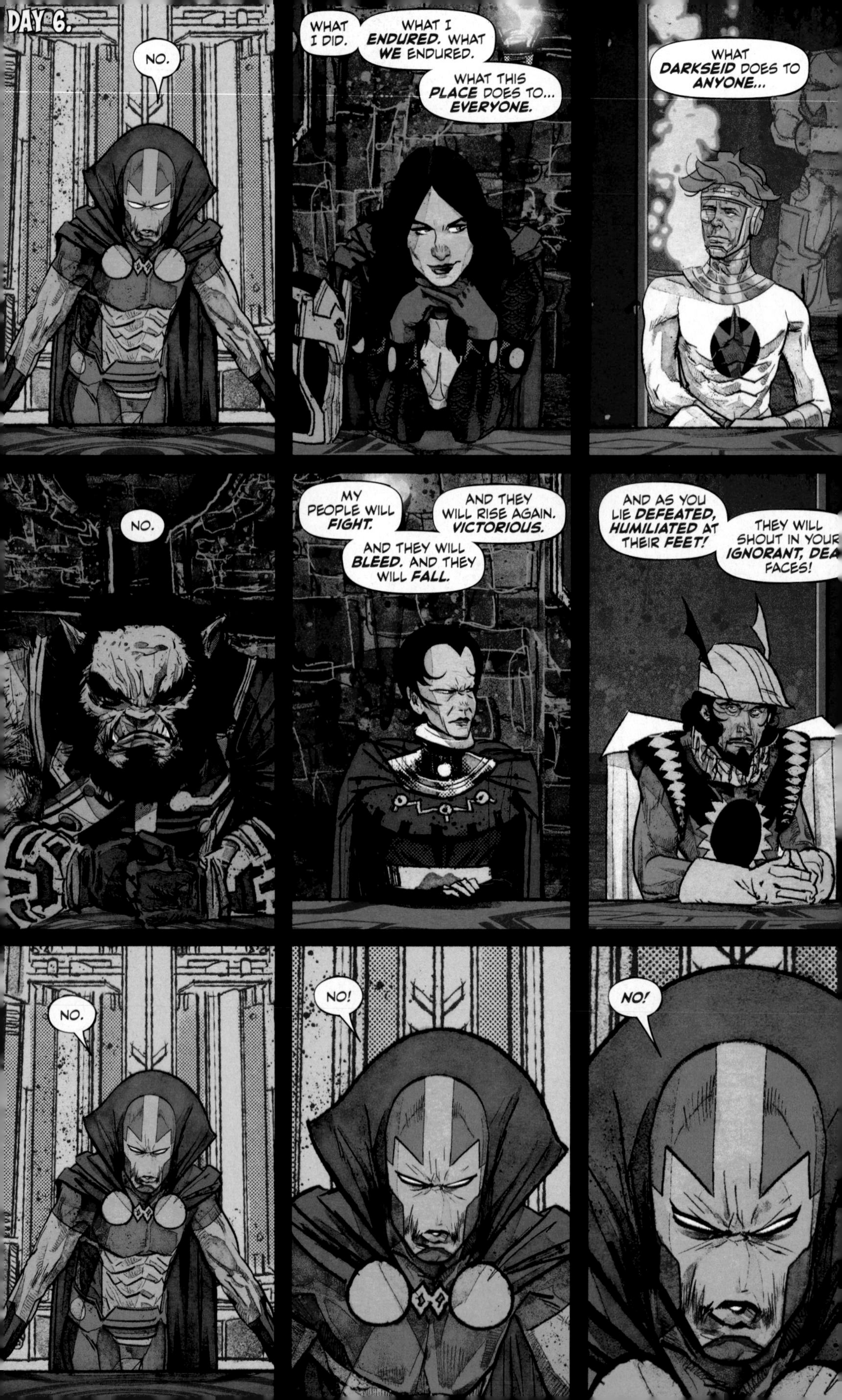
DAY 6.
NO.
WHAT I DID.
WHAT I ENDURED. WHAT WE ENDURED.
WHAT THIS PLACE DOES TO... EVERYONE.
WHAT DARKSEID DOES TO ANYONE...
NO.
MY PEOPLE WILL FIGHT.
AND THEY WILL BLEED. AND THEY WILL FALL.
AND THEY WILL RISE AGAIN. VICTORIOUS.
AND AS YOU LIE DEFEATED, HUMILIATED AT THEIR FEET!
THEY WILL SHOUT IN YOUR IGNORANT, DEA FACES!
NO.
NO!
NO!

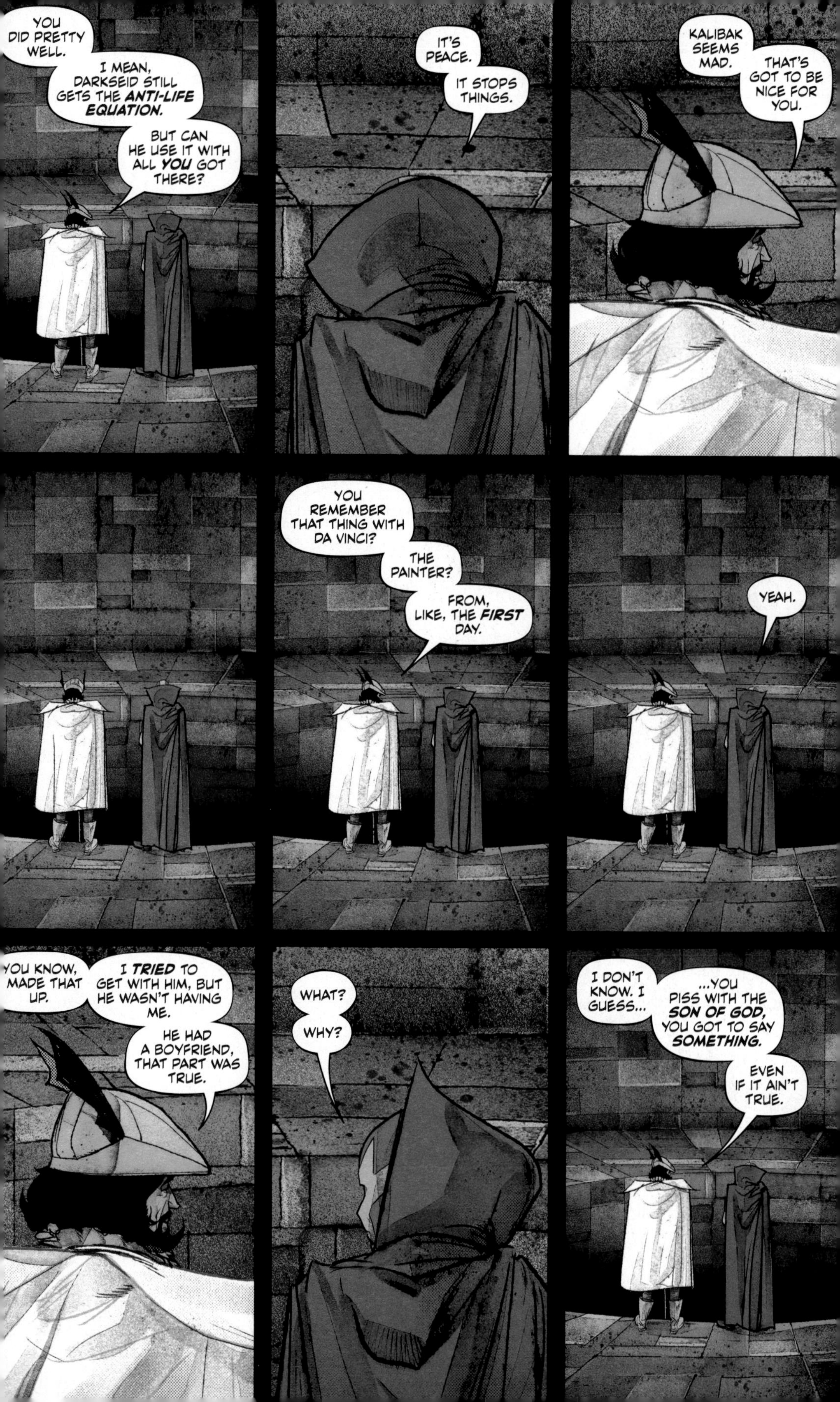

YOU DID PRETTY WELL.
I MEAN, DARKSEID STILL GETS THE ANTI-LIFE EQUATION.
BUT CAN HE USE IT WITH ALL YOU GOT THERE?
IT'S PEACE.
IT STOPS THINGS.
KALIBAK SEEMS MAD.
THAT'S GOT TO BE NICE FOR YOU.
YOU REMEMBER THAT THING WITH DA VINCI?
THE PAINTER?
FROM, LIKE, THE FIRST DAY.
YEAH.
YOU KNOW, MADE THAT UP.
I TRIED TO GET WITH HIM, BUT HE WASN'T HAVING ME.
HE HAD A BOYFRIEND, THAT PART WAS TRUE.
WHAT?
WHY?
I DON'T KNOW. I GUESS...
...YOU PISS WITH THE SON OF GOD, YOU GOT TO SAY SOMETHING.
EVEN IF IT AIN'T TRUE.

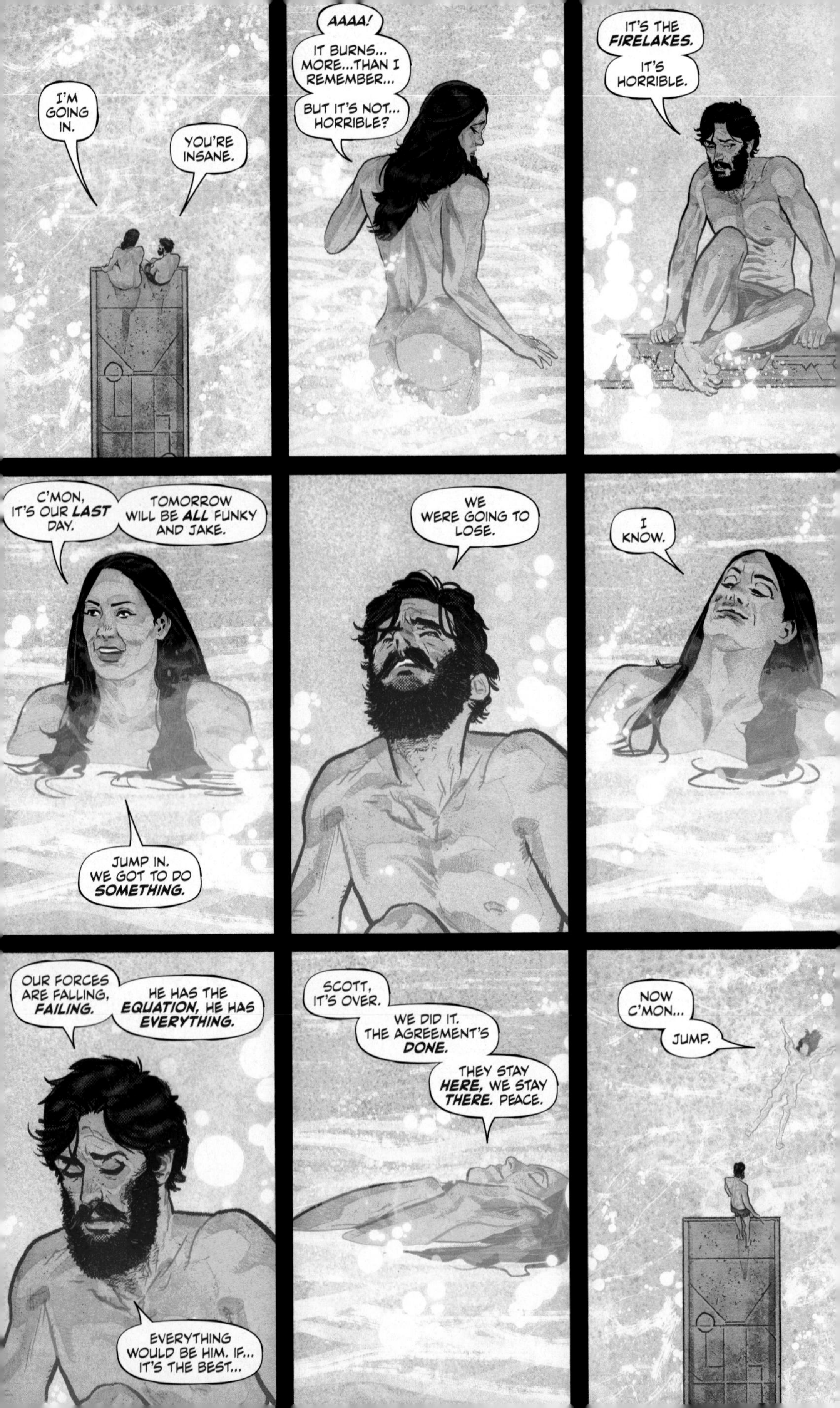

I'M GOING IN.
YOU'RE INSANE.
AAAA!
IT BURNS... MORE...THAN I REMEMBER...
BUT IT'S NOT... HORRIBLE?
IT'S THE FIRELAKES.
IT'S HORRIBLE.
C'MON, IT'S OUR LAST DAY.
TOMORROW WILL BE ALL FUNKY AND JAKE.
JUMP IN. WE GOT TO DO SOMETHING.
WE WERE GOING TO LOSE.
I KNOW.
OUR FORCES ARE FALLING, FAILING.
HE HAS THE EQUATION, HE HAS EVERYTHING.
EVERYTHING WOULD BE HIM. IF... IT'S THE BEST...
SCOTT, IT'S OVER.
WE DID IT. THE AGREEMENT'S DONE.
THEY STAY HERE, WE STAY THERE. PEACE.
NOW C'MON...
JUMP.

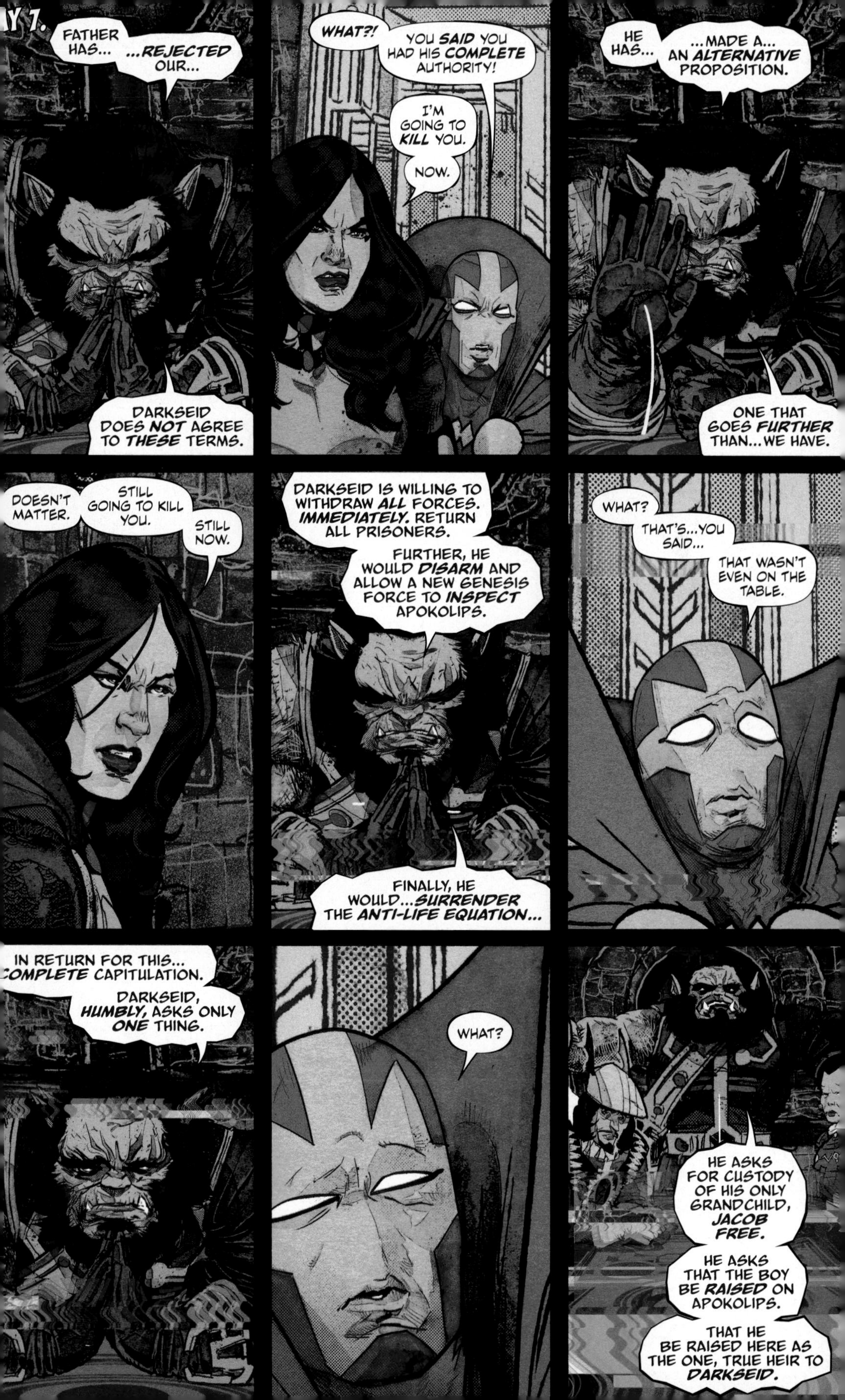
Y 7.
FATHER HAS...
...REJECTED OUR...
DARKSEID DOES NOT AGREE TO THESE TERMS.
WHAT?!
YOU SAID YOU HAD HIS COMPLETE AUTHORITY!
I'M GOING TO KILL YOU.
NOW.
HE HAS...
...MADE A... AN ALTERNATIVE PROPOSITION.
ONE THAT GOES FURTHER THAN...WE HAVE.
DOESN'T MATTER.
STILL GOING TO KILL YOU.
STILL NOW.
DARKSEID IS WILLING TO WITHDRAW ALL FORCES. IMMEDIATELY. RETURN ALL PRISONERS.
FURTHER, HE WOULD DISARM AND ALLOW A NEW GENESIS FORCE TO INSPECT APOKOLIPS.
FINALLY, HE WOULD...SURRENDER THE ANTI-LIFE EQUATION...
WHAT?
THAT'S...YOU SAID...
THAT WASN'T EVEN ON THE TABLE.
IN RETURN FOR THIS... COMPLETE CAPITULATION.
DARKSEID, HUMBLY, ASKS ONLY ONE THING.
WHAT?
HE ASKS FOR CUSTODY OF HIS ONLY GRANDCHILD, JACOB FREE.
HE ASKS THAT THE BOY BE RAISED ON APOKOLIPS.
THAT HE BE RAISED HERE AS THE ONE, TRUE HEIR TO DARKSEID.

DON'T GET JUMPY!

IT HASN'T HAPPENED YET.

THOUGH DARKSEID IS ABROAD...

...THE FUTURE IS STILL FREE TO ALL!!

THUS, FROM THIS *HEAVY* FRAGMENT OF "MISTER MIRACLE--PAST!"

WE MOVE TO THE MOST *EXCITING* AND *DANGEROUS* CHAPTER OF...

"MISTER MIRACLE--

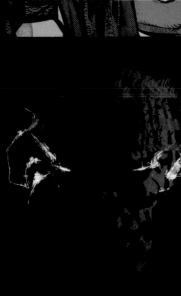

"--TO BE!"

WHAT?

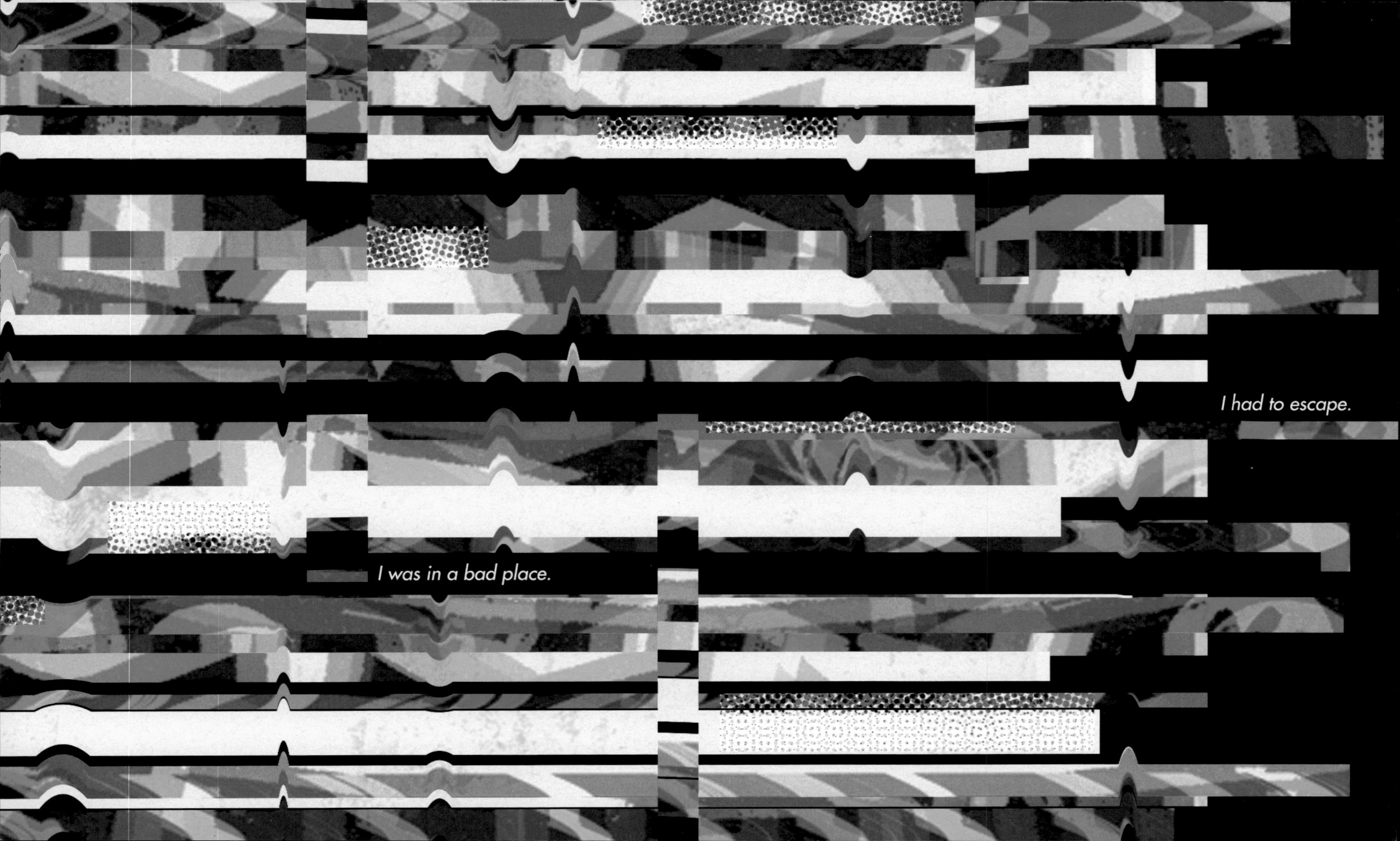
I was in a bad place.
I had to escape.

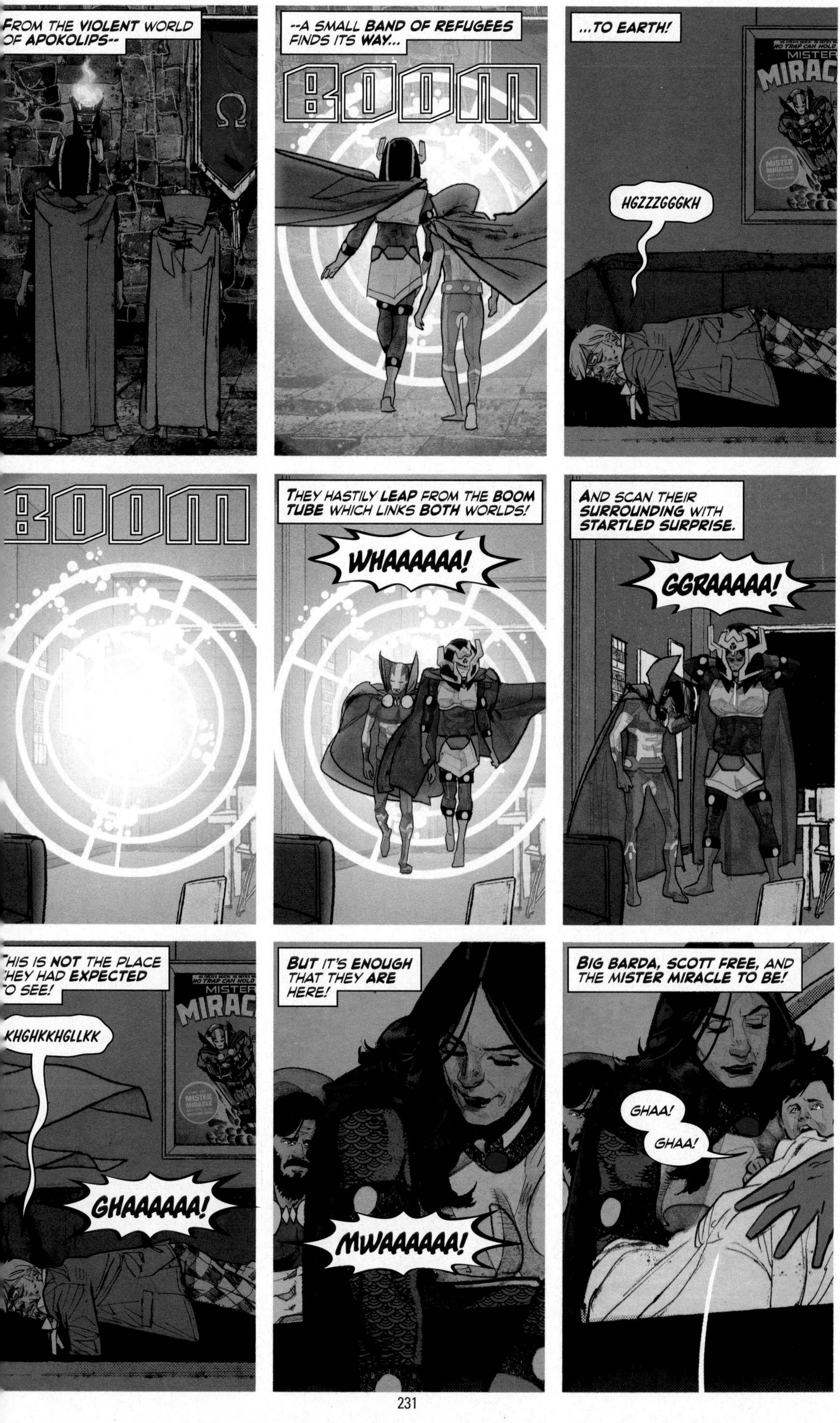
FROM THE VIOLENT WORLD OF APOKOLIPS--
--A SMALL BAND OF REFUGEES FINDS ITS WAY...
BOOM
...TO EARTH!
HGZZZGGGKH
BOOM
THEY HASTILY LEAP FROM THE BOOM TUBE WHICH LINKS BOTH WORLDS!
WHAAAAAA!
AND SCAN THEIR SURROUNDING WITH STARTLED SURPRISE.
GGRAAAAA!
THIS IS NOT THE PLACE THEY HAD EXPECTED TO SEE!
KHGHKKHGLLKK
GHAAAAAA!
BUT IT'S ENOUGH THAT THEY ARE HERE!
MWAAAAAAA!
BIG BARDA, SCOTT FREE, AND THE MISTER MIRACLE TO BE!
GHAA!
GHAA!

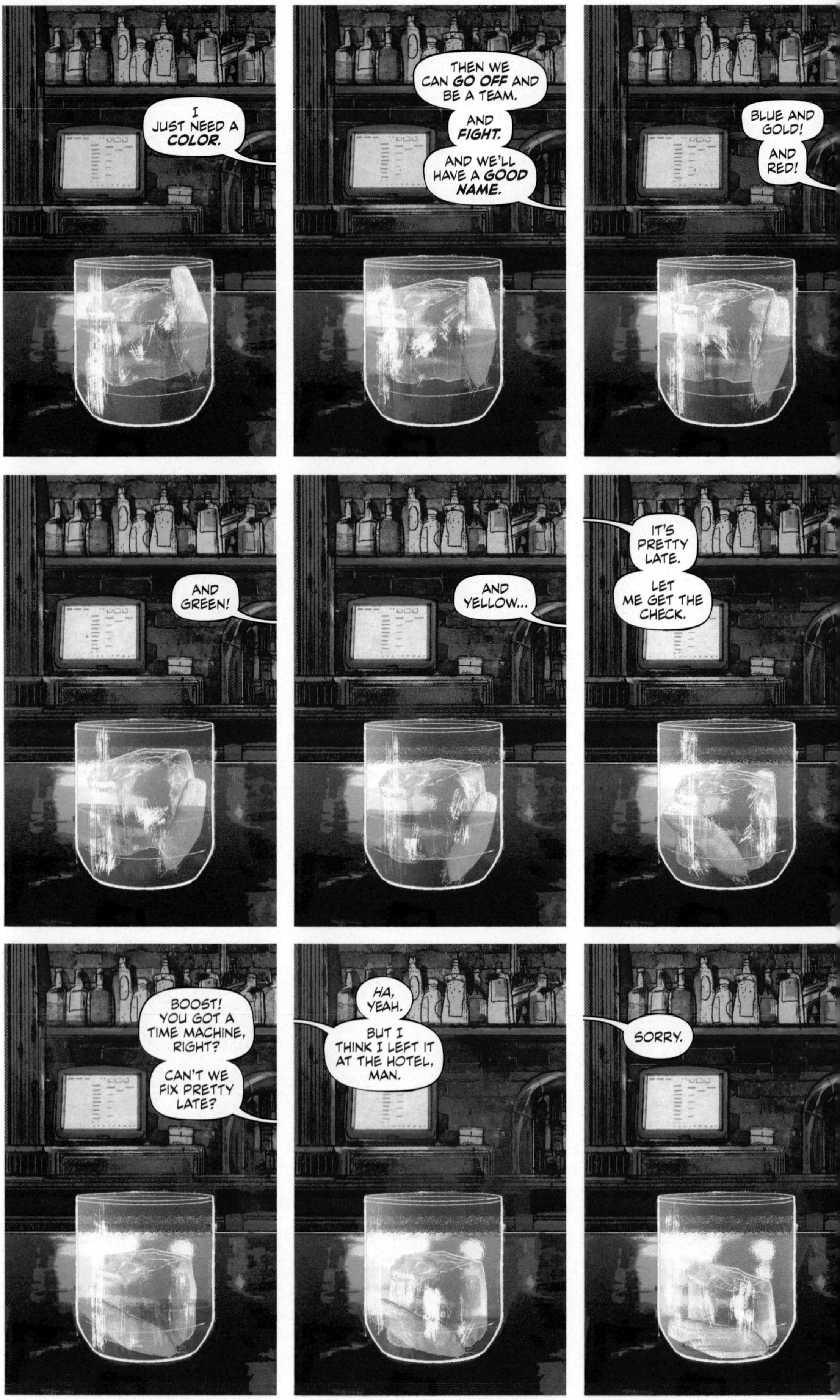
I JUST NEED A **COLOR.**
THEN WE CAN **GO OFF** AND BE A TEAM.
AND **FIGHT.**
AND WE'LL HAVE A **GOOD NAME.**
BLUE AND GOLD!
AND RED!
AND GREEN!
AND YELLOW...
IT'S PRETTY LATE.
LET ME GET THE CHECK.
BOOST! YOU GOT A TIME MACHINE, RIGHT?
CAN'T WE FIX PRETTY LATE?
HA, YEAH.
BUT I THINK I LEFT IT AT THE HOTEL, MAN.
SORRY.

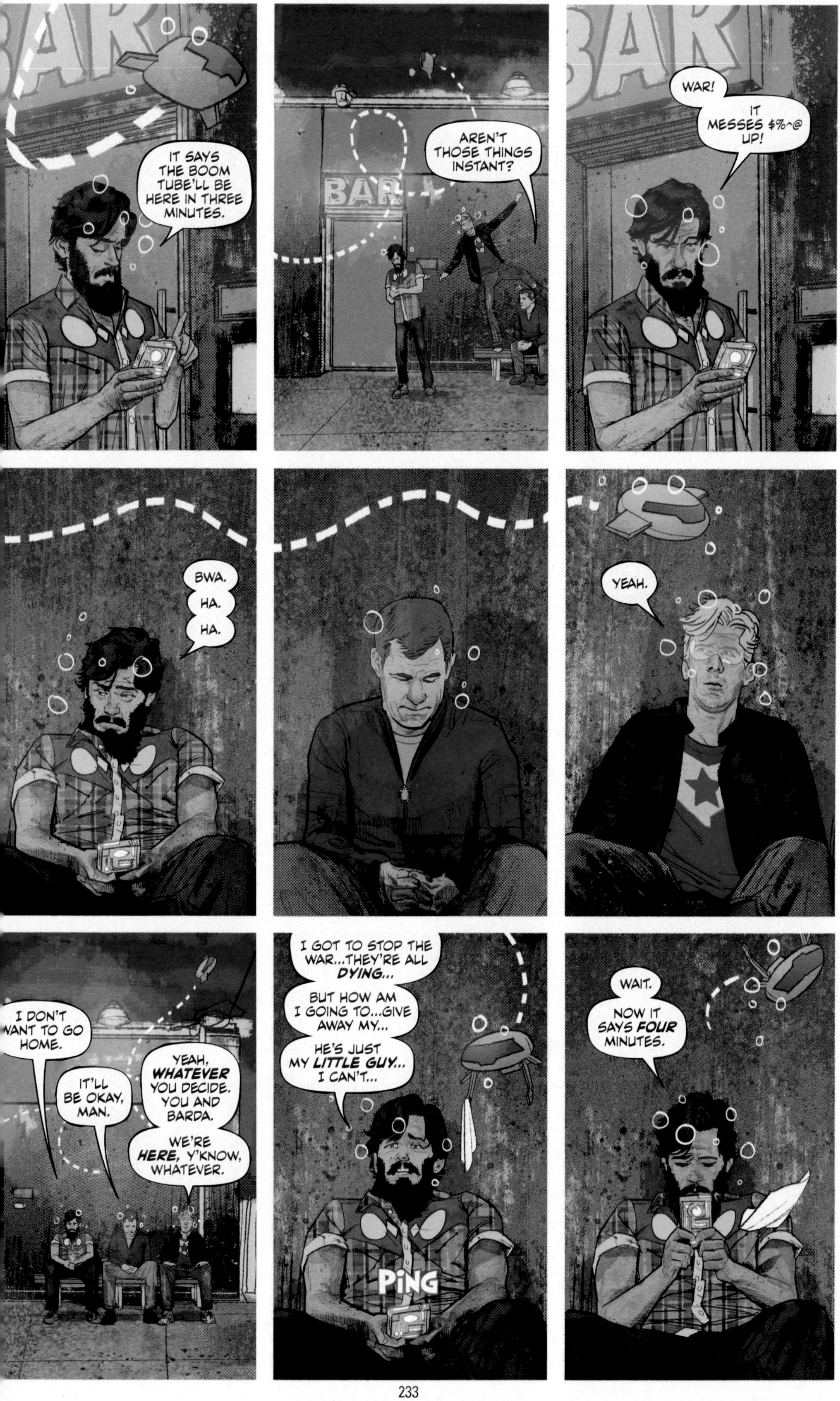

IT SAYS THE BOOM TUBE'LL BE HERE IN THREE MINUTES.
BAR
AREN'T THOSE THINGS INSTANT?
WAR!
IT MESSES $%^@ UP!
BWA.
HA.
HA.
YEAH.
I DON'T WANT TO GO HOME.
IT'LL BE OKAY, MAN.
YEAH, *WHATEVER* YOU DECIDE. YOU AND BARDA.
WE'RE *HERE*, Y'KNOW, WHATEVER.
I GOT TO STOP THE WAR...THEY'RE ALL *DYING*...
BUT HOW AM I GOING TO...GIVE AWAY MY...
HE'S JUST MY *LITTLE GUY*... I CAN'T...
PING
WAIT.
NOW IT SAYS *FOUR* MINUTES.

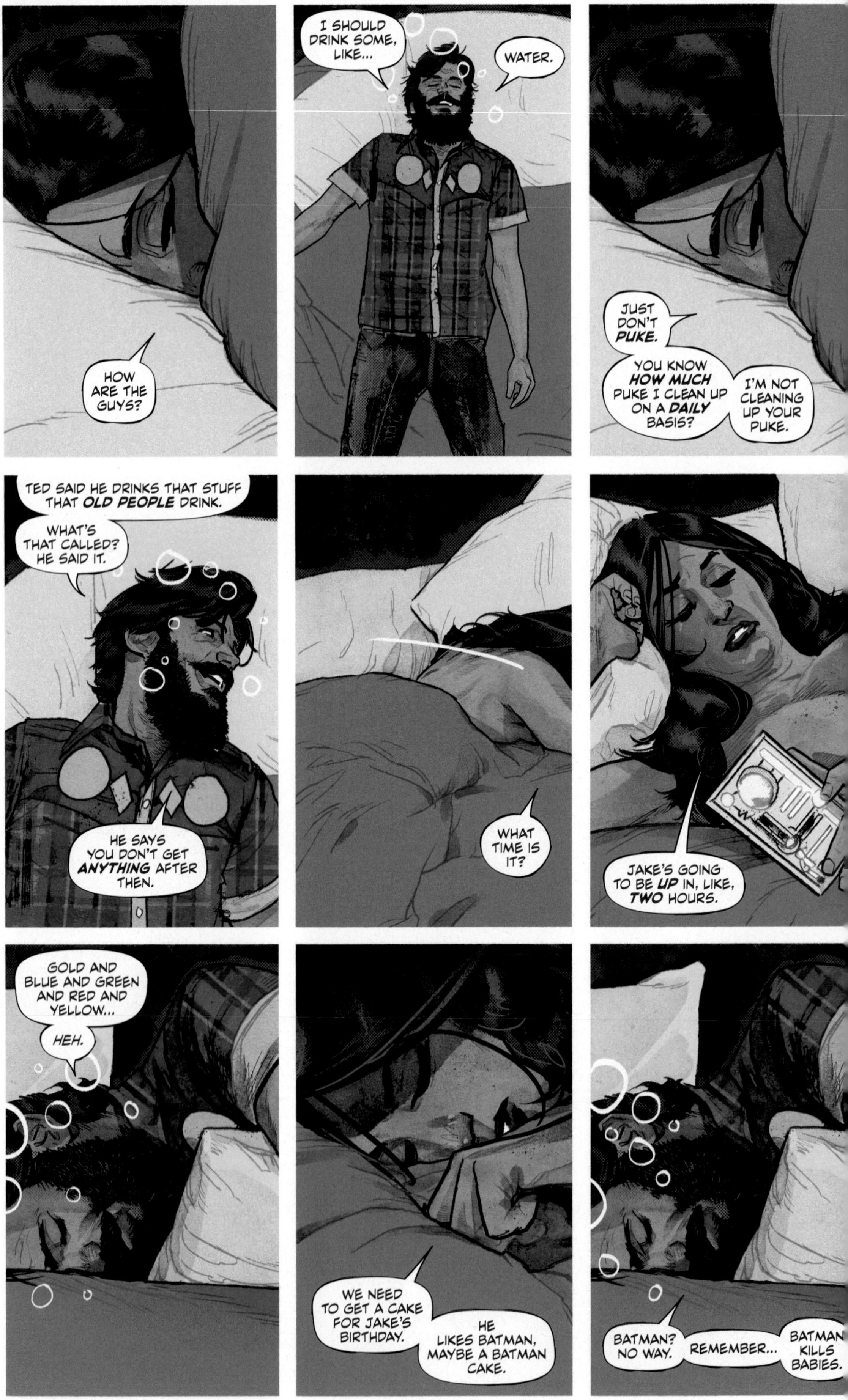
HOW ARE THE GUYS?
I SHOULD DRINK SOME, LIKE...
WATER.
JUST DON'T PUKE.
YOU KNOW HOW MUCH PUKE I CLEAN UP ON A DAILY BASIS?
I'M NOT CLEANING UP YOUR PUKE.
TED SAID HE DRINKS THAT STUFF THAT OLD PEOPLE DRINK.
WHAT'S THAT CALLED? HE SAID IT.
HE SAYS YOU DON'T GET ANYTHING AFTER THEN.
WHAT TIME IS IT?
JAKE'S GOING TO BE UP IN, LIKE, TWO HOURS.
GOLD AND BLUE AND GREEN AND RED AND YELLOW...
HEH.
WE NEED TO GET A CAKE FOR JAKE'S BIRTHDAY.
HE LIKES BATMAN, MAYBE A BATMAN CAKE.
BATMAN? NO WAY.
REMEMBER...
BATMAN KILLS BABIES.

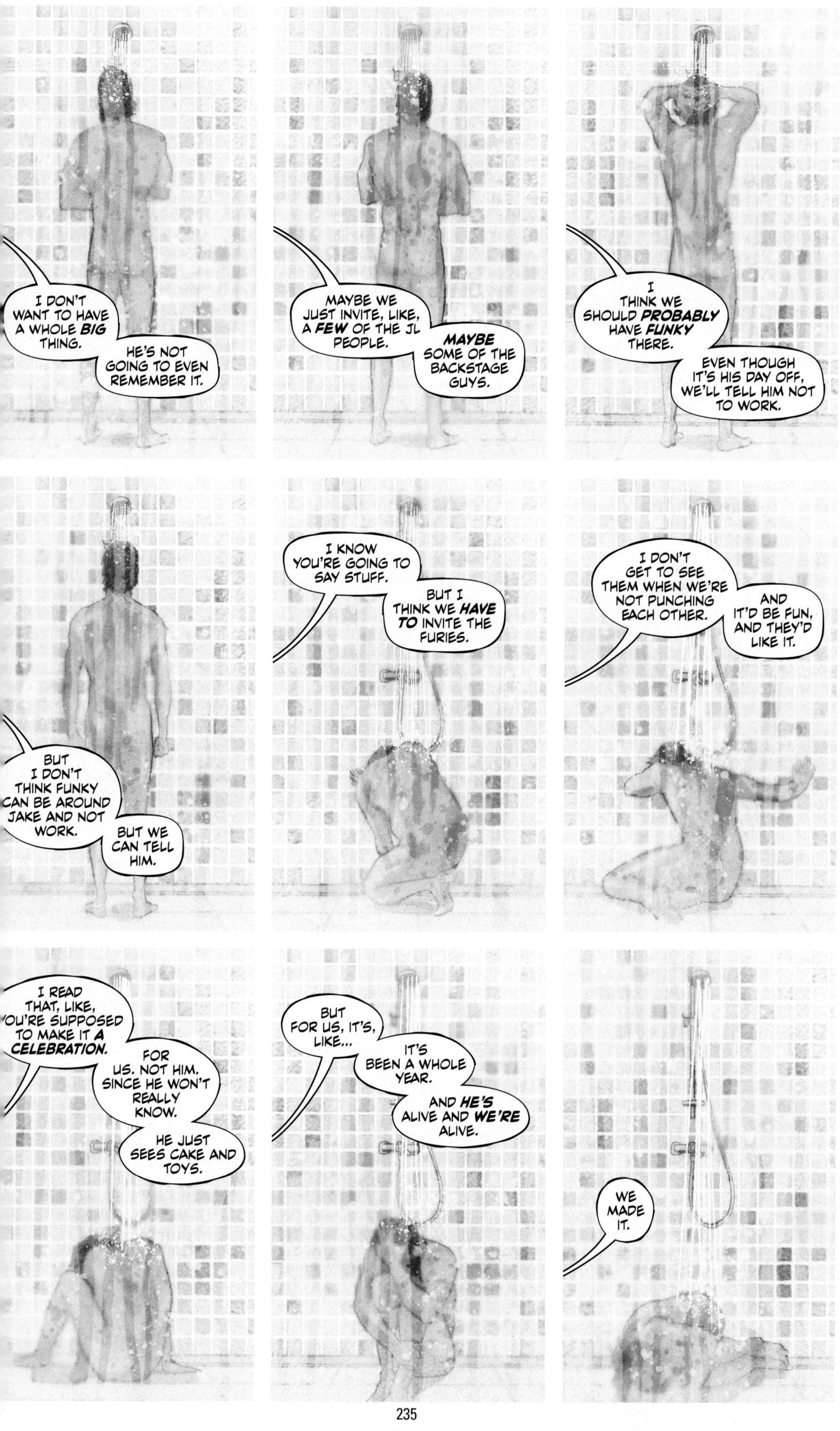

I DON'T WANT TO HAVE A WHOLE BIG THING.
HE'S NOT GOING TO EVEN REMEMBER IT.
MAYBE WE JUST INVITE, LIKE, A FEW OF THE JL PEOPLE.
MAYBE SOME OF THE BACKSTAGE GUYS.
I THINK WE SHOULD PROBABLY HAVE FUNKY THERE.
EVEN THOUGH IT'S HIS DAY OFF, WE'LL TELL HIM NOT TO WORK.
BUT I DON'T THINK FUNKY CAN BE AROUND JAKE AND NOT WORK.
BUT WE CAN TELL HIM.
I KNOW YOU'RE GOING TO SAY STUFF.
BUT I THINK WE HAVE TO INVITE THE FURIES.
I DON'T GET TO SEE THEM WHEN WE'RE NOT PUNCHING EACH OTHER.
AND IT'D BE FUN, AND THEY'D LIKE IT.
I READ THAT, LIKE, YOU'RE SUPPOSED TO MAKE IT A CELEBRATION.
FOR US. NOT HIM. SINCE HE WON'T REALLY KNOW.
HE JUST SEES CAKE AND TOYS.
BUT FOR US, IT'S, LIKE...
IT'S BEEN A WHOLE YEAR.
AND HE'S ALIVE AND WE'RE ALIVE.
WE MADE IT.

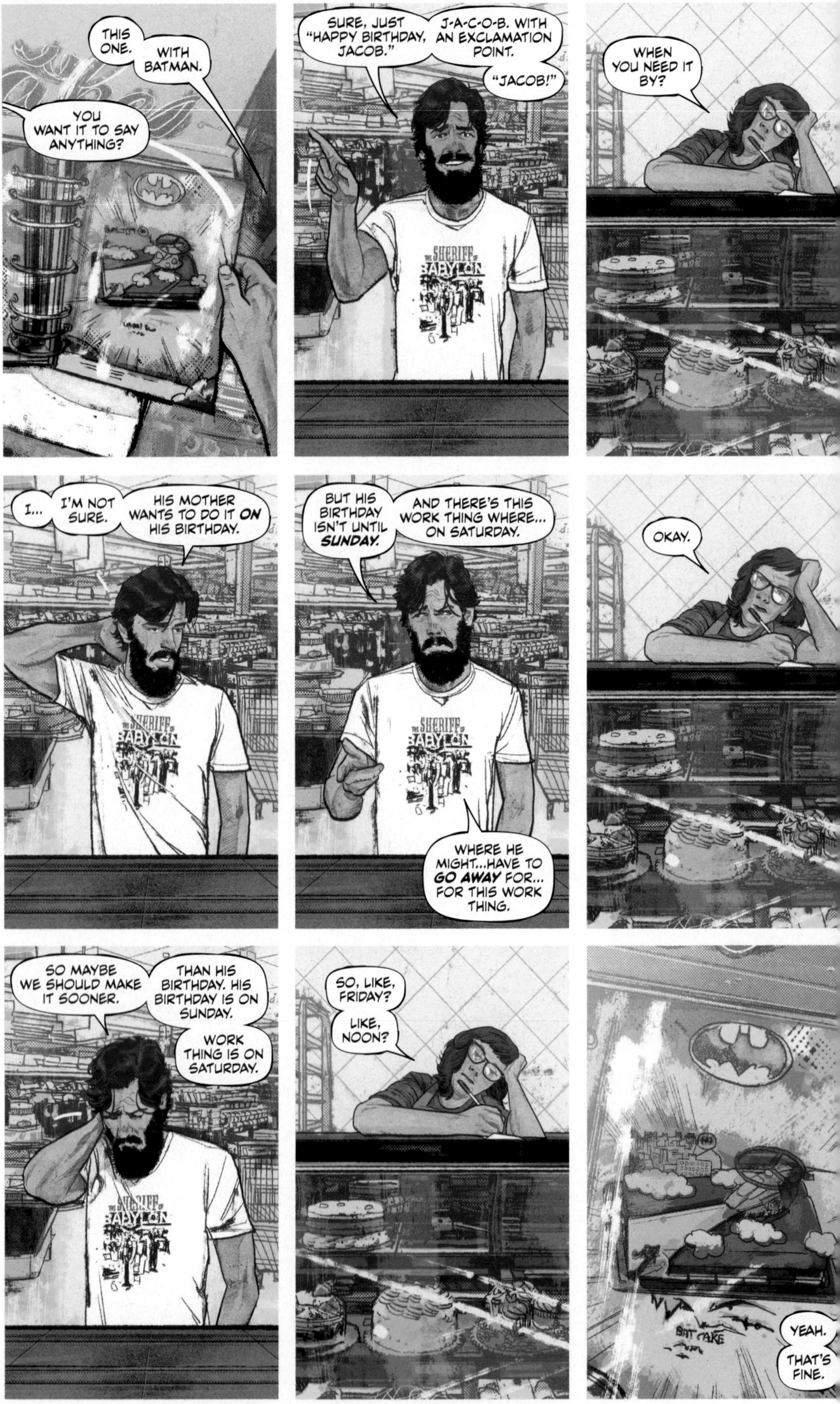
THIS ONE.
WITH BATMAN.
YOU WANT IT TO SAY ANYTHING?
SURE, JUST "HAPPY BIRTHDAY, JACOB."
J-A-C-O-B. WITH AN EXCLAMATION POINT.
"JACOB!"
THE SHERIFF OF BABYLON
WHEN YOU NEED IT BY?
I...
I'M NOT SURE.
HIS MOTHER WANTS TO DO IT **ON** HIS BIRTHDAY.
BUT HIS BIRTHDAY ISN'T UNTIL ***SUNDAY.***
AND THERE'S THIS WORK THING WHERE... ON SATURDAY.
WHERE HE MIGHT...HAVE TO ***GO AWAY*** FOR... FOR THIS WORK THING.
OKAY.
SO MAYBE WE SHOULD MAKE IT SOONER.
THAN HIS BIRTHDAY. HIS BIRTHDAY IS ON SUNDAY.
WORK THING IS ON SATURDAY.
SO, LIKE, FRIDAY?
LIKE, NOON?
BAT CAKE
YEAH.
THAT'S FINE.

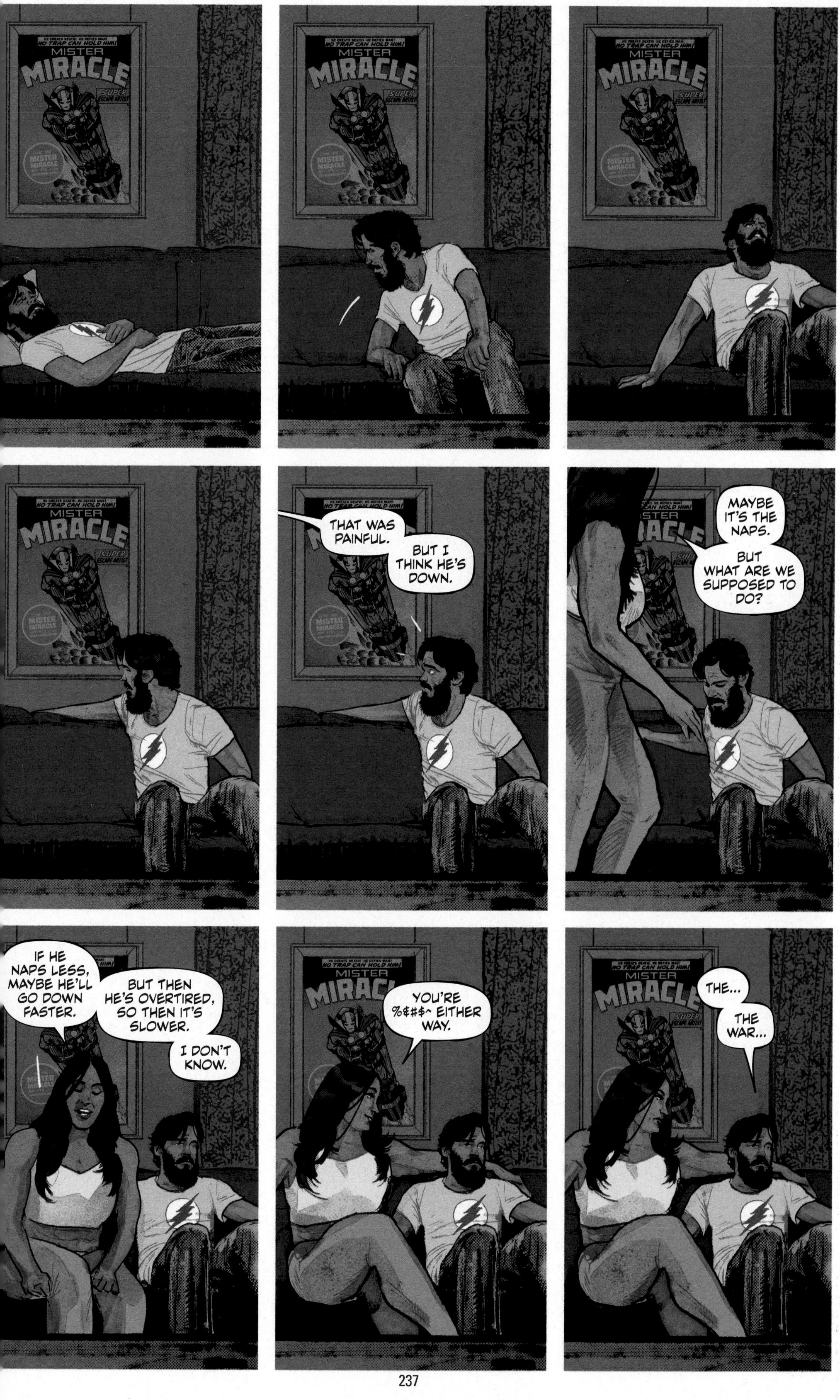
HE CHEATS DEATH! HE DEFIES MAN!
NO TRAP CAN HOLD HIM!
MISTER MIRACLE
SUPER ESCAPE ARTIST
THAT WAS PAINFUL.
BUT I THINK HE'S DOWN.
MAYBE IT'S THE NAPS.
BUT WHAT ARE WE SUPPOSED TO DO?
IF HE NAPS LESS, MAYBE HE'LL GO DOWN FASTER.
BUT THEN HE'S OVERTIRED, SO THEN IT'S SLOWER.
I DON'T KNOW.
YOU'RE %$#$^ EITHER WAY.
THE...
THE WAR...

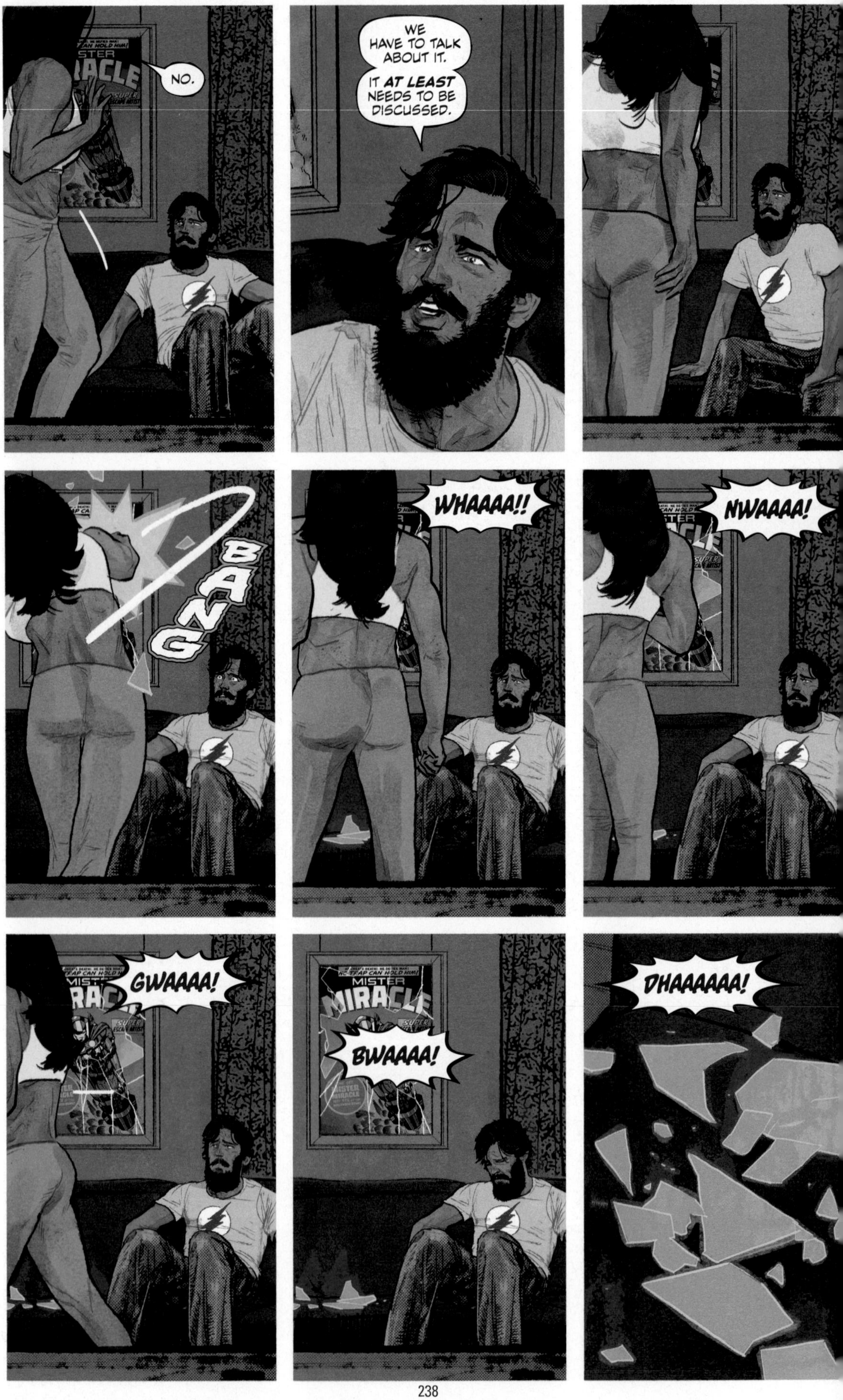

NO.
WE HAVE TO TALK ABOUT IT.
IT **AT LEAST** NEEDS TO BE DISCUSSED.
BANG
WHAAAA!!
NWAAAA!
GWAAAA!
BWAAAA!
DHAAAAAA!

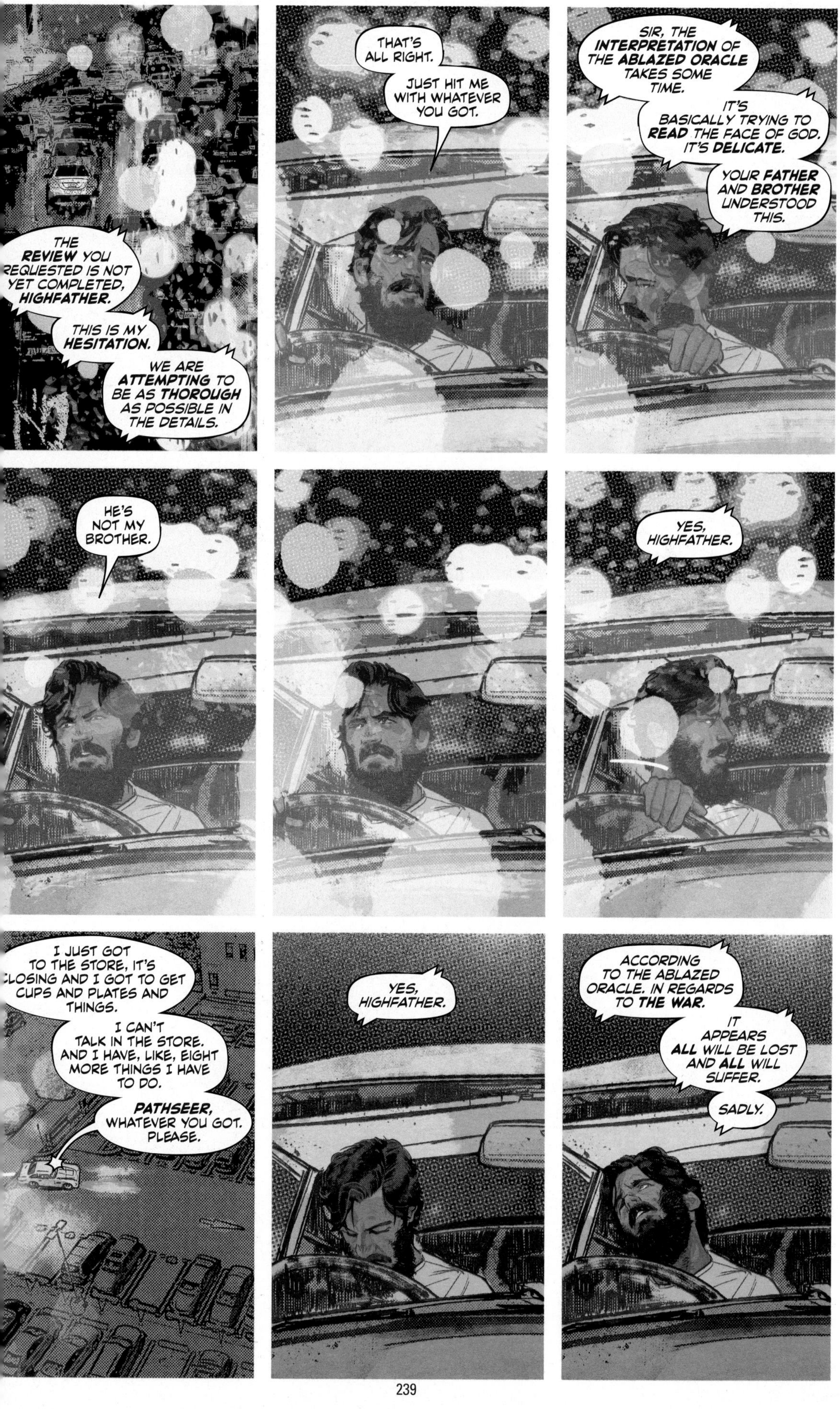
THE REVIEW YOU REQUESTED IS NOT YET COMPLETED, HIGHFATHER.
THIS IS MY HESITATION.
WE ARE ATTEMPTING TO BE AS THOROUGH AS POSSIBLE IN THE DETAILS.
THAT'S ALL RIGHT.
JUST HIT ME WITH WHATEVER YOU GOT.
SIR, THE INTERPRETATION OF THE ABLAZED ORACLE TAKES SOME TIME.
IT'S BASICALLY TRYING TO READ THE FACE OF GOD. IT'S DELICATE.
YOUR FATHER AND BROTHER UNDERSTOOD THIS.
HE'S NOT MY BROTHER.
YES, HIGHFATHER.
I JUST GOT TO THE STORE, IT'S CLOSING AND I GOT TO GET CUPS AND PLATES AND THINGS.
I CAN'T TALK IN THE STORE. AND I HAVE, LIKE, EIGHT MORE THINGS I HAVE TO DO.
PATHSEER, WHATEVER YOU GOT. PLEASE.
YES, HIGHFATHER.
ACCORDING TO THE ABLAZED ORACLE. IN REGARDS TO THE WAR.
IT APPEARS ALL WILL BE LOST AND ALL WILL SUFFER.
SADLY.

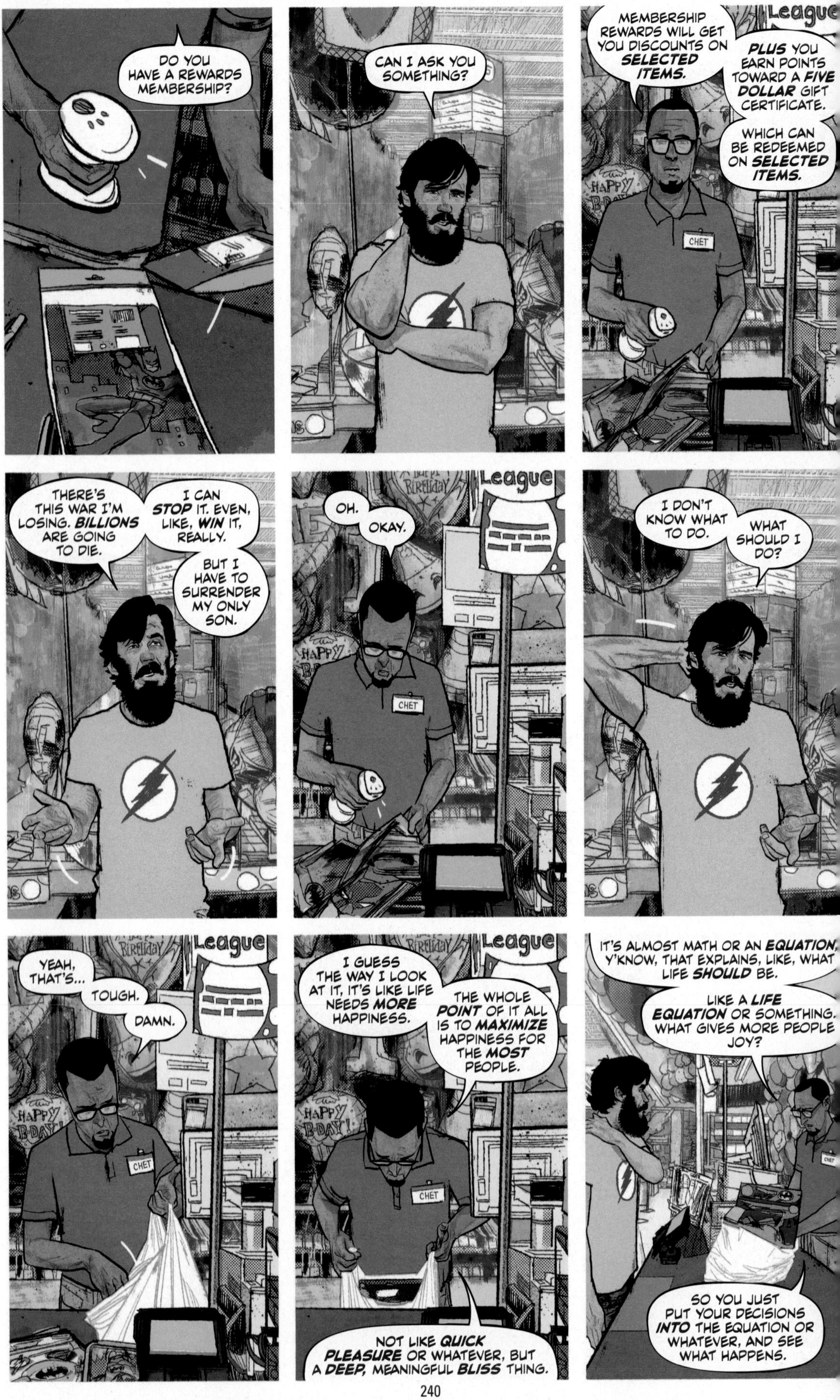
DO YOU HAVE A REWARDS MEMBERSHIP?
CAN I ASK YOU SOMETHING?
MEMBERSHIP REWARDS WILL GET YOU DISCOUNTS ON SELECTED ITEMS.
PLUS YOU EARN POINTS TOWARD A FIVE DOLLAR GIFT CERTIFICATE.
WHICH CAN BE REDEEMED ON SELECTED ITEMS.
CHET
THERE'S THIS WAR I'M LOSING. BILLIONS ARE GOING TO DIE.
I CAN STOP IT. EVEN, LIKE, WIN IT, REALLY.
BUT I HAVE TO SURRENDER MY ONLY SON.
OH.
OKAY.
I DON'T KNOW WHAT TO DO.
WHAT SHOULD I DO?
YEAH, THAT'S...
TOUGH.
DAMN.
I GUESS THE WAY I LOOK AT IT, IT'S LIKE LIFE NEEDS MORE HAPPINESS.
THE WHOLE POINT OF IT ALL IS TO MAXIMIZE HAPPINESS FOR THE MOST PEOPLE.
NOT LIKE QUICK PLEASURE OR WHATEVER, BUT A DEEP, MEANINGFUL BLISS THING.
IT'S ALMOST MATH OR AN EQUATION, Y'KNOW, THAT EXPLAINS, LIKE, WHAT LIFE SHOULD BE.
LIKE A LIFE EQUATION OR SOMETHING. WHAT GIVES MORE PEOPLE JOY?
SO YOU JUST PUT YOUR DECISIONS INTO THE EQUATION OR WHATEVER, AND SEE WHAT HAPPENS.

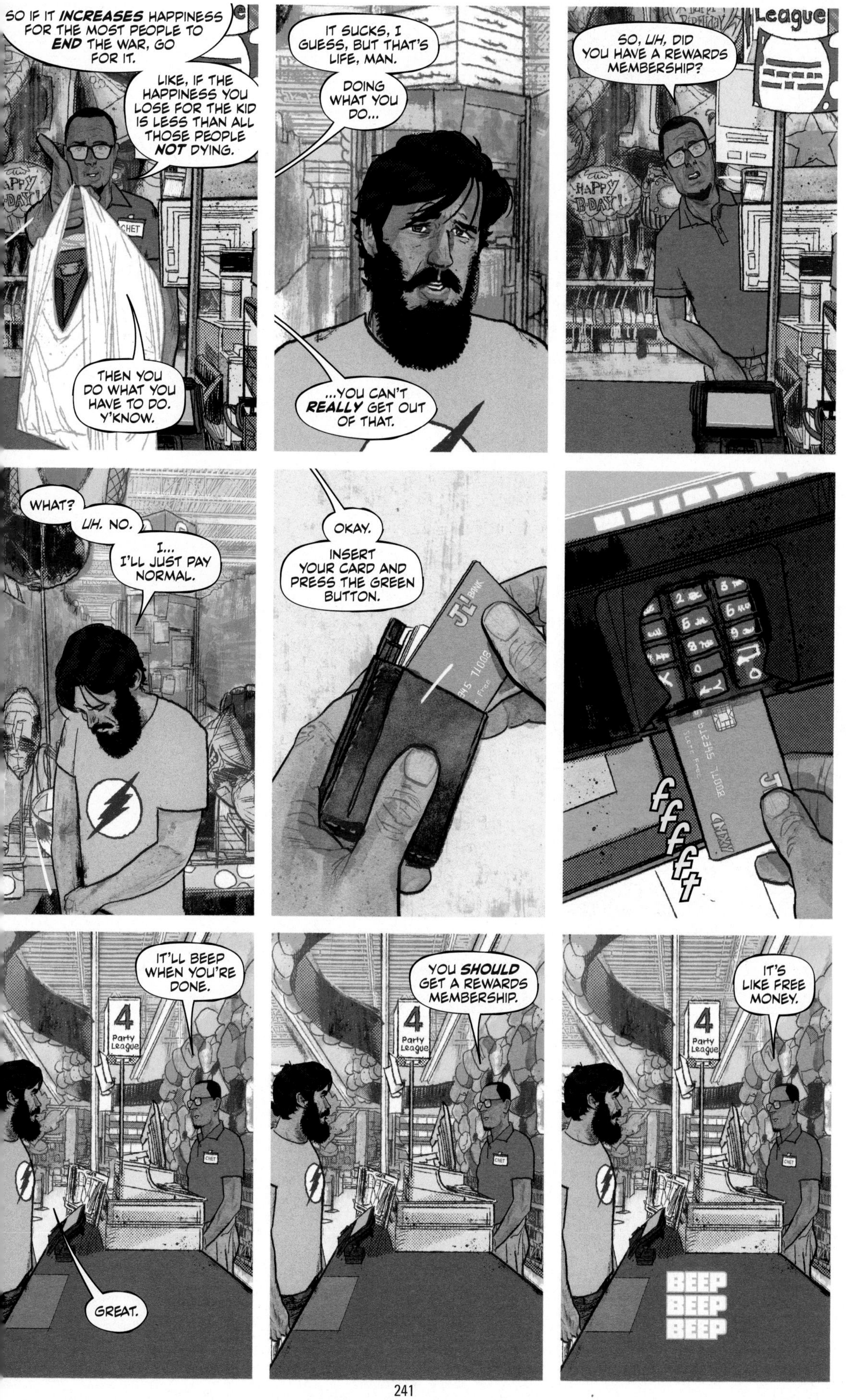
SO IF IT INCREASES HAPPINESS FOR THE MOST PEOPLE TO END THE WAR, GO FOR IT.
LIKE, IF THE HAPPINESS YOU LOSE FOR THE KID IS LESS THAN ALL THOSE PEOPLE NOT DYING.
THEN YOU DO WHAT YOU HAVE TO DO. Y'KNOW.
IT SUCKS, I GUESS, BUT THAT'S LIFE, MAN.
DOING WHAT YOU DO...
...YOU CAN'T REALLY GET OUT OF THAT.
SO, UH, DID YOU HAVE A REWARDS MEMBERSHIP?
WHAT?
UH. NO.
I... I'LL JUST PAY NORMAL.
OKAY.
INSERT YOUR CARD AND PRESS THE GREEN BUTTON.
ffff
IT'LL BEEP WHEN YOU'RE DONE.
4
Party League
GREAT.
YOU SHOULD GET A REWARDS MEMBERSHIP.
IT'S LIKE FREE MONEY.
BEEP
BEEP
BEEP

clkkk

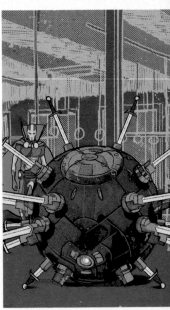

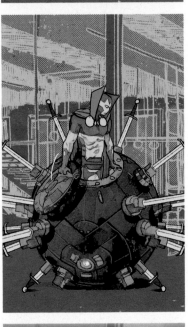

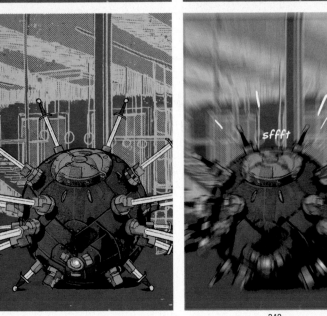

sffft

GODDAMMIT.

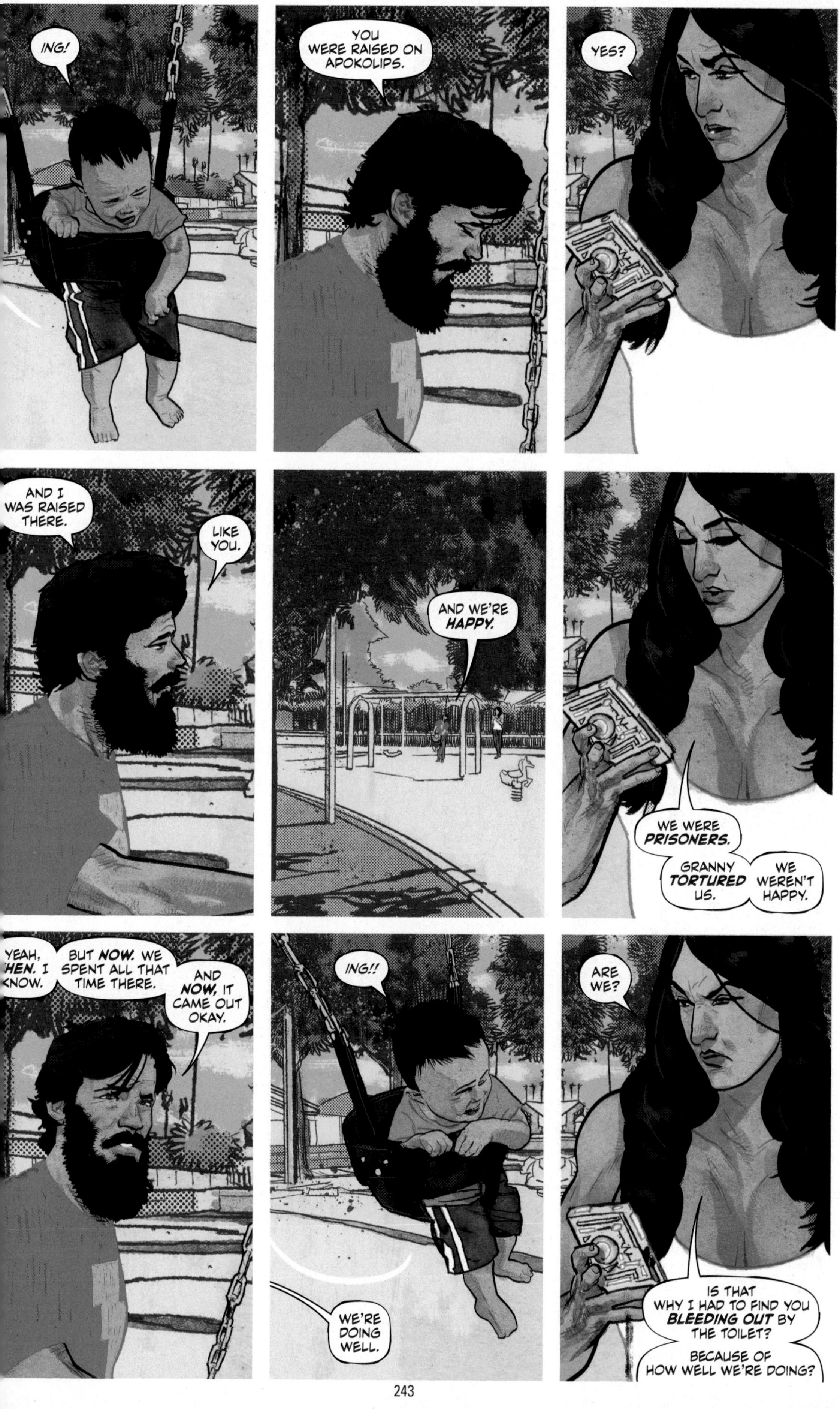
ING!
YOU WERE RAISED ON APOKOLIPS.
YES?
AND I WAS RAISED THERE.
LIKE YOU.
AND WE'RE HAPPY.
WE WERE PRISONERS.
GRANNY TORTURED US.
WE WEREN'T HAPPY.
YEAH, THEN. I KNOW.
BUT NOW. WE SPENT ALL THAT TIME THERE.
AND NOW, IT CAME OUT OKAY.
ING!!
WE'RE DOING WELL.
ARE WE?
IS THAT WHY I HAD TO FIND YOU BLEEDING OUT BY THE TOILET?
BECAUSE OF HOW WELL WE'RE DOING?

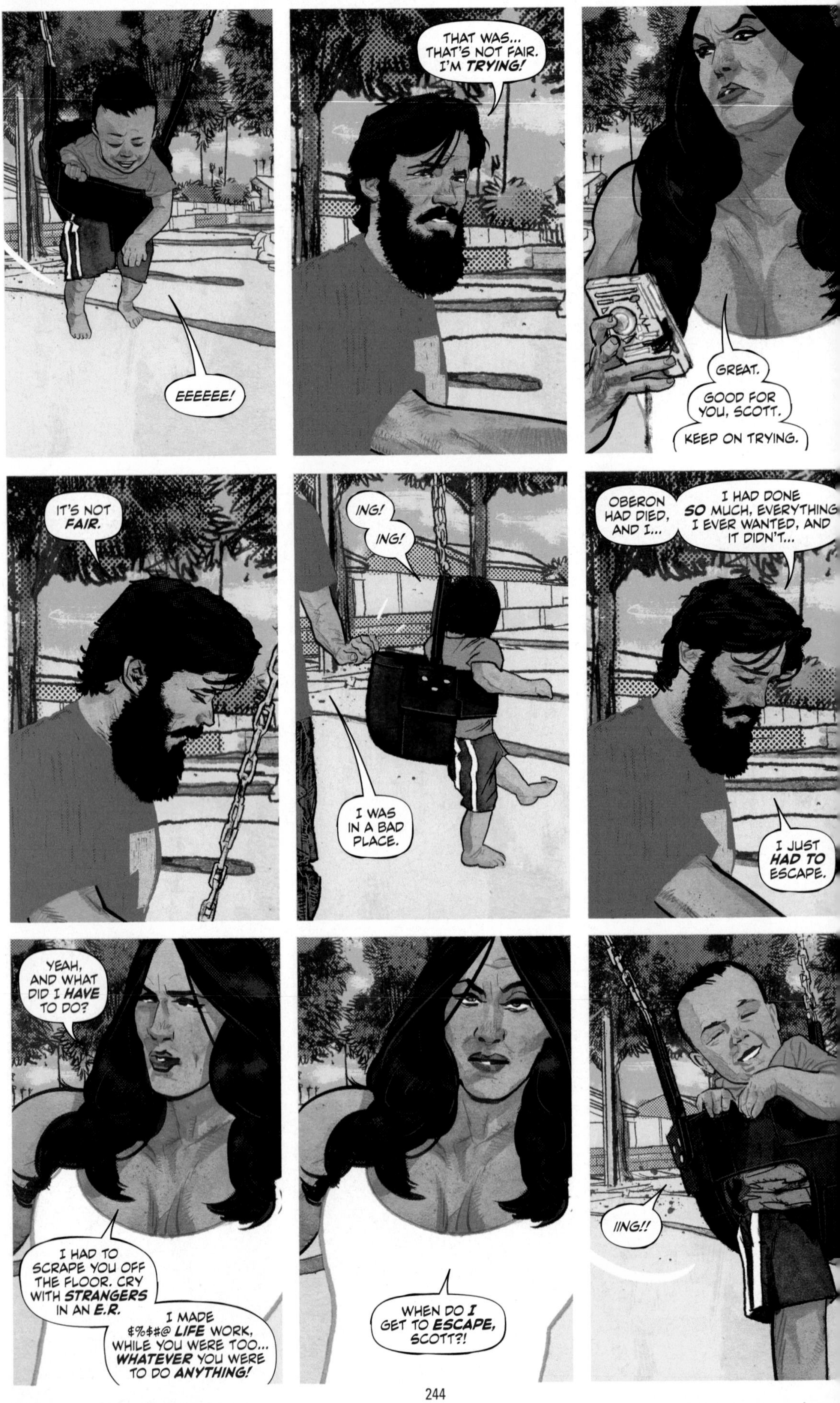
EEEEEE!
THAT WAS... THAT'S NOT FAIR. I'M TRYING!
GREAT.
GOOD FOR YOU, SCOTT.
KEEP ON TRYING.
IT'S NOT FAIR.
ING!
ING!
I WAS IN A BAD PLACE.
OBERON HAD DIED, AND I...
I HAD DONE SO MUCH, EVERYTHING I EVER WANTED, AND IT DIDN'T...
I JUST HAD TO ESCAPE.
YEAH, AND WHAT DID I HAVE TO DO?
I HAD TO SCRAPE YOU OFF THE FLOOR. CRY WITH STRANGERS IN AN E.R.
I MADE $%$#@ LIFE WORK, WHILE YOU WERE TOO... WHATEVER YOU WERE TO DO ANYTHING!
WHEN DO I GET TO ESCAPE, SCOTT?!
IING!!

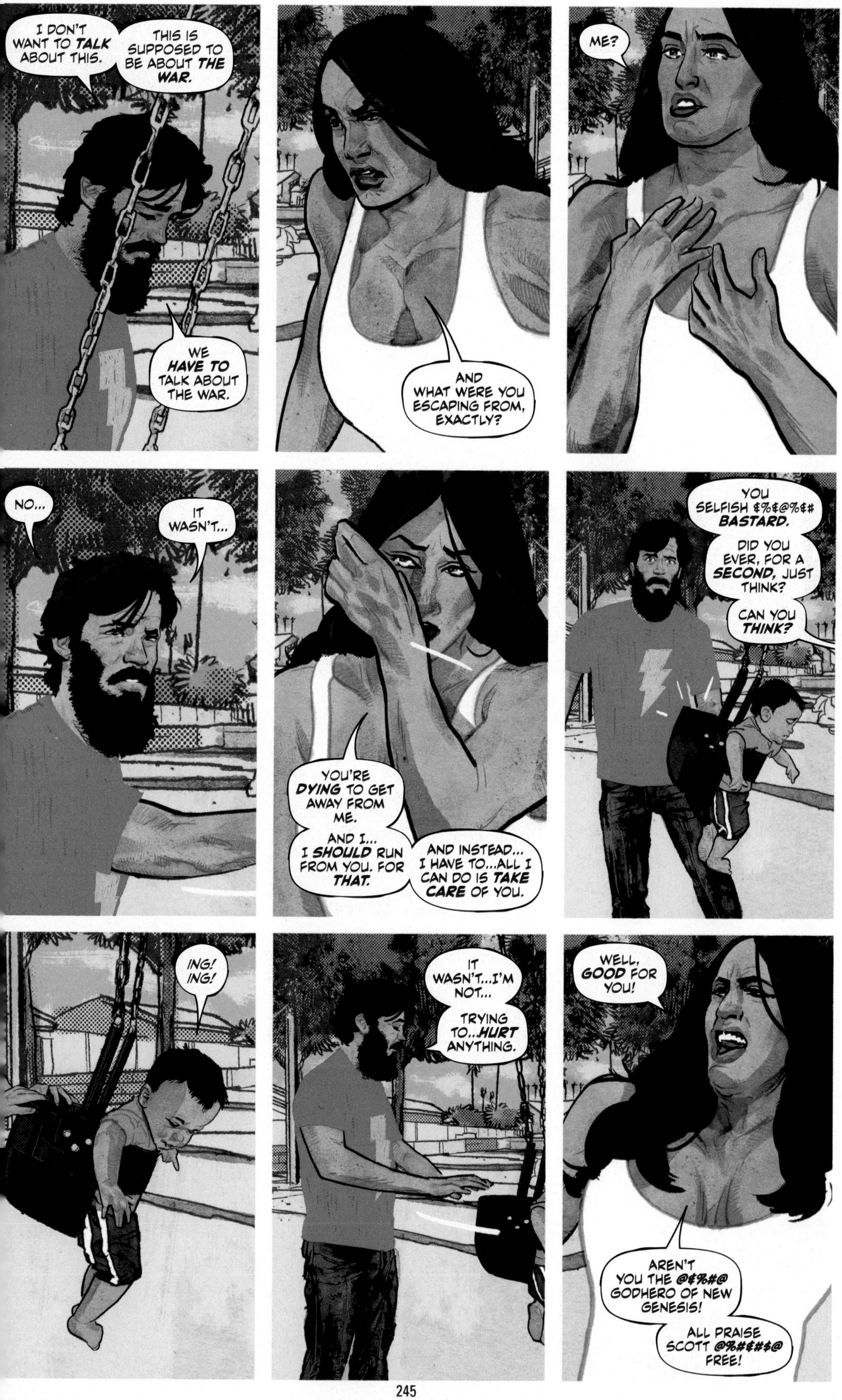

I DON'T WANT TO **TALK** ABOUT THIS.
THIS IS SUPPOSED TO BE ABOUT **THE WAR.**
WE **HAVE TO** TALK ABOUT THE WAR.
AND WHAT WERE YOU ESCAPING FROM, EXACTLY?
ME?
NO...
IT WASN'T...
YOU'RE **DYING** TO GET AWAY FROM ME.
AND I... I **SHOULD** RUN FROM YOU. FOR **THAT.**
AND INSTEAD... I HAVE TO...ALL I CAN DO IS **TAKE CARE** OF YOU.
YOU SELFISH $%$@%$# **BASTARD.**
DID YOU EVER, FOR A **SECOND,** JUST THINK?
CAN YOU **THINK?**
ING! ING!
IT WASN'T...I'M NOT...
TRYING TO...**HURT** ANYTHING.
WELL, **GOOD** FOR YOU!
AREN'T YOU THE @$%#@ GODHERO OF NEW GENESIS!
ALL PRAISE SCOTT @%#$#$@ FREE!

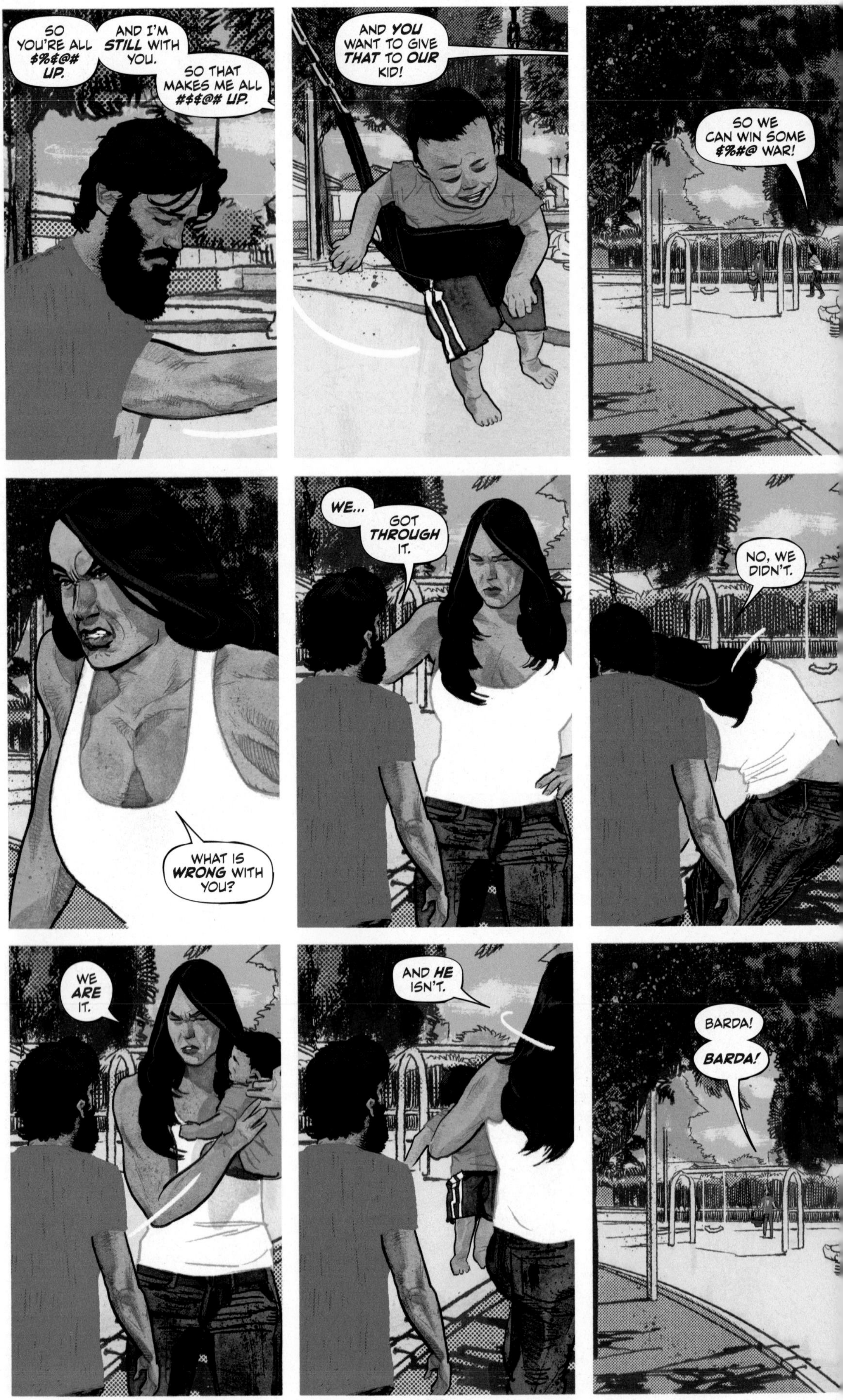

SO YOU'RE ALL $%$@# UP.
AND I'M STILL WITH YOU.
SO THAT MAKES ME ALL #$$@# UP.
AND YOU WANT TO GIVE THAT TO OUR KID!
SO WE CAN WIN SOME $%#@ WAR!
WHAT IS WRONG WITH YOU?
WE...
GOT THROUGH IT.
NO, WE DIDN'T.
WE ARE IT.
AND HE ISN'T.
BARDA!
BARDA!

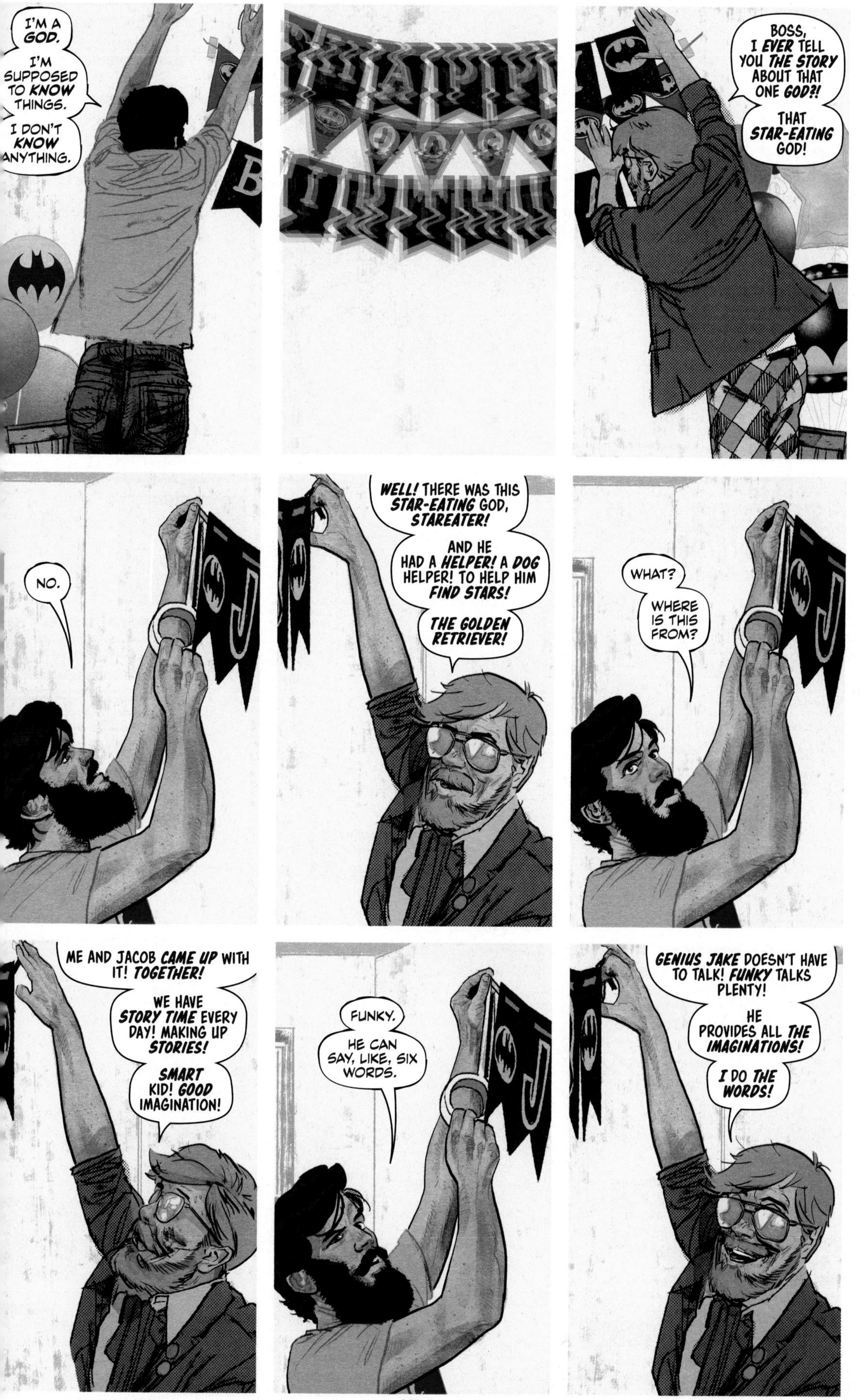
I'M A GOD.
I'M SUPPOSED TO KNOW THINGS.
I DON'T KNOW ANYTHING.
HAPPY BIRTHDAY
BOSS, I EVER TELL YOU THE STORY ABOUT THAT ONE GOD?!
THAT STAR-EATING GOD!
NO.
WELL! THERE WAS THIS STAR-EATING GOD, STAREATER!
AND HE HAD A HELPER! A DOG HELPER! TO HELP HIM FIND STARS!
THE GOLDEN RETRIEVER!
WHAT?
WHERE IS THIS FROM?
ME AND JACOB CAME UP WITH IT! TOGETHER!
WE HAVE STORY TIME EVERY DAY! MAKING UP STORIES!
SMART KID! GOOD IMAGINATION!
FUNKY.
HE CAN SAY, LIKE, SIX WORDS.
GENIUS JAKE DOESN'T HAVE TO TALK! FUNKY TALKS PLENTY!
HE PROVIDES ALL THE IMAGINATIONS!
I DO THE WORDS!

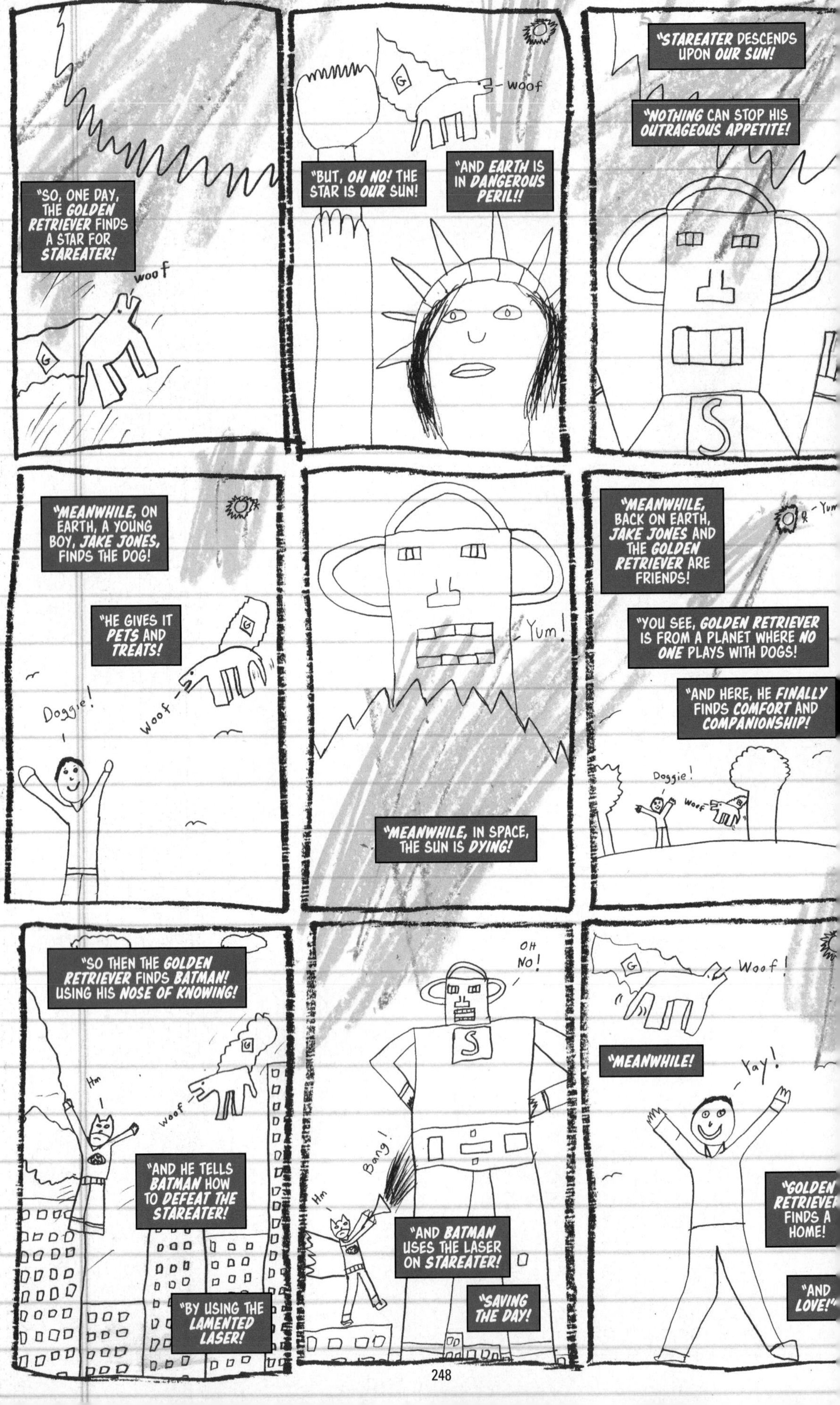
"SO, ONE DAY, THE GOLDEN RETRIEVER FINDS A STAR FOR STAREATER!
woof
"BUT, OH NO! THE STAR IS OUR SUN!
woof
"AND EARTH IS IN DANGEROUS PERIL!!
"STAREATER DESCENDS UPON OUR SUN!
"NOTHING CAN STOP HIS OUTRAGEOUS APPETITE!
"MEANWHILE, ON EARTH, A YOUNG BOY, JAKE JONES, FINDS THE DOG!
"HE GIVES IT PETS AND TREATS!
Doggie!
woof
Yum!
"MEANWHILE, IN SPACE, THE SUN IS DYING!
"MEANWHILE, BACK ON EARTH, JAKE JONES AND THE GOLDEN RETRIEVER ARE FRIENDS!
"YOU SEE, GOLDEN RETRIEVER IS FROM A PLANET WHERE NO ONE PLAYS WITH DOGS!
"AND HERE, HE FINALLY FINDS COMFORT AND COMPANIONSHIP!
Doggie!
woof
"SO THEN THE GOLDEN RETRIEVER FINDS BATMAN! USING HIS NOSE OF KNOWING!
Hm
woof
"AND HE TELLS BATMAN HOW TO DEFEAT THE STAREATER!
"BY USING THE LAMENTED LASER!
OH NO!
Bang!
Hm
"AND BATMAN USES THE LASER ON STAREATER!
"SAVING THE DAY!
Woof!
"MEANWHILE!
Yay!
"GOLDEN RETRIEVE FINDS A HOME!
"AND LOVE!"

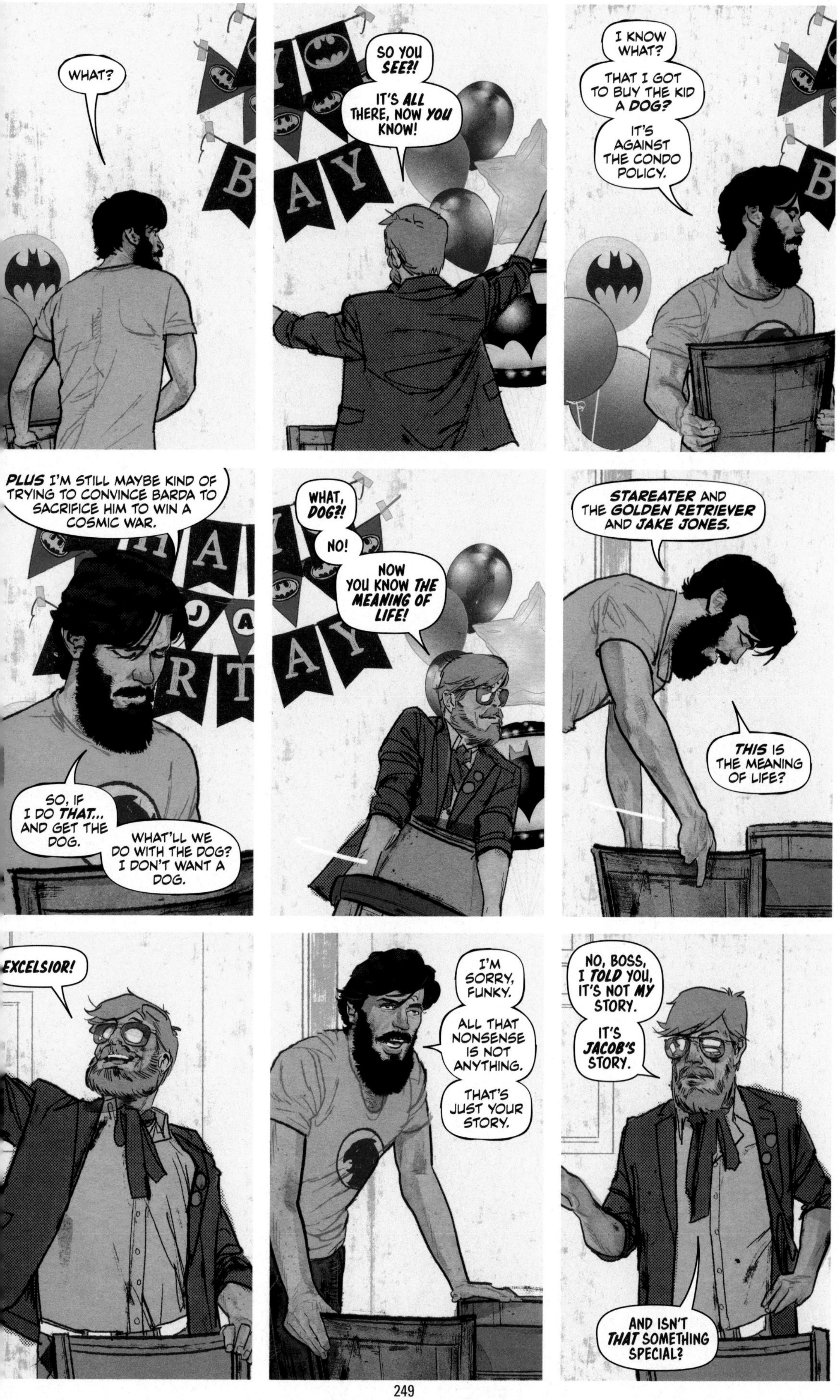
WHAT?
SO YOU SEE?!
IT'S ALL THERE, NOW YOU KNOW!
I KNOW WHAT?
THAT I GOT TO BUY THE KID A DOG?
IT'S AGAINST THE CONDO POLICY.
PLUS I'M STILL MAYBE KIND OF TRYING TO CONVINCE BARDA TO SACRIFICE HIM TO WIN A COSMIC WAR.
SO, IF I DO THAT... AND GET THE DOG.
WHAT'LL WE DO WITH THE DOG? I DON'T WANT A DOG.
WHAT, DOG?!
NO!
NOW YOU KNOW THE MEANING OF LIFE!
STAREATER AND THE GOLDEN RETRIEVER AND JAKE JONES.
THIS IS THE MEANING OF LIFE?
EXCELSIOR!
I'M SORRY, FUNKY.
ALL THAT NONSENSE IS NOT ANYTHING.
THAT'S JUST YOUR STORY.
NO, BOSS, I TOLD YOU, IT'S NOT MY STORY.
IT'S JACOB'S STORY.
AND ISN'T THAT SOMETHING SPECIAL?

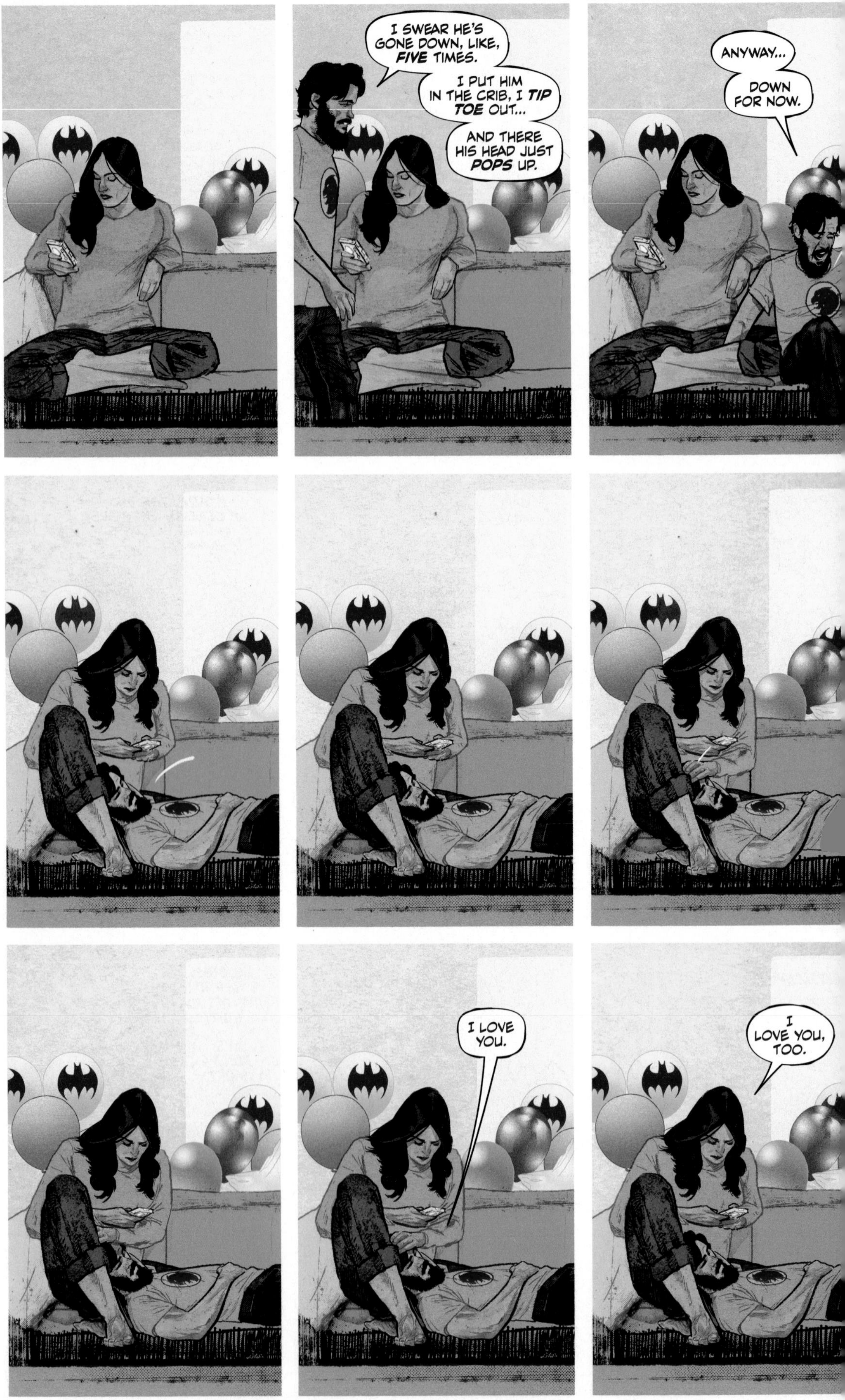
I SWEAR HE'S GONE DOWN, LIKE, *FIVE* TIMES.
I PUT HIM IN THE CRIB, I *TIP TOE* OUT...
AND THERE HIS HEAD JUST *POPS* UP.
ANYWAY...
DOWN FOR NOW.
I LOVE YOU.
I LOVE YOU, TOO.

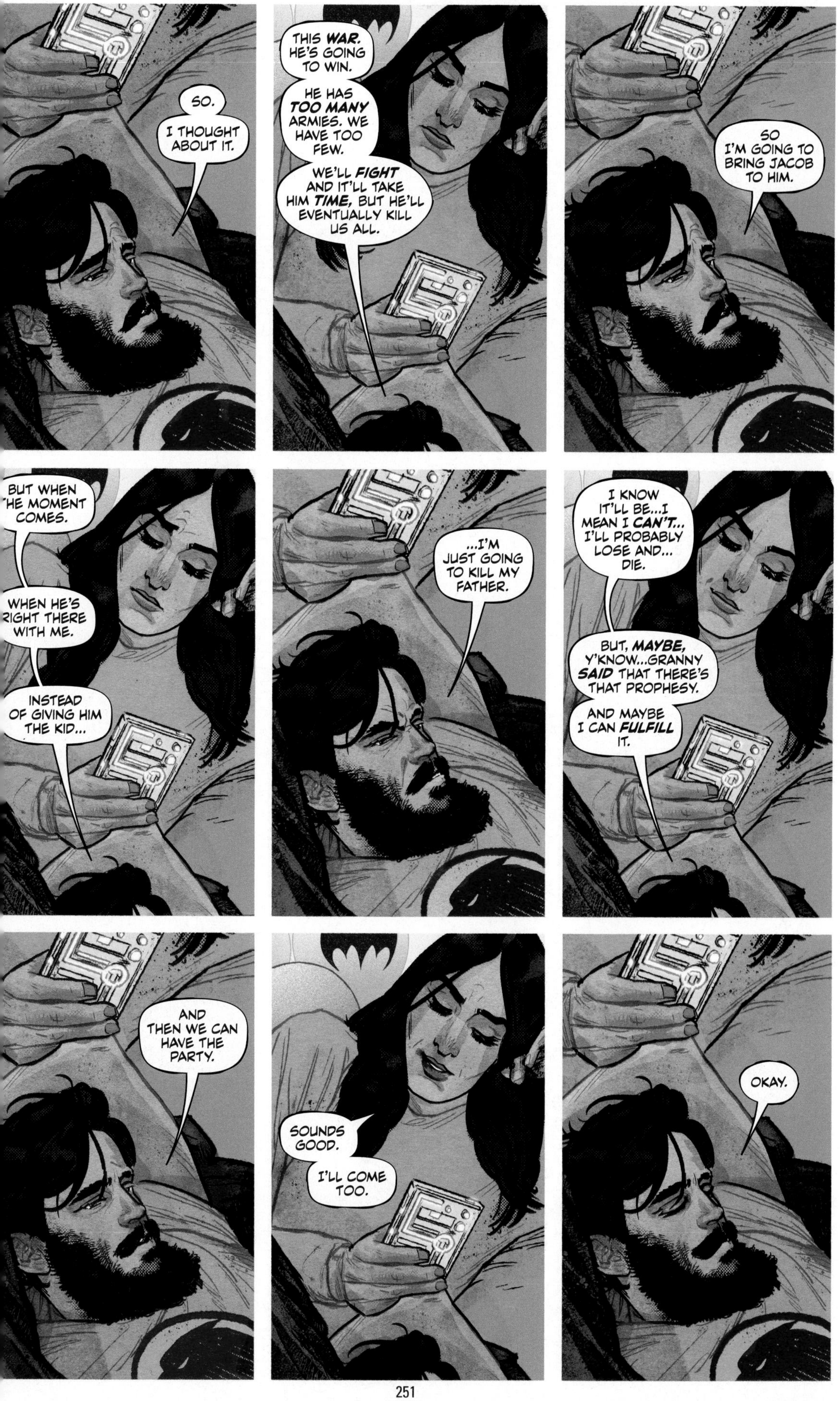
SO.
I THOUGHT ABOUT IT.
THIS WAR. HE'S GOING TO WIN.
HE HAS TOO MANY ARMIES. WE HAVE TOO FEW.
WE'LL FIGHT AND IT'LL TAKE HIM TIME, BUT HE'LL EVENTUALLY KILL US ALL.
SO I'M GOING TO BRING JACOB TO HIM.
BUT WHEN THE MOMENT COMES.
WHEN HE'S RIGHT THERE WITH ME.
INSTEAD OF GIVING HIM THE KID...
...I'M JUST GOING TO KILL MY FATHER.
I KNOW IT'LL BE...I MEAN I CAN'T... I'LL PROBABLY LOSE AND... DIE.
BUT, MAYBE, Y'KNOW...GRANNY SAID THAT THERE'S THAT PROPHESY.
AND MAYBE I CAN FULFILL IT.
AND THEN WE CAN HAVE THE PARTY.
SOUNDS GOOD.
I'LL COME TOO.
OKAY.

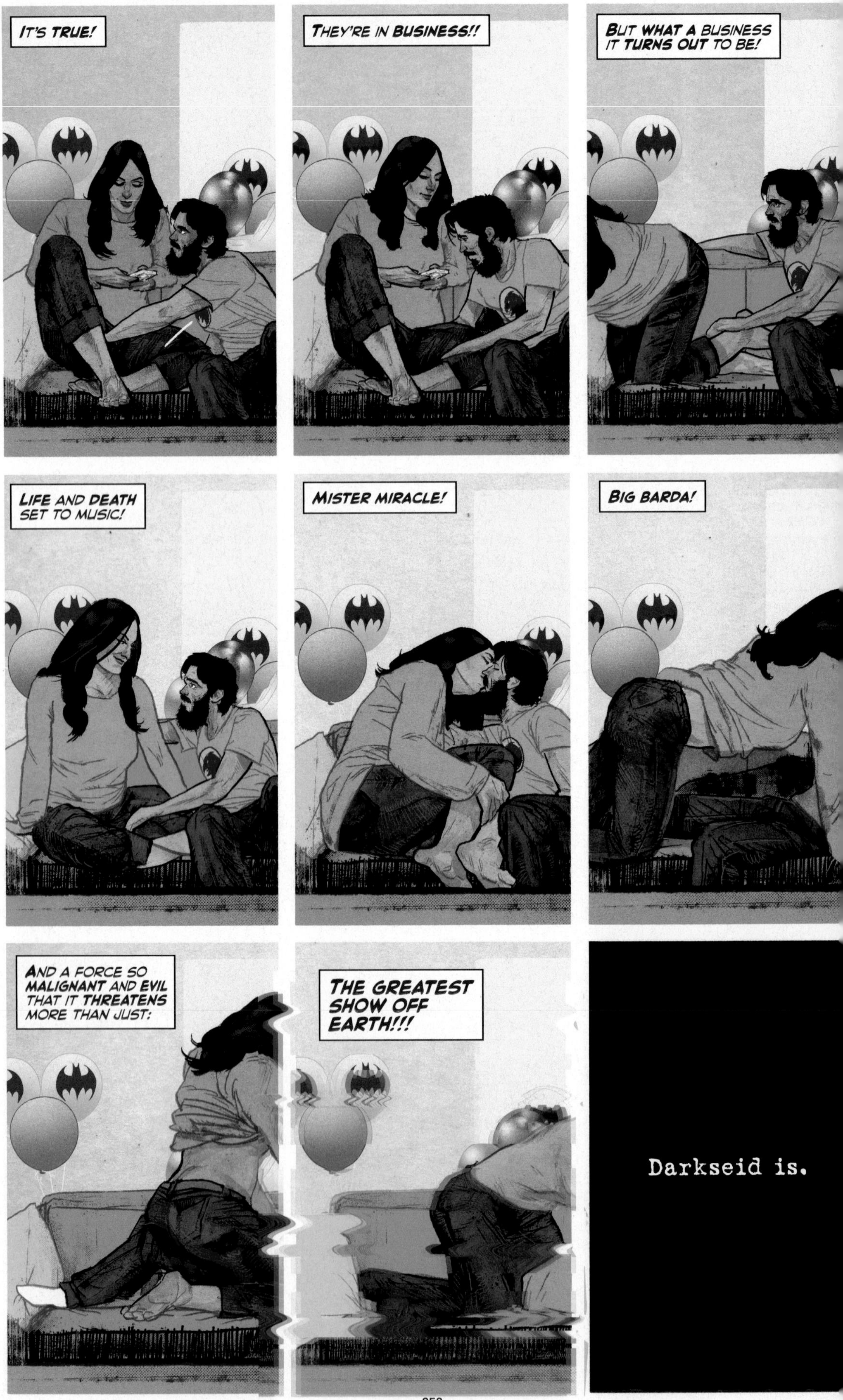
IT'S TRUE!
THEY'RE IN BUSINESS!!
BUT WHAT A BUSINESS IT TURNS OUT TO BE!
LIFE AND DEATH SET TO MUSIC!
MISTER MIRACLE!
BIG BARDA!
AND A FORCE SO MALIGNANT AND EVIL THAT IT THREATENS MORE THAN JUST:
THE GREATEST SHOW OFF EARTH!!!
Darkseid is.

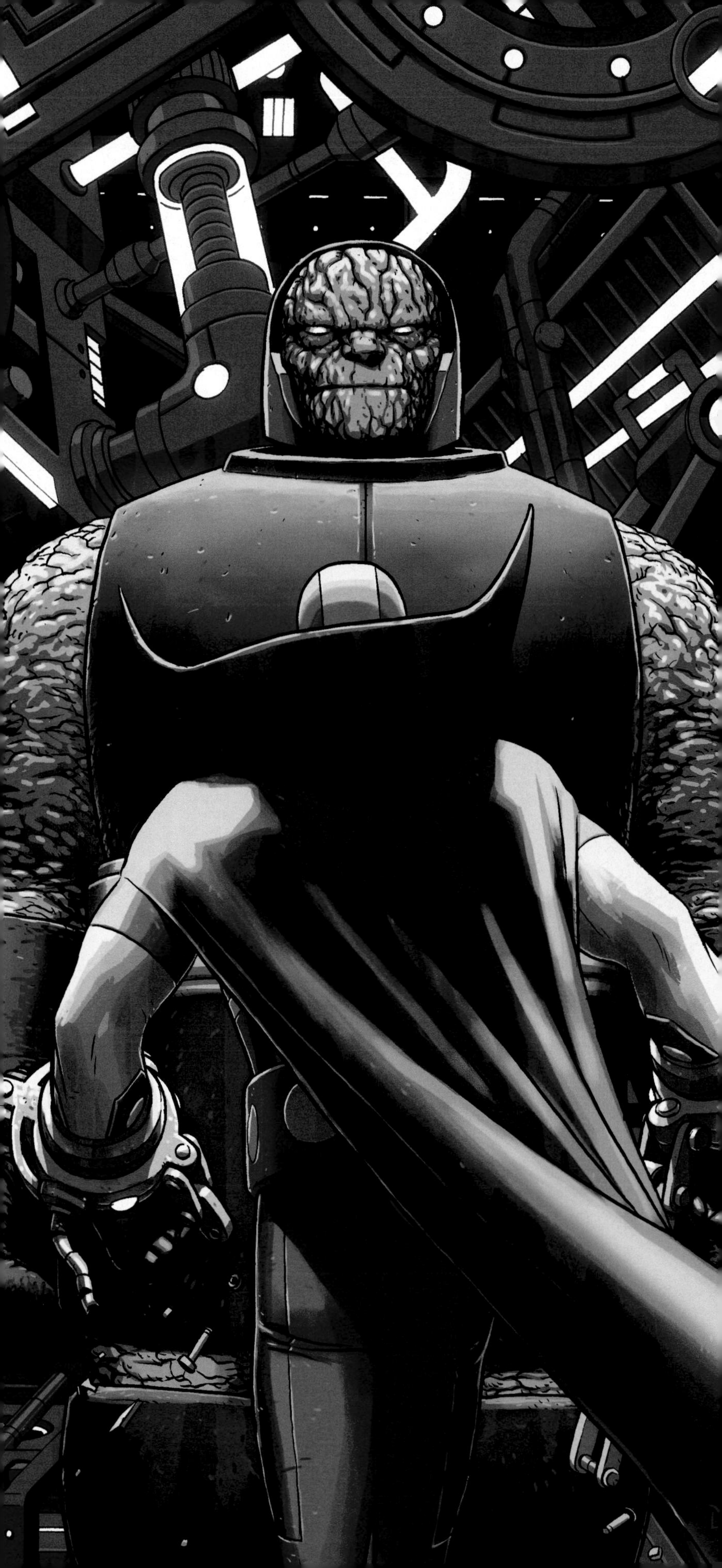

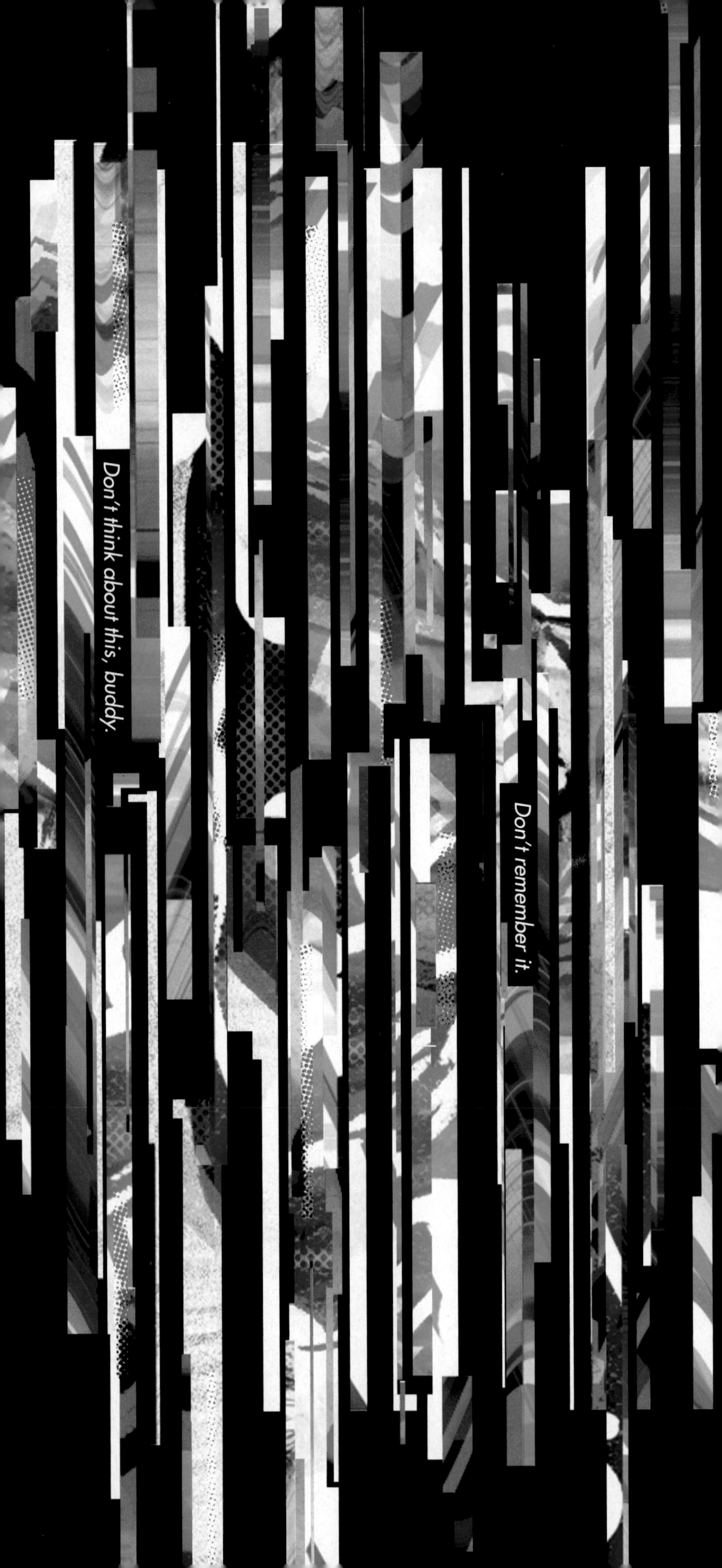
Don't think about this, buddy.
Don't remember it.

AND THIS IS HOW T BEGINS!

DON'T FORGET THE TRAY!

WITH *FLAMING DEATH* LEAPING TO CLAIM ITS *VICTIM* AND COMPLETE ITS *HORRIBLE* CYCLE!

DID YOU GET THE EXTRA DIAPERS?!

BUT, WHERE NO OTHER ESCAPE ARTIST *DARES* TO HOPE *THIS* ONE DARES *ANYTHING!!*

ALL RIGHT, I GOT THREE!

IS THAT *ENOUGH?!* WHAT ABOUT THE *BOTTLES?!*

ESPECIALLY WHEN HE HOVERS AT THE EDGE OF DOOM!

DO YOU HAVE THE *BATMAN?*

HE'LL *FREAK* OUT.

ESPECIALLY, WHEN DESTINY CHALLENGES HIM--*LURES* HIM TO THE POINT OF NO RETURN--AND BEYOND!

I FOUND IT!

BUT HE PROBABLY NEEDS A TEETHING THING, TOO!

THIS IS MORE THAN AN *ACT!*

I FORGOT! WE GOT TO GET ANOTHER CHANGE OF CLOTHES!

HE ALWAYS SPITS UP IN THE TUBE!

THIS IS THE *LIFESTYLE* OF...

ALL RIGHT. WE'RE GOOD.

TIME TO SAVE THE DAY.

BOOM.

#$^%$.

MISTER MIRACLE.

WHAT?

I FORGOT MY #$^%ING MOTHER BOX!

SUPER ESCAPE ARTIST.

MAA!

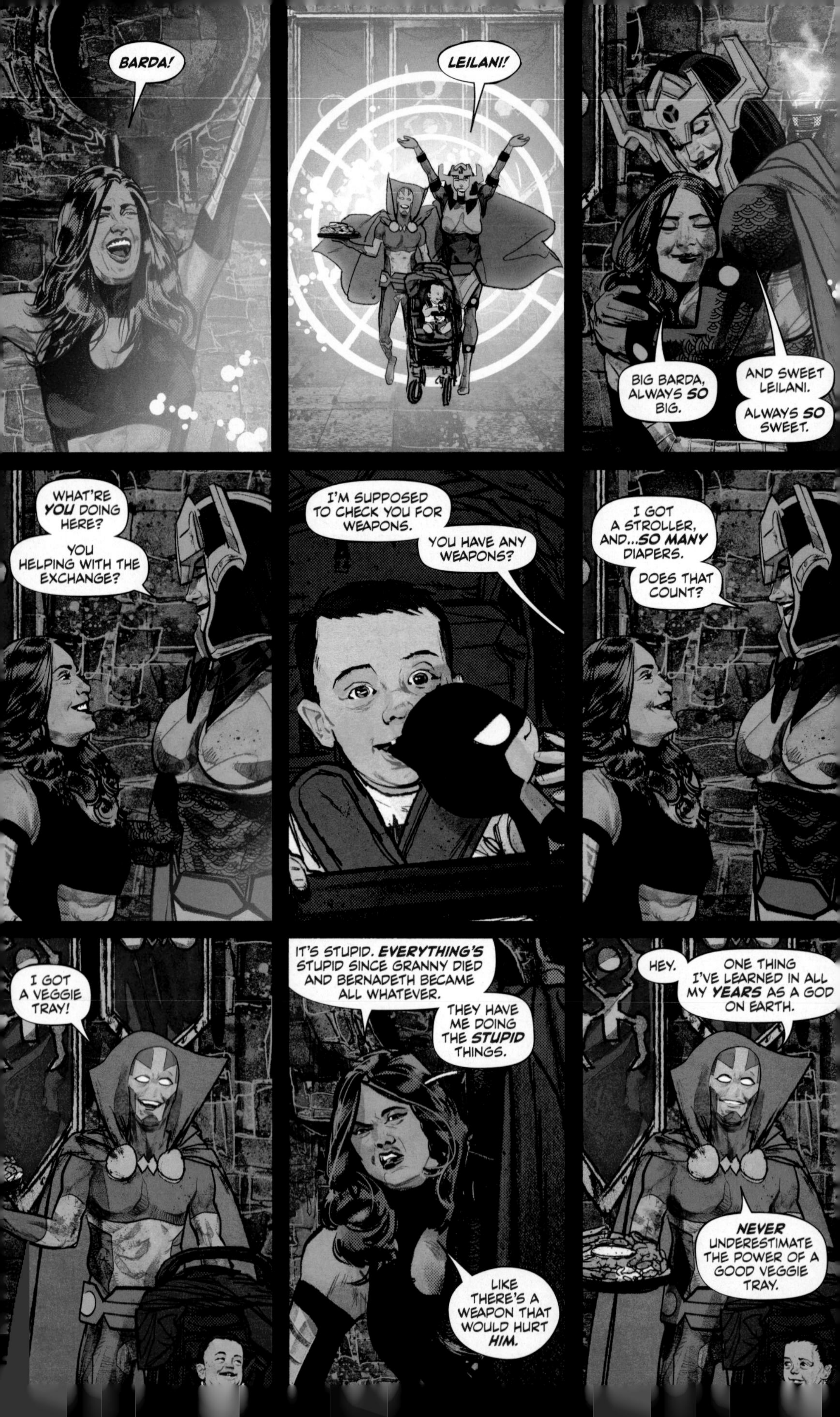
BARDA!
LEILANI!
BIG BARDA, ALWAYS SO BIG.
AND SWEET LEILANI.
ALWAYS SO SWEET.
WHAT'RE YOU DOING HERE?
YOU HELPING WITH THE EXCHANGE?
I'M SUPPOSED TO CHECK YOU FOR WEAPONS.
YOU HAVE ANY WEAPONS?
I GOT A STROLLER, AND...SO MANY DIAPERS.
DOES THAT COUNT?
I GOT A VEGGIE TRAY!
IT'S STUPID. EVERYTHING'S STUPID SINCE GRANNY DIED AND BERNADETH BECAME ALL WHATEVER.
THEY HAVE ME DOING THE STUPID THINGS.
LIKE THERE'S A WEAPON THAT WOULD HURT HIM.
HEY.
ONE THING I'VE LEARNED IN ALL MY YEARS AS A GOD ON EARTH.
NEVER UNDERESTIMATE THE POWER OF A GOOD VEGGIE TRAY.

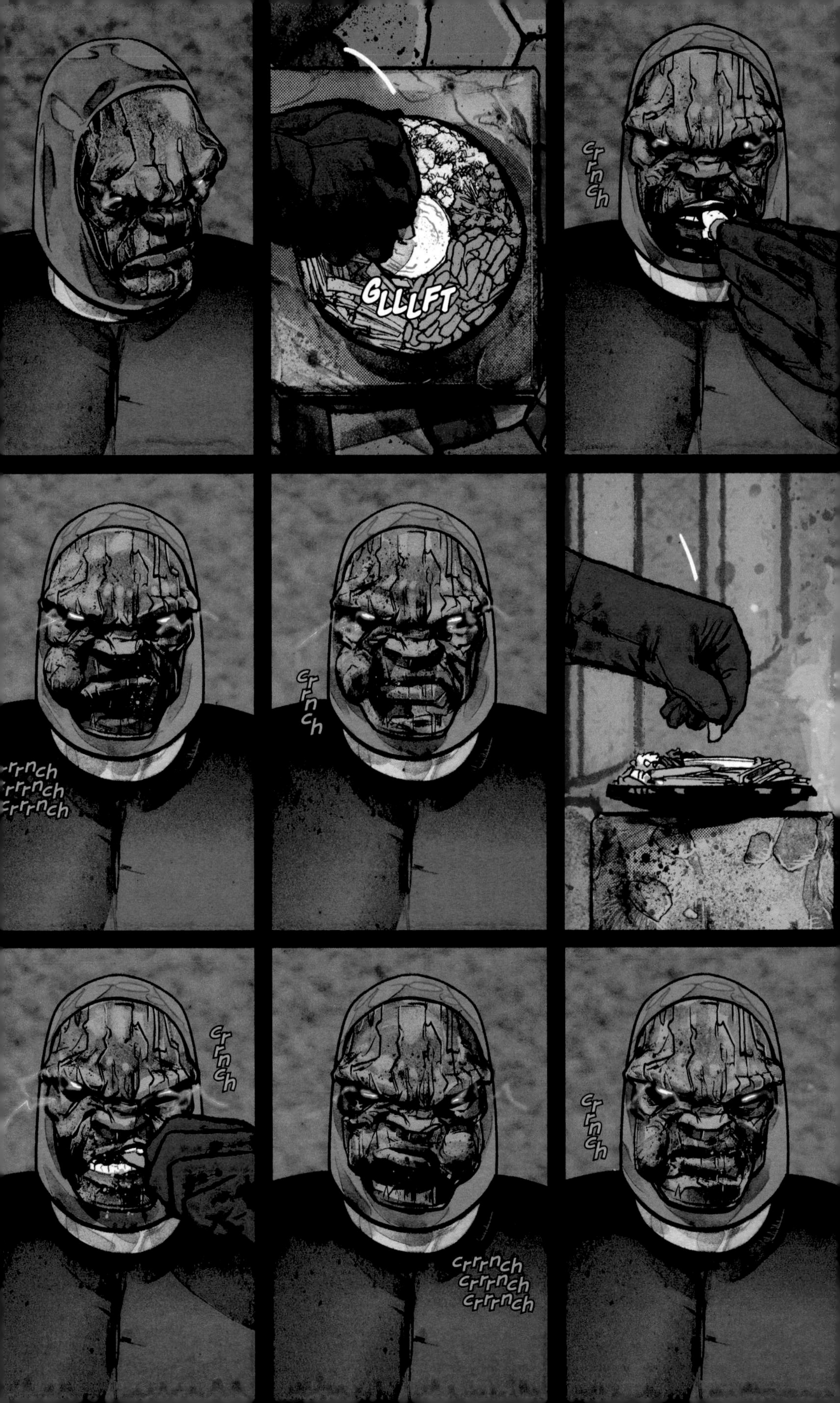
GLLLFT
crrnch
crrrnch
crrrnch
crrrnch
crrnch
crrnch
crrrnch
crrrnch
crrrnch
crrnch

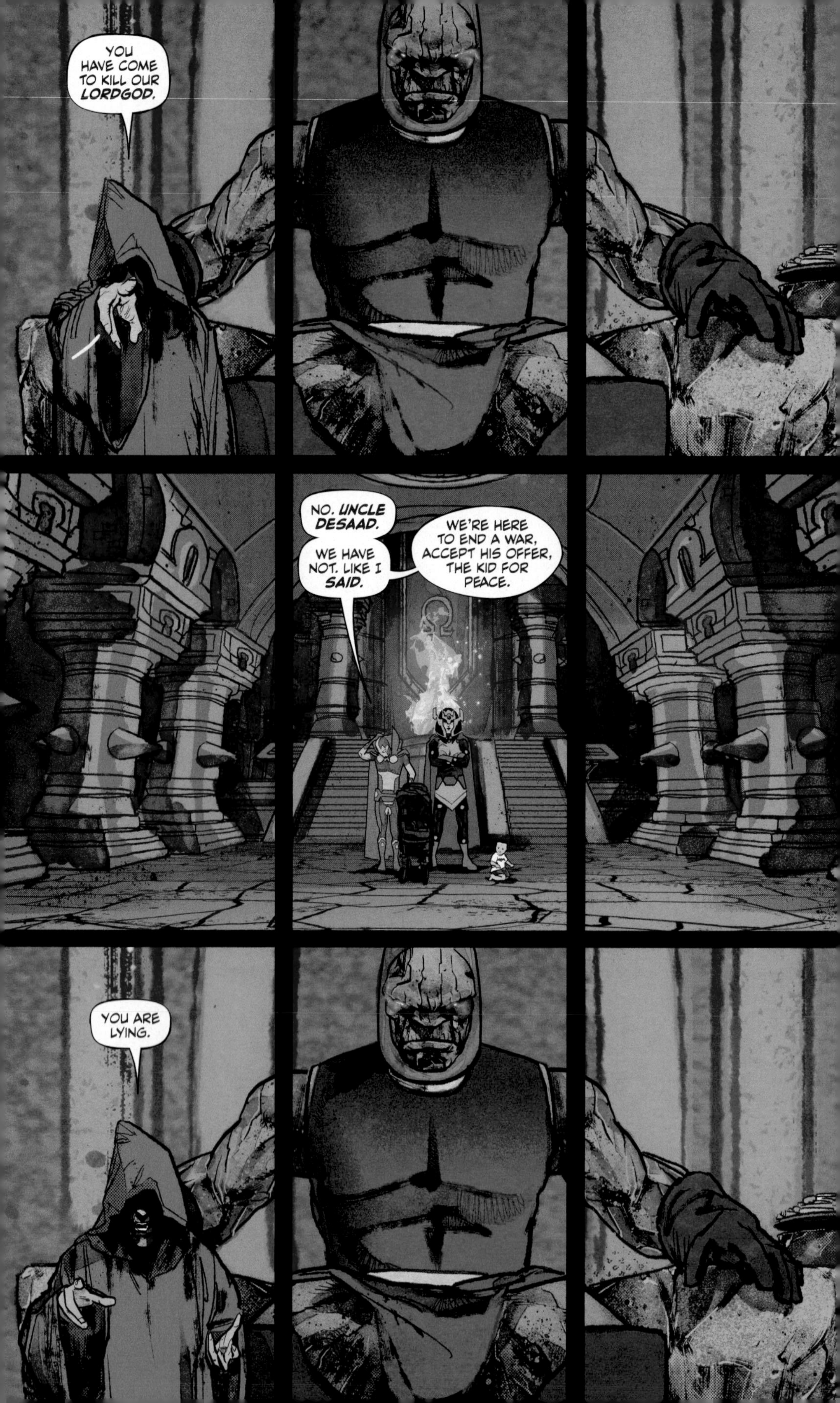
YOU HAVE COME TO KILL OUR LORDGOD.
NO. UNCLE DESAAD.
WE HAVE NOT. LIKE I SAID.
WE'RE HERE TO END A WAR, ACCEPT HIS OFFER, THE KID FOR PEACE.
YOU ARE LYING.

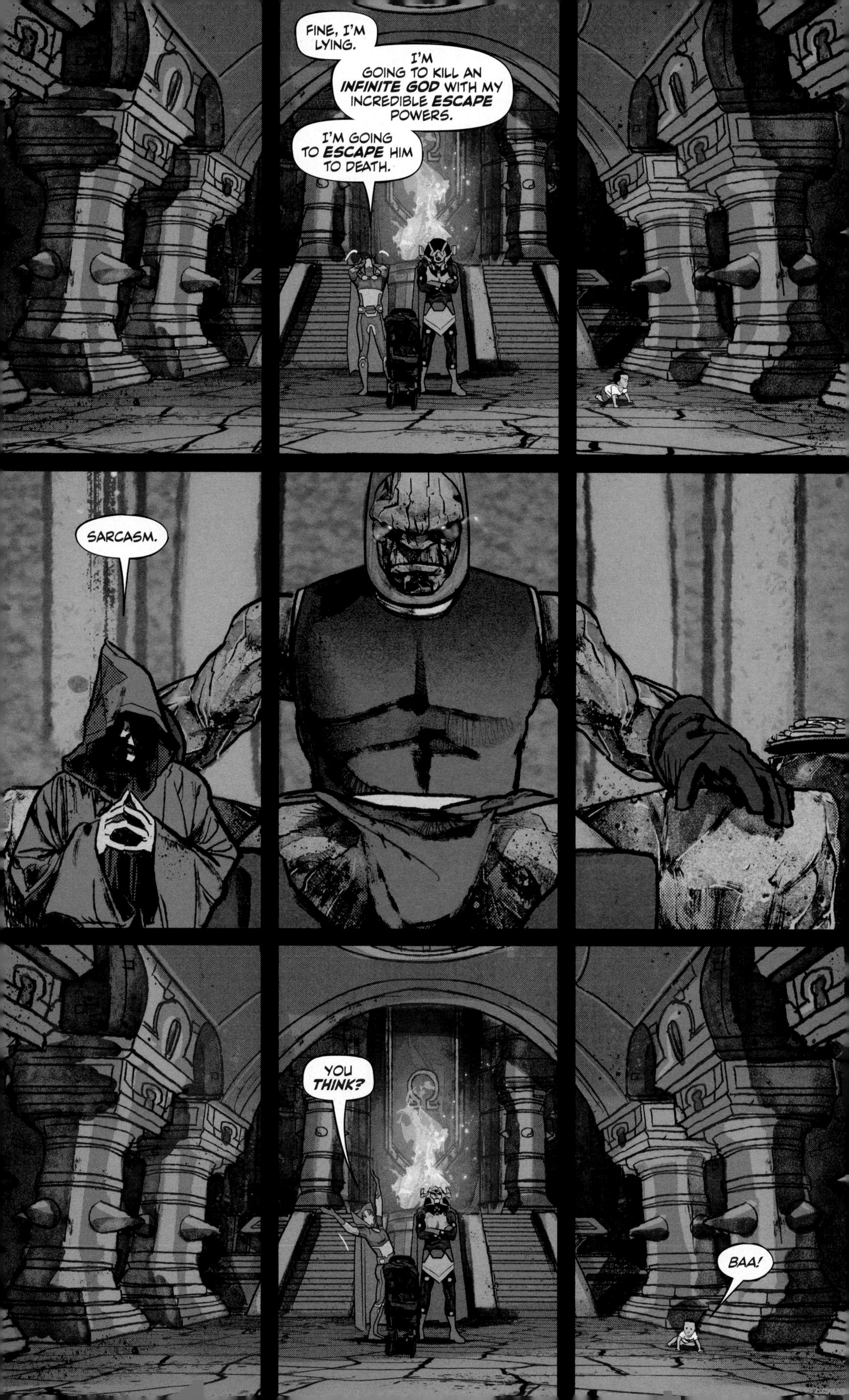
FINE, I'M LYING.
I'M GOING TO KILL AN INFINITE GOD WITH MY INCREDIBLE ESCAPE POWERS.
I'M GOING TO ESCAPE HIM TO DEATH.
SARCASM.
YOU THINK?
BAA!

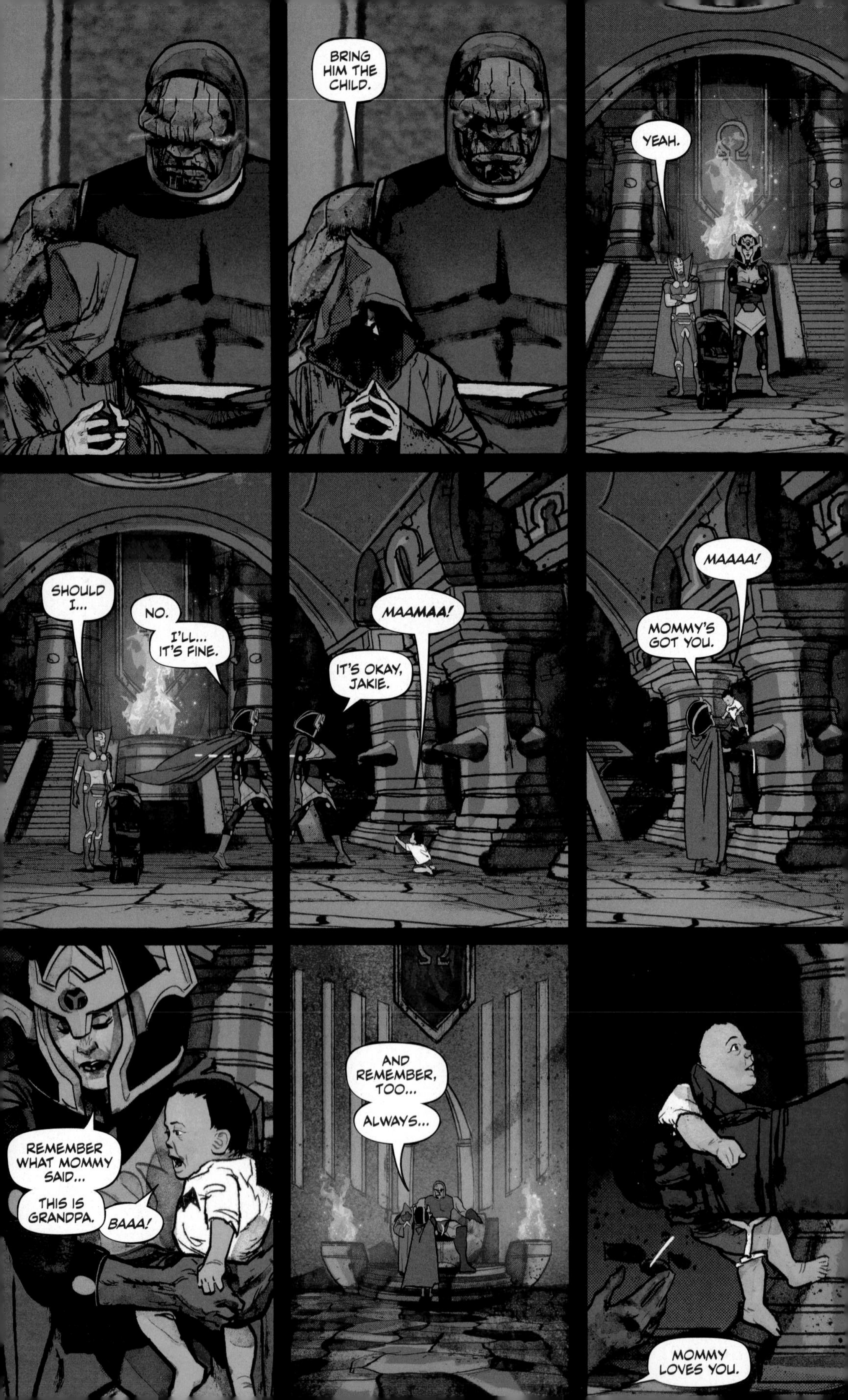
BRING HIM THE CHILD.
YEAH.
SHOULD I...
NO.
I'LL... IT'S FINE.
MAAMAA!
IT'S OKAY, JAKIE.
MAAAA!
MOMMY'S GOT YOU.
REMEMBER WHAT MOMMY SAID...
THIS IS GRANDPA.
BAAA!
AND REMEMBER, TOO...
ALWAYS...
MOMMY LOVES YOU.

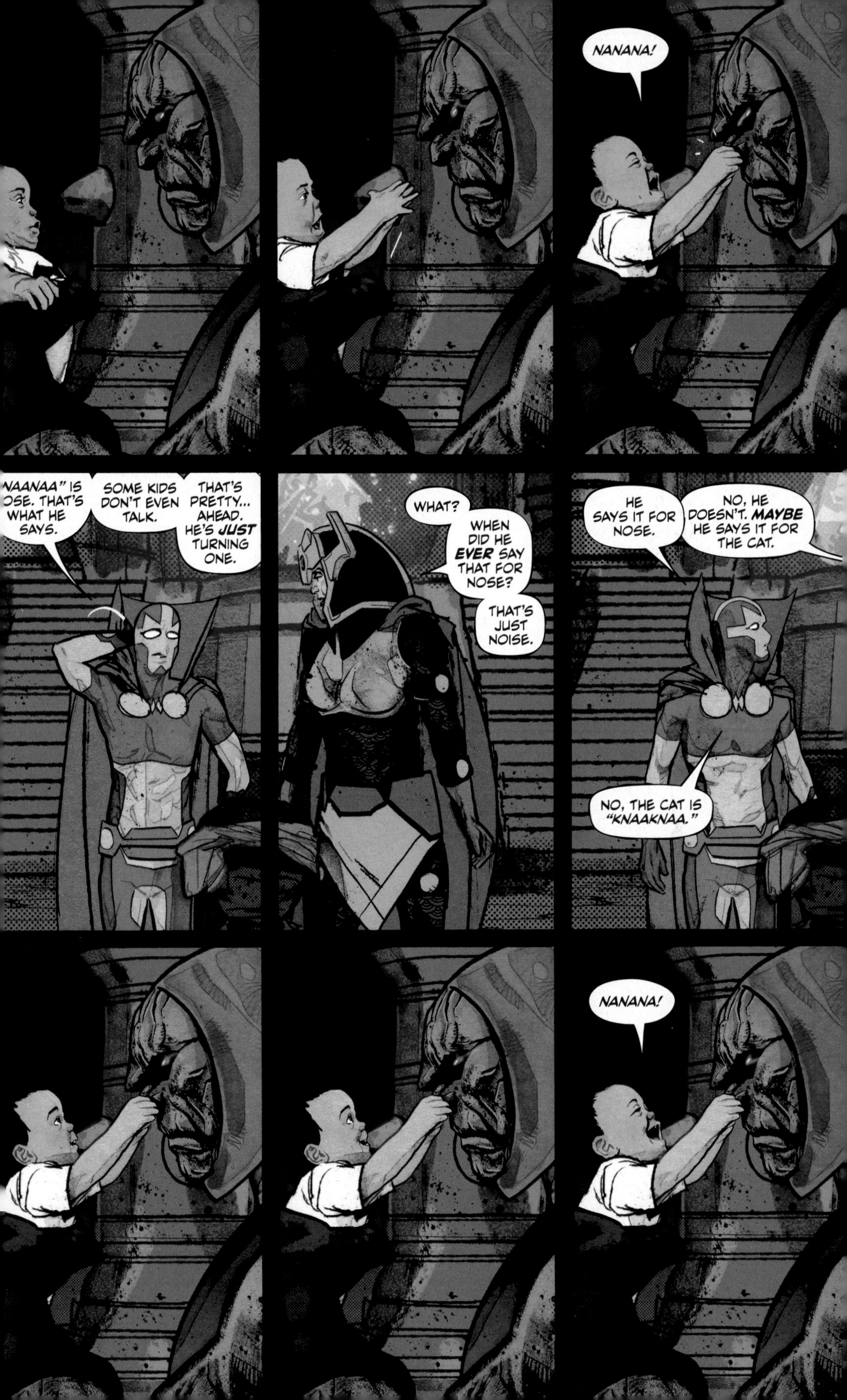
NANANA!
"NAANAA" IS NOSE. THAT'S WHAT HE SAYS.
SOME KIDS DON'T EVEN TALK.
THAT'S PRETTY... AHEAD. HE'S JUST TURNING ONE.
WHAT?
WHEN DID HE EVER SAY THAT FOR NOSE?
THAT'S JUST NOISE.
HE SAYS IT FOR NOSE.
NO, HE DOESN'T. MAYBE HE SAYS IT FOR THE CAT.
NO, THE CAT IS "KNAAKNAA."
NANANA!

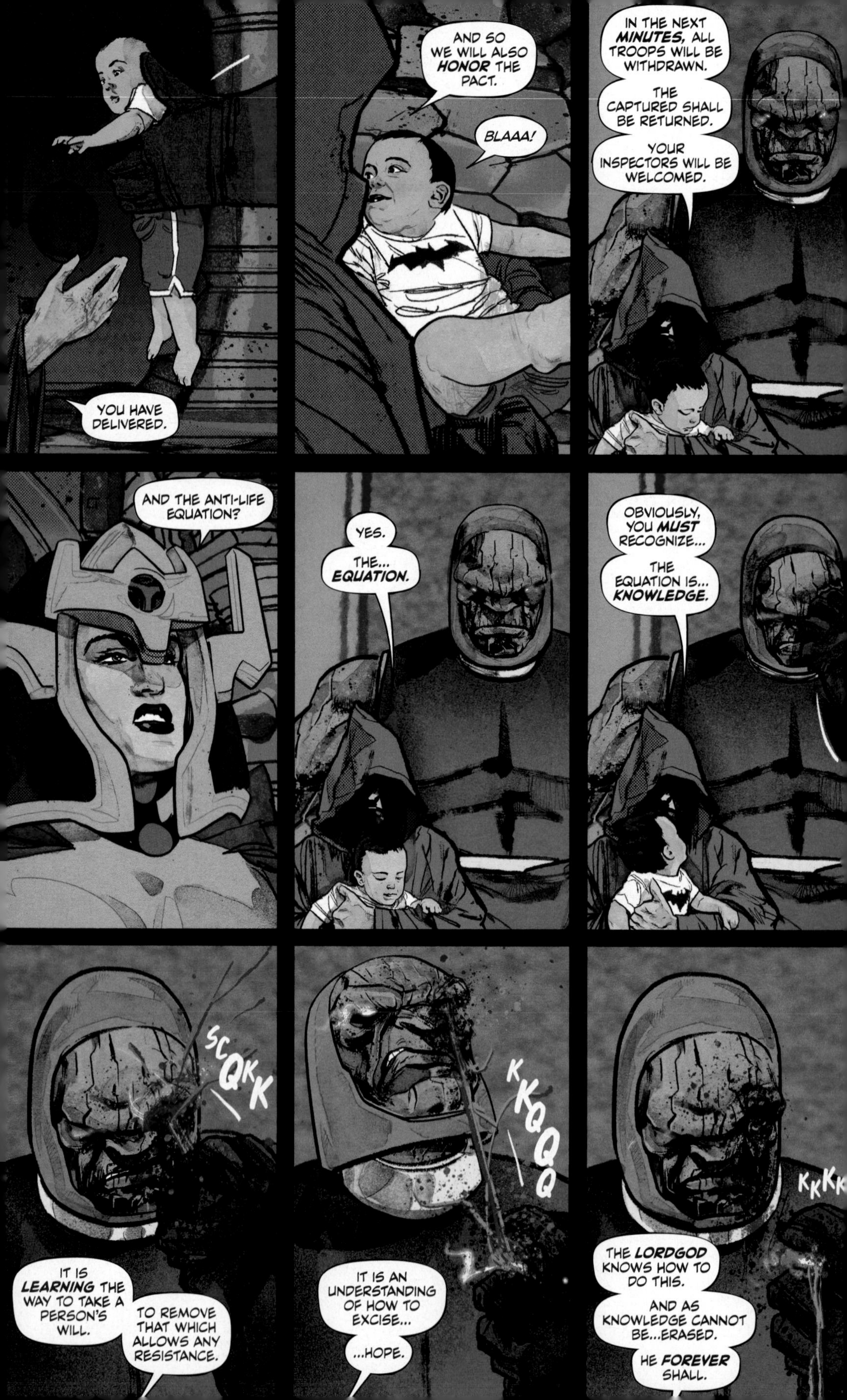
YOU HAVE DELIVERED.
AND SO WE WILL ALSO HONOR THE PACT.
BLAAA!
IN THE NEXT MINUTES, ALL TROOPS WILL BE WITHDRAWN.
THE CAPTURED SHALL BE RETURNED.
YOUR INSPECTORS WILL BE WELCOMED.
AND THE ANTI-LIFE EQUATION?
YES.
THE... EQUATION.
OBVIOUSLY, YOU MUST RECOGNIZE...
THE EQUATION IS... KNOWLEDGE.
SCQKK
IT IS LEARNING THE WAY TO TAKE A PERSON'S WILL.
TO REMOVE THAT WHICH ALLOWS ANY RESISTANCE.
KKQQQ
IT IS AN UNDERSTANDING OF HOW TO EXCISE...
...HOPE.
KKKK
THE LORDGOD KNOWS HOW TO DO THIS.
AND AS KNOWLEDGE CANNOT BE...ERASED.
HE FOREVER SHALL.

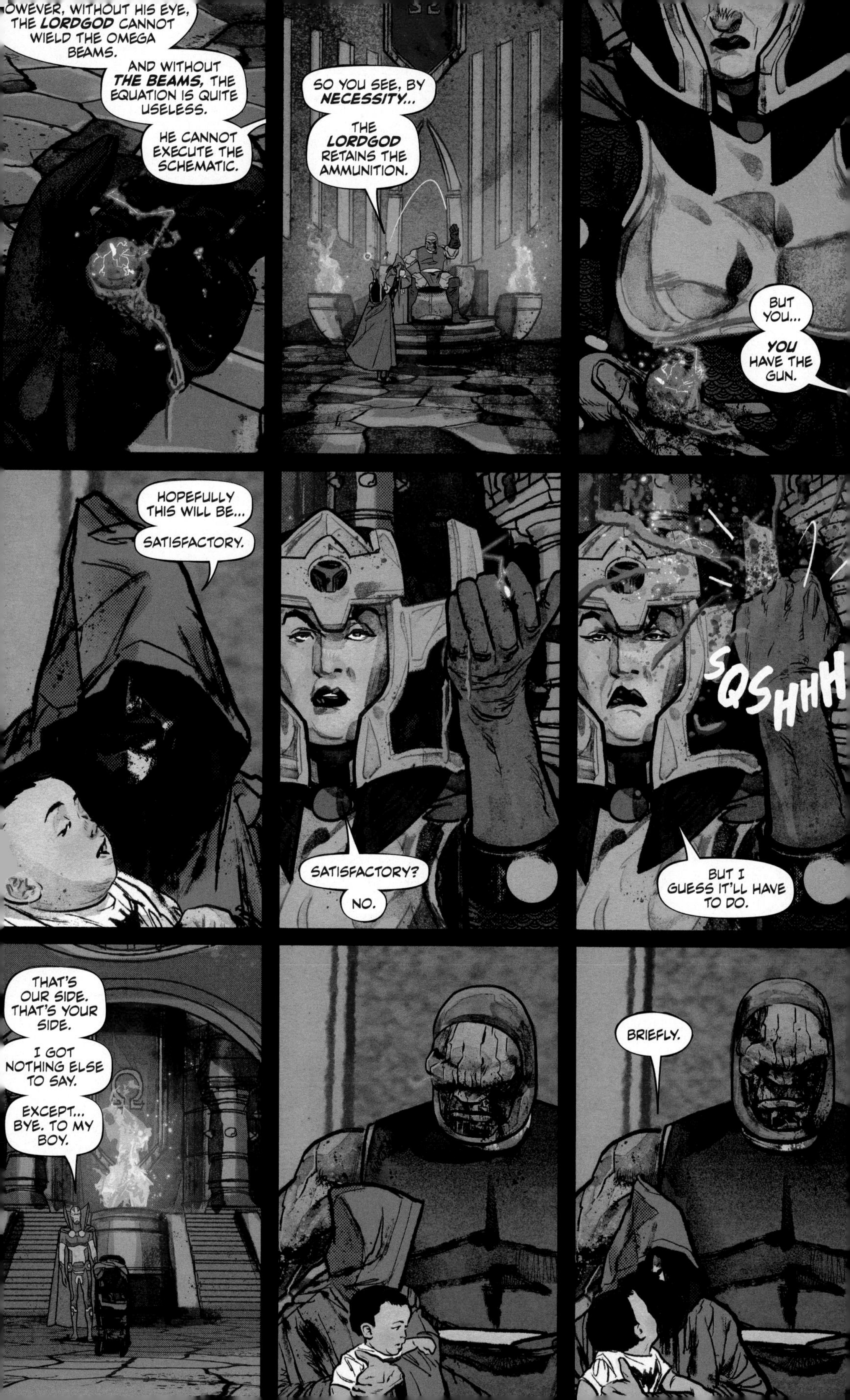
OWEVER, WITHOUT HIS EYE, THE LORDGOD CANNOT WIELD THE OMEGA BEAMS.
AND WITHOUT THE BEAMS, THE EQUATION IS QUITE USELESS.
HE CANNOT EXECUTE THE SCHEMATIC.
SO YOU SEE, BY NECESSITY...
THE LORDGOD RETAINS THE AMMUNITION.
BUT YOU...
YOU HAVE THE GUN.
HOPEFULLY THIS WILL BE...
SATISFACTORY.
SATISFACTORY?
NO.
SQSHHH
BUT I GUESS IT'LL HAVE TO DO.
THAT'S OUR SIDE. THAT'S YOUR SIDE.
I GOT NOTHING ELSE TO SAY.
EXCEPT... BYE. TO MY BOY.
BRIEFLY.

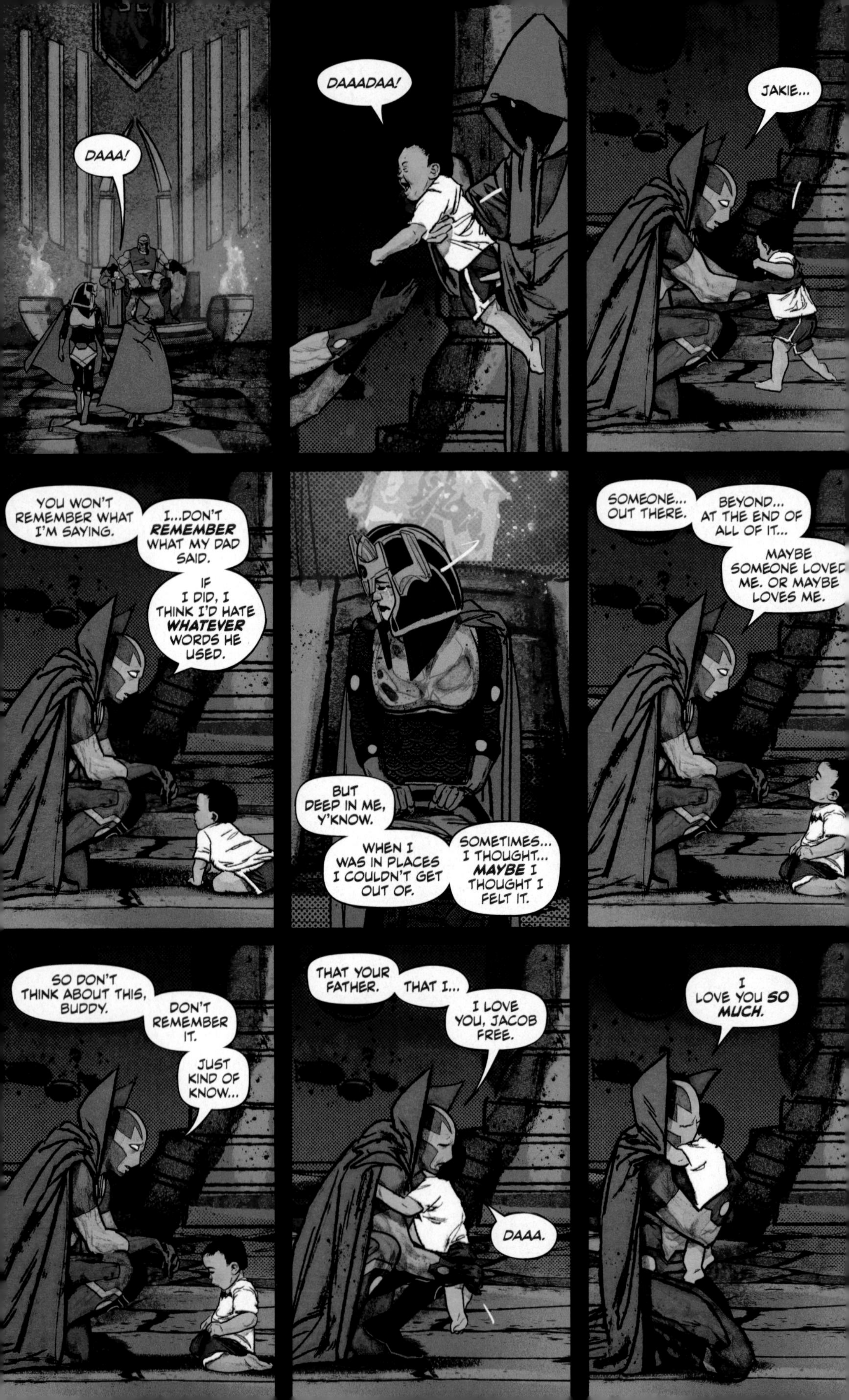
DAAA!
DAAADAA!
JAKIE...
YOU WON'T REMEMBER WHAT I'M SAYING.
I...DON'T REMEMBER WHAT MY DAD SAID.
IF I DID, I THINK I'D HATE WHATEVER WORDS HE USED.
BUT DEEP IN ME, Y'KNOW.
WHEN I WAS IN PLACES I COULDN'T GET OUT OF.
SOMETIMES... I THOUGHT... MAYBE I THOUGHT I FELT IT.
SOMEONE... OUT THERE.
BEYOND... AT THE END OF ALL OF IT...
MAYBE SOMEONE LOVED ME. OR MAYBE LOVES ME.
SO DON'T THINK ABOUT THIS, BUDDY.
DON'T REMEMBER IT.
JUST KIND OF KNOW...
THAT YOUR FATHER.
THAT I...
I LOVE YOU, JACOB FREE.
DAAA.
I LOVE YOU SO MUCH.

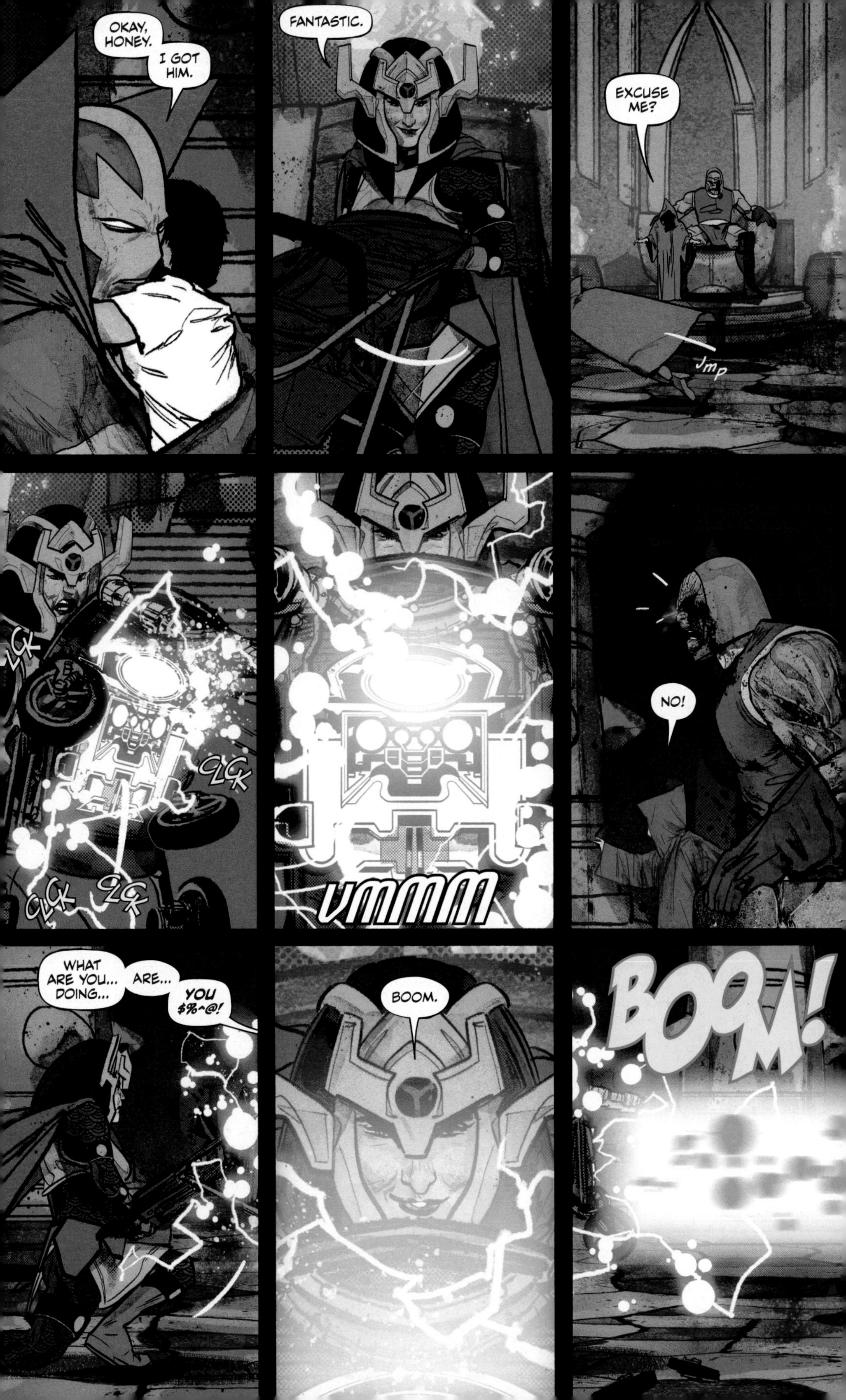

OKAY, HONEY.
I GOT HIM.
FANTASTIC.
EXCUSE ME?
Jmp
CLCK
CLCK
CLCK
CLCK
VMMMM
NO!
WHAT ARE YOU... DOING...
ARE...
YOU $%^@!
BOOM.
BOOM!

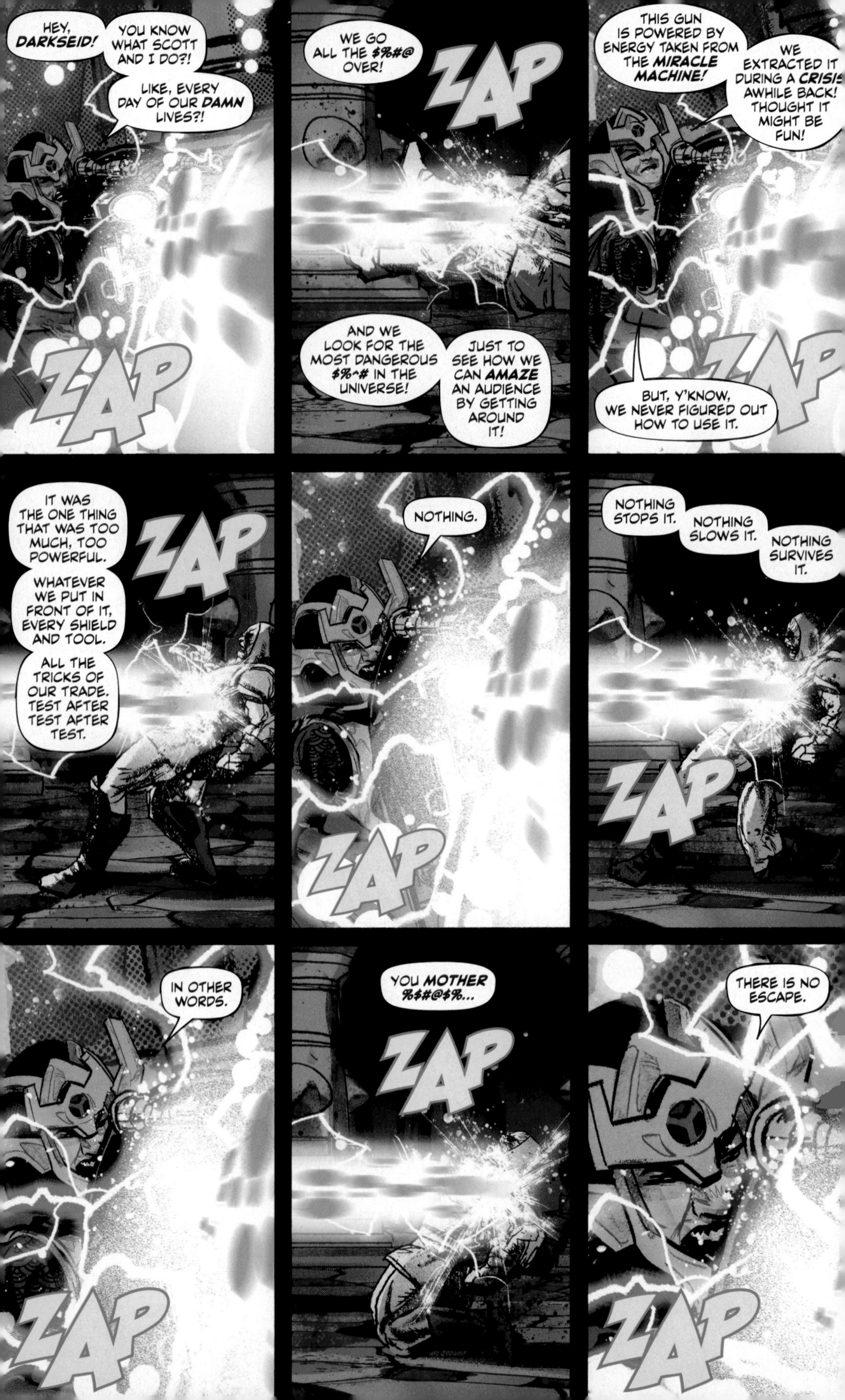
HEY, DARKSEID!
YOU KNOW WHAT SCOTT AND I DO?!
LIKE, EVERY DAY OF OUR DAMN LIVES?!
ZAP
WE GO ALL THE $%#@ OVER!
ZAP
AND WE LOOK FOR THE MOST DANGEROUS $%^# IN THE UNIVERSE!
JUST TO SEE HOW WE CAN AMAZE AN AUDIENCE BY GETTING AROUND IT!
THIS GUN IS POWERED BY ENERGY TAKEN FROM THE MIRACLE MACHINE!
WE EXTRACTED IT DURING A CRISIS AWHILE BACK! THOUGHT IT MIGHT BE FUN!
BUT, Y'KNOW, WE NEVER FIGURED OUT HOW TO USE IT.
ZAP
IT WAS THE ONE THING THAT WAS TOO MUCH, TOO POWERFUL.
WHATEVER WE PUT IN FRONT OF IT, EVERY SHIELD AND TOOL.
ALL THE TRICKS OF OUR TRADE. TEST AFTER TEST AFTER TEST.
ZAP
NOTHING.
ZAP
NOTHING STOPS IT.
NOTHING SLOWS IT.
NOTHING SURVIVES IT.
ZAP
IN OTHER WORDS.
ZAP
YOU MOTHER %$#@$%...
ZAP
THERE IS NO ESCAPE.
ZAP

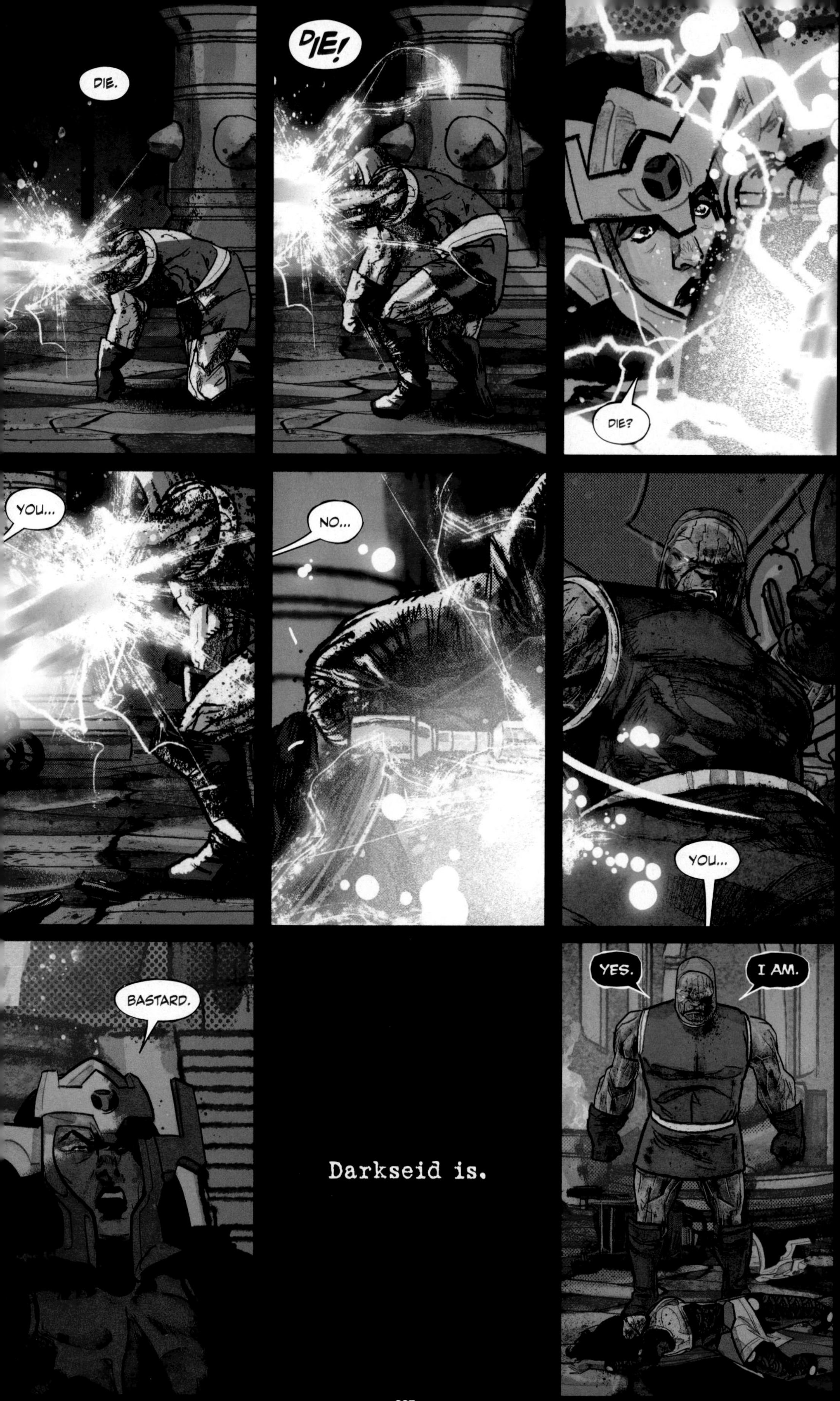
DIE.
DIE!
DIE?
YOU...
NO...
YOU...
BASTARD.
Darkseid is.
YES.
I AM.

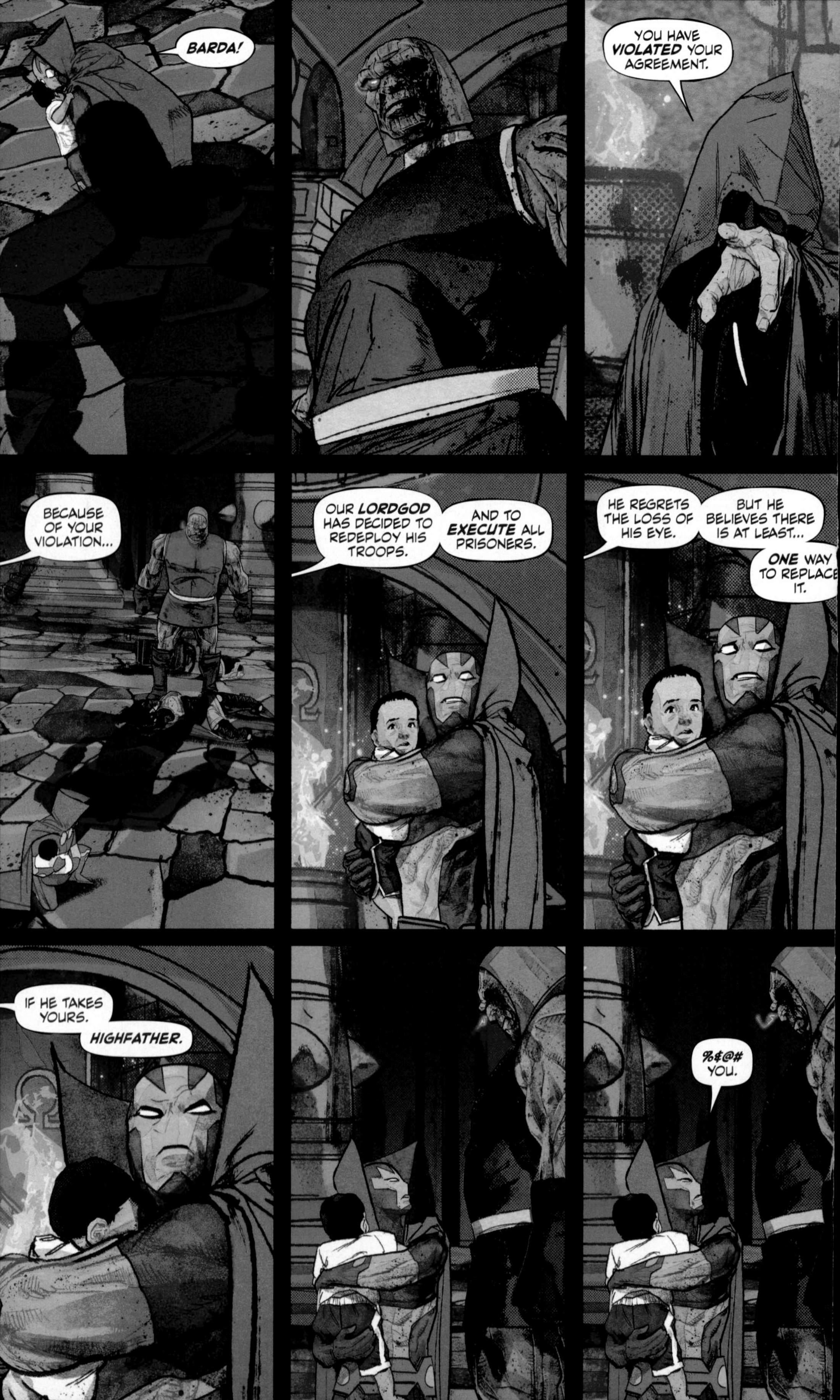
BARDA!
YOU HAVE VIOLATED YOUR AGREEMENT.
BECAUSE OF YOUR VIOLATION...
OUR LORDGOD HAS DECIDED TO REDEPLOY HIS TROOPS.
AND TO EXECUTE ALL PRISONERS.
HE REGRETS THE LOSS OF HIS EYE.
BUT HE BELIEVES THERE IS AT LEAST...
ONE WAY TO REPLACE IT.
IF HE TAKES YOURS.
HIGHFATHER.
%$@# YOU.

YOU ARE A DISAPPOINTMENT, SCOTT FREE.

YOU WERE GIVEN THE GREATEST GIFT ONE CAN RECEIVE.

YOU WERE GIVEN *PAIN.*

POW

PAIN MAKES YOU STEADY, STRONG.

ABLE TO CONQUER, RULE.

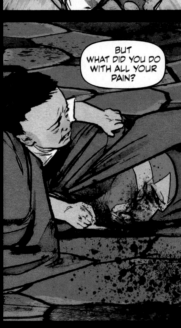

BUT WHAT DID YOU DO WITH ALL YOUR PAIN?

PERFORMED. MARRIED.

POW

BRED.

SWSHHHH

WHAT A WASTE.

WHAT A PITY.

WAAAAAA!

KQRSHH

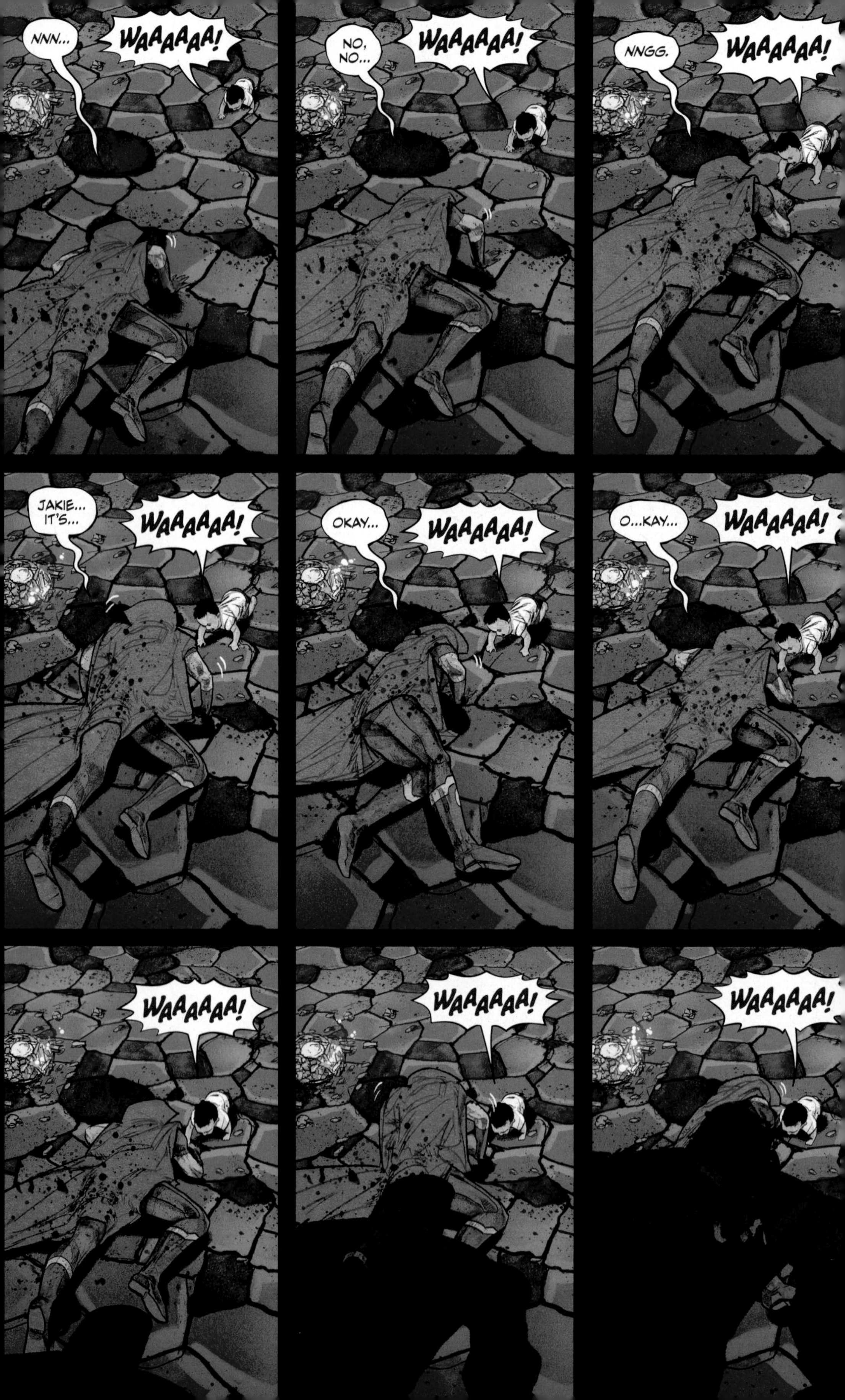
NNN...
WAAAAAA!
NO, NO...
WAAAAAA!
NNGG.
WAAAAAA!
JAKIE... IT'S...
WAAAAAA!
OKAY...
WAAAAAA!
O...KAY...
WAAAAAA!
WAAAAAA!
WAAAAAA!
WAAAAAA!

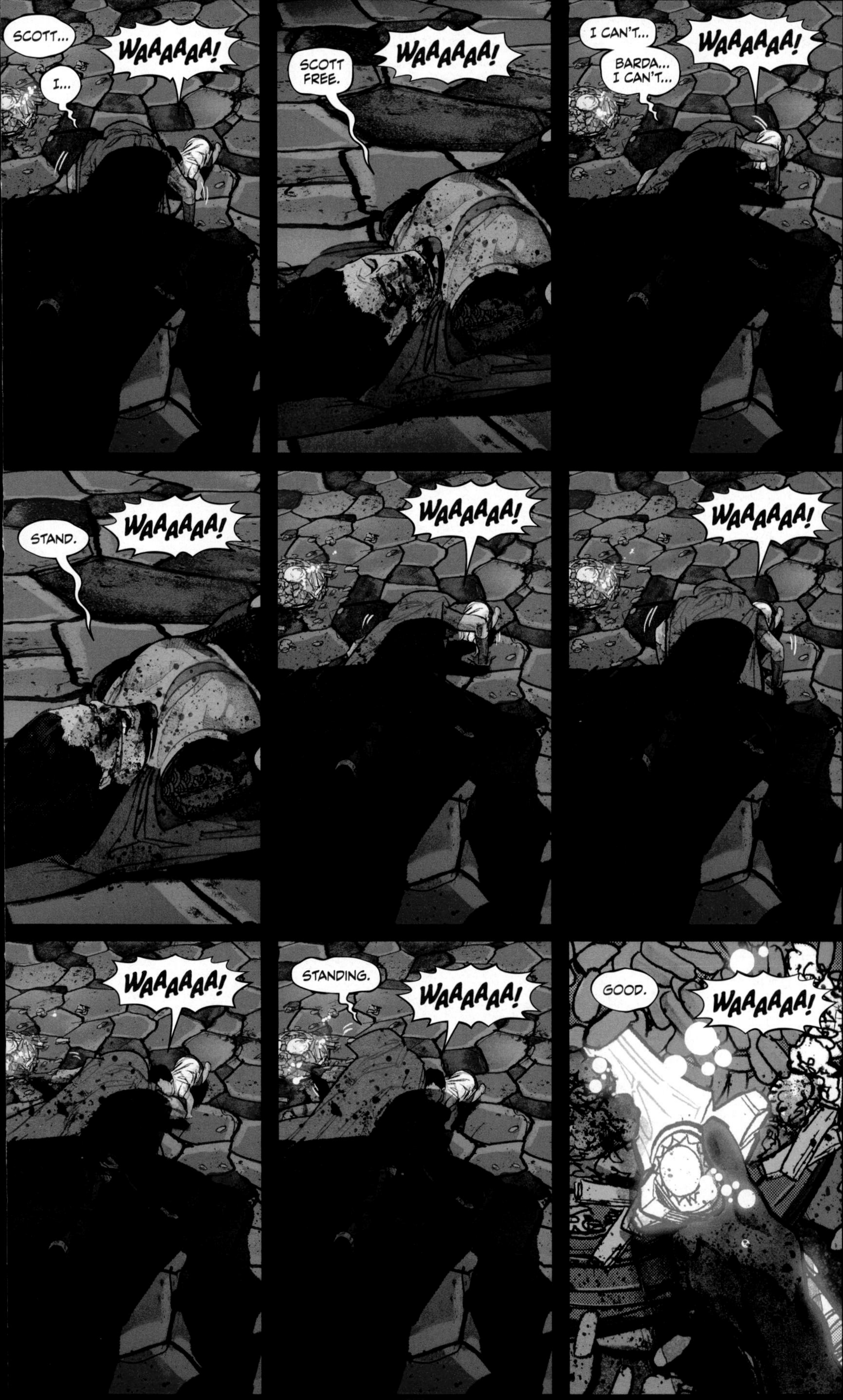
SCOTT...
I...
WAAAAAA!
SCOTT FREE.
WAAAAAA!
I CAN'T...
BARDA... I CAN'T...
WAAAAAA!
STAND.
WAAAAAA!
WAAAAAA!
WAAAAAA!
WAAAAAA!
STANDING.
WAAAAAA!
GOOD.
WAAAAAA!

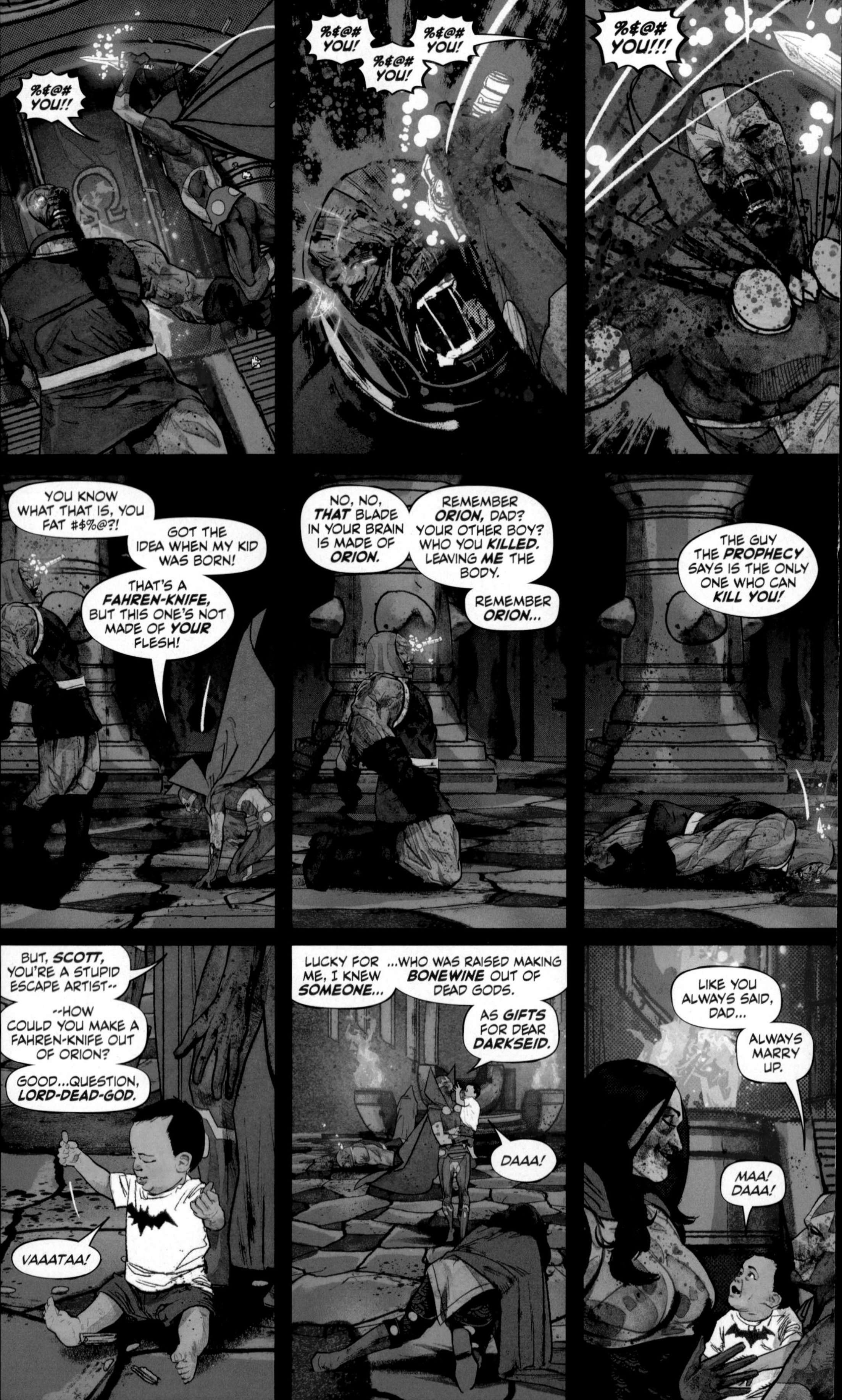
%$@# YOU!!
%$@# YOU!
%$@# YOU!
%$@# YOU!
%$@# YOU!!!
YOU KNOW WHAT THAT IS, YOU FAT #$%@?!
GOT THE IDEA WHEN MY KID WAS BORN!
THAT'S A FAHREN-KNIFE, BUT THIS ONE'S NOT MADE OF YOUR FLESH!
NO, NO, THAT BLADE IN YOUR BRAIN IS MADE OF ORION.
REMEMBER ORION, DAD? YOUR OTHER BOY? WHO YOU KILLED. LEAVING ME THE BODY.
REMEMBER ORION...
THE GUY THE PROPHECY SAYS IS THE ONLY ONE WHO CAN KILL YOU!
BUT, SCOTT, YOU'RE A STUPID ESCAPE ARTIST--
--HOW COULD YOU MAKE A FAHREN-KNIFE OUT OF ORION?
GOOD...QUESTION, LORD-DEAD-GOD.
VAAATAA!
LUCKY FOR ME, I KNEW SOMEONE...
...WHO WAS RAISED MAKING BONEWINE OUT OF DEAD GODS.
AS GIFTS FOR DEAR DARKSEID.
DAAA!
LIKE YOU ALWAYS SAID, DAD...
ALWAYS MARRY UP.
MAA! DAAA!

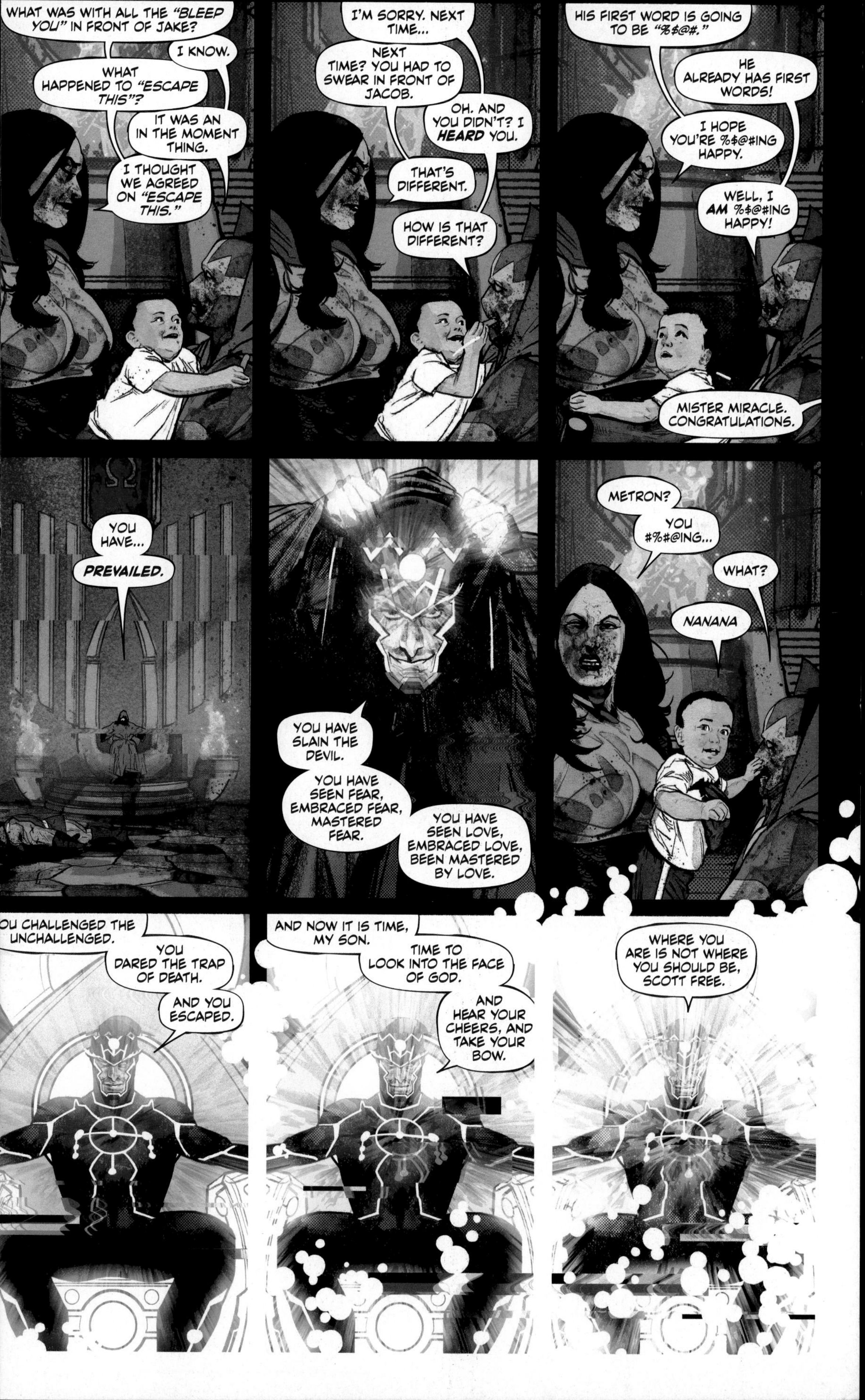
WHAT WAS WITH ALL THE "BLEEP YOU" IN FRONT OF JAKE?
I KNOW.
WHAT HAPPENED TO "ESCAPE THIS"?
IT WAS AN IN THE MOMENT THING.
I THOUGHT WE AGREED ON "ESCAPE THIS."
I'M SORRY. NEXT TIME...
NEXT TIME? YOU HAD TO SWEAR IN FRONT OF JACOB.
OH. AND YOU DIDN'T? I HEARD YOU.
THAT'S DIFFERENT.
HOW IS THAT DIFFERENT?
HIS FIRST WORD IS GOING TO BE "%$@#."
HE ALREADY HAS FIRST WORDS!
I HOPE YOU'RE %$@#ING HAPPY.
WELL, I AM %$@#ING HAPPY!
MISTER MIRACLE. CONGRATULATIONS.
YOU HAVE... PREVAILED.
YOU HAVE SLAIN THE DEVIL.
YOU HAVE SEEN FEAR, EMBRACED FEAR, MASTERED FEAR.
YOU HAVE SEEN LOVE, EMBRACED LOVE, BEEN MASTERED BY LOVE.
METRON?
YOU #%#@ING...
WHAT?
NANANA
OU CHALLENGED THE UNCHALLENGED.
YOU DARED THE TRAP OF DEATH.
AND YOU ESCAPED.
AND NOW IT IS TIME, MY SON.
TIME TO LOOK INTO THE FACE OF GOD.
AND HEAR YOUR CHEERS, AND TAKE YOUR BOW.
WHERE YOU ARE IS NOT WHERE YOU SHOULD BE, SCOTT FREE.

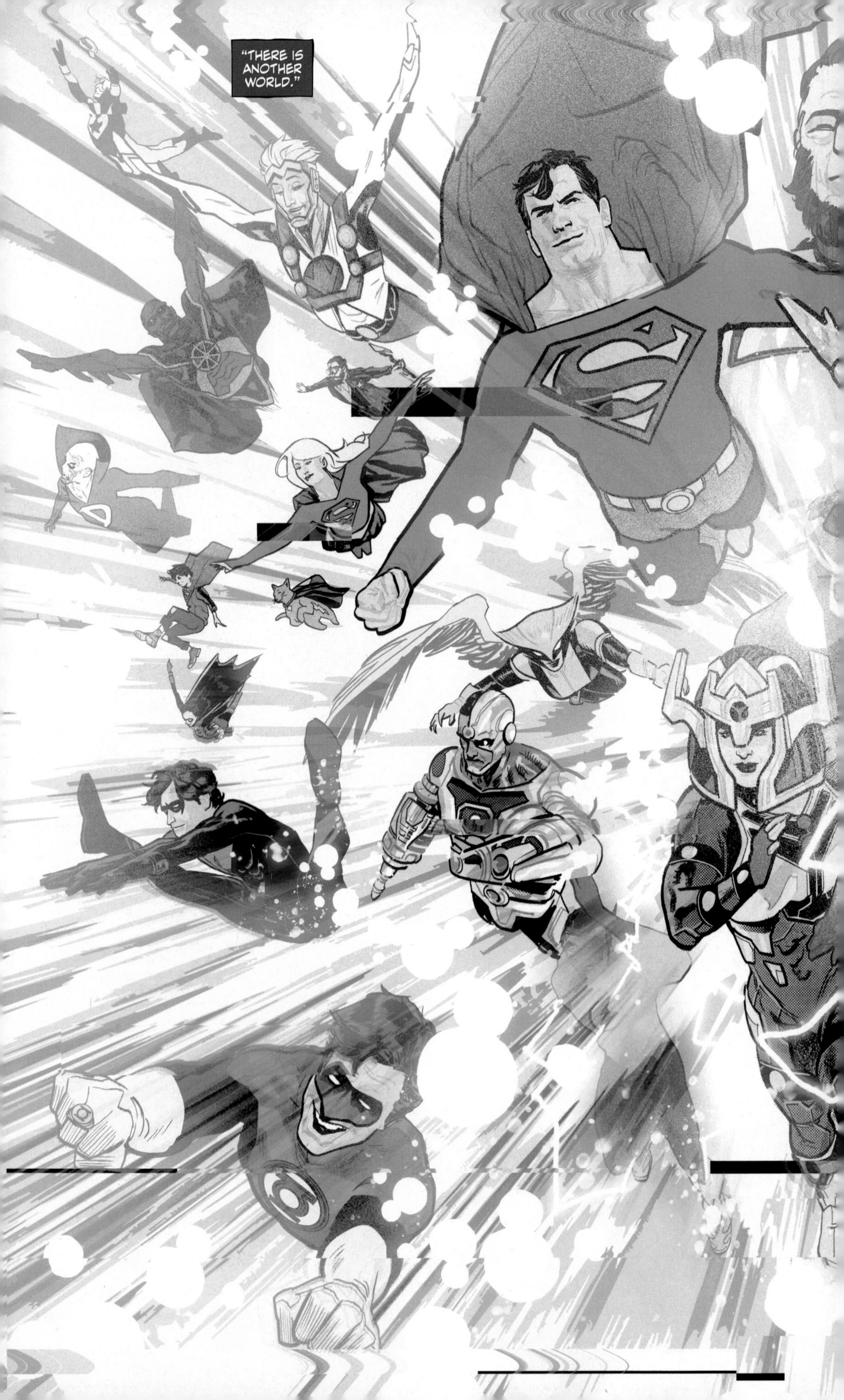
"THERE IS ANOTHER WORLD."

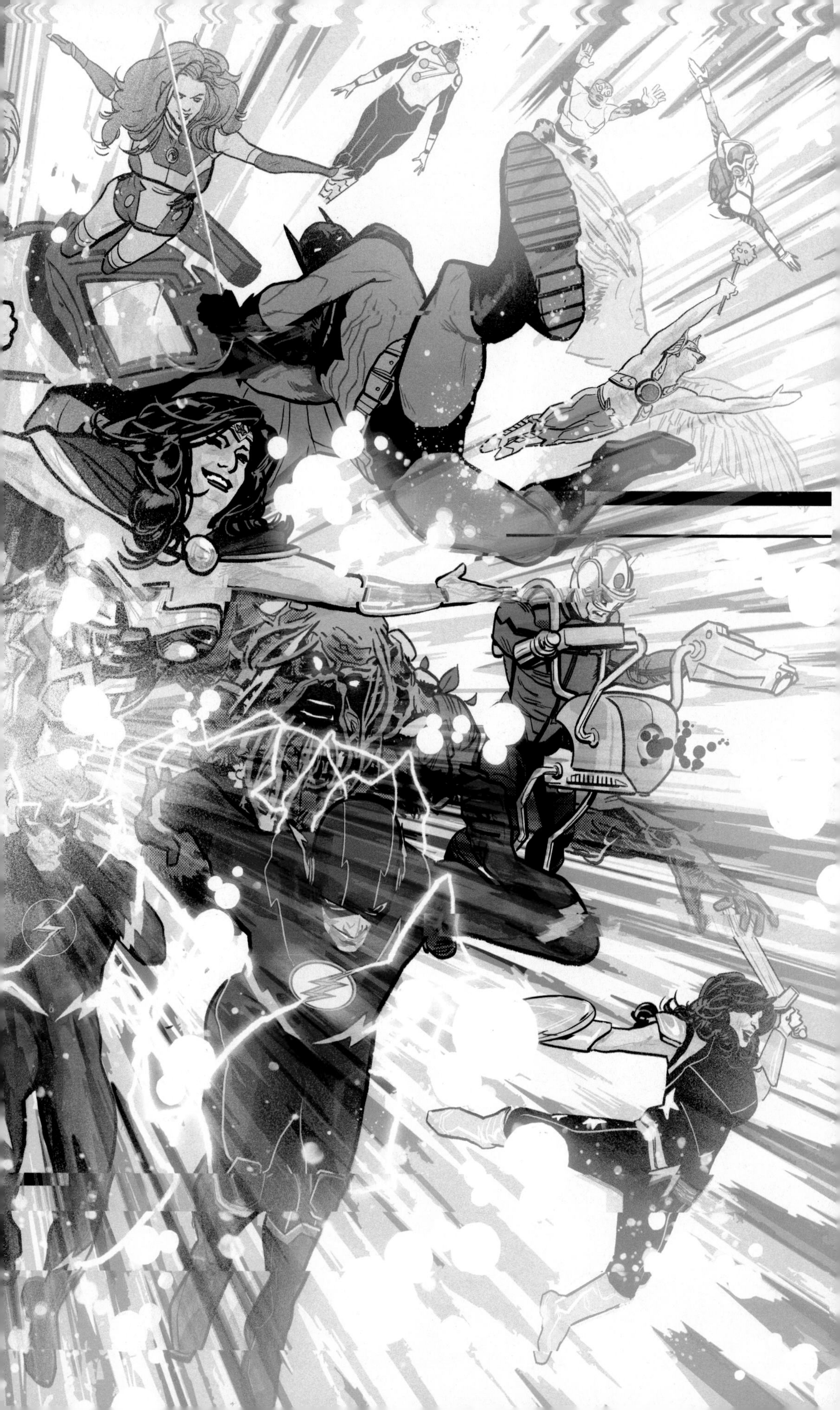

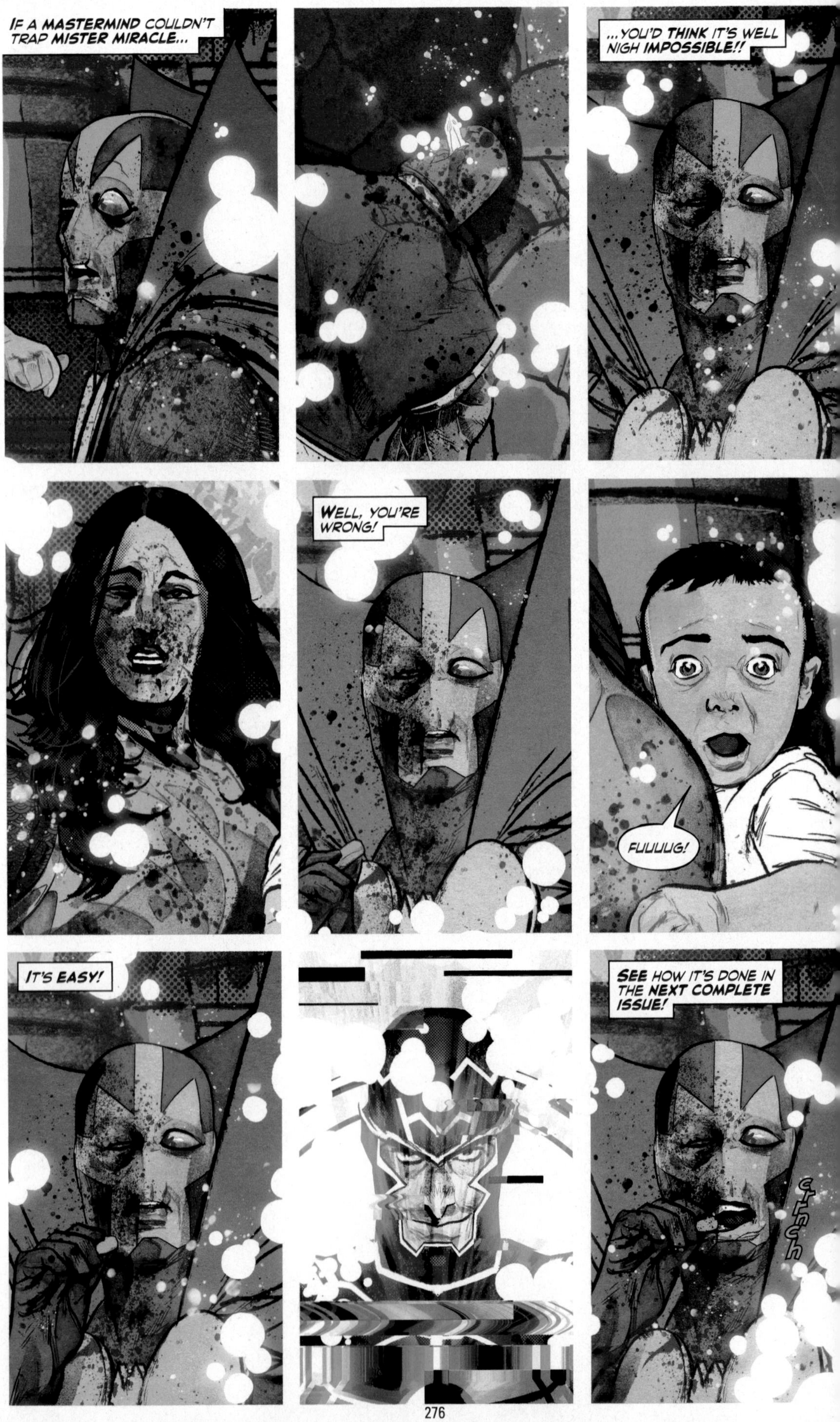

IF A MASTERMIND COULDN'T TRAP MISTER MIRACLE...
...YOU'D THINK IT'S WELL NIGH IMPOSSIBLE!!
WELL, YOU'RE WRONG!
FUUUUG!
IT'S EASY!
SEE HOW IT'S DONE IN THE NEXT COMPLETE ISSUE!
crnch

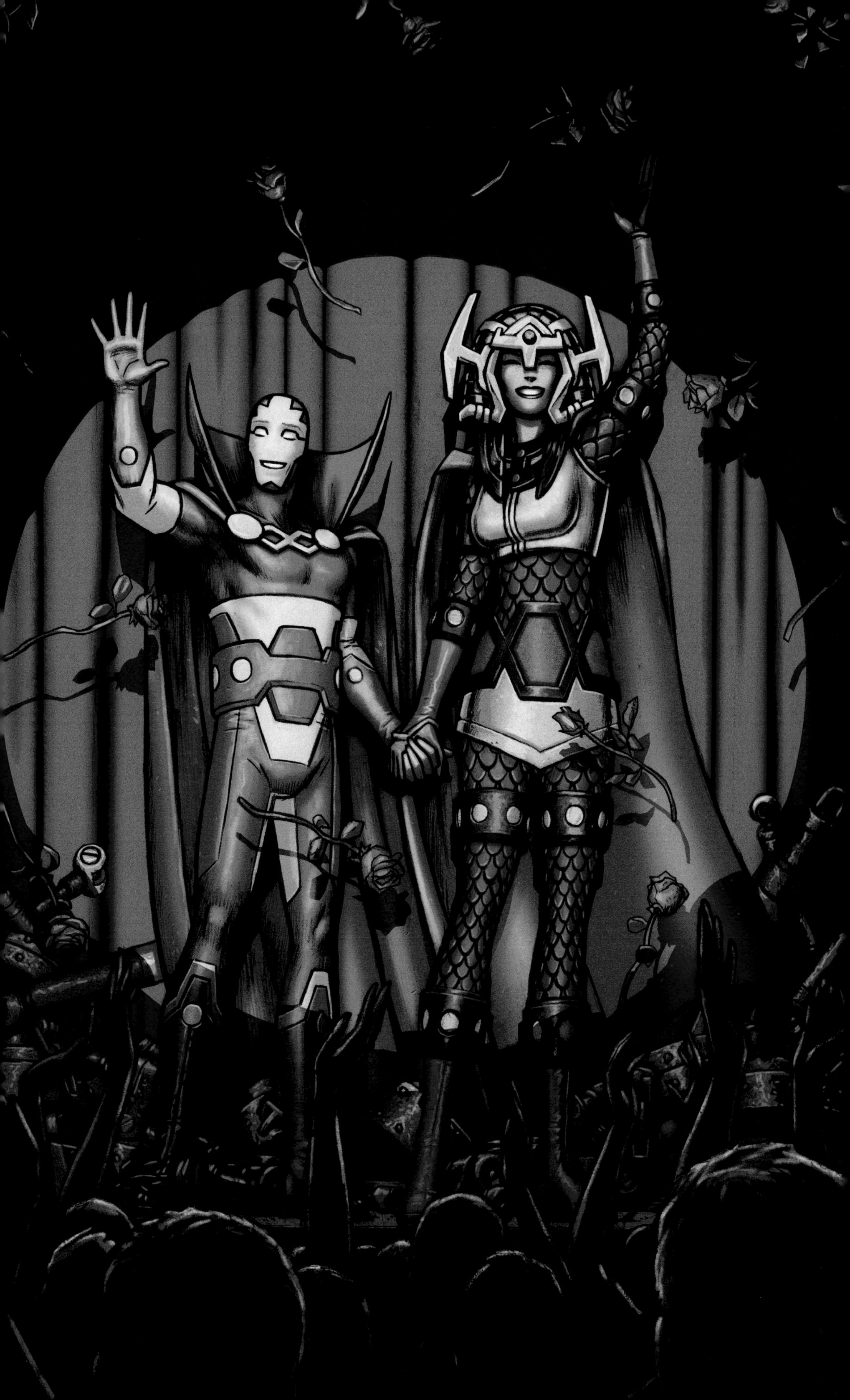

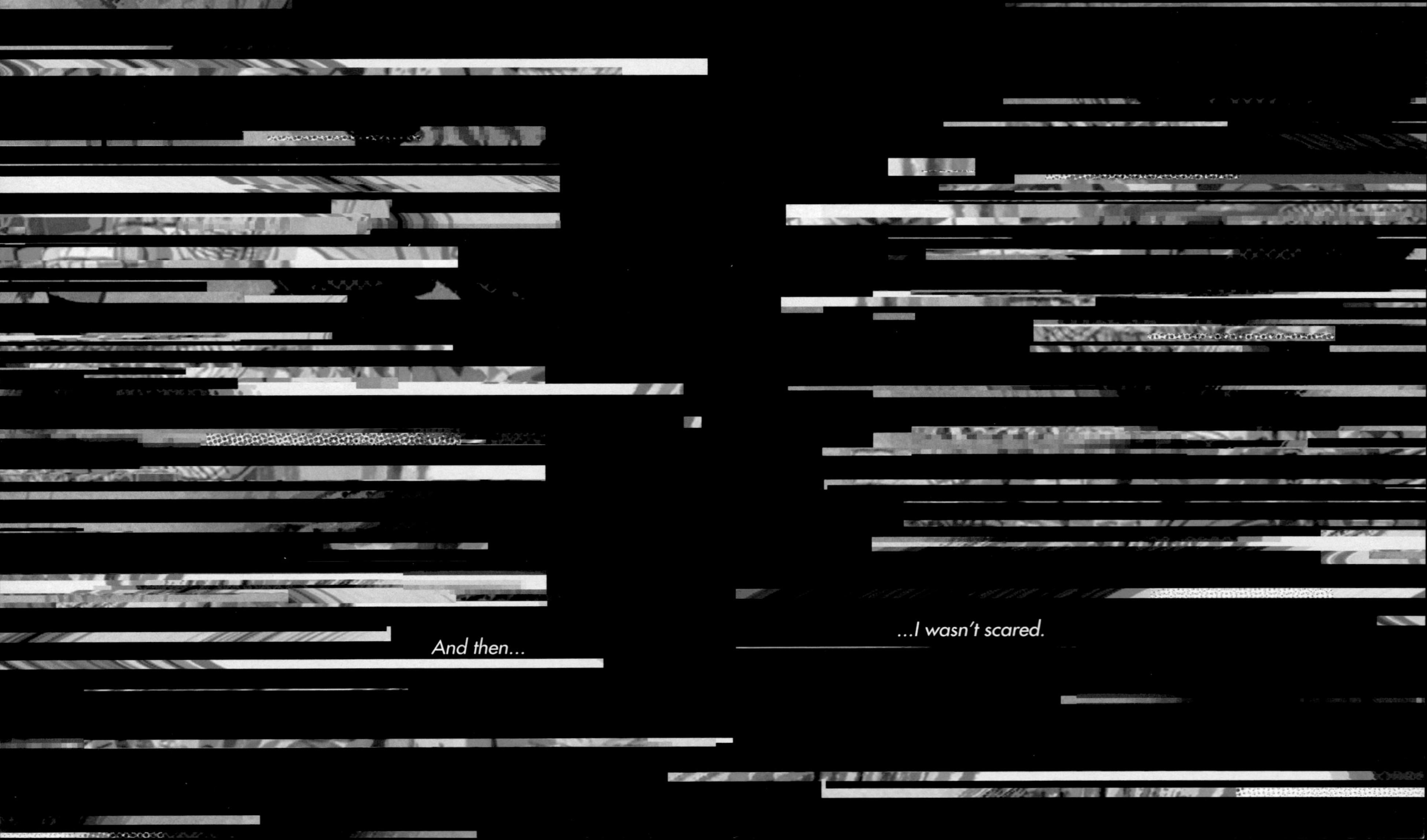
And then...
...I wasn't scared.

SUCH IS THE **CURSE** OF **FAME!**

EVEN IF IT IS IN ITS **EARLY STAGES!**

NEVER **DREAMING** OF INVOLVEMENT WITH THE **STRANGE** PERSONALITIES THAT **LURK** IN THE **UNSEEN** AUDIENCE NOW ATTRACTED BY HIS **EXPLOITS...**

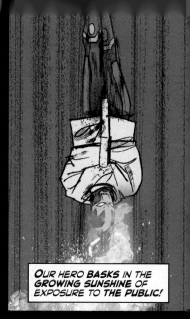

OUR HERO **BASKS** IN THE **GROWING SUNSHINE** OF EXPOSURE TO **THE PUBLIC!**

BUT--

--THIS IS TO CHANGE **QUICKLY!**

A **TRAP** IS ABOUT TO BE **SPRUNG** ON **SCOTT FREE!**

A **TRAP** WHICH IS **DIABOLICAL** IN ITS **SIMPLICITY!**

A **TRAP** MEANT FOR THE **MASKED CHALLENGER OF DEATH!**

A **TRAP** SCOTT MUST FALL **VICTIM** TO--

FOR SCOTT FREE IS.

MISTER MIRACLE

SUPER ESCAPE ARTIST!

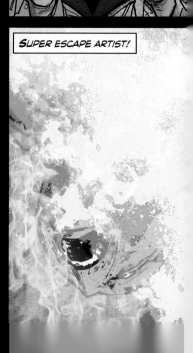

SHHHHHHSHHHHHH
SHHHHHHSHHHHHH
SHHHHHHSHHHHHH
SHHHHHHSHHHHHH
SHHHHHHSHHHHHH
SHHHHHHSHHHHHH
SHHHHHHSHHHHHH
SHHHHHHSHHHHHH
SHHHHHHSHHHHHH
GOOD MORNING!

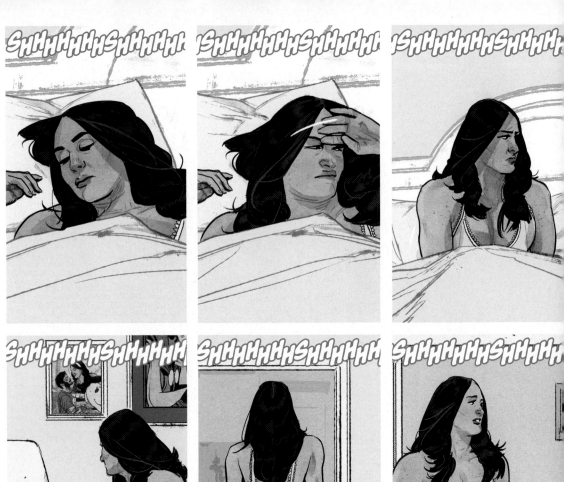

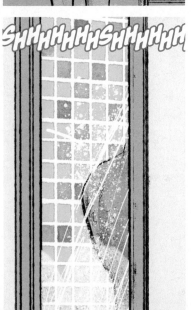

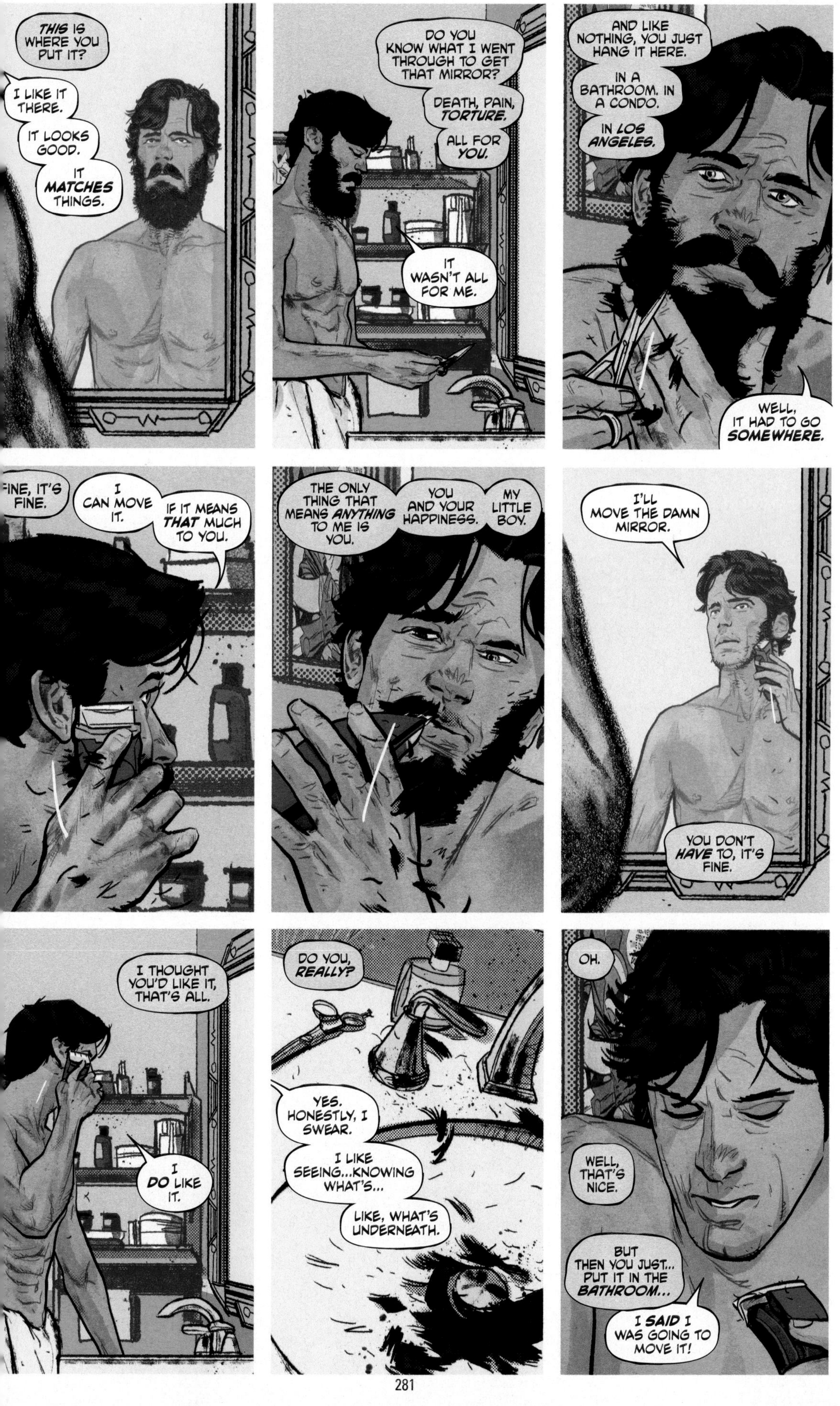

THIS IS WHERE YOU PUT IT?
I LIKE IT THERE.
IT LOOKS GOOD.
IT MATCHES THINGS.
DO YOU KNOW WHAT I WENT THROUGH TO GET THAT MIRROR?
DEATH, PAIN, TORTURE.
ALL FOR YOU.
IT WASN'T ALL FOR ME.
AND LIKE NOTHING, YOU JUST HANG IT HERE.
IN A BATHROOM. IN A CONDO.
IN LOS ANGELES.
WELL, IT HAD TO GO SOMEWHERE.
FINE, IT'S FINE.
I CAN MOVE IT.
IF IT MEANS THAT MUCH TO YOU.
THE ONLY THING THAT MEANS ANYTHING TO ME IS YOU.
YOU AND YOUR HAPPINESS.
MY LITTLE BOY.
I'LL MOVE THE DAMN MIRROR.
YOU DON'T HAVE TO, IT'S FINE.
I THOUGHT YOU'D LIKE IT, THAT'S ALL.
I DO LIKE IT.
DO YOU, REALLY?
YES. HONESTLY, I SWEAR.
I LIKE SEEING...KNOWING WHAT'S...
LIKE, WHAT'S UNDERNEATH.
OH.
WELL, THAT'S NICE.
BUT THEN YOU JUST... PUT IT IN THE BATHROOM...
I SAID I WAS GOING TO MOVE IT!

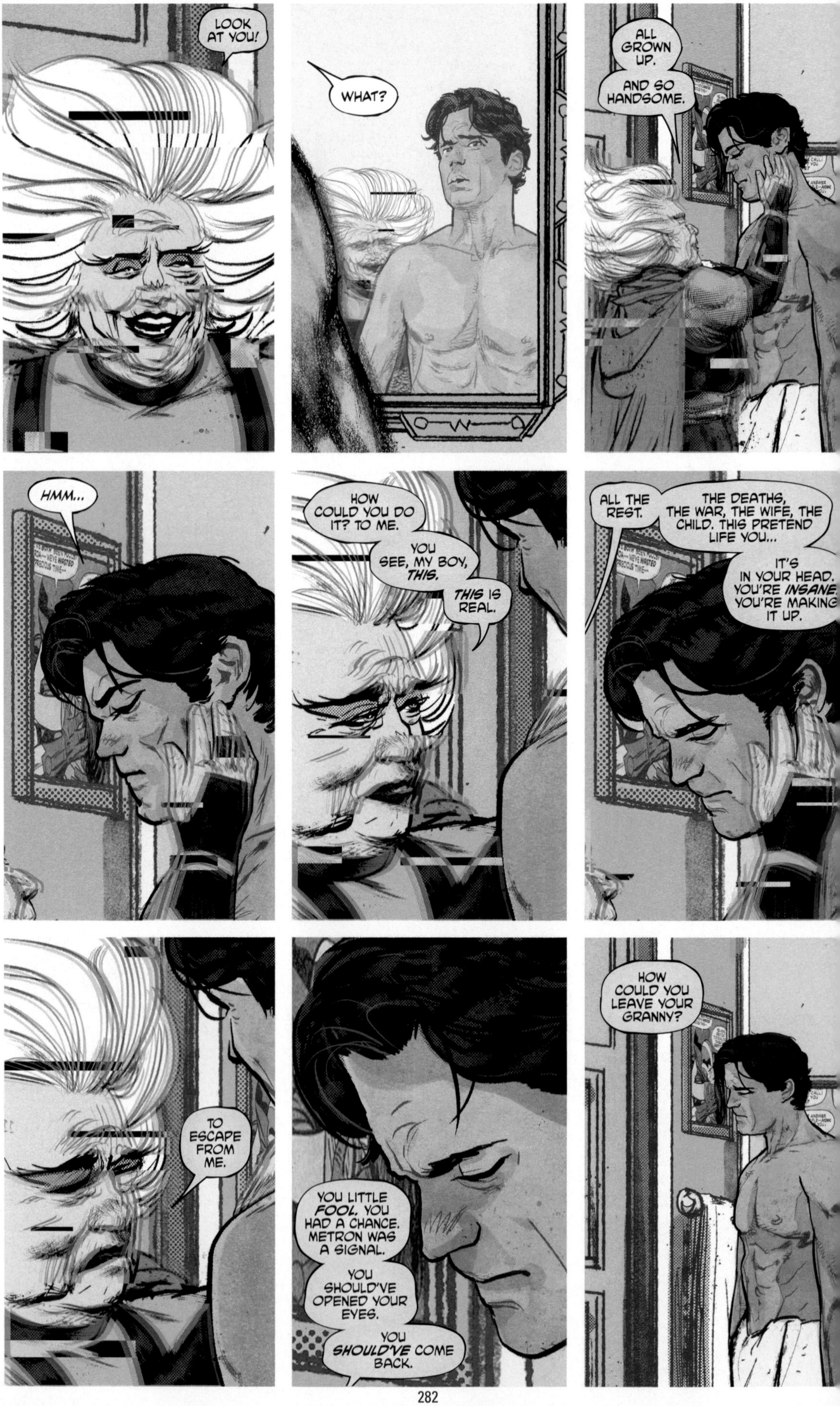
LOOK AT YOU!
WHAT?
ALL GROWN UP.
AND SO HANDSOME.
HMM...
HOW COULD YOU DO IT? TO ME.
YOU SEE, MY BOY, *THIS.*
THIS IS REAL.
ALL THE REST.
THE DEATHS, THE WAR, THE WIFE, THE CHILD. THIS PRETEND LIFE YOU...
IT'S IN YOUR HEAD. YOU'RE *INSANE.* YOU'RE MAKING IT UP.
TO ESCAPE FROM ME.
YOU LITTLE *FOOL.* YOU HAD A CHANCE. METRON WAS A SIGNAL.
YOU SHOULD'VE OPENED YOUR EYES.
YOU *SHOULD'VE* COME BACK.
HOW COULD YOU LEAVE YOUR GRANNY?

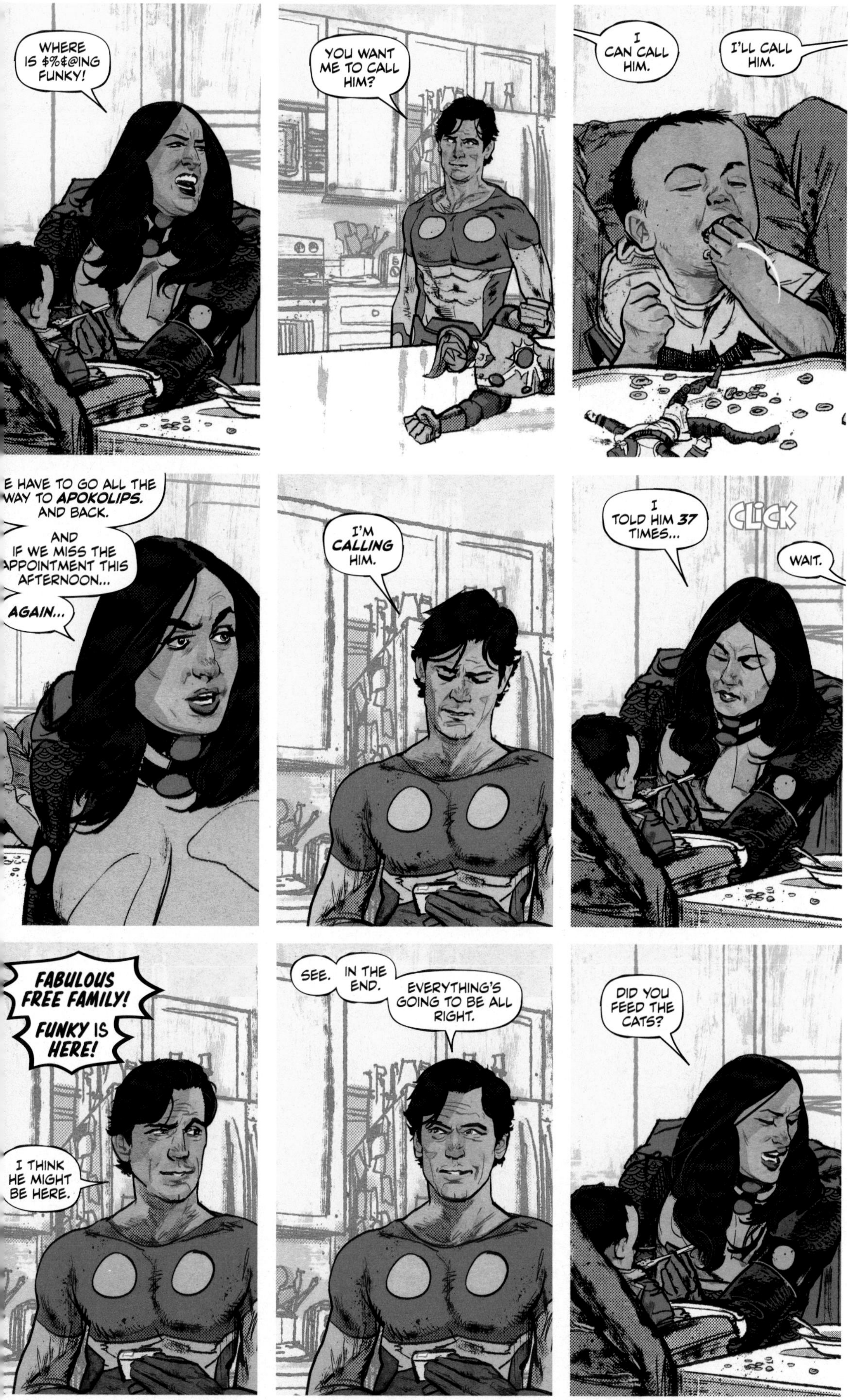

WHERE IS $%$@ING FUNKY!
YOU WANT ME TO CALL HIM?
I CAN CALL HIM.
I'LL CALL HIM.
E HAVE TO GO ALL THE WAY TO APOKOLIPS. AND BACK.
AND IF WE MISS THE APPOINTMENT THIS AFTERNOON...
AGAIN...
I'M CALLING HIM.
I TOLD HIM 37 TIMES...
CLICK
WAIT.
FABULOUS FREE FAMILY!
FUNKY IS HERE!
I THINK HE MIGHT BE HERE.
SEE.
IN THE END.
EVERYTHING'S GOING TO BE ALL RIGHT.
DID YOU FEED THE CATS?

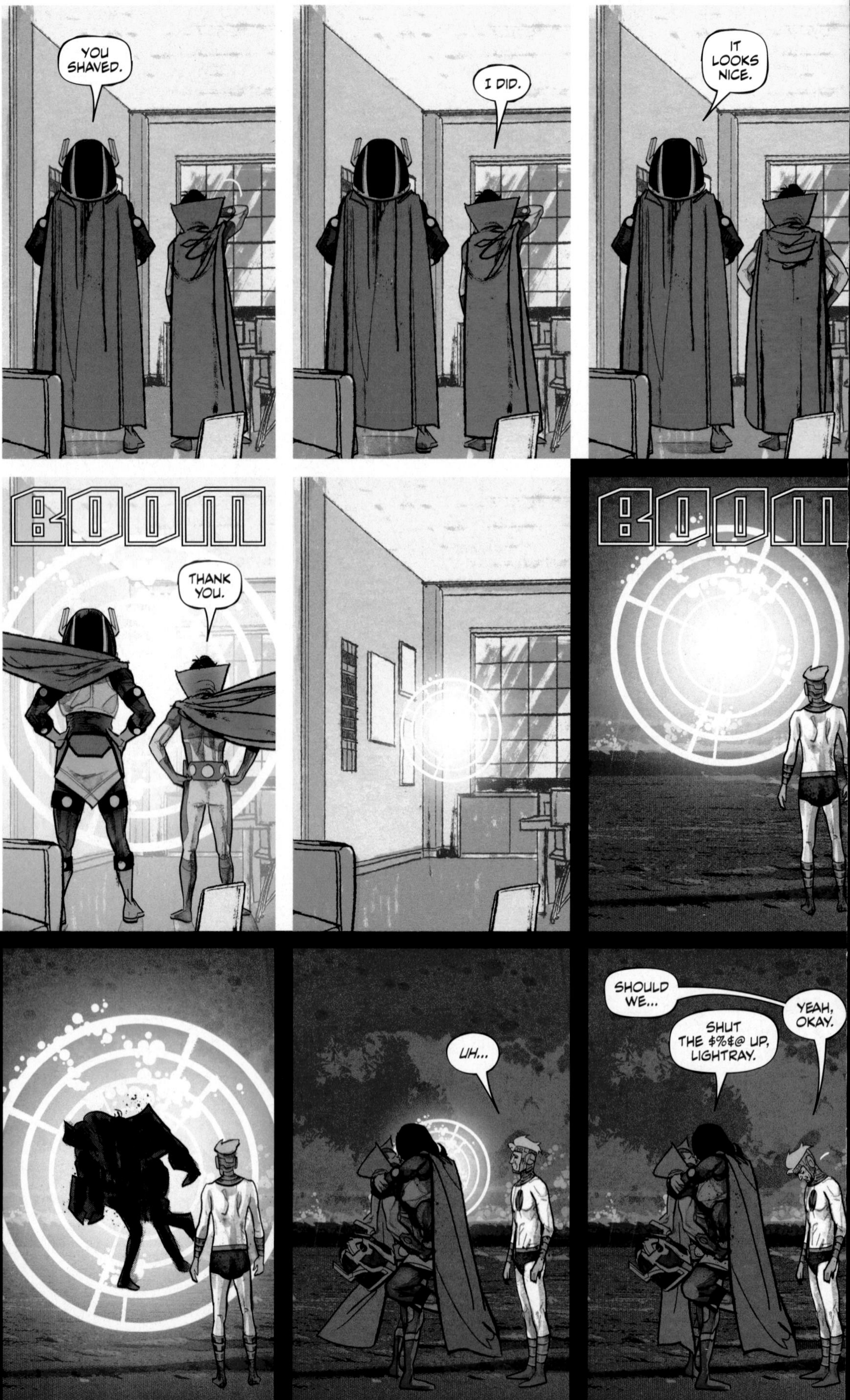
YOU SHAVED.
I DID.
IT LOOKS NICE.
BOOM
THANK YOU.
BOOM
UH...
SHOULD WE...
SHUT THE $%$@ UP, LIGHTRAY.
YEAH, OKAY.

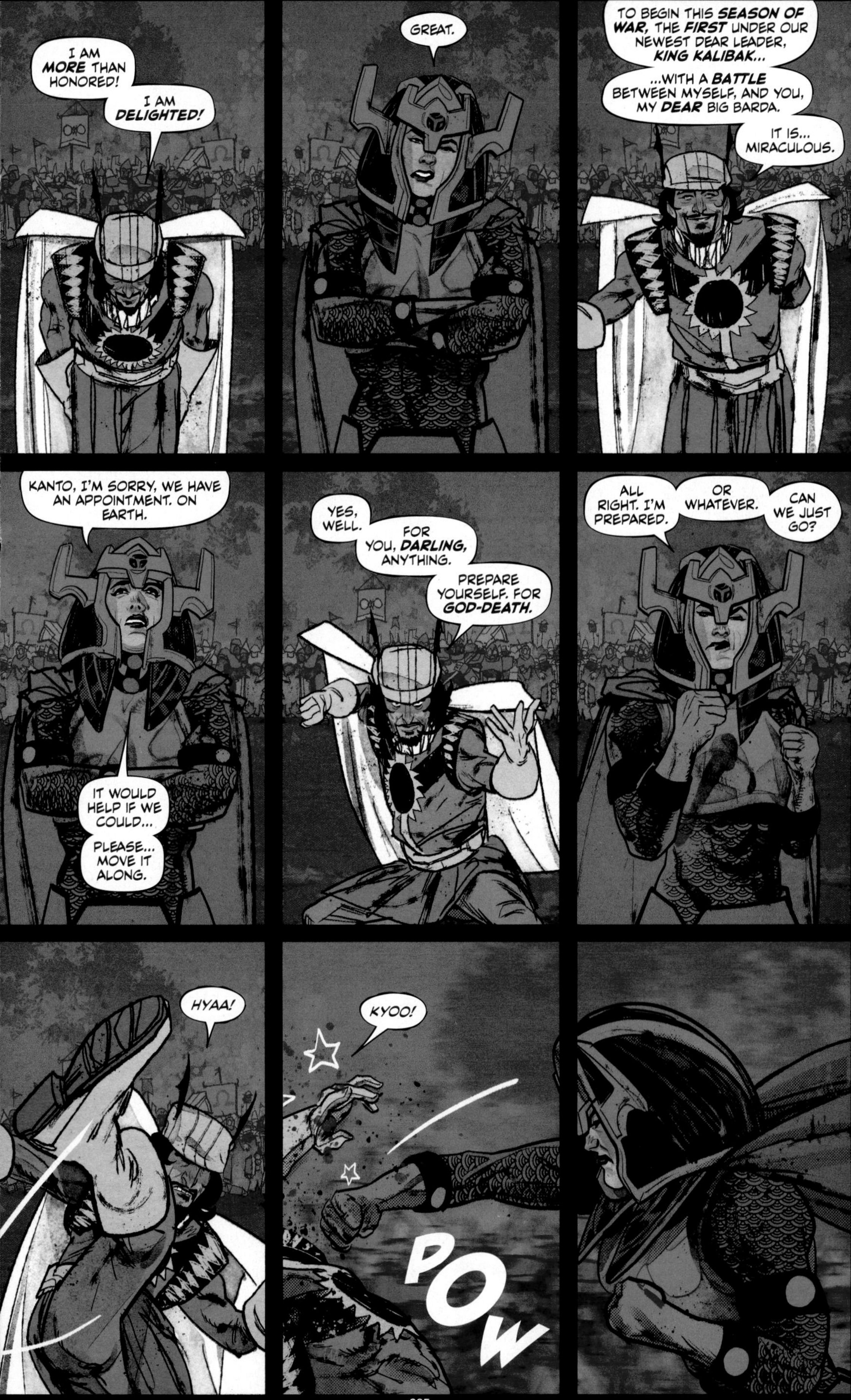
I AM **MORE** THAN HONORED!
I AM **DELIGHTED!**
GREAT.
TO BEGIN THIS **SEASON OF WAR**, THE **FIRST** UNDER OUR NEWEST DEAR LEADER, **KING KALIBAK...**
...WITH A **BATTLE** BETWEEN MYSELF, AND YOU, MY **DEAR** BIG BARDA.
IT IS... MIRACULOUS.
KANTO, I'M SORRY, WE HAVE AN APPOINTMENT. ON EARTH.
IT WOULD HELP IF WE COULD...
PLEASE... MOVE IT ALONG.
YES, WELL.
FOR YOU, **DARLING**, ANYTHING.
PREPARE YOURSELF. FOR **GOD-DEATH.**
ALL RIGHT. I'M PREPARED.
OR WHATEVER.
CAN WE JUST GO?
HYAA!
KYOO!
POW

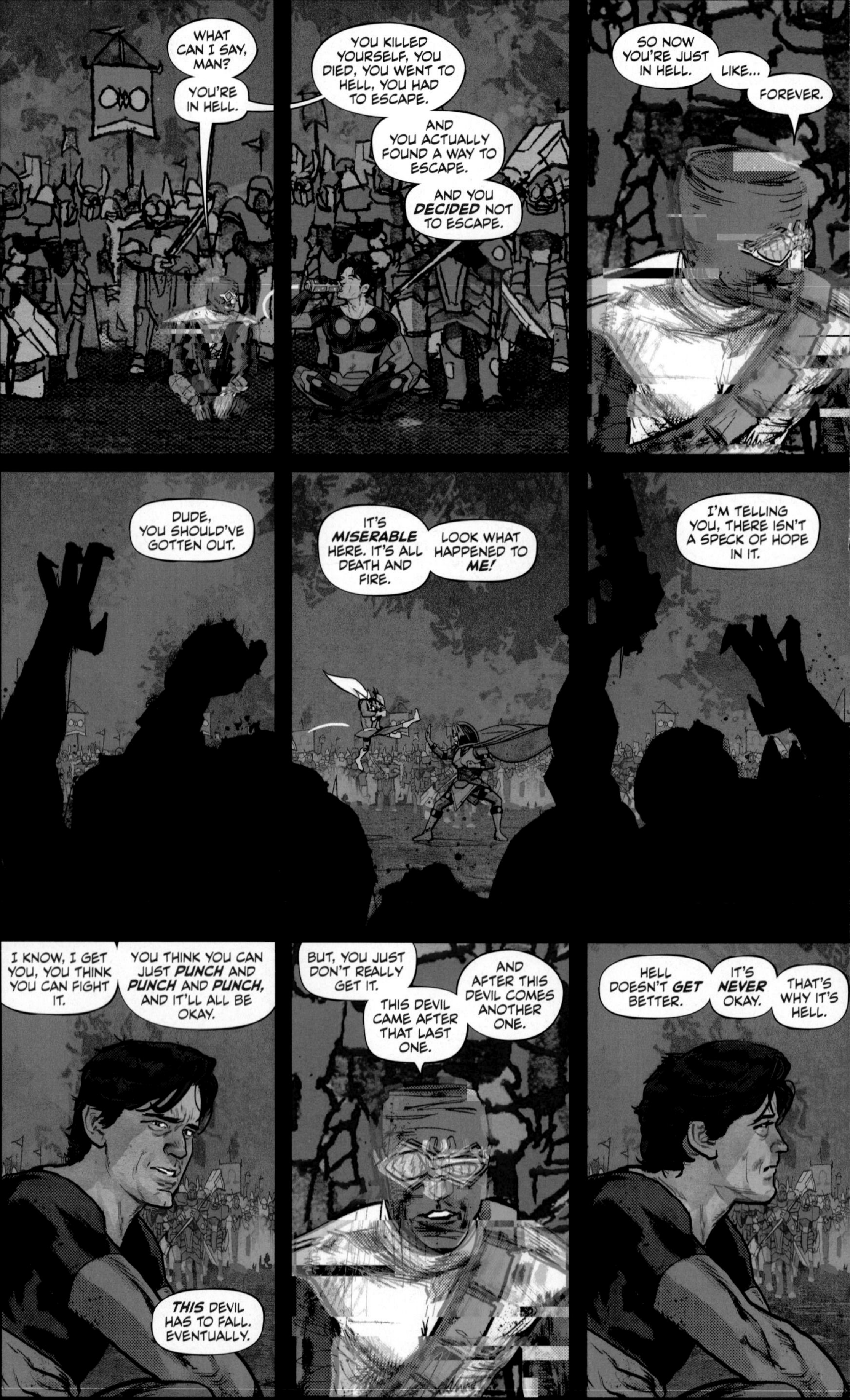

WHAT CAN I SAY, MAN?
YOU'RE IN HELL.
YOU KILLED YOURSELF, YOU DIED, YOU WENT TO HELL, YOU HAD TO ESCAPE.
AND YOU ACTUALLY FOUND A WAY TO ESCAPE.
AND YOU *DECIDED* NOT TO ESCAPE.
SO NOW YOU'RE JUST IN HELL.
LIKE...
FOREVER.
DUDE, YOU SHOULD'VE GOTTEN OUT.
IT'S *MISERABLE* HERE. IT'S ALL DEATH AND FIRE.
LOOK WHAT HAPPENED TO *ME!*
I'M TELLING YOU, THERE ISN'T A SPECK OF HOPE IN IT.
I KNOW, I GET YOU, YOU THINK YOU CAN FIGHT IT.
YOU THINK YOU CAN JUST *PUNCH* AND *PUNCH* AND *PUNCH,* AND IT'LL ALL BE OKAY.
THIS DEVIL HAS TO FALL. EVENTUALLY.
BUT, YOU JUST DON'T REALLY GET IT.
THIS DEVIL CAME AFTER THAT LAST ONE.
AND AFTER THIS DEVIL COMES ANOTHER ONE.
HELL DOESN'T *GET* BETTER.
IT'S *NEVER* OKAY.
THAT'S WHY IT'S HELL.

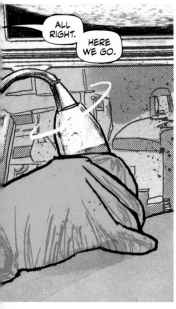

ALL RIGHT. HERE WE GO.

IS EVERYTHING...

IT'S FINE. SO FINE. I'M SURE. AND IF IT'S NOT...IT'S FINE.

WE'RE JUST WAITING FOR A HEARTBEAT.

SOMETIMES THIS CAN TAKE A SECOND.

ONE SECOND...

IT'S GOOD. SHE SAID ONE SECOND.

PLEASE. GOD...

beepbeep

THERE WE GO.

ARDA BIG F (GOD)
VM -OB-
...BEING VERY COOPERATIVE.
WE'VE GOT A GOOD VIEW. DO YOU WANT TO KNOW THE SEX?
UH...
OR... I...
WHAT?
YES.
PLEASE.
IT'S A GIRL.
CONGRATULATIONS.
WHAT, REALLY?
THAT'S AWESOME.
I MEAN.
I MEAN, AWESOME.
IS SHE--
IS EVERYTHING...
WELL, WE'RE GOING TO DO SOME MEASUREMENTS TODAY.
BUT SHE LOOKS GOOD. IF ANYTHING...MAYBE A LITTLE...
BIG.

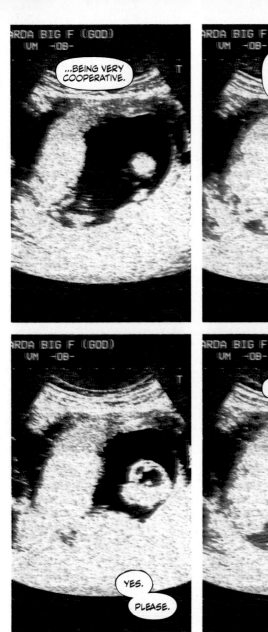

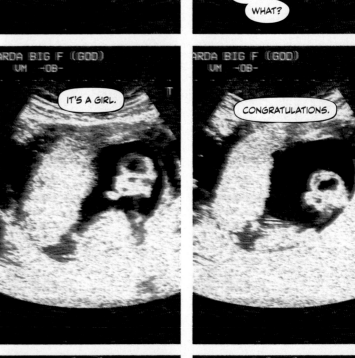

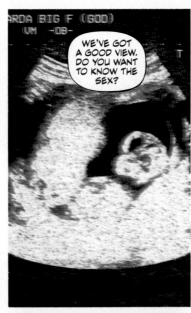

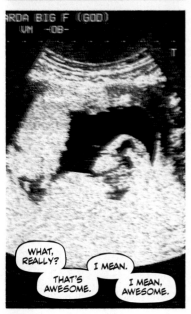

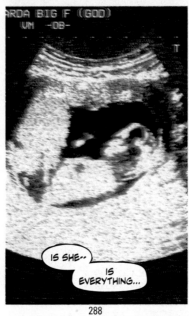

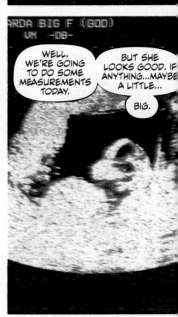

DARKSEID'S GONE. I
M GONE. YOU ARE
HIGHFATHER.

YOU HAVE
THE FAMILY
OF YOUR
DREAMS.

YOU
ARE...IN
HEAVEN.

YOU KILLED YOURSELF.
WENT TO PARADISE.

TRIED TO
ESCAPE. FOUND
A WAY.

DECIDED
TO STAY.

I CAN'T
THINK OF ANY
GOOD GIRL
NAMES.

WE PROBABLY
SHOULDN'T EVEN
DO NAMES.

I DON'T
KNOW WHAT I'M
SAYING. I DON'T
KNOW. NEVER
MIND.

TRAPPED IN
YOUR OWN PERFECT
WORLD.

I CANNOT SAY
THAT I BLAME YOU,
BROTHER.

I'M
NOT YOUR
BROTHER.

BUT
I CAN
SAY...

I'M
DISAPPOINTED
IN YOU.

WHAT ABOUT
ROSALIND? ROSALIND
THE GOLD.

THAT
WAS MY
GRANDMOTHER.
SHE WAS VERY
COOL.

I
THOUGHT LIFE WAS
SUPPOSED TO BE THE
CHALLENGES.

THE
STRUGGLE.

THE
MOMENT BEFORE
THE BOW.

IF
EVERYTHING
IS EASY AND
NICE.

LIKE
HOW NOW
EVERYTHING IS
EASY AND
NICE.

YOU MIGHT
AS WELL BE
DEAD.

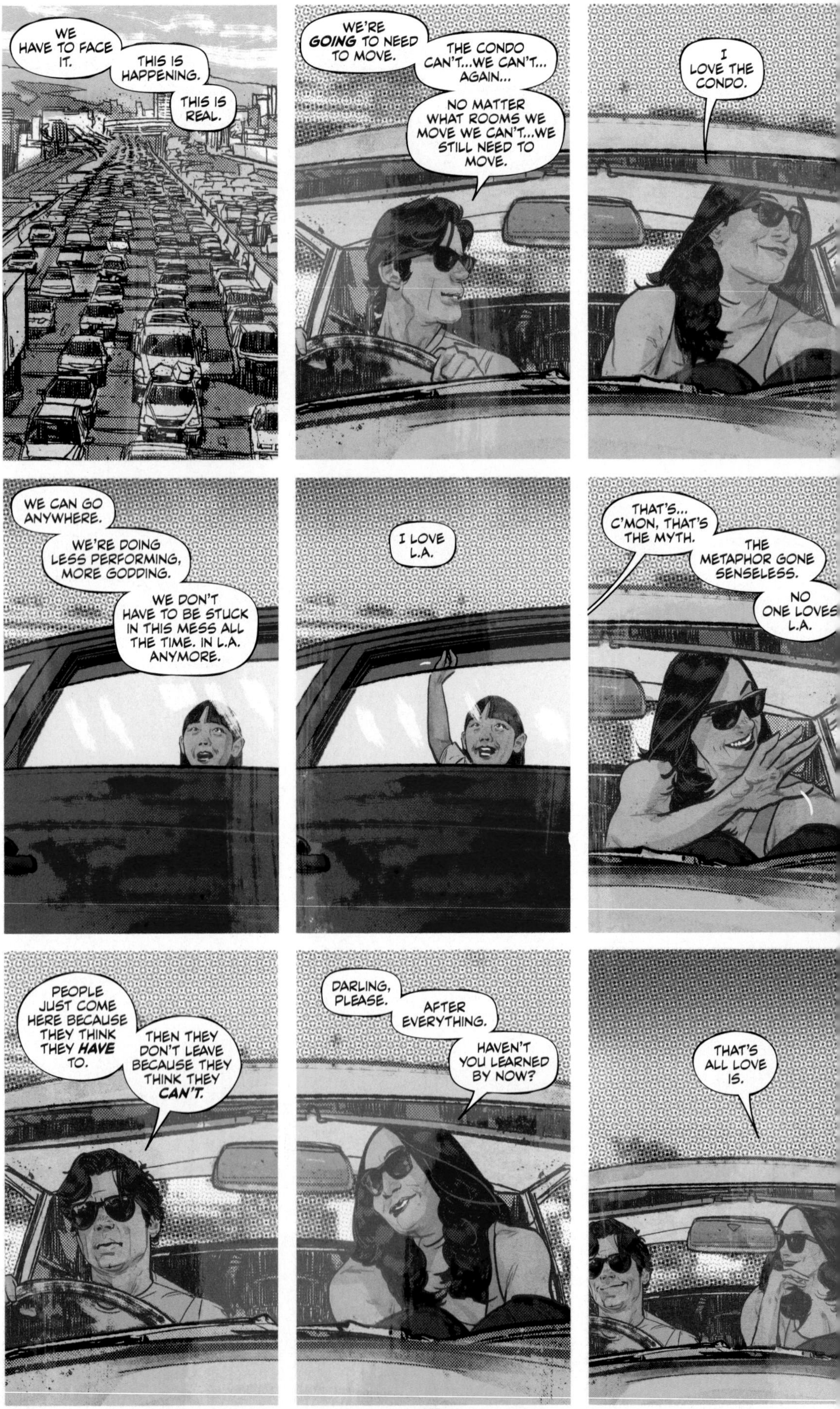
WE HAVE TO FACE IT.
THIS IS HAPPENING.
THIS IS REAL.
WE'RE *GOING* TO NEED TO MOVE.
THE CONDO CAN'T...WE CAN'T... AGAIN...
NO MATTER WHAT ROOMS WE MOVE WE CAN'T...WE STILL NEED TO MOVE.
I LOVE THE CONDO.
WE CAN GO ANYWHERE.
WE'RE DOING LESS PERFORMING, MORE GODDING.
WE DON'T HAVE TO BE STUCK IN THIS MESS ALL THE TIME. IN L.A. ANYMORE.
I LOVE L.A.
THAT'S... C'MON, THAT'S THE MYTH.
THE METAPHOR GONE SENSELESS.
NO ONE LOVES L.A.
PEOPLE JUST COME HERE BECAUSE THEY THINK THEY *HAVE* TO.
THEN THEY DON'T LEAVE BECAUSE THEY THINK THEY *CAN'T.*
DARLING, PLEASE.
AFTER EVERYTHING.
HAVEN'T YOU LEARNED BY NOW?
THAT'S ALL LOVE IS.

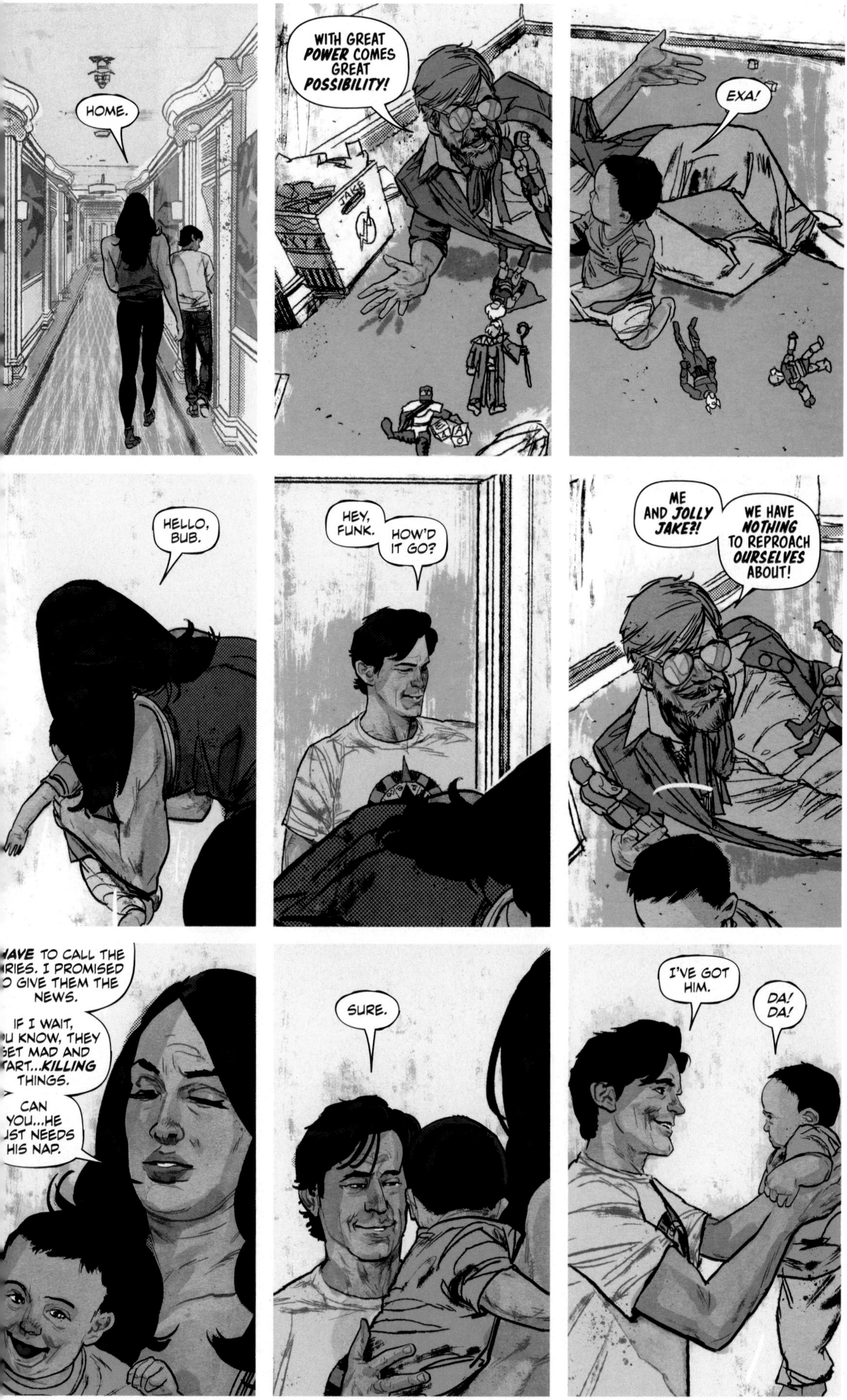
HOME.
WITH GREAT POWER COMES GREAT POSSIBILITY!
JAKE
EXA!
HELLO, BUB.
HEY, FUNK.
HOW'D IT GO?
ME AND JOLLY JAKE?!
WE HAVE NOTHING TO REPROACH OURSELVES ABOUT!
AVE TO CALL THE RIES. I PROMISED O GIVE THEM THE NEWS.
IF I WAIT, U KNOW, THEY ET MAD AND TART...KILLING THINGS.
CAN YOU...HE ST NEEDS HIS NAP.
SURE.
I'VE GOT HIM.
DA! DA!

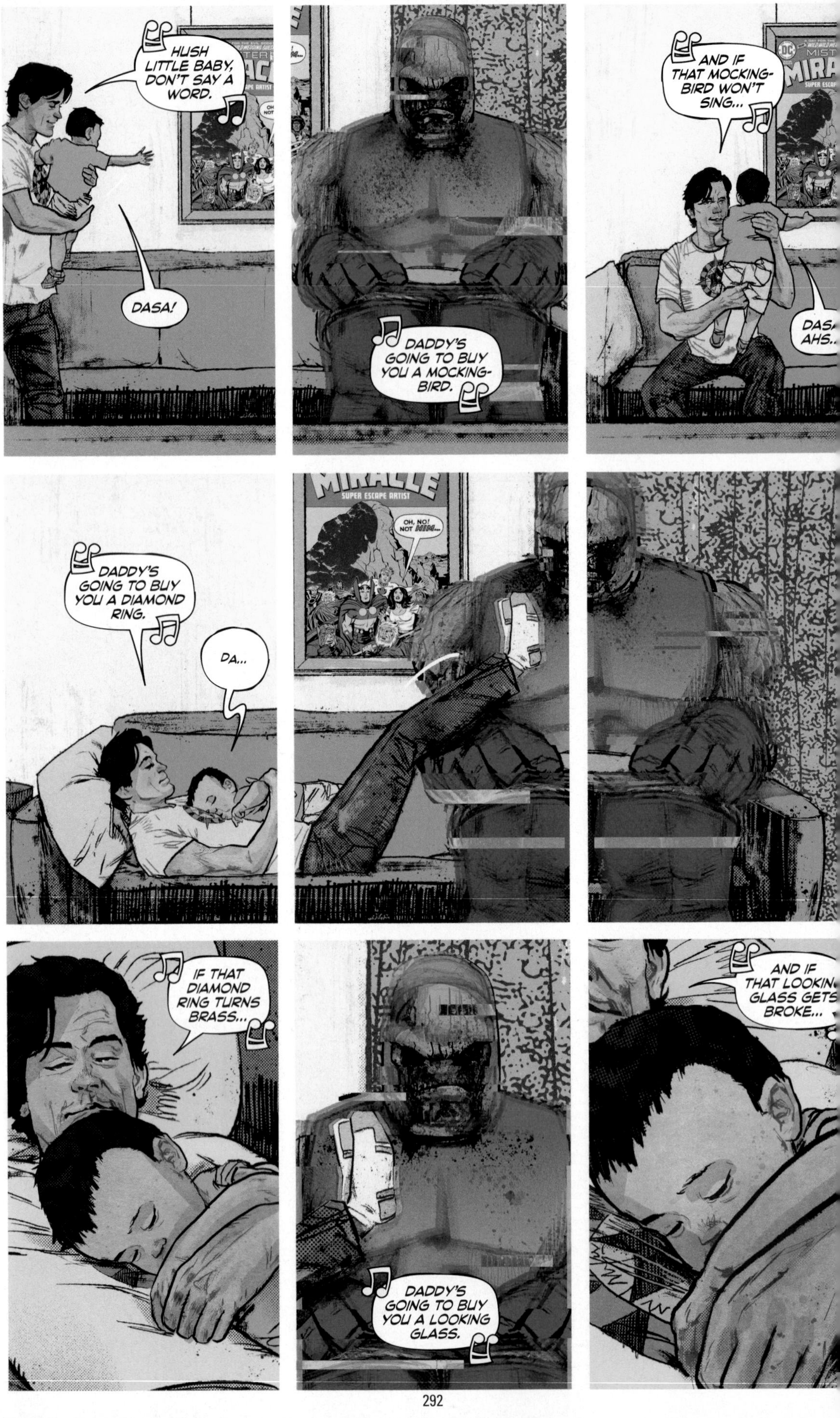

HUSH LITTLE BABY, DON'T SAY A WORD.
DASA!
DADDY'S GOING TO BUY YOU A MOCKING-BIRD.
AND IF THAT MOCKING-BIRD WON'T SING...
DAS/ AHS..
MIRACLE
SUPER ESCAPE ARTIST
OH, NO! NOT HIM...
DADDY'S GOING TO BUY YOU A DIAMOND RING.
DA...
IF THAT DIAMOND RING TURNS BRASS...
DADDY'S GOING TO BUY YOU A LOOKING GLASS.
AND IF THAT LOOKIN GLASS GETS BROKE...

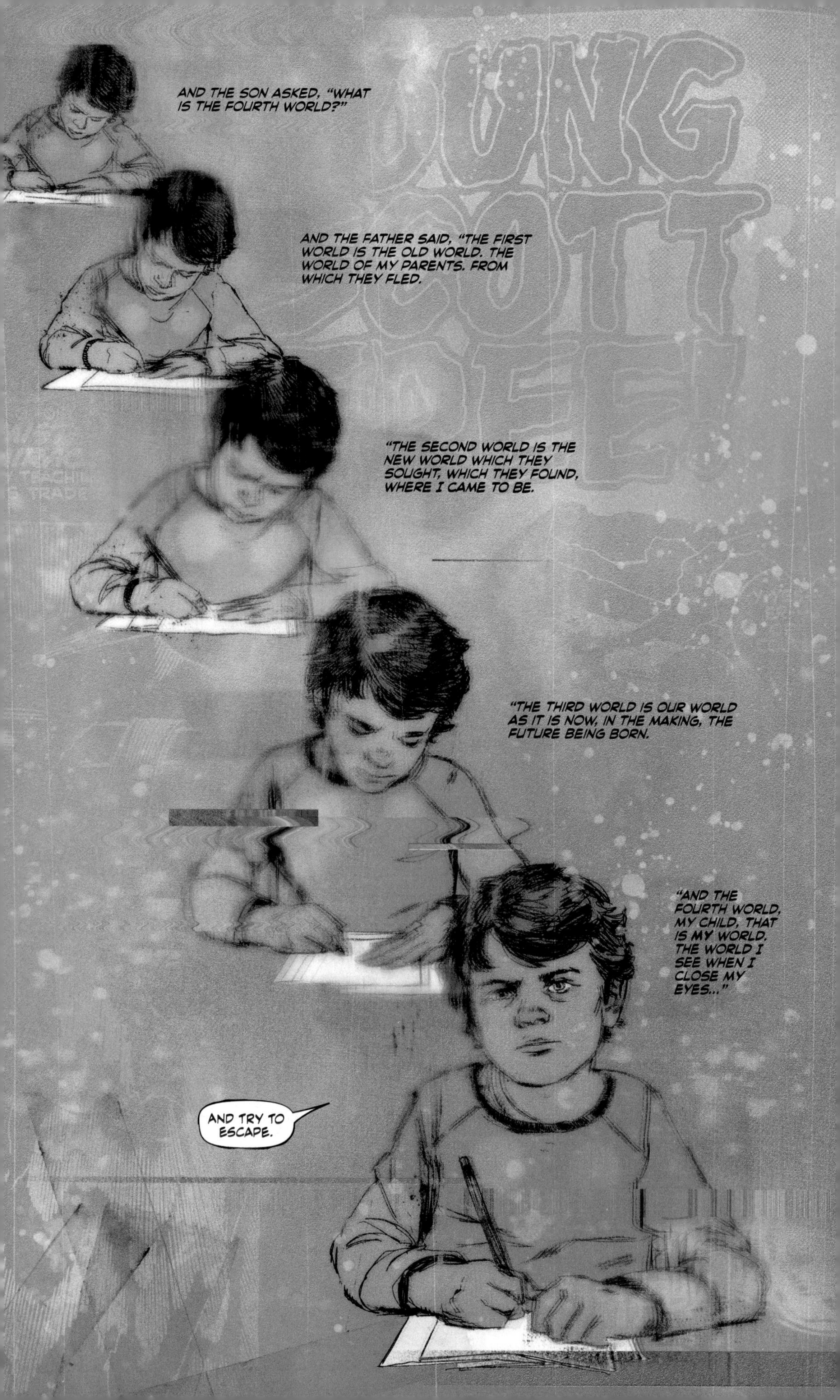
AND THE SON ASKED, "WHAT IS THE FOURTH WORLD?"
AND THE FATHER SAID, "THE FIRST WORLD IS THE OLD WORLD. THE WORLD OF MY PARENTS. FROM WHICH THEY FLED.
"THE SECOND WORLD IS THE NEW WORLD WHICH THEY SOUGHT, WHICH THEY FOUND, WHERE I CAME TO BE.
"THE THIRD WORLD IS OUR WORLD AS IT IS NOW, IN THE MAKING, THE FUTURE BEING BORN.
"AND THE FOURTH WORLD, MY CHILD, THAT IS MY WORLD. THE WORLD I SEE WHEN I CLOSE MY EYES..."
AND TRY TO ESCAPE.

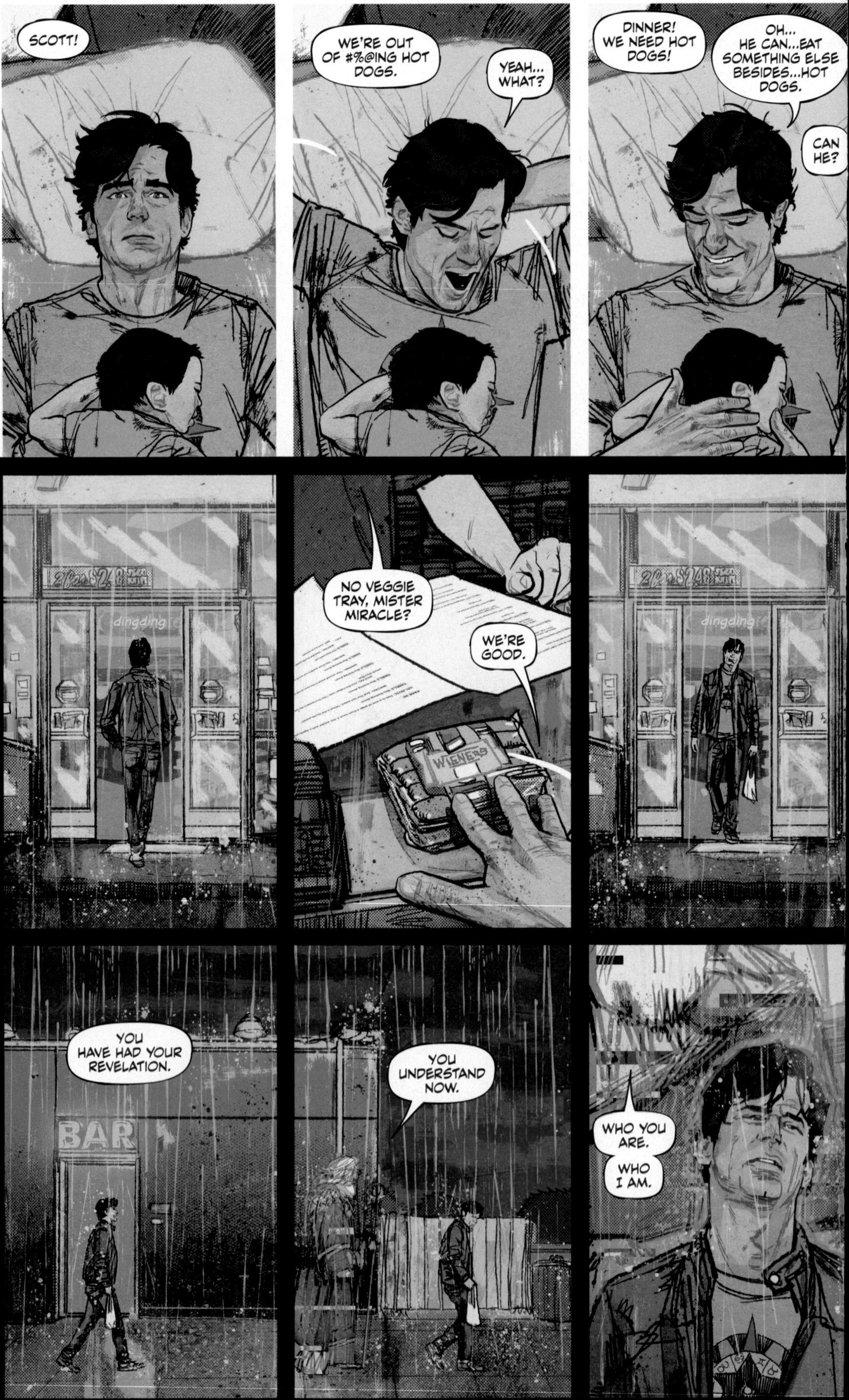
SCOTT!
WE'RE OUT OF #%@ING HOT DOGS.
YEAH... WHAT?
DINNER! WE NEED HOT DOGS!
OH... HE CAN...EAT SOMETHING ELSE BESIDES...HOT DOGS.
CAN HE?
dingding
NO VEGGIE TRAY, MISTER MIRACLE?
WE'RE GOOD.
WIENERS
dingding
YOU HAVE HAD YOUR REVELATION.
BAR
YOU UNDERSTAND NOW.
WHO YOU ARE.
WHO I AM.

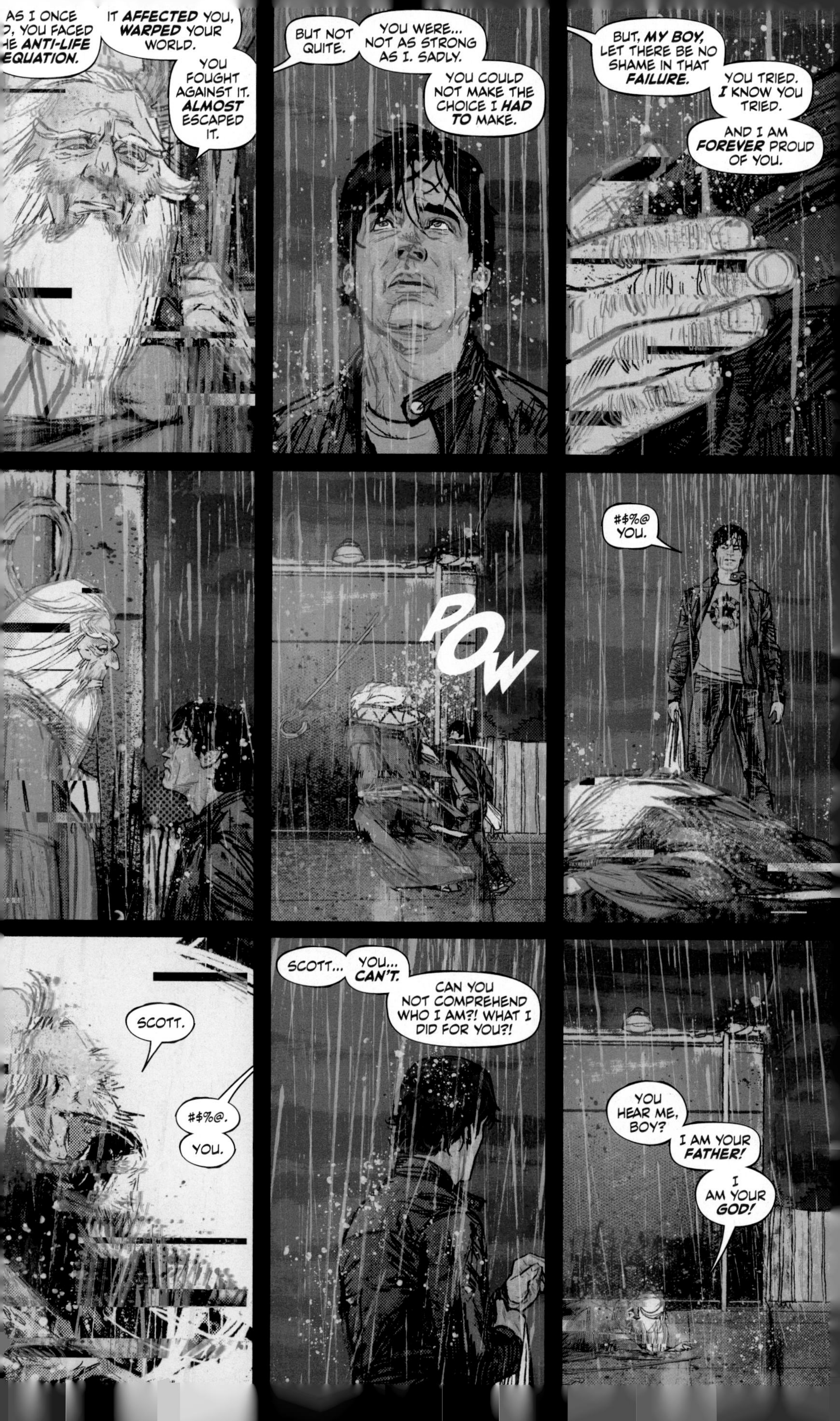
AS I ONCE D, YOU FACED HE ANTI-LIFE EQUATION.
IT AFFECTED YOU, WARPED YOUR WORLD.
YOU FOUGHT AGAINST IT. ALMOST ESCAPED IT.
BUT NOT QUITE.
YOU WERE... NOT AS STRONG AS I. SADLY.
YOU COULD NOT MAKE THE CHOICE I HAD TO MAKE.
BUT, MY BOY, LET THERE BE NO SHAME IN THAT FAILURE.
YOU TRIED. I KNOW YOU TRIED.
AND I AM FOREVER PROUD OF YOU.
POW
#$%@ YOU.
SCOTT.
#$%@.
YOU.
SCOTT...
YOU... CAN'T.
CAN YOU NOT COMPREHEND WHO I AM?! WHAT I DID FOR YOU?!
YOU HEAR ME, BOY?
I AM YOUR FATHER!
I AM YOUR GOD!

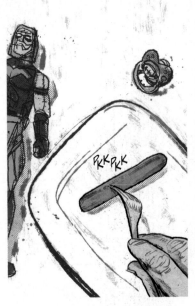

whrrrrr

DUG!

MOMMY AND DADDY HAVE SUPER BIG NEWS, JAKEY.

YOU'RE GOING TO HAVE...ARE YOU READY?

A LITTLE SISTER!

DUG!

HE'S TAKING IT WELL.

HE'S SO YOUNG.

HE WON'T REMEMBER THE WORLD WITHOUT HER.

WHATEVER CAME BEFORE.

THIS'LL JUST BE HIS WORLD.

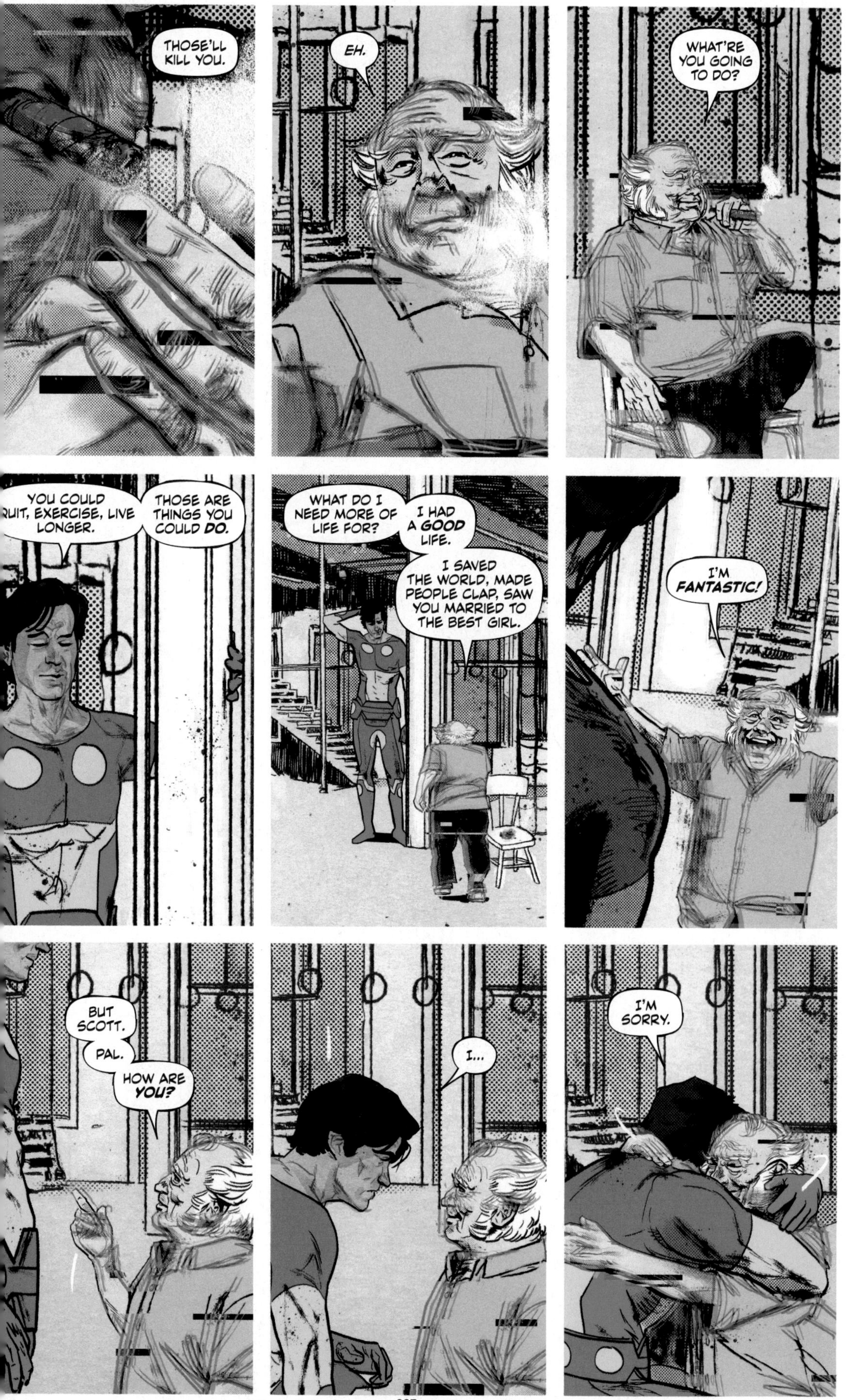
THOSE'LL KILL YOU.
EH.
WHAT'RE YOU GOING TO DO?
YOU COULD UIT, EXERCISE, LIVE LONGER.
THOSE ARE THINGS YOU COULD *DO.*
WHAT DO I NEED MORE OF LIFE FOR?
I HAD A *GOOD* LIFE.
I SAVED THE WORLD, MADE PEOPLE CLAP, SAW YOU MARRIED TO THE BEST GIRL.
I'M *FANTASTIC!*
BUT SCOTT.
PAL.
HOW ARE *YOU?*
I...
I'M SORRY.

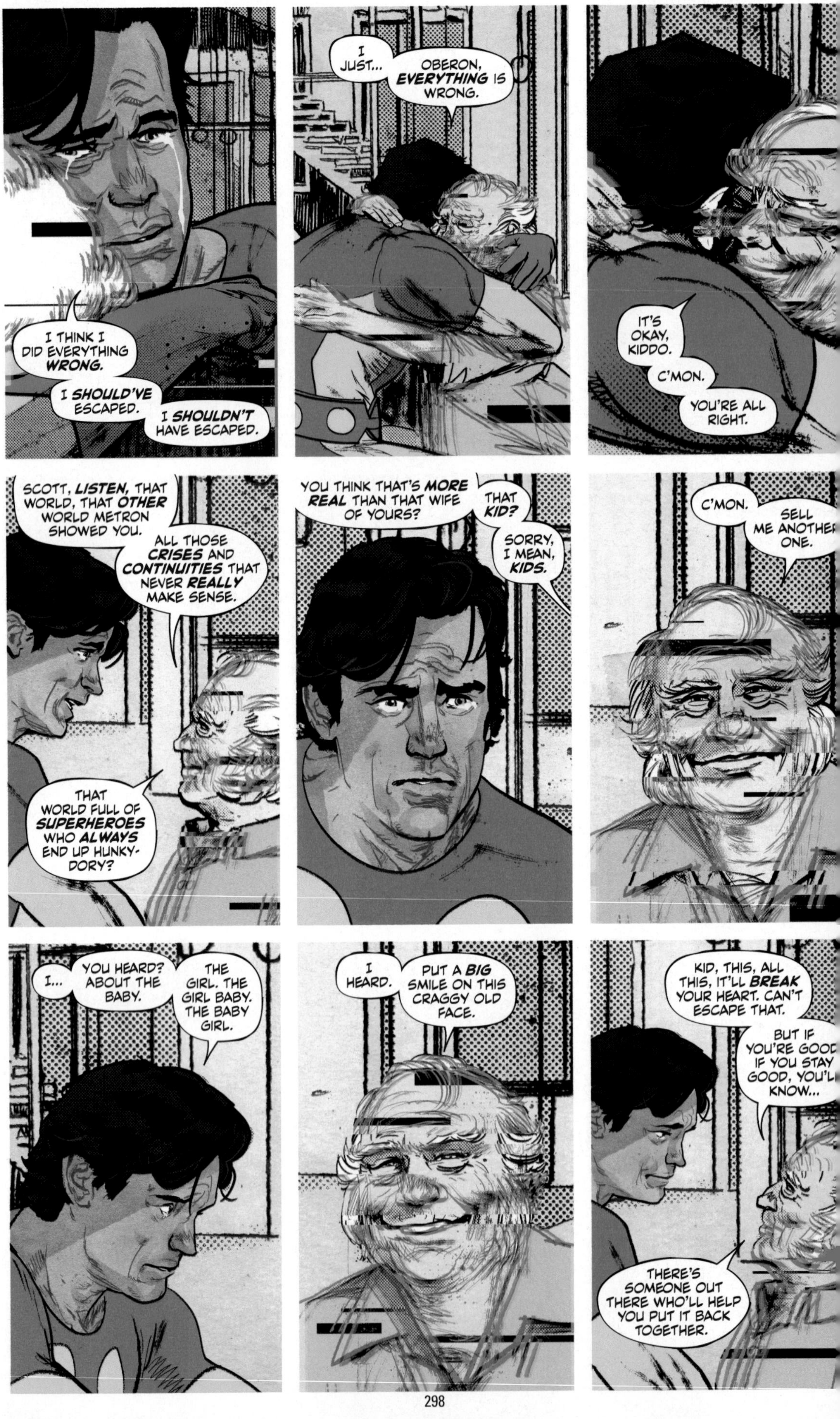
I THINK I DID EVERYTHING WRONG.
I SHOULD'VE ESCAPED.
I SHOULDN'T HAVE ESCAPED.
I JUST...
OBERON, EVERYTHING IS WRONG.
IT'S OKAY, KIDDO.
C'MON.
YOU'RE ALL RIGHT.
SCOTT, LISTEN, THAT WORLD, THAT OTHER WORLD METRON SHOWED YOU.
ALL THOSE CRISES AND CONTINUITIES THAT NEVER REALLY MAKE SENSE.
THAT WORLD FULL OF SUPERHEROES WHO ALWAYS END UP HUNKY-DORY?
YOU THINK THAT'S MORE REAL THAN THAT WIFE OF YOURS?
THAT KID?
SORRY, I MEAN, KIDS.
C'MON.
SELL ME ANOTHER ONE.
I...
YOU HEARD? ABOUT THE BABY.
THE GIRL. THE GIRL BABY. THE BABY GIRL.
I HEARD.
PUT A BIG SMILE ON THIS CRAGGY OLD FACE.
KID, THIS, ALL THIS, IT'LL BREAK YOUR HEART. CAN'T ESCAPE THAT.
BUT IF YOU'RE GOOD IF YOU STAY GOOD, YOU'LL KNOW...
THERE'S SOMEONE OUT THERE WHO'LL HELP YOU PUT IT BACK TOGETHER.

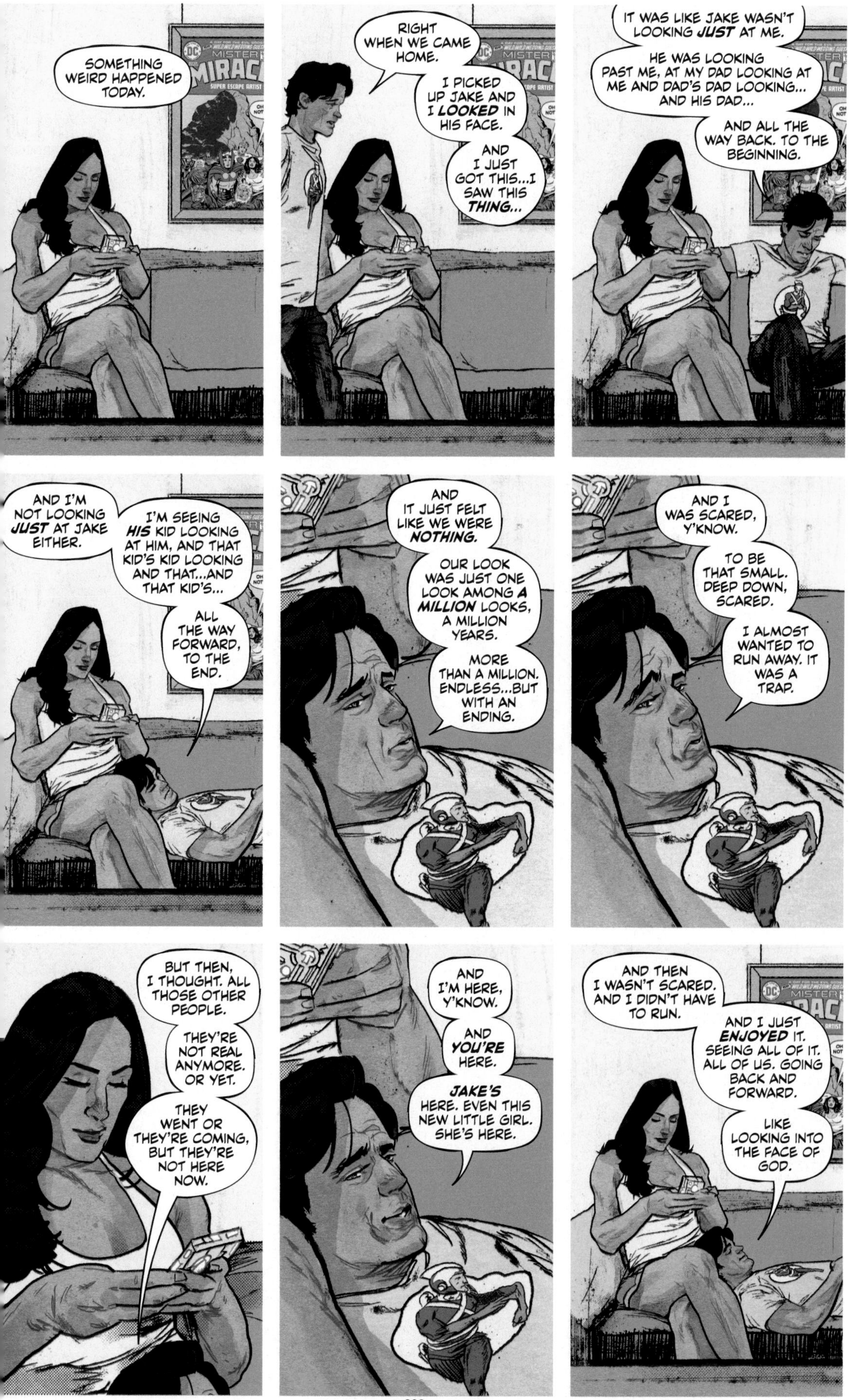
SOMETHING WEIRD HAPPENED TODAY.
RIGHT WHEN WE CAME HOME.
I PICKED UP JAKE AND I **LOOKED** IN HIS FACE.
AND I JUST GOT THIS...I SAW THIS ***THING...***
IT WAS LIKE JAKE WASN'T LOOKING ***JUST*** AT ME.
HE WAS LOOKING PAST ME, AT MY DAD LOOKING AT ME AND DAD'S DAD LOOKING... AND HIS DAD...
AND ALL THE WAY BACK. TO THE BEGINNING.
AND I'M NOT LOOKING ***JUST*** AT JAKE EITHER.
I'M SEEING ***HIS*** KID LOOKING AT HIM, AND THAT KID'S KID LOOKING AND THAT...AND THAT KID'S...
ALL THE WAY FORWARD, TO THE END.
AND IT JUST FELT LIKE WE WERE ***NOTHING.***
OUR LOOK WAS JUST ONE LOOK AMONG ***A MILLION*** LOOKS, A MILLION YEARS.
MORE THAN A MILLION. ENDLESS...BUT WITH AN ENDING.
AND I WAS SCARED, Y'KNOW.
TO BE THAT SMALL. DEEP DOWN, SCARED.
I ALMOST WANTED TO RUN AWAY. IT WAS A TRAP.
BUT THEN, I THOUGHT. ALL THOSE OTHER PEOPLE.
THEY'RE NOT REAL ANYMORE. OR YET.
THEY WENT OR THEY'RE COMING, BUT THEY'RE NOT HERE NOW.
AND I'M HERE, Y'KNOW.
AND ***YOU'RE*** HERE.
JAKE'S HERE. EVEN THIS NEW LITTLE GIRL. SHE'S HERE.
AND THEN I WASN'T SCARED. AND I DIDN'T HAVE TO RUN.
AND I JUST ***ENJOYED*** IT. SEEING ALL OF IT. ALL OF US. GOING BACK AND FORWARD.
LIKE LOOKING INTO THE FACE OF GOD.

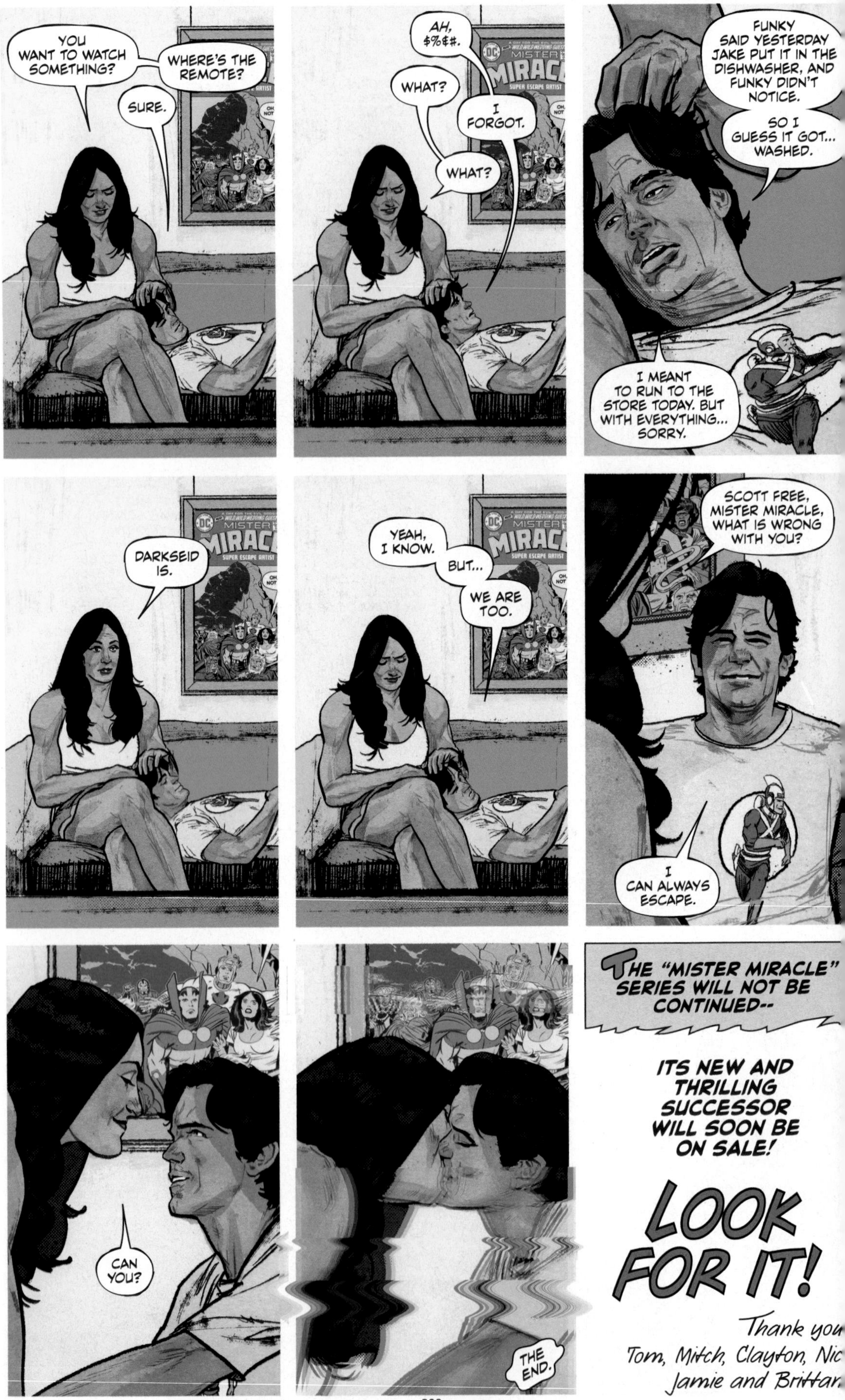
YOU WANT TO WATCH SOMETHING?
WHERE'S THE REMOTE?
SURE.
AH, $%$#.
WHAT?
I FORGOT.
WHAT?
FUNKY SAID YESTERDAY JAKE PUT IT IN THE DISHWASHER, AND FUNKY DIDN'T NOTICE.
SO I GUESS IT GOT... WASHED.
I MEANT TO RUN TO THE STORE TODAY. BUT WITH EVERYTHING... SORRY.
DARKSEID IS.
YEAH, I KNOW.
BUT...
WE ARE TOO.
SCOTT FREE, MISTER MIRACLE, WHAT IS WRONG WITH YOU?
I CAN ALWAYS ESCAPE.
CAN YOU?
THE END.
THE "MISTER MIRACLE" SERIES WILL NOT BE CONTINUED--
ITS NEW AND THRILLING SUCCESSOR WILL SOON BE ON SALE!
LOOK FOR IT!
Thank you Tom, Mitch, Clayton, Nic Jamie and Brittan

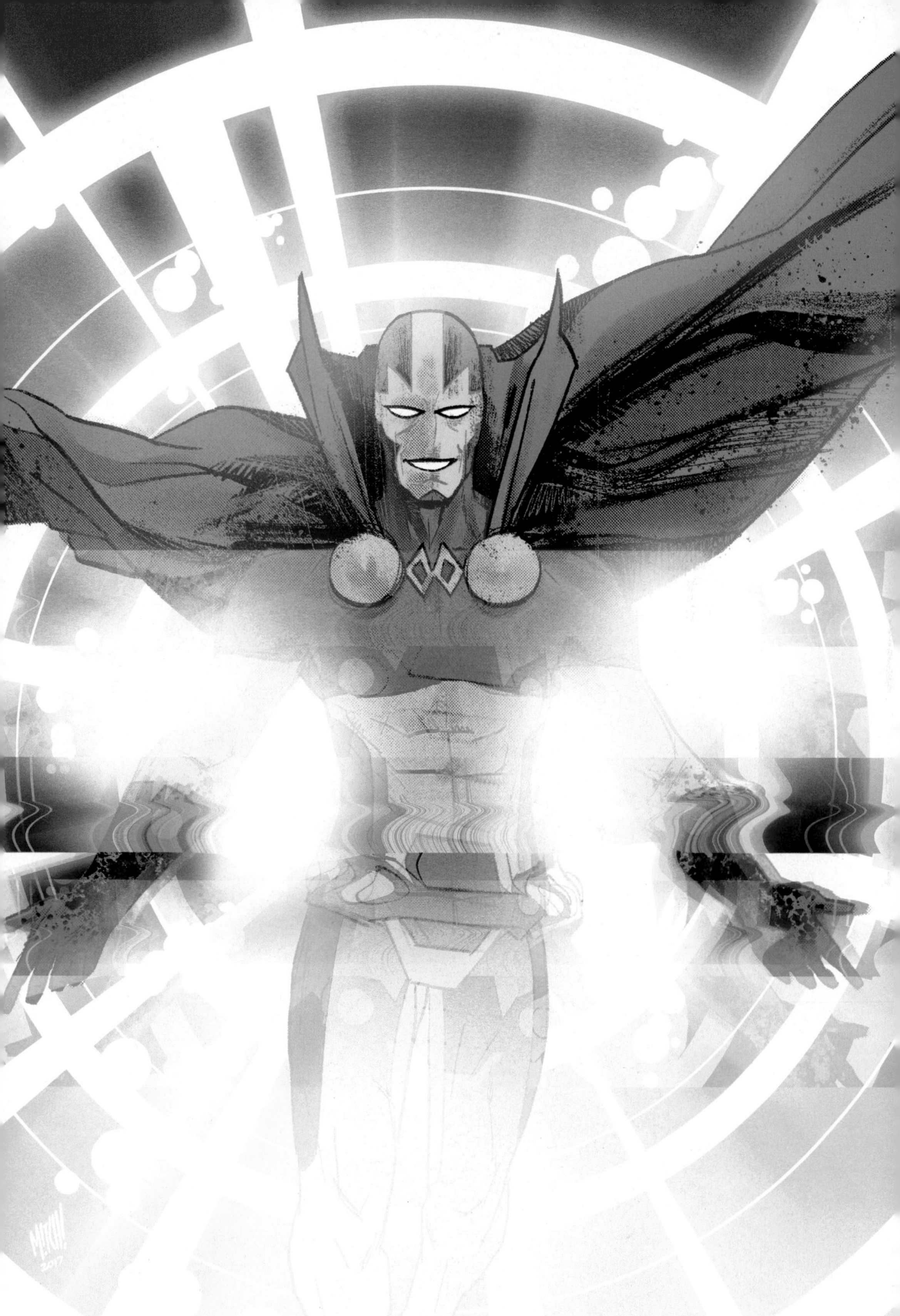

VARIANT COVER GALLERY

BY MITCH GERADS

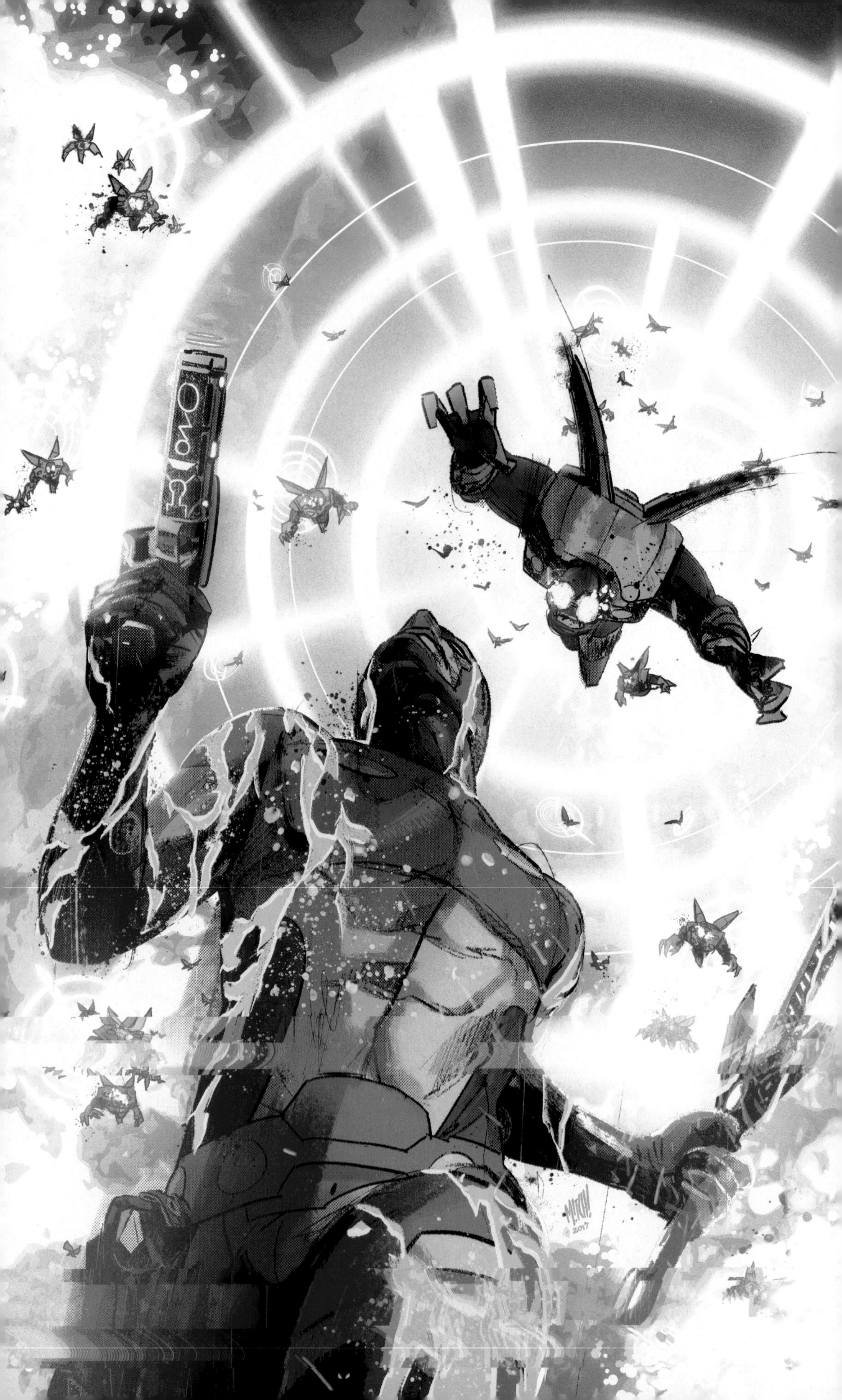

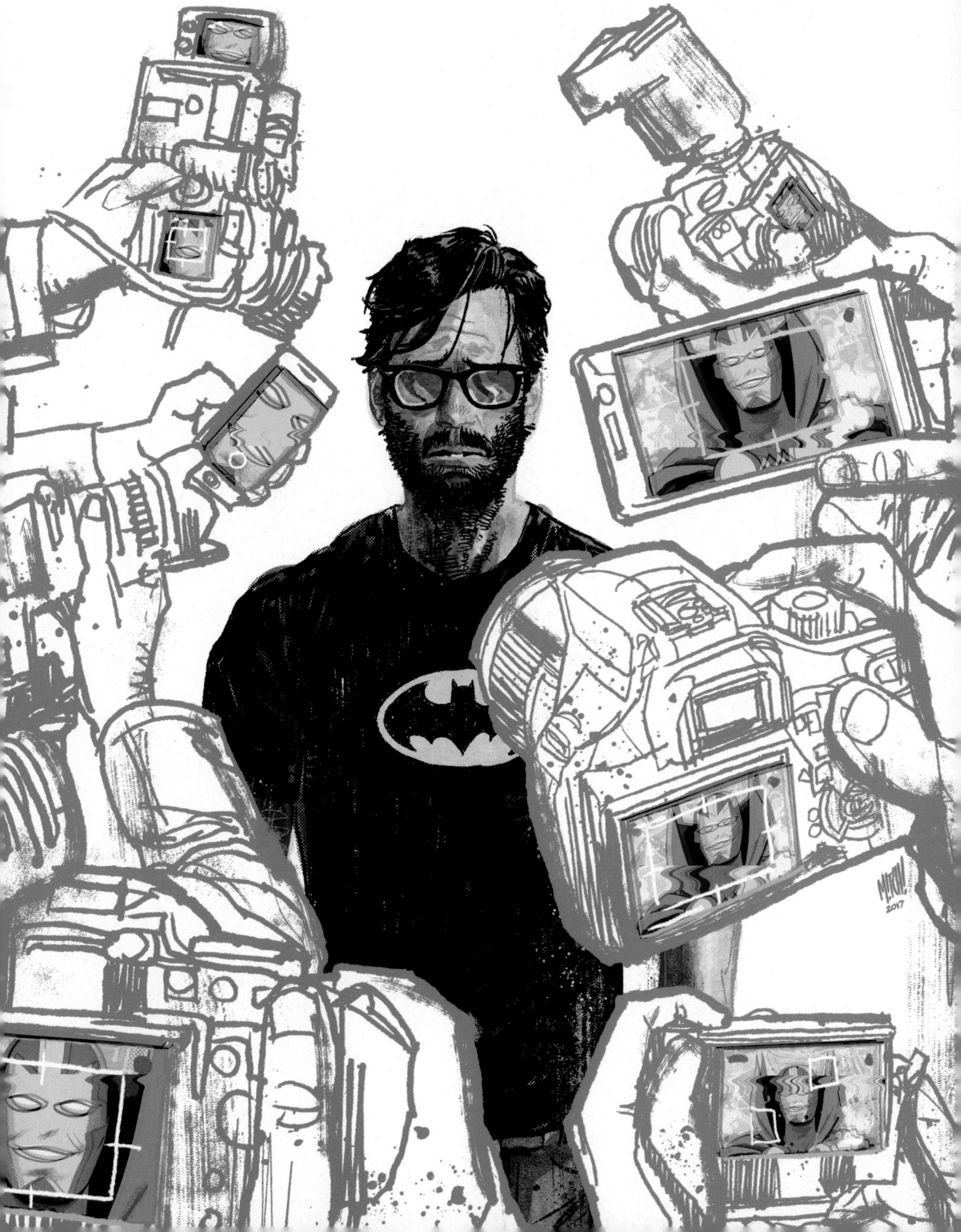

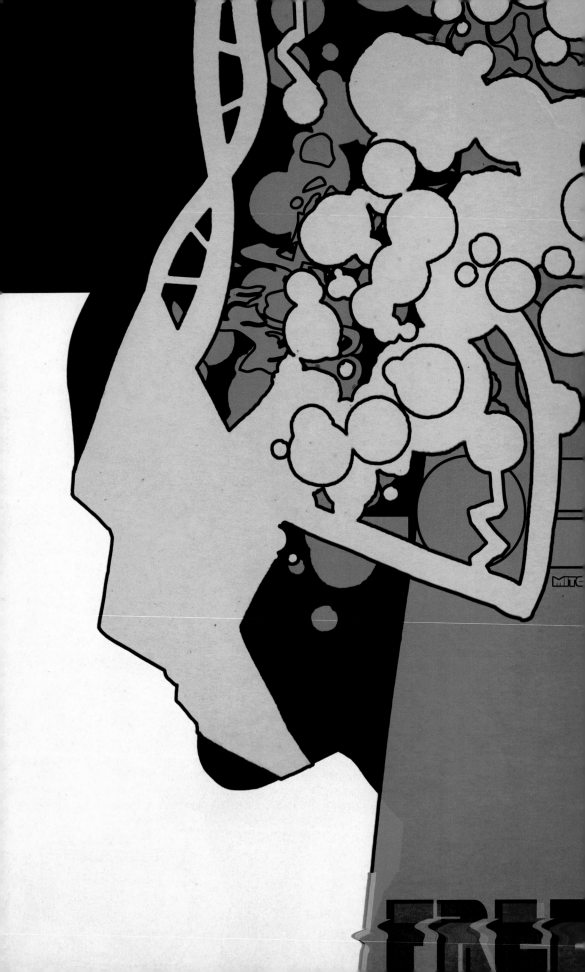

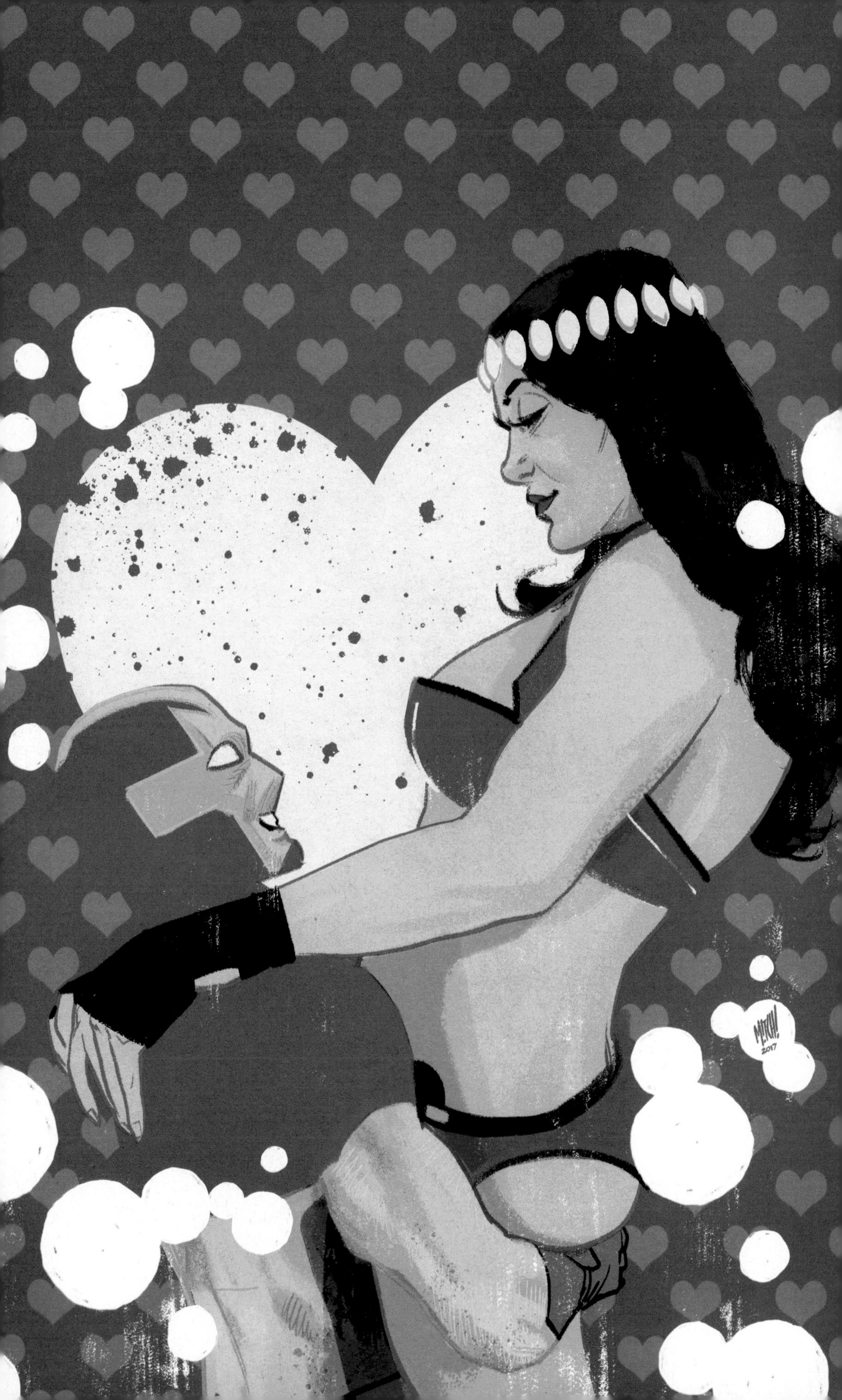
MITCH!
2017

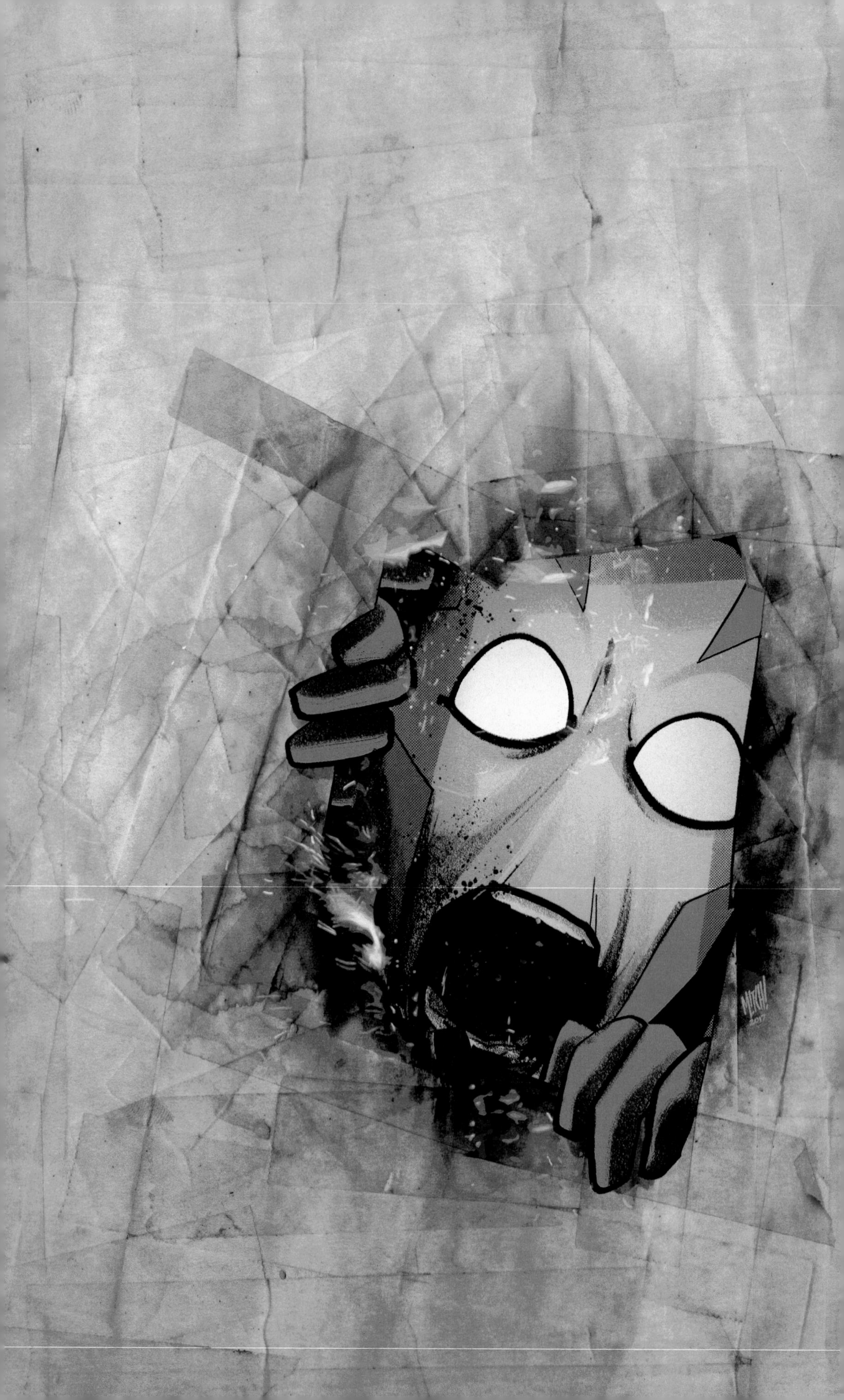

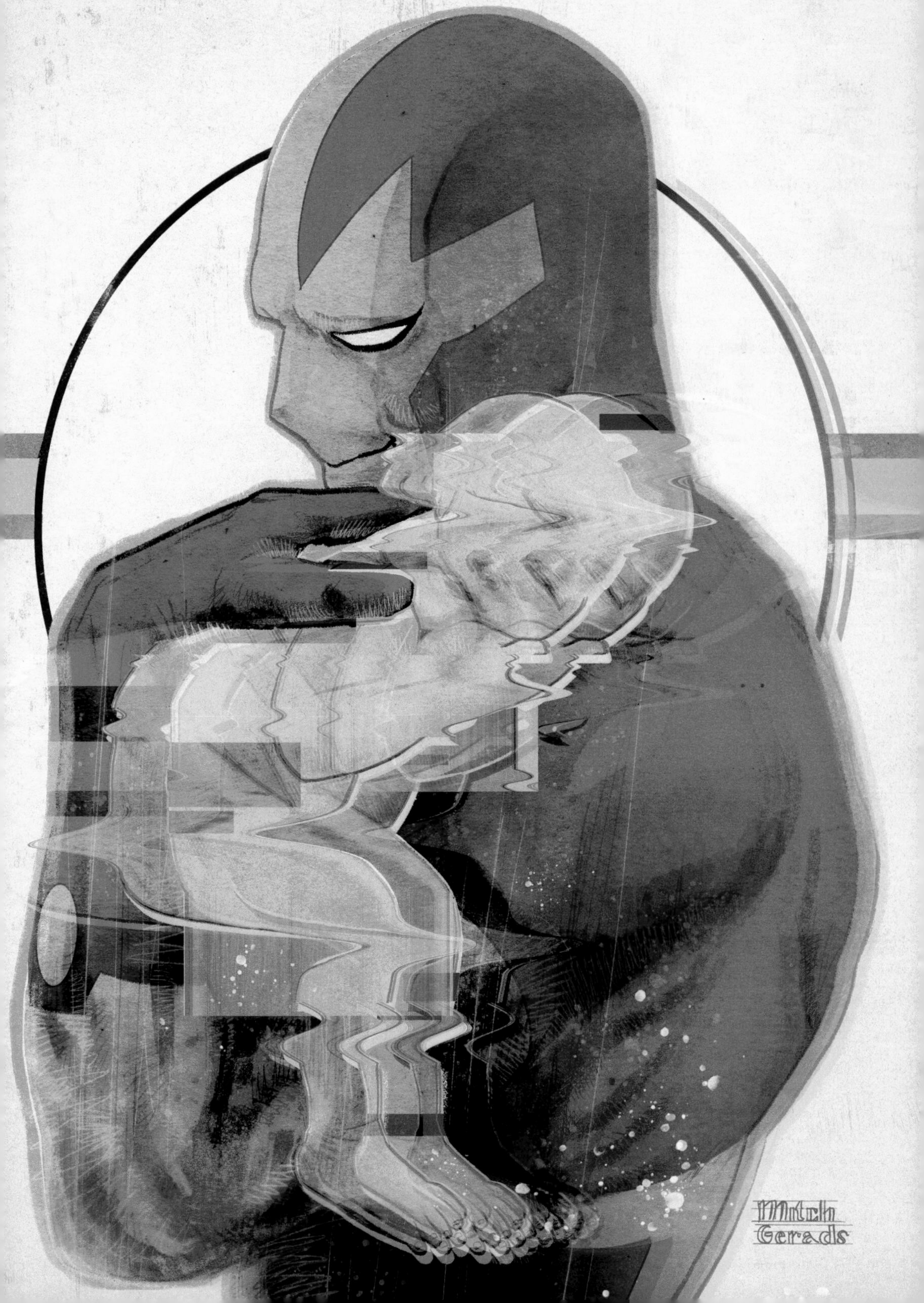
Mitch
Gerads

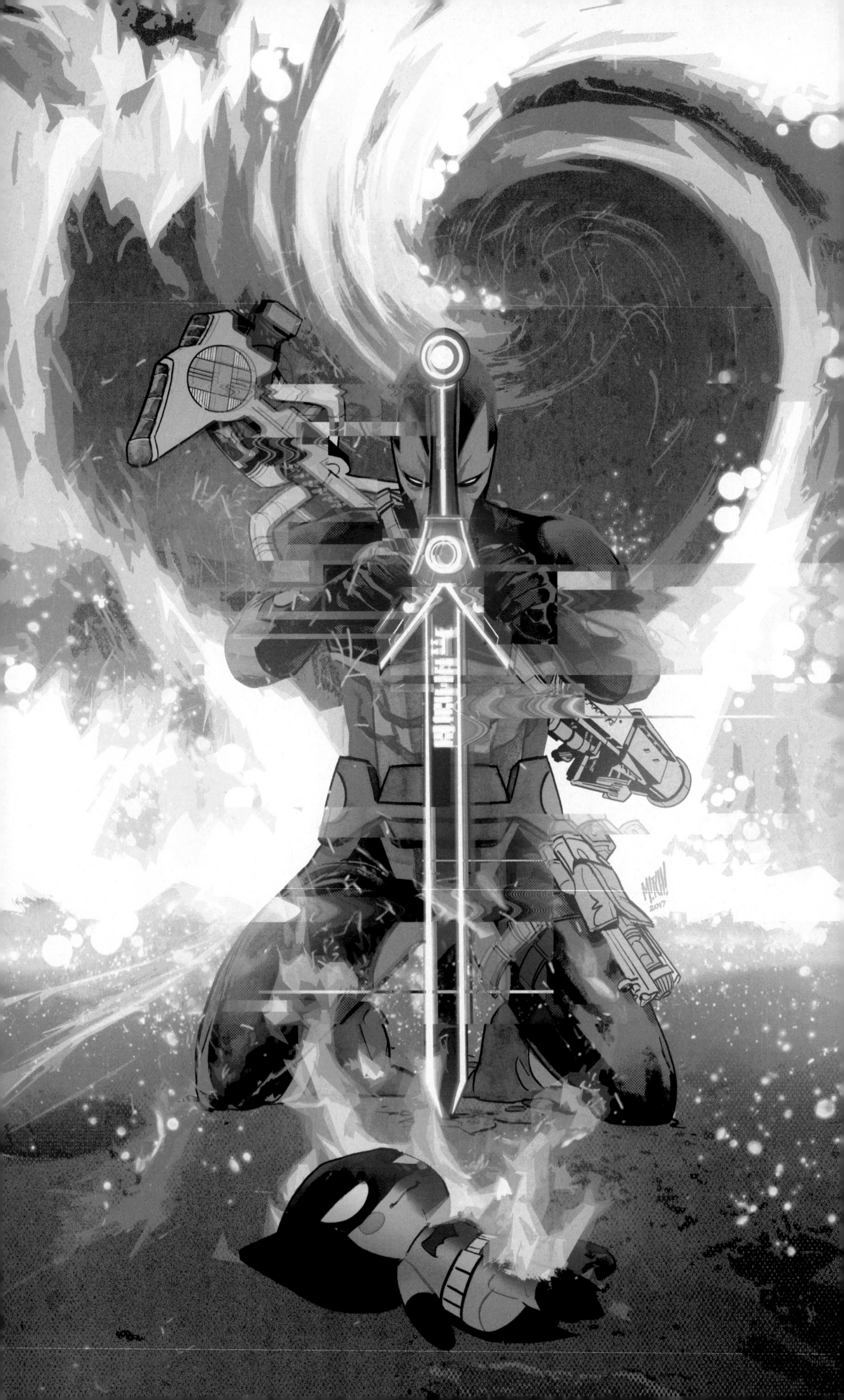

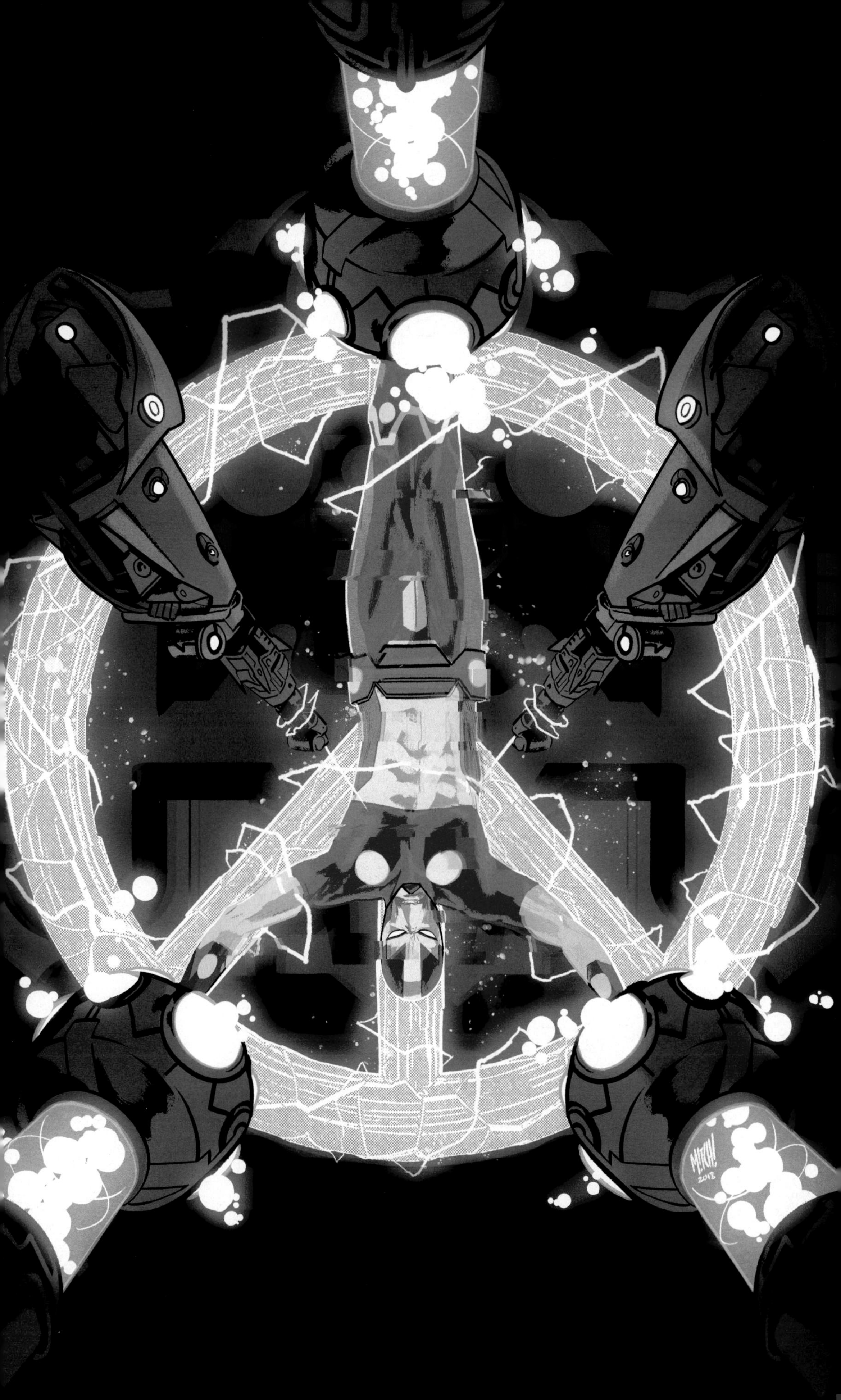

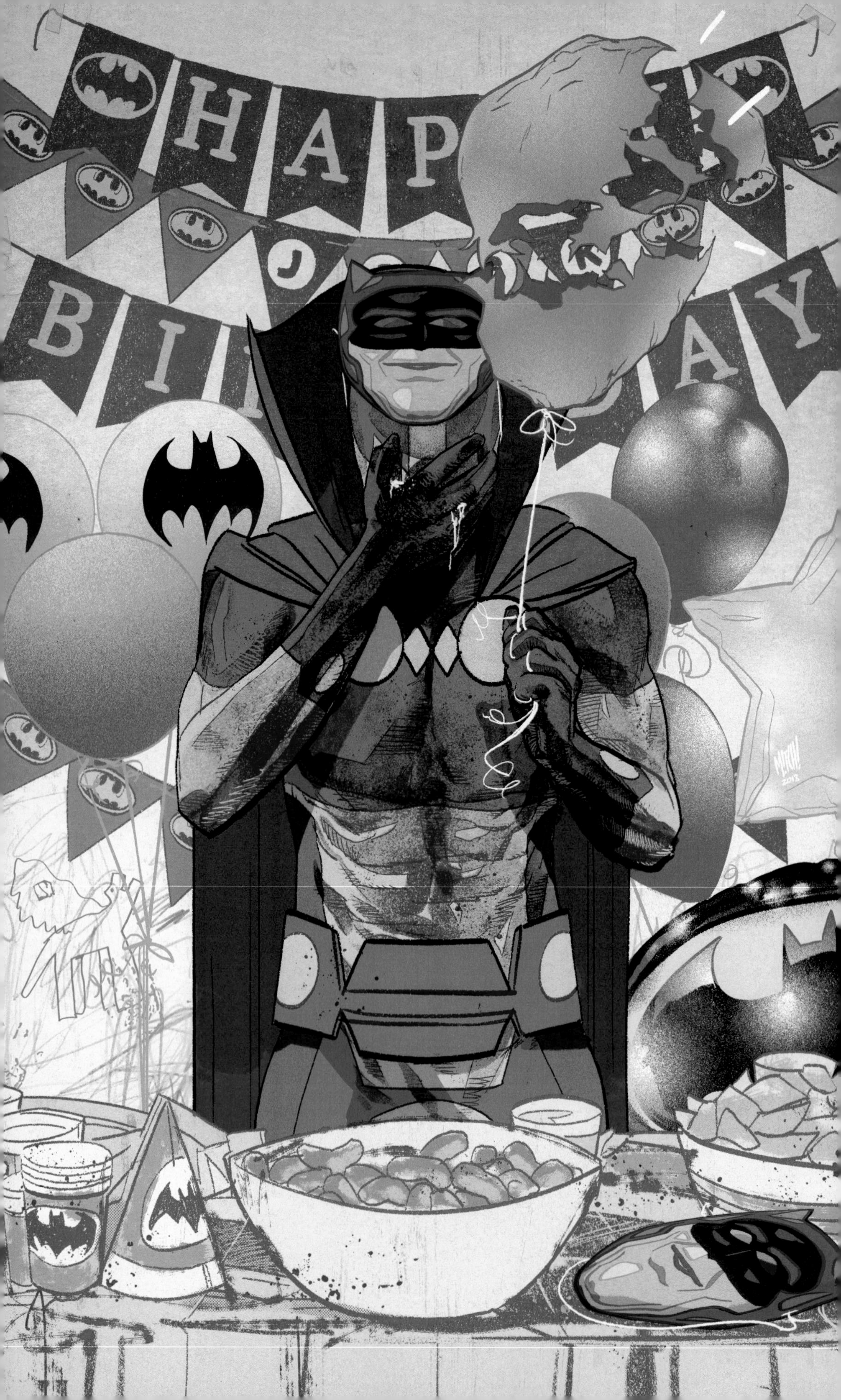

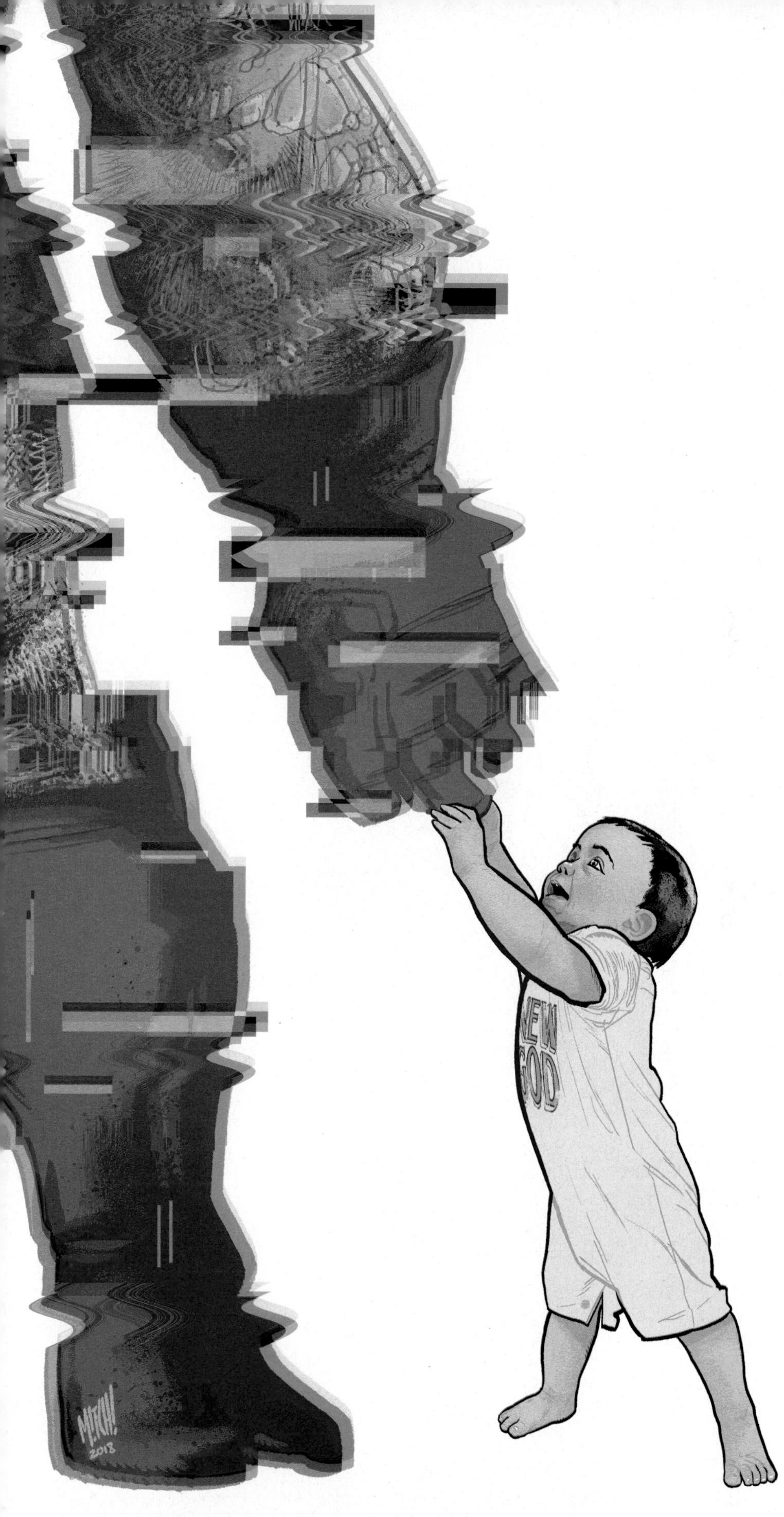
NEW GOD
MITCH! 2018

Darkseid is.

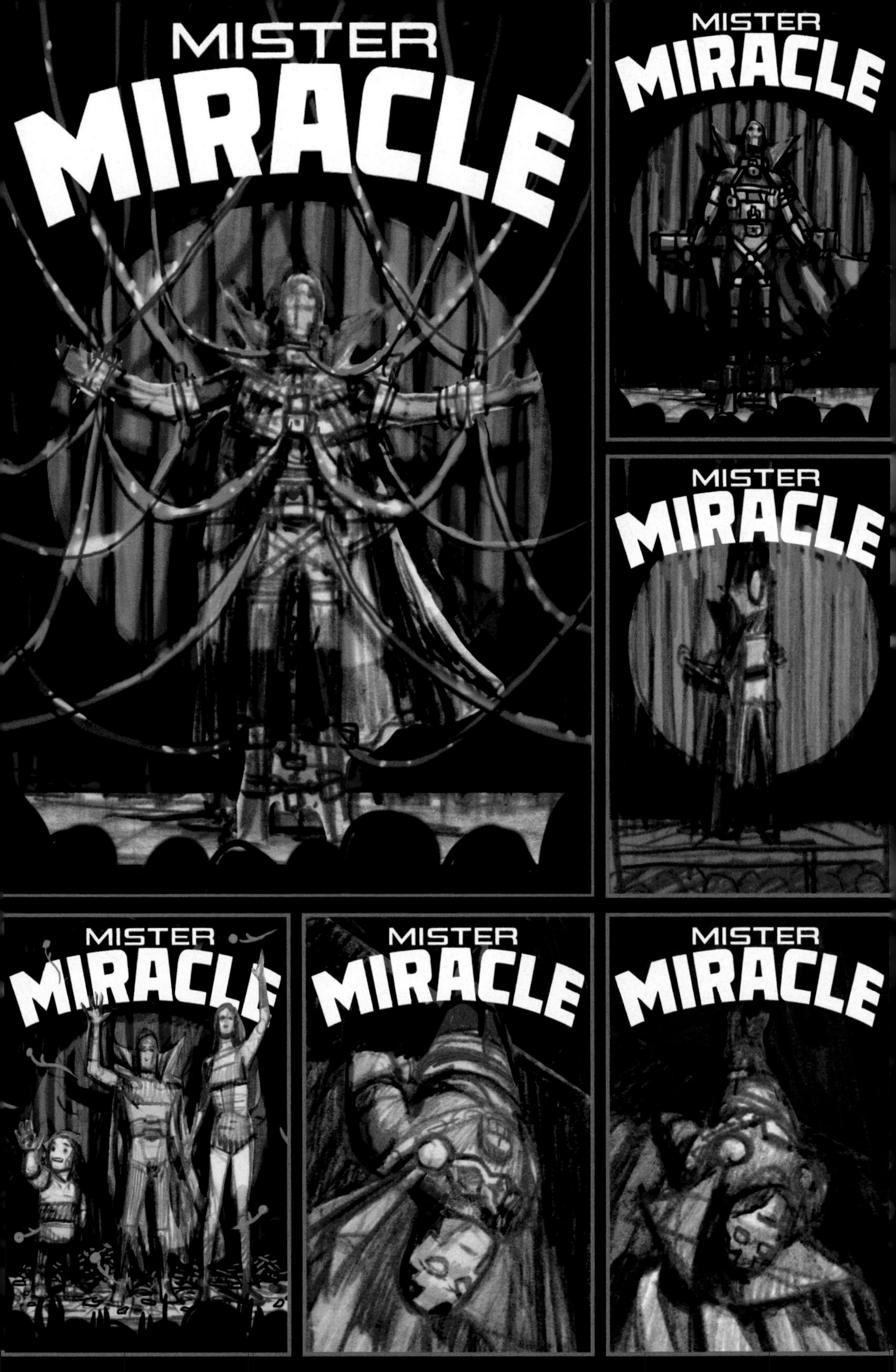
MISTER
MIRACLE
MISTER
MIRACLE
MISTER
MIRACLE
MISTER
MIRACLE
MISTER
MIRACLE
MISTER
MIRACLE

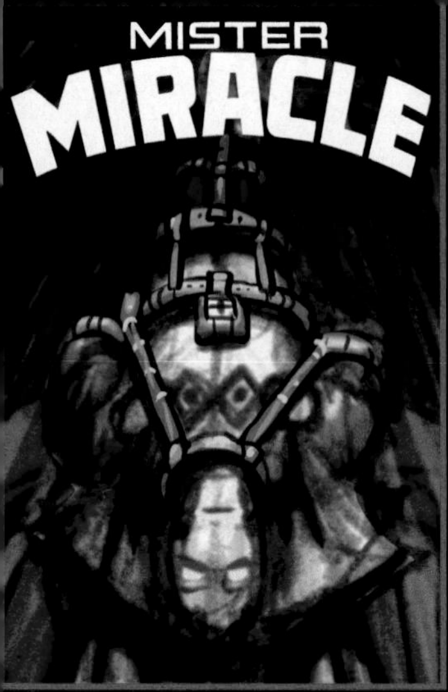
MISTER
MIRACLE

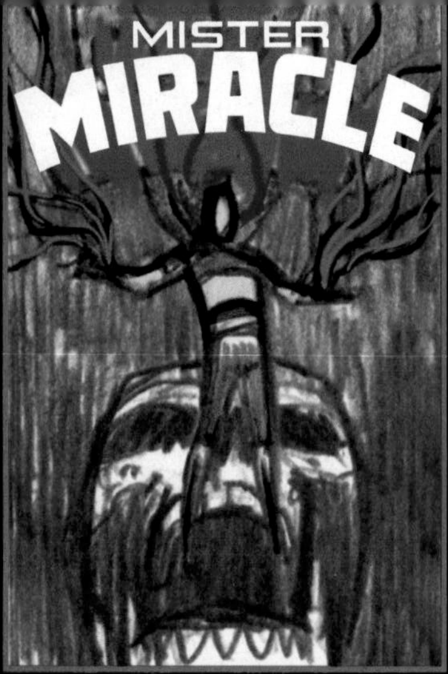
MISTER
MIRACLE

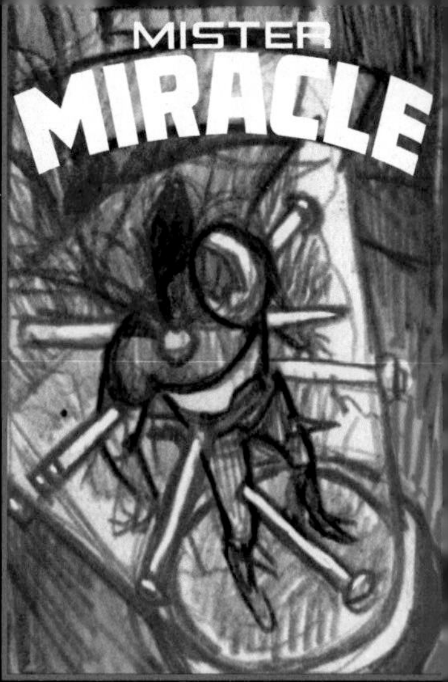
MISTER
MIRACLE

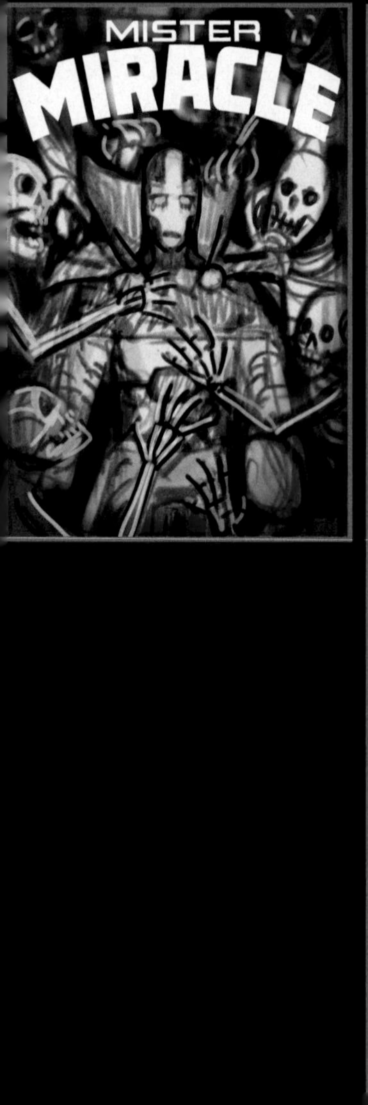
MISTER
MIRACLE

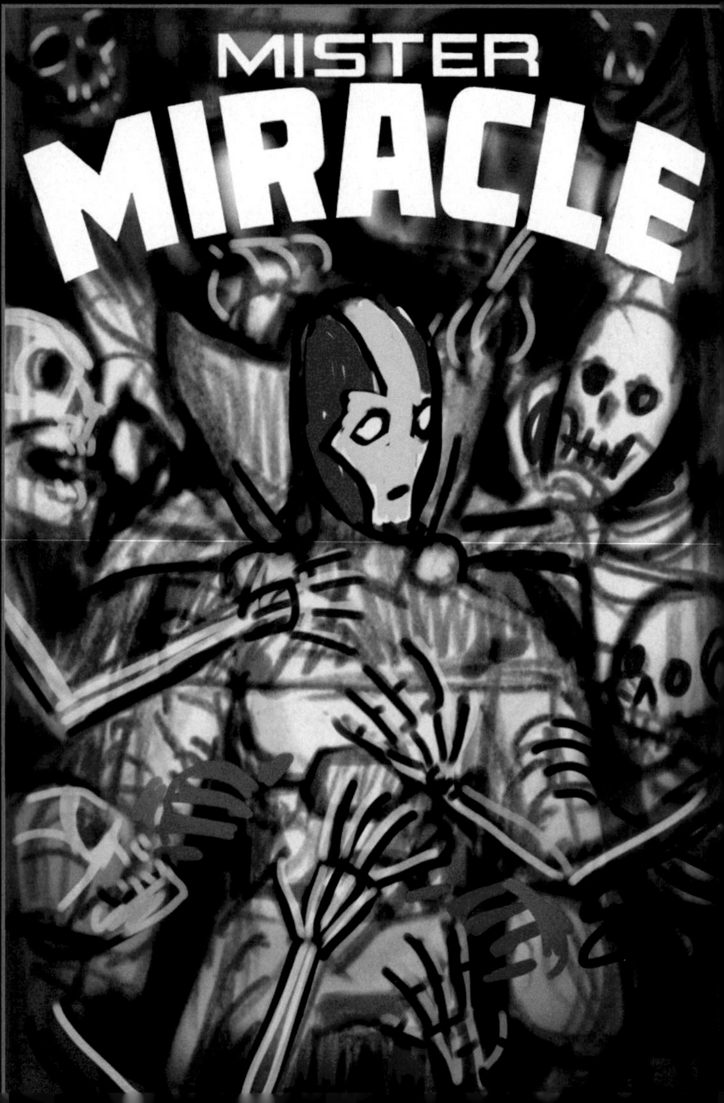
MISTER
MIRACLE

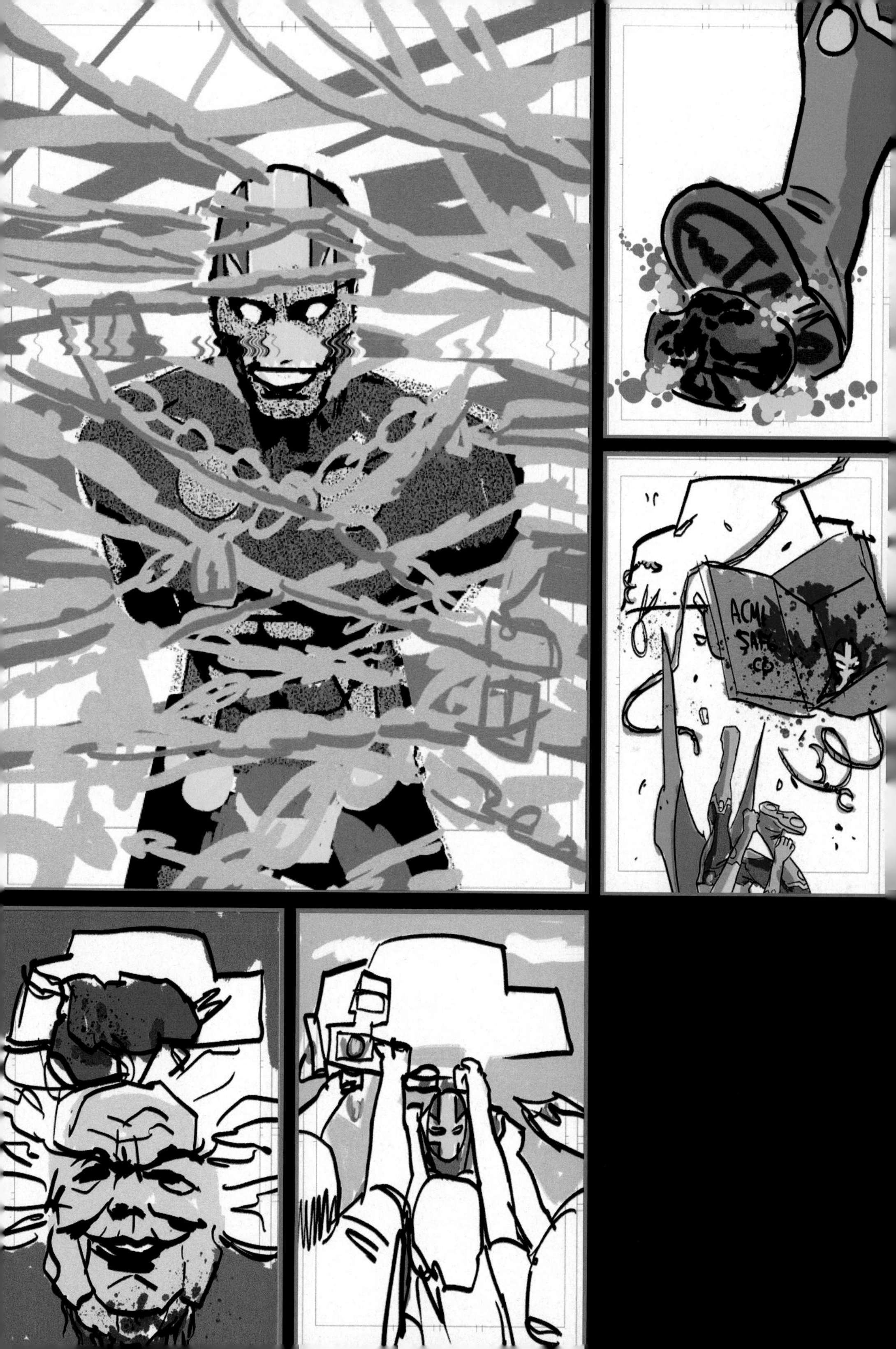

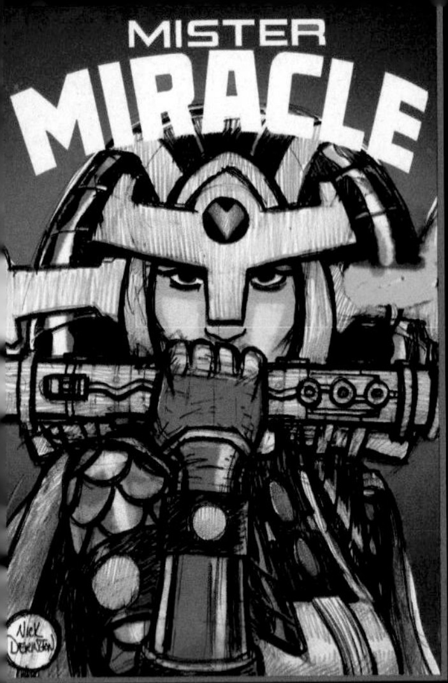
MISTER
MIRACLE
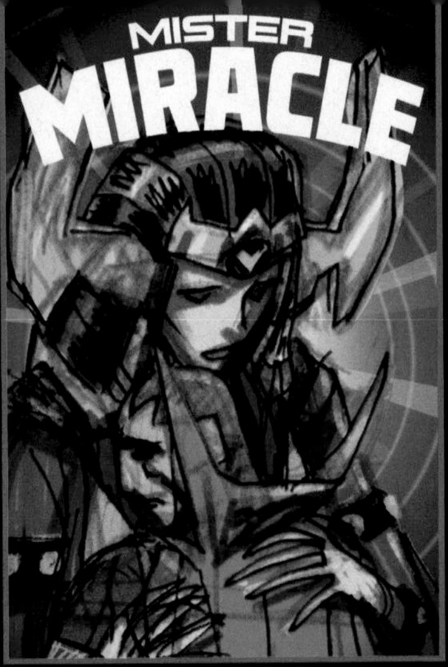
MISTER
MIRACLE
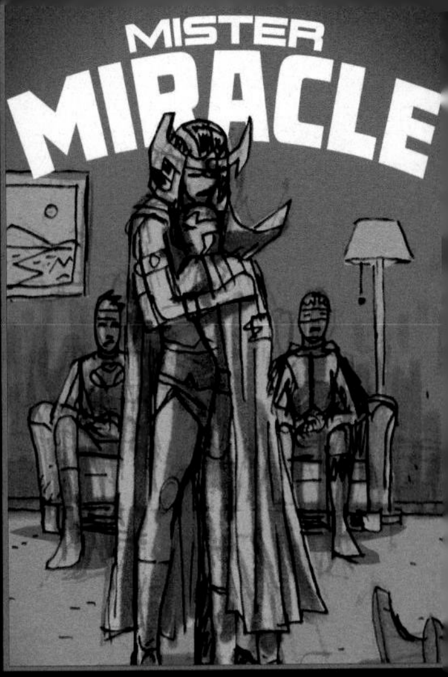
MISTER
MIRACLE
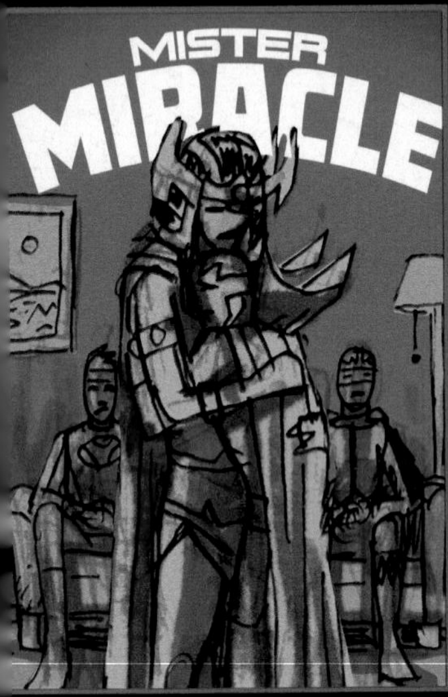
MISTER
MIRACLE
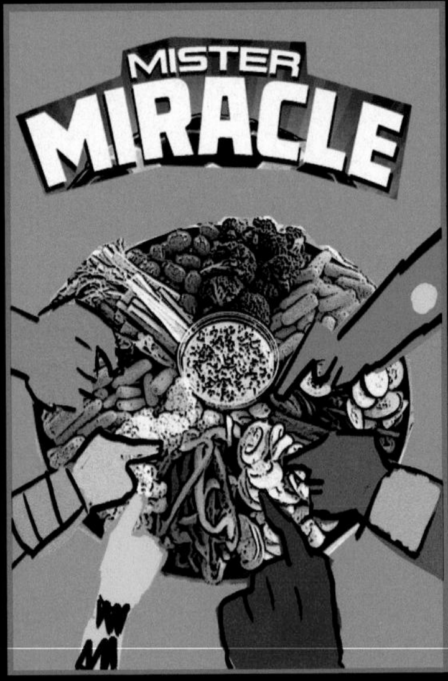
MISTER
MIRACLE
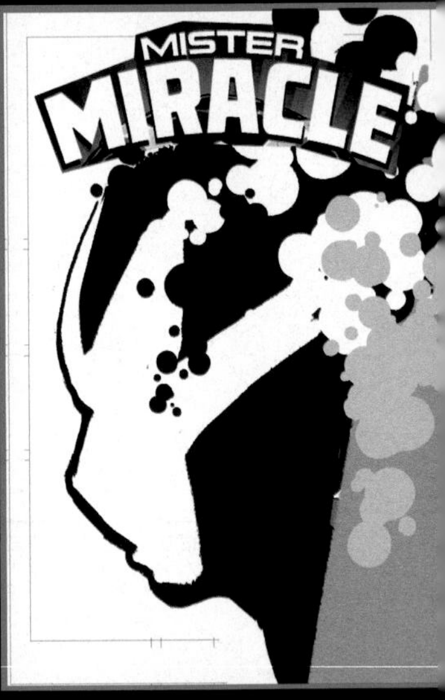
MISTER
MIRACLE
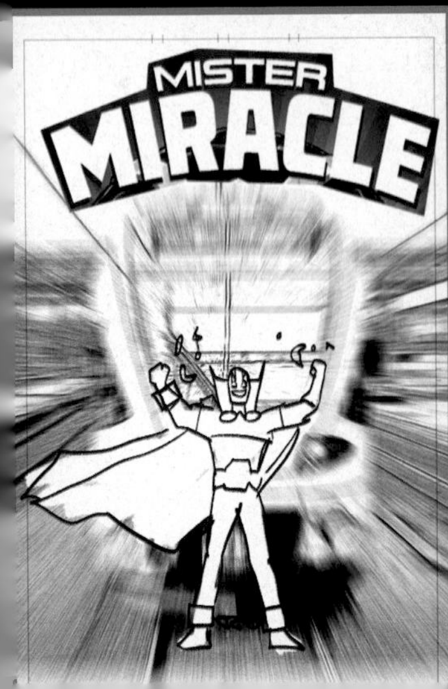
MISTER
MIRACLE
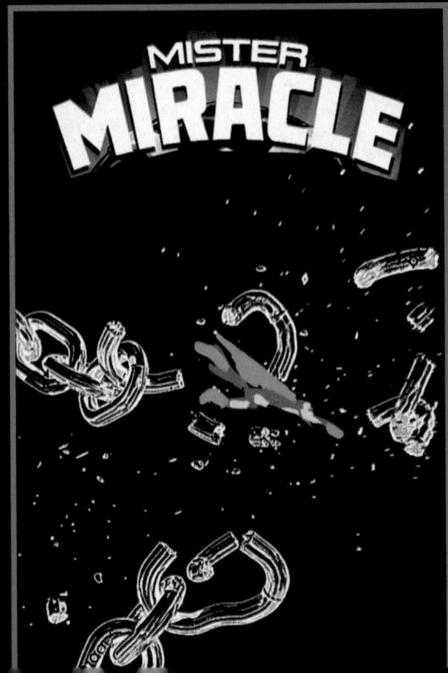
MISTER
MIRACLE
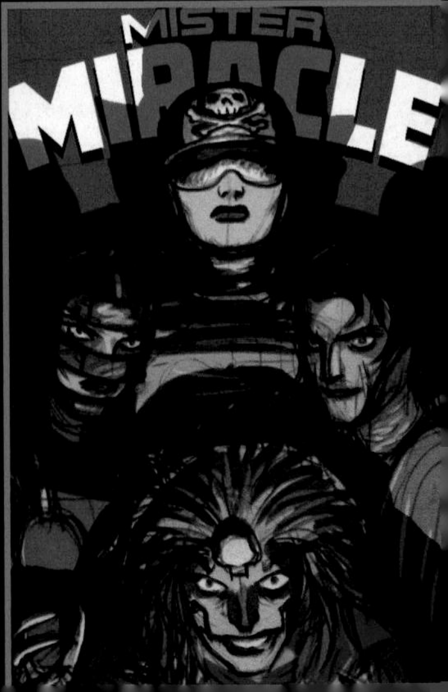
MISTER
MIRACLE

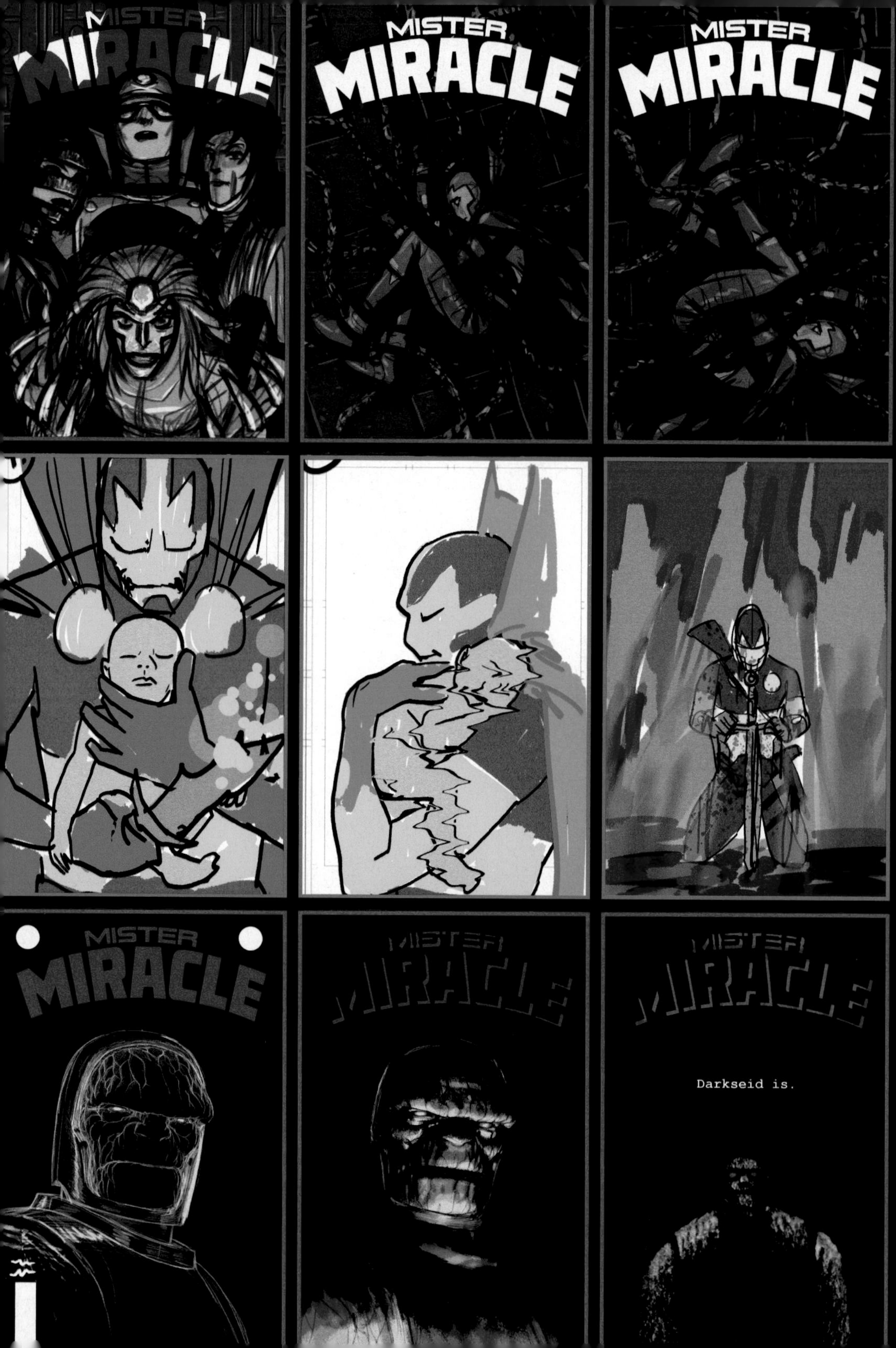
MISTER MIRACLE
MISTER MIRACLE
MISTER MIRACLE
MISTER MIRACLE
MISTER MIRACLE
MISTER MIRACLE
Darkseid is.

Darkseid is.

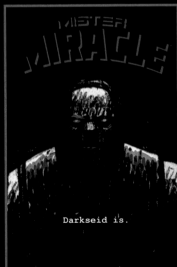

Darkseid is.

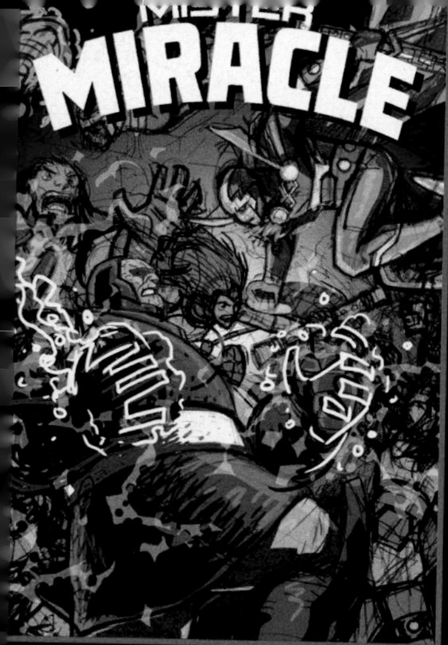
MISTER
MIRACLE
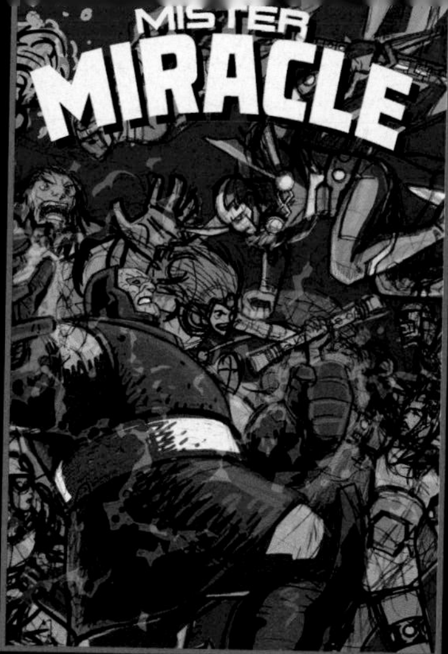
MISTER
MIRACLE
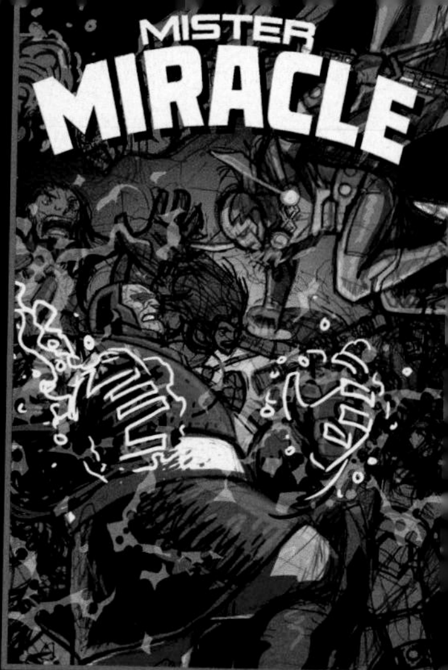
MISTER
MIRACLE
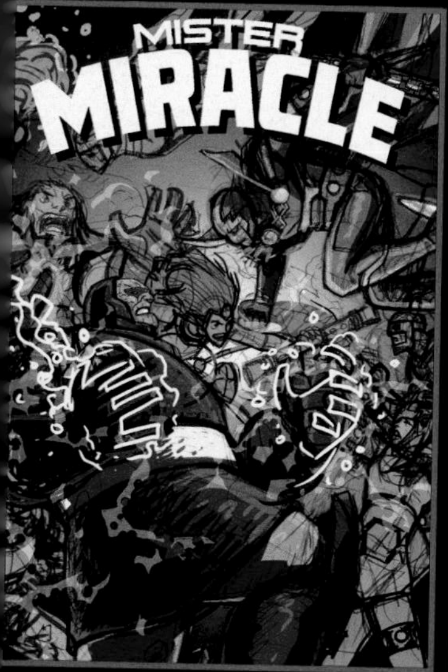
MISTER
MIRACLE
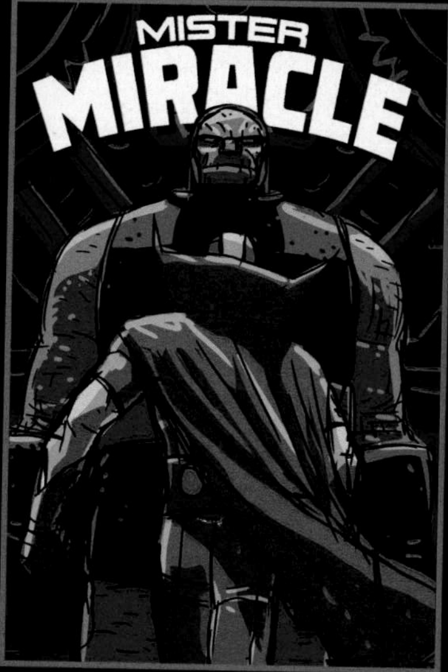
MISTER
MIRACLE
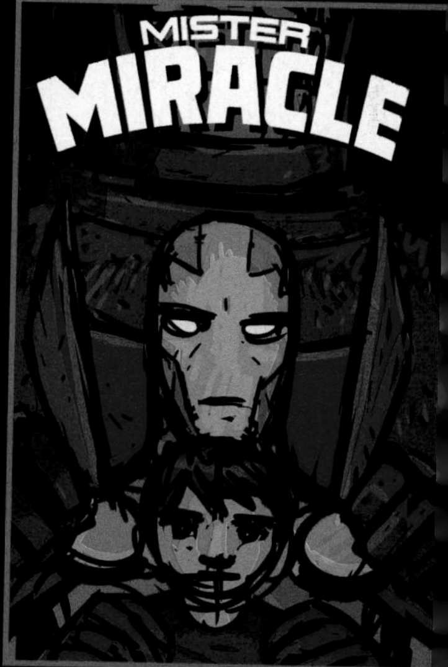
MISTER
MIRACLE
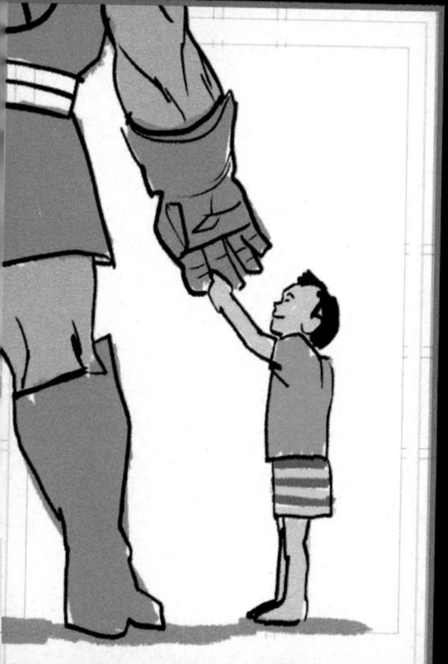
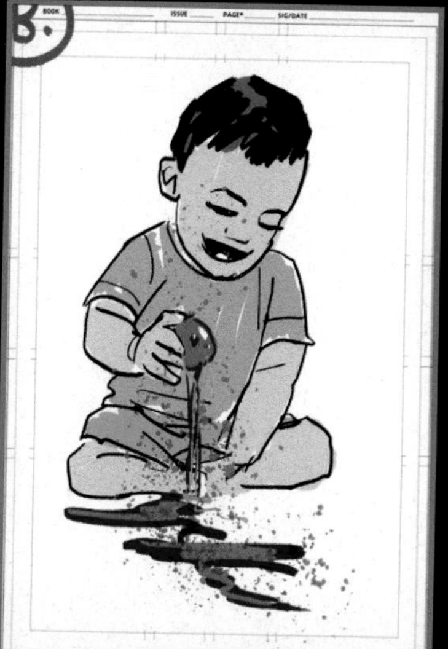

TOM KING is a *New York Times* best-selling and Eisner, Harvey and Ringo award-winning writer. He is best known for his acclaimed work on BATMAN, *The Vision*, THE OMEGA MEN, MISTER MIRACLE and THE SHERIFF OF BABYLON. Prior to becoming a writer, King worked at the CIA as an operations officer in the counterterrorism center, where he served overseas in the Iraq and Afghanistan theaters of war. He currently lives in Washington, D.C., with his wife and three children.

MITCH GERADS is an Eisner and Ringo award-winning illustrator who has made a career out of bringing humanity and realism to the superhuman and unreal. He is best known for his critically acclaimed work at DC Comics with writer (and friend) Tom King on MISTER MIRACLE, BATMAN and THE SHERIFF OF BABYLON. He lives and draws in Phoenix, Arizona, with his wife and son.